Mean Ol' Mr. GRAVITY

Mean Ol' Mr. GRAVITY

Conversations on Strength Training

Mark Rippetoe

The Aasgaard Company
Wichita Falls

The Aasgaard Company, Wichita Falls 76308

Published 2009
13 12 11 10 09 1 2 3 4 5

Printed in the United States of America

ISBN-13: 978-0-9825227-1-4
ISBN-10: 0-9825227-1-1

The older I get, the more I realize how fortunate I was to have made the acquaintance of Bill Starr when I was a young lifter. He taught me how to train, how to coach, and how to compete. He also taught me how to party, how to tell a story, and he encouraged me to write and thought it was fine that I stayed self-employed. He was a bit "wilder" at times than I am prone to be, but he was a good counterbalance to my precious mother Judy Rippetoe, who was a perfect angel every day of her life, who never had a cross word for or about anyone (except Nikita Khrushchev), who raised me to be a very good boy, and whom I miss very much. This book is dedicated to them.

Contents

Preface

Back in 1985 when Bill Starr was staying with me for a while out at my little rent house on the Bondurant in Wichita County, I brought home a video one night. He was already asleep in the middle bedroom when I got there, so I cooked a batch of stuff to eat and put the tape in. It was "Hey Vern! It's My Family Album" starring the most underappreciated American comic actor in modern history, Jim Varney. We were watching a lot of movies and at the time the concept of movie rental was new enough that we had burned through most of the interesting stuff at the store in front of the gym. This one looked interesting, but I had no idea what I was about to see. The first part of the tape was a collection of his commercials, which at the time composed most of his work (this predates the Ernest Goes To… movies). The rest of the tape was a series of sketch comedy put together by the agency he worked for, Carden and Cherry. All of it is brilliant, the work of a master character actor with an extraordinary talent for voice control, comic timing, and facial expression.

One of the sketches remains to this day the funniest short piece I have ever seen, featuring Varney as Uncle Lloyd Worrell, the Meanest Man in the World. I was on the couch watching it after I ate supper, and got to laughing so hard that I fell off the couch onto the floor. This woke Bill up, and he walked out of the bedroom, blinking in the light of the kitchen, wondering what the hell was going on. All I could do was point at the screen. He said he'd just watch it tomorrow, which he did after I left for the gym the next day. He called me from the couch, laughing his ass off, and to this day the lines from this sketch remain an inside joke amongst us and our friends that have enjoyed it for the past 25 years. It is not nearly popular enough to suit me, so I've included glimpses of it in this book.

It was about this time that I came into a position of actual responsibility for other peoples' training, when I bought Anderson's Gym from David Anderson and changed the name to Wichita Falls Athletic Club. I made this rather sudden transition from trainee to gym owner in 1984, on April 1 as a matter of actual fact. Going from asking for help to providing it for a fee should be a humbling experience for any psychologically normal person that realizes his limitations. Although I had worked in a couple of clubs off and on since 1978, there is just something different about being The Gym Owner. I proceeded rather carefully, sticking to what I knew while trying some things out that I felt might be helpful, keeping the stuff that worked and eventually accumulating what might be termed a "method" for dealing with new members that was quite a bit different from the things we'd all been told in the magazines.

I began to read as much technical material about physiology and exercise as I could find, prepared to understand it by a fairly broad science education in geology and biology. I found that the method I was developing was different than what I was reading as the accepted practices of those with advanced degrees in Biomechanics, Exercise Physiology, Kinesiology, Physical Therapy, and Physical Education. It took many years to purge myself of the doubt I had about what I was doing with my members, the result of my respect for the advanced degrees, published research, and academic gravitas that forms the basis of the conventional wisdom to this day. For instance, in contrast to the entrenched idea that it was only possible to gain 7-10 lbs. of muscle a year, I found that my members could easily gain 30 lbs. of lean bodyweight in 6-8 months with correct diet and adherence to my program of regularly increasing work set weights on the basic barbell exercises.

Some gained much more than that in a year. Virtually every male that even tried to eat correctly gained 5 lbs. the first week. This was, of course, impossible according to both the magazines and the textbooks. I stopped reading the magazines many years ago, and I learned to take what I read in the textbooks and journals with a big tablespoonful of salt.

The process of learning about my little corner of applied physiology continues to this day, as I teach our barbell training seminars and answer questions for people about their training problems posted on the web. This book is essentially a compilation of examples of the interactive process of my helping and learning at the same time. As anyone who has coached can attest, the explaining of a movement pattern to someone who has never done it teaches something about it to the coach as well. Questions about training work the same way, in that every time I have to process even familiar concepts into an explanation specific to a personal question, that synthesis teaches me.

In July of 2007 Phil Hammarberg began hosting my Q&A board on his Strengthmill.net site. The readership has grown steadily over the past 2 years, and as of tonight the board has accumulated over 3200 threads and almost 19,000 posts. This representing a tremendous amount of information and a pretty decent investment of my time, I decided to edit the material into a book. Now, this may seem incredibly stupid, since the information is obviously already available free on the web, and will continue to be. But the editing is the key here. With the help of my buddy David Patrick, who initially did the grunt work of pulling all this text off the website, I have ingeniously removed all the posts that primarily pertain to the many videos that are posted for me to critique, which you'll have to admit would be pretty damned useless in this format. The posts have been much further edited for redundancy, stupidity, and uselessness, and in certain instances my replies have been updated, cleaned, revised, corrected, or otherwise improved. But pretty much, this is the good stuff from the entire corpus of the board, arranged in a helpful, interesting way into what we believe to be the first book of its type - a printed volume compiled from internet posts. My hope is that you will find it interesting even if you have been reading the board for a while, and that the organization will provide the added value that makes it worth the money you've spent over and above the computer electricity.

Some people have expressed enthusiasm for the type of humor I sometimes employ in dealing with the people on the board. It is, ah, *coarse* at times. This coarseness is herein preserved, not because I necessarily think it is worth preserving in the sense that the work of Mark Twain is worth preserving, but rather that most of the writing on exercise topics could use a little less *"if you track the vertical movement along the horizontal axis concentrating on moving the weight in a linear fashion towards peak overhead natural contraction you will note that the movement is linearly opposite the concentric definition of the elbow peak"* and a little more *"Quit asking for my fucking data, and let me, finally, see yours."* I say this in the interest of your psychological well-being, so that you may just give this book away now if you bought it by mistake. But please, I BEG YOU, don't buy it for a kid and then attempt to assign to me the responsibility for any subsequent deviations from accepted behavior.

Anyway, here's the book. Just leave it in the bathroom and read it a little at a time. Know what I mean?

Freshman Orientation

Read this stuff first, if you want to. We all have to start somewhere. I started at the Midwestern University weight room in 1978 doing half-squats.

Early stall

Casbah: Yesterday was my fourth workout (B) and I struggled on my squats. On the third workout last week the squats started to feel heavy so I anticipated failure, I was close to it but just about made the 3 sets. My form wasn't ideal either. Since I started I have been increasing the weight 10lbs for the squat, too much perhaps considering I've hit this wall already. Aside from that, I started feeling a pain on the outside of my knee over the weekend, and on my last set yesterday the pain was there. I might have to miss the squats in the next workout and resume them on Friday, depending on how it feels. When I resume, should I reset or do the same weight again?

Mark Rippetoe: Sounds to me like you are taking too big a jump for your bodyweight, or that you're not getting recovered (maybe not drinking your milk?), or both. There is no possible way to be stuck on the 4th workout unless you have done something wrong.

Casbah: I'm 126lbs, so certainly on the light side of the spectrum! What should I do from here; start over when my knee has recovered? If that is your recommendation should I start much lighter than last time and increment by half the amount?

Dave76: Rip, as you might suspect, I've answered a lot of questions just like this one. The "something wrong" is usually a case of starting out with too much weight. No one wants to believe me when I tell them that the average male novice in your gym starts squatting at 85 to 105 lbs in your gym.

Mark Rippetoe: Dave is right. So, how tall are you, how old are you, what did you squat the 4th workout, how many calories are you eating every day, and how much milk do you drink?

Casbah: I'm 20, 5'10, 126lbs. Was a late developer so have a very young complexion for my age. I get about 2500-3000 calories a day. I have milk several times a day. Diet for a day includes oats, milk, eggs, brown bread / pasta / rice, veg, fruit, chicken, tuna, post workout supplements, etc. The diet side of things is something I know I'm doing right. I get plenty of sleep too.

I started on 30kg squats (not including the bar which is only a standard, not Olympic) and added 5kg each workout until the 4th. The 4th workout I done 42.5kg, I added half the weight due to how 40kg felt in workout 3. If I started too heavy for squats, I have no doubt I've started too heavy for everything else too. The first set of squats at 30kg felt easy but it got hard very quick.

Mark Rippetoe: As a general rule, if you let go of an object and it falls, it weighs something, so we always count the bar. By "standard, not Olympic" what do you mean? How much does the bar weigh? Reading the rest of this, it is apparent to me that your form was bad the first day, that you do not eat 3000 cal/day, that you are not drinking a gallon of whole milk a day, that you do not eat red meat, and that you need to weigh 200 lbs. as soon as possible. Get busy.

Volume in SS

Stu: Should the total volume (i.e. warmup and work sets) in each successive workout always go up in SS? My total volume in workout one was 4450kg, but only 3960kg in workout three. Granted it's only been three workouts so far for me, and my work sets have all increased.

Mark Rippetoe: Volume in the sense of total tonnage is not the primary concern for the novice program in SSBBT. Volume goes up slowly as work set weights accumulate. Work set weight is the focus, and warmups will taper to facilitate better work sets as you get stronger, so tonnage might actually go down if you've been doing 5s all the way up.

Sit-ups on starting strength program

tiptop: I'm following your starting strength program which was recommended to me on various sites. My question concerns the type of abdominal assistance exercise advised on the program. It says to use the sit up on an incline board of 45 degrees. Is this exercise potentially damaging to the back and is it the best exercise to activate the abdominal muscles. I have no problem performing it, just want to know if its the best abs exercise or if there are other ones that can be used. I find the program excellent by the way and like the way the info is given in a clear manner with no bs.

Mark Rippetoe: I don't remember advocating a specific sit-up method, so you must have gotten this somewhere else, and you have therefore not read the book. Sit-ups on a board are no more damaging to the back than 400 lb. squats and 500 lb. deadlifts. In other words, if you can do them, you are strong enough to do them without **Damaging Your Back**. There is nothing wrong with using hip flexors in a sit-up, unless for some reason you have chosen to omit strengthening your hip flexors.

Squat Weight Progression

bigmike000: Mark, I just bought Starting Strength last week and began a few days ago on the program. I'm 5' 8" and around 142lbs. I know in the text you say people usually will add 10-15lbs to the squat per workout, but what if someone is only starting at 95-100lbs on the squat? I did my third workout with 105lbs (5lb progression) and it was beginning to get challenging with a 2 minute rest.

Mark Rippetoe: Then rest longer. Where in the hell did you come up with a 2 minute rest?? I believe I specifically state that you need to rest long enough to let the fatigue from the previous set dissipate. The idea is to do whatever you need to facilitate the increase in work set weight. This means that you are going to have to eat a lot more than you obviously have been, and rest long enough between sets to get all the reps of the next one.

SS workout length

cskolnick: How long do SS workouts tend to take and do they get longer as the trainee progresses (because of longer rest periods and more warm up sets)?

Mark Rippetoe: You should be spending between 45-90 min for a novice program, warmup to finish. Longer than that indicates socializing, shorter indicates something left out, usually rest between sets.

Texas Method

sci-muscle: I have almost 2 years of consistent barbell training under my belt and have been stalled for awhile. I want to try the Texas method to build strength on the slow-lifts (big 3 PLs), but I am not sure how to set it up. This is the best I can come up with, does it look effective and if not how would you fix it? *(3-day workout that omits cleans)*

Mark Rippetoe: Looks pretty close to me, save for the standard omission of cleans, which I guess I'd better get used to.

sci-muscle: I would love to do cleans, but I train at home and don't have bumper plates...is it safe to do them if I can't drop the bar? One idea I had is to front squat the bar down to the power rack and then reverse deadlift it from there...but that would be a major pain in the ass to do after every rep of course.

JMT: Your "if you're not squatting you're a pussy" argument seems to have driven people to squat more. Perhaps you could utilize a similar motivational tactic to get people to do power cleans.

Mark Rippetoe: Cleans should be done instead of RDLs in that sample program. They can be done without bumpers if you just catch them at the hang and then lower them to the floor, and that could be your RDL. How do you think we did them in the 1970s? I don't know why people are afraid to learn how to clean. Rows got subbed very early in the internet versions of the program, so I know there must be a visceral dislike for doing complicated explosive movements. But think about it: what does the modern health club industry teach? And where do most people train and learn about this shit? Is it any surprise that most people won't do what they are not allowed to do, and have been taught is unnecessary, dangerous, and unproductive?

Warm set rest periods

Cskolnick: For my warm ups, is the time spent adding plates to the bar between sets generally the amount of time I would want to spend between sets?

Mark Rippetoe: It would be for the first few, but as you get stronger and the work sets get very heavy, you need to rest more between both work sets and last warmups. Remember that warmups facilitate work sets – they should not interfere with them, because they are the whole point of the workout.

Lowering the weight after a power clean

howardw: I workout in my house so I don't want to drop my bumpers and therefore lower and catch the weight around the thigh after each rep and lower it to the floor from there. Is there a weight at which this becomes dangerous? And is there any physical benefit to catching the weight in this manner (just curious)?

Mark Rippetoe: This is the way it was done for decades, before God made bumper plates, and is one reason the old guys were stronger. The negative work is the other half of the stimulus that we have given up for the convenience of dropping the bar. Lower away.

Improving pull-ups on SS

bango skank: I'm getting my strength back up after a 2 month hiatus and using the orthodox Starting Strength model. I started with about 75% of my previous 5RMs and am not hitting old PR's until Week 6. I'm currently on Week 3. I'm 28, 5'8" and 150 lbs, last I checked. It's possible I'm heavier. I doubt I'm any older.

I want to improve my pull-up numbers (dead-hang, not kipping) while doing SS. My previous bw chin-up pr (~2 months ago) was 20 unbroken reps with full ROM. I'd still like to alternate deadlifts and power cleans every other workout, so basically I want to add them on as supplementary... well, actually, I already have: I've been doing 3 sets of bodyweight pull-ups, taken near or to failure, after Workout A, and 3 sets of bw chin-ups (near/to failure) after workout B. Everything else is the same, no additional ab work or anything. At the moment my 3 sets of pull/chin-up numbers are in the neighborhood of 12-7-5, with about 3 minutes rest taken between sets. I was planning on adding 10 lbs. once all three sets got up to 45 total reps (if they ever do). Would you change anything?

Mark Rippetoe: It may be a problem for recovery if you chin/pullup every day, especially at that light bodyweight. But it might work if you are eating enough to keep some bodyweight gain accumulating. Any reason why you're still this light after a previous go at the program?

bango skank: Well, when I first started I weighted about 140 and I got up to 170 on SS including a fair amount of bodyfat, then I got down to a lean 155 and stayed around there. I'm currently eating pretty generously. I guess the subtextual question is; will SS alone improve my pull-up numbers? Need I even add in specific pull-up work? And if so, to what effect?

Mark Rippetoe: You need to do pullups/chinups if you want them to improve, yes. They have to be specifically worked. Your bodyweight is, of course, your business. But I am 52, 5'8", 215, and have recently done 19 dead-hang chins. My point is that it is possible to be good at chinups at a heavier bodyweight that facilitates a more efficient squat, press, and deadlift.

Press/bench's sensitivity to weight change

Stu: I recall you mentioning in an earlier post that presses are more sensitive to bodyweight changes than other lifts. I've found once again than my presses seem to be stalling, while my other lifts are not. I assume that if I'm resting enough to keep gaining on the squat, dead and clean, that I'm also adequately rested for the presses. Would it then be most likely that I'm not eating enough?

Mark Rippetoe: Not necessarily, because the press is also the hardest of the main lifts to improve because of the size and number of the muscles that constitute the prime movers of the lift. For this reason the jumps for the press are smaller than for the other lifts, and progress usually stalls there first. This also means that microloading the press is more important than for the other lifts.

New lifters

casbah: As a new lifter last year I started SS and like many others had crap squat form. Thanks to getting misinformation on the bb forum I started adding weight and ended up with bad knees and back. I posted on here asking for advice but it was too late, I had already f*cked things up. I studied the descriptions in the book over and over yet still didn't understand the concepts of a proper squat. You'll have something humorous to say, but I am an intelligent lad and yet no studying could translate into proper form without the guidance of a skilled trainer. It just isn't that simple when you don't know how, when you have no experience and you really don't understand the exercise or lifting in a general sense.

I think realistically, months are needed to study and learn a safe squat. Then an additional month just for form adjustments. After all that is what's most important, right? Yet clearly hardly anyone is aware of this at the beginning and therefore go through long stages of lifting with bad form picking up bad habits along the way.

Mark, how dangerous do you see lifting beginners squatting with no PT or expert guidance at the gym? I've watched countless videos on here and most of them have the same old issues; sliding knees, looking up, butt tucking etc. It seems very few beginners can get sufficient understanding of the physical requirements of the squat in the early stages of their lifting career, putting them in danger. Thoughts?

Mark Rippetoe: My thoughts are that for many years I have successfully shown many people how to squat correctly the first time I worked with them, that I do this with 25+ people at our Basic Barbell seminars, and that my book quite thoroughly explains the basics of correct form and has enabled lots of people to pick it up by themselves in far less time than you seem to think is necessary. All these people can squat with significant weight almost immediately, and therefore begin to get strong that day. The process you are describing sounds more like Tai Chi than barbell training, and – being polite here – I would dispute the necessity of the timeline you advocate.

Understanding assistance exercises

sdds: My question is how assistance / ancillary exercises tie in for say a bodybuilder. I mean looking at the average trainee split it's mainly just a bunch of assistance exercises rammed together with the exception of bench. A bodybuilder needs the 'main lifts' I guess because this is what drives the progression. The assistance exercises complement by adding workload/strengthening - fixing a week point for a lifter / refining a bodypart for the bber. So for someone like me adding assistance work is pointless because everything is weak and I need general training.

Also from a general strength training perspective what makes a complete lift, e.g. why is the barbell row an assistance exercise and the bench press a complete exercise?

Mark Rippetoe: The word "bodybuilding" immediately makes me stop paying attention to most questions, but your assessment is correct about the use of assistance exercises in that particular activity and how they relate to people who actually train. Your question about rows vs. bench is interesting. The BB row is an assistance exercise because it doesn't train anything that can't be done with other exercises, while the bench press trains upper body strength in a way that no other exercise does, and makes a significant contribution to upper body strength.

---

2 Q's: Grip width on Bench; small plates on DL

Drewfasa: 1) In SS (p.80) you recommend a bench press grip between 22-28 inches wide at the index fingers. I understand that the scoring is 32" apart on a power standard bar. I had been used to gripping the bar with index fingers around this scoring - I was uncoached and this felt comfortable. Having just finished SS 1st ed. (2nd ed. is on the way over the Atlantic right now) tonight I adjusted my bench press, including narrowing the grip so as to keep my entire hands about 1" inside the scoring. This feels 'weird' and a bit wobbly.

Are my shoulders wide enough to warrant my earlier grip? (32" between index fingers) I measured my shoulders and they are 21" measured across the chest from the widest points. Or is my discomfort simply the result of bad habit?

2) My university gym is rather pitiful and doesn't have Olympic discs. I believe the 20KG plates are Olympic standard, but the rest are smaller depending upon weight. Having last week deadlifted 170kg with what I know now is terrible form, I know find that I cannot quite DL 60kg without losing lower back position when using proper form (or at least, more proper). This means I have to use the smaller 10kg plates for deadlifts, and cleans. Am I better off just bending lower to start properly, from the floor (because of the shorter plates)? Or should I compensate by not setting the weight down but stopping a few inches short? Should I just man up and start with 60kg and hope my form will improve as the weeks pass? Or is there a solution I haven't thought of?

Mark Rippetoe: 1. I'm 19" in that dimension, and I use a grip about 27". Try using your little finger on the score mark. That should be wide enough for a behemoth such as yourself.

2. I find it hard to believe that a 170kg bad deadlift is so bad that 60kg is your new work set weight. What is wrong with your form that lowering the plate height would not make worse? The vast majority of people having DL form problems are not flexible enough to get in a good extended lumbar position, and lowering the plate diameter would make this worse. Stopping short on the way back down just keeps the problem from getting solved. You just have to stretch out your hamstrings, fight your back into a good position, and make your form better with the equipment you'll be using from now on in every gym you train in, the standard diameter 20kg plates.

Absolute Novice Needing Advice

gannimal007: I'm a 34 y/o complete novice to strength training. I'm 6-1, 203 lbs, 34 y/o (20% BF) and have read SS. I have been through 4 workouts (5th Wed. Morning) and after reading hundreds of threads here I need to change some things and need help.

1 - I am failing on the 3rd or 4th rep already on BP and SP, sometimes in the 1st set (BP - 125 lbs, SP - 95 lbs). Should I continue at that weight until I hit all of the reps or drop a few pounds and reset?

2 - I have soreness in quads - probably due to leg pressing instead of squatting them b/c of knees forward, ass not back, etc ... I'll fix it.

I began at 165 lbs and have progressed to 195 but was failing yesterday and couldn't get past 3 or 4 reps in all of my squat sets - should I start over w/ correct squats at a lower weight?

3 - I read in another post that many male novices at your facility begin at 105 lbs on the squat - did I start entirely too heavy on all my lifts?
Starting weights ...
BS - 165 (failed at 195 last wo)
SP - 85 (failed at 95 last wo)
BP - 115 (failed at 125 last wo)
DL - 245 (succeeded 265 last wo)
Clean - 95 (succeeded at 115 last wo)

Mark Rippetoe: I think that all your problems are the cause of starting too heavy and accepting less-than-adequate technique on your work sets as a result. The 3 sets have to be done with absolutely correct technique, especially at first, or any subsequent increase will be building on an inadequately prepared base. You CANNOT be at failure intensity your first weeks on this program if you have chosen your weights correctly. Reread the programming part and start over before you fuck something up that cannot be unfucked later.

How to know what jump to use doing simple progression?

Ganondorf: In your simple progression advice in PPST you recommend making jumps of 10-15lbs. for squats, 15-20 lbs. for deadlifts, and bench presses, overhead presses and cleans 5-10 lbs. per workout. I started lifting again for the third time about 3 months ago. I lifted for 4 weeks, took a week off, 4 weeks then took another week off. These workouts consisted of 3x15 lunges and DB squats (holding dumbbell on chest). Then I followed the SS program verbatim for about a week and a half before I had an issue and couldn't train except with the bar for a week. I started back SS again, and my 6th workout will be Saturday.

Before I stopped SS I felt that I could move up 10-15 lbs. on the 3x5 squat weight; it did not feel heavy enough. When I came back, I only got 2 reps on the last set at that weight. Next two workouts I did the weight for all the reps. Workout after that, went up 10 lbs. and then the workout after that another 10.

Should I keep moving it up by 10 until I can't get all the reps on the last set, and then add another set of 5 at 10-20 lbs. less weight to get the volume in? Or would it be better to at some point, I guess going off how I feel, start tapering the increases down so I always get all reps in a set? I wonder about the second option as going by how you "feel" doesn't always seem to be useful in defining your limits.

Mark Rippetoe: You should do the program as written. You should carefully plan your increases so that you always – and for a long as possible – get all the reps in all three sets across. This is how long-term progress is accomplished. "Feeling" is untrustworthy for a novice, because it is not based on experience. Stick to the program, grow stronger, and you'll eventually develop the judgment to vary the program. But not now. Just do it as written.

Progress

maritime: I am doing the program by the book and drinking as much milk as possible (sometimes 1 gallon, sometimes less. stomach does not like it so much.)

12/11/08 6'4" 198.2 lbs ~17% bodyfat
12/26/08 209.8 lbs

Squats 115 lbs > 160 lbs
Bench 80 lbs > 125 lbs
Dead 170 lbs > 245 lbs

Press 75 lbs > 85 lbs
Clean 45 lbs > 95 lbs

The last 3 days of squats I have done 2X5 and then failed on the last set on rep #4 and had to dump. I have still been going up 5 lbs each workout though... I think i might need more rest time between sets. Deadlifts are going up strong, bench is going up strong, cleans are getting better, I am working on technique. Muscle is going up, but bodyfat is definitely going up as well.

Mark Rippetoe: If you have been doing the program, you have had time to do about 7 workouts since you started. The last three of them you have failed to get all of your work sets. I would submit that failing to do all of the work sets on what is essentially half of your training is NOT DOING THE PROGRAM. Something is wrong, whether increases or rest time or form. Fix it.

Training volume and dieting

sdds: I wish to drop some of the fat gained over the last few months so have reduced my calorie intake and added a little cardio, as one does. I realize by doing this I am reducing my recovery and ability to put weight on the bar. My squats seem to be the most affected exercise so far with deadlifts next in line.

My question is (I don't want to mess with the plan still being a novice) should training volume reduce at a time like this when an athlete wishes to drop bodyfat?
Would stepping back for 6 weeks help in maintaining or allowing slow progress in my lifts, would you just reduce work sets? I don't really have any experience of dieting with a strength programme.

Mark Rippetoe: You can either moderate your volume, a requirement if your diet is not supporting your training load adequately, or you can reevaluate your desire to drop bodyfat at this point in your training progression. I would submit that if you are making good progress on your strength with a linear progression, and that since you know this pace of progress will eventually slow, that this might not be the best time to alter the program. Fat is easy to take off, easier than strength is to gain. Do it later.

Power Clean versus Snatch

Brandon E: I would assume that you include the power clean in the program instead of the snatch because of technique concerns. Would you recommend someone with exposure to Oly lifts and is following the program simply to increase their numbers to sub snatches for the clean? Or do you think a certain weight should be hit first, i.e. being able to perform a body weight power clean before advancing?

Mark Rippetoe: I wouldn't sub them completely, since if you do you don't get to clean. Just alternate them.

Draco: Yes, this is my question too. I want to learn power snatches at some point down the road, but how strong should my power clean be before I consider them? Like Brandon suggested, is being able to clean one's bodyweight a good marker?

Mark Rippetoe: There is nothing about snatches that requires that you be able to clean any particular weight before you learn them. How do you think junior Olympic weightlifters start?

Definition of "failure" w/ chin-up's & pull-up's

Stevo: Per your coaching, I now do chin-up's & pull-up's using the full ROM. With the rumblings in previous posts, there was talk about how to program exercises using "bodyweight" & going to "failure". Is "failure" defined as a) starting at the bottom & not being able to go up at all or b) just not being able to clear the chin above the bar or c) your shoulders becoming dislocated?

Mark Rippetoe: "Failure" means not getting your chin over the bar. Now, this doesn't mean that you get to raise your chin up to the level of your eyes by tilting your neck back. You have to keep your neck in normal anatomical position when you chin too.

Plate size on deadlift

Volador: I've recently been thinking about this: My gym has two types of 20kg plates; one variety is thicker and smaller in diameter and the other one, the opposite. I'd say, approximately, the smaller ones measure 12" in diameter and are measured in kilograms, and the bigger ones are 16" and are measured in lbs (45). I had never thought about this until I read the deadlift chapter in SS and saw it mentions specifically the importance of the starting height of the bar on a deadlift. I really don't know which of these two are of the standard measure you mention. I've been using the smaller ones, just because, but I suppose I could lift more weight with the bigger ones. Do you recommend any plate type in particular between these two?

Mark Rippetoe: Standard plate diameter for both barbell sports is 45 cm or 17 11/16". Make your plans accordingly.

Starting strength for "Starting Strength"

tonester: Just wondering what is the initial status of the young trainees you deal with. Do they come to you with some semblance of exposure to physical activity? Do they come to you straight off the couch and Playstation? The reason I ask is because I tend to steer raw beginners towards developing strength and stability with bodyweight work before loading them. Your take on this would be appreciated (as well as educational for me).

Mark Rippetoe: I have started very young underweight kids with the same program I use in the book. The advantage to barbell training over bodyweight training is that barbell training intensity is almost infinitely scalable, and bodyweight training is not. Squats are usually within the ability of most people, but I have trained many overweight people who could not do an air squat and who had to be started on a leg press machine. Most everyone can manage a deadlift with some weight. Lots of people can't do pushups – everybody can bench press and press *something*.

Best way to progress?

banderbe: Is it better to continue from workout to workout using the same amount of weight increment for a given exercise until you miss reps and then reset, or would it be better to anticipate failure by noting when the weight gets very heavy and you barely get the last rep, and drop the weight increment down for that exercise at the next workout? I don't believe this is covered in BBT but my apologies in advance if it is.

Mark Rippetoe: It's not mentioned specifically, but you can do it either way. If you're sharp enough to know that the next 10 lb. jump is not going to go, use 5. If that was ridiculously easy, you were wrong but you're not stuck.

Been lifting for 3 years-SS?

Trojan50: I have been training for several years now and I've run numerous cycles of 5x5 and other bodybuilding (worthless) programs. I even tried SS a couple of years back, but was too stubborn to think I could get some size gains in that rep range.

With that said my numbers flat out suck, and I would like to change that.
Bench-195
Squat-250
Deadlift-315

I'm 5ft 7, 170, at roughly 15% bodyfat and I know I need to get stronger in the big 3 if I ever want to have a solid muscular build. Even though I've had a few years of training do you feel I could still benefit from Starting Strength? I'm sure you're sick of hearing this, but I'm also an endomorph at 15% and I don't really want to gain a lot of fat (which is what would happen if I drank 1 gallon of milk a day).

Mark Rippetoe: The thing I'm sick of hearing is that you want to gain muscular bodyweight, you know the program works to that end for everybody that's tried it, yet you think that your need for a svelte waistline supersedes the correct application of the program. Boys, fat is just not that hard to lose, while muscle mass is damned hard to gain. Bodybuilders 30 years ago all knew this, and incorporated it into their training year, at least until it became more important to be available year-round for photo sessions; this is when exogenous hormones became so important.

If you've trained for a few years but never done a linear strength progression, it has the potential to work for you for several months. I've said here before that a linear progression is always your default training mode, even if you are advanced and coming back off a layoff.

Deadlift frequency and DL/Squat ratio

David: I'm a little confused as to how the DL should keep pace with squats using SS if DL and PCs are alternated (e.g. the Onus Wunsler workout). For a two week period, a trainee squats six times and at best deadlifts twice. If we assume a 20 lb increase/session for DL and a 10 lb increase/ session for Squats, this leaves a total increase over two weeks of 40 lbs for DL and 60 lbs for Squats. How is it that deadlift should remain stronger than squats over a period of months (years)? Are my increases per workout off?

Mark Rippetoe: You are assuming that the DL and the squat started off at the same weight, and that would be incorrect. The deadlift for everyone I've ever trained is always about 1.5 to twice as strong as the squat at first, so the squat needs to catch up anyway.

Connor Mc: In line with that, for the average trainee (say, intermediate), what relationship do you tend to find between them? (How much stronger does DL continue to be than the squat, I mean.)

Mark Rippetoe: Remember that linear increases slow by 6 months or so for most people, and for essentially everybody in 9 months, so by the time linear increases for the squat have stopped and the deadlift has slowed too, the squat will have approached the deadlift. And most normally proportioned people that have no grip problems and train the deadlift effectively will always pull a little more than they squat without a suit and wraps.

Benching without spotters

tscw1: I'm coming to the point where my bench press is about to hit the limit and although it's not at a weight where my arms will snap and drop the bar on myself, eventually I will be unable to finish my sets. The issue is I have no spotter, so if I do get stuck I'll have to roll the bar down me, which would be unfortunate, painful and a touch embarrassing. Do you think I should switch to dumbbells which I could just drop to the floor if I get stuck, but is harder to get in position to bench press?

Mark Rippetoe: You can avoid being stuck on the bench by learning how to gauge whether or not your next rep will go. This requires that you be conservative but observant. BUT, if you train by yourself and there is the slightest danger that you could get stuck, NEVER COLLAR THE BAR. This way you can always dump one side off and get it off of you before darkness closes in for the last time. This is very important: the bench press is where virtually all of the fatalities associated with weight room activity occur, usually guys training alone that get a crush injury or suffocation. So, **TAKE THE COLLARS OFF THE BAR IF THERE'S ANY DANGER AT ALL OF GETTING STUCK UNDER THE BENCH PRESS**.

Texas method and bodybuilding body

hockmasm: Most of what you preach is for strength training. Your PP book talks about doing sets of 10 reps for hypertrophy and is geared for bodybuilders. What if that is what I want to do as opposed to strength? Look like a bodybuilder? Will the Texas method or Bill Starr method work to do that? Even if they use sets of 5?

Mark Rippetoe: If you want to look like a bodybuilder, that's fine with me. That is a matter for you to discuss with your God and your psychologist. But even a bodybuilder is a novice strength trainee until he's an intermediate. The fastest way to gain muscular bodyweight – the supposed goal of a bodybuilder – is with a linear progression on the basic barbell exercises. And 5s are the way this progression works best.

New old kid

one_one_six: I am a 79 year old male. 5'10", 195 lbs. about 27-30% fat and very out of shape. Cleared by doctor to begin Starting Strength. I will be working at home, with a non-Olympic barbell (15 pounds)and about 130 lbs in plates, no cage, no bench; no room for them in condo. In future possibility of joining YMCA where would be available.

Plan is to do the SS routine, squat or deadlift, bench (with dumbbells), press, and bent row (don't really follow the procedure for the clean - plus I am on second floor and don't feel jumping would be acceptable). Starting at very low weights (dumbbells 20 lbs, bar 25 lbs) and slowly work my way up, aiming for say 145 DL, , squat with whatever I feel comfortable with sans any way to get on my back other than lift it up (65-75?), db bench maybe 50, press maybe 75 and bent row 145. Did some searching for info on seniors, over 60s, 70s, couldn't find anything. Do you think this is a good plan?

Mark Rippetoe: I'd strongly encourage you to change your situation to one of adequate equipment, for safety and program effectiveness. Specifically, if you don't have a squat rack and plan on getting all your weights overhead, you are eventually going to hurt yourself, not to mention the fact that a linear increase in load will become quickly unmanageable and progress will stop.

one_one_six: Thanks for your input Mark. Re-joined the YMCA today *before* reading your post. Y has the benches, cages, etc., should be good to go. The plan is to go very, very light, so much that if I were 50-60 years younger I would be laughed at. Expect some of the younger guys will take pity on me and bail me out if I get in trouble.

Mark Rippetoe: Fuck those younger kids. You'll be fine.

Too out of shape for Starting Strength?

RVD: I guess I'll start with my stats first. I'm 33 years old, 5 foot 7 inches, and 223 pounds. My waist is about 40-41 inches. I estimate I should really lose approximately 40 pounds of fat. Not too strong for my size. I can Bench about 150lbs. x 10-12 reps. Best Squat was 13 x 170lbs. (no belt).

Anyhow, I think my problem is that my work capacity is just terrible. For instance, I could start the routine in Starting Strength with about half the weight I am capable of using, and I wouldn't last more than a week! I've even had problems with routines that were very similar to yours, but only 2 days per week. I would start light and try to be conservative with my poundage increases. And yet, I would burn out within about 3-4 weeks. When I say "burn out", I mean headaches, dizziness, loss of appetite, can't sleep well, etc. I've literally been through this several times now, and didn't really get anywhere, didn't even get a chance to lift heavy. Please don't get me wrong. I can certainly push myself very hard, but it was always on a routine that was very low volume/frequency (like 1 set per exercise, training less than 2x per week).

My question is, other than trying to ease my way into the Starting Strength routine with ultra light weights, is there something that I could do to bring myself up to speed? Someone even suggested that I should forget about lifting weights for 2-3 months, and focus exclusively on cardio. I have access to plenty of cardio equipment at my gym, and I can also run/walk if you need me to. Although, I would like to keep lifting if possible. So, what would you suggest?

Mark Rippetoe: There exists a weight at which you can start each of the exercises in the program, although they may be very light. And there also exists an increment by which each of those weights can be increased each workout, although it may be very small. But the laws of physiology apply to you just like they do to everybody else. You will adapt to stress applied in a linear progression, and it may take longer than for other people but it will occur. The only reason it would not occur is the presence of a profound metabolic disorder like uncontrolled diabetes or muscular dystrophy. The only reason it would occur more slowly than for others is the presence of profoundly terrible genetics, or a failure on your part to eat and rest correctly. Other than that, get busy.

Form limitations on strength?

rmscott_75077: I've been lifting for a long time (over 10 years). My results are pitiful for the amount of time I've put into it. Anyway, if it matters any I'm 42, 6' 1", 215lbs about 25% body fat (24 hour fitness measurement). One more thing, my arms are a bit short for my height. I've decided to follow the beginner program. It seems all these years, my squat form has been wrong (well way off). It seems a bit difficult to correct some of these learned patterns. I seem to be limited by flexibility, lower back, and hips. I'm using less than half the weight I used to. I'm really concentrating now on proper form with lower weights.

So my question is, how long does it usually take to start getting weights up higher for someone in my circumstance? How long can I expect to retrain myself to use proper form on squats? Deadlifts, I am using very little weight. I actually have never done them before and really have to think a lot about my form. Right now, I'm deadlifting less than my bench to try to get my form down.

Mark Rippetoe: Your progress will follow a linear trend for a shorter time than a true novice, but it will nonetheless progress faster if you stick with a linear progression. This is because you have previously just fucked around, and now you are actually training, working hard over a full ROM with increasingly heavy weights that force an adaptation where there has been no adaptation before. I don't know how long this process will continue since it depends on many factors, not all of which you control. I see no point in babying your deadlift either; if your form is correct, just train it normally as the program calls for and let it get strong so that your back strength will improve along with your squat.

And your gym is typical of most commercial clubs. You'll eventually outgrow it.

rmscott_75077: I finished my 3rd week. On the squats I'm starting to feel much more natural. My old training partner looks at me a bit funny. I used to do about 315 20 times, but at least 8 inches higher, now I'm doing 175 all the way down with 5 reps but good form. I'll keep adding the prescribed weight each workout. My deadlift still feels a little hard at the bottom hitting the form right. I'm also finding more concentration required on the descent.

Dumb question after the working set, is it okay to lower the weight to the bar and keep practicing the form for a couple more sets? I find myself becoming fanatical and practicing my deadlift and squat form a couple times a day with no weight at my desk.

Mark Rippetoe: If you get dependent on backoff sets for perfecting your form, when will you get correct form on your work sets? I'd discipline myself by making my work sets the best sets, with no opportunity to do them better at lighter weight.

Elbow Pain

Notorious: I started having elbow problems from squatting a little more than a week ago. I wasn't really paying attention to my wrist and elbow position, and as it turns out, they were way off. I'm now squatting thumbless, with a much wider grip, and making sure that my wrists are straight. 2 days ago, I had a relatively pain free workout, but today my elbows were killing me during the workout. I made sure my wrists were straight -- there was no pressure on my wrists, so I'm not sure what went wrong. Pressing movements were also painful (I attempted both). However, I have a feeling they would be fine if my elbows weren't first aggravated from squats.
So what do you suggest I do if the pain continues? Obviously load up on ibuprofen, but should I work through the pain or work around the pain? I'm pretty sure I can do front squats with no pain, so I'm considering just switching to those until the pain subsides.

Mark Rippetoe: You're probably carrying the elbows too low. Raise them so that they are not under the bar holding up the weight. But there's another problem here, one that runs through lots of posts on this board: where did you people get the idea that nothing was supposed to hurt when you train?

Notorious: Haha, so I take it from your response that if the pain continues, I train through the pain as opposed to the front squat option? I should also mention that I'm pretty sure it's mild tendonitis, since it also hurts outside of workouts occasionally (but you probably already knew that).

Mark Rippetoe: When something hurts when you're doing a core exercise, you just stop doing it? No, you fix what's wrong with it, because it's important enough an exercise to be one of the 5 we do.

Power cleans and missing thumb-skin

Drewfasa: I was wondering if you have any home-remedies for the wear and tear that occurs to the thumbs with heavy power-cleans? When I do my 8x3 PC workouts the skin between the webbing and knuckle of my thumbs gets completely scraped off and ends up tucked under my thumb-pads and I get blood everywhere. I'm using chalk, which is also good for soaking up the blood and pus, but the irritation is interfering with my last few sets.

Mark Rippetoe: This is why God made athletic tape.

Squat and Power Clean

jicjac: 1. When squatting, should the out-spreading of the knees occur during the descent or right as you near the hole?

2. When performing the power clean, during the jump portion, if the bar is "banged" by the thighs during hip/knee extension doesn't this propel the bar away from the body and therefore make it harder to keep near your torso during the shrug phase?

Mark Rippetoe: 1. It should occur from the top down, but it is often useful to think about it at the bottom if depth or rebound are your problems.

2. Not if you learn the clean from the top using the jump. The bar touches your thighs as an artifact of the re-bending of the knee, and the cue to "Bang" your thighs against the bar is useful *after* it has been learned well enough that the bar is going up strongly already. What actually occurs is that the shrug counters any forward momentum that may be imparted to the bar by the bang against the thighs, and this forward force is minimal due to the fact that the jump is directed upward.

Recommended speed of SS repetitions?

rmscott_75077: What is your recommended speed for each repetition (squat, bench, press, deadlift)? Should it be slower for beginners learning the correct form and faster for intermediate to advanced lifters? Or does it matter at all? I'm currently doing slow on the downward movement of squats, but thinking about the ascent. I go faster on the ascent.

I hear you must train fast to be fast type of stuff. Just curious on your take, I'm sorry if this has been answered before I didn't see it when looking over the book or by the search function, but it may be previously covered.

Mark Rippetoe: Movement speed in the slow lifts should be controlled and slow until they are learned well and being executed with good technique. Then they should be done as explosively as good form at 5RM weight will permit – slower on the way down and fast on the way up – to maximize motor unit recruitment and power production. Cleans obviously are always fast.

Use a belt or keep going?

Sawol: I'm up to 335x5 on deadlifts but I haven't put on a belt yet. My work sets don't feel particularly difficult, especially when I warm up properly and apply the Valsalva maneuver, but I do usually feel soreness in my lower back for about a few hours after the session. Many people, especially my friends and people at bb.com, say to put on a belt, but isn't it better for my strength to deadlift without one?

Mark Rippetoe: No, a belt is a damned useful tool if you are judicious about its use. You can make a harder ab contraction against a belt than you can without one, and it allows you to safely lift more weight than you can without it. I'd use it if I were you.

A few questions, Coach

fisch: 1. When I squat, my lower back rounds right before I hit parallel. Should I just do some stretching for a while to stop this? I hurt my lower back because of this, so I'm taking a week off and I am kind of nervous to start back up with weights with a rounded back, and was wondering what you would recommend I do to fix this problem.

2. I did get 3 weeks in, but after bumping my lifts up 5 pounds every workout, I couldn't increase the weight for 2 workouts for the bench and the press. (I only have 2.5 lb plates) I don't think I should be stalling so early, so from your experience, do you know what would be causing this? I think I should be still progressing every workout, since my numbers are pretty low. (125 lb 5 RM bench, 75 lb press)

3. If I bought squat shoes, would it be best to only wear them for squats and get another shoe for the other lifts?

Mark Rippetoe: 1. This is usually due to your knees not being shoved out of the way at the bottom. The thighs will block your trunk drop at the bottom if you don't shove your knees out. This is sometimes related to hamstring and adductor flexibility, but usually you can just jam your knees out laterally at the bottom and fix it immediately.

2. Jesus Christ Jumping Up And Down On A Stolen Pogo Stick. It is being caused by your failure to get some small plates, as has been pointed out about *3 million times*.

3. How many other lifts are you planning on doing that don't involve your standing on the floor with a bar somewhere on your body? Yes, you may change your shoes when you bench, although it seems odd to regard this as worthy of an answer on this highly respected – and I might add, busy – forum.

Should I be tired on rest days?

Kyle5000: I've been doing the novice program for a few weeks now, and I'm seeing progress in all of the lifts. I've been going up in 5 lb increments every workout on Press and Bench. I'm doing deadlift every third workout and though I've only deadlifted 3 times, I've gone up 20 lbs each time. I had a minor setback with my squats with a quad injury, but that's gone now and I feel a lot better about my squat form, and I'm increasing that 10 lbs every workout. I've gained about 5 pounds, and I'm still able to do more pull ups and chins each workout. I'm going to try power clean for the first time tomorrow I think.

Thing is, I don't feel tired or sore at all on my rest days. I want to go to the gym. Does this mean I'm not working hard enough when I am at the gym? I feel like I could deadlift more often. It sucks only doing it once a week. I'm 22 years old, 5'8", and 170 lbs. One other question that doesn't deserve a separate thread: At my height and weight, should I be doing GOMAD? I've been drinking slightly less than a gallon a day of 2% so far. I have a little bit of a gut and I'd love to stay at the same weight but cut that down.

Mark Rippetoe: At your age, you should be able to recover well enough that you might very well not be tired on rest days. Enjoy this while it lasts. Perceptions of fatigue are not always useful for planning one's training – it's like the "pump" that physiquers like so much, and may not tell you a damn thing. The only thing that counts right now is that your strength is increasing in a linear manner.

More weight each workout = you getting stronger.

The thing that will ruin your progress is your (hopefully) latent preoccupation with your gut. If I were you – and I wish I was – I'd quit worrying about this silly aesthetic shit and enjoy the fact that you are now making the fastest gains in strength you will ever make in your entire training career. So yes, drink the GOMAD. The gut can be taken off later.

Legs

poiuytrewq: I have been doing the SS program for 2.5 weeks now and I have been pretty steadily upping weight each workout. My legs have definitely grown and I am going to have to buy some new pants because they're all really tight in the thigh area now. However, I haven't really noticed much change as far as upper body goes. Is it normal for legs to quickly get larger and upper body to lag behind like this?

Mark Rippetoe: Of course it is, since the leg muscles are larger to start with and thus have greater growth potential.

Learning the hook grip

stronger: I've decided to start using a hook grip to see if it helped my deadlift at all. I have a hunch that it's affecting my ability to gain in the lift. I tried it yesterday and it seemed to work pretty well. I am right handed, so my right handed hook felt a lot better (it was double overhand to try and get my strength up). Is this typical to have a non-dominant hand's hook feel a bit off? I've looked in SS:BBT and your hands don't look incredibly large, rather similar to mine. Can you make an effective hook?

Mark Rippetoe: I actually have large hands and can make a good hook. But I do not feel the difference between my dexterous and non-dexterous hands in the hook. I assume you are using a double-overhand hook as opposed to an alternate hook.

JLascek: Should it be standard to deadlift with the hook grip? Does that hold true when you use the alternating grip?

Mark Rippetoe: The standard grip has traditionally been an unhooked alternate grip, because the hook hurts enough at heavy deadlift-level weights that it can be a distraction. This may be because a heavy deadlift takes about 8 times longer than a heavy clean to do. But many lifters have used the hook grip, the alternate hook grip, and the monkey grip for heavy deadlifts. Do what works for you.

Win: What is the monkey grip?

jacob cloud: Rip, did you use the hook during meets?

Mark Rippetoe: I did not hook at a meet, because I never had grip problems. I can still double-overhand 405. A monkey grip is where the bar rides down in the fingers below the level of the thumb, either double-overhand or alternate. Gives you about an inch you don't have to pull.

Routine for 30+ Lifter

ruzg: What routine (or rough guideline) would you recommend for a 33 yr old lifter interested primarily in improving the squat & deadlift while maintaining bench & press?
5'9-170lbs
squat 5RM - 175lbs, deadlift 5RM - 225lbs, bench 5RM - 195 lbs, press 5RM - 140lbs
Been going between SStrength and Texas periodization - for a year - gains have stalled.

Mark Rippetoe: These numbers at your bodyweight indicate either a testosterone deficiency or an incorrectly followed novice progression.

Ruzg: Some of it may have to do with the fact I had never squatted prior to doing SS, also I have not been regular for more than 1 month at a time because of work travel. But the squat and dl numbers are alarmingly low I agree. My bench actually peaked at 225 1RM and dl peaked at 255 2 RM. Squat has always been abysmally weak. Perhaps an imbalance that requires preparatory work which I have never done - not sure what prep work to do actually or how to get "diagnosed" - as for the test deficiency, recent blood tests returned normal levels.

Mark Rippetoe: The preparatory work necessary would be your Novice Progression. Let's see: 5 lbs. per workout x 3 workouts per week = 15 lbs. per week. Then, 52 weeks per year x 15 lbs. per week = 780 lbs.!!!!! My god, *this didn't happen* now, did it?? In fact, no part of it happened at all, right? Had you done your Novice Progression with 1 lb. jumps per workout for a year like you said you did, had you started with the 45 lb. bar you would still be 26 lbs. stronger than you are now.

Your testosterone may be normal, but you seem to have wasted it. My diagnosis is that you have not followed the program.

Light touch to box

38SS: Is it OK to squat down to a light touch on a box simply to confirm proper squat depth? Specifically, I tend to struggle being consistent with the depth of my squats. One set I go too deep, the next slightly too high.

I don't remember where I picked up from but I find that if I do my squats over a small cardboard box about 12 inches high, go just go down to a light touch, it solves my consistency problems. I hit just below parallel every time. Instead of worrying depth I can focus on hip drive, etc. With good timing, I really don't have a pause at the bottom. Horrible thing to do?

Mark Rippetoe: If you get in the habit of feeling for the box, you will never learn to feel for the bottom of the squat.

KSC: I sometimes use a band across the bottom of the rack or a Dynamax med. ball but not for too long. People tend to relax a bit at the bottom of the squat when they are reaching for an object instead of rebounding against the tension in their hamstrings. This sometimes causes the knees to get shoved forward and also slows down progression to heavier weights.

Mark Rippetoe: KSC, as usual, is dead on the money. The "bottom" is felt when everything in the posterior chain gets tight and the rebound occurs. If you have done everything correctly – knees out, ass back, back angle correct – you will feel it at the bottom and know you're there. If you lose tension in the hamstrings, your knees have dropped forward and probably in.

Expectations For Overweight Individuals

jwm79: Have you ever trained extremely large (300 +) people on SS? I am starting the program. I have bought a bench and Olympic weights and plan on buying your book and a squat rack in the next couple of weeks. You recommended The Zone diet, so I'll also be doing that. At 1800 calories a day, can I expect to stall out pretty quickly being in a caloric deficit? Is it still possible to build some muscle and get stronger? Were you a hard gainer as a beginner? Thanks for your time.

Mark Rippetoe: So you're not doing the program yet. You're going to wait a couple of weeks for your equipment and book to come in, and you want to know stuff about what will happen without actually doing it to see for yourself. You figured you'd wait until conditions were perfect to do this thing. This pattern of behavior didn't just start recently, did it?

Gordon Bombay: What, planning ahead and strategizing? Bit harsh perhaps Mark? Maybe I'm missing something...

jwm79: Point taken. Do the fuckin' program.

Mark Rippetoe: Yes you are, Gordon. But jwm is not.

How long a pause between squat reps?

JohnFraz: The title pretty much says it all, but how long is too long to stop and breathe? Or is there no such thing as too long a pause, if it helps get that next rep?

Mark Rippetoe: It varies with the length of the set. 5s or fewer get a breath between reps to reset. Longer sets might take 2 breaths. During the last few reps of a true 20RM squat, just do what Jesus tells you to do.

Ryan: I always aim for a maximum of 2 breaths on my last rep of five. And one breath for the previous reps. There is no science in it, but if I plan how many breaths I take, it stops me being a pussy and taking too long.

Mark Rippetoe: Good point: breathing can be used to actually time the set and enforce your rhythm.

JohnFraz: Dang, I think I just lost a few pounds off my 5 RM.

Mark Rippetoe: Howzat?

JohnFraz: Because I was taking a lot more than one breath between reps ... being strict on that will give me an honest, but probably lower, 5 RM ...

Oh well, had to deload anyway.

Mark Rippetoe: No, no, no, things aren't this simple. There is never an absolute answer to everything, except of course that you have to do your squats. If you are working with enough weight that you need multiple breaths to get each rep, take them, but don't just stand there and pray that the next rep will be easier. If you need 2 or 3 between, take them. A novice should only be using one breath between, and I assumed that a question like this would come from a novice. My mistake.

JohnFraz: Thanks, Coach -- will keep the "stand there and pray" limit in mind during my sets as I work up again this time.

Ryan: Is there a difference between the breathing patterns you should use for squats, and the one you should use for deadlifts? The way I see it, is that whilst in between squat reps, you are still holding a heavy weight on your back. In between deadlift sets you do not get this benefit. Is there a line between a set of 5, and 5 consecutive singles?

Mark Rippetoe: You'll tend to breathe more between heavy squat reps than DL, because the weight is laying on your back making you tired while squatting, and unless you let go between DL reps (thus making it 5 singles instead of a set of 5) you really can't breathe down there anyway, so you might just as well go ahead and get it over with.

Hip Drive

Blah3: When I'm squatting I have the hip drive working but as I'm driving up with the hips and them coming up first this is causing my torso to lean forward and it feels that the weight is shifting onto my toes. Is it right for my torso to be leaning forward as my hips drive up? If not how could I stop this?

Mark Rippetoe: The back angle is not supposed to change as the hip drive is initiated. You have to keep the chest up as the hips drive. This is a common misunderstanding of hip drive, and we see it all the time at our seminars. Your cue must be "keeping the chest up", not *lifting* the chest.

Meaning & Implication of failure of workout sets

GregKee: It seems to me that when I fail on the second or third set of my workout sets that what is really happening is that I failed to give myself enough time to recover between sets. Since I've lifted that weight before (in the prior set), then I have the muscle to move the weight and the only reason I failed was muscle fatigue, not from too much weight.

If this is mostly true then as I figure it the implication is that if I get most of my work sets in, say I failed on rep 4 or 5 on the last set I ought to continue the progression and add five pounds on my next workout. And, of course give myself additional recovery time between sets. Does this make good sense? I am sure it is simplistic. Are there any rules of thumb on how to deal with this situation?

Mark Rippetoe: It makes sense on paper if you assume that the only variable is inter-set fatigue. The fact is that a weight that is too heavy to do for 3 sets across even with sufficient rest is too heavy to add to on the next workout. If the goal is 3 sets across, the first two sets must be light enough that the 3rd can be done in the context of ATP replacement allowed by the rest period and the tissue damage and nervous system depletion produced by the first 2 sets (substrate depletion is not a factor for sets of 5, and that's one good reason to use them instead of higher reps). If the weight is too heavy, these factors will override the recovery provided by even an extended rest between sets, and the last set will not be 5 reps. Furthermore, if you don't get all three sets today, the same conditions will exist next time, and you'll get 5,4, and 3, and it goes down the toilet from there. Try it and see for yourself. No better way to halt progress.

Deweighting between Deadlifts

Dave(DBD): I'm an intermediate lifter, lifting for about a year and a half. I'm about 5'8", 170lbs with 1RM dead in the early 400s. I've been having trouble pulling 385x5 recently. When I tried a different approach where I simply let the weight hit the ground and come back up under the same reflex I was able to do 385x5, I also did it under a single breath making the best of the Valsalva maneuver. The reflex motion was kind of similar to the way SSBBT would suggest to come out of the hole on a squat (the eccentric to concentric change). I know in SSBBT you stated this defeats the purpose of the deadlift but could explain what exactly this robs the deadlift of? I've been researching the mechanics of the deadlift lately and I think this explanation would solve a few things for me.

Mark Rippetoe: The deadlift is defined as starting from a concentric position. This is what makes it hard. And dead. By turning it into an RDL, you have made it easier by using the floor and the eccentric rebound for a bounce. If you want to do this, it's fine, but it's not a deadlift. You don't get to redefine classic exercises to make your training poundages heavier. Please don't make me elaborate on this.

Problem with hand position in squat

freefall68: As recommended in SS-BBT, I have tried keeping my wrists straight in line with my arms, but I cannot. May be my lower arms are longer or may be it is a flexibility issue, but my wrists get bent under the bar. So far this was not a problem since my squat weights were light. However, as I have started lifting heavier weights my wrists are getting sore under the weight. Only way I can keep my wrists straight is by taking a wider grip on the bar, which again is not recommended per the book. My question is if I have to make a compromise and choose between a bent wrist and a wide grip, which one is preferable?

Mark Rippetoe: The wider grip, obviously. You can't allow mindless adherence to advice that doesn't apply to you to be an impediment to progress. *Think.*

1st month of SS

baboseki: I've been doing the original SS program for a little over 4 weeks now (13 workouts total). I'm 6'0" and I started at 165 lbs and I'm 176 lbs now. I've been doing the GOMAD thing but my weight gain kind of stalled, so I started eating more to get the bodyweight up. I know you hate spoon feeding information to people, but I guess I'm too much of a beginner to know what to do next. I really don't want to stall so early. Is there anything other than eating more that I can do?

Mark Rippetoe: If your form is correct on everything, growth must occur for progress to occur. You got a problem with eating more?

Baboseki: Not at all. I just weighed myself and I'm 182 after a big meal. My goal for right now is hitting 200 and probably more once I get there. I guess I was just wondering if there is some super duper ultra secret programming trick that I could do in **addition** to eating more and not being a pussy.

Mark Rippetoe: You mean one that I know and failed to put in the book? Now, why would I have done that?

Baboseki: Point taken. I've been making things more complicated than they need to be. I'll just shut up and go train now.

Mark Rippetoe: An excellent idea.

Alternate technique for BB rows

LCN: Wondering if you have an opinion about the technique described here, where the pull off the floor is initiated by middle back extension rather than hip extension:

"Rows: Well, the best way to do them is to start with the bar on the floor every single rep. Your middle back will have slight bend to it. You pull the bar off the floor quickly with the arms, and by a powerful arch of your middle… (whole bunch of detailed shit about barbell rows and how they work, emg studies, muscles used etc.) ...getting an erector workout."

This was quoted by madcow2 on some other forum. I don't know who the original author is.

Mark Rippetoe: I do. My opinion about barbell rows is as follows: fuck barbell rows. Really. Fuck them. Stop wasting time worrying about barbell rows and get your deadlift up to 500. By then you'll have your own opinion and you won't have to worry about mine.

Can weak lats hold back a deadlift?

Sawol: I deadlift 375x5, squat 315x5, bench 190x5, but I cannot even do a single chin up at 206lb @ 20% body fat. Will strengthening my lats (or more generally, will strengthening my chin up strength) help my deadlift? I feel that I have somewhat strong legs, but my upper body, especially upper back, is pretty weak.

Mark Rippetoe: I know good deadlifters that cannot chin themselves. The lats are intimately involved in the deadlift, but they work isometrically during the pulling movements. Getting them strong concentrically/eccentrically is not absolutely necessary for a good deadlift, but it will help. And a guy ought to be able to do some chins.

How do you deem a deadlift a failure?

LCN: If you can get the weight off the ground in what looks like approximately correct deadlift form, but you can feel that you do not have lumbar extension, should you give up and try a lower weight? I think the answer is yes and that this sounds like a dumb question, but the reason I ask is I have seen a 1 RM video from a powerlifter who had pretty bad thoracic flexion, and someone who seemed knowledgeable told me that it still 'counts' as a deadlift if you have thoracic flexion, but not if you have lumbar flexion.

Mark Rippetoe: Are you doing the deadlift in a meet or at the gym? Are you a novice or an advanced lifter attempting a new PR? Can you normally hold spinal extension in your work sets, or is all your work done with a flexed spine? These are important considerations.

Ending novice phase and still relatively skinny?

b33k4y: I am 6 feet tall and weigh approximately 165. I am too fucking skinny. My issue is that my lifts are starting to stall and they are approaching the intermediate values you note at the back of PP:ST. I have never tested for 1RM's, but my last sets of 5 were 275 for deadlift, 225 squat, 165 bench, 140 clean (lower I know, I added these in later and they aren't stalling quite yet) and 110 presses. I eat 4000 cals minimum daily and I sleep around 8 hours. I thought by the time I was almost ready to move to intermediate I would weigh more for my height. Should I start eating 5000 minimum? Or should I start microloading then move to intermediate?

Mark Rippetoe: Why do you not just eat 5000 calories and grow some levers to see if you're really stuck instead of just too skinny? Hmm?? Maybe drink a gallon of milk a day?? Hmmmm????

b33k4y: I am an idiot.

Mark Rippetoe: It is possible that you are. But many people who are not idiots will not do the program because they want to "personalize" it for themselves. Since you are a tall skinny young male, it has already been personalized Just For You.

Dead lift grip strength

eleazar: I have been on the SS program for about a 6 weeks now and on my last 2 dead lift workouts I have nearly dropped the bar out of my left hand. I am pulling the weight up fine so my weakness is clearly my grip. I have tried flipping my hands around but that doesn't seem to help either. Do I continue to lift the same amount till my grip catches up? Go with straps? Work on my grip with some sort of assistance exercise?

Mark Rippetoe: An alternate grip did not fix the problem, for a novice lifting novice weights? I find this hard to believe. How much weight did you drop?

Eleazar: I didn't actually drop the bar yet, but it ended up rolling towards my fingertips on reps 4 and 5 when pulling 255. Then I switched up my grip on my next dead day at 265 and I had the same issue. I am just using a regular grip (thumb over knuckle) and I grab the bar near where my fingers meet my palm. Should I be using chalk?

Mark Rippetoe: Yes, eleazar, you should be using chalk. This is why it's provided in actual gyms and why serious trainees carry it into gyms where it is not.

Lifting on asymmetric surface

Egrof: My rack is in my backyard and the surface I lift on is called "crazy paving." After several weeks of doing the program I started to notice that I sometimes emphasize one side over the other - it might have been there before and I can't say for sure that it's the surface fault - although it probably is. There is also a slight slope but that is something I can fix. The main issue is the height difference between the blocks themselves. There is no gym in town and I have no other surface to lift on. Since it's not my house and the backyard is used to host people - I favor a solution which isn't permanent - but if anyone has a permanent one I will like to hear too. Should I worry about it or just alternate sides each workout?

Mark Rippetoe: Less-than-optimal training situations usually result in less-than-optimal you-know-what.

Maybe some Sackrete and a level would improve the situation.

KSC: Maybe you should move your bed into the back yard and your squat rack into your house.

Mark Rippetoe: Yes, it is important to prioritize.

High bar squats

pamparius: My shoulders are pretty busted, due to martial arts-training and things of that nature. The low bar position aggravates my shoulders something fierce, especially when I try to elevate my elbows. Should I do the novice progression using the high bar squat?

Mark Rippetoe: If you can't get in the low-bar position, you'll have to use the high bar. It's not optimal, but many people have done it that way for a long time now.

Will single work sets allow linear progression?

pnp_pc: If a trainee has limited time to train, (45 minutes max per session) is progress in a linear fashion possible doing 1 or 2 work sets on the SS routine? (Sort of like combining it a bit with Starr's beginner where the weight is ramped up to a single work set whether it's five or a triple.) More to the point: if you have to adjust something for time's sake do you cut sets or exercises?

Mark Rippetoe: Single work sets will work for a short while for a rank novice, but will not serve to exhaust the actual potential of the novice linear progression. So, if something must be sacrificed in the weight room, it would have to be exercises, not work sets.

pnp_pc: I appreciate you taking the time to reply to this. Length of workout becomes an issue as the rest times between work sets increases. A workout that consisted of Squat and Bench/Press 3x5 is acceptable then if time is a factor for the trainee. Deadlifts/PC and any needed assistance exercises would be done as time permits.

Mark Rippetoe: Yes, but you should go to great lengths to ensure that time permits.

Judotaffy: Could you add volume by adding an extra training day, i.e. squatting 2 works sets 4 times per week instead of 3 work sets 3 times per week? Are there any downsides to adding an extra training day as opposed to doing more work sets?

Mark Rippetoe: You could do anything you wanted to, but 4x/week means that there is a workout without a rest day once/week, thus fucking up the premise of novice progression.

Thomas: Time is a problem for many of us with families and jobs who try to balance our lives. It took me 83 minutes to get through the prescribed SS # 1 yesterday, and that didn't include transit time or locker room time. It was a Saturday so I got away with it. Resting takes longer than the actual exercises. One thing that I have tried (and I don't know if The Boss will approve): you can probably recover from pullups or chinups faster than you can from cleans or deadlifts, so when pressed for time, do the squats and the presses and then try pulls or chins.

Mark Rippetoe: You could also recover faster from wrist curls than you can from deadlifts and cleans.

Maybe that would be okay too, huh? I'm sorry, but the program is what it is because its constituent components do what they do, and they have a callous disregard for your personal situation.

Bench press arch

quack23: Just bought your book and tried benching with an arch after years of benching with a flat back. Afterwards I felt much more soreness in the upper back than the chest/shoulders. Just curious if this is normal because my back was significantly sorer?

Mark Rippetoe: It is generally regarded as normal to experience soreness in areas that have never been trained before that are now being trained.

Dumbbell Press Form

Axegrinder: What are the key elements to good dumbbell press form?

Mark Rippetoe: Getting them out of the rack and cleaned into pressing position without tearing up your shoulders in the process, controlling the dumbbells at the top, and not hitting yourself in the head on the negative.

Silly question about lumbar extension

elVarouza: This may seem silly, but I've noticed something about placing my lumbar in extension. You know how the spinal erectors are approximately shaped like a Christmas tree? Well, it feels that I can tighten my lumbar in two different ways: flexing the bottom (the tree stem) or the top (the branches). Sometimes when I squat or deadlift I can feel that the "upper" erectors (the branches) are nice and flexed, but I'm unsure about the "lower" area (the stem).

So this may seem silly, but is it possible for one area of the lumbar erectors to be flexed while another area is relaxed, or is it that if I feel a strong contraction in the "upper" area that it is also strongly contracted in the "lower" area?

Mark Rippetoe: The only thing silly here is your Christmas Tree analogy. In all my years in this business it has never once occurred to me that your erectors and Santa Claus had anything in common at all. The lower back is indeed hard for some people to consciously put into contraction, and assuming that it will stay that way if you contract the muscles superior to it is not a safe assumption at all. One of the most common kinesthetic deficits is a lack of ability to voluntarily contract the lower lumbar erectors, and if you can't squeeze your low back into extension because you can't feel the muscles contract, you can't really tell when it's extended or flexed, and you certainly can't keep it that way if you don't know the difference in the two positions. Setting the low back into a hard "arch" is a very basic piece of motor awareness and control that all lifters and athletes should have.

It is amazing how many people don't know how to do this. Every time we have a barbell seminar I will introduce the participants to our program by standing everybody up and determining whether or not they have voluntary control of their lumbar spine position. I always find 2-3 people that don't, and we go through a series of movement cues I use to teach the movement. We always get it done, and the reaction is always the same: the light goes on and they are genuinely surprised – "I have never felt my back do that before." It is immediately put into use when we squat, and it never fails to improve the quality of the movement. Without a rigid lower back, power transfer up the spine to the load on the back or hanging from the arms is not as efficient as it could be, and the lower back squeeze is a critical thing to know how to do.

Long term progression and goals

scotts: I lift in the silence and solitude of my basement, and though this arrangement suits me, it does have one major disadvantage: I have no one's experience to draw upon. A few weeks ago, I had a conversation with someone who informed me that, given my time under the bar, I was not lifting the kind of weight I should be. Although I have no particular reason to give this man's opinion any credence, it did get me to thinking: *how the hell am I doing, and could I be doing much better?*

I am 33 years old and 182 lbs. I have been lifting for a little over 2 and half years. I did SS and have now moved onto Bill Starr's intermediate program (as described in PP). My current PRs are: deadlift-410; squat-330; bench-260; press-180; power clean-215. I'd like be deadlifting 500, squatting 400, and benching 300 before the end of the year. I figure I'll need to be close to 200 lbs to accomplish this. So, am I progressing poorly or well, and are my goals reasonable?

Mark Rippetoe: The weights you're lifting are not the criterion – it's the progress you've made and how you made it. There are few absolutes here. I don't think these numbers are bad, but I don't know where you started. Your goals are reasonable and attainable, but you might be doing lots of things wrong with no input on either the fact that they are wrong or any way to fix them. As a general rule, the only people that can train by themselves productively are older bodybuilders who are not concerned with form on isolation exercises and who have already decided that their only training criteria are how the workout felt and how they look in the mirror.

Scotts: I didn't start out doing the SS routine. I also took a three month period in I which I went from 210 to 160, after becoming determined to lose my gut before concentrating on strength gains again. Here are the details of my last complete cycle of SS.

Late July 2008 (160 lbs): Deadlift-280; Squat: 210; Bench-185; Power Cleans-140; Press-100.
Late Feb 2009 (182 lbs): Deadlift-410; Squat: 330; Bench-260; Power Cleans-215; Press-180.

Mark Rippetoe: You're doing pretty well. But it will soon be time to get some input from somebody with a coaching eye. The weights you're handling now will soon demand a spotter, and it's a good idea to let somebody else judge your depth and your form on a regular basis.

Measurements

Goat: I have, a little more than a week ago, started the SS novice program and GOMAD. All is going well (still working on the power clean technique, but I'll get it). This may well make me sound a bit crazy, but already (I swear) I've seen a noticeable size increase, especially in my legs and my shoulders. Being the guy I am, I'd like to know if it's for real or if I'm just bullshitting myself, so I'm going to take some measurements, and track the progress.

This brings me to my question. I've never done this before, and don't know how it's typically handled, or if there is even a typical way. For instance, I would assume that I would measure my thigh at its largest point, but would I flex the muscles or leave them relaxed? I guess that's really my only question, unless there is something I didn't ask but should know.

P.S. Just for the record, I am doing the program for strength increases, hypertrophy is not my goal. But I'm curious.

Mark Rippetoe: If you want to track size increases, I'd measure the thigh at the largest circumference (up by the crotch) in an uncontracted state with a tape that does not stretch. This way, you'll be measuring the same thing every time and can see an actual change. The chest is measured at the nipple line, unexpanded. Arms are measured at the peak of the bicep, elbow at 90 degrees with the muscle contracted. Calves are measured at the largest circumference, waist at the navel. That's enough measuring.

Warm-up Sets

shibalnom: I have a hypothetical (pointless?) question. All things being equal, if you had a trainee do SS with the warm-up sets and another trainee jump straight to the work sets with no warm-up would there be an appreciable difference in strength levels between the two after say 6 months? Just curious if the extra practice from the warm-up sets would measurably increase performance.

Mark Rippetoe: There'd be a measurable increase in strength, yes, because the stupid idiot that didn't warm up would be injured and unable to train.

Unhappy with my deadlift. Advice?

TravisRussellDC: I feel like I do a pretty good job keeping the thoracics locked up to the 450. But, once I hit 500, I lost it. I'm still having issues bringing my hips into play. I really only feel work in the hamstrings and lumbars, never in my glutes or adductors. I know I need to work on the "chest up" cue, but I've obviously got some work to do to get the hips involved more.

Would you think that the loss of extension is an issue of erector strength/awareness? Or could it be a problem with the hamstrings not doing their job to keep the hips in place, which would decrease the adductor activity since they're so closely related? Or, am I just completely missing the boat on something else entirely? I have a habit of not seeing the things that are right in front of me, which is why I'm hoping a non-biased set of eyes can shine a little light on it all.

Mark Rippetoe: The problem is your start position. The bar is in front of where it needs to be in order for you to be efficient off the floor. On the second rep the bar clearly moves forward at the start of the pull, from a position that was already forward of the mid-foot. Here is our method that we teach every weekend:

1. Take your stance, feet a little closer than you think it needs to be and with your toes out more than you like. Your shins should be about **one inch** from the bar, no more. This places the bar over the mid-foot (not the mid-instep).

2. Take your grip on the bar, *leaving your hips up*. DO NOT MOVE THE BAR.

3. Drop your knees forward and out until your shins touch the bar. DO NOT MOVE THE BAR.

4. Hard part: squeeze your chest up as hard as you can. DO NOT MOVE THE BAR. This establishes a "wave" of extension that goes all the way down to the lumbar, and sets the back angle from the top down. DO NOT LOWER YOUR HIPS – LIFT THE CHEST TO SET THE BACK ANGLE.

5. Squeeze the bar off the floor and drag it up your legs in contact with your skin/sweats until it locks out at the top. If you have done the above sequence precisely as described, the bar will come off the ground in a perfectly vertical path. All the slack will have come out of the arms and hamstrings in step 4, the bar will not jerk off the ground, and your back will be in good extension. You will perceive that your hips are too high, but if you have completed step 4 correctly, the scapulas, bar, and mid-foot will be in vertical alignment and the pull will be perfect. The pull will seem "shorter" this way.

Try this during your warm-ups next time and let me know what you think.

The 101 Program: 101 Exercises for 101 Sets of 101 Reps at 101 lbs. Works Every Time.

At Anderson's Gym we had a running joke about the 101 Program. I suppose I shouldn't be amazed that some version of it has actually been tried. Just so you'll know, it was a joke. Really. Don't do it.

Throwing, Injury and Starting Strength

aussiethrower: I used your training protocol in Starting Strength for 12 weeks to rehab myself back to 70% of pre surgery strength (I had knee surgery to realign my knee cap in Feb, I returned weight training at start of April). I have since moved on to my specific throwing training I followed before knee surgery. However I am still using your protocols for some exercises.

A few questions
1. I have a trainee who simply can't get into a squat position while holding the barbell correctly. It seems his shoulders and hips are very inflexible. Can you suggest any exercises that will help him get more flexible in these areas?

2. Can I use the clean or snatch high pull instead of the power clean for this individual?

3. Is it ok to add some single-legged exercises to the Starting Strength program? Or should I remove a squat session a week and add the single legged splits squats, lunges or Bulgarian squats?

4. Would rotating Deadlifts, Snatch Grip Deadlifts and Trap bar deadlifts every 6 to 8 weeks still work with the Starting Strength Protocols?

5. My guys are coming up to an important competition at the end of October – would it be wise to de-load a few weeks out, that said how to I do de-load using the Starting Strength Protocols?

Mark Rippetoe: 1. The squat itself is the best stretch for the squat. Jam him into the correct position and make him do the squat as correctly as possible to the extent that he is capable, enforcing position like you would if you were having him do a stretch, and making as few accommodations to his lack of flexibility as you can while still getting a squat out of him. He will improve quickly.

2. You can, but it is a lower quality exercise. No one approaches a hi-pull the same way they approach a clean

or snatch, not even an advanced lifter, because you know you're not actually going under the bar and the commitment to completing the pull is not there. The answer to this problem is to get better at teaching the clean, and there is no better way to do that than with a kid that doesn't move well. Hard cases are the best teachers of teachers, so jump right in there.

3. Single-legged stuff is not part of our program. These are relatively advanced movements that, as far as I am concerned, apply to few athletes. Asymmetric work is best done in the context of sport practice, not strength work, and the attempt to make strength work so specific that it applies very precisely to sport reflects a misunderstanding of why we train for strength and how it applies to overall sports preparation.

4. Trap bar deadlifts are silly, IMO. Just deadlift and see if the guy will give you your money back for the trap bar.

5. Novice lifters don't really need to taper for a contest, and intermediate- level trainees just reduce volume and up intensity a couple of weeks out.

Strength and BP splits?

Reform: My understanding of intermediate programming, from your book Practical Programming, is that a trainee must organize multiple workouts within a week to disrupt homeostasis and spur progress. The Texas Method example uses Volume, Active Recovery, and Intensity days to achieve this end. This makes sense, and I enjoyed great progress on the TM, but my question is: What then of people gaining strength on Body Part Splits?

Inherently, they are (or should be) on the intermediate or higher level in their training stages, yet they are able to gain strength with only a 1x per week frequency. What enables them to do this? Or, does the super compensation and hypertrophy they develop enable the gains? Would the strength gains necessarily be slower?

Mark Rippetoe: Novices can gain strength on body part splits, just like they can gain strength on an actual full-body strength training protocol. The actual question should be: why would a person who is sufficiently unadapted that they are capable of making linear progress like a novice want to use a programming model that limits their ability to make rapid progress? And the answer to that question is that they wouldn't if they understood that body part splits waste training time for novices. If you can squat 3x/week, you can make faster progress than on a split that only has your squat 2x/week. And body part thinking is not performance thinking, so I don't usually do it.

Texas Method

dred807: I understand how the Texas Method works and you outlined how to set up a routine for pressing and squatting. For pulling, I am not so sure.... Would you recommend a top set of 5 on the loading day? If so, then would Friday be a heavier triple in the deadlift? Maybe a max double or triple in the power clean?

I guess what I am getting at is how do you load for deadlifts and cleans successfully after squats on Monday and how would Friday look?

Mark Rippetoe: I get these questions all the time, and they indicate to me a widespread problem: you people are always asking permission instead of forgiveness. Look, try it several ways and see what works best for you, and get in the habit of learning for yourselves. The guidelines in PPST are meant as a starting place, as illustrations of principles, not as a surgical template for everybody's training.

I appreciate that you trust my judgment. But I don't have exclusive jurisdiction over the Texas method, and you may find a better way to do it than I did. What is certain is that you won't if you aren't willing to trust your own judgment, and this means depending on yourself to reason your way through your own training. Try it several ways, and let me know how it goes.

Maximizing the deadlift

PMDL: Mark I was curious as to how you'd program for someone at the intermediate stage with an interest in improving the deadlift specifically. I can't see the Texas Method working all that well for it, considering how the deadlift seems to fight back when it's exposed to higher volumes of heavy work (I know, I've tried hahaha), but hell maybe you've seen different. I'm mainly curious as to whether you've had anything that's worked well for that goal, or have anything in mind that might be productive. Main reason I ask is that the lift seems so all over the place....once you're past a point you just have to hope for the best and if you get lucky something you tried will be productive.

Mark Rippetoe: I used a deadlift program that did not involve deadlifting. For the reasons you describe, I found it impossible to make progress by using the full movement, so what we did was alternate the halting deadlift and the rack pull (described in detail in BBT) every other week, using cleans and snatches for light day every week. They were easier to recover from and responded to the same slow weekly progression that squats did. Starr gave us this program, and it worked well enough to get me to 633 on two occasions.

Craigrasm: Can you elaborate a bit of the specifics of how you used the halting DL and the rack pull in preparation for a meet. In particular:

1. I think you mentioned in the new book that you like to use 5's on the rack dl, and you like to use 8's on haltings. Did you ever pull any singles or triples on either version in a training cycle for a meet?

2. Did you only use 1 work set on each movement for the duration of a cycle?

Mark Rippetoe: I looked up some of my old workouts just to be sure, and

1.) I never did anything but 5 x rack pulls or 8 x HDL, unless I missed a last rep, and

2.) I never did sets across, just one heavy work set after warmup. My records are sketchy from that time, but for an 8-week cycle I think I might have started with 3 sets across very early in the cycle for a couple of weeks only, but for various reasons I just let the one work set ride up to the end of the cycle.

Craigrasm: Thanks for looking that up Rip. Just to be clear, am I correct in assuming that you would go right to the meet having only done 5's on the rack pulls and 8's on the haltings in preparation for the deadlift? In other words, you did no regular deadlifts at all before the meet, correct?

I am curious about how you went about selecting your openers if you didn't do any regular deadlifting (to "gauge" things) prior to the meet. I would imagine that nothing felt "heavy" in your hands due to the all rack pulls.

Mark Rippetoe: I could usually do a single DL with my 5RM rack pull. I opened about 17.5kg down from that and only counted on two attempts. Really, I only deadlifted in the warmup room, DLs not being a particularly technical lift that needed a lot of weekly drill. But then again, I was not a particularly good lifter.

Plateau in different exercises - heterochronicity

Mladen: I didn't have a clue how to name this thread/question... so bear with me. What would be your approach in solving the 'phenomena' of reaching plateau and thus different programming need for different exercises for a novice or even intermediate? In other words, what if progress stalls in bench press sooner than in squat for the novice lifter? What to do then? You will almost never ever 'switch' from novice to intermediate (or upper level of programming) for all core exercises at the same time, but rather there will be some sort of heterochronicity 'phenomena'.

Mark Rippetoe: I sure do like the term "heterochronicity". Yes, if different exercises plateau at slightly different rates, it's obviously necessary to move their training along at corresponding times. However, if there is marked variance between the rates at which the basic movements are plateauing, there may be some discrepancies in the efficiency with which they have been programmed. The novice/intermediate demarcation is a systemic feature, and individual exercise components – although demonstrating some limited variation in advancement – should not reflect wildly different rates of progress if they are programmed correctly. In other words, if your squat plateaus to intermediate 3 months before your press does, you got in too big a hurry with your squat or were too conservative with your press advancement.

Various Questions Regarding Training

corz422: Dear Mr. Rippetoe, I had several questions after reading through your books.

1. You wrote that a good way to train was to cycle a 5x5 through the movements of squat/press/bench. How would I go about incorporating this into my program in terms of weight to use relative to my usual 3 sets of 5?

2. How would you recommend that I learn to do the dumbbell bench as you posted somewhere that other than powerlifting it may be a superior exercise than the standard barbell bench? What is the best way to go about transitioning in terms of technique/weight used/and programming?

3. What are the benefits of pursuing Oly lifting because in your section on the power clean most if not all the benefits can be obtained my training the power clean and power snatch? Are you planning to write any sort of book on Olympic lifts in the future?

4. I've been doing power cleans and my find that my form degrades severely if I do them after squatting and pressing. I'm doing 5 sets of 3 for cleans. Would it be a better idea to do them first after warming up?

5. I've been following your program where I do 1 set of deadlifts at the end of one of my workouts. Under what circumstance would I need to do possibly 2 sets? If I were to do deadlifts on a day without squatting and pressing would it be safe to assume that I can do more than my usual work set since I am not pre-fatigued? If so how much should I do relative to my normal deadlift weight?

6. What can I do to increase upper body explosiveness? The only way I can think of is the dynamic effort method used by Westside gym. Is that what you would advocate as well and how would I incorporate that into my program?

7. I find that on my last set of deadlifts it takes me a few seconds 4-6 to pause and reset myself for the last few reps. Is this bad?

8. Can I use an ab-wheel as isolation to strengthen my abs? If so how would I incorporate this into your program?

Mark Rippetoe: 1. If you are ready to progress to 5x5, the first week use the weight you used for 3x5 three workouts before you got stuck, to give yourself a little room to run before things get too hard.

2. Take the dumbbells out of the rack, figure out how to get down on the bench with the dumbbells in position above your chest, and do the exercise. You're a bright guy, and with me not there to show you you'll have to wing it. I usually recommend them as an assistance exercise for more advanced lifters, and in this context they are done for higher reps.. Try to run up the reps on each set of dumbbells to a predetermined number, then jump to the next heaviest pair. Let's say you started with the 59s and did 3 sets, 8, 7, and 6. When in three weeks you get 12, 11, and 9, go up to the 64s, if 12 reps was your goal.

3. You pursue the Olympic lifts if you want to be a weightlifter, or if you like to do the full movements. They are fun, not boring, and weed out the fools. No book is currently planned.

4. Yes, do them first if you want to focus on them.

5. Do 2 sets if you feel you need the extra work. Yes, it would be safe to assume that you'd be stronger if you were not tired. If this is the case, do as much more as you think you can, based on your familiarity with your training – a familiarity which I do not possess. But remember that deadlift fatigue accumulates quickly to levels from which it is hard to recover, so 2 sets is plenty, and probably too much for most people. I'd recommend you just up the weight a little and do one set like you meant it.

6. Upper body explosiveness is certainly the purview of the Westside people. I use it myself. I've used it effectively on benches, presses, and chins.

7. No, it is not bad to do what is necessary to finish the set, unless it involves actually turning the set into a series of singles.

8. An ab wheel can be used as an ab exercise, and it's actually not a bad one. L-pullups are better, but any hard isometric ab exercise is more functional than a situp. Incorporate them into your workout like you would situps, only do them instead.

corz422: 1. Just an area of clarification. I was asking in regarding to what you wrote in your book. To which I interpreted as doing a 5x5 sets across alternating between bench/squat/press. I wasn't asking in regard to the 5x5 programs. Would you recommend using this before I'm stuck to prevent being stuck?

2. So basically you're saying use higher reps for dumbbells? What's the best way to determine the predetermined number?

3. I do enjoy the O-lifts a lot. You are, however, saying that other than my enjoyment there are no additional strength/power/athletic benefits to be derived from the full lifts relative to the partial versions? I was reading somewhere that the squat clean teaches you how to receive force better.

5. Would doing 2 sets make my overall deadlift ability increase at a faster rate?

6. Could you point me in the right direction as to where I can find a reliable starting point into Westside's methods in that regard?

7. In your opinion at what point does it become excessive and turn into singles?

8. I guess I should flip through the Practical Programming book to figure out where to add ab work?

One more question: I was reading that heavy work 5 reps or below in the compound lifts is very CNS intensive. HIIT training via the indoor rower or sprinting is also CNS intensive. In that case, would it be safe to assume that doing HIIT before a lifting day or afterwards would be a poor move for performance or recovery respectively?

Mark Rippetoe: 1. I'm sorry, but this reads as gibberish. Do you speak English as a second language, a situation which might explain this?

2. Yes, I'm basically saying that since DBs do not lend themselves to lower reps you should use higher reps. The predetermined number will be determined by you, and I believe I gave an example for you to use that might aid in the predetermination phase of the workout.

3. The full Olympic lifts provide many benefits, among which is a longer range of motion over which explosive force is applied. I do not know what force reception you are referring to, except that you may mean racking the bar on the shoulders or overhead, which the power versions of both of the movements incorporate. Your actual problem is convincing someone to teach them to you.

5. No, doing 2 sets will be much harder to recover from, and is too much for most people who have progressed according to the program. If 2 sets were generally better, I would have used 2 sets in the program. I, however, did not.

6. I would check with Westside, if I were you.

7. It becomes singles when you release your grip on the bar between reps.

8. PPST does not address the issue of where to put abs into your workout. It fails miserably with respect to this topic. Maybe you should experiment for yourself and determine where they work best for you.

And yes, it would be logical to assume that activities which interfere with the optimum performance of basic exercises are best not done in close enough proximity to those exercises to interfere with their execution.

Amu: 1. I think he is asking whether you have recommended (in your book) doing 5 sets of 5 as part of the beginner routine in order to prevent stalling.

Mark Rippetoe: Then we'll just let him clarify. But if he is asking this, he hasn't read the book, and he promised that he has.

corz422: 1. BBT p293 "In fact, one of the most effective intermediate strategies for the squat, bench, and press is five sets across of five reps, done once a week as one of the three workouts, increasing the weight used by a very small manageable amounts each week."

Unless my understanding of this is incorrect, I interpreted this to mean to do a 5x5 squat one week followed by a 5x5 bench press followed by a 5x5 press in the weeks after. However, not every squat/bench/press will be a 5x5 as most of them will be done with 3x5. Is this what you meant? In your earlier response you implied to use the weight 3 workouts before becoming stuck on 3x5. My later question was whether or not I could do an occasional 5x5 to prevent getting stuck.

2. Ok. Are you also saying that it would be better to use descending # of reps instead of sets across?

3. Does training the power snatch offer any sort of tangible benefit versus training the power clean only for power?

6. I'm not sure I follow. Maybe this is the wrong approach but I was more wondering along the lines of whether there was a website or book on how to get started and incorporate Westside principles in the work outs.

8. How would I quantitatively gauge how well extra ab work is for me?

I apologize for any confusion I may have caused.

Mark Rippetoe: 1. No, because if you do it this way you're only squatting on Monday once every three weeks. And, if you nearly double your tonnage for the workout by going from 3x5 to 5x5 at the same weight, you're likely to produce enough fatigue that you *do* get stuck, since you were only adapted to the 3 sets.

2. If you go to failure on the first set, your next set will obviously be with fewer reps, or you didn't go to actual failure.

3. Power snatches make you pull through a longer range of motion, and thus strengthen a longer range of motion. They are a little harder to learn, you can't use as much weight since the ROM is longer, but they are a useful thing to know since knowing more stuff is better than knowing less stuff.

6. Consult Google. That's what Google is for.

8. You don't speak English as a first language, do you?

corz422: What I meant to say is that how do I quantitatively gauge to see whether ab work is paying off for me or not? Sorry I'm a bit incoherent but my English is usually better.

Mark Rippetoe: I suppose that if you are able to keep your spine stable under a heavy squat or pull, it's working just fine. In what way would you possibly be able to quantify the benefits of ab training? You can quantify a strength increase with your weighted situp progress, but aside from that I am really puzzled.

One rep max

Langolier: What's the best way to warm up for a one rep max? Sets, reps, weight increments. Looking at the strength standards chart has me curious how to go about this.

Mark Rippetoe: A 1RM warmup depends on several things, including but not limited to the weight of the 1RM (455 vs. 155), your experience (reflected largely by the 1RM relative to your bodyweight), your injury status, your age (22 vs. 51), your sex (male vs. female vs. Big Heather D), the temperature in the gym, the lift you're doing (SQ, PR, BP, DL, PC) and your level of psych about the 1RM.

As a general rule, outside a meet situation, you will know what your 1RM will be. At least you should have a very good idea. Back off from that number about 8% for a boy, and about 6% for a girl not using drugs, and this will be the last warmup. Then divide the space between that last warmup and the empty bar into roughly even increments -- the number of which will depend on the aforementioned factors -- and do most of the actual warmup reps with the first two or three lightest weights. Then single up to the 1RM.

F'rinstance: Me doing a 355 squat: 45 x 5 x 5, 135 x 5 x 2, 225 x 1 x 2, 275 x 1, 325 x 1, 355 x 1.

Girlfriend doing 225: 45 x 5 x 2, 95 x 5 x 2, 135 x 1, 165 x 1, 195 x 1, 210 x 1, 225 x 1.

SS combined with sports

progressiveman1: For athletes who do sport specific workouts outside of weight lifting, do you usually still have them do the typical SS routine? If the typical SS routine with sport specific training is too demanding, what are valid ways of fixing the problem to allow a combination of those workouts?

Mark Rippetoe: Younger trainees – high school freshmen and sophomores – can effectively do a novice progression during sports specific training, because their recovery capacity is such that sports training will not interfere with strength gains. Most other athletes will need a different approach.

A novice linear progression doesn't take that long to do, a few months at most, and most athletes benefit quite a bit from being significantly stronger. Given this, I feel as though it makes good sense to approach a linear novice progression in the off-season, when sports-specific training will not interfere with what will be an extremely important addition to athletic ability. Once this is accomplished and strength levels have increased to the point where linear progress slows, the athlete is an intermediate lifter and strength training can be effectively integrated into sports-specific training without compromising important initial strength acquisition.

progressiveman1: For the sport specific training to not interfere with weight lifting, are you suggesting doing a very small amount of sport specific training and focusing more on weight lifting during the off-season? And will you give your opinion on how to incorporate sprints into off-season training (frequency, volume, intensity- not numbers but an explanation) to, once again, not compromise results from the weight lifting program?

After one has finished the novice phase in the off-season, are you suggesting they should seek consistent progress during the intermediate phase when their sport is in-season, or should they just maintain during the season and wait until the off-season to begin progressing with the intermediate phase?

Mark Rippetoe: I am suggesting that, for the novice, the linear progression model should be followed for the few months that it will work without any other training at all. There will be time later for sport-specific training, and the strength gains are beneficial enough that other training should be avoided during this phase to let the trainee get as strong as possible. No sprints, no nothing.

In-season training for an intermediate should be designed primarily to maintain the gains that have previously been acquired. This is in contrast to what a novice can accomplish during in-season training if he is forced to both play the sport and pursue a linear progression: the novice can make progress while the intermediate will have trouble, and the intermediate is strong enough that maintenance of that strength keeps him functional in the sport while the novice *must* get stronger to be functional.

progressiveman1: I don't want to assume, so I want to ask you if the best way to maintain the gains from off-season weight lifting is to do the same workout throughout in-season as was done lastly in the off-season? For example, the athlete finished the off-season doing X frequency with X exercises with X weight, etc., should he just do that same workout throughout the entire in-season?

Mark Rippetoe: For an athlete for whom in-season strength maintenance is appropriate, I advise that each major lift – squat, press, deadlift, clean, bench press – be done 1x/week, with no assistance work.

progressiveman1: 1. At what intensity?

2. If I rid my weight lifting of those accessory exercises after I have completed the beginner's stage, won't I get weaker in the accessory exercises and then also weaker in the main lifts?

Mark Rippetoe: 1. At a weight that can be managed for 3 sets of 5 across, and using a significant percentage of 5RM, say 95%, so that strength does not decay.

2. The assistance exercises aren't keeping you strong. They are allowing you to make progress after the basic movements stop working in a linear fashion. Leaving them out allows you to recover from football practice *and* the basic exercises you'll use to stay strong.

SS combined with Muay Thai

Regielya: I have recently read your book and I have to admit this is the most interesting book I have ever read. I like your simple yet very effective approach to training. I have recently moved to 5x5 program as I am intermediate now, but a few friends of mine (from a competitive MT team) would like to try your program, but I'm afraid they wont have enough recovery between workouts as we train for 2-3 times a week, 1.5-2 hours each. What are your thoughts of this? Thanks :)

Mark Rippetoe: Thanks for the kind words, but if SS is the most interesting book you've ever read, you must have just started reading a couple of weeks ago. If your team guys are novices, I think they'll be fine with both types of workouts, at least for a few months until they get stronger. Novices are generally hard to overtrain unless insanity is being approached.

Progress to Intermediate?

Astro: I'm a little confused about the different figures you give here on the forum about results some of your trainees have achieved on the SS model so I want to clarify in my own context. I have been on the Novice linear progression for 3 months now and my lifts reached a weight just above the Novice strength standard for my weight class and stalled. (For example, the squat 1RM standard is 93kg for a 75kg trainee and my 5RM squat is 97.5kg.) I reduced the load by 10% and worked back up to another stall at the same load. Does that mean that I have come as far as the Novice programming can take me?

Mark Rippetoe: Not unless you have unusually poor genetics. Getting stalled at 200 x 5 for a 165lb lifter is not common, and usually indicates diet problems or incremental increases that are too big. You say that it took 3 months to get to 200, so it is probably not the increases. How much weight have you gained on the program?

Polynomial: I'm curious what you think about novices using belts. I finally received a copy *Strong Enough?* Today and after reading the article on gear I got a sense that you think that using belts is justified in many cases. So I decided to bring one with me today, and even though I was still sore from Wednesday and had some irregularities in my schedule, I got a PR of 3x5 of 225 with much better form than on Wednesday or Sunday, when I was only able to pull 225x5x2 and 220x5 respectively. I'm drinking my milk (making my way up to a gallon - I'm at about 1/2 - 3/4 of a gallon now, and I switched to whole milk today), but it feels like the belt will really help to drive my squats up a lot and get past those novice sticking points.

Mark Rippetoe: That's why the belt is helpful. It helps us get stronger by making the spine more stable by enabling the abs to contract harder against the resistance of the leather. Now, quit hijacking the thread.

Astro: So, the way the strength standards tables work is you should get to about Intermediate weight before you need Intermediate programming? Up to now, the lightest plates I've had access to are 1.25kg pairs, so I've been incrementing by 2.5kg. My order of a pair of 0.5kg plates just arrived so I can use them when I need them. Well, I wasn't actually following the program and that was my mistake (I know, I'm an idiot), I was doing 5x5 instead of 3x5. I gained 3kg on 3000Cal a day. Although I can't justify doubling my intake by adding a gallon of whole milk a day, I understand that I do need to eat more. I will also start the program with the prescribed volume on Monday and that should also leave some energy for growth.

Mark Rippetoe: So, you have gained a total of 6kg on the program, while not actually doing the program. You can't justify drinking enough milk to gain enough weight to get stronger, even though you know it works. Read PPST again, ask better questions, and decide whether you're willing to do what's necessary to attain your stated goals.

Astro: Hold on Mark, I never said I was doing your program, in fact I just told you that I wasn't doing it. In my original post I only said that I was doing a linear progression. I did not say I can't justify drinking "enough milk", I said I can't justify doubling my daily energy intake. I can justify eating more to gain weight and I did add 1000Cal to my daily diet when I started training. And now you've helped me realise it's time to increase that again.

I said 3kg not 6kg, read my post again. I'll try to rephrase. I asked you to clarify how the strength standards are supposed to be used. I understand that "when the training overload of a single workout and the recovery period allowed for by the 48- to 72-hour schedule does not induce a performance improvement, the novice trainee needs a change of program." I just didn't know how I am supposed to know whether I have reached that point or whether something else is wrong (as you pointed out) without having a rough estimate of how much can be achieved by doing that particular program. In other words, if a 5RM squat of 97.5kg is not a common point for a Novice to stall at, is 113kg (250lb - the intermediate standard for a 165lb trainee) a common point for a Novice to stall at? Let me know if I'm still not making myself clear.

Mark Rippetoe: Astro, your post asked *"So, the way the strength standards tables work is you should get to about Intermediate weight before you need Intermediate programming?"* Which is asking if a level of training advancement corresponds to a particular strength level; of course it doesn't, and had you read PPST you'd know why. The strength standards are supposed to be used as a general guideline for someone training for general strength and conditioning, not competitive lifting.

And if you've only gained 3k instead of 6k, as my admittedly too-hasty reading of your post missed, then here's the deal: stalling is a combination of genetics and adherence to the program. More often than not it corresponds to the general guidelines provided by the Standards, sometimes it doesn't, especially when you don't eat and train like you want to get strong.

Maybe I'm expecting too much, but you're supposed to know that guidelines are applied generally, that their value lies in the trends they indicate, and that mitigating factors will affect how well they apply. Why would a set of generalized standards be applied specifically to any one particular situation?

How many reps for chins?

Umholtz: Hello Mr. Rippetoe. How many reps do you recommend for heavy chins? I can do more than 20 without weight. Today I did 3 sets of 5 with 30 pounds with no problem. Do you recommend using higher reps even if I am using weight? My biggest concern is to avoid injury and continue to progress.

Mark Rippetoe: As a general rule, I think that more than 15 dead-hang reps means it's time to start adding weight. Chins/pullups can be used for two different purposes. If used as an upper-body strength exercise, the need to be fairly strict, done without a lot of other movement. If used as a conditioning exercise in met/con workouts, kip the hell out of them for high reps, as many as possible. So it depends on what you're doing them for.

Strength Standards

Stu: I'm a little confused with the strength charts that appear in Practical Programming. Assuming I achieve the typical gains you've mentioned on earlier threads, I'd be in the 198 lb limit, and have a 5RM squat in excess of 400lb, before the end of the year. But this puts me past the advanced average for a 1RM squat: confused.

On an unrelated note, I can't find much bio information about Bill Starr online, at least not about his early years. What sort of shape was he in when he started weightlifting? Only wondering because I'd like to know whether a mortal like myself could ever get near his 350lb press shown in SSBBT.

Mark Rippetoe: You're going to have to clarify this question. And Starr was damned strong, primarily because he worked as hard as any human being ever has. He was not a genetic freak, but his balls were huge, and he applied himself to his training like few people have ever done.

Stu: Assuming the typical gains, I'd have a 5RM of 410 pounds by the end of the 9-12 months at a bodyweight of about 190-195lb. I'd be at the end of linear progression, and classed as an intermediate lifer. But that squat weight at that bodyweight would be past advanced for a 1RM at that bodyweight range on the charts.

Mark Rippetoe: Here is the statement: *"Assuming the typical gains, I'd have a 5RM of 410 pounds by the end of the 9-12 months at a bodyweight of about 190-195lb."* Now, the fact that I say "It is not uncommon for novices to gain 40 lbs. of bodyweight and 300 lbs. of squat strength on this program ...That is for a 5RM, in the first 9 months. If you'll just do the program." seems to be confusing some of you. The fact that something is not uncommon does not mean that it's typical. I have had talented athletes who were diligent about their training and diet gain this much on many occasions, but this does not meant that it is typical. It means that it has happened many times, and that it can happen if you are diligent and have the right genetics. But not everybody that does this program will see these results.

Stu: Okay, so "it's not uncommon" maybe didn't imply that there's only a few guys that will get to this level. No worries. So Rip, you said you've had guys gain:
300 on the squat
350 on the deadlift
150 on the bench
75 on the press

Could you suggest more common gains on the lifts, or does no such average exist? I'd assume that there is a pretty normal distribution of gains, with a reasonable standard deviation.

Mark Rippetoe: Yes, we've had results like these many times over the years. But as for the statistics on what is actually average, that's hard to say. I haven't done the statistics on it, and I'm quite sure no one has. The statistics types don't even believe that this can occur.

Novice or Intermediate

Jake: Alright so currently I am 155 lbs, 5'7", with around 15% bodyfat. I have been lifting seriously for about 2 years for bodybuilding purposes. I have done various routines with my most recent routine being Bill Starr's Intermediate 5x5 Routine with a slight variation taking out the Olympic lifts like cleans and snatches. Recent I purchased your Starting Strength book and read it. I realized that for those 2 years I have been doing squats and deadlifts wrong. I have high bar squatted 330 lbs. for 5 reps with bad form, benched 275 lbs. for 5 reps with pretty good form, and deadlifting 370 lbs. with bad form. About 2 weeks ago I started your Starting Strength routine for novices and started my bench at 225, squat at 165, and deadlift at 310. I'm still working on the squat technique since the whole low bar position feels uncomfortable and awkward. I'm doing 235 lbs. now with squats with decent form that still needs improvement. I'm benching 245 for 3 sets of 5 with good form and deadlifting 330 for a set of 5 with good form. Power cleans are a bitch and I'm still working on them. This is my first time doing this exercise. I tried squatting 245 lbs. for 3 sets of 5 today and did it but it felt quite heavy even though I've high bar squatted 330 for 5 before with bad form. Would you classify me as a novice or intermediate? I just bought Practical Programming and I was wondering if I should do a novice program or intermediate program.

Mark Rippetoe: So your strength went down when you started using better form? This means that you were doing some pretty sloppy shit before. As a general rule, everybody should exhaust the potential of a simple linear progression before going to more complicated programming. This is true for advanced athletes coming back after a long layoff as well as intermediate lifters making a radical change in programming.

Jake: I don't think my strength went down. I think that now I'm just using the correct muscles more dominantly for the lifts. Example, on squats now the emphasis is on the hamstrings, before it was quads.

Mark Rippetoe: Let me rephrase: the weight you were able to lift went down, which prolly means your range of motion increased, which means you were squatting high, and prolly deadlifting with a round back.

Please let me know if this can be improved

corz422:
Current Programming:
A)
Power Clean 5x3
Bench Press 3x5
Back Squat 3x5
Push press 2x8
Pullups 2x8

B)
Front Squat 5x3
Press 3x5
Deadlift 1x5
Incline Bench 2x8
Dip 2x15

Is there anything that you would recommend I do in order to improve this program? One thing I noticed is that while my cleans and squats are improving linearly at doing sets of 210 and 310 respectively and still going up almost every other workout I find that my press and bench tend to stall much lower at around 125/190. Is there something that I'm doing wrong here? I am planning to add assistance movements push press/inc bench in there hoping that it will. You wrote in BBT that assistance movements are better done at higher rep ranges and that push press would be a good addition to the bench day. With that being said is there anything I could do to better improve this? I find that my pullups are stalled at 2x8 for a month or two now.

Mark Rippetoe: Quit doing inclines. They're not worth a shit anyway. As a general rule, most motivated people get stuck because they do too much, while most lazy people get stuck because they don't do enough. And if your pull-ups stay the same as you gain weight, they are not stuck. Right?

corz422: Did you change your opinion of the incline bench? You wrote on p234 BBT "On the other hand, the incline can be a useful bench press variation." I also remember reading somewhere in SS/PP that for sports like football and shot put incline bench uses a favorable angle. So having my bench stuck and playing some football and rugby I thought the incline bench would be good assistance work for me to progress benching strength. If I was incorrect in this line of thought what can I do to further improve my bench? The other exercise you wrote about was the narrow grip bench. Should I use those instead?

Also as far as pullups goes I've been at the same weight for the past 3-4 months of the program and while all 5 of the lifts in SS/BBT have gone up the pullup count has remained constant. I'm thinking that I might adopt of different approach of doing a lower number of pullups weighted to see if I respond better that way and since I can do 2 sets of 15 for dips it would be good to add weights to that according to BBT. Can you be a little more clear on what kind of belt I should be looking for if this were the case?

Does the rest of the program especially the placement and the set/rep count of the push press look okay to you? Would you consider providing a little more information for us in terms of which assistance exercises to select and how to determine the right weight/sets/reps to use based on the 5 major lifts?

Mark Rippetoe: And the next sentence says: *"It should be said that if you're doing both bench presses and presses, everything that the incline press accomplishes is redundant; there is no aspect of shoulder and chest work that these two exercises do not adequately cover."* You're doing presses and bench presses, and not paying close enough attention to what I said, and what I meant.

Read and absorb carefully the information about chinups on page 259, at the top. The type of belt you use MUST be a belt that a weight can be suspended from. Figure it out. And I don't provide a lot of information regarding assistance exercises because my programs DO NOT USE a lot of assistance exercises. So no, I won't even consider it.

corz422: Lol. Sorry I didn't realize that was a commonly asked question around here. What can I say, you got another person wanting to buy stuff you make, that's a good thing I assume. I'd also like to thank you for encouraging power cleans. Ever since I added them to my program my squats and deadlifts have improved considerably.

I'd like your input on something on something else as well if possible. I ran into a weightlifting coach and he mentioned to me that a lot of the bars at gyms are unsuited for Oly style lifting. That it's possible for the bar to not twist/spin during a clean and I could potentially damage my wrist. In your opinion is this a legitimate concern? As for the pullups and bench press if I'm doing them every other workout and not progressing. Is it possible that I need an intermediate style program for those while remaining on a novice linear program for clean/squat/dl? Thanks again.

Mark Rippetoe: Shitty bars are more common in most gyms than good bars, and lots of people have learned to clean with them. They are mainly a problem for people who have learned to lift on good bars that find themselves having to lift on a bar that won't spin, because they're out of town, at a strange gym, etc. Shitty bars can be managed easily if you understand how to use your grip correctly when you rack the bar. Oly WL coaches tend to be rather elitist about some things, especially if they also happen to sell equipment.

And it is entirely possible that different exercises can halt their linear progression at different times during a lifter's novice progression, due to the efficiency with which they have been trained, injury, or genetics. It is also possible that you have not progressed them correctly.

My lifting situation

Gordon Bombay: I hope you can give me some input on my situation. For the record, I'm 23, 5'10" and weigh just over 160 lbs at around 10 or 11% bodyfat. This is the routine I've been following for about three months now:
A: Squats 3x5, Bench Press 3x5, Weighted Chins 3x5.
B: Squats 3x5, Press 3x5, Rows 3x5.

This has made me a lot stronger and bigger (used to weigh 140 lbs before I started this routine) but now I've stalled on most of my lifts, with pretty weird numbers too; 230lbs 5RM for Squats, 210lbs 5RM for Bench and 120 lbs 5RM for Press. I haven't been doing Deadlifts and Cleans like you prescribe, and this is because when I started lifting I had a lot of lower back pain, and doing Deads just destroyed it (my body proportions don't help either). However, I am looking to implement them into my workouts as Low Bar Squats have strengthened my lower back a hell of a lot and I hardly ever get back pain any more. I figure doing these will help me get better at Squats too.

So basically, at this moment in time I would consider myself almost intermediate in some lifts (Bench, Press, Squats to a lesser extent perhaps), but a stone cold novice in others (Deads and Cleans). What sort of routine do you think I should use from now on?

Mark Rippetoe: I don't know. You have so thoroughly fucked up the initial novice period that your pulling strength never developed and never contributed to your squats, or consequently to your bodyweight apparently. Go back and start deadlifting in a normal workout sequence with a little reset of the squat and see what happens as your pull strengthens.

Speed work on Texas Monday?

RRod: I've been on the Texas Method since last December. I finally hit a bit of a wall 2 weeks ago: tired, scared under the bar, missing reps on M and F. Monday of last week I was totally drained, couldn't even do 50% squats with any vigor, so I'm looking into changing up Monday and Friday a bit.

I've been becoming more interested in the Olympic lifts, but my technique is not quite up to snuff yet to make them the cornerstone of my routine. I'm thus considering using speed sets as my main Monday workout, rather than keeping with 5x5 on M and dropping the volume. The intent is to improve my power output and get my damn speed up (bar's been slowing down for a while now). Here is my current regime as illustrated by my last good week:

Mon: Squat 225x5x5, Push Press 125x6x3, Rack Pull 365x1x5
Wed: Clean 135x5x2, Press 100x2x5, Front Squat 195x3x3, Overhead Squat 95x3x3

Fri: Squat 285x1x2, Press 127.5x1x1, Clean 165x1x1
(note: I took squats down from the previous week since I had started doing 'standing leg presses' for some reason.)

Current 1RMs, (@ 5'4", ~ 150 lb)
Squat 285, Deadlift 380, Clean 165, Press 127.5

Here's the routine I'm considering for next week:
Mon: Squat 170x10x2 (speed), Push Press 127.5x6x3, Deadlift 225x1x15 (speed)
Wed: Clean 135x5x2, Press 102.5x2x5, Front Squat 200x3x3, OH Squat 95x3x3
Fri: Squat 280x3x1, Push Press/Press 150x1x2/127.5x1x2, Clean 167.5x1x1

Does this look sound? If so, here are a couple of questions:
1) Is the goal for Monday to keep the weight but increase the speed?
2) Is the goal for Friday to keep the singles across going up in weight?
3) Would some singles across on rack pulls/haltings be a good addition to Friday?

Mark Rippetoe: All 3 things are right. But it occurs to me that you have described a guy who may simply need a week off to sleep more and eat too much. You are doing well for your bodyweight and height, and you may just be a little overtrained. This program you have suggested is good and will work well, but not if the reason the first one stopped working was because you were overtrained. So either way, I'd take a week off/sleep more/eat more and 1.) try the old routine again for a couple more weeks to see if that fixed the problem, or 2.) go ahead and change programs if you want to after you've rested a week.

Progression to Texas Method

Travis: Going from the novice 3x5 (working sets) to the Intermediate 5x5 (working sets), the jump is a lot more painful than I thought it would be. I believe I read on this forum that you said when moving into an intermediate program, you should start using the weight from three workouts prior to the Novice program. Now that I think of it, you may have been talking about resetting the Novice program. Regardless, that's what I used.

I ended my Novice program doing 3x5@267.5. I started the Texas method at 5x5@255. And it was much harder than I expected. I know you don't necessarily judge things based on total tonnage, but 3x5@267.5 is 4012.5 total pounds. 5x5@255 is 6375 total pounds. This is quite a jump. Now, I did get it done. But I had to decrease what I thought I could use for my bench, and decided to decrease power clean poundage as well, just to be safe. I am very concerned about stalling out early (as you said, its better to undertrain than it is to overtrain), but would have no problem progressing in very small increments per week, if necessary.

Basically, I want to know if discrepancies between total tonnage of Novice and Intermediate workouts of this magnitude are common/normal, and if it's okay? I also realize that Monday is the volume workout, and I won't be doing near as much volume throughout the rest of the week, which could explain the ball-busting on Monday. But being on set 4 and feeling my hamstrings spasm freaked me out.

Mark Rippetoe: The difference in the tonnage between 3 x 5 and 5 x 5 is significant. That's why we only use the 5 x 5 for intermediate trainees, and why they're only done once/week as opposed to the three times/week a novice does 3 sets across. The more advanced trainee is capable of lifting enough weight that 5 x 5 across requires more than just the break between two workouts to recover from. The novice is actually using a higher tonnage for the *week* than the intermediate, but the intermediate is using more tonnage in one workout of 5 x 5, so recovery is built into the program.

Deadlift and Squat on Same Day

Jason AUS: What is your opinion on Deadlifting and Squatting heavy on the same day? I hear you should alternate between the lifts (heavy squat one day, heavy deadlift the next), but the program has you squatting 3 times a week heavy, and doing deadlifts in there. I feel great doing it, but what is the theory behind those who argue that deadlifting and squatting too much is detrimental? Is it because they are such exhaustive exercises on your CNS when performed at high-intensity?

Mark Rippetoe: I suppose the argument against squatting and pulling on the same day is reflective of a lack of understanding about the mechanisms of adaptation. The ability to adapt is itself trainable; you can get used to pulling and squatting on the same day. There are lots of very strong European and American weightlifters that have adapted to heavy snatches and C&Js, squats and front squats, several times per week, and often on the same day, with up to 4 workouts per day being common. Maybe they just don't know about this.

But then again, those who argue against squatting and deadlifting on the same day may just be pussies.

Some direction for an advanced trainee

mrjack: I've been training around 16 years. My best lifts are 130kg bench, 87.5 kg overhead press, 150kg Back Squat and 180kg deadlift for six reps (pre injury - now 170kg for 1 rep) at a bodyweight of 84-86kg. I have tried many routines over the years and I think I am probably guilty of working too hard. I was gaining quite well on Westside-inspired routines over the last three/four months or so but I think the ME workouts are taking their toll on me and they wipe me out. I have generally found that I am stronger training two days per week, but even then I stall and don't know where to go next!

Am I an advanced trainee? My numbers are not huge but I have trained for many years (never juiced). I was considering trying the Texas method for six weeks or so. Do you have any advice for me? I am determined to get a double bodyweight squat (rock bottom) and a 200kg deadlift, 100kg Press and a 150kg bench, I just don't know how to achieve it.

Mark Rippetoe: Training advancement is not determined by strength, but rather your level of adaptation. You are an advanced trainee, no doubt. And it may be that a short regression to an intermediate program like the Texas method would work for a while, as long as you understand that an advanced trainee doing an intermediate program will exhaust the potential of the program much faster than a true intermediate would. Start light, and ride it up as long as you can, but be ready for it to stall in 6-8 weeks. Then pick another intermediate program to try. Do this a few times and see what happens.

Mrjack: What do you think about infrequent training, such as every 10 days or so? I'm so confused when I see that advanced trainees should train with more frequency?

Mark Rippetoe: If you mean working out once every 10 days, that is not training. That is the behavior of most commercial gym members.

I kinda broke your programming rules

Irishman301: See, when I was following the linear novice progression before, I started at a very light weight - 135 lbs. and I added 5 lbs. per workout. Once I got to about 185, my shoulder started bothering me really badly (not due to the squatting, but because of poor form in the press). Also, a 185 lb. squat felt really heavy to me, and I felt like I was going to stall shortly. Because of this shoulder injury, and because of previous knee problems due to poor squat form I decided to take a break from heavy lifting for a bit.

What I did was used the same exercises from your novice routine (squat every workout, alternate bench/press every other, alternate power clean/deadlift every other), but I applied a different rep range to the workout. I did 2 weeks of 2x15, 2 weeks of 3x10, 2 weeks of 3x8, 1 week of 4x5, and then onto the 3x5, which I've been doing ever since. Essentially, I worked my way up to your brutally hard program. I started out with everything pretty light (135 lbs. for the squat, 65 lbs. for the press, etc...), and I went and added 5 lbs. every workout. Now I'm squatting 255 lbs. for 5 reps with room to keep going! My deads are much stronger, and all other lifts except the press have much room to keep going at 5 lbs./workout.

Basically what I'm asking is, was this a completely pointless thing to do? It just seems that it made the sets of 5's easier to do since I was previously doing higher reps before hand and gradually decreasing. And it also allowed my injuries to heal up in the process since I went a while using lighter weights while working on my form.

Mark Rippetoe: Linear progression works quite well for novices, even if it is used in sub-optimal ways, and this is a good example.

Irishman301: Hey, I don't mean to challenge your ideas on what the optimal way to get strong is. Obviously with the numbers you can squat and clean, and you're background, you know much much more about the subject then I do. But just for my own personal knowledge, I was just wondering what exactly makes starting out the linear progression with higher reps and gradually working your way into the 3x5 novice program sub-optimal?

If I start out a linear squat progression using 135 lbs. for sets of 15 and add 5 lbs. per workout until I can no longer get all 15 reps. Then I reduce the target number of reps so I'm able to hit them all with the higher weight until I again reach a point where I can no longer hit all the reps with the continually0increasing weight. Then again, I lower the reps once I can no longer complete all the reps with the given weight.....and so on...... I continue to do so until the "target rep range" is 3x5, and I stick with that rep range for as long as physically possible until I can no longer add weight from workout-to-workout, and at that point I am no longer considered a novice.

So I could just start with 135 lbs. using 3x5 and adding 5 lbs. per workout, or I could start using reps of 15 and adding 5 lbs. per workout and gradually reducing the reps on a bi-weekly basis until I eventually get down to doing 3x5's, I will eventually get me to the same stalling point... I think. The only thing about starting with the higher reps and gradually reducing the number as weight increases linearly is that it just makes it seem 'easier' to complete all the reps every time the rep range is reduced. So say that the point where I add an additional 5 lbs. to the squat is the same time I reduce the reps from 8 reps to 5 reps. Those 5 reps seem easier to achieve since I was previously used to doing 8 reps. The idea that I can stop at 5 just makes the higher weight seem a bit easier.

I'm thinking that you consider the latter way to be sub-optimal because either a.) The volume is too high with the higher reps, thus not allowing for proper recovery, or b.) the starting intensity is too low, and therefore by the time I hit the 3x5's, I've already wasted a bunch of time that could have been better spent lifting heavier weights, or c.) Both.

Mark Rippetoe: It has to do with the effects that different rep ranges have on adaptation and technique. Long sets of many reps get sloppy, even for experienced lifters. And high-rep sets produce a different adaptation than we want to see for a novice, for whom we're trying to produce a balance of strength and hypertrophy that 5s provide quite well. So your program has an inexperienced lifter finishing every work set with sloppier technique than he started with, and practicing perhaps 1/3 of his reps with a form different than he started the set with, at a time when learning correct technique is of more importance than it will ever again be, with a weight so light it fails to stimulate optimal strength gains at a time when a rapid increase in strength is crucial for building the foundation of the program.

Big difference between 5RM and 5x5 across

tongzilla: Does a big difference between what an athlete can do with his 5RM and 5x5 across (best effort) indicate that he is not ready to be an intermediate? From your experience Mark, how does the percentage of 5RM with 5x5 vary for different levels of athletes?

Mark Rippetoe: The difference between 5RM and 5x5 work set weight increases with experience and the ability to produce a maximal performance at 5RM. Novices will be able to do their new 5RM for 2 or 3 more sets when they first start training, and as they become more adapted a 5RM becomes a better indicator of their actual RM ability, and thus a bigger number than weights that can be done for 5 sets across.

Back-off sets

progressiveman1: I'm maintaining my strength right now but when I start back up I'll probably be able to get a bit more out of the novice program. I'm thinking about adding a back-off set to the main exercises once I exhaust the options of resetting the weights and adding assistance exercises. Do you think this is a valid option to consider at that point in a training career? Have you seen people get stronger at this point by adding back-off sets?

Mark Rippetoe: Back-off sets at a lighter weight can only add volume to the workout, and are usually done to focus on a technical problem within that lift that can benefit from some concentrated attention being paid to correcting it. A lighter weight done as a back-off set cannot drive up the weight on the work sets.

progressiveman1: Is it somehow different for an intermediate? At the bottom of page 185 in PPST you say: "If progress simply stalls...the stress needed to spur progress is probably not being applied on Monday...The addition of one or two higher-rep sets done after the regular work sets is another option; these are referred to as back-off sets." Aren't you saying that volume can drive progress here?

Peter_k: I was interested in this as well, because I thought it might offer a way to stay strong while losing weight. Could it be worthwhile for a novice to do 3x3 (heavy) and 1x8 (medium) instead of 3x5? Not as if I'm an expert by any means, but I figure the heavy triples would keep the strength and the back-ff set would add a little extra volume to maintain muscle mass.

Mark Rippetoe: Volume can drive progress for a short while, but the main work must be done in the rep range and with the weight called for by the adaptation you want to drive. If you want strength, 3s-5s are what you have to do and lighter 12s will not make that adaptation occur, whether done as a back off or as work sets. If you begin to rely on your back-off sets as the primary stimulus, you will stop progressing. But why would you want a novice doing 3s and 8s instead of 5s, when 5s work so damned well?

Dropping reps vs. fractional plates

Stu : Can you explain why exactly using fractional plates is better than dropping a rep or two on the work sets and then building up to the whole 3 x 5 in the next workout?

Mark Rippetoe: Because 3 reps has a different effect than 5 reps, and the tonnage difference between 185 x 3 = 555 and 183 x 5 = 915 is too profound to ignore, and will have an effect on your linear adaptation.

Warm up for deadlift?

Banderbe: I was wondering if it's necessary to do warm up sets for the deadlift. I feel like after the squatting and benching, my body is pretty warmed up. I am not sure if there's any advantage to doing warm up sets for deadlifting or if I'm just wasting my time.

Mark Rippetoe: If you have already squatted, the deadlift would not require a warmup for the tissue. But warmup does more than prepare the tissues – it prepares the movement pattern. Motor pathway warmup is always necessary. I only did a couple of sets before I deadlifted at a meet, but I would NEVER have gone out on the platform with the movement pattern cold.

Drcra: Say after max squat and max bench or press with warmup from bar up to work weight, how is this deadlift warmup for 5rm?
135x5
185x3
225x2
275x2
315x1
345x5
As I get higher, say to 405 for 5rm I would probably ramp up the same but go 315x1 365x1 405x5, so continually adding sets. Would that seem like too many sets?

Mark Rippetoe: I'm talking about this for 345 x 5: 135 x 5, 225 x 5, 275 x 2, 315 x 1, 345 x 5

Banderbe: Is that 135 lbs. on the bar? Or is it 135 including the bar? I would think anything not using both 45 lb. plates is going to require excessive ROM and thus not really prepare you for the lift properly. This is probably a stupid question, but is it standard to state weight lifted to include the bar or is it the weight on the bar??

Drcra: Interesting warmup: is there some sort of template for that? I've always followed the warmup idea with starting with the bar x2x5 and adding 30-50lbs doing 3s, 2s and 1s up to the work set and applied that to squat and everything.

Mark Rippetoe: **As a general rule, if you let go of it and it falls, it "weighs" something. So it would need to be counted as part of the "weight". Anytime I name a weight for a BARBELL EXERCISE, the bar is going to be included. And yes, there is a template, and now that you know you can derive it yourself from this example. Post the results of this assignment here.**

Drcra: Just to make sure, after looking at your warmup: sets should not exceed too many regardless of weight, but always start with empty bar? I guess I'm just confused after reading from varying sites on warm-ups.

Mark Rippetoe: **You can't practically start with an empty bar on deadlifts, so you'll have to use either 40 kg (10 kg bumpers of regular size) or 135. The idea for warmup is to start as light as the lift will allow and then take a few even jumps up to your work set weight, enough to get warm, not enough to get tired.**

Jason L: I've noticed during my last couple of workouts that inevitably my first set of the day (squat, of course) is a whole lot crappier than my 2nd and 3rd set. This problem of crappy first set more of less disappears when I move to the second movement of the day (press/bench press) I wonder if this is due to incomplete warm-up or some sort of "system shock" when the body encounters its first serious stress that day and freaks out a little ...

MadDwarf: I've dropped the empty bar warmup for squats as well, though I do some air squats while focusing on keeping everything tight. 45lb doesn't seem to be enough mass for the bar to fit cleanly into its groove, and the little changes needed to pull it into position seem to muck up the process of reminding my hips and knees what they're supposed to be doing.

That's not contradictory to the numbers Rip gave below, since they didn't start at 45lbs either, just a comment on the spreadsheet. I would suggest that warmup weights for all the lifts should scale to match working weight. There's nothing particularly magic about an empty bar, so I don't see why you would need to waste warmup time on 45 pounds if you're working up to 345, whether it's a squat or a deadlift.

Mark Rippetoe: **Most people have noticed that the second set of 5 squats always feels better than the first, unless the weight is just too heavy and none of the sets are going to go. And there is nothing magical about the empty bar, Sean. I do it because I'm old and beat up and it takes several sets with 45 before I can even do 135. For a novice not yet strong it's a part of the normal warmup progression. But if a more advanced lifter wants to start with 135, they certainly can, and they're going to anyway. Lots of very strong contest PLers start with 225. To them, it's an empty bar.**

Frequency question and 1RM question

Dan F: 1) In the next two months (until late August) I think I'll be able to train only two times a week or, at best, once in three days (I'm too busy with family and extra work these months). Have I to change something in my current program not to slow too much my progress? That is already slow now because I think I'm not far from the end of the novice period. My routine is actually:

A: Squat Press Chins
B: Squat Bench DL/PC

2) Has it sense to add in the meantime a "cardio" workout like GPP drills (with jumping jacks, split jumps, squat thrusts, burpees and similar) once a week to maintain general fitness? Something I could do everywhere, also in a hotel room and only with BW.

3) I'd like to confront my lifts with the 1RM tables at the end of PPST, to understand where I am. Do I risk some 1RM tests or is there, from your experience, a percentage I can add to my 5x3 PR (5x1 for DL) to grossly infer the 1RM? 10% is realistic? (I'm 46 years old -- if it's of use).

4) Is it easier to recover from a "volume" workout (like 12reps x 4sets) or from an "intensity" workout (like 3reps x 8sets) when the total tonnage of the workout is similar? (I had a discussion with a friend, he says from a "volume", I from an "intensity" -- perhaps it's the same... Perhaps it's a bit stupid question... Pardon! :D)

Mark Rippetoe: 1. For two days/week this is optimal.

2. I don't think you "need" cardio unless you are a heart patient. It will not hurt you to do some metcon in your hotel room, but your strength work will keep you fit.

3. If you'd like to test 1RM, go ahead. There is no absolutely reliable conversion table or formula due to the high degree of variability with which individuals convert reps to 1RM.

4. It depends on the difficulty of the sets. If the 12-rep sets are very close to 12RM while the 3-rep sets are being done with your 5RM, them the 12s will tap in more, and vice versa.

SS & Traveling

Trip: Sometimes I end up having to travel for work. I usually try to find a gym to lift at while out of town, but that does not always work out. Given that I may have a 5 day lapse of training is it best to just try to pick back up where I left off? Also, if I am home for 3 days and then back on the road again is it best to try to do my normal SS on 2 of those days even though it might be another 4-5 days before I can lift again?

Mark Rippetoe: In a situation where you cannot control your schedule, you will experience less-than-optimum results. But we don't always have the luxury of complete schedule control, so you'll just have to make do with the training opportunities you have. Just stay as close as you can to the schedule, and if the breaks between workouts end up being longer than 5-6 days, just repeat the last workout and make your increases the next time.

This may not necessarily be true for a rank novice, who very well might be able to make an increase every workout despite a screwed-up schedule.

When to add accessory exercises

Strengthmill: I've been following your SS workout and I'm really enjoying it (yes even the power cleans). It's been over a month now and I haven't stalled yet, so I guess I'm still making progress. Is now a good time to add some accessory exercises? In your book you recommend some good exercises to add on to the workout, the problem is I don't know which ones to add and how to add them for the best results.

Mark Rippetoe: If you are making progress, don't change anything. There'll be plenty of time for assistance and ancillary exercises later. Plenty of time.

Robert: How do I know when to add these assistance/ancillary exercises? You say (in PP I think) that they are good for getting extra work in, but how do I know if I need this extra work?

Mark Rippetoe: Assistance exercises are always the first thing you drop ***from*** a workout (like when you're tired or overtrained) and the last thing you add ***to*** a workout (like when you perceive that you need more *exercises* when in fact you just need to work harder or more productively on the exercises you're already doing.

Time between sets

pnp_pc: I saw a youtube of you doing a set of 10@315. Your pauses between reps were around 4 seconds. Is that due to the high rep set you were doing? How long between reps should one pause / reset etc.

Mark Rippetoe: It's because I'm 52, fat, balding, and not very strong; the weight was heavy for me. If you're doing a set of 10 with no pause between reps, it's nowhere close to a 10RM.

pnp_pc: IMO 315 is still pretty f-in strong for 10 reps. I was asking because after I saw the clip I started pausing - I am not exactly a kid at 41 (and hope before I keel someday to be able to do what you did in that clip) and surprise surprise, I was able to lift more weight with much better form. So I am counting to 3 at the top, taking a deep breath and dropping. Unfortunately it's a bit tougher to use that technique on the bench. Speaking of bench: is it acceptable to do 2x bench 1x press each week instead of alternating? Really trying to get the bench up and I seem to lose some on the weeks when I alternate and it's a 2x press schedule that week.

Mark Rippetoe: As long as you're doing some benching and some pressing, whatever balance suits your needs is fine.

pnp_pc: What have you found to be the ideal length of time to pause between reps? I imagine if its too long a pause it would enable one to have a false sense of how much they should be lifting in their work sets? Is a 3 count acceptable-or should it be shorter/longer etc?

Mark Rippetoe: This obviously varies with the intensity of the work, the length of the set, the object of the workout, and the proximity to RM limits. In general, hurry up and get out from under the bar, but don't hurry so much that you miss a rep.

Measuring workset tonnage/volume

Stevo: When measuring worksets for the novice routine, should the BW exercises be included in the total amount of weight? For example, my last workout was the following:

Squat - 3 x 5 @ 200 = 2,800 lbs
Press - 3 x 5 @157.5 = 2,363 lbs
Chin's - 8, 4, 2 @ 180 lbs = 2,520 lbs

Total 7,683 lbs or 3.8 tons. This includes Chin's. My guess is you'll say, "...Stevo, you retard, of course you include the BW work!" If you have a more colorful, insulting or viscious response, please give both barrels! BTW, it gets my girlfriend all hot-n-bothered when I tell her how much tonnage I move! That is, of course, nullified when I follow-up by cutting a loud juicy milk rat.

Mark Rippetoe: I'm surprised that you have a girlfriend, considering your inability to spell "vicious". If I were calculating tonnage, I'd probably use bodyweight for my chin calculation like you have done here. The purpose of calculating tonnage is to track work done over the course of a week, month, or year, and you can't leave it out if it comprises a significant part of your upper-body training, so yeah, add in your bodyweight stuff. But pushups will be a problem in terms of tonnage due to the difficulty of determining how much of your bodyweight you actually lifted, and in fact chins might be the same problem. What would be wrong with just leaving it as reps done? It would just depend on what you're going to do with your tonnage calculation.

Light back squats

Draco: Rather than have front squats on a Wednesday workout, I know light back squats can be done, 2x5. I also know that "light" would be 80% of my 5RM. Instead of testing myself to find my 5RM (which might not be a true 5RM anyway), how can I use Monday's 3-sets-of-5 to determine "light?" I was thinking that 90% of Monday's weight would be about right. Or is that too high?

BTW, things are going well with my workouts again. A girl at work told me that my ass looks bigger.

Mark Rippetoe: 85-90% of your 3 x 5 weight would be a good light day. If you're tired, drop a little more. And for every girl at work that tells you about your ass, there are 3 older ladies thinking the same thing.

Questions about the Starr Model

Flying Fox: I'm currently doing a program based on the Starr model for bench. I have a heavy day (ramp up to a set of 5) on Monday, a light day with seated press (ramp up to a set of 5) on Wednesday and a medium day with bench (ramp up to a five with about 90% of Monday). A very basic workout schedule. But I have a few questions:

1) What exactly is the use of a medium day? I understand that the heavy day causes homeostasis disruption, and light day aids recovery. But what is the purpose of the medium day? Does it add to the disruption in homeostasis? So that the medium day, followed by the medium day induce the disruption through cumulative fatigue?

2) If I do overhead presses instead of bench presses on a light day (like front squat vs back squat and power clean vs. high pull), how does it still serve his purpose? In Practical Programming, you say the light day should not induce an overload, and should work through the movement pattern to prevent loss of fitness. Don't heavy OH presses cause an overload? And the movement pattern is different from the bench, so how do I prevent loss of fitness in the bench?

3) A very small question: am I right in my observation that the Texas Method is nothing more (and nothing less) than the Starr Model with 2 heavy days (one volume, one intensity)? It caught my attention that you first describe the TM in practical programming, and later the Starr Model. In the chapter about the Starr model, you speak of several heavy days with different set/rep schemes, which is the Texas Method again.

4) Do you feel the deadlift contributes to lat strength and size?

5) How exactly is your name pronounced? Is it "Riptoe" (2 syllables) or do you pronounce the 'e', ripp-e-toe (3 syllables)?

Mark Rippetoe: 1. It adds to the general workload (for hormonal purposes), aids in directing the remodeling of the tissue stressed during the heavy day, and reinforces the motor pathways used in the primary movement without the same level of stress as a heavy day.

2. Heavy presses would be a poor choice for a light day exercise.

3. How have you arrived at the conclusion that even though the two programs are different, they are really the same?

4. The deadlift works lats isometrically, like it does the traps and the trunk muscles. To the extent that the lats will respond in an untrained novice to this type of work, they contribute to lat size and strength. Chins reinforce this effect concentrically, and are included in the program for this reason.

5. My last name is pronounced with 3 syllables.

Texas Method Squats Setup

notbuff: I'm about to start a routine which follows the Texas Method to some extent. Currently I have planned 4x5 squats on Monday, 2x5 light on Wednesday, and 1x5 heavy on Friday. However, I also have 1x5 heavy deadlifts on Friday which I can't really move to another day. I was thinking that doing 5RM squats and deadlifts on the same day might be a bad idea so I was wondering if it is fine to move all the squats up a day so that Monday is 1x5 heavy, Wednesday is 4x5, and Friday is 2x5 light. My concern is going from the 1x5 heavy to 4x5 on only two days rest. Will this be a problem, or is this manageable because Monday would be so little volume?

Mark Rippetoe: You can do this if you adjust your 4 x 5 down to a load that you can complete. The ratios between the workouts will obviously have to be adjusted to be doable no matter what the workout calls for.

Notbuff:

When you say 'adjust the load down', do you mean decrease the weight or the number of sets? Also, I know in SS you have kids power cleaning and then deadlifting two days later. Could this little separation become a problem as the deadlifts get heavier? I'm inclined to separate them by 3-4 days in my TM workout.

Mark Rippetoe: Lower the weight. If you drop reps you change the effect of the set, if you lower the sets you drop the tonnage back to a novice one-day workload. And by now you should be pulling every 5 days as with the program on page 300 of BBT.

Program recommendations for twice weekly training

weinstev: I purchased Starting Strength just under a year ago, and have been able to safely learn squats, deadlifts, power cleans, and overhead presses. However, as a 34 year old father of a young child working a full time job, making it to the gym three times a week with plenty of rest and enthusiasm for training is not a reality for me. Instead, I have been able to commit to training twice/week which gives me the flexibility to adjust for busy days at work when I can't make it to the gym, to give me an extra day of recovery, or allow me to participate in some other form of exercise as time permits.

I think that simply working to get stronger all around would allow me to pursue other goals such as being able to do full range handstand pushups, to be able to do muscle ups on a bar, 20 pullups, become faster for pickup sports, and to have a strong and healthy back, something that I've had a difficult time with for more than 15 years. I have been a competitive cyclist and will likely resume that activity to some degree when I have more free time. I'm giving you the "I also enjoy moonlit walks on the beach" background because I feel like my goals aren't all that different from others who might also be interested in your writings and training productively.

My current strength level is as follows:
Bench press 3x5 155lbs
Overhead press 3x5 95lbs
Squat 3x5 215lbs
Weighted chins 3x5 + 40 lbs
Power cleans 5x3 85lbs (still a lot of easy progress to be made as I've only incorporated these more recently and am finally comfortable with the technique)

I'm 6'0" tall and weigh a little more than 190lbs. My weight has increased about 10 pounds in the past year. Given that I'm at a fairly low strength level, but will not be following your standard recommended novice plan, I'm in search of an intelligent compromise. Should I scrap the attempt to train explosively and just do the A and B Starting Strength days two times/week until I've become quite a bit stronger? Does PPST address how to set up a training program using less than three days per week? As someone with limited time to train I want to make sure that I'm making the most of it. I've hesitated to purchase PPST because I'm not sure whether it's flexible or general enough for me to be able to apply its concepts to my level of commitment and to reaching my goals.

Mark Rippetoe: One of the most frequent complaints about PPST is that it is too general, and as a result I am deluged with questions about how to precisely apply one or another of the (quite intentionally) diagrammatic programs to a specific situation. PPST covers the why and the how, with the what, when, and where left up to the individual. I get paid lots of $$$ for doing this part for you, and nobody seems to have the money. At least not on this board. So I think PPST might just be your book.

That having been typed, I think you may have jumped ahead in line with your explosive stuff, because your numbers don't indicate that you're through with your novice phase. Even at twice/week you should still be able to increase the basic numbers beyond where you are without getting exotic. I'd back off the fancy stuff and just try a simple A/B rotation a little longer, and try to eat more.

---

2 questions for the coach - weight jumps and belt use

gallo_blanco: I have reached a point in the Starting Strength program where my Squat and Deadlift are slowing a bit. I am wondering whether it's time to slow down the jumps in weight or to continue as is (10lb jumps) or if I should wait until I hit my first failure set. Although I am not sure if actual weight is a determining factor for this decision, I am squatting 355 and deadlifting 385.

I've just started using a belt for a little reassurance to keeping form, but, it almost feels as though I am cheating when using it. Is there anything to say for not using a belt at point to practice keeping form without assistance? Or, is performing the warm-up reps without the belt good enough?

Mark Rippetoe: If you have not missed any jumps, how do you know if you are slowing down? Just your perception? Sometimes this is correct, and if you're getting recovered well I'd drop to 5 lb. jumps to keep the progress going as long as possible. These weights are pretty good for a novice progression unless you're at a 250+ bodyweight, and it is probable that you're correct in your assessment.

The belt is a perfectly legitimate tool. You are not cheating: in fact your abs are working harder with it on since they have something to contract "against". This is a proprioceptive thing, with the belt giving the abs something to push against while they contract. Your abs don't just go to sleep when the belt is on, I promise. If you are going to use it, put it on for your last warmup set, because it is dumb to introduce a new variable into your work set that hasn't been warmed up in the "practiced-with" sense.

gallo_blanco: By slowing down, I am referring to rep speed. I am not really exploding out of the hole as I have been. As for my weight, I am 5'7" and fluctuate between 214-217lbs....unsure of my BF%. Getting a little concerned about my midsection, still trying to clean up my diet. My primary concern has been to bring in enough calories to have energy and eating enough protein to allow my muscles to recover.

Mark Rippetoe: At your bodyweight, your progress can continue like this a while longer, and then just drop to 5 lb. jumps. Bar speed will always slow down as your work sets approach your true 5RM, because as the weight gets heavier you'll normally slow down, right up to the point where you get stuck. This is normal, and unavoidable if progress is to continue. If you insist on limiting your training to weights can be handled explosively for the absolute strength exercises, especially at the novice level, you'll never handle the weights necessary to get strong.

Deadstopped squats and other

Dan F: 1) I read in your SS about the "deadstopped" squat variant (similar to box squat but with bar stopped on rack pins at bottom): i like this variant because it's impossible to cheat with depth (in last reps of heavy sets of normal squat I tend to go deep not enough - it's something common I think and "unconscious"). I'm thinking to start from top, stopping the bar at bottom at full depth (not a partial squat) -- the depth I usually reach in first good reps of my heavy normal squats - - and go up without bouncing on the pins. I tried it and can lift about 10% less than normal squat (for 5 reps). In an intermediate program like TM could be a not so bad idea to use it in volume and light days? Or only in light days?

2) What about doing only shoulder presses and not benching in my first intermediate program using TM? That because OP is absolutely my weakest movement. I could do:

Monday 5x5 OP
Wednesday 3x3 Push Press with same weight of Monday (it's light day)
Friday 1x5 (or 1x3) OP

Mark Rippetoe: 1. If you're going to do this, it will have value only if it improves your ability to get deep on all the reps of your other squat workouts, so just do it on light day. The point is to fix your other days' squats, and to fix them you have to keep doing them.

2. The bench press strengthens the press. Your press will get stronger if you do it M-F and bench press Wednesday.

Dan F: Thanks for the clear answers.

About 2) I think the BP on Wed would be a max effort of 3 sets of 5 reps or similar, not a "light" bench workout. Is it right?

Mark Rippetoe: Exactissimo

When to switch to intermediate

Drewfasa: I've gone back to a linear novice progression since getting microplates, and also because I've thrown caution to the wind and am eating like a pig (and as you said, at 5' 11", 209lbs, I'm not skinny). I was wondering at what point it is best to switch to a weekly progression. The obvious answer is after reaching a stalling point. However, I have plates that allow increments as small as 250g to be used, and it seems that a weekly progression of 2.5kg (on squat) is obviously better than a 3x per week progression of 250g (at least, mathematically speaking).

Likewise, my deadlift is at 191kg x5 and adding 1kg per week is becoming quite difficult, but adding less than that seems pointless (am I right?). Should I start using partial movements to train deads?

Mark Rippetoe: But 5'11" at 209 is not big enough either. Nobody's linear progress is going to hold together for 250 gram jumps. When things are moving this slowly, you've exhausted the potential for linear increases that actually add up to meaningful weight. But more importantly, when you're this advanced, you have developed the ability to stress the system sufficiently that your recovery ability gets "wavy" and won't be able to resolve against very small increases on a reliable basis, workout to workout. You will get stuck before 250 gm jumps accumulate into anything useful. Just go on to weekly programming.

Stalling squats on SS

Beast: I've stalled on squats at 80kg for 3 consecutive workouts. This is my second stall at 80kg after deloading to 70kg. My bodyweight is 87kg (192 pounds) so although not heavy I still believe I am defiantly not an intermediate and there should be more linear progress. Though what should I do deload again or what?

My eating is good GOMAD etc., and plenty sleep, and my form I think is proficient enough. Deadlift is progressing still however am stalling on presses but that is expected and not as important?

Mark Rippetoe: I guess I'd need to see your progression before I could say what the problem was. If you are trying to make large jumps, you will in fact get stuck.

Beast: Started doing squats at 40kg after starting with the bar in first workout, this was incredibly easy and could have definitely added more to the bar. Anyway went up in 5kg progressions per workout. Once up to 70kg the weight definitely starts to feel heavier however still managed 75, then went up to 80kg from here I started stalling. I felt the 5 kg steps should have been manageable especially when only in the 80 kg range.

Mark Rippetoe: It may be that 1.) you're actually not eating enough, most people don't. 2.) You're not resting enough between work sets. Most people think this is metcon – it's not, take all the time you need to make damn sure the next set gets finished. 3.) If the previous points don't apply to you, then the jumps are too big. You may need 2.5 kg jumps.

Beast: Thanks, I think I'm going to take smaller steps, today did 77.5 and made all reps then going to go up in 2.5 kg steps instead. I think my rests are about right, typically I rest no less than 2-3 mins first set, then 3-4 mins second and 5 mins or so for last set. Regarding the standing press, I presume its best to take 1 1/4 kg steps instead of 2.5kg steps if I'm stalling?

Mark Rippetoe: Take the jumps that allow you to continue to make progress every workout, until this stops working. But 2-3 minutes between sets is not long enough if the weight is even remotely heavy. Are you in a hurry for some reason? This is strength work, not metcon, and there is not supposed to be a conditioning effect. You're just supposed to make your increases.

Less is more? (...a lot less...)

pnp_pc: About 2 weeks ago due to time and schedule constraints I had to scale back the routine a bit. I was following the SS model without any assistance exercises, alternating PC and DLs, and the gains were coming (albeit slowly). My workouts were getting close to 2 hours due to the extended rest times that were necessary. But due to temporary work demands in the past 2 weeks I have had to compress my schedule a bit in order to stick with a regular S/Tu/Th that I have been on since May.

What I have noticed during the time that I have reduced the workout to Squats 3x/wk alternating with Presses and Bench is that my gains have increased more rapidly on the Squat and the Bench(Press remains the same) than they ever have before. For the first time in my life I am squatting more than my bodyweight, and my bench is approaching my bodyweight. The one week I managed to squeeze in some Chins my next bench session was much harder than the one preceding the chin session, so I skipped the next Press workout and my Bench was good again. Is this a legit model to follow (throwing in power cleans when I can)?

Mark Rippetoe: It is quite likely that for some people even a rather simple novice workout is too much volume. If you are stuck, or even slow, it is more likely that you are doing too much work instead of too little. McRobert, Steiner, and others have written of abbreviated workouts that may be very effective for you. Less may very well lead to more.

Smallest increments one should use

Drewfasa: What are the smallest increments you would use with a healthy male trainee for: Squat; Deadlift; Bench press; and Press? I have microloaders as small as 0.125 kg but that seems pointless.

Mark Rippetoe: I'd say anything less than 5 lb. is not suitable for the squat or deadlift, because the jumps stop adding up to more than can be obtained with intermediate programming (5 lbs./week). For presses, benches, and cleans, and assistance stuff, anything that adds up to an increase will work.

Vanessa: So, should a woman then switch to intermediate programming after she can no longer add 2.5 pounds per workout on squats?

Mark Rippetoe: If she makes it that far. Most don't, unfortunately.

Texas Method Friday Question

djl236: On Friday I'm going for PRs, but when I first start the program, how do you know where to start on Fridays? For example, I know on Monday I should start with my 5x5's at around 80% of my 5RM for week 1 and keep moving up about 5 lbs a week, but where do you start on Friday for a 1, 2 or 3RM? At 80% of your 1, 2 or 3 RM, or just start going for PRs right off the bat? I've re-read the chapter in PPST and it doesn't say.

Mark Rippetoe: Anytime a program calls for PRs, it will involve titrating up to the PR with your warmups. They cannot be calculated accurately – they must be empirically determined. But if you think your 5 x 5 Monday workout is to be done with 80% of your 5RM, you have not read carefully. See the top of page 174.

djl236: Ok, I just re-read it and I see it says for example if your 5RM is 355, start with 340 or 345 for 5x5. So basically just drop 10-15 lbs off your 5RM for your 5x5, meaning a 5RM of 270 is about 255-260? Maybe I'm over thinking this way too much, I have a habit of doing that. It seems like I would stall out quickly.

The question is, while doing this TM, would it be a good idea to not deadlift for PRs on Friday but rather start lighter and use a simple linear progression Friday to Friday to get back up to strength on them? It dawned on me as a good idea today but I wanted to run it by you.

Mark Rippetoe: Yes, it might stall out quickly if you don't pay attention to recovery. But the jump is 5 lbs/week, and lots of people do this for quite a while before stalling all the time. And you can permute the workouts to fit your rehab schedule any way you want to. You have my permission.

djl236: Do a lot of people have success with starting a little lighter than normal to stave off an eventual stall (i.e. instead of 255, maybe 235-240 for 5x5 and work up 5 lbs/week?) or is this starting too light?

Mark Rippetoe: Yes, it is also permissible to use your own judgment in these matters.

---

53 Year Old Needs Some Help!

slideman: I have been lifting haphazardly for a little while with mediocre results, as you say a novice can get results even with a bad program. Any way, recently I started you program. The problem is, I am having a hard time recovering, from workout to workout. It seems I am constantly moving into overtraining. Even though I am definitely a Novice I wonder if I need to go to periodization work to allow for more recovery. Certainly stick to the 3 sets of 5. But maybe heavy, medium, heavy or something like that. I am 5'11 @ 175, 53 years old, and fairly athletic.

Mark Rippetoe: Just because you are old and creaky does not mean you need more training complexity. If anything it means you need a more simple program. I'd just do the novice program progression and only train 2x/week before I got into an intermediate program prematurely. It might help you to gain a few pounds while you're at it.

The importance of Wednesdays -Texas method

drcra: How important are they? Sometimes I have not recovered enough from 5x5 for some retarded reason (nutrition and sleep most likely) and on Wednesday I can barely do a body squat without my adductors ripping into shreds. Are they integral to progression and should I still lift on Wed. despite soreness?

Mark Rippetoe: You want to drop your Wednesday training day so you don't have to pay attention to recovery? Sure. Fine with me.

Question about SS and volume

Thomas: Enjoying your SS book, and have been on the novice program for a bit more than two months. Background: am 5'10" / 167 Lb / 63 / M (with military experience in my jaded youth) and now with an international job that makes me travel a lot and causes me to miss SS 3 days a week from time to time (hotels gyms). Have always been an athlete, but have never "seriously strength trained." Came to SS from CrossFit to try to get stronger for the C/F program. For many years, off and on, I did what you call "working out with weights" as well as B/W calisthenics, not strength training per se.

Am bumping up against my limits, I think. I had to restart my squats once when I failed at 5x5x97.5K, and will probably have to restart presses as I am stuck completing 5x5x47.5K. Bench, Dead and Clean are all still creeping upward. Comparative levels track your expectation (deadlift stronger than squat, etc.) I always restart at the last level when I miss a week of SS workouts due to travel.

Looking for clues, I analyzed my volume. It's all over the place - as a result of inconsistent warming up. Some days I warm up more than others, some days I start warming up at a higher weight. The question is whether the volume matters? By your standards, the volume probably isn't high. On 26 Aug (when I started record keeping), total volume for "SS#1" (S,B,D) was 4565K (S75/B50/D90 K). On 4 Oct it had doubled to 9245K (S97/B66/D106 K) and that was when I stalled on the squats (97.5). On 25 Oct, volume was 6622.5K (S95/B68/D108 - I restarted the squats at 90). My increases 5x5s have been consistent and I took your advice to get light (0.5K) plates.

Should I try to manage the (warm up) volume more carefully or do you see something else that's fixable.

Mark Rippetoe: It is pointless for a masters guy to count total volume including warmup, since the requirement for it is so variable. It will depend on injury status, sleep quality, and nutrition, and this applies doubly to you since you're on the road so much. Warm-up might vary as much as 4x between individual workouts, but it's light and does not function as an adaptive stress. And I don't see the value in calculating work set volume for a novice, since volume is not really a variable you should be manipulating anyway. Just make your increases on a regular basis in whatever way you can that fits your schedule, and stop worrying about programming variables that just don't apply to your situation.

The Press Progression

Notorious: About a month ago, after hitting 115x3x5 on the Press (took at least 3 workouts after 110x5), I moved up to 120. I hit 3x4 the first workout and stalled after that -- my reps were only decreasing. I finally decided to invest in some 1.25lb plates and went down to 115 again and increased calories. I got 115x3x5 the first workout, but it took me 3 workouts to get 117.5x3x5. When I got to 120 again, I got 3x4 again. Today I finished my third workout of 120, and I only got 5, 5, and 4 reps (reps increased by 1 each time).

So my question is this -- is there even a point of increasing weight by 2.5lbs a workout at this point, as opposed to 5? It seems I basically wasted 3 workouts on 117.5, since I got the same number of reps of 120 after that anyways. I'm pretty sure I am only somewhat stronger now because I bumped up calories.

Mark Rippetoe: Since you didn't include the info, I have to ask your bodyweight/height. But since there are lots of other questions to answer, let me just say that if the 2.5 lb jumps on the bench have been working fine, and the press is not as strong as the BP, then it follows logically that smaller than 2.5 lb jumps should work on the press. This is especially true if you are at a light bodyweight for your frame; I would assume that a guy 5'8" @ 198 had a form problem with this problem, but I think you just need smaller jumps. Do the math on 1.25 lb jumps unstuck over the same time and you'll see the point.

Appropriate weight increases Novice to TM

David: In at least one previous post, you mentioned some thing to the effect that increasing DL by less than 5 lbs per workout on a novice program (DL once per week) is not productive and that one should switch to more advanced programming (read: intermediate) where weight increases could be made more effectively. Here are my questions:

1) Is there a minimum increase that should not be used on an intermediate method, ie after several months when things get hairy is there any reason not to microload the DL?

2) When considering loading of the squat, would it be more appropriate to use 2.5 lb/wk increases on an advanced novice program (5 lb increase per week) or 5 lb/wk increases on an intermediate method (like TM)?

Mark Rippetoe: 1. It has been my experience that microloading the deadlift is not as productive as other methods, since you're only going to be doing it once/week at that point and it only amounts to a 10 lb./month or less increase. There are better ways of strengthening the pull at this point.

2. At that point, it's you're call since the math is the same. Try them both and see which works best. If you're wrong, we don't kill you, so experiment and learn.

---

20 Rep Squats

theuofh: After reading Strong Enough, I have decided to give a 20 rep squat routine a try. My motivation for giving it a go was to add some size to my legs first of all and secondly to pay my prospective dues to the hard men who have come before me in the strength training world.

Anyway, I'm having a hard time finding programming information on the subject. I have Strossen's book, and I have all your books, but haven't read Practical Programming all the way through though. From skimming, I have found no mention of any information related to 20 reppers in there. I was wondering if you could give any suggestions on how to set up the rest of the routine in 20 rep squats? Stick to 5 reps for upper body work or up it to the hypertrophy rep ranges? How much more lower body work to add w/ the squats? Can power cleans be added before hand?

I'm 5'7" up to about 183 lbs, squat 1rm at probably a little over 305. I'm doing 2 squat workouts a week, and one deadlift, with another day for some kb swing/snatch conditioning w/ about 3500-4000 kcal a day. I started at 205, got 215, then 225, then 230. I think I'm going to stick w/ the 5 lb jumps and hopefully add 10 lbs a week. It's hard, but hasn't gotten Talk-to-Jesus/puke/collapse/pray for death-hard yet. Also I remember your 315x10 video not too long ago and I'm assuming your 20 RM PR is above that, if you wouldn't mind sharing it.

Mark Rippetoe: Since the 20-rep squat routine only lasts a few weeks if it's done correctly, the rest of the routine is almost irrelevant. I'd just maintain things with 5s so as not to create other stress to recover from. And I'd have to look up my PR on this, but I think it was about 345.

Tiburon: Good luck. Last person to try this was fluxboy, and we haven't heard from him in months.

Skuhr: Can you give any more information about a plan of attack for 20 rep programming? I am training for heavy backpacking/mountaineering and it would seem like a good fit after hitting the end of the novice phase. I'd be particularly interested to see how 20 rep training affects stamina.

Mark Rippetoe: It basically involves doing a set of 20 with a weight close to what you had previously assumed was your 10RM, once a week for as long as your psychology holds up. Get through the first 10 reps, and then just stand there and do them until you're through, however long that takes, with 10 lbs/week added. It's been written about elsewhere. It does work well for what you're describing.

Tor: Yeah, what the hell happened to Fluxboy?

Mark Rippetoe: Fluxboy may not be the most stable element in the periodic table. And it's hard to tell your 20RM based on your 10RM until you've tried it, because of the way that the 20s are done. You get through with your first 10 reps, and then the last 10 are essentially done as 10 singles, done with enough breathes in between the reps so that you can get them done, no matter how long it takes.

Why sets across?

JPostSam: I have a question about sets across, and it's basically this: why? You're critical of pyramiding because, as you say, it wears you out before you can get your work in. in that case, if you're doing 3 sets of an exercise with the same weight and for the same number of reps, aren't those first two sets just like really heavy warm-up sets? Wouldn't you be better off doing each set as heavy as you safely can? For example, if you're doing three sets of 5 reps with 175 pounds, as in the bench press example from the programming chapter of Starting Strength, doesn't that mean that you really could do about 190 for 5, then 180 for 5, then 170 for 5? (or something close to that?). And if so, wouldn't that be better than 3 sets of 5 at 175? it would certainly mean more power output, especially at higher weights...

I know I'm opening myself up to the usual "just do the program!" or some other kind of response that points out that I don't know what I'm talking about. But I'm not trying to sound like a jerk. I really am interested in learning about what makes one way better than another.

Mark Rippetoe: Experience has proven that the 3 x 5 works for novices and that 5 x 5 works for more advanced lifters. The reasoning is as follows: there is a weight you can train with for 5 reps that allows all the sets across to be done. This weight is light enough that the first sets can be done with good form and the last set to be done with acceptable form. This weight can be increased in a linear fashion, thus driving the adaptation upward in a linear fashion. On the other hand, descending sets would start with a weight at which the form was merely acceptable and the intensity was maximum, thus making all the subsequent sets a max effort due to the fatigue and the form increasingly bad. Bad form due to fatigue for squats usually means a lack of depth. Therefore, descending sets generally equals sloppy form, less than full ROM, and a very quick halt to progress.

Moved the weight up too fast/the Bent Press

max_power1.2: Just started SS last week...I was supposed to squat 165lbs today, but since I'm an idiot I accidentally put 175 on the bar (I added 10lbs to each side expecting the weight to increase by 10lbs in total...god I'm dumb. That's what happens when you workout first thing in the morning). The first two sets felt HEAVY, and I realized my mistake and lowered the weight to 165 for the third set. Should I put the weight to 175 next workout, or should I jump to 185 since I managed 175 for this workout? I'd assume the former, but I just want to make sure.

Also, what is your opinion on the old strongman favorite, the Bent Press? Do you think it's a good lift for building additional abdominal strength? I don't think I've seen it mentioned in any of your books.

Mark Rippetoe: I'd back up to the weight you were supposed to use. You'll get stuck very soon if you don't, since you have exceeded your adaptive ability through the misloaded jump. That's why you noticed it feeling heavy. You might get away with this once, but I'd correct it now and not get cocky about my ability to disregard my mathematical shortcomings.

The bent press is not a good exercise for an old guy with an old-guy spine. It is at best a more advanced exercise and at worst a subsidy program for chiropractors and neurosurgeons. There are better ways to train asymmetrically.

Deadlifting, erector spinae, and other things

tikuane: 1) My left erector spinae is significantly larger than the right
- Doctor said it was natural variation. Found no scoliosis.
- Resuming training again, left erector spinae is sore after front squats and deadlifts and right one isn't.
- I call bullshit on doc's explanation now. This appears to indicate the left one is being 'favored'?
-This is not in my head, in some close fitting shirts I can feel the left side pressing against the shirt whilst the right isn't and has been noticed by others during massage.

2) For volume day, has anyone tried using 6 x 4 as follows: 2 x 4 Press, 2 x 4 Dips, and 2 x 4 Bench? Or 4 x 4 Press and 2 x 4 Bench for 2:1 press/bench training ratio as indicated for CF Total improvement. Is this useful? Why or why not?

Mark Rippetoe: 1. Scoliosis is not necessarily the only cause of an imbalance in erector size. Even if your spine is straight unloaded, anything that might cause an asymmetry under load – a short leg, for instance – would produce a muscle belly asymmetry over time.

2. No one has ever done this because it is illegal. If you do it, be sure that you are alone; sets of 4 reps, again, are illegal.

Thruster/Squat Death

BWR: Did some heavy work last week, 3RM Thruster and the following day 3RM squat. Weights aside, I tweaked my back on the last set of thrusters, trying to get to full extension. Leaning back into what turned into a press my lower back hyper-extended a little I think, just a sharp pinch. Squats next day couldn't have helped. Other than overall being weak, what is the best way to finish off a pressing movement like that? Working the press should improve my thruster, but would like to avoid this again since the back still bugs me.

Mark Rippetoe: Now that you know, wear a belt next time you do 3RM thrusters. Rehab the back with higher reps on your normal back training. The belt will help with lockout on heavy presses, as will the ab strength that comes with regular 5x5 pressing, which you probably haven't been doing enough of. If the only time you press heavy is when you're actually locking out a pushed press or a thruster, then you are not really prepared for the task, either with strength or technique.

Reset on TM?

Albert987: So I've been doing TM for about 3 months now and my weight has gone up to about 192 lbs. Last week I went home for spring break and kind of got tired of eating so much... I ate maybe no more than 2000 calories a day. Sometimes I just had cookies and milk. I also didn't weight train, but I did stop by a CF gym and did a workout that made me puke for about an hour straight. My appetite was gone for the rest of the week after that. Anyways, I went today to weight train, I still weigh the same, about 2 lbs lighter, but my lifts were horrible, particularly squats. The last time I completed them I got 315-5x5.

Today I got:

315-1x3(fail)
295-1x3(fail)
295-1x1(fail)

I'm not sure what to do. I've never done a reset on TM before. It seems like if I did a 10% deload, it would take several weeks to get back to 315-5x5, if I go up by 5lb increments as I have been doing. It makes me sad to think my training actually regressed several weeks. Your advice would be appreciated.

Mark Rippetoe: I'm sorry you're sad. Were you a good boy about your recovery recently? The TM works for longer than 3 months, so I'd attribute your stall to either improper application of the programming or a recovery issue before I reset or changed programs.

Albert987: Yes sir it was. Unless that metcon workout killed me so much that I needed more time to recover? I was feeling pretty shitty for a couple days after.

Mark Rippetoe: A metcon workout that was hard enough to make you talk on the Big White Telephone for an hour could easily disrupt recovery for days. Be more respectful of metcon next time, and plan your training better. Hey, now you know.

Textbook form vs. adequate form

Joel: Rip, I had been struggling with the deadlift for several months. The loads were about the same as my squat loads, which I knew was a warning sign that something wasn't right. I had my squat depth verified by two different people. I focused my energies on the deadlift, and two points allowed me to immediately add weight to my working set: 1) the "chest up" cue 2) allowing for adequate form vs. perfect textbook form.

Addressing the second point, I believe I was too focused on textbook form to really lay it out there and go for a big weight. I had been squatting for years so I was comfortable with bigger weights on my back, and I instinctively knew what I could get away with form-wise when attempting a max set. The deadlift was relatively new to me, and I was trying to be very strict with my form.

When attempting a max working set (assuming a person has adequate experience), do you believe in always going as heavy as possible (each workout) with passable form? Or, do you believe in keeping textbook form most of the time and reserving passable form for the occasional max attempt?

Mark Rippetoe: I believe in progressing safely, with emphasis on progressing. If you always handle weights that can be done with textbook-perfect form, you will never handle weights heavy enough to cause a progression. Rank novices need to use textbook form, because for them this is not a limiting concern and they need to embed the elements of lumbar and thoracic extension and correct pulling mechanics as reflex from the beginning. As things get heavier, some deviation can be tolerated, but never enough that the movement becomes inefficient or dangerous. How much? This is a matter of experience, the judgment about which is acquired through the process and through good coaching.

---

101 rep bodyweight back squat

Jim: I just completed this challenge that I have had in the back of my head for over 2 years. I squatted 190 x 101 at 189lbs bodyweight. I have been talking to people about this type of training and have gotten mixed emotions. My question is: Do see any value in ultra high rep squats in a normal training routine aside from "seeing how much you can take". I am surprised though (not that surprised, just disappointed) that the carryover from high rep squats does not really affect lower rep high load #'s. Do you ever have your athletes do high rep squat workouts, and if so, about how often?

Mark Rippetoe: Other than manhood development, 100-rep sets of anything is merely a good way to get a nice dose of some sort of tendinitis. Now, I have used high-rep deadlifts – 100 reps with 30 sec between them – for work capacity development, but to leave the bar on your back for 101 reps is actually a joke workout we used to laugh about 20 years ago: The 101 Program = 101 sets of 101 reps with 101 pounds in 101 different exercises. It was a very complete approach, really. But we never actually *did* it. Because we were trying to get *strong*. And a weight you can do for 101 reps is not heavy enough to make you *strong*. Like kettlebell training, it's good for something but not for getting *strong*.

Human Biology

As upsetting as this may be to some in the religious community, humans are actually just little piles of biology – stacks of organic reactions, gobbets of various complicated types of proteins and fats, heaps of cellular goo organized in an interesting way. Mostly over my head, but that has never stopped me from writing about anything.

Morning lifting

Corey: I read that doing heavy lifting first thing early in the morning is not the best time because the CNS needs a little time (hour or two) to "wake up". Do you know if there is any truth to this claim?

Mark Rippetoe: I'll go out on a limb here and say that training first thing in the morning is for crazy people. And my CNS takes more than just time to wake it up. But depending on your reason for training, it might behoove you to slap it around a little, especially if job requirements dictate that you are not always able to control the time when you have to use the aforementioned sleepy CNS. Combat personnel, firefighters, law enforcement types, etc., often do not have the luxury of choosing when to exert, and are best prepared for this contingency by doing an occasional workout very early.

Corey: *"....training first thing in the morning is for crazy people."* ? Haaaa...I love it. Mark, I've had two minor shoulder/upper back muscle strains and both times it happened at crow p*ss. I'm a Fire Protection Engineer and like yourself get extremely busy. I have to get my workouts in when I can, but my apprehension to pulling 400lbs off the floor at 6am is now confirmed by the Master. Everyone is different, but it's good to know I at least share something in common with you (certainly not strength)....a sleepy CNS.

MISSINGLINK: I lift early in the morning and the thought of deadlifting heavy weight or doing the Smolov squat routine is the last thing I want to do, but once it is over you are done for the day. All my friends say I am half a bubble off so I guess working out in the mornings suits me just fine. Once you get over the groggy feeling it is all good. Bite your upper lip and get in there and lift some heavy weights. A lot of people do it.

Mark Rippetoe: Corey: I'll bet you a fire extinguisher that you're waaaay stronger than me.

Link: A lot of people also buy U2 records, but that doesn't mean I'm going to start wearing purple sunglasses. I applaud your nads. Now, run along and have fun doing heavy things at 6am.

MISSINGLINK: You don't like U2?

Mark Rippetoe: I don't like Bono. He needs to train more.

Galapogos: Isn't the reason why you shouldn't lift within 1 hour of getting up because of the spinal synovial fluid issue? This is the first time I've heard about the CNS issue...

Mark Rippetoe: Tell me about the Spinal Synovial Fluid Issue.

Galapogos: I'm quoting from someone else here
Quote:

Best Time to Train
… according to Olympic Strength Coach Charles Poliquin, your joints (specifically, the synovial fluid that lubricates your joints) require about 3 hours to reach an optimal level of warmth which will help improve performance while decreasing the likelihood of injury.

Mark Rippetoe: How is it possible that the rest of you gets warm but your synovial fluid takes 3 hours? Is it somehow insulated from the rest of your tissues? Does it not conduct heat as well as the other tissues, all of which have about the same water content? How would the same processes that prepare the rest of the surrounding tissue fail to also prepare the synovial fluid?

Front Squats and Hip Flexor Tendonitis

Anonymous: I've been front squatting regularly for a few months, and I've noticed that my right hip flexor is getting increasingly sore right where it attaches to my hip. In the squat chapter, you said that this is caused by letting my knees slide forward at the bottom. However, in front squats, isn't that supposed to happen due to being very upright? So I don't know what to do.

Also, I don't really understand the explanation that well. While standing up, I can flex my knee and grab my foot (standard quad stretch). So in that position, since my knee is flexed and my hip is extended, my rectus femoris is fully lengthened. Now, at the bottom of the squat, even though my knee is flexed, my hip is flexed as well. So I don't understand why my rectus femoris would pull so hard at its attachment, since it still has more room to lengthen.

Anyway, the fact of the matter is that my hip flexion ROM is very limited due to a pinching feeling right there at the hip flexor attachment. It's always been like that. I can barely flex my hips more than 90 degrees without feeling that pinching sensation. I can't do regular back squats or conventional deadlifts (I've been doing sumo) due to not being able to achieve enough hip flexion. It feels like the top of my thigh is simply running into my hip bone.

Mark Rippetoe: I think the first thing I would do is quit front squatting, because for you they are an assistance exercise. The hip flexor problem happens because of the tension applied to its insertion points on the ASIS (the anterior superior iliac spine) and the AIIS (the anterior inferior iliac spine) as the knee drops forward. It doesn't matter that the muscle belly is not fully stretched, because it is contracting eccentrically – it's not relaxed – and as it resists lengthening it is applying tension at its insertion point. This is always obviously the case, but when the hamstrings relax and allow the knees to drop forward, the tension at the insertion becomes more dynamic. It happens for the same reason you get knee tendonitis from plyometric movements. Not everybody has trouble with this, but when one does, this is usually the reason.

But you seem to have something else going on. Find an intelligent PT if you can and get it evaluated. I can't tell from here.

(As is often the case, I have learned, or read more carefully, since this was posted. The thing he is describing – hip "impingement", analogous to the same thing that happens to a shoulder – is simply fixed by getting the knees out of the way by shoving them out at the bottom of the squat so that the femur clears the ASIS. This works for both front and back squats. In combination with a locked lower back, it forms a technique we now call "active hip", and is fundamental to the way we explain good squatting and pulling mechanics.)

PP Cardio question

Jamie J: In PP, you say that cardio training should be done at least 5 hours after strength training and that it a negative effect on strength and size. This statement is in regards to Long Slow Distance (LSD).

My question is on the effects of sprinting and middle distance (300 - 800 meters) on strength development? Would the same 5 hours time frame apply? Could you suggest a training protocol for sprints and middle distance running to compliment SS program or a basic Texas method? If not, could you suggest a source for such information?

Mark Rippetoe: LSD is really not good for humans. Middle distance efforts and sprints can be quite useful for metabolic conditioning. If you are working up through your novice SS progression, I'd recommend holding off a while until your initial plateau is reached; this linear strength improvement will be more valuable in the long term than met/con, which is easier to obtain and comes more efficiently when you are strong. If you are already an intermediate-level trainee, you could add a sprint day to your week, and then add your middle distance day a month or two later after you have had time to adapt the rest of your training to the added work.

Jamie J: How do you draw the line between LSD and more useful training? Heart rate, speed, RPE?

Mark Rippetoe: As a general rule, if you can keep doing it for more than 20 minutes at the same intensity, it's slow.

Reasons why we're different and respond better to different training

britlifter: Ok I know this, we're all different and what may be an optimal way to train for one person isn't going to be the best way for everyone. I would like to ask about the things that actually make us different with regard to training for strength and size. Would you mention some things that actually make us different and therefore respond better to one form of training as opposed to another?

Mark Rippetoe: The things that are primarily responsible for the differences in individual genetic capacity for the ability to excel at strength sports depend on the sport. Anthropometry is a big consideration. Most very good weightlifters are either of normal proportions with relatively long arms, or tend slightly towards longer torsos/shorter legs. Longer arms can be a liability for powerlifting, where the bench press is adversely affected by long arms but where the deadlift benefits. Squatting ability is benefited by balanced leg/torso proportions. Bodybuilding is not a sport, but still lives and dies by anthropometry: normal balanced proportions, thin skin, low propensity to store sub-Q bodyfat, and long muscle bellies are all anthropometric characteristics.

The second most important characteristic would be neuromuscular efficiency, a thing which is unfortunately quite dependent on genetic endowment. The density of motor unit innervation, fast twitch/slow twitch ratios, and CNS efficiency are all controlled by genetics, and to a large extent are not trainable. The abilities they control can be improved within the boundaries imposed by their limitations, but you can't train a kid with a 10" vertical to have a 20". These factors are not visible in a bodybuilder, but the effects their limitations impose on his training are.

Getting Sarcoplasmic?

RRod: In your experience, what role (if any) does sarcoplasmic hypertrophy training have in the program of aspiring barbell competitors? Does a focused effort on increasing the capacity of the sarcoplasm yield any tangible benefit (in either performance or recovery), or does it just make you look like a vascular marshmallow? Throughout all this I mean that the trainee (intermediate or better) focuses on efforts in the 10+ rep range, as opposed to the lower ranges associated with strength and power building.

Mainly I wonder if having more squishy stuff around would a.) improve recovery ability by aiding the transport of nutrients into the muscle fibers and/or b.) improve leverages for more efficient force transfer, and if these benefits (if they exist) ever warrant taking time away from lower rep training.

Mark Rippetoe: Sarcoplasmic hypertrophy and myofibrillar hypertrophy compliment each other in the ways you mentioned, and depending on your anthropometry, it may make perfect sense to do an occasional hypertrophy cycle as an intermediate trainee. A novice, of course, cannot hypertrophy any faster than the linear progression model facilitates, and done correctly this will be the period of fastest growth a lifter ever experiences.

Active rest

bango skank: Should rest just be rest? What's your take?

Mark Rippetoe: Depends, as most things do. It must be for me, because I'm old and don't sleep well. Active rest will not benefit my recovery, but for a younger man it usually helps IF it is applied correctly. Correctly means light enough and short enough to constitute a "flush" and not another stressor.

Steven Q: Would that be a stressor to the muscle itself or to the CNS? I was told that some of the non-weight lifting movements (bodyweight squats, pushups, kipping pullups done at relatively low reps, as not to completely fatigue the muscle) were not particularly stressing towards the CNS.

Obviously the only way to find out is to test these things out, but would doing high rep work on air squats, a Tabata for instance, be helpful? Doing even 10 or 15 air squats has my legs burning; would increasing my threshold on higher reps benefit my lower rep squats, or is one too specific to benefit the other?

Mark Rippetoe: Any stress to which you are not adapted will produce a stress response – an adaptation. If you are capable of recovering from it. There is nothing magical about high reps that makes them active rest, especially if you are not adapted to high reps. There are few ways to get more sore than Tabata squats if you're not used to doing them, and the process of getting used to doing them would be an adaptation, and during that adaptation they would not be rest. It doesn't matter if the CNS or the contractile organs are subjected to the stress; the only thing that could constitute active rest would be a sub-adaptive stimulus.

Approach to bad sessions

Patrick: My question, most generally, is how you approach a workout you know is going to be god-awful. Specifically, I have chronic insomnia and that means there are times when I'm going on a couple hours of sleep for three or four consecutive nights. It doesn't happen all that often anymore and unless I think I'm risking injury by lifting I don't allow it to prevent me – my doctor agrees with this approach, shockingly. Nevertheless, the situation has arisen once or twice a month for the past year that I'm damn nearly gassed when I get to the gym so I just man up and grind out the reps until I'm done.

My problem is that I'm getting to the point where I can no longer perform maximal effort lifts on these days because it just takes too much juice. My working squat is 275 and the rest of the lifts are on par with my squat at my bodyweight. With weights like that I feel like I need all the strength I have at my best to move the bar. If it's a heavy squat day and I go at full intensity, I have nothing left by the end of the workout. On the one hand that's fine, because my important stuff is done up front but on the other hand I give really short shrift to everything but the first one or maybe two lifts, sometimes skipping them after the first set fails horribly. In either case I'm going to be slowing the progression plan I have set up but I'm not sure which one strikes me as better.

I think I might try just doing 75% of what I had planned, in terms of weight. At least then I can get through a full workout as written, and give all of the lifts some decent attention. Does this sound reasonable? Would I be better off doing the primary lifts at full effort and scaling back on the later stuff? Or am I overthinking it and need to just keep my head down and do whatever I can?

Mark Rippetoe: Training when you're all used up like this is best avoided. You run a higher risk of injury during the workout itself and the benefit of the training is muted because the work you do get done further depresses your already depleted ability to recover. Suboptimal training plus suboptimal recovery tends to be an unrewarding combination. I'd just skip a day.

If you decide that you have to train under these circumstances, I'd recommend you keep the intensity the same and drop the volume. This means triples instead of fives for the primary "slow" lifts after as little warmup as you can tolerate, decrease the number of sets on power clean and drop any assistance work.

Arms fall asleep

banderbe: Wondering if you have had experience with trainees who had their arms fall asleep at night while sleeping. I notice that it starts whenever I start doing flat bench pressing on a regular basis.

Mark Rippetoe: My hands do that due to a little carpal tunnel constriction, but not my whole arm. How far up does the numbness go?

Banderbe: Well, actually last night it was just my hands, primarily my right hand. And I'm right handed. But in the past I have woken up with essentially a dead arm, and when I stopped benching it went away, although my weight was dropping (and now I'm gaining) so it could be related to those sorts of body comp changes too. I'll try some heat on it tonight and have my wife (chiropractor) work on it some.

Well, actually last night it was just my hands, primarily my right hand. And I'm right handed. But in the past I have woken up with essentially a dead arm, and when I stopped benching it went away, although my weight was dropping (and now I'm gaining) so it could be related to those sorts of body comp changes too. I'll try some heat on it tonight and have my wife (chiropractor) work on it some.

Baldr: My hand goes numb rarely, but when it does it stays numb for at least two weeks. This could be due to the ganglion cyst in my wrist, perhaps the cyst is restricting normal blood flow.

Mark Rippetoe: Numbness has nothing to do with blood flow; it's not "cut-off circulation" as we were told when we were kids. It is a conduction block of some type affecting the nerve supply to the numb area. A whole arm asleep implies something in the shoulder, possibly a brachial plexus issue. If a ganglion cyst on the wrist is big enough and you sleep with your hand in a position in which the cyst presses against the nerve for an extended period, it might very well be damaged enough to take a couple of weeks to heal.

Stuck on the bench press

hithebeach: 15, 5'8, 145.2lbs. And I have a major problem regarding the bench press.
I'm stuck with the same weight for 2 month and am doing your program by the book for 3 1/2 month. All the other lifts are GREAT. Before starting the program I was 112.2lbs, now I'm 145.2 and still gaining weight. First squat workout was 66lbs, now 162lbs. First deadlift workout 66lbs, now 154lbs. First press workout 49.5lbs now 82.5lbs. Never thought clippers could be used as plates to prevent stalling! Figured it out about the middle of may and since then I'm increasing the weight by 2.2lbs almost every single workout.

I was benching a little without any program before starting, 55lbs, after starting your program I was gaining weight on the bar every workout, 5.5 lbs each workout to the bench... UNTIL I GOT TO 110lbs, ALMOST NO WEIGHT GAINS ON THE BENCH SINCE THEN. I've reset this damn exercise 3 times and it still doesn't help! What to do?

Mark Rippetoe: The main things to consider is that you are 5' 8", 145, and 15 years old. You're doing very well, but you're rather young to be expecting gigantic progress in such a short timeframe. The best thing you can do for your progress is to grow. To the extent you can control this, eating more is your primary tool. You're doing very well, just calm down and enjoy the fact that you're not 53.

Elevated Cardiac Enzymes

KSC: I have an issue with a client of mine. Brief history: Male, 43 years old, recently had his annual physical... got back a report from the MD's that he had high/elevated levels of cardiac enzymes in his blood stream (Creatine-phosphokinase and troponin, I think). He was told that this was not good and could be a sign of a damaged/unhealthy heart?

I am skeptical of this. I am no doctor but isn't the only way the heart can get damaged thru an actual heart attack? And wouldn't he know if he had had a heart attack???? I have also read that CPK levels can be elevated due to strenuous exercise. If so, is this okay or is it dangerous? He basically works out with me twice per week doing one basic barbell workout each week and one metcon workout each week. The doctors scared him though, and now he is very apprehensive about working out cuz he thinks he is gonna have a heart attack any minute now. Thanks for any help you can provide.

Mark Rippetoe: An undulating elevated CPK is a normal thing for someone who trains heavy. Depending on the proximity of his last workout to the blood draw, he will always show an elevated CPK, and his SGOT (AST) and SGPT will also be elevated. As a general rule, if you are muscle-sore when you are drawn, you will show elevated "heart" enzymes, because muscle repair is what they indicate. To the extent that the heart is a muscle, the non-cardiac-specific "cardiac" enzymes are always periodically elevated in an athlete that trains hard. It is odd that doctors always practice CYA in lieu of asking relevant questions, but this is the norm. There are certainly instances of occult CVAs, but they are more common in women. And how is it possible that an unhealthy heart could tolerate a hard metcon workout weekly? Get him a better doctor, if you can find one.

Q: nicotine & effect on strength training

Airborne RU: Occasionally I like to smoke a nice cigar. Lots of my compatriots like to dip. Question, does nicotine inhibit or adversely effect strength training & muscle growth? I've read and heard that nicotine constricts blood vessels (something about inhibiting blood flow to the skin), but do these side effects (albeit minor) change the body's chemistry or hormonal balance with regards to a SS regimen?

Mark Rippetoe: There has been little if any work done on nicotine's effects on anabolic processes. It provides a general CNS stimulation, similar to caffeine. The problem is probably not the nicotine, it is the delivery systems, all of which cause other problems.

Trying SS but with interesting problem

DarkKnight91: When I was born, my left foot came out crooked (bent in towards the right) while my right was fine. I had an immediate operation as a kid and they straightened it out (by breaking some bones and rearranging some stuff), but now it's okay and straight. The only problem is my left foot is smaller than my right and my left calf is noticeably weaker and smaller than my right (everything under the left knee). I have modified the SS training I've done to include calf exercises for my left leg alone (2 times a week).

What I wanted to ask you was if it's okay to do SS (i.e. squat, deadlift, etc, etc). when one of my legs is weaker than the other. My left and right quad are about equal in strength, and my right hamstring is just a little more stronger than the left... I only notice big discrepancies below the knees as far as mass and strength goes....what do I do? I don't want to build to a point where I'm going to have joint problems and have my legs fall apart.

Mark Rippetoe: Chad Vaughn, a member of our US Olympic weightlifting team at the 2008 Games, has a similar "problem", one that has not stopped him at all. Just train normally, paying special attention to the maintenance of perfect symmetry, and the structures that are weaker will receive proportionately more work, thus bringing them into eventual balance. I don't think doing an intentional asymmetrical load on the weak side is of value, because it does not address the problem of symmetrical performance which is your base issue.

Only 20 pounds of muscle on a normal man?

fluxboy: Sorry if this is off topic a bit, Rip, but with all this interest in gaining weight, and putting on muscle, I'm curious if you have on thoughts on this: Years back, I read that Arthur Jones (yah, I know) made a claim that no one had ever actually determined how much bodyweight actual muscle is responsible for. If memory serves, I think he estimated it at only about twenty pounds or so. That sounds a little on the light side, but anyway ...

I bring this up, just because sometimes it's hard not to get a little gloomy over the prospect of only adding a few pounds here or there. But if one does manage to put on twenty pounds of quality muscle, that is (if we are to believe Art) literally doubling the muscle mass of the body.

Mark Rippetoe: If I am a 210 lb. man with 20% bodyfat, my non-fat bodyweight is 168 lbs. What are the chances that 148 of those pounds are guts, brains, and bone? Maybe they were for Arthur, but not for someone who actually trains.

KSC: It's easy to hate on old Art, but I did like the old Nautilus pullover machine with the bike chain. Anyone ever use that? No other manufacturer was ever able to replicate that one. Feel free to rip me apart for this one, but I will admit that if I came across one today that was priced reasonably I'd buy it. Then I'd have to hide it from all my hardcore trainees.

Mark Rippetoe: Me too. Our little secret...

Lon Kilgore: There were two cadaver dissection studies from where we get data to estimate how much muscle mass is on the average frame. One study from the 40's (can't remember the authors name) and one in 1984 by Clarys. Muscle was estimated to comprise 40-60% of body mass. Neither study included any athletes or hard training individuals. The average individual's skeletal elements made up about 21% of body mass.

Hey Rip! How about 6 week, 20 rep squat cycle?

fluxboy: Tonight I started doing a few singles in the squat, just out of curiosity. Got up to 350 lbs, and could have done more (I'm certain) but for some reason my hip drive took flight at 355. But here's what I'm thinking:

What if I drop the weight big time, say down to 225 doing 20 rep breathing squats, and then over the next six weeks, add five pounds a workout, 90 lbs in total, so that come October 1st ... I'm doing 315 x 20. Now, that 225 is a big drop. Traditional folklore says that I'm to do twenty reps with a ten rep weight, which is probably closer to 275 lbs. However, I'm not greedy. Dropping to 225 will give me a chance to build up plenty of momentum to hit 315 x 20.

Current lifts:
Squat: 320 x 5, 335 x3, 350 x 1
Deadlift: 345 x 5
Bench: 205 x 5
Press: 140 x 5
Power Cleans: 185 x 3
Bodyweight: 215 lbs

I'd really appreciate your thoughts on this. And maybe, if possible, a Rip sanctioned, 20 rep squat routine?

Mark Rippetoe: Jesus, flux, why don't you do it and *then* I'll tell you what's wrong. That will be more fun for me. But I'll give you a hint: I don't think you're going to turn 320 x 5 into 315 x 20 in six weeks. At least not the pure, wholesome way.

Training Volume and Blood work

Alpha Zulu: Next Friday I am going to be getting some blood work done with my annual physical, including total/free/bound Test levels. By the time the appointment rolls around, I will be finishing up my third week in a block of very hard training.

I am still an intermediate, making weekly gains, but usually by about 3-4 weeks of hard training, I begin to feel a little rundown, workouts are not as productive, I have a little bit of a harder time sleeping, etc... so I am wondering if I should backoff the training next week, and maybe even the remainder of this week, to ensure that I am not at that point and that my Testosterone levels are not adversely effected by hard training. Is even an issue for someone who is not an advanced lifter?

Mark Rippetoe: Your test levels will be elevated in all likelihood, but if they do a cortisol level it will be elevated as well. Their ratio is important, and a higher C than T would indicate some degree of overtraining. But a more conventional concern will be your CPK and SGOT (possibly AST on your panel) levels, which will almost certainly be elevated as a normal effect of hard training. Don't let them bother you about this. Do a little reading in advance and be prepared for poor levels of understanding by the lab/nursing staff.

zephed56: I was thinking about getting a blood test done for shits and giggles, then eating a ton of eggs, whole milk and red meat (paleo-ish except for carne asada days) for the next several months, and then getting the test done again to compare.

I just looked up blood tests and I found the chem7 test and a comprehensive blood test as two common tests performed, but neither had anything to do with what you wrote above. Would an HMO typically approve any of the tests you mentioned above or do you need some compelling reason to get them done? I'm pretty sure I can get the basic tests done through an HMO. Is there anything else I should know before going in? Also, I intend to make a prop bet with someone over my test results, any good ideas here?

Mark Rippetoe: The tests vary according to the type of equipment the lab is using. A partial lipid panel used to be included in the Series 20, but is now a separate test in many labs. And I don't know what an HMO pays for because I always just pay cash for the tests I need after I get them called in by a doctor friend. It is MUCH cheaper that way.

zephed56: Thanks. So I assume tests aren't all that expensive. Good to know. I'll probably get a physical or annual checkup done sometime soon and ask about it then. Perhaps I'll drink a GOWholeMAD for a certain time period and compare before and after test results.

Mark Rippetoe: I once ate a half-pound of liver and went in 2 hours later for a lipid panel. Total cholesterol was 188.

Osteoarthritis of the knee

dirkh: I would like to know your opinion on strength training with osteoarthritis. Seems like I have pre-stage osteoarthritis in my knees, they are clicking and crunching when I squat etc. and sometimes hurt. Until now, it's not that excessive, more a discomfort than real pain but I am worried what it will be like in 5 years or so. I think the cause might be my fallen arch in both feet.

Since I don't want to stop training of course, I talked to my lecturer at the university who is PhD in sports physiology and he told me that it would be very difficult to identify the intensity where there is too much stress on the cartilage and that especially if I'm more advanced chances are high that I will damage the cartilage with my training more and more because of the heavy weights that will be necessary to cause an adaptation.
So he told me I should reduce the intensity on the exercises which put stress on the knee and be careful with them so that a strength base is maintained but no further damage is done to the cartilage. What would you recommend?
My stats: age 24, 5'9", 174 lbs., squat 249, deadlift 286

Mark Rippetoe: I recommend that you go to a school that hires professors who are smarter than their students, one who understands that the articular cartilages adapt to stress just like all the other tissues – like muscles, bones, ligaments, meniscii, and tendons – do. Osteoarthritis of the knee usually involves a trauma, and I have never seen it occur from just squatting. And I have taught more people to squat than he has. How does your professor think that powerlifters get to a 600 lb. squat? How many people has he made strong? You have been diagnosed with pre-osteo by whom? By a guy that doesn't like the way your knees sound? Does he know that many people have thicker synovial fluid, depending on chronic hydration status and other factors that make their perfectly healthy knees noisy? Does he understand that pre-osteo is by definition a healthy knee? Do you understand that everybody's knees hurt sometimes if they train? Are you sure your form is correct? Are you using weightlifting shoes to keep your goofy flat feet stable when you squat?

Dirkh: This surprised me a bit because I was told that osteoarthritis is a degeneration of the cartilage caused by overuse over a longer period of time. I don't think it occurs just from squatting but maybe developed over time from the defective position of my feet. I already felt some discomfort in the knees before I started to squat I think. To defend my professor, he doesn't think that squats cause these problems in general and he is not one of these guys who just tell you "quit weight training" when you have any pain or so. It was just his recommendation to cut down intensity to make sure that the cartilage is not damaged any further (I have no ambitions to compete in WL or PL but just train for my personal fitness and he suggested that maybe I should just maintain my current strength level to keep my knees healthy as long as possible).

And OK, I didn´t get an MRI to check it, but I thought that the symptoms indicate this diagnosis (knees cracking almost every time I bend or extend my legs, slight pain that seems to get worse when staying in a position for a longer time, e.g. standing around or sitting at my desk).

Mark Rippetoe: I don't think you are "wearing out" you knees. And I'm not sure you don't have osteo; I'm just sure you don't have osteo from squats, which are very good in your case. I'm surprised that you aren't aware that most osteo comes from trauma. Wouldn't this mean that everyone eventually gets knee osteo? And this statement: *"It was just his recommendation to cut down intensity to make sure that the cartilage is not damaged any further."* reflects a lack of understanding of the adaptive processes upon which training is based. Specifically, cartilage develops into bone, and loading inhibits the change from cartilage to bone; the thickness of cartilage is greater where there is more loading because of this.

Dirkh: So, would you recommend that I just continue with my training as long as it causes no problems? In fact, I often have the impression that my knees feel better after the workouts. As far as I know, nearly everyone is more or less affected by osteoarthritis in the course of time. Many resources on the internet state that about 80% of the people over 50 or so have radiographic evidence of osteoarthritis (although only 60% of them are symptomatic). I was under the impression that most osteo comes from abrasion caused by defective positions of joints or overweight.

Mark Rippetoe: That's exactly what I'd recommend. But isn't it far more likely that most people over the age of 50 have suffered some type of trauma in the course of being a human than it is their knees just grind themselves away in the absence of an adequate repair mechanism?

Full Squat Safety Question

Neil G: In the full squat, a trainee has to pass through the quarter and half squat positions on the way to the correct depth. Why is it that these positions are not considered dangerous to the knees when they are part of the full squat movement?

Mark Rippetoe: The main reason is that on the way down through these positions that would be bad were you to stop there, you're not stopping. Your posterior chain is tight in these positions because the descent of a deep squat is not the same position as you assume if you intend to do a partial squat. And you are in a very different position at those points in the descent of a full squat than you are in the equivalent partial squat, so your knees are protected. That, and the fact that the change in direction occurs below parallel and distributes the force more equitably makes the deep squat much easier on the knees than any partial.

Good weight for CrossFit?

Brian: You say that 200 or more pounds is good for someone that is 5'10". Is this for powerlifters, CrossFitters, or just any average person?

Mark Rippetoe: I don't know that there is a "valid weight" for CrossFitters. I just know that big motors make cars go faster, especially when towing a boat.

sasquatch989: Except those same big engines only get 12 mpg. Some of those longer battles in CF really punish you for having extra weight to bear, especially in monostructural and bodyweight centered events. I've found that extra weight makes some CF workouts better, others slower. Grace (135# Clean and Jerk x 30) is at 3 mins when I weigh 115kg, but my Cindy (5 pullups, 10 pushups, 15 squats, 20 mins max rounds) never goes above 15 rounds. The concept of strength-to-weight ratio is one that gets passed over in the NSCA Essentials and I've never read anything in the journal about it. I think it is a far greater indicator of fitness, and it's definitely more impressive when a 60kg guy puts up a 110kg C&J rather than a big oaf like me does. I think the key is your BW to strength ratio. If you're 200lbs. and can DL 400 and there is someone who is 150lbs. and can DL 400 chances are that person can outperform you on the BW exercises, can run faster, etc.

Rip, any thoughts on ideal strength to weight ratios for CF, PL, OL, and general athletic development? Could there possibly be an ideal S:W ratio rather than an ideal weight? Any good exercise science (oxymoron?) published on this?

Mark Rippetoe: These are all rather obvious observations. They all boil down to the fact that the stronger you are, the better you are at CF. A guy that's 5'3" at 138 may be strong for his weight, but a guy 5'10" that weighs 150 is just not going to be able to hang, because his MOTOR ISN'T BIG ENOUGH. Strength/weight ratio is going to be dependent on skeletal dimensions, since there is an optimum amount of muscle mass and bodyfat that makes the skeleton work effectively, and "effective" is determined by the nature of the task. CF strives for balance among several disparate skills and abilities, since the point is not to specialize. But the common factor all good CFers have is that they are very strong. If you are 200 and can DL 400, but your buddy is 150 and can DL 400, you are not as strong as he is. You need to get stronger. But what if you are 6'7" and he is 5'4"?

I don't know of a table that details a bodyweight/strength ratio for anything. There would be different values for each fitness parameter, and there would be enough people that performed well outside the "norms" that they would be of little value anyway.

But much more important than any consideration of strength/bodyweight ratio is that usually the Universe does not care about this. If a 200 lb. man is down and needs to be moved NOW, the S:W ratio of the guy that has to move him is absolutely irrelevant. In the field, the task usually encountered is not scalable for bodyweight or strength – it merely is what must be done, and you are either strong enough to do it or you are not.

Tight Back & Crack

kayno: I'll give you some background to better help you with my query:

Age- 34. Weight- 88 kg. Height- 5' 9.
Training- Texas Method, spent 3 months learning Oly Lifting at a state association.
Flexibility- crap. Injuries- never.
So, I found that my lower back was becoming increasingly tight at rest, not sore as such but just really tight. If I went for a run for a warm up before training then it just got unbearably tight and would have to stop about 3 minutes in. So I saw a physio who told me I was a tight arse in so many words, and tight hammys too, so he gave me stretches for those as well as the hip flexors. My query is:

1-With all the movements being done with a lower back locked hard under load particularly with pulls, why does there not need to be a counter-balance with some more torso flexion built into these type of programs. The only one I can think of is sit ups which don't seem to rate terribly high in the programs hierarchy.

2- What do you think is an effective way for me to avoid this problem in the future?
Thanks again mate.

Mark Rippetoe: Here's the deal: when you are experiencing your early growth spurts, it is frequently reported that the lower back becomes "tight" as you describe upon exertion that involves postural muscle isometric contraction, like running. It happened to me as well. My theory is that it is a form of muscle compartment syndrome, where the muscle belly has grown faster than the fascia around it can accommodate. It will go away eventually, but a myofascial release might help. I didn't know about MF release when I was in this phase, so I just dealt with it. Find a massage therapist and give it a try.

Kayno: Thanks mate. That could be it because another time the pain gets real bad is when I do the dishes (hips in slight flexion). On a related topic, since I have already made those initial increases in body weight and strength and am on an intermediate program, is GOMAD still the best way to go? My nutrition quality and amount of calories has never been a problem. My body weight 88kgs -deadlift 3RM 150kgs -squat 3RM 125kgs -press 3RM 65kgs -bench 3RM 105kgs -clean 60kgs/3rep

And an unrelated topic, you say in PPST pg.149 that "focused abdominal exercises may be the most important assistant movements to include". So if we give the trunk musculature a stimulus while doing all of our functional compound movements with a decent load, why is it then necessary to do isolation exercises for the abs? Thanks again mate, stoked for your input.

Mark Rippetoe: I think that at 5'9" you can carry quite a bit more than 88 kg. I'd try the milk for a while and see what happens to your numbers. If you're intermediate and find you're getting too fat, back off. And I don't think it will hurt to do an occasional set or two of knees-to-elbows or weighted situps. It is true that heavy pulls, squats, and presses keep your abs strong, but it still won't hurt.

Kayno: Re: abs, sorry to be persistent on this one Rip, but "why not" was the response I got when asking another friend who I regarded knowledgeable. I'd like to know what you think are the actual benefits to adding isolated ab work to this type of programming. I've been doing the program to date without any ab stuff, and I was just wondering if I could get added benefits by bringing them into the routine or could they be a waste of time.

Mark Rippetoe: Try them and see. People have been using heavy brief ab work quite productively for a long time because a little extra ability to stabilize the spine is never a bad thing. And the flexion work might pertain to your initial question 1. The thing I actually dislike about most ab work is the tendency most people have toward high reps. Like the military, f'rinstance, which seems to be under the impression that if 20 bodyweight situps is good then 200 must be better.

Patella and squat?

Oleg21: A good friend of mine, who had done an anatomy course told me that squats cause the patella to move forward, and that is very likely to cause a severe injury. I do not intend to stop squatting, but I would like to hear what you have to say about that.

Mark Rippetoe: It should be obvious that your friend is a fool, who does not understand either anatomy or statistics. Be more careful with whom you associate.

Do deadlifts damage your spine?

Paradigm Shift: I was talking to someone who knew quite a bit about working out today (soon to enter competitions, great body, wealth of knowledge). He said that he does not do deadlifts as they put hundred of pounds of pressure on your spine (even when done correctly and in good form). And I'm not referring to getting injured after working out. He was saying more in the long run it would be bad for your back. Can anyone comment? I know Rip wouldn't tell us to do something that would hurt us in the long run but I was just wondering if there was any truth to this.

Mark Rippetoe: Deadlifts do put hundreds of pounds of pressure on your back. This could only become a problem if you're actually strong enough to lift hundreds of pounds. Your bodybuilder friend is apparently not, so he doesn't really know. I'd ask someone who's actually done them, if I were you.

Polynomial: It's nice to see that your friend has avoided having more weight on his spine by keeping his head up his ass.

Exercising lumbars in full ROM

ia1234: I would like to know your opinion on exercising lumbars in full range of motion, using exercises like straight leg deadlift or back extensions. Some coaches argue against it (e.g. Eric Cressey, Mike Robertson), some for it (e.g. Bill Starr).

Mark Rippetoe: The function of the trunk muscles is neither concentric nor eccentric, but rather isometric – their job is to maintain constant stable intervertebral relationships under a load. So the concept of full

ROM for the lumbar muscles in terms of their normal function is rather squishy. The erectors and abs can be worked with extension/flexion exercises like back extensions and situps, but their normal function is that which is manifested in the squat and deadlift. Direct extension/flexion work is useful for injury rehab or light day work for intermediate/advanced lifters. Machines for this purpose are just made to sell club memberships to the general public.

Cortisone

9S3RQ9: The diagnosis: hip bursitis (right). Doc's recommendation: local cortisone injection. Any opinion on cortisone? Is it catabolic? Will it weaken my right leg? Damn it!

Mark Rippetoe: Of course it's catabolic. That's how it works. I'd damn sure try an IT band release before I let them inject it. The reason they want to inject it instead of doing the release is because they can charge more for the injection, and because they don't know how to do the release.

TravisRussellDC: Cortisone is a very powerful anti-inflammatory. Bursitis is inflammation of the bursa (a fluid filled sack). It seems logical that an anti-inflammatory would take care of the inflammation. However, what caused the bursa to become inflamed in the first place? If that cause isn't addressed, will the bursa become inflamed again when the cortisone dissipates? With the catabolic effects of the cortisone shot (cortisone pretty much eats away the connective tissues around the injection site) are you essentially creating a weaker and less stable joint? Will this instability cause problems in and of itself later on? Why do they only allow 3 cortisone injections per location?

These are questions you need to ask yourself and perhaps your doctor. If it were me, I would do whatever I could to avoid injecting something into the joint that pretty much destroys whatever it comes in contact with. Find the cause of the bursitis. Treat the cause and the body will reduce the inflammation on its own. If the cause is coming from the IT band, get it stripped out. It's pretty painful, but incredibly effective. If the cause is from a hip joint dysfunction, get it adjusted. If the cause is from any number of other reasons, get it taken care of. But the cortisone shot is the "magic pill" solution. But it really doesn't solve anything except for some immediate pain relief. It's more of a band-aid really.

Lower back weakness

Jamie J: I'm back on the SS program after being laid up from surgery (UP3, tonsils and uvula removed, palette reshaped). I'm having a hard time with my lower back. When I'm squatting, it feels like the weak point and when I deadlifted today, one of my trainees mentioned that my back curved much more dramatically then it usually does. I've started doing lower back training at the end of a session (curved back deadlifts/Straight leg deadlifts) and heavy abs (suit case deadlifts/weighted decline situps). I raise weight if I get to 10 reps, I try to keep it between 5-10 at 3 sets.

Does this programming seem like it will produce enough of a training response without going into overtraining considering the program I am on? Are there other exercises you would suggest instead of the ones I am currently doing?

Mark Rippetoe: A snoring boy, eh? I can just imagine the noise level in the room. Your low back will get strong again even if you don't do any exotic shit for it, unless there was something wrong with it before the blessed surgical event occurred. Just focus on keeping it locked in extension when you pull and squat and it will recover to its previous level. Really, why wouldn't it?

Dizziness

eekrazyk: The other day I experienced some dizziness during my first workset of OH Press. I did the first rep and felt a little dizzy with the weight in the top position, so I racked the weight and about fell over. I got this weird blurred vision/tunnel vision and a warm, tingly sensation all through my body. The rest of the sets were fine. It happened again during my heavy set of power cleans on the next workout. Do you have any ideas what I'm doing to experience that? Is it just hypoxia from holding my breath? Am I impinging a nerve somehow?

Mark Rippetoe: You are mashing the bar into your carotids a little too hard, causing what is called a vaso-vagal syncope. It can also be the result of your Valsalva if you've taken too big a breath. Carry the bar a little further away from your throat. Blacking out can be dangerous if you fall on something, so take a knee if you get too wobbly. The blackout itself is harmless, and the response – especially to the Valsalva – is trainable.

Tjayarmyguy: This happens to me when I try to fly right into my Presses after murdering myself with squats. I find it useful to take a couple of minutes to catch my breath after I re-rack the squat plates. I have also done the carotid artery smashing thing too. But usually when I get dizzy on presses it's because I'm already huffing and puffing. Perhaps I'm jamming my arteries up and huffing and puffing. All I can offer is that when I calm down and relax for a couple of minutes the dizziness stop and my presses can continue.

Mark Rippetoe: It may be that every time you exhale you are relaxing a little into the bar, and that this is when it mashes your carotids.

jep6095: tjay, you may want to try taking your quick breath at the top (while the bar is overhead) utilizing your stretch reflex at the bottom. This will ensure that you're not resting the bar anywhere near your arteries and will move along the set.

Tjayarmyguy: I've tried that. I get really loose if I try to breathe at the top. I need the stability that the held-breath provides inside my torso, but thanks for the advice. I really do find that if I just calm down a bit and work through my press warmups deliberately instead of flying through the warmup sets I don't get dizzy.

Mark Rippetoe: JEP, you might elaborate on what you mean by breathing at the top. He doesn't understand the concept.

jep6095: Will try: First off, you should stay tight no matter where you are taking your breath, it sounds as if you're not in either position. Take your first breath, unrack and press. While the bar is overhead prior to your second rep-take a breath and press. Continue this pattern, staying tight, throughout the set. Using the stretch reflex at the bottom, much like in the bench press, is useful in a heavy work set of pressing.

SS, weight gain, legs falling asleep

JakePat: All right, I did the Onus Wunsler program from Starting Strength for a large portion of 2008 and I put on around 50 lbs. I went from ~190 to ~240 without a huge increase in fat, so I feel great about my gains. Since putting on the weight, I've noticed that my legs are prone to falling asleep more often than they did when I weighed less. This usually happens while sitting -- I've noticed that sitting on the john too long induces "sleeping" legs, and generally sitting without shifting my legs regularly will do the same.
I'm not too concerned that this represents some kind of real problem, but have any of you experienced the same thing? What's the cause? Bigger legs make it easier to pinch nerves? More physical mass means my heart has trouble with pumping blood? I have no idea, and I figured this would be a good jumping-off point for research and discussion.

Mark Rippetoe: When you say "asleep", I assume you mean numb skin. I hope you're not suggesting that you have to recover from paralysis every time you sit down.

JakePat: Yes, by "asleep" I simply mean a tingly, numb sensation. It's akin to falling asleep with your arm twisted and waking up with a "sleepy" arm. This doesn't present a problem for me, I'm just curious if anybody else has experienced it, why it happens, and if there's a correlation between gaining body weight and a more frequent sleepy sensation in my legs.

Mark Rippetoe: Anytime you produce numbness with pressure, you have mashed a nerve into submission. It is almost always a superficial dermal nerve. You will notice the sensation proceeds from numbness to tingling to normal. I hate to be the pot calling the kettle black, but maybe you shouldn't enjoy yourself so much on the toilet. I'd never get any reading done if I didn't do it on the can, but then again, numbness below the waist has never been my problem.

How to heal hip flexor

Sabin: It seems that I have been bouncing off of my hip flexors at the bottom and that has fucked them up. I also bounced off of them doing high bar squats as well, and that may have initiated the problem, but I haven't done that recently. What do you suggest to heal the hip flexor? Massage, Advil, NO stretching I assume?

Robert: I was discussing this recently on a couple of other forums. The short of it was that front and high bar back squats both have a greatly reduced hamstring contribution to the lift and as such the quads and hip flexors must work harder to make up the difference. My question would be, if this is true wouldn't that make low bar back squats a good alternative for Oly lifters who are frying their hip flexors from all the front squats, cleans and such?

Mark Rippetoe: Robert, why do you think the hip *flexors* are involved in an exercise that consists entirely of an eccentric and then a concentric hip *extension*?

KSC: My hip flexors first got the tendonitis when I introduced front squats to my program. I was going super deep and relaxing too much at the bottom which allowed my knees to slide forward. I was doing it some too on the back squat but not as bad as fronts. I tried training through it for a while then eventually just had to take about 10 days off from any type of squatting along with lots of NSAIDs. IMO, if you got it bad, then just rest for a while, Ibuprofen a bunch and read the book while you are resting.

Sesami: I was under the impression that hip flexors have two functions: hip flexion and knee extension, the latter of which is used in the squat. Is this correct?

Mark Rippetoe: The hip flexors are the rectus femoris, the sartorius, and the tensor fascia latae, only the first one of which has any knee extension function. But in this capacity the rectus femoris is using its distal function, and is thus not a "hip flexor". We don't actively "flex" our hips when we squat, any more than we use our lats to lower the bar when we press overhead. But when you allow your knees to travel forward at the bottom of a squat, the distal tension pulls against the proximal insertion of the rectus femoris and makes your anterior pelvis sore.

Robert: So in a front squat with the knees traveling much further forward than a low bar back squat and little hamstring involvement the rectus femoris has to work much harder at knee extension and this would lead to increased tension against the proximal insertion of the rectus femoris thus requiring more work by the hip flexors (even if it is isometric)? Or would this only occur when you have shitty form on front squats?

Mark Rippetoe: It only occurs even in the front squat if the forward knee travel occurs at the bottom.

Hernia question

bg1968: I know in your previous threads you said you were not answering any more hernia questions, but this is not about the hernia directly, I know I have one, I have had it for about 5 or more years. I regularly pull 500+ for reps on DL and 400+ for reps on back squat without any discomfort; this is without belt or other supportive gear. But I would like to add to these lifts, maybe get my DL to 600+ and squat to 500+.

My question is this: you suggest wearing a belt, should It be worn lower than usual? Also I was thinking of buying some of the Inzer squat briefs or power pants, or similar product, do you think those would provide a little extra support? I will eventually get this fixed, but I am a doctorphobe and avoid them at all costs so I will probably wait until a catastrophic failure of my yam sack to have the needed work.

Mark Rippetoe: Just wear the belt in the normal way, because 1.) you can't wear it otherwise effectively, and 2.) it won't work to support your back any other way. The belt is worn primarily for back support, and braces your hernia only tangentially. An inguinal hernia is a flaw in the abdominal floor, and the belt will not really take any pressure off of that. The reason you can train the deadlift with a hernia is because the load is static – it usually takes a dynamic load to squirt the thing. I'd use the belt to decrease the likelihood of a wiggle during the pull that might get turned into a dynamic situation.

Deadlift Question. Balls Get In the Way

Powerlifter48: Hi Rip, this is a serious question. I have noticed here lately when I do the deadlift upon lifting it from the floor to the completed lift position it ends up right where my balls are and I in my concentration to keep it close to the body I end up smashing my balls. I end up grinning and bearing it and then bringing the bar back down to the floor. It's as if I am scooping up my balls as I complete the lift as my arm length settles in that area. I wear the proper underwear support and it still happens. Any suggestion on what to do outside of having a sex change operation?

Mark Rippetoe: You have short arms. In fact, a pretty good way to define "too short" – in terms of arms – would be if your deadlift smashes your balls. Damned if I know what to do about that, if you're sure your grip is narrow enough. Sumo may be your only option.

Lean Strength/Power Athletes

Neil G: I am curious to know how so many top strength/power athletes maintain their strength but stay so lean e.g. 100m sprinters, track cyclists, etc. For example, Chris Hoy has squatted 500lbs at a bw of 93kgs and he is very lean. Is his a case of superior genetics, dietary regime, copious amounts of performance enhancing drugs, or all three? Or is there another explanation? I am approximately the same weight as him and about 2 inches shorter and I know that if I don't keep a little puppy fat on my midsection I lose strength dramatically!

Mark Rippetoe: Genetics, my friends. Well, mostly genetics. There are lots of strong guys that carry 20% that you haven't noticed, and strong guys that train in sports that demand a lot of training volume tend to stay leaner. But genetics has a lot to do with it.

Mass Gains

ben23: I'm coming to the end of my strength and conditioning cycle (6 months) have seen great gains and improvements in fitness, appearance, strength and power. So couldn't be happier. However as I am not an athlete, and an 18 year old guy, I want to give a good size cycle a good go. As although I give advice for those to choose strength routines over size routines, I think it's only fair I give a size routine 110% and see what happens, so I can use that to back up my knowledge and also experience. The goal I have from this is to generally just get bigger, I've pretty much ran 5x5 into the ground, so want a change. Any ideas on a good routine for it?

Mark Rippetoe: How much milk are you drinking?

ben23: erm? About 3/4 of a gallon a day.

JLascek: Ben, does this mean you have exhausted your potential on the novice progression? Or you just completed some sort of obscure six month long 'strength and conditioning program'?

Mark Rippetoe: Ben fails to realize that the "size" cycle he wishes to perform could have been halfway complete by now had he actually done the program correctly as a novice. Boys, I'm not kidding: ***if you're a novice***, do the novice program just like it's written in the book, and you're doing the best muscular bodyweight-gaining program in existence. Better than steroids, faster gains that you will ever experience again.

ben23: Sorry for not being clear, but I am in the intermediate, if not, advanced stage, not the novice stage. So, I already have quite an aesthetically pronounced size and shape, however, with my strength coming to a stand still after periodization, increasing calories, rest and deload weeks. I've read about the use of hypertrophy routines in order to produce more motor units, and then allowing a greater strength potential.

Mark Rippetoe: It is impossible that you are an intermediate/advanced lifter having said *"However as I am not an athlete, and an 18 year old guy, I want to give a good size cycle a good go."* in your OP. Get the book. It's explained there.

ben23: Well it's not impossible, as my lifts are in the advanced/intermediate brackets. I used to play basketball, and was given UK under 21 trials. But have given up with it, and want to focus on weightlifting.

Mark Rippetoe: It doesn't matter how strong you are. It matters how much you have already adapted. There are strong novices and weak advanced lifters. Buy the book.

Stakehoagy: I am afraid to say that I was also reluctant to drink the gallon of milk per day for one reason: a whole gallon of milk contains about 4800 mg of calcium which exceeds the upper limit of calc. intake by 2300 mg. suggested by most dieticians. Too much calcium has been said to produce excess calcification of some tissues, constipation, and other minor issues. I suppose it is improbable that all of it would be absorbed in the first place or that it even matters, but I know you will come up with an intelligent response to this.

Mark Rippetoe: Sure. Here: Fuck dietitians. Fuck 'em.

Muscle mass gains linear?

BreezerD: Forgive me if the nature of this question defies basic logical thinking patterns, but do novice lifters lose the ability to gain muscle mass in a linear fashion as they lose that ability with strength gains? Or will muscle mass gains remain linear, assuming the caloric surplus is sufficient?

Mark Rippetoe: If muscle mass gains remained linear, I would weigh 785 lbs. at my same svelte 22% bodyfat.

BreezerD: But you're only 585lb. Hmm. Now I feel like the guy who suggested that people simply crapped out excess calories. Damn.

Why does so-called indirect DL training methods work?

paulr: At 40 years of age and first doing a deadlift exactly 7 months ago, I've taken my deadlift from 135 to a new PR of 400. I will understand if that special bottle of wine you've been saving for a special occasion remains uncorked. In spite of how satisfying it would have been to finally get my money's worth out of purchasing those 8 used 45s for my garage, I stopped at 400 because my lower back began to round during the lift to the point where, for once, I showed what may be the first glimmerings of wisdom in the gym.

The day following this new DL PR, in a clear and immediate regression from this new gym wisdom PR, I undertook a workout involving 5 rounds of (among other sadisms) 25 back extensions and 25 32kg kettlebell swings. The sensations shortly after, and continuing into today, have caused me to reflect on what more intelligent people than me have warned regarding overtraining the lower back, as it is said to be very slow to recover. As with too many things, I understand the warning now, but after the point where it would have been useful.

As I have every intention of eventually setting a PR of (at least) 500 on the deadlift, mainly to redeem the first 40 deadliftless years of my life and earn the right to something on my gravestone such as "He was for a time not entirely a pussy". It would seem I need among other things a stronger lower back. In thinking through what it's going to take to get there, I can't help but think there's a paradox in the advice on deadlifts and lower backs. How exactly can one train the lower back to be strong enough for a heavy DL without actually working the hell out of the lower back with ever heavier weights?

I would be the first to admit less than perfect readings of your three fine books, as many a stupidity and error on my part been corrected by a subsequent more thoughtful reading. But one thing I thought I understood clearly is to build strength in a muscle, you must stress that muscle beyond what it has been stressed before for it to adapt. Sure, it's not always linear progression, but we certainly don't get a muscle stronger by coddling it. It must be pushed further, to boldly go where that muscle had never been before, stress-wise.

How, then, can so-called indirect methods of training the deadlift as described by say Starr or Simmons actually get the lower back strong enough to pull a 500+ deadlift and earn one a reasonable gravestone without actually overtaxing the lower back as one would via deadlifting more? We're either stressing the lower back with a new, heavier-than-before weight, or we're not, as I thought I understood. The whole point of this preamble is to show I don't doubt the lower back is easily stressed. And I believe I understand your Star Trekkean principles of gaining strength. So what special trick about these indirect training methods for deadlifting am I failing to understand? Is it just as simple as we must take it a lot slower with the lower back, and there's nothing special to figure out?

Last thing, *why* is the lower back so slow to recover? What's the physiology behind that? This fact alone is what remains between me and my embrace of evolutionary theory, as it seems so goddamn counter-intuitive to have something so useful as a lower back so easily overtaxed. And I don't recall ever seeing an "older guys only" disclaimer on this lower back warning.

Mark Rippetoe: I don't know that this explanation rises to the level of physiology (or even correctness), but it probably has to do with the nature of low-back muscular contraction. The erectors' job is to maintain the intervertebral positions of the column of bones in the back so that they act like a rigid bar capable of transmitting force instead of the spine of a Member of Congress. The point is to be able to generate force with the hips and legs that can be transmitted up the back and down the arms to the bar, and if the torso is not rigid then force transmission is not efficient. The function of these muscles is isometric: they do not act to change the positions of the bones to which they are attached, but to maintain the positions of those bones relative to each other. A developed erector is a rather large round bundle of muscle that therefore doesn't move much during its work. It doesn't change length, doesn't get much skinnier or fatter, even when it's not deadlifting, and as a result doesn't "flush" itself as effectively as a muscle whose primary function is to cause motion around a joint and in the process lengthen and shorten. My guess is that this influences low-back recovery.

The "indirect" method of training the pull (I've never heard it called that, and it's not indirect at all) merely shortens the distance over which each exercise causes the erectors to work isometrically, easing the amount of stress applied in terms of time under contraction, albeit definitely not in terms of the weight handled. Rack pulls are very heavy -- I could do 625 x 5 from below the knee when I was good for my PR of 633, and halting DLs were very heavy too. But they could be recovered from in a week when a comparable deadlift effort would take longer. So it's not as simple as just applying a stress overload; it has to be an overload from which you can recover in time to train hard again in a length of time that works best for progress. Lots of people got strong with just deadlifts, so that works too, but I did it the other way and it worked. Why, I'm not sure, but maybe you'll like my stab at it, or maybe somebody else has a better explanation.

Paulr: Could you comment on how flushing may be affected by using a reverse hyper? I have looked for a concise explanation of why the RH is said to be effective. As you point out in SS, the shearing force on the spine is removed from the exercise, and hence makes it useful for rehab in some cases. More to the point, I've been staring at the final part of the second to last paragraph on the reverse hyper: ", and special equipment is required before they [back muscles] can be exercised concentrically". As you point out in the book, access to a proper reverse hyper that can be done weighted is rather rare. Assuming one is available, might this help somewhat with the flushing (presumably of blood?) of the lower back, and hence improve recovery? Is this the general idea? If it is, do you have an opinion on how effective this might be as part of one's training program?

I've seen a product promotional video out of Westside where the claim was made (who escapes me, but I can find out -- it was not Simmons, but I believe a PhD/chiro guy) that the discs in the spine have no direct blood supply. Hence, the flexing of the spine while performing the reverse hyper exercise helped draw in nutrients, which of course sounds very wholesome and good. But it seems safe to say this has nothing whatsoever to do with the flushing you mentioned, and is more useful in the rehab and so-called prehab roles?

Mark Rippetoe: The flushing I am talking about is muscular, but the only comments I could offer is that RHs and Glute/hams and back extensions use the muscles concentrically/eccentrically, which probably aids with flushing, if such a thing actually happens. Remember, this is just my guess. I'm pulling this out of my ass, and it may be wrong. Exercise science in general is at best a poorly educated guess and at worst the ravings of unqualified people with something to sell you.

Gallon of milk a day... makes you go bald?

Applesaucemcgee: I have been drinking a gallon of whole milk a day since early January 2009. So far I went from 170lbs to 197lbs. All of my lifts have increased drastically as well (I have been doing the 5x5 program for 4 months now). HOWEVER...a guy in my gym told me that his friend did the gallon of milk a day diet...and ended up losing all his hair. He claimed that the doctors told his friend it was because of all the milk he was drinking.

Do you know if there is any truth to this? I am a first year medical student, and have access to tons of medical journal websites through my school, and could not find anything regarding this topic. I also asked two fourth year med students, they did not know why this would happen either. I love this diet...it has done wonders for me and I don't want to quit it.

Mark Rippetoe: Hmm, the only adverse effects I actually know about the GOMAD is the fact that it makes your dick shorter, but I never considered it important enough to mention. I'll have to add the baldness warning to the list immediately, because *THAT'S* not something to be taken lightly.

Applesaucemcgee: So............really though. Do you know anyone that has a full head of hair that has done this diet for a long time? I just don't know where else to find the answer to this. I mean I'm sure it doesn't make you go completely bald within a short period of time...but if a lot of people that happen to use this diet have thinning hair or receding hairlines...then maybe there is some truth to this. Anything?

Mark Rippetoe: You will not be graduating from medical school, I predict. I hope.

Applesaucemcgee: Ok, you don't need to be a dick about it. It was a completely reasonable question...and stranger things have happened in this world than excessive whole milk causing you to lose some of your hair. Our skin and hair are reflections of our health and diet...when we are unhealthy or deficient in vitamins, our hair and nails get brittle, etc.

Its known that your diet can influence premature baldness, and there's plenty of research out there that's related weight training to accelerating baldness due to DHT...so I didn't know if this would help accelerate that even more, or if you had anything to say about it from observing other people who went on the same diet.

Ok...from my most basic knowledge of medicine, here is my understanding/deductive reasoning of why whole milk would contribute to premature baldness:

-Excessive testosterone leads to hair loss.

-Testosterone is derived from Cholesterol.
-Presumably, high levels of cholesterol would make it easier for one to reach high levels of testosterone...since a large supply of cholesterol is available to create the testosterone. These high levels of testosterone would be initiated by intense weight training.

-Diets with high levels of saturated fat (a gallon of milk has 80 grams of saturated fat. That's 400% of your daily value) lead to high cholesterol levels. High saturated fat = high cholesterol in the body, is a basic fact in biochemistry. (On an unrelated note, our liver creates 3-8 times more cholesterol than a normal diet contains....and if we happen to ingest an unusually high amount, our livers will simply create less to equalize the amount. ... if you want to reduce your cholesterol levels...stay away from saturated fat, not diets high in cholesterol).

My question is really not that far fetched. Drinking a gallon of whole milk every day is not a normal thing to do...so I don't get how its so strange to you people that maybe something not very normal (hair loss) could result from it. It's not like I'm asking if normal things like eating 2 apples a day will cause your nuts to shrink, or if 3 bananas a day will make u go bald. This is an unusual diet...and for an unusual side-effect to come out of it is not too outlandish of a thought. Fuck.

Also...to people who are so surprised that a medical student would ask this: I am a first year medical student. I am not a doctor. I am 7 years away from that. We don't learn anything clinically relevant until the second year at the earliest. The only knowledge I have is in the most basic of sciences: anatomy, physiology, genetics, immunology, biochemistry, etc.

Mark Rippetoe: I am not questioning your level of education at this point, but rather your reasoning ability. First, has any of your hair fallen out since January? You didn't mention this rather obvious thing.

You say,

"-Excessive testosterone leads to hair loss.

-Testosterone is derived from Cholesterol.

-Presumably, high levels of cholesterol would make it easier for one to reach high levels of testosterone...since a large supply of cholesterol is available to create the testosterone. These high levels of testosterone would be initiated by intense weight training."

So it follows logically that everybody with high serum cholesterol has high serum testosterone levels. See my appraisal of your reasoning ability above.

"-Diets with high levels of saturated fat (a gallon of milk has 80 grams of saturated fat. That's 400% of your daily value) lead to high cholesterol levels. High saturated fat = high cholesterol in the body, is a basic fact in biochemistry."

No, ASM, it's not. This may be an educational matter, finally, especially since you are a young product of the government schools.

"(On an unrelated note, our liver creates 3-8 times more cholesterol than a normal diet contains....and if we happen to ingest an unusually high amount, our livers will simply create less to equalize the amount. ... if you want to reduce your cholesterol levels...stay away from saturated fat, not diets high in cholesterol)."

These are unrelated? Did you proofread this statement?

"My question is really not that far fetched. Drinking a gallon of whole milk every day is not a normal thing to do...so I don't get how its so strange to you people that maybe something not very normal (hair loss) could result from it. It's not like I'm asking if normal things like eating 2 apples a day will cause your nuts to shrink, or if 3 bananas a day will make u go bald. This is an unusual diet...and for an unusual side-effect to come out of it is not too outlandish of a thought. Fuck."

GOMAD is no more abnormal than lifting heavy weights. But you finally said something right: Fuck. Let me second that: Fuck. FOK. FECK.

TerriblyUsefulBlockOfWood: Troll?

Mark Rippetoe: Never attribute to malice that which is adequately explained by stupidity.

- Robert A. Heinlein

Kids Training

ThatGuy: I just got out of an interview with a gym that claims that barbells are bad for kids... even those at 17 years old. They say the spine is more fluid or some crap, that something I think was referring to the upper back (not lats) isn't strong enough, etc. Basically, they pride themselves on NEVER putting a bar on anyone young's back (or anyone at all, really) because it compresses the spine and so forth. What do you SAY to someone like that? Better yet, can you point me toward any good studies and science and stuff that proves them so very wrong?

Mark Rippetoe: I say, "Quit asking for *my* fucking data, and let me, finally, see *yours*. You stupid fools keep telling us that it stunts a kid's growth, or injures the growth plates, or makes them all require back surgery, or turns their hair red, or all this other fantasy shit. I am not interested in your opinion, since it has no basis in fact. SHOW ME YOUR DATA, OR *SHUT THE FUCK UP*."

You may quote me.

Hamstring Activation

DB5: This question concerns the active use of the hamstrings during the squat. The reason I ask is that my squat seems fine when I don't think about the hamstrings – as in, knees out, butt back, stand up while keeping back angle with the ground constant. However, when I actively flex the hamstring on the way down my bottom position is much tighter. To my mind, this tighter position should give me a better rebound out of the bottom. On the other hand, when I flex my hamstring on the way down they seem tighter but not as stretched (not as long) -- does this make sense?

So my question is: Do you actively flex your hamstrings anytime during the squat or do you just try to squat down by showing your knees out and stand up without actively flexing the hamstrings. Or, do you flex the whole thigh right before or after the rebound?

Mark Rippetoe: 1.) Joints "flex" and "extend", muscles "contract".

2.) If your squat feels better when you don't think about active use of one muscle group over the others, good. This is normal. If you place yourself in the correct position at the top, on the way down, and on the way back up, the correct skeletal position will cause the right muscles to be used in the right way without you having to micromanage. This is the primary advantage of the use of major exercises, but you insist on bringing a little bodybuilding with you when you squat. The squat is valuable precisely because you cannot and should not think about a muscle group when you do it – your body thinks about all this for you, leaving you to just think about driving your ass up.

Lifting with a shorter leg

Gerrich: My question is related to my left leg which is 3/4 in. shorter than my right. I had a serious motorcycle accident in my twenties resulting in a rebuilt left leg between the knee and ankle. On x-rays, my pelvis is visibly tilted and my spine compensates by going left then curving right before straightening out. I have had no unusual problems lifting, but I wonder if at some point I may. The question is should I take any special measures lifting? Some have suggested something to raise my left foot when doing squats or deads to even out. What do you think?

Mark Rippetoe: I have always recommended a shim under a short leg, especially one this asymmetrical. Shim either the platform with a piece of rubber mat, or take your lifting shoes to a shop and have the shim added to the sole. It is important for your long-term spinal health that your pelvis be loaded evenly when you train.

Gerrich: Thank you Rip, you verified what I was starting to believe. I just received my first weight lifting shoes (Rogues). I can add some height to the left shoe. I can't add the full 3/4 inch to it because it will screw up the fit. However, I can add half and then use a rubber pad as well. I have been using a 5lb plate, but I'm squatting heavy now, and I don't want the issue of trying to get situated over the plate. The rubber mat sounds excellent.

Mark Rippetoe: A small difference is not usually significant, but how does a 3/4" shim on the bottom of the shoe alter the fit?

Gerrich: I was thinking of an insert which would raise the heel too much. That is what I am used to wearing. However, I could certainly have the shoe altered and the shim put on the bottom. Should the shim be 3/4 inch the whole length of the shoe or tapered down towards the front with any more heal lift? I am assuming a flat 3/4 shim, because the shoes already have elevated heels (Rogues). I just want to be sure before paying the "exorbitant fee."

Mark Rippetoe: Since people with symmetrical leg length squat with both ankles at the same angle, you'll want to do the same. The shim is the same thickness for the length of the sole.

Hearing question

Matt604: Sometimes when doing a particularly hard squat, when I am in the hole pushing with everything I have and the bar has slowed to a near stop, my hearing (actually probably my perception of what I'm hearing) changes slightly. I lift at a Globogym with Top 40 music blaring all the time, and at the moment of maximum intensity, it seems like the music slows down. Pitches become lower and the rhythm becomes elongated. The effect lasts only for that moment -- as soon as I am out of the hole and moving again, the music goes back to normal.

Do other people experience this? I have been assuming that it is a CNS effect that is just new to me because I have never lifted heavy enough before to really tax my neuromuscular connections. Sound right? Any research on this that you're aware of?

Mark Rippetoe: I think we all have noticed it. The most logical explanation is that the pressure increases the tension across the eardrum (the tympanic membrane), which drops the frequency of the sympathetic vibrations and lowers the pitch you perceive.

About 5 reps for 14.5 year old

Guy007: I'm about 14.5 year's old, (well closer to 14.9), and well, the coaches at my gym, who would like to deload my training weights, says that 5 reps places stress on the bones, etc.., As far as I know its BS. Can you confirm their or my statement?

Mark Rippetoe: Stress on the bones is kinda the point. That's how they get stronger. It's hard to make adults smarter, isn't it?

Deep squats and femur degeneration

TommyEurope: I had a discussion with my friend who is a human kinetics major, about squats. Basically, he said that that deep squats (we'll define deep as your definition of deep i.e. the hip crease dips below the knee) will grind and degenerate the femur which will lead to problems in the future. He said he had a discussion with a physio about it. Can you comment on the merit of what he said?

Mark Rippetoe: Sure. Ask him to show you his data.

TommyEurope: I was actually asking because my friend is very much against deep squats. When he had the discussion, he said something about elite athletes being injured over time because they do deep squats (I think he was referring to the femur). Anyways, aside from the data comment which I will ask him to provide, can you please, using biomechanics, explain how deep squats won't screw up your femur/hips.

Mark Rippetoe: No, I can't, because it would be answering a question that is not valid, and I don't have time since there are about 60 questions in line here. Just because some jackass asserts a thing does not mean that it is worthy of refutation. If the same guy tells you that every space shuttle launch perturbs the Earth's orbit, and that the cumulative effects are just about to start the process of the loss of the atmosphere into space, thus creating a vacuum that will destroy all life on the planet in approximately 36 hours, would you deem this necessary to refute? How much time would you spend explaining to him why this cannot happen? Would not your time be spent better doing other things? And if you devise a concise explanation, why would you assume he would understand?

“Today, the gravity is pulling back and to the left.”

I actually had a chiropractor tell me this one time about ten years ago, as his version of an explanation of why my back was bothering me. In response to my further inquiry into this fascinating revelation, he stated that, “It’s the ionosphere” in a very matter-of-fact way. “They’re heating it with microwave towers, seven of them in all. One is in Alaska, another one is in Russia – Gdansk, I believe.” Perfectly straight face; dead-ass serious. He even charged me full price for the adjustment. Tuition, I suppose.

I hope that my little explanations here make somewhat more sense.

Power Clean Q

Kyle: Over the years of your coaching and teaching of the lift I'm sure at one stage or another you've come across somebody who lacked the flexibility to properly rack the barbell at the top of the clean. I'm wondering what you do to correct this situation? What type of drills/stretches do you have your clients do in order for them to be capable of racking the weight correctly?

Mark Rippetoe: Flexibility for racking the clean can depend on wrist, elbow, shoulder, or tricep flexibility, all of which can be stretched in several ways – usually by just shoving the elbows up under the bar in the rack and holding that stretch.

What is often unappreciated is the fact that forearm/upper arm dimensions can have a lot to do with racking ability. A person with long forearms relative to upper arms will be anatomically unable to rack the bar with the elbows in an elevated position with the same ease as a person with the opposite anthropometry. A person with longer forearms will have to take a wider grip to get the elbows up into the same position, and this may be the only way to get the bar in a secure position on the shoulders.

Racking the weight correctly is important to learn very early. You have to commit to slamming the elbows up into position, and never settle for catching the bar with the elbows pointing down. Learning the rack in the context of the squat clean makes you do this (since if you don't, the bar falls off), but the power clean can also be successfully taught correctly with the proper emphasis on high elbows.

Push Press/Jerk and Flexibility

Lifting N Tx: I've read your reply to Kyle's question about power cleans, as well as your discussion in *Starting Strength.* It seems that many of the same issues would apply to flexibility needed for proper performance of push presses and jerks.

I have gotten to the point where I can rack the bar and perform front squats by doing exactly what you mentioned in the "Power Clean Q" thread:

Flexibility for racking the clean can depend on wrist, elbow, shoulder, or tricep flexibility, all of which can be stretched in several ways - usually by just shoving the elbows up under the bar in the rack and holding that stretch.

It took some time, and I still need more flexibility, but at least I can perform power cleans and front squats. However, that is with elbows at less than a 90 degree angle from my torso, and the bar on my fingers, not on my palms. When I do military presses I find that I cannot hold the bar securely in my palms and also rest it on my deltoids. Moving my grip out somewhat wider than what you recommend in *Starting Strength,* I can perhaps hold the bar so that it barely touches my deltoids. However, I can't both hold the bar securely and also de-weight it on my deltoids sufficiently to transfer leg drive to the bar in a push press or jerk.

Are there any stretches or pointers useful for developing the ability to properly perform push presses and jerks that differ from what I quoted above?

Mark Rippetoe: Since you're not going to press or push press with your upper arms at right angles to your torso anyway, your lack of flexibility there is not critical. You just need to get the bar onto your delts for force transfer from the dip in a push press, and even that is not necessary for a decent press. A grip width adjustment should allow the bar to sit on your delts for push pressing, but if you've already tried that and still can't get it down there, just do it as best you can and let it function as the stretch. You don't need perfect flexibility to use either exercise effectively.

ATG Squatting

Dave76: Ass to grass squatting seems to be all the rage these days. There are many people who believe that you teach ATG squatting. Could you comment, please?

Mark Rippetoe: Thanks for bringing this up. Squat depth is critically important, but so is correct form. ATG-level depth most usually requires that the lumbar muscles relax the lordosis and that the hamstrings relax before extreme depth can be reached. It doesn't sound like a good idea to me that *anything* be relaxed in a deep squat, since doing this kills your good controlled rebound out of the bottom and risks your intervertebral discs. Those rare individuals that can obtain ass-to-ankles depth without relaxing anything might be able to get away with it, but as a general rule you should squat as deep as you can with a hard-arched lower back and tight hamstrings and adductors. This depth will be below parallel, but it will not usually be "ATG".

VikingMan: I've always considered my squat to be ATG, but really, it's more along the lines of what you recommend. I go till my hams are touching my calves and I get that stretch reflex and then blast out of the hole. Problem though is that my lower back will generally flatten out a bit, loosing some of its arch. What is the problem there, and how do I fix it?

Mark Rippetoe: It is sometimes easy to confuse a position cue with an anatomical position. Just had a row with a buddy about this last week, in fact. I don't usually have any problem getting good depth with a decent back position. I agree with you about decent: perfect lordotic extension is not necessary, and that's not my criteria. Decent is safe, and safe need not be perfect. Coaches who insist that perfect flexibility in the hamstrings be present before loading up the squat 1.) will never get much done with novice athletes, and 2.) ignore the value of the loaded squat as a stretch.

It has been my experience that most people who have decent hamstring flexibility can get below parallel if their thighs are kept out of the way; the knees should track straight over the toes, the toes should be pointed out at about 30 degrees, and this allows the hips to drop into good depth 95% of the time.

PMDL: I've noticed from looking at my squat vids that I get some serious hip-tuck/back rounding going on at the bottom of my squats, from parallel on down. But it's never once caused me any problems, and feels normal to me. So I've never given it much thought really. I know that, from a technique standpoint, it's not a good thing, but considering it's never really messed with me, I've not bothered doing much to correct it.

Mark Rippetoe: The butt-wink Nazis don't like it, but as long as it causes no problems, I'd never yell. I'd like to see a little stiffer lumbar in a novice, but 325 x 5 done easily in a more advanced lifter is not a big deal. "The perfect is the enemy of the good", one of my favorite pithy aphorisms.

VikingMan: On the subject of the "butt wink", how do you fix it? I've got the same issue with my squats, but I want to do something about it, given that I've had past back issues. If I'm not mistaken, it's cause is weak hip flexors, correct? And the hams overpower the flexors at the bottom? So, if I'm approaching this correctly, the way

to fix it is to focus on pushing the knees out and engaging the flexors as much as possible towards the bottom, and an increased emphasis on abdominal/flexor work. Thoughts?

Also, do your athletes ever struggle with tightness in the lower back? I've been having issues with that for quite some time. What is generally it's cause, and what do you usually do about it? I'm finding that HEAVY abdominal work and a reverse hyper seem to be having a positive impact on it, but wanted to get your opinion. I also have an ortho appointment coming up, but the best sports doc I could find can't see me till October.

Mark Rippetoe: Okay, someone needs to explain to me how weak hip flexors are involved in this. How is it that resisting the load on a heavy bar as you perform an eccentric contraction down to the bottom of your squat involves active hip flexion? Yes, the hips and knees are coming into the position of flexion, but do you think you are actually *pulling* 405 down into the bottom with your hip flexors? I thought the weight pushed you down. Or is there some arcane, esoteric aspect of biomechanics that eludes me here? I see these comments occasionally, and it appears to me that we are using our hip *extensors* rather thoroughly when we squat, and that the hip *flexor* muscles (flexion in this case being the proximal function of these muscles, the rectus femoris, sartorius, and tensor fascia latae) are working distally to resist knee flexion, and then to actively extend the knee.

As for fixing butt wink, it usually involves stretching out tight hamstrings, the primary cause of a lack of hip extension ROM. It is more usually addressed by just shoving the knees out. And tightness in the lower back could mean several things, from a lack of flexibility in either flexion or extension to a persistent feeling of "pump" upon initiation of work.

VikingMan: Certainly not. But, hip flexors do connect from the top of the femur to the inside of the lower back, right? As you approach the bottom of the squat and the hamstrings are getting tighter, engaging the hip flexors at that point could help keep the arch, right? Maybe I'm wrong.

And I've stretched my hamstrings till I'm blue in the face and that hasn't helped the butt wink issue. Am I simply stretching wrong?
Quote:

> *And tightness in the lower back could mean several things, from a lack of flexibility in either flexion or extension to a persistent feeling of "pump" upon initiation of work.*

Totally NOT the kind of tightness I'm talking about. I mean, a week after I squat, my lower back feels tight. Not, "pumped because I just did a set of 50 reps of 45 degree hyper extensions" tight, but, "something's not quite right" tight. Know the kind of tightness I'm talking about?

Mark Rippetoe: I have always been of the opinion that the erector spinae were the primary muscle group involved in keeping the lumbar spine erect (and extended). Trying to actively pull the lumbar into extension with the psoas at the bottom of a squat seems a rather inefficient way of doing what should have been done at the top of the descent, and what will stay there just fine if the hamstrings are sufficiently extensible and

the knees are out of the way. This last point may very well be your problem – knees out frees up depth by taking the thigh contact away from the lower trunk as the bottom is approached. An active shoving-out of the knees may fix butt-wink better than anything else you've tried. Give it a shot.

Locked out?

azx: Should I lock out my knees at the top of the squat? I lock my knees at the top at the movement because it gives me time to breathe in and out before I descend. And generally I think it's easier to complete the set this way. However I'm unsure whether this is a safe practice, especially when the weight gets heavier. I have read the book

however I don't think this issue is addressed. If the answer is no, why do we lock out the bench press but not the squat?

On an entirely different note, I haven't done any weight training for a while but am looking to get back into it. But I feel extremely inflexible especially in the lower back and legs. Are there any stretching routines that you would recommend? Is it a bad idea to stretch statically before a set?

Mark Rippetoe: Yes, lock your knees at the top. That's how you rest between reps. Same with bench, press, deadlift, cleans, snatches, and every other exercise that uses a barbell, and this is obvious to everybody except people who use Swiss balls. I suspect you glanced through SS rather quickly and failed to notice that all the pictures at the top position showed locked joints.

If you're too tight to correctly perform the exercise, stretch. If you're sufficiently flexible, don't. And if you're not training with weights right now, why are you asking me these questions?

What are my 'limiting' muscles in the deadlift?

FROGGBUSTER: I squat 230x5 to parallel comfortably and feel I can still add weight every time for awhile before I stall. Deadlift, however, is another story. I sumo-deadlift 225x5, and this is an incredibly strenuous effort for me. (the reason I sumo-deadlift is because I had a knee injury that prevented me from conventional deadlifting; however, that injury has since healed)

According to your standards in practical programming, I'm between intermediate and advanced in squat and still a novice in the deadlift. I'm trying to find out why there is such a disparity between these 2 lifts that seemingly have so much in common (many of the same muscles are used). Is it hamstring/lower back/glutes that need work or is it quads that need work? Or both? But if it's both, then why do I have a relatively strong squat? I'm very confused.

Also, I've taken a 2-week break from squatting and deadlifting (groin injury) and I start back on Monday 9/24. My plan was to drop to 200 on deadlift and increase every workout by 5lbs because 225 was so hard. How much do you think I should drop down on squats? Progress has been slow recently (I replaced Wednesdays with front squats because i just couldn't recover quickly enough), and I really want to increase weight. But on the other hand, I know I can't go back to directly squatting 230 after a 2-week break.

Mark Rippetoe: The problem is the sumo. But I don't really understand why you started using it, because the vast majority of the time a knee injury is not affected by conventional deadlifting due to the abbreviated ROM for the knees. Seems to me like sumo would be harder on a knee injury than conventional.

The problem with sumo is that it leaves out a lot of the back work that the deadlift is supposed to include. The sumo position gets the feet and knees out of the way so that a steeper back angle and a shorter bar path can be used. The steeper back angle reduces the load on the erectors by decreasing the distance between the bar and the hips, and because the nearer the back is to vertical the shorter the lever arm between the load and the hips. The sumo position allows these leverage improvements to be made while keeping the scapulae directly over the bar, the necessary configuration for pulling.

But the advantages of sumo also make it the wrong style for training, because you can't get as strong. In my day, the best sumo deadlifters only did sumo at the meet. This is probably your problem, and I would immediately switch back to conventional and stay there until you lift in a meet. Everything you have described indicates to me that your posterior chain is weak, and I'll bet that a squat video of you would show a quad-dominant squat style. So, if you get your deadlift fixed using conventional form and learn to use your hips to squat, good things will occur.

I'd go down to an easy weight and do 3 sets of 5 deadlifts for about 3 workouts, increasing 10-15 lbs. each time, and then go to our usual one heavy set of five, as described in the books.

Row Substitution

Dave(DBD): Hey Rip, I was just wondering about your opinion on the substitution of Pendlay rows on Starting Strength. From what I've seen it's by far the most common sub I've seen on SS. I personally used barbell rows instead of cleans and I know it worked well for me. I was just curious to hear your opinion on it.

Mark Rippetoe: My opinion is that you need to learn how to clean. There are a couple of reasons why cleans might not be used: if your gym won't allow you do them, or an injury prevents your racking the bar on your shoulders, you'll have to sub something for them. The injury angle is legit, but if the gym won't let you clean but *will* let you row, well, somebody needs to explain that to me.

Usually, people just feel intimidated by anything that resembles a technical exercise and just would rather not do them. This is just being a pussy, and sets a bad precedent for the management of both training and life. I think that Starting Strength includes an understandable method for learning to power clean. You don't really need bumper plates to do them if you don't have access, so that doesn't wash either. They are in the program because an explosive movement is a valuable contribution to power production, and they make deadlifts get stronger faster.

So my advice is to learn how to power clean. And since you mentioned it, Glenn did not actually invent the barbell row. I don't think he ever said that he did. The standard way to do barbell rows is to pull each rep off the ground. So the actual name of a barbell row should henceforth be "Barbell Row". Please try to remember this.

Adas75: The BB.com Rippetoe forum \ post recommends replacing with rows (which I have been doing) as it say's you need a coach to learn Power Cleans. Looks like somebody needs to put them right, it also mentions that you could use chin ups \ pull ups first to build up your conditioning before introducing Power Cleans. Is this bull as well?

Mark Rippetoe: You don't need a coach to learn power cleans, because we fixed things up so that you can learn them out of the book. And what exactly is the downside of trying to learn them and failing? Firing squad? The bodybuilders making fun of you from the safety of the dumbbell rack? Loss of wages? Just try them before you decide you can't learn them without a coach.

As for pullups/chinups being a necessary pre-strengthening movement for the clean, what does a movement that is primarily a jump with a barbell hanging from the hands have to do with a bodyweight pull in the opposite direction? They are both very important exercises, neither of which depends on the other for anything.

There is no danger from doing rows. I just consider them an intermediate level assistance exercise that should be done long after cleans are mastered. Power cleans are a terribly important exercise because they develop skill, explosion, and a better deadlift. Barbell rows are a moderately useful assistance exercise. That's why cleans are included as one of the Five exercises in SS and rows are not.

Squat forward lean

pmb: When the weight gets close to maximal on the squat, I tend to lose form coming up out of the bottom, in that I lean forward excessively. This in turn necessitates something more like a good morning to get the bar up. It has been suggested to me that part of the problem may be that my glutes are not firing like they should. Naturally, I will go down in weight and work on form, but if the culprit indeed is too little involvement in the movement by the glutes, is there any point in supplementing by specific assistance exercises like RDL or some such? Is there some other focused work that I can do to address the weakness in the most time efficient manor?

Mark Rippetoe: Look at it this way: if you lean way over in the squat and your back angle gets more horizontal, your knees have extended without moving the bar, right? This means that the posterior chain muscles – the glutes and hamstrings – now have to do all the work of lifting the bar without the help of the quads. They are obviously strong enough to do this, so it's not glute strength. It's failure to maintain the correct back angle – failure to keep your "chest up" – while the hips drive up out of the bottom. This is the result of more than just a glute problem; it's erector/lat/ab/hamstring/glute/quad and brain. Same thing happens in a deadlift if you stick your butt up before the bar leaves the ground: muscles that should be doing their part don't because of a form problem, forcing other muscles to do the job in a way they aren't supposed to.

The fix is to lower the weight and keep your back angle constant as you drive hips up from the bottom. If you make your form perfect, whatever is weak in the chain will get more work and will thus catch up. I don't advocate the use of assistance exercises to fix the basic lifts, since this doesn't address the primary problem.

Jerks

Troy: Coach Rippetoe, I'm interested on what your take would be on substituting jerks for the standing press?

Mark Rippetoe: Jerks are not a good sub for presses. While they include the supporting-the-weight-overhead part of the movement, the job of driving the load up is accomplished with the lower body as opposed to the target muscle groups. Jerks make a damned fine assistance movement for everybody except Olympic weightlifters who do them as a primary lift, but you have to press too.

Why power cleans?

FROGGBUSTER: I was just wondering why you suggest we incorporate power cleans in your SS model, as opposed to full cleans, full snatches, power snatches, etc. Don't all of these develop explosive power equally? The starting position to the jump is virtually the same for all of these. So why power cleans specifically?

Mark Rippetoe: Because they're easier to learn, and they don't interfere with the back squat movement pattern that a novice should be learning. Snatch movements are fine if you've got a coach, but I can't even get these people to try a power clean without a babysitter; this is why you see so many people wanting to sub barbell rows for cleans in my program. The problem with full squat cleans is that the front squat part of it gets confused with the back squat a novice needs to learn, and quite often novices taught to squat clean never learn how to back squat correctly as a result.

The difference between pullups and chinups

FROGGBUSTER: In SSv2, you say the main difference between the two is that chinups incorporate more biceps, and as a result, pullups have more lat involvement. However, why can most people do more chinups than pullups? Lats are a bigger and stronger muscle than biceps, so if they are used more actively in pullups than in chinups, shouldn't it be the opposite way around?

Mark Rippetoe: If you leave out a muscle group, it doesn't matter how big the other ones are. The ones that remain have to work harder (and get more work), but the addition of another muscle group will make any exercise stronger.

Overhead squats

garrett: My question is about overhead squats. Could and should they be implemented into your program? If so, when and how should they be included? From my limited experience OHS seem to be a great full body strength exercise. Also do you have any advice on technique for performing this lift? How does it compare with the other lifts you have included in your books.

Mark Rippetoe: OHSs are a very good light-day intermediate exercise, and work well when following front squats on Wednesday's workout in the Texas method. They are performed with the bar balance over the mid-foot, and are kept directly above the scapulas just like a press. The arms attach to the scapulas and the traps support the scapulas, so the bar, scapulas, and mid-foot are in a vertical line, with the back angle accommodating this configuration. They use much lighter weights, and therefore don't provide as much leg work, so we use them after front squats for this reason.

Dingas: Are OH Squats doable without bumper plates?

Mark Rippetoe: As long as you don't drop the bar.

On OH pressing

Markus: Should you try to pull the bar apart? To pull the shoulder down, or squeeze them? Should you try to are the lats? I'm pretty good at them (press 176 at 198) but am not so sure on the technique.

Mark Rippetoe: At the top in the lockout position you shrug up and squeeze the traps and triceps to support the bar. The arms attach to the scapulas, and they are hung from the traps, so that the traps essentially support the load at lockout. Triceps straighten the elbows, and traps shrug up to support the load.

Markus: One more quick question, on OH squats should you flare the lats and pull the shoulders down? Cause that is how I do it, I pull the bar apart, flare the lats, keep the wrists straight and pinch the shoulders down but not together. Is it right?

Mark Rippetoe: I thought I just told you. Look, you're supporting the bar overhead, right? Why would you support it differently when locking it out at the top of the press than when you were planning on carrying it down into a deep squat and driving it back up? The scapulas are still supporting it, and you still have to shrug the traps up to support the scapulas no matter what you're doing with the bar overhead.

---

10 questions

Pnigro: Hi Mark! I have a few questions if you don't mind.

1) This has been killing me for a few days. I've seen some of your videos in youtube instructing people on how to overhead press. Most of them keep the wrists the same way during the whole repetitions, that is, not straight. I wonder if this isn't a problem in the future when pressing heavy weights. I try to grip the bar as close to the palm of the hand.

Why is it that you recommend keeping the wrists straight during the squat (where you demonstrate using a tape on the hands) and the bench press (which are not completely straight but definitely more straight than overhead press), but at the same time it's correct to keep the wrists bent during overhead press?

My only worry with this is a wrist injury when pressing heavy weights, but I feel weird straightening the wrists on my way up in overhead press. So I guess it's ok to keep them bent as long as the bar is on the palm and not toward the fingers?

2) During a squat, what's the thin line between too much hip drive and a good morning? Would you prefer someone who rises his/her butt too much over someone who has no hip drive at all?

3) Can you recommend me any book on nutrition? I feel I know better than 99% of the instructors in my country after reading both Starting Strength and Practical Programming, but my nutrition knowledge is ZERO. I am a skinny guy and want to get HUGE so I just have to eat like a lion, but not everyone is like me or have my same goals, so I find myself clueless when friends ask me about nutrition advice.

4) Is there something I should not eat in huge quantities? I heard you recommend milk. I'm a little intolerant but I can manage to drink up to a liter per day. What about eggs? Is it ok to eat 5 eggs per day? What juices would you recommend? I love orange juice.

5) Can someone who has been diagnosed with scoliosis do exercises such as squats and deadlifts? How much

scoliosis is too much for these exercises? Should he ask his doctor first?

6) I have been doing your starting strength program for some time now and I still get super sore. Why do you think this is? I go Monday, Wednesday and Friday and I work out sore Wednesday and Friday, is it ok?

7) While lowering the bar during the deadlift, the bar goes a little forward when they reach the knees. Is it ok or should it go straight down? Should I wait until the bar reaches my knees before flexing my legs?

8) Is it ok if I still have butt wink when going below parallel? I'm working on my flexibility and lumbar muscle contraction, but I'm worried if it may cause some injury when squatting heavy weights.
9) Is it possible for an extremely flexible person to overarch their lower back during the squats loading the spine in the posterior side?

Phew, I'm sorry for all these questions. If you don't have the time to answer all of them it's ok.

Mark Rippetoe: If these weren't decent questions that are easy to answer, I'd send this post down the road with a carrot in its ass for being too long. But here goes:

1. The distance between the bar and the wrist has to be as close to 0 as possible to shorten the lever arm against the wrist. The bar will fall out of your hand if you try to keep it vertical, so you have to carry the bar over the ends of the bones in your arm with the wrist bent just enough to accommodate this position. I find that a little pronation of the hand just before the weight is taken out of the rack helps with this position.

2. The line is the point at which the lever arm between the bar and the hip increases. If the back angle changes enough to increase the horizontal distance between the bar and the hip, it's too much. There should be a visible *very slight* change in back angle upon the initiation of the hip drive, but not very damn much.

3. There is no book that I know of that can elaborate much more on the GOMAD thing than you've already read about here.

4. Vince Gironda used to have his trainees eat 3 dozen eggs a day fried in certified raw butter, for some reason. They all lived. Juice is a glass of sugar and water, with a few vitamins. It will just make you fat. Stick with milk, meat, eggs, vegetables, and fruit and you cannot fuck up.

5. Scoliosis is bad if it's bad, not so big a deal if it's not bad. If you have been diagnosed, and if your back hurts every time you train and does not improve, you may not be able to train heavy. But Lamar Gant pulled a ~725 deadlift with *severe* scoliosis, so there you go. And if you have to ask your doctor's permission to do anything, you have a poor understanding of the economics of this relationship.

6. Excessive, prolonged soreness is most usually a nutritional problem. Eat more, and eat more protein.

7. Yes, you should.

8. No one does a heavy squat with a perfectly motionless lordotic curve. You need to try to maintain a motionless low-back position, and that is the mechanical model. But no RM effort will be executed with absolutely perfect form – if it was, it's not a true RM effort. Try like hell to keep it tight; if it's excessive, fix it; if it's a little round, well, you've been doing it wrong anyway and you're still okay.

9. It is possible for some people to overextend their low backs. This is due to flexibility and a lax anterior torso musculature (notice that I did not use the term "core" because I'm tired of hearing it on infomercials). The abs have to be cued and attention paid to the back position so that this does not become a problem. But really, I've never seen anyone but a rank novice do this, so I suspect that the problem fixes itself over time and before the weight gets heavy enough to kill you.

A question about power cleans

Irishman301: As of right now I suck at them. I've been practicing and practicing with the bar, but my form still sucks. I have been substituting rows for them (I know it's not what you're supposed to do, but I love rows), but I've still been practicing the cleans with the empty bar.

Considering that I cannot yet do power cleans with proper form, should I still try to do them on the power clean day at the end of my workout with whatever form I can, although it's bad form? Basically I'd be doing 5 x 3 power cleans with the bar, but with crappy form (until it gets better of course). OR would you suggest that I do squats, overhead press, and rows, then just spend like 20 minutes or so working on my form for power cleans and eventually replace the rows when I have my form down much better?

Mark Rippetoe: It may very well be that you need to add some weight to the bar to practice your cleans. If you have followed the instruction in the BBT power clean chapter, and know that a clean is a jump with the bar in your hands that racks on the shoulders, you probably need to be using a weight that is heavy enough that it cannot be done terribly wrong. Light weights can be done quite badly, while heavier weight won't rack unless you clean it correctly. Quite often form gets better when the weight goes up.

Irishman301: Okay, I'll try adding some weight then. I figured that I was supposed to wait until I had my form perfected with just the bar before I started to add weight, but I'll give some weight a shot. Thanks.

Mark Rippetoe: Quite often, for many exercises, form improves with the addition of weight – within the boundaries of reason. This is sometimes due to the opportunity to stretch afforded by the weight, as with a squat, or the inability to do it terribly wrong, as with a clean or a snatch. Now, this does not mean that it is always better to add weight, but sometimes it helps stretch into position or motivates a better explosion.

Squat form Q-

Rahbah: My question is in regards to Squat form as to when to perform the "knees out" action? In BBT you suggest to start the squat movement with an active knees bending and out action followed by hips back and down - is this correct, because in an earlier thread you mentioned just one down that "knees out" should be at the bottom?

As well, second question - when out of the bottom - I raise the hips straight up. Is it done with a simultaneous chest raise or hips up and then followed by chest raise after a few inches?

Mark Rippetoe: As is usually the case, different problems require different cues. I cue the knees out at the bottom to fix a depth problem, since this is usually enough to get another 2" of depth for a person cutting off the bottom but not otherwise doing anything wrong. Knees going forward at the bottom is another problem, and for that I like to cue the knees out at the top, since the forward knee travel at the bottom indicates a release of hamstring tightness, and if forward knee travel is finished before the first 1/2 of the descent then the rest of the movement will be hips back. Other problems may be addressed differently as well.

Raising the hips out of the bottom is always the focus. The object is to make the back angle stay constant as the hips drive up, not to let the chest fall forward which would change the back angle to more horizontal. If the hips are the cue, most people will keep the back angle constant to keep from falling over. It is seldom necessary to cue a raising of the chest, since this would change the back angle by making it more vertical, which drives the knees forward and which therefore kills hamstring drive. At no time during a back squat is it useful to raise the chest and let the knees drop forward. Just keep driving the hips up the whole time, and when the knees need to finally straighten and the chest needs to lift, it will.

Lack of balance with no-weight squats

progressiveman1: I just started learning to do squats how you describe in your book, and you say one should first start practicing with just the barbell alone. I'm pretty sure that I'm following all your technique instructions, but for some reason I keep falling backwards near the bottom. Is this probably because of the lack of weight being used, or is it possibly bad form?

Mark Rippetoe: It is because you're not leaning forward enough. It is safe to say that anytime you fall over backwards, you were off-balance backwards. The bar is in balance when it is over the mid-foot, and if you fell back you didn't have it there.

progressiveman1: Okay, that seems to help.

I have another problem. For depth, I can't get all the way down. As I near the bottom, I can feel my low and middle back get really tight and my body just won't go down any further.

Mark Rippetoe: This is generally fixed by shoving the knees out as you approach the bottom. Are you sure you have the book?

progressiveman1: I think I figured out the problem, but it might contradict what you say about stance in your book. You explain that stance width can vary for each individual depending on things like height or flexibility; that a tall person will probably need a wider than usual stance. However, you also explain why non-powerlifters shouldn't use a powerlifting (extremely wide) stance since it omits the quads. When I widened my stance to about 28 inches (from the inside of each foot)(and I'm 6'2"), I could finally consistently maintain balance and get proper depth. But I'm wondering how do you know when a wide stance is too wide?

Mark Rippetoe: Excellent question. A stance is too wide when it "binds" the hips and limits depth. A narrow stance limits depth by placing the thighs in contact with the gut at the bottom (at least for people of normal bodyweight – the emaciated may be exempt from this rule), keeping the last bit of depth from being attained. A wide stance stretches the hip joint ligaments into a position where they are very tight at the bottom, useful for powerlifting where you'd like to be very tight at a parallel squat but not useful for squatting when the criterion for depth is full hamstring and adductor stretch. The stance I suggest allows depth to be trained without any other anatomical constraints other than muscle extensibility in the posterior chain.

If your balance and depth are working better at 28", use it. Just what I like to see: successful problem solving.

Upper back rounding in deadlift

LegsLegsLegs: I am a newly minted intermediate trainee whose results are consistent with the tables in PP. I am currently following a version of the Texas method where I do rack pulls and halting deadlifts alternating weeks according to the approach you have described here previously. Rack pulls are progressing fine, but on the halting deadlift my weakness that keeps me from progressing is my upper/middle back: I have no problem separating the bar or finishing the movement, and my lower back always stays protected. However, my upper/middle back rounds noticeably after a few reps of halting deadlifts.

Questions: What can I do in terms of assistance exercises to remedy this? Are rows the only option? The amount of weight that can be rowed seems a lot lower of a stressor than what is needed to hold the upper back isometrically under a heavy load, so my worry is whether there is enough carryover. Is there some other approach I should take to remedy this?

Mark Rippetoe: I'm not a big fan of assistance exercises to fix problems with primary movements, especially those that use the muscles in different ways than primary exercise does. If your upper back is rounding during a pull, it's not holding a good isometric contraction. How about front squats with very strict form? I think you'll find that they work better than rows. Or just lower the DL weight to a point where you can just keep flat, and let that be a direct exercise for the upper back.

Front squat biomechanics

Polynomial: Can you discuss the forces on the knees during a front squat? I'm curious because the hamstrings, which help to protect the knees during a back squat, are not as engaged in a front squat.

Mark Rippetoe: The correctly positioned front squat places the hamstrings in a contracted position at the bottom. Since they are already contracted they can't really contract any more and are thus not involved in hip extension out of the bottom. This is why your glutes get sore but your hamstrings don't. But likewise, since they are contracted, they are contracted *against something* and are thus placing tension on the origin and insertion, the ischial tuberosity of the pelvis and the tibia. This provides an anchor for the back angle and knee support to counteract the anterior tension produced by the quads. So at the bottom of the front squat, the hamstrings function in an isometric capacity to hold the back upright and to protect the knee while they aren't actively involved in extending the hip.

Cleans + Bruising

Jeffo: After years of being a pussy, I'm finally trying to learn the Power Clean. I've had a handful of sessions and I seem to be pulling and racking decently. Two things are of a concern though;

1) Racking the bar is leaving a pretty good bruise on my right collar bone. Elbows are up high, but it still wants to slam into my right collar bone. Left side is fine.

2) I'm getting some decent burns up my thighs and some bruising on my upper thigh where the jump occurs.

The collar bone bruising is painful and therefore annoying, and I'd like to fix it somehow. The thigh bruising is not painful and is therefore only a cosmetic concern to the missus. Have you seen these problems before and are they normal? If they're not normal, am I doing something obviously wrong that should be fixed?

Mark Rippetoe: The collarbone is probably a function of your particular morphology. If your elbows are up, you'll have to learn to shrug your shoulders up and forward when you rack the bar, to get the bar away from your chest. Your wife will have to learn how to appreciate the bruises on your legs. At least you're not a pussy anymore, huh?

How long did it take you to perfect your squat form?

Irishman301: I was just wondering how long it took you until you finally had it figured out. Some days I feel like I'm doing great - Back arched, eyes down, knees aligned with toes, driving up with the hips, wrists straight, etc... Great form altogether. Other days, like yesterday, I kept having the feeling that my back was rounding and I was leg pressing the weight up. And other days I can't seem to find a comfortable stance width.

It's weird. I watch lots of videos on here, and carefully listen to your critiques. I keep going back to the squat chapter in SS too to try and pick up more useful tips and tricks. I also practice all the time in the gym and out of the gym with no weight. I just can't seem to get the feeling of perfect squat form. I have a feeling that other people may be in the same boat as me on this one. I ask some of the more experienced people at my gym to critique my form, and they usually say that it looks good, but I don't know how creditable their opinions are.

I keep trying though, and I'm going to get it one day. Who knows when? But I was just wondering how long it took you to learn how to perfectly squat. Also, how long does it usually take the typical, new-to-squatting, trainee to learn?

Mark Rippetoe: My personal squat form is not perfect, and neither is anybody else's who is not constantly coached. I know what is supposed to look like, but because I can't see it while I'm doing it, my form will drift over several workouts from good to bad. It will settle into a stable, bad technique and will remain there until I get it corrected again. This is called "form creep", and affects all uncoached athletes to varying degrees.

Everybody needs a coach, no matter how accomplished they are. A coach provides a good set of eyes and the experience to know what to say to get you to do a movement correctly. This is the primary problem with training alone at home, not the lack of some asshole yelling that it's "All you, man!" You can't see it as it's being done, and you can't correct it as it happens if you can't tell what's wrong. Video is useful, but it's no substitute for a coach's correction in real time, your feeling the correction and incorporating it into the movement pattern, and then your feeling the difference the correction made from wrong to right during the set.

Robert B: This being the case, wouldn't the best arrangement for a well-appointed squat station be a video monitor set on the floor 6' away from the squatter, tilted up at say 45 deg, with the camera on a tripod set at an angle oblique to the squatter? Then the squatter could 1) maintain proper gaze direction and 2) get continuous real-time visual feedback on his/her form. Is there any reason NOT to have such a set-up (except for the expense, of course)?

Mark Rippetoe: It is very hard to look at something while you're trying to feel it being done correctly at the same time. If you watch yourself do something while you're doing it, you will slow yourself down and ruin your focus on performing the movement. And if you can afford all that equipment, you can afford to come to our seminar.

Weighted Push Ups

XTrainer: In the dip section of "Starting Strength," you mention how push ups would be an excellent movement if only they could be weighted conveniently, since they share many of the same "ground-up" kinetic chain aspects of the press and core stabilization requirements.

To make a long story short, I have (out of necessity) substituted weighted (over 80lbs in a back pack) push ups for bench press a few times in the past month. Both my press and my bench have increased, and when I perform these weighted push ups, I can't help but feel like I am performing something of more of an athletic movement, in the same way a chin or pull up is much more athletic than a lat pulldown. Not quite to that degree, but you get the idea.

Now, I'm not saying weighted push ups should replace bench press. That'd be stupid. Bench allows for more weight and slightly greater ROM, among other things.

I am wondering why weighted push ups should not be considered to be a viable exercise. I have a multi-compartment back pack which allows for an even distribution of weight. I secure the pack high on my shoulders by tightening the straps and trust it to stay there. I have no trouble loading/unloading this exercise myself. It seems to combine a lot of the best aspects of the bench press and the press.

Mark Rippetoe: If you have figured out how to make weighted pushups into a viable exercise, I'll help you promote them. Sounds like you might be ready to go public. A Pushup Vest.

Jake: What's wrong with sticking a weight plate on your back out of curiosity? Not stable enough?

XTrainer: I was just wondering if you have an issue with using a back pack to load push ups. Is there something I'm missing here that should prevent back pack push ups from being considered a safe, convenient, and most of all, *effective* movement?

Mark Rippetoe: A plate sitting on your back tends to fall off, and needs another person to put it there. A pack that can be loaded is still not a stable load on the back, and the mass of the plates or load tends to interfere with shoulder ROM at the bottom of the pushup. And there will rapidly reach a point at which your ability to maintain the plank will be the limiting factor, not your ability to press the weight with shoulders, chest and triceps. This makes the weighted pushup a very good exercise, but limits its use for upper body strength. The truth is that most people could stand to just do weighted pushups, presses, and chins, if only the logistical and equipment limitations could be overcome.

Deadlift Grip Question

SlyBlackDragon: Thanks to your books my deadlift is steadily improving week to week, the bad part is that my grip is not keeping up. Last workout my last warmup set was 315 and I barely held onto it for the duration of the set, and had to use straps for my working set. My question is should I back down to a weight I can hold and let my grip catch up, or just use straps so that I can keep challenging the rest of my body?

Mark Rippetoe: Are you using a double-overhand grip for your warmups, or are you alternating all the way up to work sets?

SlyBlackDragon: I use double overhand through my all of my warmup sets. I also usually use a double over for the first rep or so on my working set until I feel I wouldn't be able to do another rep without dropping it.

Mark Rippetoe: Are your fingers short for your hand size? This makes an efficient grip very tough to develop.

SlyBlackDragon: I don't think so, how can I tell?

Mark Rippetoe: When you grip the bar, how close is the tip of your middle finger to the meat of your thumb? An efficient grip will place the middle finger in contact or very nearly so.

SlyBlackDragon: Just a thought, but I am the proud owner of a 2" diameter thick bar that I made after going bonkers for old strongman training. Would doing say rack pulls or static holds on power clean days on the thick bar be beneficial without killing my grip for the next deadlifting session?

Mark Rippetoe: No, the fat bar is specifically used to TIRE your grip, and if you've trained it much you know that it takes a relatively long time to recover a tired grip. The fat bar works well, but not right before another grip-dependent workout.

Hamstring inflexibility

Emp: If poor flexibility were a crime, I'd get the chair. I'm pretty confident your recommendation is to shut up and keep doing the damn exercises until flexibility comes– and this has worked terrifically for my clean grip. However, after ~2 months of SS, my HS flexibility is still shit. I'm a good 3-4 inches short of touching my toes (5'8", typical anthropometry), and my back rounds like no other when I try. The funny thing is, I can maintain a reasonably good arch in the hole; there's some slight rounding, but with some concentration, I can correct it. Among scads of other HS stretches, the most useful I've found is to simply start in the hole and work on holding a tight arch for ~30 sec. x 5.

Can you recommend a more aggressive method of improving HS flexibility, or should I continue taking it millimeter by agonizing millimeter? ...For that matter, are toe-touches even a good index of flexibility?

Mark Rippetoe: If your hamstrings are extensible enough to permit good form in the squat and the deadlift starting position, why does it need more work? If I understand your post, you are merely short of touching your toes, a rather arbitrary and non-functional criterion. If your flexibility is good enough to permit correct technique and full ROM in the movements you perform in training and in sports, as far as I am concerned you don't need to spend training time improving it any more.

Scapulae Imbalance

craigmeister: I was reading on article that stated both the bench press and rowing movements tend to put the scapulae in a position of retraction and depression. They then went on to state that this could lead to an imbalance in the muscles that control the scapulae. Do you agree with their assessment? If so, what do you think is the best way to offset this imbalance?

Mark Rippetoe: I'd have to read the article. But offhand, I don't see how.

Brandon: Well... let's say you only rowed and benched. Are there any muscles that manipulate the scapulae (I don't remember all the different articulations, but there's plenty) that would be left out? Traps, maybe?

Mark Rippetoe: If you bench and row, and that's all, and a "muscle imbalance" occurs, that would not be terribly surprising. That's why I always balance bench pressing with an equal volume of pressing, and why chins are also a major exercise in my programs. In other words, if you construct a goofy training scenario – say, leg extensions and leg curls, pec decks, crossover cables, and seated behind the neck presses – you shouldn't be terribly shocked with goofy results like "muscle imbalances".

Lack of hamstrings involvement in deadlifts?

SMN: I'm 21 and I weigh 170lbs. I've done the Starting Strength program from October 2007 to February 2008. (However I wasted two of these months trying to "cut"). Two months ago I switched to a program with 2 upper days and 2 lower days, as my bench press and press were stuck for good on SS. Right now my squat 5RM is 265, which wasn't particularly hard. My deadlift 5RM is 300, and my whole body was shaking on the last rep. However, according to the "Strength Standards" charts, my deadlift "should" be higher than this compared to my squat. I figured this wasn't a big deal. I don't see what could be wrong with my deadlift form. (I've read BBT) Or maybe my squats aren't deep enough.

What prompted this post is that today, for the first time in months, I did leg curls... and they weren't any stronger than when I last did them, 7 months ago, when my deadlift was around 150lbs. If anything, they were weaker. This seems strange to me. Is it possible that my hamstrings aren't involved much when I deadlift? What form problem could cause this? BTW, I'm wearing flat sole shoes (chucks) if that makes any difference.

Mark Rippetoe: I had to laugh at this: "*Right now my squat 5RM is 265, which wasn't particularly hard.*" If it wasn't hard, it wasn't a 5RM. Which I guess means your ratio is even worse.

I can't tell without being there what's wrong, or if anything *is* wrong. It might be that your deadlift is not as good as you think it might be due to your anthropometry being not optimum for deadlifting.

Anyway, there isn't anything particularly shocking about not improving a leg curl after strengthening your hamstrings using compound movements like the squat and deadlift. You've been practicing using your hamstring function from the proximal end and it not surprising that this would not transfer well to a movement such as the leg curl that is designed to focus on the distal function of the muscle group. But as leg curl strength is not a relevant test of hamstring strength, just calm down. That's like bitching about masturbation not being fun anymore since you started dating a porn star.

SMN: Thanks for the reply. As for the squat 5RM not being hard, that was a bit of an exaggeration. I meant that form and speed were pretty good. I didn't increase the weight further since a 5lbs increase per workout seems reasonable. It's hard to monitor my form when using maximal loads, but it seems that I try to extend both the hips and knees right off the ground, instead of extending only the knees at first. Does that actually make any difference in the weight I can pull?

I also forgot to mention that I fail when trying to break the weight off the floor, which isn't the way it should be if I understand correctly.

Mark Rippetoe: The first thing that happens in a deadlift is the knees extend. This allows the quads to get the bar moving, and the hamstrings facilitate this knee extension by "anchoring" the hips at their insertion on the ischial tuberosity so that the quads can extend the knees and the force of that extension actually gets up the back and down the arms to the bar. If the knees extend and the hips are not anchored, the ass just comes up without the bar moving. When this occurs the quads don't help lift the bar – they just straighten out the knees.

Now, if the opposite of this happens – if you actually try to use your hamstrings to extend the hips right off the floor instead of just using your hamstrings to just maintain your back angle – you actually cause the bar to travel forward, out around your knees, to a position of imbalance forward of your mid-foot. So yeah, this would make it hard to get the bar off the floor and cause what you describe as your problem. Set your back at the right angle, and just think about pushing the floor with your whole foot.

Few things of concern

Jason AUS: I really need to pick your brain again; here are a few issues which have been concerning me for a while…

- the DB Snatch and DB Clean, good or bad for training? The reason I ask is because in the deadlift, balanced loading across both sides is stressed. However, when we explode up with a DB I can imagine the spine is being rotated towards one side.

- Twisting DB Deadlift: another concern about adding a twisting motion to picking up a heavy weight

- Lunges: does it really matter if your knee goes past your toes? All my EP teachers have said never let it go in front, but my argument is when we squat our knees travel forward, and in the sporting context this movement is unavoidable.

Mark Rippetoe: The DB snatch and clean are good examples of movements we use to train asymmetrically. This is intentional, is quite useful for post-novice sports conditioning, and is designed to prepare you for stabilizing the asymmetric stresses that are always a part of sports.

I'm not familiar with a twisting DB deadlift, but unless you have a really big dumbbell, I don't see it as a particularly valuable exercise, especially when DB snatches and cleans can be done instead. Heavy stuff is better done symmetrically for general strength, and asymmetrical stuff is best done light and explosively with technically challenging movements.

If your knees are not injured or prone to injury, lunges can go past the knees. I just don't tend to regard lunges as a terribly useful exercise for most trainees, when squats are so much more useful a way to spend training time. There is nothing inherently bad about them, they are useful at times for the reasons mentioned above, but I seldom use them in my programs.

Deadlift injury

Jamieb: A couple of days ago I began my first work set of deadlifts and felt a sharp pain between the upper medial border of the right scapula and the spine. The pain occurred on the first rep just as the bar came off the floor.

Physiotherapist says I've sustained a costovertebral joint injury in said area. My neck is as stiff as a board and my head is permanently leaning to my right side. Just moving around is not easy.

Ever heard of this kind of injury occurring before in relation to the deadlift? Is there any obvious technique error that could cause this? Some people recommend retracting the scapula but I don't see you mention this in SS. My chest was up and my shoulders were in front of the bar with shins in contact.

Mark Rippetoe: Sounds more like a C7 injury to me, as opposed to a rib-head dislocation. I've had some experience with these before, and you'll feel it all along your c-spine down to about T4-5 on one side. What did he do about it? Did he try to shove it back in or did he just do soft-tissue stuff? I'd see a well-recommended chiropractor first when this happens again – and it will, sorry. You may not have done anything wrong, but these things tend to recur once they happen.

Jamieb: Just soft tissue manipulation. Gave some mild and transient relief. If it turns out to be a C7 injury, would you recommend dropping the deadlift or carefully reintroducing?

I'm interested in your thoughts on retracting the scapula as I mentioned before.

Mark Rippetoe: I don't recommend scapular retraction because I don't believe it is a useful cue. The traps and rhomboids will hold the scapulae in place correctly without a conscious effort, because the traps and rhomboids are in isometric contraction through the pull. They don't work in a shortened position; they hold the scapulae in place in normal position relative to the spine. If you consciously pull your scaps back, the heavy weight is going to pull them forward anyway, and this motion will not be as helpful to you as perfectly set, still shoulders.

Jamieb: I've since come to the conclusion that I've probably strained some attachments to the superior angle of the scapula. Palpation of this point is sore, with no soreness when palpating the adjacent rib joint or t-spine, nor any pain in the c-spine. ROM in neck is much better with the only restriction coming from pain in this scapula region. I've tried pressing and squats and they're fine.

I'm just not sure how to proceed with re-introducing the pulling exercises. Once again your thoughts would be much appreciated (in the full knowledge of the limitations of talking about this stuff over an internet forum).

Mark Rippetoe: If you're confident in your diagnosis, then I'd say the scapular retraction cue was probably the cause. Start back with the rehab program detailed in the sticky, using deadlifts for the exercise, and expect the improvement to happen in a shorter timeframe than a full-blown muscle belly tear. Be sure to just *set* your shoulders in normal position.

Few questions

SilverBlue: 1. If the weight of the squats and deadlifts starts to be really heavy, should I use belt?

2. In the book you said to take your shoulder blades back and raise the chest up during bench pressing. When I bench I feel that in the middle my tightness starts to loosen, so how can I fix it?

3. Another question about the bench press, do I need to unrack the barbell with locked elbows? I find it difficult to do that in this position.

Mark Rippetoe: 1. Use a belt when you need to. It will not cause any problems and it may prevent several.

2. You may have to re-set the shoulder blades each rep until you get better at keeping them tight.

3. You should always move the bar over your face and neck with locked elbows. Try to get close enough to the bar to do this so that the bar doesn't fall on you.

Captainpicard: When do you know you need a belt? If you do all the lifts right won't your back get strong enough to perform the lifts safely without one? I know that the abdominals and erector spinae don't just relax and do nothing with a belt on, but the belt has got to prevent them from doing *some* work, or else it wouldn't help would it?

If you have to use a belt to squat your PR, then it really isn't your PR is it? It is more like you and your belt's PR. Also, for the deadlift wouldn't a belt be counterproductive as the deadlift is the main exercise for back strength and hypertrophy?

Mark Rippetoe: I always squat in my squat shoes, because they help me squat better. Do I have to share my squat PRs with my shoes?

Captainpicard: But couldn't you have the same firm surface if you were barefoot?

Jamie J: Don't forget the chalk; you have to remember the chalk. And the milk.

Mark Rippetoe: So the floor gets credit too?

Captainpicard: A belt is something external that aids in the lift. Similar to, but not nearly as bad as powerlifting gear. Shoes are only there so you don't drop a weight and lop a toe off; you have always had your own non-compressible heel. Food is natural and necessary to survive. Chalk just dries your hands out; you could produce a similar effect by wiping them on your shorts them rub them together very quickly (producing heat from the friction). Chalk is much easier though. If you are going to be really strict, a deadlift with the use of straps does not count either. The point of a deadlift isn't mainly grip strength though, it is primarily back strength, and then following that leg strength

Jamie J: The floor, my wrestling shoes, what's left of my chalk, the squat rack, a collection of cotton t-shirts and

2 pairs of shorts thank you for helping them get much stronger using Starting Strength.

Thank you,
My stuff

Mark Rippetoe: Maybe Jamie's stuff could explain these subtleties to the Captain.

Make it so.

Jamie J: Captain,

I don't know if the belt helped me lift more weight, but it helped do it safer. If my back is not feeling right, if I need some help tightening up my midsection, the belt gives me something to push against. The belt doesn't help with any of the muscles that are moving the weight, just the ones that stabilize. But used properly, unlike the straps, it doesn't cause a muscle imbalance. Knee wraps, when used too tightly, stores the energy you produce on the way down and helps you lift the weight. That, like a suit, helps you actually lift the weight.

There is a much better description of this in Starting Strength. It's a wonderful book; I suggest you pick it up.

I hope this helps,
Jamie's shorts

Calf-muscle strength

Drewfasa: I have recently begun training with a novice partner and we are both doing your SS:BBT program. This has involved a lot of explanation to my friend about why we do compound lifts and skip isolation exercises - i.e. explaining how all the muscles are used in the basic 5 exercises. I have done this by using the information about lifting mechanics from your book. However, when he asked me how the calf-muscles get stronger through the training I realized I didn't know. In fact I don't believe the muscles of the lower leg are mentioned in SS:BBT (please correct me if I'm wrong).

What part do the muscles of the lower leg play in the basic lifts? I presume they do get stronger through the lifts, is their role mainly isometric? Is the plantar flexion produced in a clean sufficient to produce adaptation?

Mark Rippetoe: Yes, they primarily function in an isometric and short ROM capacity. They adjust your position against the ground and maintain balance at their distal function on the foot, and they anchor against the femur in their proximal function to help control knee angle. The discussion of the glute/ham raise touches on this in BBT. The issue is clouded by the old “triple-extension” idea of the clean. I don't think that active plantar flexion contributes to the clean; I think that the momentum generated by the knee and hip extension carries you up onto your toes, and that calves – being composed of predominantly slow-twitch fibers and low-threshold motor units – don’t really have the potential to help much with explosion. They do have the important function of controlling foot position and stabilizing the foot as the knees and hips explode, and in this way they ensure maximum efficiency of the hip/knee explosion by controlling the ground reaction.

Bench press? Why not dips instead?

Robert: In SS:BBT you say that regarding full body involvement, pushups are better than bench presses, and dips even more than them. Since the weight on dips can easily be modified considering they are done with more than bodyweight, why do they not have the place in your novice program that the bench press does? I have heard you say that the bench press translates into greater pressing ability, which helps with the press, but couldn't dips do the same albeit more effectively, or do dips generally use less weight than the bench press and are therefore not as useful in that regard?

Mark Rippetoe: Because lots of novices can't do a bodyweight dip, and they are therefore too hard to program for the 3 sets of 5 linear progression.

Jamie J: For someone who can do greater than body weight dips for sets of five, which would be the more useful exercise? Assuming the trainee wasn't planning on competing in powerlifting.

Robert: Aside from having to be careful around the sensitive male area with a weighted belt would there be any reason not to do dips for the main lift instead of bench press? The only other things I can think of are: I have heard that dips are generally more prone to injury, especially shoulder/rotator cuff injuries than the bench press. Is this true considering they are done with correct form (not going too low and/or dropping to the bottom really quickly)?

Mark Rippetoe: The easy answer here is that SS is a barbell training program, and that dips are not a barbell exercise. But since that is a weasel, I'll just say that heavy weighted dips are way easier to get hurt doing. A dip belt is the traditional way of loading them incrementally, and the weight swinging around at the bottom presents a bunch of technical problems for both the execution of the movement and the management of the weight itself before, during, and after the set. The apparatus has never been standardized, the form is subject to ROM problems due to lockout and depth issues, and the bench has become the reference lift. Dips are a very good assistance exercise, and I've used them myself as a bench sub when I couldn't bench due to some weird injury, but I'm afraid they will never be able to replace the bench on a long-term basis.

KSC: We like using heavy chains draped around the neck/trapezius for performing weighted dips as opposed to a heavy dumbbell or plate swinging around your waist. Just FYI.

Mark Rippetoe: Further illustrating the lack of standardization. This works fine, I'm sure, and I'll bet it looks really cool, but it makes small jumps quite impossible.

Phil: In terms of extra resistance for dips, what do you think of powerlifting bands and chains? I agree that the dip belt is both cumbersome (putting 4+ 45 plates between your legs is never fun) and the swinging motion at the bottom throws off the center of gravity of the motion.

Mark Rippetoe: I think they are great ideas for making the dips more useful, but not for making the dips a sub for the bench.

Presses

SHMENT: I have a question about bench press and standing press. When I bench press my feet is on the floor and my lower back hyper extending. Does it hurt my lower back? Or this is fine? I thought to put my legs on a box so my lower back will be flat. About the standing press, in the heavy sets I am using my hips to gain momentum and by doing that my back is hyper extending. Again does it hurt my lower back?

Mark Rippetoe: A big arch in your back on the bench press doesn't hurt your back because it's not loaded in compression. But on the press it is, and if your lumbar is overextended your abs are not doing their job of stabilizing your back. The movement comes from hips, not lumbar flexion/extension.

Squat: hips up before shoulders

Dan F: I noted that sometimes, specially the last reps of heavier sets of squatting, my hips begin going up before shoulders (so back becomes slightly more horizontal), I feel this also in the bar on my back that have a tendency not only to "go up" but also to slide/roll forward, direction traps (it's a "tendency" I feel in hands, not real movement). Is this a sort of exaggerated hip-drive (if possible) or instead no hip-drive at all and a symptom of something other wrong? When this happens I feel the weight more on toes than on heel and going up is harder because there is a light pause in the meantime.

Mark Rippetoe: It is probably not an exaggerated hip drive, but rather a failure to keep the low back and hamstrings tight. If this occurs and the back angle becomes excessively horizontal, you increase the length of the lever arm at the hip and fuck up the mechanics. Hip drive is apparent when you see a little suggestion of a back angle change, but a full-blown leaning over is not at all what I look for out of the bottom.

Jamie J: My girlfriend just started doing this as the weights got a bit heavier, also as fatigue sets it. First set isn't bad, last set is not so good. I just don't know what cues to use to get her to stop it. She's aware of it, but she doesn't know what to do either. I looked through the squat videos and can't find anything else like it. Her head is up while looking down, elbows are raised, hip drive is decent and just is up. Any suggestions Mark? And no, getting a new girlfriend is out of the question.

Mark Rippetoe: I'd have to see it, Jamie. Sorry, but this is exactly why internet coaching is not something you pay money for – too many things that need to be seen and not read about.

Steven Q: I'm still struggling with extending the knee and moving the hips backwards/making the back more parallel to the ground. I was wondering if there are any cues you have used in lifters who took the idea of hip drive too far and screwed up the mechanics of the lift.

I've been trying to simply will myself not to do it, but as you've said before, in the absence of enough yelling, fewer things get done. One thing that helped a bit was actually thinking about driving the bar up now, which helped eliminate some of the good morning of the weight. If I think about hip drive, I get exaggeration. If you have any cues you've used in the past with people who extend the knee and raise the hips without moving the bar that you think might be helpful, please let me know. If not, I suppose I'll just continue willing myself to not screw up. While I've gotten better at not shooting the hips back, I still do it in an effort to get hip drive.

Mark Rippetoe: This particular problem would be a good example of something in need of a cue that would otherwise be wrong. A "Lift the chest" cue would normally be the wrong thing to hear in a squat, because it would typically cause a change in back angle that is detrimental to hip drive, but in this case it is appropriate because the error would be "averaged out" in response to the cue. It is important to know when to cue in this way, and that comes with experience

---

Ab work

Drewfasa: What's the best ab exercise I can do if I only have access to the following equipment: bench; power-rack; barbells and plates; chinning-bar; dip bars; decline ab-board. I can only do a couple chin-ups right now so L-sit chins are out of the question (although I can do lots of dips, if there is such thing as L-sit dips?).

Mark Rippetoe: Knees-to-elbows, done as best you can, are very good. But there's nothing wrong with situps.

Rocko: There isn't much in your SS book about it, but could you give us some tips on doing a proper situp? I understand that a badly performed situp can have negative side effects on the back. I have worked so hard to master proper form on the big lifts that I would hate to get injured doing an assistance exercise.

Mark Rippetoe: There is no magical way to do a situp that takes the strain off of the low back. The psoas has an anterior insertion on the lumbar and a medial attachment to the femur, so that when you perform the hip flexion component of a situp the psoas pulls the lumbar anteriorly into what might be overextension if it is extreme. But this is countered by the rectus abdominis contracting the anterior ab wall into flexion when the situp is correctly performed, meaning that the movement is understood correctly and performed by pulling the chest towards the pelvis. So if you do them right they shouldn't really hurt your back at all. Weighted situps are done with a plate held on the chest or behind the neck, and if they are too hard or hurt too much you're not ready to do them heavy.

Stronger: What is your opinion on planks, where you basically hold a prone position with your elbows for ab work? This seems to me that since it's a stabilizing exercise it would translate into benefiting other exercises where ab stability is needed (squats).

Mark Rippetoe: They are fabulous if you can do them. But then again, if you are strong enough to do a plank you probably don't need any more ab work than you already get.

Draco: Um, is it okay to just never do ab work?

Mark Rippetoe: I seldom do situps anymore myself. I like to do a few reps of L-chinups when I chin to get the work done, but it's been a long time since I regularly incorporated situps into my training, and my abs stay strong from the other work. There are many ways to do situps, so try them all if you want to and see which make you the most sore/strong.

Hang Cleans vs. Power Cleans

progressiveman1: Why are power cleans more beneficial than hang cleans? I've read that people are equally as strong or possibly stronger with hang cleans. I see that there is a longer range of motion with power cleans, but the extra distance at the bottom is just moving a light weight into position for the jump. Some timing is required for power cleans, but I can't say whether this has any benefit since I don't understand the importance of timing in weight lifting regarding it transferring over to a sport. Can you fill in the gaps for me on this topic?

Mark Rippetoe: You're not just moving the weight through a longer range of motion. You are *accelerating* through a longer range of motion, and the acceleration is why we do the clean. The longer ROM requires that power be produced over that longer ROM and that you control the position of the bar and your back while this is occurring. Hang cleans are easier to teach, so any excuse for not teaching the harder movement will apparently do for some coaches.

Polynomial: I'm not sure if this generalizes to other people, but I found that past a certain weight, getting set up for a hang clean is a lot more taxing than doing a clean from the floor.

Mark Rippetoe: It very well may be, due to the full deadlift and the lowering back down to the jumping position. More actual work (the force x distance type), even done more slowly.

JPC: I don't understand how hang cleans allow some to use more weight (I've heard that rumor before too). I can certainly lift more from the floor, since by the time I hit the second pull position, the bar has some momentum.

progressiveman1: Is that acceleration through the extra range motion important mostly for the carry-over effect to the deadlift?

Mark Rippetoe: I've never seen anybody that knew how to power clean correctly lift more from the hang. And the full range of motion is important for getting strong and explosive over the whole range of motion.

Brandon: Under the thinking that the first pull of a clean is more for positioning than power, you may theoretically hang clean the same as you clean. But the only way you should be hang cleaning MORE is if your form is iffy and eliminating the first pull makes the movement simpler, and therefore better. Kinda like how you might power clean more than you squat clean; it's a beginner's phenomenon rather than an advanced one.

Mark Rippetoe: But Brandon, the bar accelerates into the second pull, thus entering the jumping phase of the lift at a higher velocity that it would from the hang. This makes for more than just a positional consideration, even in a novice (but maybe not a rank novice).

Progressiveman1: But how specific is that adaptation with its transfer over to sports? In other words, does increasing your power in the extra distance at the bottom have much importance with baseball, or other sports?

Mark Rippetoe: It is only important if you use the whole range of motion in baseball or other sports.

Push Press not main exercise?

progressiveman1: Why do you choose the press instead of the push press as the main exercise? The push press involves the entire body more so, and you can use more weight and move the bar more quickly over the same range of motion, generating more power. Not that you don't know that, but I want to make sure you understand why I'm asking the question.

Mark Rippetoe: Because it's quite possible to be very good at the push press and not have a very good press, since it leaves out the bottom of the movement with respect to the pressing muscles. Power is not our only concern – the press is a strength exercise. If our only criterion is that heavier weights can be lifted faster, the jerk would be even better than the push press.

Knees out too much?

DB5: The question is how do I know if I'm pushing my knees out too much? The feeling I get is somewhat off balance, as if the weight is on the outside edge of my feet. I feel much better when I don't intentionally push out my knees but simply try to stay in balance on the way down. I did the drill suggested in SS where I look between my feet on the way down and the knees are not going inside, but how do I know if they are too far outside?

Mark Rippetoe: The purpose of knees-out is twofold: keeping the knees from twisting, and placing the femurs in a position using the external rotators (glutes and the deep rotator muscles) in which the adductors can also be used most effectively. If your femurs are parallel to your feet, you are correct, and if your knees are outside your toes you are shoving them out too much.

DB5: Part of this problem might be the geometry of my legs. When standing straight, heels close together (maybe 6 inches apart), my feet naturally point slightly out. While walking, too, I notice that my feet are not lined up straight but are slightly out.

While sitting in a chair, if I try to make either the feet point straight or make the knee go right over the foot I feel tension in the knee. However, if my knee goes a little to the inside of my feet then it feels alright.

Mark Rippetoe: Well, it is certainly relevant that you are duck-footed. If your feet and femurs are not naturally straight, the angle between them has to be preserved in your squat stance or you'll have torsion on the knee, as you've observed.

DB5: If that is the case, how would I figure out what the right angle is?

Mark Rippetoe: If it is anatomical (and it usually is if a few weeks of correct squatting have not changed the relationship) then correct will be the foot position that stays constant when you squat with your knees in the position that would be parallel to your feet at about a 30 degree stance. In other words, when you warm up, place your feet at the normal angle of about 30 degrees, keep your knees at that angle, squat down, and see where your feet end up as the toes rotate out to accommodate your asymmetry. That will be your stance.

Experience training swimmers with shoulder injuries?

JLascek: Do you have experience training swimmers with shoulder injuries? Swimmers, as a whole, are incredibly overtrained and typically have overuse injuries (which coaches continue to ignore). I'm not a swimmer, but I have friends that are collegiate swimmers.

I'm convinced that if pressing was incorporated into their training appropriately (which I use the term loosely, since many other variables would need to be changed in order to make their training "appropriate"), it would strengthen the integrity and ability of their joint to some degree (barring injury that requires surgery). I'd like to see your thoughts on the matter. If we're on the same page, when would it be best for implementation? Off-season or as soon as possible?

Mark Rippetoe: It is common to see shoulder injuries in athletes whose overhead ROM is unweighted, like swimmers, basketball and volleyball players, and in the racket sports. Impingement is usually the problem, and is dealt with in *Strong Enough?*. Pressing correctly prevents these injuries, and the way to incorporate them into the workout would vary with the sport and the level of training advancement of the trainee. But there is no time like the present to start.

Brandon: How does pressing prevent these injuries?

Mark Rippetoe: It strengthens the structures that usually get hurt, teaches proper scapular position, and makes the stuff that's already hurt a little heal up.

Brandon: My understanding of the impingement problem (mainly from the explanation in that article) is that it's caused by the acromion digging into the soft tissue of the arm when it's elevated without the scapula coming along with it. Can strengthening the surrounding muscle, etc. really prevent a bone from sticking into things? That seems illogical.

And I assume that if proper form in a sport doesn't involve an elevated shoulder, it's not going to happen when you practice it, whether you know about impingement or not.

JLascek: I believe you've made this clear before, but is your view that having an appropriate bench press to press ratio more beneficial for the previously mentioned athletes (with problems in the shoulder) than the typical "external rotation" band exercises?

Mark Rippetoe: If the structures are physically tougher, they're harder to injure. If the scapular position is established when pressing, it can carry over to the repetitive activity, but this is not really the deal. Not everybody who swims, plays volleyball, etc., has impingement problems, so it's not that big a deal anyway. What is it about the people who get injured vs. the people who don't that makes the difference? Is it the shape of the acromion, the condition of the soft tissue, or the way they use the shoulder? It might be all three, but pressing can help the last two. Band exercises are a waste of time for a healthy shoulder; just get your press strong and that is about the best investment of your time for prevention.

Shins torn up from deadlifting

banderbe: Looking for suggestions on how to protect shins when deadlifting. I have scabs that keep getting reopened and bleed when I deadlift. I tried some skin tight new balance running pants but the material is too thin..

Mark Rippetoe: Cut some shin guards out of a 1 liter 7UP bottle, or any other smooth-sided plastic soft drink bottle, and put them in your socks before you deadlift or pull. Fixes it every time.

Banderbe: Great (and cheap) idea! I'll try it out.

JLascek: I was under the impression that if you begin the pull off the floor by opening the hip angle first (as opposed to opening the knee angle first), this will pull the bar into the shins. I think there was a quote in the deadlift chapter saying "the blood on the bar will tell you this is wrong". Wouldn't fixing this form cue prevent the bar from dragging on his shins, or is it acceptable with abnormal segment lengths? Or is it that dragging the bar is better than the alternative of not keeping it close to the shins at all in the first place?

Mark Rippetoe: While it is quite true that correct form minimizes shin damage, some people are unable to keep the shins from getting scraped, even with good form and especially after they are already bloody, scabbed, and sore. Cheap shin guards keep blood off of the bar, and if you are in a commercial gym, this is more important than even getting the form correct.

Power Clean Question

Andrew: I am having an extremely difficult time learning power cleans. For the past month or so I've been doing the variation of SS with chins/pull ups and it's been working fine. I figured it's time to step it up though. When I try to put the bar in the rack position I am finding it extremely difficult to keep my elbows up. I also am still really unsure as to how the bar is supposed to sit on my shoulders. For some reason this position seems beyond uncomfortable for me -- it just seems unnatural, and I'm not really sure how I can get it to feel right. I've watched videos and read the section in SS over and over again. It doesn't seem like it has anything to do with me being inflexible. I just don't think I'm "getting" it. How high are my elbows actually supposed to be? Where should the tips of my fingers be in relation to my shoulders? Should I have someone "load" the bar onto my shoulders while I have my elbows up so that I can get used to the position?

Mark Rippetoe: Rack position problems are quite often the result of anthropometry. If your forearms are long relative to your upper arms, this geometry will always result in a lower elbow position with a typical close clean grip. We want your elbows pointing more or less straight forward, and if your forearms are long you're going to have to widen your grip to accommodate the longer forearm dimension. There's just no other way to fix it, and it's not flexibility. Widen your grip a finger width at a time until the rack position works with your elbows in the right place.

Andrew: Thanks for your response. The bar is supposed to sit on my shoulders right? And my fingers are there only to support the bar and keep it in place? Should I be forcing my wrists to turn outward as I widen the grip? The only thing I have in my room right now close to a barbell is a lacrosse stick. I just tried to hold in the rack position and no matter how much I widen my grip, my elbows won't point forward. I really want to learn power cleans... this is just really frustrating for me.

Mark Rippetoe: The bar should be sitting on the meat of your deltoids, and the fingers do not support the weight. They just trap the bar between your elbows and your shoulders. You don't have to force you wrists to do anything; once your grip is correct you just think about driving your elbows up and in toward the middle. Widen your grip until this is possible. And you won't be able to do this with a light stick, so just wait till you train again.

Fixing a squat

Bleve: I'm sorry I don't have a video of this yet Rip, but I'm working with a masters age track cyclist doing your squats, and we're running into a problem. He's a 44 y/o guy with great leg speed but poor strength, so squats & deadlifts will help him a lot. We're using a modified PPST program to build him up and mixing it with track sprint work on the bike.

He has two problems I'm not sure how to fix.

I hope my description is clear :

Firstly, no matter how much we demand that he reach back with his hips in the squat, his hips drift forward at the bottom, his knees come way forward and he turns it into an almost front-squat squat, all quads. He's watched your

video on squats with me, we've gone over SS ad nauseum, but it just doesn't matter what we do he drifts forward, after an initial good hip movement to initiate the descent once he gets to about 80 degrees of knee bend his hips and knees come forward. We've done the "get down and jack the knees apart with the elbows" thing, I've loaded him up with weight to get him deeper but it's just not happening at the bottom. His flexibility is junk, but I don't think it's a flexibility thing, I think it's confidence and posterior strength.

He spoke to his osteopath today and they discussed squats and this is his report :

I asked him to look at my squat position and why he thought I can't easily get into the correct position and why I can't get back and why I get that pain/soreness in the front which confused you and Merv on Wed. night.

Basically my gluteals are very weak and I am using my quads to support me. If I try to push back, it recruits more of the gluteals but because they are weak I want to come forward to prevent losing balance and toppling backwards. It's the gluteal media and gluteal minor which are at fault. This is just his opinion of course, he is no weights guru.

He suggested we come up with additional exercises/ drills/ lifts - whatever it takes to strengthen the glutes. During this time he really emphasised keeping the weight down and making sure technique is spot on. He mentioned something about during squats the main muscle groups need to activate and fire in order - A,B,C. That may not be happening and you may know more about what he was talking about than me.

So the osteo at least isn't saying "squats hurt your knees"! I'm not a huge fan of osteos, but he is and this one at least doesn't seem like a complete twit.

Now if that's the case (and I'm not sure that it is, but I'm at a loss) would you suggest that deadlifts might be a useful thing to do to get his posterior chain to work? Maybe even SLDLs to get the quads right out of it at first to build up his backside? He deadlifts reasonably well, at least in terms of technique, it's acceptable and we're improving it, but I have to fix his squat somehow.

The second problem is that we have a lot of trouble keeping his feet under his knees, his feet drift right out beyond 30 degrees as he goes down and his knees cave in, so there's no power out of the hole (what little hole there is because he doesn't go down and back far enough to really get into it!). Again, even doing unweighted squats onto a ball or bench doesn't seem to help this, I'm not sure if it's some weird hip flexibility thing. He explains that it's his anterior hip muscles that tighten up, but I can't see why, they're not really loaded or stretched much?

I will get a video of him doing this this weekend I hope, so we'll be able to show it to you, but in the mean time, your suggestions are much appreciated.

Mark Rippetoe: Problem 1: Both you and the osteopath, and lots of other people, are confused about how to fix a problem within a major multi-joint exercise. Let's assume for a second that your cyclist's glutes are weak – and I'm not entirely sure that most of this problem is not merely the fault of flexibility, since cyclists are such notoriously inflexible fuckers, and even though the vast majority of humans are flexible enough to squat below parallel correctly, your cyclist might not be – and then let's figure out a way to get those weak glutes strong enough to help us squat. What "glute" exercise for the medius and minimus are we going to select that will produce strength usable in the squat? Some weird cable deal? A new form of hip extension on the GHD? How will this work, since he also wants the lifter to micromanage the "firing order" of the now-stronger constituent components of the kinetic chain?

The reason we do the squat is because it is a normal human movement that requires the use of all the skeletal components of the body and therefore all the muscles that move them. If we are careful to make our movement pattern reflect the correct use of the skeletal components moving with the physical system provided by the loaded barbell sitting on the shoulders – correct technique – then all the muscular components work the way they have to to move the skeleton "correctly" within the constraints of that physical system. Correct meaning the most efficient way to move the bar through space while using the most muscle mass possible and therefore making the most possible stuff strong. In other words, the neuromuscular system solves the problems of skeletal position, which muscles to use, how much to use them relative to each other, eccentric/concentric/isometric, their "firing order", all this shit that is too complicated to actually keep track of with your brain. If your movement is correct, then the use of the muscles that produced that movement is correct too. It's like an economy – there are too many parts to micromanage, and every time you try you fuck things up. You just set up a framework of laws to enforce contracts, safeguard the value of the money, and the damn thing runs just fine.

Excuse the tangent. The answer is that you make him squat correctly and the "gluteals" will get strong in exactly the way they need to, because they got strong in the context of the movement pattern they are designed to perform.

Now, Problem 2 is really just more of Problem 1: the guy can't produce a position that actually lets him use his posterior chain because all its components are so tight that he can't – or he won't – get into a position to use them correctly in the movement. Sure, you can use RDLs to show him how his hamstrings and glutes are supposed to work, but that doesn't show him the femoral external rotation necessary for the squat, and if you can't get a correct squat out of the guy, what makes you think you can coach him through an RDL or an SLDL?

So, the problem is either severe flexibility inadequacy, best fixed by a vicious massage therapist and myofascial release, or your ability to coach the guy into a correct position. You cannot fix the strength of a section of the kinetic chain of a multi-joint movement by isolating that component, making it stronger, and sticking it back into the movement. The whole movement has to get strong, and when it does all the components of the movement are strong in the way they normally function together. AND then if they need to be used in ways that are different from the big movement, they're still strong; this is how the low-bar squat improves the front squat. Leg extension will improve nothing but the leg extension, the pec-deck won't make your bench press stronger, and if you figure out a way to make the osteopath happy and isolate some of the glutes, that won't improve the situation either.

There is a way to coach the guy into position, I'll bet. You can figure it out.

DB bench vs. BB bench

BIGGUY6FT6: Is DB bench as effective as BB bench if you have DB's with 2.5 lb increments? Also, if you have a heavy bench day and no spotter would DB's be better or worse than BB as long as you stay consistent with one or the other? Thanks in advance.

Mark Rippetoe: There are 2 problems with this. 1.) Nobody has dumbbells in 2.5 lb. increments, because they're not made this way. At least not heavy ones. And this would still be 5 lb. jumps, which is too heavy toward the end of a linear progression. 2.) You cannot handle heavy dumbbells any more safely without a spotter than you can a barbell. Have you ever tried to get in position on a bench with 122 lb. dumbbells? It's no party, and you can really hurt a shoulder or two.

Jamie J: If you could make smaller jumps (some ferromagnetic washers, a 60 amp dc power supply, a pretty serious electro magnet and physics degree), are there any issues with the dumbbell bench?

Mark Rippetoe: There is still the problem of handling the heavier dumbbells, and your physics degree didn't prepare you for that.

Sticking point

Jeroen: I am now at a point that I have to make small increases on the squat to keep making progress. I have no problem getting out of the bottom position but I have a sticking point about ½ way up on the last 2 reps of the last set. By watching the vids I make I can see that by that point I stop looking down and lift my chest just to finish the rep. Is this just a matter of bad technique or normal for a limit attempt squat? I was thinking that getting out of the bottom would/should be the hardest part.,

Mark Rippetoe: When you lift your chest, you let your knees come forward. When this happens, your knee angle closes a little, and the hamstring shortens as the distal insertion approaches the proximal origin. This kills hip drive by killing tension in the posterior chain. Believe it or not, hips are still extending 2/3 of the way up, and anytime knees go forward at this point your bar speed will drop. So don't look up and don't lift your chest.

What's wrong with situps?

Shaka: I read this on the bodybuilding.com forum:

Q5: What's wrong with situps?
Traditional situps emphasize sitting up rather than merely pulling your sternum down to meet your pelvis. The action of the psoas muscles, which run from the lower back around to the front of the thighs, is to pull the thighs closer to the torso. This action is the major component in sitting up. Because of this, situps primarily engage the psoas making them inefficient at exercising your abs. More importantly, they also grind the vertebrae in your lower back.

They're inefficient because the psoas work best when the legs are close to straight (as they are when doing situps), so for most of the situp the psoas are doing most of the work and the abs are just stabilising.

Putting the thighs at a right angle to the torso to begin with means that the psoas can't pull it any further, so all of the stress is placed on the abs.

Situps also grind vertebrae in your lower back. This is because to work the abs effectively you are trying to make the lower back round, but tension in the psoas encourages the lower back move into an exaggerated arch. The result is the infamous "disc pepper grinder" effect that helps give you chronic lower back pain in later life.

Do you agree?

Mark Rippetoe: No, I don't. The situp is not my favorite choice of trunk exercises, but in the absence of the ability to use the trunk muscles in their normal isometric function as spinal stabilizers when lifting a load heavy enough to work them, they may be all you've got. Novices can strengthen the abs quite effectively with situps and then progress beyond them later. And if the psoas and iliacus get strong at the same time, how can this be bad? As for saying that the psoas does all the work in a situp, well, this is just plain old stupid, and anyone who has ever gotten their abs sore from situps *knows* this is stupid. It is not necessary to challenge the effectiveness of traditional exercises using a brand-new anatomical analysis just because it's 2008 and somebody just looked at *Netter* and discovered that the psoas is a hip flexor and decided that a situp involves hip flexion. The abs are in a much better position of leverage to produce a spinal flexion than the psoas is to produce a hip flexion, so the abs will get worked harder if the situp is done correctly.

And as for destroying the low back, that's what deadlifts are for. I think I remember that there are intervertebral discs between the vertebrae, and that in a situp there is no compressive load on the spine, so that "grinding" is probably an exaggeration.

Win: The argument that situps are less efficient because multiple muscle groups are involved strikes me as backwards. It sounds like part of the "isolation is better" school of thought. I would think situps are a decent exercise (compared to crunches) *because* multiple groups are used to perform the situp, and that makes them more natural and functional.

1369phil: So what is your favorite exercise(s) for the trunk?

Mark Rippetoe: Situps are better than crunches because you know when you've done a whole situp, and a crunch is just a partial spinal flexion – never really finished, just started; we can quantify situp work, but we're always just playing with ourselves when we do crunches. And I like weighted bent-knee situps, or Roman chair situps. L-pullups are very good, and knees-to-elbows are maybe the best unweighted exercise. But if your presses are heavy, your abs will be strong.

Small question on the power clean

gallo_blanco: As I move up in weight on the power clean, I find my feet not leaving the floor as much and find myself really thrusting my hips forward as I am powering the weight up past my waist. This causes the weight to travel away from my shirt a bit, but, I am also extending my back a bit more, so that is causing me to move away from the bar, too.

Is this exaggerated thrust a normal part of the movement as I move up in weight or does this sound like a very horrible mistake that is leading to great failure and pain in the future?

Mark Rippetoe: Focus on your stomp – the resetting of your feet on the floor after the jump. You have stopped jumping enough, a movement composed of both hip and knee extension. You are probably not emphasizing the knee extension enough, and the symptom is the exaggerated hips-forward and no stomp since the feet never left the ground. Make yourself stomp and you will have made yourself jump first.

Breathing on bench

Lord Burly: I'm working hard to eliminate some bad habits I acquired before discovering your books. I have tried to fix my breathing patterns, among other things, and have grown comfortable with the Valsalva maneuver on most of the lifts.

I still have one question about breathing during the bench press. I understand that a huge breath precedes the first rep. Should this breath be taken just before I unrack the weight, or should I take it once the bar has reached the correct position over my chest?

Mark Rippetoe: That depends on whether you have a spotter giving you a hand-off or not. If you do, take the bar from the spotter, set the chest up, take the breath, and then start the rep. If you have to take it out of the rack yourself, you'll need to do it on a breath before you move the bar, then you can decide whether to just hold the breath during a short set-up or take another one before the rep starts. If it doesn't take long to set the chest, I'd just use the same breath as the take-out.

Single arm snatches

dan302: What are your views on singles arm snatches with either a dumbbell or barbell? I realize they may not be suitable for a novice but how about as a pull on a light day for an intermediate?

Mark Rippetoe: I like them, and I do them occasionally. They are not hard to learn. I much prefer the dumbbell version, which is much easier with my revolving-sleeved dumbbells I had made for the purpose.

A belt question

lukeBW: I finally decided to get a belt a 4"wide all around, not because I needed it but to get used to it since now I am deadlifting nearly 300lb and squatting 240lb I figure it can't hurt to try. So my question is with placement and tightness; I remember reading something in here but I cannot find the post.

For squats I place the belt just about in the center of the abs, suck in my belly and tighten it just enough so that it's supported but I can still breath, when deadlifting I place it a little lower to cover the lower back and lower abs. Again I try to tighten it but not so much that it becomes difficult to breath. Since it was all guessing, am I doing something wrong? Is there a better way to set the belt to maximize its purpose?

Mark Rippetoe: I wear my belt a little higher in back and lower in front for the deadlift than the squat, but these things are dependent on your proportions. I have found that if the belt is so tight that I had to relax my abs to get it in that hole, it is too tight. Trial and error is the method here.

Yunstr: Is having the belt the same width all the way around helpful or is it completely necessary? I guess I mean does having a belt with a wider back mean just a waste of material or does it actually hinder movement? Basically I want to know if I need to buy a new belt.

Mark Rippetoe: Since the primary function of the belt is anterior, any belt that is wider in the back was produced by someone who does not know this. Powerlifters use a 4" all-the-way-around belt.

Back can't support squats

yunstr: I am 19, 5'4", 140 lbs. I have been trying to use the correct form on squats but when I am doing heavy weights (245 lbs. for sets of 5) I absolutely cannot keep the arch in my back. I can do about 285 lbs. for 5 reps on the deadlift. My hamstrings lose tension when my back isn't tight and the lift is screwed up (also having trouble using the stretch reflex with heavy weight).

I have been trying to do "knees out" and "sit back" simultaneously but "sitting back" makes it feel like my torso just wants to fall forward. A pretty good powerlifter I know says that I should be looking straight forward or slightly up (he says if you look at the best squatters they do this) with squats and that I should move the bar farther up than the low bar I am currently using so my back won't have as much weight to support (with regard to torque). He also says since my back is weak I should do good mornings to make it stronger because they don't take as long to recover from as deadlifts. He also objects to your SS routine as has mentioned that I should try some more advanced Louie Simmons style speed work too.

I used to like squats but now I feel like I can't do them right unless I use a weight about 20 lbs. than my legs can handle. I can deadlift more, but the back angle I have in deads is more upright than my squat (and I am fairly certain my deadlifts are good form-wise). I try to think about the "hips up" cue but even in conjunction with "chest up" I feel as if my torso just wants to tilt forward excessively. Do you have any tips to help me with my back/squat problem?

Mark Rippetoe: You can't keep your back arched with your work sets, but this guy wants you to do high-bar squats with advanced Westside programming? I think you should back off, learn how to get voluntary control of your lumbar muscles, and work back up to 245 with better form. Don't confuse a lack of progress with a lack of programming complexity. And your back angle for a squat should be more vertical than for a deadlift unless you're pulling sumo.

Front Squat Rack Problems

Albert987: I haven't had any problems with the rack position when I do power cleans or front squat. Lately however, I find it really hard to keep proper form doing front squats now that my working sets have gone up to 255. When I hit the bottom, the weight makes the bar roll forward, which sometimes causes me to drop the set. How can I fix this? Do I need even more wrist flexibility? Maintain a more vertical back while squatting?

Mark Rippetoe: Heavy front squats get missed because the bar gets too far forward in front of the mid-foot. You're rounding your upper back or dropping your elbows. The cues for coming up out of the front squat are "lift the chest" and "lift the elbows" as you come up, like hip drive for the back squat.

Equipment Questions

Bergie: Although this does not relate directly to training methods, it is the forum I read most often, so here it goes.

1) Should the plates always be collared, except for the bench?

2) Is there any maintenance that should be done to the bar? My work out area is outside but not directly exposed to weather. I have noticed some rust showing up on the bar. Do the bearings need to be lubricated?

Mark Rippetoe: 1. If the plates slide off the bar frequently, due to the sleeves being manufactured with little ridges on them instead of a proper flat surface, or due to your inability to handle the bar in a level, balanced manner, the bar will have to be collared. It can be collared for the bench too, but **NOT IF YOU DON'T HAVE A SPOTTER**. People who train alone get killed doing this.

2. Bar maintenance depends on the bar. If the bar is an expensive stainless or plated bar, it will not have surface rust and will therefore need no cleaning, unless excessive chalk has built up in the knurl; this comes off with a wire brush. If it is unplated steel – my personal favorite due to its feel in the hands – the knurl will need an occasional wire brushing in humid weather. Best to not use WD40 or a lube-based solvent to remove the rust dust; plain thinner or mineral spirits work best and leave no residue on the bar. Bearing mounted sleeves require no maintenance, but bushings require a drop of oil at both ends of the sleeve occasionally, when the spin gets sticky.

Overhead squat

kayno: This overhead squat exercise is really starting to grow on me. The dynamics of this exercise challenges me in so many ways, but the main reason I like this exercise is that when performing it you can feel everything (proprioceptive), and for me if something isn't switched on, it doesn't happen.

My question is this: I am considering using the o.h.s. on a light day in Texas method. Do the glutes and hammys contribute to the exercise in a way that serves the back squat heavy days? I ask because I am under the impression that the front squat does not and wondered if it was also the case for the o.h.s. My main goal is to continue linear progression on my back squat for as long as possible.

Mark Rippetoe: The OHS can be done in two ways, depending on your flexibility. Many people do it with an upright torso, so that it essentially uses front squat mechanics, but the same back angle used in the back squat can also be employed, so that the posterior chain gets pulled in more. But either way, the OHS will never constitute enough of a percentage of your back squat to serve as a strength exercise for the lower body because the limiting factor is your ability to keep the bar overhead, not your ability to squat it. You could do it on light day after front squats, but not instead of.

Front squat vs. overhead squat

isis: I have the bad combination of body proportions for the front squat: long legs, short torso, long forearms. I have been trying to learn it for a couple weeks with just the bar, trying to get the elbows up higher and my upper back strong enough to hold the position. I'm improving but slowly. On the other hand, I've tried the overhead squat, and while it's not easy either, I don't feel like I'm fighting my body to do it. Besides, it makes me feel like someday I could be as sexy as those CrossFit girls doing overhead squats on youtube.

What are the pros and cons of replacing the front squat with the overhead squat in the advanced novice program?

Mark Rippetoe: The short torso/long legs combination is famous for frustrating attempts at front squats. I mentioned in another post tonight that there are two ways to Overhead squat, and you are doing the second style, the one where your back angle is the same as the back squat. In any overhead bar position, the bar is in balance when it is directly above the shoulder blades, and it is stable when you shrug your traps up to keep it there. I also mentioned the limitations of the OHS. But if you just can't front squat because of anthropometry, you'll have to do something else, and OHS might be that something.

Front Squat 'Knees Forward' Question

tescott: On page 45, in the chapter on squats, you talk about the problem of knees sliding forward, which seems to be a common problem in many trainees (including myself!). You say:

Now, if at the bottom of the squat the knee should be allowed to move forward, tension is increased on these muscles [the hip flexors which cross the hip and knee] and their attachment at the hip as the knee angle becomes more acute. The ASIS (the attachment of the rectus femoris is actually the Anterior Inferior Iliac Spine, as more careful attention paid to hip anatomy after the 2nd edition was published has revealed. – Rip) *is pulled on very hard by these muscles at their attachment, and a marvelous dose of the weirdest tendinitis you have ever seen can be the result.*

Also:

it [knees forward] is inefficient and increases the risk of injury

Later on, in your section on Front Squats, it seems that it's ok for knees to go forward in front squats, and that (as in a recent previous post) hip drive isn't the focus. If avoiding 'knees forward' in the back squat is merely to preserve the hip drive focus, I can understand the difference, but it seems to me (according to the quotes above) that it's also because of possible hip/knee injury - so why isn't 'knees forward' a problem for front squats too?

Sorry for the technical question, I've just been thinking about it and would like to know the answer.

Mark Rippetoe: Technical questions are good questions, as opposed to questions about my favorite color. Forward knee travel on both back and front squats has to take place during the initial phase of the descent or there will be problems at the anterior pelvic attachment of the rectus femoris. If the hip flexor comes under proximal tension, as it will when the knee flexes, and then the tension markedly increases, as it does if you relax the hamstrings and let the knees slide forward at the bottom, the sharp tug on the proximal tendon attachment can make it sore. If the forward knee position is established early in the descent, tension is rather uniform during the whole movement. This true for both front and back squats. Due to the back angle, a front squat requires a much more forward knee position than the back squat, but it is not trouble if the forward position is established well before the bottom is reached.

Position of the Scapula on the OHS

Doofuswhack: On this Board I came across a statement made by you twice (at least), that the Overhead Squat can be done with to different back angles (Front Squat and Back Squat like). Could you explain this in detail or kindly direct me to an article where this is elaborated?
Also the placement of the scapula in the Overhead Squat is of particular interest to me, as I have seem to aggravated chronic bicipital tendonitis in my left shoulder (Funnily enough I did OHS to give my lower back some rest...). It

went from chronic to acute pretty damn fast actually. I'm not sure if I kept the scapula just a tad too low; shrugging up fully just seemed impractical even though load was low.

Mark Rippetoe: I doubt you'll find an article on this other than my references to it here on the board. Nobody seems terribly interested in this. The salient point is that the scapulas hold up the arms, and thus the bar. The traps hold up the scapulas, and if the traps are to do their job well they must be shrugged up to support the load. And since the bar is over the scapulas, any lateral deviation from a vertical line over the glenoid constitutes a moment acting on the joint. This can be accomplished with a more horizontal back angle if you want to use hip drive, or with a more vertical back angle if you want to "quad" the thing up like a front squat. Hips are stronger, if you are strong enough to hold very heavy weights overhead, i.e. you are a competitive weightlifter.

There's your article.

Squats

joseph: I am having real trouble squatting due to lack of flexibility. I have tried to use a low weight and squat as low as I can as a stretch but have found that this is starting to cause a pain on my knees - inevitable from what is basically a partial squat I guess.

I am working on stretching but it is a very slow process to gain much flexibility. I know that the squat is the foundation of SS but is there something I can do as a replacement until I am in a position to do the squat safely and with half decent form?

Mark Rippetoe: How do you propose to become capable of doing the squat without doing the squat? I have seen a vanishingly small number of people that were so inflexible that they couldn't squat below parallel with correct form, meaning correct stance, knees out, and the hips active. What remains to be stretched out after this is accomplished in the process of going up to work set weight.

Joseph: I completely agree about being needed to do it to become capable of it and I have tried but since I can only go so far down I think it is putting too much pressure on my knees (I believe). I cannot even do it without any wait properly. I have tried goblet squat and variants but my hips are not flexible to stop my back tilting backwards and losing balance.

I have seen an osteopath and he seems to think that apart from having very tight hamstrings the problem is with my glutes and tensor fascia latae. Since these are so tight that they are rubbing against my hip and causing an ungodly amount of pain when I squat or even stretch. I will start squatting again with very light weights though and hope to make more progress with an added stretching routine.

Mark Rippetoe: You're not paying attention.

Joseph: Weighted squatting with knees out and an active hip should provide all the stretching I need?

Mark Rippetoe: You have begun to pay attention.

Weighted Ring Dips vs. Bench Press

Tsypkin: We haven't got a bench in the gym right now. I intend to get a couple eventually regardless, for my athletes to do certain CF WODs, but I greatly prefer training the ring dip...not really because I know whether or not it's better or even equivalent, simply because I enjoy them more. Am I losing a significant amount as far as strength development goes if I'm only doing weighted ring dips and never benching?

Mark Rippetoe: You are losing the ability to scale the effort, for the more novice trainees especially. Weighted ring dips makes my shoulder hurt when I type the words, and even bodyweight ring dips are an advanced exercise for most people. The bench is too useful to omit from your equipment list.

KSC: What is with the unfounded hatred for the bench press among the CF community? I guess it is just because there is a bench involved? I feel like I'm seeing this more and more.

Mark Rippetoe: I think it is an overreaction to the bench press masturbation that occurs at Gold's.

Tsypkin: I know benches are too important to omit...I'm asking here about my training specifically, just because I don't really like benching that much. I absolutely agree that the benches are something we need, and we will get them...I'm just wondering if I need to do them, if I am capable of heavy enough ring dips that I can scale the effort easily?

Mark Rippetoe: No, you don't have to bench, especially if you 1.) are strong enough to do weighted ring dips and 2.) you really don't want to. Just don't make your novice members the subject of this advice.

Jumping Backwards - Power Clean

Randy T: What causes someone to jump backwards on a power clean? Is it acceptable or is it considered a fault? I think I've heard you say on here before that it is better than jumping forward, but should it try to be avoided or fixed? If so, how do you correct it?

Mark Rippetoe: I usually encourage it, because it is the artifact of a good pull. If the bar is in front of you and you don't pull in a way that produces a slight jump back, you will most usually have started your jump (second pull) early and jumped forward. A cue to jump back fixes many things that are wrong with an early/low jumping position, and as long as the jump back is not excessive it is considered good technique to do so.

Low-bar position and powerlifting squats

wecoyote: First. When I start my low bar position, I create the "shelf" by bringing my elbows back and up. However when I load the bar onto my back, it feels like the bar wants to roll up my back towards the traps. Am I raising my elbows too high or is this just an idiosyncrasy with my anatomy?

Second. What are the differences between competitive powerlifting squats and low-bar squats for strength training? In videos, I see some powerlifters with a really wide stance, wide hand positions, and a head up position.

Mark Rippetoe: First, since most people don't have this problem I'd say you're doing something wrong. I doubt it's the fact that your body is completely different from everyone else's body. It's probably due to placing the bar too high, above the spine of the scapula instead of underneath it.

Second, the differences are a really wide stance, wide hand positions, and a head up position, due to the fact that they are coached to do this. Why this is done probably has a lot to do with the way the suit and wraps are thought to be best used by the lifters involved in the sport. I disagree with lots of this, but then again I don't train powerlifters for competition, as I've pointed out many times.

Row vs. Chinups

ghoff1: I'm 6' 242. Have been on Texas Method for about a month from SS. I love to do rows and chinups but am so gassed by end of workout I can't get any volume of chinups in. I usually do 3x5 @ 170 for rows and/or 3x2 chinups. Does one exercise put on more muscle than the other?

Mark Rippetoe: Well, you'll have to admit that chinups are harder to cheat, what with the fact that everybody in the gym can see you not getting your chin over the bar and that this is a rather easily verified and understood criterion for a complete rep. And since rows can be done pretty much any fucking way you want to do them and still be considered rows, my default would always be towards the chinups/pullups. Particularly if you can only do 2 of them at a time.

Bands and pullups

MrTambourineMan: I am going to do The Wichita Falls Novice Program. The thing is that I am very weak. I can't even do one pullup. I have bought some bands and I was wondering if it is appropriate to use them on your program until I get strong enough to do this exercise without them. My concern is that when you use bands it takes away the core stability out of the movement.

Mark Rippetoe: You don't have any Core Stability to worry about right now, so just do them with the bands as best you can. Everything will get stronger, including your chinups.

The "Science" of Exercise?

I recently got to meet Kary Mullis, Nobel Laureate in chemistry in 1993. He has written some very important things about the way science is and should be done, and I recommend that you don't compare the following gibberish to his stuff. I do recommend that you read his book Dancing Naked in the Mind Field, *and that you also read Gary Taubes's* Good Calories, Bad Calories, *and that you also refrain from comparing it to the following material.*

It is perhaps important that I do not have a formal education in the "exercise sciences." I did not develop an interest in this topic until after my actual science education in geology was well along, and the mentorship of Dr. Philip Colee had influenced me for what is hopefully the better.

Hamstrings and squatting

Craigrasm: I was curious if you saw the last NSCA Journal article on the squat titled "Optimizing Squat Technique" from December 2007. It was stated on page 12 in regards to hamstring activation on the squat, *"Research suggests that the squat, regardless of technique variation, produces minimal activity in hamstring muscles."* My initial thought (without going through the references given), is what kind of "technique variations" were used in the studies? I unfortunately don't have easy access to the references so it will be some time before I can check them out. Did you see this article, and any thoughts on this statement?

Mark Rippetoe: This kind of shit is why I am no longer a member of the NSCA. It is literally impossible that this study was performed correctly, and a quick reading of the paper would reveal why, but since I am not a member – and have not been since this time last year – I do not have this volume of the Journal. If anybody involved with this "study" had ever personally done squats themselves using correct technique and as a result gotten sore hamstrings, this embarrassing paper would not have appeared in this poorly reviewed form. And if peer-review actually worked as it was supposed to, instead of merely functioning as peer-approval, it would have been sent back to the authors for revision. They probably used a Smith machine in the study. Seriously, I have read such things in their journals.

This type of thing has been a common feature of both of the NSCA's journals for quite some time now, ever since the Physical Therapists took over the organization. I commented on it specifically in an article for the CrossFit Journal entitled "Silly Bullshit", and that appears in my book *Strong Enough?* I fully expect a revised position statement on the Full Squat any day now. Bad for the knees, you know.

So, I'm probably going to drop my credential. If they can't design a study to reflect the experience of millions of people who get hamstring sore, hamstring size, and hamstring tears when they squat, they can be wrong about eye gaze too. And I can't see the value of a credential granted by an organization that publishes such silly bullshit. This has been coming for a long time.

(I later obtained a copy of the paper. It was a review paper that cited ten journal articles to substantiate the position that the squat does not involve hamstrings, all of which were apparently written by groups of "researchers" that have never attempted to squat with a hamstring tear.)

Polynomial: Would it be difficult for you to get a response published in the same journal?

Mark Rippetoe: I have published several articles in that particular journal over the years. Judging from the difficulty I had getting as simple a thing published as the suggestion that novices require different programming than advanced athletes, it would be prohibitively aggravating to try. And I have no interested in convincing anyone in the NSCA that I am right about anything.

NSCA "Study"

KSC: To expand on our conversation from a few weeks ago about the growing lack of validity of the NSCA...here is another example from this month's NSCA Journal. The study was titled: "No difference in 1RM strength and muscle activation during the barbell chest press on a stable and unstable surface."

"*The results showed that there was no difference in 1RM strength or muscle EMG activity for the stable vs. unstable surface.*" Here is the kicker....."*these results further indicate that there is NO REDUCTION IN 1RM STRENGTH FOR THE BARBELL CHEST PRESS WHEN PERFORMED ON AN UNSTABLE EXERCISE BALL WHEN COMPARED TO A STABLE FLAT SURFACE.*"

It's getting bad. Do the people that write these things actually train for anything themselves, or train actual clients or athletes in a practical non-laboratory environment??? What's going on at headquarters, Rip?

Mark Rippetoe: There will be "studies" conducted by people this unaware of the realities of barbell training, and people that have a vested interest in the use of special equipment. The problem is that the highly-respected peer review process was somehow unable to sort this particularly embarrassing piece of chaff from the rest of the priceless wheat of exercise science. It tells you that the reviewers aren't any better at this than the guys that did the study, and that everything in the journal is therefore suspect.

This is from some accounting done by Dr. Kilgore, which first appeared in my article in the CrossFit Journal, now included in *Strong Enough?*:

Further complicating this matter is the sad fact that the academic exercise science community is also in the business of conventional wisdom. Biomechanics/kinesiology/exercise physiology/physical education has contented itself for many years with creatine studies and peer review of each other's work. For example, Volume 20, number 4 of the NSCA's Journal of Strength and Conditioning Research published a total of 42 papers, five (12%) of which list the editor-in-chief as a co-author, and 17 (40%) of which list associate editors (the ones doing the peer-reviewing) as authors, either singly or in groups. One associate editor is listed on five papers. Another associate editor has 11 of his 14 published papers (according to the National Library of Medicine's catalog) published in the JSCR. The editor-in-chief has published 11 of his past 25 authored or co-authored articles in this journal. This level of cronyism is not the norm for reputable peer-reviewed scientific journals, most of which are concerned less about the number of papers they publish and more about their quality and academic reputation.

KSC: "*It tells you that the reviewers aren't any better at this than the guys that did the study, and that everything in the journal is therefore suspect.*"

I think that is the crux of the problem right there....if they are publishing studies that state that there is no difference between a regular and a stability ball bench press, then what else in there is jacked up.....it leaves the coach or trainer (like me) who is very VERY hungry for quality information unsure of the information he is getting on subjects he may not have all that much experience with. I was able to easily identify the absurdity of this statement because I am a fairly experienced lifter, but what if I was looking for information on the dry land conditioning of swimmers, 400m sprinters, or any other area where I don't have a lot of expertise?

I guess this is where we should all be thankful for Greg Glassman; even if you aren't a CrossFitter, you can appreciate that he has gathered and brought back some notoriety to the most effective forms of training and given a bigger voice to some of the better minds in the field....I would even venture to say that USAW owes him something for bringing the clean and snatch back into the conversation.

Mark Rippetoe: I have recently voiced my opinion to many of the people associated with USA Weightlifting. CrossFit is responsible for more people actively practicing the two lifts right now than at any other time in history, and USAW has done its best to completely ignore this fact. This situation should be made right. It is also responsible for more sales of Olympic weightlifting equipment in the past two years than any other person since Bob Hoffman, a fact that has also been ignored and has gone unappreciated – at least publicly – by many of these same people. CrossFit has the potential to change the popular cultural perception of what exercise actually means over the next decade, and I will watch with delight as selectorized leg machines are melted down into more useful items like re-bar and manhole covers.

Milk

Rawr: All my life I've been drinking quite a bit of milk. All of the sudden, these last few days I've been getting stomach aches after drinking milk. Have you ever had anybody develop an intolerance to milk just all of the sudden? I'm 15, and I don't always notice it but I have noticed it several times recently. Are there certain things that I might have recently added to my diet that could be causing this?

Mark Rippetoe: There are many reasons this could have happened, including a bad batch o' milk, a little stomach bug, you drank too much at one time, wrong combination of other foods, etc. Just lay off a couple of days and start back.

Ucbmathgsi: I'm lactose intolerant, and your experience describes mine exactly. All of a sudden (literally overnight), I had vicious stomachaches, accompanied by deathly (and I mean deathly beyond any deathly you have produced before) farts and diarrhea.

Rawr, if you have the gaseous/bowel disturbance(s) I have just described, then maybe some lactaid pills are in your future. Of course, it could just be a bad batch of milk. But be aware that all mammals will eventually become lactose intolerant, if they live long enough. Evolutionarily speaking, we are only meant to drink milk as infants, and then only from our mothers' breasts.

Mark Rippetoe: You are probably not lactose intolerant, just unused to drinking lots of milk – like lots of people that don't drink lots of milk. And it is not true that all mammals will become lactose intolerant if they live long enough. Lots of old people drink milk quite easily. This adaptation is one of the features of human physiology that indicates that evolution in response to the environmental stresses of cultural influence is still in operation: when we developed pastoralism many thousands of years ago and milk became a common food for people of all ages, we obviously redeveloped the ability to produce lactase (if we had ever lost it). That's why I can drink milk at 52 with no problems at all. And really, 52 is pretty damned old, at least as far as adaptive reproduction is concerned.

Ucbmathgsi: I'm sorry Mark, but this post is factually wrong. Saying things like "lots of old people drink milk" and "I drink milk" does not reinforce the position that the average person is not lactose intolerant. Also, the reference to pastoralism as a "trigger" for an evolutionary response betrays a serious misunderstanding of the theory of evolution. I am guessing you haven't actually taken a class in evolutionary biology?

What is in fact much more likely is that the phenomenon of lactose intolerance has only recently been recorded accurately, since it ISN'T A LIFE THREATENING PHENOMENON. Welcome to evolution 101: genetic adaptations only occur in the event that there is a differential ability to reproduce. (Ignoring the fact that farts during sex hinder the mood.) You may instead be referring to the general ability for the human body to adapt; meaning, a person who has been drinking milk for his/her whole life is very likely to be able to drink it healthily for a long time in the future. This is quite different from the generation to generation evolutionary adaptation that you seem to refer to.

In general, yes, the human animal will adapt to stress. This is a quite general evolutionary adaptation that has been present (and is still present) in virtually all living things. This has to do with our DNA being fundamentally redundant, etc. Saying something like "mankind can now enjoy a lifetime of drinking milk because a few thousand years ago we started domesticating cows, and since then we have adapted to the situation" is absurd.

And the fact is that Rawr, according to statistics, IS PROBABLY lactose intolerant. I'll quote Wiki: "According to Heyman (2006), approximately 70% of the global population cannot tolerate lactose in adulthood."

http://en.wikipedia.org/wiki/Lactose_intolerance

Mark Rippetoe: Well, my undergraduate degree was geology, my minor was anthropology, and I have had both invertebrate and vertebrate paleo, the latter under Walter Dalquest, so I have had some exposure to evolutionary biology (although no formal training in process, merely 30 years of independent reading).

Here's my link: http://evolution.berkeley.edu/evolibrary/news/070401_lactose

I stand by my point, despite the fact that my presentation may have been a bit clumsy and imprecise.

Jcf: I'll guess ucbmathgsi hasn't taken an actual college course on statistics. Well, I have and it is absurd to ignore the fact that you have enough information about the OP to know that he is from a sample with different characteristics than "the global population".

It is also absurd to make a desperate appeal to authority (or rather a desperate criticism of someone else's authority) and then paraphrase wikipedia for us. I'm sure that despite his lack of college courses on evolutionary biology, Coach Rippetoe is more than capable of paraphrasing wikipedia for himself. Since you are so interested with other people's credentials, I am surprised you didn't share your own with us.

Ucbmathgsi: You are right, I did not look into the specifics of the relevant distribution; had I done so, I would have seen that the Chinese population overwhelmingly skews the global results. So yes, I am wrong when I say that the OP probably is lactose intolerant, viewed solely from the perspective of statistics among Americans (for example).

I was mainly responding to Rip's misapplication of evolution. I get irrationally "nerd angry" when I see people claim that evolution accounts for certain changes that have only occurred over a few thousand years. The choice of suggesting that he has "never taken a course in evolution" was a poor choice of words; I fully grant that one does not need coursework to understand a subject, and this sentence was out of line. However, to suggest that the ability to enjoy a lifetime of drinking milk is a consequence of us domesticating cows, and to cite evolution as the culprit, is simply a mistake.

Anyway, this is ultimately beside the point. People, drink your milk, it will make you strong, Prof. Rip has declared it, etc. etc. The beneficial nutritional profile of milk does not get negated simply because of the trivial matter of mammals (sometimes) not being able to digest a sugar present in it. If you are lactose intolerant, then buy some cheap pills that will let you eat normally. Thank your lucky stars that you live in a society where these pills can be bought at every drugstore.

If you are wondering if you are lactose intolerant, try the pills FIRST, since it is so easy, and if they don't work, then look into other explanations. This is the point I should have made to begin with, and I apologize for being stupidly unclear amidst my nerd rage.

Ok, so now for some real nerd rage, since I have to respond to the quoted post. Mr. jcf, I have in fact taken a course in statistics. Had you paid attention in your course in statistics, then you would have known that Bayes' theorem is relevant here. I.e., since we already know that the OP is experiencing digestive difficulties, then his likelihood of being among the victims of lactose intolerance is skewed considerably, since lactose intolerance is among the most common explanations of digestive discomfort.

I wouldn't call what I wrote an appeal to authority, although I admit I am attacking Rip's authority in matters of evolution. And wikipedia is a useful tool that I do not apologize for using. I obviously misapplied an article to "back up" my point; in retrospect, I should have left it out, and used Bayes' theorem instead. Since you will probably knee jerk if I post a link to the wiki article on Bayes', I won't post it.

Mark Rippetoe: Okay, fine. Statistics, math major, all that shit. But here: "*I was mainly responding to Rip's misapplication of evolution. I get irrationally "nerd angry" when I see people claim that evolution accounts for certain changes that have only occurred over a few thousand years. The choice of suggesting that he has 'never taken a course in evolution' was a poor choice of words; I fully grant that one does not need coursework to understand a subject, and this sentence was out of line. However, to suggest that the ability to enjoy a lifetime of drinking milk is a consequence of us domesticating cows, and to cite evolution as the culprit, is simply a mistake.*"

You have not addressed the point made by my source. Evolution can and does occur over short time spans. It happens frequently, and this is a very good example of it having done so. The use of milk as a food in post-natal humans is adaptive reproductively in cultures that raise cows, the gene is there from infancy anyway and the mutation just keeps it turned on, the adaptation does not require that we evolve another arm or eyeball, and it is quite well explained in this article, which I shall now give you again: http://evolution.berkeley.edu/evolibrary/news/070401_lactose

Hell, man, they're right down the hall from you. Go talk to them sometime.

Ucbmathgsi: Did you know that the same DNA template yields both worker/drone ants and queen ants? The difference between the two lies in the proteins that the insect is fed during development. Did you know that more than one gene can code for lactase production in human beings, and the activation of these genes can depend on what you are fed during development? Apparently the author of this article did not, or at least wished that it weren't true. More precisely, the authors' logical flaw comes when they assume that they have identified THE gene that produces lactase.

My point is that redundancy in phenotype activation is a much more likely explanation for modern man's ability to drink milk, rather than random mutation. Whether or not you prefer to call this "evolution" is up to you, I guess. I agree that modern man is much more equipped to drink milk than his ancestors.

Mark Rippetoe: If some groups have the mutations and others don't, the phenotypic expression of these mutations is obviously dependent on ... what? They got there somehow, they get selectively turned on somehow, and their differential phenotypic expression is dependent on culture. You seem to think that there is only one mechanism by which evolution occurs – mutation. There are several, and mutation is one of them.

Are you familiar with the cichlid radiation in Lake Victoria? This is a perfect example of rapid, diverse evolution using all the tools at the disposal of nature, due to an opportunity created by environmental factors that did not respect the slow pace of mutation. You seem to think evolution always takes a long time, because random mutations have to accumulate into adaptive change over a long time, and that is just not the case.

Gaining weight and type II diabetes, CVD

progressiveman1: Are you concerned about developing type II diabetes or CVD from having to bulk regularly for weight lifting?

Mark Rippetoe: Are you asking me personally?

progressiveman1: Yes. All of the studies I've seen show an increased risk associated with being overweight. Do you agree with the evidence and does it concern you about having to bulk on a regular basis for weight lifting?

Mark Rippetoe: You're not looking at all the *evidence*. You're citing the conventional wisdom, which is quite literally always wrong. And I haven't "bulked" for anything in a couple of decades.

progressiveman1: 1. http://content.nejm.org/cgi/content/abstract/346/6/393?ijkey=3b56b399cde9a731c8f78f6fc50294ce9557b872&keytype2=tf_ipsecsha

Combination of weight loss and increased physical activity resulted in improvements in diabetes compared with a diabetes drug and control group.

2. http://www.ncbi.nlm.nih.gov/pubmed/16391903?dopt=Abstract

Similar setup of study with same results.

3. http://content.nejm.org/cgi/content/abstract/344/18/1343?ijkey=68bb920fb4b6395bcd3c600cac7563a8c494c092&keytype2=tf_ipsecsha

Similar setup of study with same results.

4. http://aje.oxfordjournals.org/cgi/content/abstract/132/3/501?ijkey=05de7eba474689238582ba8043ec9efe1255b9eb&keytype2=tf_ipsecsha

A cohort study examining the correlation of BMI and diabetes in women. Their results show that as BMI increased, so did risk of developing diabetes. However, I don't think it's strong evidence, considering as a woman's BMI increases, it usually means she's physically inactive.

5. http://www.ncbi.nlm.nih.gov/pubmed/15649575?dopt=Abstract

Two groups: the one that lost more weight had better improvements in diabetes. However, that group probably exercised more often to create a larger caloric deficit, which may have been the contributing factor for its success. So, Rip, do you think the increased physical activity is the sole contributor to the improvements and prevention in diabetes, with bodyweight being a non-contributor?

Mark Rippetoe: I'm glad you posted these. They are an excellent representation of exactly what I mean about the conventional wisdom. Granted, all we're seeing here are the abstracts, but the whole paper won't show anything we need to see. All these studies attempt to correlate bodyweight with the likelihood of developing type II diabetes. The first 4 studies do not mention anything about bodyweight or bodyfat loss at all in the intervention groups. They just say that lifestyle modification lowered the risk of developing the disease. The last study attempts to correlate the reduction in bodyweight with the lowered risk, but omits any consideration of the processes that produced the bodyweight reduction as possible factors in the risk reduction. Yet you are ready to conclude that bodyweight increase = elevated diabetes risk, and bodyweight decrease = reduction in risk, without any consideration given to about 3000 other factors that are obviously involved.

And this doesn't even begin to address the fact that their little chickenshit lifestyle intervention consists of walking and a reduction in the number of donuts. There is essentially *no such thing* as type II diabetes in conditioned athletes, irrespective of bodyweight. This is because type II diabetes is a disease of carbohydrate metabolism, and training and a clean diet specifically addresses this metabolic domain (recreational distance runners and road cyclists are not conditioned athletes). And doesn't matter how much you weigh while you're doing it. At all. The hilarious thing about this is that even the most casual attempt at resistance training immediately has a positive effect on blood sugar, so it's really not necessary to be an elite lifter or competitive track athlete to get the benefit of training. In short, your concern for me is misplaced, albeit appreciated.

It is a sad state of affairs in science education when cause-and-effect and correlation are indistinguishable in the minds of both the public and the assholes publishing these studies, and truly frightening when these minds belong to public officials, bureaucrats, and legislators.

progressiveman1: The clinical studies here isolated weight loss and physical activity as the main differences between the groups, and they produced similar results with all the trials. I think it proves that at least one of these two factors improve diabetes. I'll try to find some hard evidence proving which one or if it's both of them.

Mark Rippetoe: An excellent idea.

Arterial Stiffness

Coldfire: I don't know if this question should be directed at you or Dr. Kilgore, but I'll try anyway. I've heard from a few sources that resistance training is associated with increased arterial stiffness which increases the chance of a heart attack, stroke and World War III. I've looked at some articles and found that this is not an established fact, but a few claim this to be true. This sounds like some silly attempt to make weight training dangerous once again, but I would like to know your opinion. There is also a funny part in the article:

Quote:

Maximal muscular strength in the intervention group was tested before and after resistance training using the following exercises: half squat, bench press, leg extension, leg curls, lateral row, and abdominal bend. After 10 warm-up repetitions, 1-repetition maximums (1RM) were obtained according to the established guidelines. Because of the potential risks involved in 1RM testing, this test was not performed in the control group.

Mark Rippetoe: Typical idiotic medical types doing studies about a training method they do not understand. Both studies show no increases in blood pressure with this "decreased carotid arterial compliance" and no femoral arterial "stiffening". Sounds like a perfect adaptive response to strength training to me. They seem to be poor understanders, failing to distinguish the differences between arterial stiffening due to disease processes and an increase in tone as an adaptation to the higher temporary pressures encountered in training. Standard worship of aerobics in evidence. I'll get Dr. Kilgore to respond.

Lon Kilgore: Little snippets of information extrapolated to the real world are only occasionally accurate and useful. I think everyone needs to read this article:

BMJ. 2008 July 12; 337(7661): 92–95. PMCID: PMC2453303
doi: 10.1136/bmj.a439.

Association between muscular strength and mortality in men: prospective cohort study
Jonatan R Ruiz, research associate,[1,2] Xuemei Sui, research associate,[3] Felipe Lobelo, research associate,[3] James R Morrow, Jr, professor,[4] Allen W Jackson, professor,[4] Michael Sjöström, associate professor,[1] and Steven N Blair, professor[3,4]
[1]Department of Biosciences and Nutrition at NOVUM, Unit for Preventive Nutrition, Karolinska Institutet, Huddinge, Sweden
[2]Department of Physiology, School of Medicine, University of Granada, Spain
[3]Department of Exercise Science, Arnold School of Public Health, University of South Carolina, Columbia, SC, USA
[4]Department of Kinesiology, Health Promotion, and Recreation, University of North Texas, Denton, TX, USA
Correspondence to: J R Ruiz, Email: ruizj@ugr.es
Accepted June 16, 2008.

Abstract
Objective To examine prospectively the association between muscular strength and mortality from all causes, cardiovascular disease, and cancer in men.

Design Prospective cohort study.
Setting Aerobics centre longitudinal study.
Participants 8762 men aged 20-80.
Main outcome measures All cause mortality up to 31 December 2003; muscular strength, quantified by combining one repetition maximal measures for leg and bench presses and further categorised as age specific thirds of the combined strength variable; and cardiorespiratory fitness assessed by a maximal exercise test on a treadmill.
Results During an average follow-up of 18.9 years, 503 deaths occurred (145 cardiovascular disease, 199 cancer). Age adjusted death rates per 10 000 person years across incremental thirds of muscular strength were 38.9, 25.9, and 26.6 for all causes; 12.1, 7.6, and 6.6 for cardiovascular disease; and 6.1, 4.9, and 4.2 for cancer (all $P<0.01$ for linear

trend). After adjusting for age, physical activity, smoking, alcohol intake, body mass index, baseline medical conditions, and family history of cardiovascular disease, hazard ratios across incremental thirds of muscular strength for all cause mortality were 1.0 (referent), 0.72 (95% confidence interval 0.58 to 0.90), and 0.77 (0.62 to 0.96); for death from cardiovascular disease were 1.0 (referent), 0.74 (0.50 to 1.10), and 0.71 (0.47 to 1.07); and for death from cancer were 1.0 (referent), 0.72 (0.51 to 1.00), and 0.68 (0.48 to 0.97). The pattern of the association between muscular strength and death from all causes and cancer persisted after further adjustment for cardiorespiratory fitness; however, the association between muscular strength and death from cardiovascular disease was attenuated after further adjustment for cardiorespiratory fitness.
Conclusion Muscular strength is inversely and independently associated with death from all causes and cancer in men, even after adjusting for cardiorespiratory fitness and other potential confounders.

Being strong means you are less likely to die from all causes. This study is a large, long one and clearly shows this. You get strong from training with weights. So I'd say that a large scale and big picture study (there have been 3 similar large studies that I know of) that actually measures death rates trumps the hypothetical relationship between training, the microphysiology of the vasculature, and risk of disease.

Coldfire: Thanks Dr. Kilgore. That's a nice article which confirms that strong people are harder to kill and are more useful in general.

EIC: Dr. Kilgore and Rip burnt this one to a crisp already, but I thought I'd add that, if I recall correctly, weight training (particularly at higher rep ranges) essentially lays down miles of additional capillaries throughout the muscles of the body. Much like installing additional sinks in a home and turning them all on, it would seem that this would result in a relative reduction of fluid pressure (be it blood or water) at any given point in the plumbing. I doubt that such an effect could be perceived in a study of short duration, but it certainly becomes a significant factor when one adopts a prolonged dedication to the iron.

Mark Rippetoe: And the geniuses that insist on doing these studies on untrained populations will never understand why.

On Learning

Phillipo: I have a couple questions on learning the movements and authority vs. experience. I'm not sure I'll be able to explain this well but please bear with me. When one is trying to learn a new motor skill, be it a squat or golf swing, we often attempt to learn from a template passed down from authority (that would be you and Starting Strength). This form is considered best and we should work towards moving our current movement more in line with the "best" movement.

However when we try to learn on our own without a template we usually move towards whatever works best, as trial and error is a strong basis for learning. Often what works best for a trainee initially is not in line with the authoritative best model. For example, a trainee may find it so difficult to lift the proper way that he can lift very little weight at all, but lifting an improper way, perhaps by shifting more to the quads on a squat, he/she is capable of lifting more weight (due to the strength of the quads vs. the hamstrings).
Which leads to the question of how the "proper" form is determined. Usually we look at people who are the best in their fields and try to copy what they do because it works the best. However, usually these people have gone through years of adaptation through trial and error development, perhaps starting exactly with the improper form that new trainees exhibit.

So I guess my questions are:

1. How is the best form for these movements determined (specifically for your squat technique with hip drive vs. other styles)?

2. How do we trust learning on our own when the knowledge we gain from experience of what works best may lead us in a different direction from the accepted authority best model?

3. Do we lose something by trying to force ourselves into "correct positions" at the outset rather than allowing a more gradual organic learning from trial and error to take place and the trust that goes with that?

Mark Rippetoe: 1. From my Basic Barbell Seminar notes: This system maximizes
a.) control of all relevant moment arms while
b.) utilizing the most muscle mass
c.) over the greatest useful range of motion
d.) and therefore allowing the most weight to be lifted over that ROM
e.) thus resulting in the development of the most usable strength

The system we have developed is not based on my opinion, which is really not much more valuable than yours. It must be based on the optimal application of force to a barbell operating within the gravitational framework derived from the logical analysis of human skeletal and muscular anatomy. I have attempted to do this. If I have not succeeded, you should pay absolutely no attention to what I say, since I claim to have done so.

2. Trusting accepted authority ensures that you will never learn anything on your own.

3. You have to start somewhere. Your responsibility is to try, question, learn, accept and discard when your intelligence tells you it is time to do so.

Muscle Actions Question?

Theuofh: When high bar/olympic squatting, front squatting, or OH squatting for the olympic lifts, where value is placed on the vertical as possible back angle, is there some concentric muscle involvement involved when pulling in, or trying to get the hips/ass as close to the heels as possible? I don't notice it when low bar squatting w/ the forward lean, but a cue I use to myself when front squatting/high bar back squatting/OH squatting is getting my knees as far out in front of my toes as possible, then actively pulling myself down and into the bottom of the squat. It kind of gets back to the active hip concept if I understand it correctly, where the hamstrings are kept stretched in the low bar squat and act as a point of stability for the lower back to arch/maintain neutral.

In the high bar/vertical back position, do the hip flexors or another muscle group take over that role, when the hamstrings are shortened in the bottom position? Is it the case that proficient Olympic lifters just possess the flexibility where they can lower into the bottom position w/o having to think about 'drawing in' or actively try to maintain the vertical back?

Mark Rippetoe: If the hamstrings, glutes, and adductors extend the hips – open up the hip angle – and the lumbar erectors place the low back in extension, why is it necessary to invoke concentric hip flexion as a mechanism in obtaining the position at the bottom of the front squat? The hamstrings are shortened at the bottom of the FS precisely because they are holding the back angle vertical and the hip angle open.

JLascek: I just wanted to throw in the fact that you cannot "pull yourself down" in any kind of squat unless you are moving faster than gravity will allow, and this is never the case in the presence of a significant load.

TPrewittMD: Actually, you can't "pull yourself down" unless your feet are literally fixed to the floor. Simply dropping the bar to the floor is faster than any squat and is the effect of gravity.

JLascek: Indeed. But isn't it possible to actively flex the hip while dropping faster than gravity would allow you to fall when you aren't under a load? This is what I was referring to.

Mark Rippetoe: Only if you're tied to the ground. Physics time.

JLascek: I mean, I understand what you're saying. The only reason I keep pushing this is because it was a concept in a class similar to biomechanics. If I very quickly drop down into the bottom of a squat from a standing position by flexing my hips very quickly, how does this not somewhat use the flexors of the hip? If you are jumping on a trampoline and you flex your hip in mid-air, does that not use the flexors of the hip? Because it's the same thing in either case (the first scenario has my body moving downward with feet off the ground/surface for x amount of time, and the second scenario has the body moving up and/or down, but x is increased for obvious reasons).

Mark Rippetoe: It uses the hip flexors, but not against the ground. This action permits you to *fall* faster, but your hip flexors are not pulling you down – they are merely pulling your knees up against the resistance provided by your hip extensors – their antagonists. To the extent that this may dis-inhibit some extensor resistance, it may work in the context of an unweighted squat. But how can you fall faster than gravity would drop you just because your feet were off the ground? Once you're falling, gravity is why.

JLascek: I don't think I was saying that the hip flexors "pull you down" in my last post. I just meant that the flexion of the hips contribute to falling faster than gravity. It makes sense that they wouldn't actively pull you down (since they aren't attached to the floor). However, after thinking about this, I realized that you can fall down (in an unweighted type of squat) by flexing the hips, but you would still fall at a rate that gravity dictates.

Apparently I interpreted something weird from a lesson in class a year and a half ago.

Mark Rippetoe: Or perhaps your professor was a moron. This occurs with disturbing frequency.

Engineering 2nd Semester

This section is really too long. It's also pretty dry. It may not be interesting to some of you, and I won't be offended if you skip it. But I find this stuff interesting even if I'm not terribly good at analyzing it. I just hope I'm not wrong about most of it. It goes somewhat beyond the point that most coaches care to explain things, and perhaps there's a good reason for that.

Squat/Deadlift Comparison

jkt1942: I take "Starting Strength" to all the seminars that I teach and I strongly recommend it to all the students. At a seminar in Denver this past weekend a student, who had a copy of "Starting Strength" with him, had an interesting question. He discussed your explanation of the importance of "Going Deep" in the squat and that partial squats are ineffective due to the omission of the hams/glutes assistance. We certainly agree. His Question: "Does the rationale that partial squats are ineffective not apply to the deadlift which involves a partial squat?" Thanks so much for your take on this one.

Mark Rippetoe: There are obviously differences in the positions of the two lifts, and in their very nature – the deadlift starts concentric and finishes eccentric, while the squat starts eccentric and then uses a stretch reflex/viscoelastic rebound to initiate the concentric phase. But the glutes/hamstrings do a different job in the two lifts also. The rebound out of the bottom in the squat is due to adductors/glutes/hamstrings immediately opening up the hip angle along with the quads opening the knee angle from a below-parallel position.

In a deadlift, the higher starting position finds the quads in a much better mechanical position to initiate the push against the floor, and the job of the hamstrings is different; they have no rebound function at all, but rather "anchor" the pelvis in position so that the back angle – the angle the plane of the back makes with the floor – can stay the same so that when the quads extend the knees all the force gets to the bar. If the back angle changes, as it will if the chest does not stay up, the quads straighten the knees but the bar doesn't move up, so they have done no work. The hamstrings pull against the ischial tuberosity of the pelvis, and together with the rigid spine produced by the erector spinae, allow the force of the knee extension to move the bar up from the floor.

This is a much different function than the hamstrings have during the squat, partly due to the different position (depth) and partly due to the differences in initial contraction (eccentric/concentric).

But his question involves the differences in *half-squat* and deadlift. The deadlift can be a nearly pure hamstring/glute contraction if the knees extend without pushing the bar away from the floor, forcing the hip extensors to pull the entire load from the floor without the quads. The deadlift starting position is, in fact, about the same depth as a half-squat, so why no hamstrings/glutes in a half squat? Well, it's not that there is NO posterior chain in a half-squat; it's that the quads are so predominant that they leave the glutes/hamstrings inadequately trained and the knees inadequately protected. The initial downward motion in a squat that gets cut off high is typically a knees-forward motion, with very little or no posterior track for the hips that would tighten the glutes/hamstrings and place them in a position where they can be used. This standard leg-press style half-squat loads the knees so much more than the hips that it effectively eliminates the posterior chain from the movement, since sufficient depth that would otherwise make the posterior chain engage when the hips moved back is never obtained. Depth in a squat is always dependent on the hips moving back, since you can slide your knees forward until they touch the ground without ever dropping below parallel. Unless the hips move back and the hip angle changes enough, the hamstrings and glutes don't lengthen, and if they don't lengthen they can't contract.

A trained powerlifter that knows how to do a correct high-box squat can fix this by using hips down to the box the same way they would be in a deep squat, merely letting the box interrupt this correct squat above parallel. But this is not the same thing as a typical half-squat at all, which is mostly quads. In fact, a powerlifter that cuts off a squat unintentionally is actually doing something more like a goodmorning, which is a predominantly posterior chain-based exercise. So the amount of posterior chain involvement in a squat is entirely dependent on the position of the hips when it is being done.

In contrast, a deadlift – even a correct one that uses quads off the floor – inherently incorporates so much hamstring and glute that it is one of the best exercises in the weight room specifically for that muscle group.

Muscle activation techniques (M.A.T.)

Ganondorf: Have you ever heard of Muscle Activation Techniques? It finds muscle imbalances, puts pressure on "inactive" muscles and reestablishes optimal neuromuscular functioning. Then you are given isometric exercises (and maybe some dynamic) to fix imbalances. What they mean by imbalances is that certain muscular issues are compensated for with other muscles and not allowed to work optimally. They CLAIM it will improve athletic performance, strength and reduce injury.

I've heard of isolating some smaller muscles so that they aren't underworked as larger ones compensate (e.g. traps taking over rear delt) before with regular weight training. Example: If the small scapular muscles are weak in someone they would strengthen them using an isolation movement so the larger muscles of the back would have to compensate for less than optimal shoulder function. To me this sounds kind of like a chiropractor/physical therapy visit and like simply doing isolation exercises would produce the same effect. Also, the idea of isometrically flexing a muscle to get used to using it is (I believe) part of this too. Ever heard of anyone using M.A.T.?

Mark Rippetoe: Let me ask you a question: Would you agree that a technically perfect squat requires the normal anatomical contribution of all of the muscles involved in the kinetic chain? If this is the case, then a technically perfect squat will cause to be resolved any muscular "imbalances" that may exist by eliciting a greater contribution from any under-contributing muscles. If we focus on the biomechanically correct position of the skeletal components during an exercise, then the muscles responsible for controlling and moving those skeletal components through that motion will necessarily be contributing their anatomically predetermined effort to the movement.

There are major organizations that certify exercise professionals on the basis of their ability to "assess" something known as "functional movement". I would much rather focus on teaching people the correct way to perform a loaded exercise, concentrate on technically correct execution as determined by the physical properties of muscles moving loaded bones through space in a gravitational framework, and let the skeleton and the muscles sort the matter out themselves. The problem with this is that I don't make as much money as a guy that doesn't feel bad about charging you $200 for a Functional Movement Screen – in other words, assessing your ability to do an unfamiliar movement pattern in the absence of proper instruction.

Ganondorf: I do read often. Some is bullshit nonsense. I found this while I was reading about Active release. Performing a loaded barbell movement is an excellent way to improve motor control and work the body in its normal anatomical function. I am unsure if it were possible for certain muscles to not fire correctly or inefficiently limiting the true functionality/strength of an exercise.

I have heard of people doing "glute activation work" to teach the glutes to fire correctly and a personal friend of mine did this to recover from knee surgery. He's at full recovery now. I know someone who has a bum shoulder. His scapula externally rotate about 30 degrees past normal scapular functioning (winging I believe). Perhaps a muscle weakness of the scapular stabilizers, or the muscles firing incorrectly/ lack of motor control.

Even with correct form on an overhead press, wouldn't his scapular muscles still rotate? I have heard that the scapular winging is a compensation measure for decreased range of motion in the glenohumeral joint. If that is the case wouldn't light overhead pressing not work as the first step? Wouldn't you have to work on getting those muscles firing correctly before light overhead pressing would be able to make everything adapt to using it in normal anatomical function?

I know after some surgeries that people can lose motor control/good motor control of certain muscles. Would other muscles compensate for a muscle with little motor control (hamstrings taking over glutes) in a major barbell movement?

Mark Rippetoe: His scapular muscles rotated? I thought they just contracted. Scapular winging is usually a neurological defect in the serratus anterior mechanism, the muscles responsible for holding the anterior aspect of the scapula stable. Overhead pressing is such a natural movement for most humans that the only thing that interferes with it is ROM issues, not an inability to "get those muscles firing correctly".

And herein is my point: tell me a way to "get those muscles firing correctly" for the press that is better than just doing the press correctly with a coach telling you how to fix your movement pattern. Any other way involves a movement other than a press, and so fails to prepare you for the press. We are not performing brain surgery here, something that might benefit from a stepwise progression through basic surgical technique, then rats, then assisting with parts of the operation, and then doing the whole thing several years later. It's just a fucking press – you push the bar up over your head and shrug into lockout, and you don't need to prepare the separate muscles. In the absence of an injury that prevents it, you just do the movement correctly by getting coached in the correct technique, and all the muscles that are supposed to fire do so because they *have to* when you do it correctly. And this is why we like barbell exercises, and why the vast majority of everybody can derive more benefit from them than any other exercise modality when coached correctly.

Deadlift and Shoulders

Dschenck: I've been working on my deadlift form and have a question - when setting up, as part of getting my chest up and a straight back, should I retract my shoulder blades, or is it ok to let my shoulders hang naturally (which for me means they are slightly rounded downwards)?

I'm thinking I should retract them - which effectively brings my chest about an inch closer to the bar, because my arms/shoulders are not as extended - but I've read through the DL section of SS and looked at the pictures many times and am not clear on this point.

Mark Rippetoe: I do not coach a scapula retraction as a part of deadlift form. I focus instead on spinal position, which must be held in rigid thoracic and lumbar extension. It has been my observation that normal anatomical position is the best position for both the spine and the shoulders, since the traps are going to do the work of transferring force from the back to the arms isometrically anyway. A heavy deadlift will pull the scapulas out of retraction at some point during the pull, and they will end up where they would have been had they not been retracted in the first place.

The scapulas are the structures that transfer force from the rigid back to the arms and down to the bar. The traps function in isometric contraction during the deadlift (and clean and snatch) to hold the scapulas in place as the bar travels up from the ground. During this trip the back angle stays constant, anchored by the hamstrings, and the quads open the knees to push the bar away from the floor. The job of the traps is to anchor the scapulas in place so that the force can be transmitted up the rigid spine and then across the traps to the scapulas, from which the arms hang. An active concentric contraction of the traps does not aid this process, and may in fact be detrimental if the traps get pulled out of concentric contraction by fatigue from trying to stay shrugged. And if the shrug changes the vertical relationship of the scapula/bar/mid-foot line, then it alters normal pulling mechanics.

Dumbbell Bench Press

JMT: In "Starting Strength" you wrote the following regarding the bench press:

In fact, the dumbbell version of the exercise, which actually predates the barbell version due to its less specialized equipment requirements, is probably a better exercise for most purposes other than powerlifting competition. This is especially true if the weights used are sufficiently heavy, challenging the ability of the lifter to actually finish a set.

Based on the above, and given the fact that I am not a powerlifter, I've replaced the barbell bench press in my routine with the dumbbell bench press. I have a few questions about this.

1) In your opinion, is this a good idea?

2) Is programming for the dumbbell bench press the same as for the barbell bench press? (i.e. sets of 5 across)

3) Do you have any specific points on how to properly execute the dumbbell bench press? (Range of motion, bounce out of the bottom, etc.)

Mark Rippetoe: 1.) Sure. But you have to approach it as a "lift", not an assistance exercise.

2.) Programming would be the same. The main limitation in training with dumbbells is that you are usually at the mercy of the dumbbell rack in the gym, in that you have little control over your incremental increases – you have to use what's there, and the next jump up may be too big. This can be addressed with magnets in the appropriate weights.

3.) Take the dumbbells out of the rack, and learn to get in position on the bench from a standing position, NOT by lying down and getting the dumbbells off the floor or from spotters. Likewise, at the end of the set, finish the last rep and learn to stand back up with the dumbbells without lowering them to the floor. This will prevent lots of shoulder injuries. Don't slam the dumbbells together at the top (at least not MY dumbbells). Keep them in line like they are a bar and touch the inside edge of the plates to your chest right over your armpit to ensure a full range of motion. The bottom rebounds to the same extent a bench press does, which is to say you "bounce" off of your pec/shoulder tightness, not off of contact with your shoulders.

FROGGBUSTER: I was wondering what your views on dumbbell military pressing are, since it is similar to the bench press in some regards. I'm partly asking because of curiosity, but I'm mostly asking because I do not think I can barbell military press anymore. I recently took 6 weeks off from pressing and 3 weeks off from any upper body work at all because I had injured my left elbow. Shortly before it became a full-blown injury, I would notice a clicking in my left elbow (sounded like tendons were being moved around) as soon as I started the pressing motion upwards. My first press workout coming back was normal, so I thought everything was fine. However, today I started to hear the clicking again and so I immediately stopped the movement. I tried pressing 25lb dumbbells and they seem to be a lot easier on my elbow.

What do you think of this as an alternative to barbell pressing? Or would you recommend the incline bench press instead of dumbbells military press?

Mark Rippetoe: I never recommend incline anything, due to the fact that standing anything is better. Dumbbell presses are completely analogous to dumbbell bench presses, for the same reasons, and they should be programmed the same way.

Craigmeister: I remember reading in another thread that the barbell press works the external rotators in the locked out position. Is the same true for the dumbbell press?

Mark Rippetoe: Of course. The lockout position contracts all the posterior cuff muscles isometrically, and unless your humerus is quite externally rotated into some weird position named after a bodybuilder, your cuff muscles are working as hard as the weight is heavy.

Polynomial: After plateauing on SS, I've been using dumbbells with Platemate magnets and programming my dumbbell bench like the barbell bench (Texas method ideology - 5x5 Monday, and 1x5 Friday, with 5x5 press on Wednesday), and so far everything's been working great.

To get in position, I pick up the dumbbells off the floor, sit down with them on my thighs, and lay down while moving the dumbbells to my side, then press up. So the beginning position for the first rep is much different than during barbell bench, since I'm starting at the bottom of the movement. I wanted to make sure that this is the correct set up, since I've seen some guys laying down with their arms extended over their chest, albeit with smaller weights. But that seems insane.

Mark Rippetoe: I like the other guy's way much better, and that's the one I teach. I start from a standing position with the dumbbells held in contact with my thighs, back flat, knees bent, and then lay back on the bench with a rolling motion, making damn sure to keep the elbows locked. This is much safer, since you will not hurt your shoulders by starting unstable dumbbells from the bottom, and you get the eccentric rebound on the first rep like a regular BB bench.

More importantly, I finish in the top position as well, and lower the dumbbells back to my thighs with straight locked elbows in a reverse of the rocking motion that put me down on the bench. This motion stands me up into the position I started. It is MUCH safer (if you can learn how to do it) than stopping at the bottom and having to either sit up with the dumbbells or lower them to the floor at the end of a hard set. Many shoulder injuries have resulted from lowering heavy dumbbells to the floor one at a time at the end of a set to failure. My advice is to stop on the rep before you know you're going to fail with the DBs at the top and then lower them back to the thighs with straight elbows while you stand up. Of course, if you're only benching the 40s, this doesn't matter, but the 100s will hurt you if you do them wrong.

Box Squats vs. Paused Rack Squats

Vicjg: In terms of carry over to the regular back squat, is there much of a difference between box squats vs. paused rack squats (as described in the "useful assistance exercises" chapter of SS). I really want to know if I use the rack squat instead of the box squat due to space and budgetary issues + the fact that they seem safer, can I expect the same result, i.e. a bigger squat?

Mark Rippetoe: I have used both with good success. Sitting back to the box probably makes the hips fire better, since an experienced lifter might be more prone to get in a better hips-dominant position if the box was reached for by the ass. But the rack squat might tend to preserve back angle a little better at the bottom. So try both and see which works best for you.

Deadlift form question

Eric: I have a question regarding deadlift starting position. I understand the correct deadlifting position is with the bar touching the shins over the center of the foot, scapula over the bar and back in locked extension. I also understand that this is the correct position for anyone. I'm curious as to why this is the case.

I'm one of the genetically un-gifted – virtually the same as Dwayne Travelstead. (page 126 of SS) From what I can tell, a guy like Dwayne will lift less weight than an equally trained guy like Hunter. This is due to the larger torque because of Dwayne's back being almost parallel to the ground. Hunter's correct stance leaves him at a back angle of approximately 45 degrees up from the ground. Hunter is lifting more, but has a shorter range of motion.

I guess the real question is: which is more important, lifting heavier weights (like Hunter) or having a fuller range of motion (like Dwayne). It seems that both situations have a tradeoff – Hunter isn't moving as far and Dwayne isn't moving as much. Besides the fact that bumper plates are a standard diameter, why shouldn't my bar be higher off the ground based on my body proportions? (bad analogy, but my golf clubs are sized differently so that I have the same stance as someone who is 5'9") Either way I could still meet all of the requirements for a correct deadlift stance. Why do I need to worry about the increased range of motion when normal sized folks don't do it? Is there a reason besides someone a long time ago decided that 17.5" is the best compromise for the diameter of bumpers or am I missing something fundamental to the movement here?

Mark Rippetoe: You seem to have several questions.

1. Why does the bar come off the floor in this particular skeletal/muscular configuration? Because this is the

position in which the muscles hold the skeleton in balance when force is transferred to the load. Check videos of heavy deadlifts and see if you can find one being pulled differently. I've tried, and you can't. This is important because it tells you where you best position to pull will always be, and makes learning technique simpler.

2. Which is more important, heavier weights or a longer range of motion? Well, neither actually. The most important thing about deadlift training is getting strong using the deadlift. You deal with the mechanics you have and get them as strong as you can. Gifted deadlifters are generally of average proportions, and some tall people have been very strong, so height is not necessarily bad. Disproportionately short arms are. But you get as strong as possible with the tools you've got, because what the hell else are you going to do? Surgery?

3. Do you raise the bar to compensate for anthropometry that gives you a rather horizontal back in your pulling position? Seems like a lot of trouble, they won't understand at the power meet, and if you're not going to a meet anyway why do you care? Rack pulls serve this function as an assistance exercise, as does the sumo stance if you're at a meet, but given that the standard equipment is not going to change anytime soon, I don't see a reason to stop pulling from the floor unless you plan to just let that range of motion get weak.

Eric: Mark - thanks for taking the time to respond. I appreciate it. You are correct that I'm not interested in power meets. I'm simply trying to get as strong as possible. You said, "I don't see a reason to stop pulling from the floor unless you plan to just let that range of motion get weak." Since a normally proportioned person doesn't train this range of motion, why should I care about it either? Or conversely, why don't we have normal people stand on a box so that they can train that range of motion?

It is my understanding that the back, hip and knee angles are determined by the bar height vs. the lifters anthropometry. Bar height, as far as I can tell is an arbitrary height. The deadlift is basically opening the hip and knee angle so that the back is perpendicular to the floor. Regardless of the starting angles, it is called a dead lift – yet people are doing very different ranges of motion.

So if you had total control over the variables, what back angle would you like to see? In other words, you say that there is no correct set of angles for the dead lift. But there must be an optimal angle, and why wouldn't someone with odd anthropometry who isn't interested in competition make reasonable modifications to train at more normal alignments? I'm not trying to be difficult, I just really like to know why I'm doing things a certain way.

Whatupdun: Since the ground is in the same place for everyone, and the deadlift is just a movement where you pick something off the ground (which has seemingly endless practical applications), can we conclude that it's useful to train to pick stuff off the ground, even heavy things? Even if my legs are shorter or longer than yours?

I guess what I'm saying is that if you have to pick something off the ground, are you going to request that your individual anthropometry be accommodated by raising the thing up onto a mat or board before you lift it?

Mark Rippetoe: Excellent points, both of you. The reality of the ground could be regarded as rather arbitrary too, but this is often the way shit is. Eric's point deserves a response though. As it turns out, tall people and short people end up having very similar diagnostic angles, despite the fact that they have different anthropometry, and this would be true no matter what the standard plate diameter had been, because most humans occupy the center of the proportion bell curve, arm length included. There is not really that much difference between a tall guy's angles and a short guy's angles, even though the short guy has less work to do to lock out the bar. And if you want a perfect back angle specified in degrees, I don't know. I just know it when I see it.

(Subsequent research has indicated that this angle is indeed quantifiable, and was quantified in the early 1960s by David Webster. It is about 26 degrees above the horizontal for a person of average proportions.)

Squat - favoring one side?

Peter_k: I seem to favor one side when squatting (putting the weight on my left leg). Is there a good way to fix this? I'm worried that I might injure one leg if I keep adding weight and don't resolve it. I try to put my feet in a set position to keep the weight even, but it feels unnatural.

Mark Rippetoe: The vast majority of the time, an asymmetry like that is the result of uneven knees. Get somebody to watch you, or video yourself, from directly behind or directly in front, and check for your strong leg knee doing something different from the other one. It may be a subtle difference, but it will be noticeable. Then fix it. The only time that this won't be true is if you have a short leg, which is actually not that uncommon.

Piratejon: What's your recommendation if you do have a shorter leg?

Mark Rippetoe: You'll either have to shim your shoe or the platform.

Unusual circumstances

Fluxboy: I like your approach to the iron game, and I could use a bit of help. I've returned to lifting after a ten year layoff, and find myself in a rather curious environment. In brief, I'm in the middle of nowhere (Canada), far north in an isolated camp, working in the oil fields. It's currently -40. I only mention this because while I would love to do squats and chug liters of milk, the only gym available (30 miles away) has NO SQUAT RACK! A hellspawn smith machine, of course, but no squat rack.

Fortunately, the gym is open 24 hours a day, has a fair selection of Olympic weights, I have access to unlimited food, and I sit on my ass all day in a truck as a field medic. So I think I can still get bigger and stronger. Actually, I know I can. I've put on about 20 lbs in the last month with the following routine:

Bench, Deadlifts, Chins, Clean and jerk, Curls, Shrugs, Leg press (workout every second day)

Eating is pretty good, generally have breakfast (bacon and eggs), pack six sandwiches, and finish the day with two dinners spread over the evening. I started at 174 pounds and now weigh 195 pounds. Unfortunately, at a height of 6'4", I have a long way to go before I actually look big. Lifts are progressing, started at 135 in the deadlift, now at about 245x5 ... but the weight is feeling no heavier that when I began, so I suspect I can probably do three plates soon.

My question: I know there is no substitute for squats, but could you recommend any alterations, or a program, I could do for someone without access to a squat rack? My goal is to become bigger and stronger, nothing more. If you could offer some strength and bodyweight goals for someone of my height, it would also be appreciated. I think John McCallum gave a formula that suggested I should be at least 260 pounds. I find this a bit daunting.

Mark Rippetoe: An interesting situation, in many ways. If I were you, I'd just make deadlift my primary lift. I'd vary the reps and sets, and don't try to program it in a linear fashion like squats. Go to a weekly programming that has you PR every Monday on the 5s and Friday on the doubles or singles. It won't work as well as the squat, but it will be better than nothing. McCallum is probably right about your bodyweight, but that won't happen without the squats, so just do what you can on a 3 day/week DL program.

Fluxboy: Thanks Mark. I'll change the reps around a little and do as you suggest. I'll probably cut back on some of the other exercises as well; I like the brevity of your programs. Do you think I should drop the leg press altogether?

Mark Rippetoe: Leg Pressing is masturbation.

Tuesday: Oh, come on. Masturbation isn't *that* bad.

Mark Rippetoe: Oh, I didn't say it was bad. But at least when *I* masturbate, I am not under the impression that I'm making anybody else cum but me.

Galapogos: Would it be an acceptable alternative to clean, then front squat? Obviously the weights would be much lesser than if you had a rack, but better than nothing? Or, if your gym has a bench press, set the bar at the highest hook, sit on the bench and get under the bar in a half squat position, then stand up with it and walk your way out of the bench. I've done this before for warmup sets when the only rack in my gym is taken up. Again, not gonna work for really heavy weights, but better than nothing.

Brandon: Masturbation aside (that may be the only time I've ever said that sincerely), I've always wondered about the feasibility of someone in these circumstances just mastering Steinborn squats.

Mark Rippetoe: Well, my buddy Phil Anderson did a Steinborn with 500 lbs at a meet many years ago (and a Zercher too), so they can be done heavy. And a clean and front squat is possible too. But we are talking here about a guy in a temporary less-than-perfect situation (his oilfield job in the boonies will not last forever, and he may have other priorities as well), and we're trying to reinvent the wheel for him. Let's just see how he solves the problem. I'll bet that if he wants to back squat bad enough, he can get it done with an equipment purchase.

How I learned to stop worrying and love the clean

Peter_k: I was reading an old Q&A with one of the Westside people, and one of the questions posed to him was about whether "speed sets" done alone would increase strength. He said they wouldn't increase strength by themselves, but would increase power and explosiveness.

I was wondering what your take is on this, vis a vis the clean or O-lifts. Specifically, the carryover from the clean to the deadlift. Let's say someone has a 500 DL, and boosts it even higher by leaving it alone for awhile, and doing cleans. He's increased absolute strength, obviously, if he can lift more when he tests himself; his power has increased. But how did a strength adaptation has occurred in the absence of slow "strength" work?

The Westside people always have the "max effort" day along with the speed day. But from what I remember, Bill Starr increased his DL just by doing cleans, a speed/power exercise. Does that mean he was doing other heavy assistance work for the DL, or are cleans just such a versatile exercise that they alone will drive progress in heavier pulls?

Mark Rippetoe: Cleans and other explosive training modalities work by increasing the efficiency with which motor units are recruited by the neuromuscular system, which thus increases the number of motor units available to generate force at the time of highest recruitment. If more high-threshold motor units are available, and are more easily recruited because their recruitment has been more frequently practiced, they can contribute to force production even at the slow speeds typical of max efforts in absolute strength-dependent movements like the deadlift. Strictly speaking, absolute strength has not increased, but the efficiency with which the contractile force of more motor units has been recruited has increased, and this can translate into a better deadlift performance with practice.

So the way I understand it is that cleans (and explosive Westside deadlifts) contribute to the deadlift by teaching the neuromuscular system to fire more motor units when a max effort is called for. Greater acceleration requires greater force production, no matter what the load: a 300 lb. deadlift moving slowly doesn't require as much force production as that same 300 lb. DL moving faster. This is what is meant by the term *power.* The faster an object is accelerated, the more force must be applied to that object to make it accelerate, no matter what it weighs, and that rapidly produced force is what we mean when we use the term.

In my opinion, cleans and snatches are the best way to practice power production, especially for the deadlift, because they cannot be done slowly. This is also why I don't use high-pulls, even though they are explosive. A high-pull – a clean or snatch pull that is intentionally not racked – is never pulled with the same force that even a missed clean or snatch is, because if you know as you pull it that you are not going to go under it at the rack position, you will not pull it with the power you will produce if you are actually going to try to rack the bar. Even experienced lifters do their high-pulls differently than their full lifts; this makes them worse to practice than deadlifts, because the motor pathways are more similar to the lifts than deadlifts, and thus more likely to interfere with the pulling pattern.

Polynomial: Since some people won't believe you I will point out that "F = ma" (force is mass times acceleration), as Newton once pointed out in between his sessions of Alchemy.

Related questions:
1) Why do you feel that one's vertical can be improved by no more than 25%?

2) What implications does this have for people who want to get into olympic lifting?

3) Do you feel that the example computations of power that you do in PP correlate well with what people would like to call 'power' in an athlete? (vertical, explosiveness when starting a sprint, etc.,) Said another way, does the power clean measure well what different people might call power?

Mark Rippetoe: **1. Because neuromuscular efficiency is like red hair: you are either born with a well-plugged-in motor neuron/muscle interface, or you're like me. It has been the experience of most coaches that paid attention and worked with lots of kids that those that would have good vertical jumps exhibited this early, and those that had poor verticals never grew a big jump, no matter how they were trained. No one is sorrier about this than me.**

2. It implies that people with good verticals make good weightlifters, and that people with not-so-good verticals sometimes make good powerlifters.

3. There have been several good studies that demonstrate that power cleans predict vertical jump and power. The power clean measures power in a lifter that knows how to do them well, and provides a scalable, gradually increasable way to improve power production, within the confines of genetic endowment.

Criteria for Deadlift Start Position

Martinelli: Please excuse my cannonade of questions, but I read your relatively recent analysis concerning the 3 criteria common in every correct starting position for the deadlift. In my attempts to meet all 3 criteria, I found that I could not fulfill all 3 simultaneously without seeing some gross distortion of the start position. I have had my friends observe my profile during my setting of the position as well.

Touching my shins to the bar is not the problem. Neither is maintaining normal extension of the spine. What appears to be quite unnatural to sustain, however, is the 3rd criterion: keeping the shoulders forward of the knees and, consequently, the bar, so that the shoulder blades are directly above and in line with both the knees and the bar.

The criteria do make perfect sense to me. Keeping the bar in contact with the shins ensures that it is as far back as it can be, making it easier for my shoulders to reach a position in front of the bar. But put into practice, it is very difficult and near-impossible to attain such a position without consciously leaning over to bring the shoulders forward - and that means raising the hips. And although I am able to maintain spinal extension when I bring my hips up to allow the shoulders to travel forward, this poses another problem: my back is pretty near a 90-degree angle, signifying a conversion of the majority of force into torque. Contrary to what you have stated in your article, as I raise my butt, I am still able to keep my shins in contact with the bar. However, the exercise, according to you, effectively becomes a stiff-legged deadlift.

And while you have stated that as long as these 3 criteria are met, how the start position looks will not matter and will be relative to the individual, I can't help but draw a noticeable disparity between the back position I must adopt to accommodate your criteria and the diagrams that often accompany your writing that detail normal back position at the start of the deadlift. Namely, whereas my back position must be nearly horizontal, your diagrams always feature a person who maintains a moderately vertical (say, about 45-60 degrees) back angle while simultaneously meeting all the criteria (in the diagram, he maintains spinal extension, his shins are in contact with the bar, and his shoulders are amazingly forward of the bar, all while maintaining relatively vertical back angle).

The only solution I can conceivably imagine is to give up one criterion in favor of the other two. And it is made apparent in your article that the overriding criterion is that the shins must always touch the bar; "The correct starting position for any pull from the floor is always one in which the bar is in contact with the shins" (Rippetoe 3). Logically, the second-most important criterion is to maintain normal spinal extension.

One thing I have noted is that in each of the YouTube videos I watched featuring execution of the deadlift, I did not see a conscious effort by any of the lifters to keep their shoulders ahead of the bar and knees. The women in the CrossFit demos performing the deadlift very much had their shoulders either above the knees or even slightly behind them.

I know that this is overkill and a result of over-analysis, but if someone with as much credibility as yourself lays down guidelines for how to correctly execute an exercise, I obviously cannot ignore it and must ask questions. I am not educated enough in biomechanics and anatomy to make my own decision concerning exercise.

Source: Rippetoe, Mark. "A New, Rather Long Analysis of the Deadlift", *Strong Enough?* Chapter 9, p71-82, 2007

Mark Rippetoe: I like overanalysis, but I think you have missed the main point. There are 3 criteria for the correct deadlift position off the floor: The bar must be over the mid-foot, the back must be in extension, and the scapulas must be over the bar. The most efficient configuration for pulling a loaded barbell off the floor is a vertical relationship between the scapulas, the bar and the mid-foot. The primary concern for all barbell exercises where the bar is held on the body or in the hands is that for the system to be in balance with heavy weight the bar will be directly over the middle of the foot. In the deadlift, this occurs at the starting position when the bar is touching the shins with the knees slightly forward of the bar. But the knees are not the marker, the mid-foot is.

The fact that the back should be in extension is rather obvious, and the fact that many very strong lifters don't keep their upper back flat means that they are strong enough to tolerate the position. But the scapular position is not so obvious. The spine transmits the force generated by the hips and legs up to the load, the traps hang the scapulae from the spine, the arms hang from the scapulae, and the bar hangs from the arms. The scapulae are the bony components that receive the force from the back, and they are the points below which the bar hangs. In this position the arms hang at a slight angle back to the bar when the arms are loaded, and the lats keep them there so that the bar can stay under the scapulae. This position is identified by the arm angle, 5-10 degrees in most people – it is not necessary to see the scapulas to know they are in the right place if the arm angle is correct; vertical arms are not correct. And you can see this even in lifters using a round-back position.

When you see videos of lifters in their set position with the arms vertical or even behind the vertical, play the video frame-by-frame until the bar breaks the floor. If the weight is heavy (light weights can be done wrong, i.e. inefficiently) you will see the configuration described above establish itself. The back angle that you see as the scapulas settle into position over the bar is the correct angle, and will vary with the lifter. My point is that an incorrect start position wastes juice, because the correct position will be along shortly whether you want it to be or not. At 1RM weight, the scapula/bar/mid-foot alignment is the law, while the extended spine is a good idea.

Find me a heavy deadlift that does not conform to this model and we'll talk. Magnusson's and Bolton's records both do, but watch them carefully to see this. The weight is heavy and their upper backs are round, making the arms more relatively vertical – possible because of the fact that the bar is still directly under the scapulas. In both cases the bar is directly over the mid-foot. There will be examples of bad form on submaximal attempts, but my point is that from a musculoskeletal perspective there is only one efficient way to pull the bar off the ground, and any other configuration wastes energy that could otherwise be used to pull more weight.

When we teach the deadlift, we place the feet under the bar with the mid-foot directly under the bar and then point the toes out, we take a grip right outside the legs, we drop the knees forward and out along the toe line until the shins come just into contact with the bar but DOES NOT CHANGE ITS POSITION ON THE GROUND, lift the chest (placing the back in extension) and pull the bar up the legs. This results in a correct pull every time, with the knees-out position making possible the back angle that places the scapulas over the bar. If your back is "too" horizontal, it may be that you have short arms, or a long legs/short back anthropometry. But if these criteria are satisfied your position is correct.

Squats and hip flexors

Sesami: I recently bought BBT and have been squatting for 3-4 months. I am continually developing hip flexor discomfort/soreness (not really pain, but it is probably abnormal) immediately following my workout and for the next day. You mention this could be due to knees sliding forward at the bottom, which relaxes the hamstrings - however I believe I have good knee position. My question is, could hip flexor soreness also be due to rounding of the lower back at the bottom (which also relaxes the hamstrings)?

Looking in a side mirror while squatting with an empty bar I have realized that just before I get to parallel, my lower back rounds (its slight, but it's there) as I pass through parallel despite my attempts to keep it straight by contracting my spinal erectors. Keeping my lower back straight I am finding to be extremely difficult, and am not feeling any hamstring stretch throughout any portion of the squat (should I be?). I have checked my stance and made sure my thighs are not restricting my torso on the way down. I'm 5'11" 150 lbs. Would you just recommend stretching outside of the gym until I am flexible enough to perform the movement correctly?

Mark Rippetoe: 3 things:

1. The relaxation of your hamstrings has nothing to do with sore hip flexors. The thing that makes hip flexors sore is the tension applied to their origin at the ASIS and AIIS when you relax your hamstrings and your knees travel forward. If your hamstrings relax because your lumbar flexed but your knees don't travel forward, it wouldn't affect your hip flexor origins. But if your hip pointers are sore, that's probably what you're doing and why, because there's not much else that can do this to the hip flexor attachments.

2. If you watch yourself squat in the side mirror, you'll never get a true picture of what happens when you're not watching, because if you alter your position to watch you've altered your squat position.

3. In addition, an unweighted or very light squat provides so little resistance against which the lumbar muscles can tighten that most people will show a little lumbar flexion at the bottom of an empty bar squat. When the weight gets heavy enough to push against, the back can set against it and stay in a better position. For this reason also, you won't feel any hamstring stretch until the weight gets heavy enough to provide some. Lots of people can't get a good lower back set with good lumbar extension until the weight on the bar is sufficient to help them stretch out their hamstrings enough to achieve a good lumbar curve.

Bench press technique question and pullup question

solidsnake123: In SS:BBT you said to lay on the bench so that if you are looking straight up to the ceiling when the bar is racked, your line of sight will be on the foot side of the bar. If I do that I cannot even get the weight off of the hooks because my arm and torso angle is like ___ that. I have to go around asking people for lift-offs. Also, you said to keep your head about 1/2 inch off the bench to avoid a neck injury. The last two times I have tried to do that I end up with a crick in my neck and a feeling like I have pulled it, especially when trying to get the bar off the hooks with an arm and torso angle of ___

Also, I have noticed the past two bench workouts that I have either strained or done something to what feels like my rear deltoid when doing pullups. I do not warmup for back extensions or pullups on those days as I did not see any mention of warming up for them in SS:BBT. Are you supposed to warmup before doing your pullups (back extensions have already been warmed up for by doing the heavy squats)?

Mark Rippetoe: Then I guess you'd better try doing things differently. I have never seen anybody who had their eyes just past the bar on the down side in the position you describe. Never. Unless they were too far down. So move back up. And if you're getting a crick in your neck from holding your head up off the bench, try laying it down without pushing it into the bench too hard.

And if you're doing any exercises without a warmup and hurting yourself, then I guess that means that you'd better warm up, huh?

Whatupdun: I like the narrow "triangle" grip, because I can really feel it in my lats. IMO, this is also a good warmup for bench presses, since the lats are called upon when you're beginning to push the bar back upwards.

Mark Rippetoe: Please explain the mechanics of this.

Whatupdun: If this question is directed toward my assertion, here's an excerpt I feel adequately explains the mechanics of how your lats are critical for the lower portion of the bench press. If not, you can simply delete my reply.

:: oh, the delights of approving the content for one's own forum…

USE OF THE LATS IN BENCH PRESSING
An often-overlooked component of the bench press is the use and development of the muscles of the back and in particular the lats. Very few lifters utilize the strength of the lats in their bench press and when they are able to incorporate lat contraction into their exercises, immediate increase is always achieved. Here is how you incorporate the lats into your bench press: Take an empty bar or even a wooden rod and assume the bench press position. Lower the bar to the chest and pause. Instead of driving the weight up with the arms, contract or flare the lats in an outward direction. If you have decent lat development, you should see the bar move several inches off the chest. This takes practice to utilize the lats in this manner, but be persistent and practice over and over with an empty bar, gradually adding weight as you get used to the movement. The eventual goal is to use the lats as sort of a cushion or coiled spring when lowering the bar and then contracting them strongly on the initial drive at the same time you are pressing with the arms. DO NOT walk into the gym tomorrow and attempt this with your max poundage if you do you will fail. I have worked with athletes who have increased their maximum bench press anywhere from 20-50lbs within 2 weeks as a result of using this technique. This also requires strong well-developed lats, which are developed by chins and rowing.

from http://www.martygallagher.com/
(whomever the hell Marty Gallagher is :rolleyes:)

For more references, search something like "bench press lats" without the quotes on Google. Such a search produced ~88,000 results for me a few minutes ago.

Mark Rippetoe: I'd be careful about my remarks about well-known coaches with whom I was not familiar, if I were you.

That having been said, I disagree with Marty's explanation. First, it is not an explanation of the mechanics, which I requested from you, so that's your fault, not his. Second, if you'll think real hard about the origin and insertion of the lat, it is hardly possible that a muscle that pulls the humerus and the spine together can contribute in an active manner to a movement that requires that the humerus and the spine move apart. The lats don't "contract or flare in an outward direction." They adduct the humerus. If you're wearing a heavy bench shirt, you'll actually use the lats to help you get the bar down to the chest, and even if you're not wearing a shirt the lats will aid the upper back muscles in arching the chest up. They may even serve as a rebound cushion at the bottom of the movement if they're large enough, but this is only useful if we quit pretending there is a pause at the bottom in a meet.

But the motion described as "flaring" the lats is a contraction of the serratus anterior as they ab-duct the scapulas; it is a shrug forward, and although it shows us the lat belly when observed from the front, like a bodybuilding Lat Spread, it is not a lat contraction *per se*. It cannot be the lats, because when a muscle contracts it pulls the origin and insertion points together – definitely not what's happening when the bar drives up off the chest. The lats can serve to support the arch as the bar approaches the bottom – and they are very important in this respect, like the erectors in a deadlift – but they cannot contribute to the upward movement of the bar.

Now, why would I want to delete a delightful post like this?

Whatupdun: Good point, Rip – my comment wasn't meant to disparage the quoted individual, so I apologize if I was out of line. Your explanation seems solid and concise (as usual – good work). Is it accurate, then, to say that the lats *help* with the bench press, but that they're not involved in the pressing motion itself? In the bottom of the bench press, I can definitely feel my midback helping to – it's somewhat hard to explain – it's like my back is pulling my arms in to my sides, which helps the chest/shoulder contraction to move the bar upward.

Mark Rippetoe: You've got it right now.

Barbell Row Movement

RRod: In SSBBT you say that barbell rows should lead with the elbows after the initial hip extension. This got me thinking about the parallel between the row movement and the power clean. In the power clean, after the hip extension the trainee is supposed to shrug hard, which pretty much automatically brings the elbows along for the ride. I would like to think this works for the row too: hips extend -> shoulders squeeze together -> elbows finish flexing. But "lead with elbows" to me means: hips extend -> elbows bend -> shoulders finish squeezing. When I try both movement patterns for the row, the clean-type movement seems to work more smoothly and powerfully. In fact, the whole experiment made me question if I've been pulling things incorrectly my whole life (which might explain why I always sucked at starting lawnmowers...). To get to a question: does "lead with elbows" mean "flex elbows first" or "squeeze shoulders together first"?

p.s. No plans here to sub rows for cleans; simply thinking of adding rows as some upper back assistance work

Mark Rippetoe: An interesting question. This is an example of how cues for movements and actual biomechanical events are sometimes at odds. The cue for the row is "elbows", but what actually happens is that the scapulas have to retract before elbows can move back. If you are in the starting position of a barbell row with your scapulas pulled forward as you reach down for the bar on the floor, the first thing you will do is retract them into a neutral position, then the elbows will slam back, and then the scapulas adduct as the elbows reach the top of their range of motion. You *think* elbows, but all those things happen.

Question on pull ups and bench press

b33k4y: For pull ups/chins, I am aware that the arms should be fully extended at the bottom of the movement, but does this mean fully relaxed and as far down as you can go? Would it be better for the shoulders to have some tension and not let them shrug all the way up to/past your ears at the bottom?

For the bench press, is it possible for a flexible person to put too much back arch into the lift even if their butt is firmly planted on the bench and their feet are flat on the floor? By doing this an easier leverage is achieved but I am not sure if this defeats the whole point of a flat bench press. The angle isn't so severe that it becomes a decline press, though. I just find that it helps me get more under the bar if you know what I mean. I am pretty lanky and don't really enjoy benching all that much...

Mark Rippetoe: If you relax your arms at the bottom and let your shoulders slide down, the muscles that have to pull you back up from that position are the lats and upper back muscles. Since we want to work them, use the full ROM in the exercise. And the better "legal" bench position you can squeeze into, the more you can bench. This is a good thing.

XTrainer: So in your opinion, we should not use the stretch reflex at the bottom of the movement?

Mark Rippetoe: Not all the time. You don't do anything All The Time. Except squat.

Scott: One thing I've been wondering is why on the bench press do you advocate a retraction of the scapulas to reduce range of motion, whereas in pretty much all the other primary lifts you advocate maximal range of motion? Why the exception for the BP?

Mark Rippetoe: Retraction of the scapulas does not restrict the ROM around the shoulder joint. It just restricts the movement of the scapulas.

Scott: Gotcha. But I'm thinking of your reasoning for not teaching the Sumo-style squat: our objective is to get strong (including the quads), not lift the greatest amount of weight. And also how you allow some hip extension and shoulder flexion in curls, making it a more compound movement. Thus, I wonder why we don't make the BP a more compound movement that trains an expanded group of muscles.

Brad D: Mark, I'm surprised by your answer on the pullups ROM. Unless I'm reading it wrong, he's basically asking if he should abandon an active shoulder at the bottom position. My understanding is that this is about the best way to cause shoulder impingement. Am I missing something?

Mark Rippetoe: I don't understand how Scott proposes to add more muscles to the bench press, and I have no idea what Brad is talking about here. Active shoulder abandonment at the bottom of the chin?

George: Apparently by protracting the scapulae to add the serratus to the movement and increase the distance the bar travels, at the expense of shoulder stability. It doesn't seem like a good idea to me, but I haven't written any books or owned any gyms.

Brad D: Mark, I thought that active shoulder at the bottom of a pullup or chin-up was defined as keeping the shoulder in an anti-shrugged position. Am I misinterpreting this?

Mark Rippetoe: Everybody is misinterpreting. 1.) The range of motion of the bench press does not increase if the shoulders are shrugged forward, because the range of motion around the shoulder joint does not increase when the scapula is shrugged up by the serratus. The bar may move a little farther, but the angle the humerus travels around the glenoid is the same, the stability on the bench is decreased, and the scapula is placed in a position where it is more likely to impinge when shrugged forward like this. 2.) Impingement is not a problem with either overhead pressing movements or overhead pulling movements if they are done correctly, with the scapulas shrugged superiorly and medially at the top of the press and hanging that way at the bottom of a pullup, because the bony components that could impinge are separated by the shrugged position. And 3.) the bottom of a pullup and the top of a press are not equivalent positions because the pullup is applying tension to the shoulders while the press is compressive – the forces are acting in opposite directions, and countering the forces requires two different types of contractions. An "anti-shrug" at the bottom of the pullup is useful for decreasing the ROM if you are concerned about how many pullups you can do with any form in a finite amount of time, but decreasing the ROM also decreases the amount of muscle involved if you are concerned about using the pullup to strengthen as much muscle mass as possible. Using the pullup for metcon is a different thing than using it for upper-body strength.

Soreness in Glutes with Squats

Sepandee: I usually don't get any pain in my glutes when squatting. But since hitting 200lb I can definitely feel it in my glutes, a soreness that usually lasts for 24-48 hours and is felt immediately after each working set. Is this a good thing (indication of good form) or a bad thing (bad form)?

Mark Rippetoe: Good or bad I don't know, but it probably indicates that you are using a fairly upright torso which leaves out the hamstrings, and is therefore not a low-bar squat.

Brandon: What exactly is the difference in what's done by the glutes and the hamstrings in a squat?

Mark Rippetoe: Both are hip extensors, along with the adductors. The three muscle groups form the posterior chain. When they all work together to extend the hip a very powerful contraction results. But when the hamstrings are removed from the work – as they are when the knee is flexed and the hamstring shortened from the distal end, as in the front squat position – the glutes and adductors have to do the whole job by themselves. In a front squat, the hamstrings function is isometric: they just hold the back angle constant. Since they are already contracted into a short position because of the knee and hip angles and cannot contract much more, the adductors and glutes are the only remaining hip extensors. That is why your ass gets so sore when you do a lot of front squats correctly.

Brandon: So the important difference is that the hamstrings also have a distal function across the knee (and are therefore contracted when the knee is flexed), whereas the glutes only cross the hip and are unaffected by the knee? If you're doing a movement that involves only the hip (a back extension, say), they would both be engaged in one big mess, yes?

Mark Rippetoe: Exactimundo squared.

Bench Press ROM/Building Max Strength

Quintus: Regarding the bench press, and given that:

- The goal is to build maximum strength, which is not necessarily the same thing as just lifting more weight.
- Greater ROM builds greater strength, as it trains more muscle mass.
- Thoracic extension on the bench press decreases ROM.

What is the rationale for recommending thoracic extension (big/raised chest) on the bench press? Unless there's a missing premise, it would seem that a more neutral back position should be preferred, since it would increase the range of motion and (presumably) serve to better build strength.

Are there mechanical problems (impingement, etc.) with the more perpendicular line of action in a neutral back bench press that go away when the upper back is arched?

I've seen some people with hyper-flexible backs that can *dramatically* shorten the ROM on a bench press with this kind of extension (while still keeping their butt on the bench). In addition, the dramatic change in the line of action of the shoulder joint effectively turns it into a decline bench press. It would seem to me that any technique that confers an advantage by blurring the lines between two distinct movements (see also: excessive layback on the press) is something that would generally be discouraged.

Mark Rippetoe: Excellent point. We could make everybody bench in the most anatomically hard position possible by taking the arch out of the back, true, lengthening the range of motion and increasing the work done on the bar. But there are other considerations: mechanics and shoulder anatomy are at odds here, and this must be considered in any discussion of the bench press position.

Arching the chest does in fact decrease the distance the bar has to travel, and this is why many gym guys like to do declines: they can do more weight because they are really doing a partial. From a mechanical standpoint, the best position when pressing, either on the bench or standing, is where the distance between the bar and the shoulder joint – and thus the lever arm – is the shortest, and where the bar path is vertical. On the bench this would be where the bar is directly above the shoulder joint (the glenoid), and this is the place where everybody likes to lock the bar out at the top. At the bottom, however, the bar cannot be directly over the glenoid, because if it is the humerus is in full adduction (90 degrees to the sagittal plane) and internal rotation, a position which is famous for causing shoulder impingement. In this position the humerus bangs into the coracoid and acromion processes of the scapula, and you can feel this when you stand and lift your elbow up as high as it will go with your hand pointed forward. The shoulder cannot tolerate this position anatomically even though it would be the best place mechanically to press since the lever arm length would be zero.

So, what has to happen is that you drop your elbow a little from complete adduction at the bottom of the bench press into a position where the humerus is at about 75-80 degrees to the sagittal. This relieves any possible impingement, but it also produces a lever arm between the bar and the shoulder joint. And it creates a non-vertical bar path due to the lateral distance between the point directly over the glenoid at the top and the position of the elbows at the bottom, an unavoidable consequence of respecting the shoulder anatomy. Raising the chest up rotates the scapula back under the bar and shortens this lever arm even though the humerus is still not at 90 degrees. So lifting the chest up serves a function other than just shortening the bar path; it shortens the distance between the bar and the glenoid when the humerus is not in adduction, and shortens the lateral distance between the bottom and top positions, making the bar path more vertical.

In fact, lots of people whose shoulders hurt when they bench could do so without pain if they lifted their chest up high.

Looking up/down in squats

Connor Mc: I've seen you recommend (frequently) looking down during low bar squats, which I've tried to do - it feels a little odd and sometimes I end up sort of looking down and forward (halfway there or so) but I try to do it. Today though I came across a video that aimed to correct rounding at the bottom (I think this is called butt wink? My terminology's a bit behind the times) and this trainer says that keeping your head down can cause your chest to come in and your arch to relax a bit. Since it was something I was never really clear on anyway, what is the benefit of looking down during a LBS as opposed to head up or straight forward?

Mark Rippetoe: We teach the value of looking down with a very simple demonstration that we always include at our seminars in the very first phase of learning the movement. After placing the trainee in the bottom of the squat and getting the feet, knees, and back angle correct, I block the hips by placing my hand on the sacrum and telling the athlete to "drive up against my hand." This demonstrates the power of the posterior chain when it engages to drive hips up. I then tell the athlete to do the same thing again looking down at a point three feet away on the platform, and then to do the same thing while looking up, blocking the hips with my hand in both cases. Without exception, I am always told that the preference is for looking down. This is because looking down better facilitates the use of the hips than looking up, and the difference in power production is immediately evident to anybody that has done my little demonstration.

When you look up, the action of assuming the looking-up position pulls the knees forward a little, closing up the knee angle and therefore slacking the hamstrings from the distal end. If the hamstrings shorten distally, they are less able to extend the hips proximally because the tension developed against their proximal attachments on the pelvis is diminished. You can demonstrate this to yourself by standing normally, looking straight forward, and then looking up at the ceiling, paying attention to what naturally happens to your knees when you do this. So, in addition to providing a useful position reference against the floor, looking down makes hip drive dramatically more effective when you squat. I am much less concerned with "butt wink" than some people, having realized long ago that some small amount of lumbar movement is inevitable, and not a concern unless it is quite egregious. And that, my now surprised-that-I-haven't-been-a-smartass friend, is the deal.

XTrainer: Is the fact that many (most?) powerlifters prefer looking up a product of gear usage?

Mark Rippetoe: Many geared powerlifters look up because they have never tried looking down. Perhaps this is a high-school football holdover.

Connor Mc: I would be a bit puzzled as to how eye position can cause your knees to come forward. I mean I am inclined to think it is a head positioning issue rather than an eye positioning issue. But I could be wrong.

Mark Rippetoe: Eyeball and head position are intimately related for most people. When you look up at the ceiling, what does your head do? I'll bet it follows your eyes, and your neck goes into overextension right behind it. And then your knees drift forward to keep you balanced on your feet. Looking down is the opposite. There may be examples of people who don't do this, but they are the exceptions, and I have to write for the rule.

SS Questions

Powerhawk: I'm a bit confused about the transition from the first pull to the second pull of power cleans described in SS. Are the knees supposed to come forward naturally after the first pull, or does it have to be forced? I have no trouble hang cleaning, but power cleans are a hit or miss.

Also, if physique is the primary concern, are power cleans necessary, and can seated press be done? I have a few friends I've put on SS, but they have been doing rows, and they don't seem to understand that they can't lean back during heavy presses (I also have trouble not leaning back during the final reps).

Mark Rippetoe: The transition from 1st to 2nd pull is built into the teaching method in BBT, so that when I teach a roomful of people how to clean with my method all of them are doing a correct second pull without it even being discussed in the process. The correct second pull is a feature of assuming the jumping position each rep, and learning the clean as a jump with the bar in the hands.

If physique is a concern, how is it that a more powerful deadlift and squat become secondary issues? Do you think that the PC is included because it makes certain muscle groups *look* a particular way? How many times do I have to tell you people why cleans are in the fucking program before you will either come to understand why or figure out a way to do them?

And by leaning back during heavy presses, do you mean at lockout or on the way up? On the way up you can lean back a little, and will have to if you do any decent weight at all, but at the top if you lean back the bar is not balanced over the scapulas and the mid-foot.

Powerhawk: My concern was this: Power cleans would increase the squat/deadlift by reducing the amount of time the concentric part of the movement takes to execute. Even if this allows you to use more weight, time under tension and total microtrauma wouldn't be affected. I can't be sure that is how it works though. A lot of this bodybuilding theory sounds more like bullshit theory to me. The leaning back is at the top, but it seems to produce soreness in the middle back, probably because it is excessive. Should the final rep of the final set be executed if it can only be done by leaning back a great deal?

Mark Rippetoe: Time under tension?? If the bar moves 4 times faster than it does for a deadlift, TUT is obviously affected. It is just irrelevant. Total microtrauma?? Sounds like quasi-biological bullshit to me. And if the weight gets heavy enough, you will lean back to press it. This is part of doing heavy presses. You just have to control the distance between the shoulder and the bar as you drive it up.

Squat depth and the "hard" lumbar arch

Peter_k: I've got the squat down pretty well, I think, except for the lumbar position, which I can't seem to do properly for some reason. The problem I have is arching my back to the right degree. If I arch my back as much as I can (to the point of hyperextension, I guess - if that even means anything), I can't get proper depth, and it seems to prevent me from keeping my chest up and dilutes the hip drive. So, what I do is take a deep breath, push my chest out (and arch my lumbar spine slightly) and drop down. That makes it easier to reach depth, but it results in bit more butt wink than I'd like.

I guess my question is - is there such thing as hyperextending the spine too much? I'm kind of confused because the only way I can prevent it from rounding is by arching it really hard.

Mark Rippetoe: I don't know that you're doing an excessive lumbar relaxation without seeing it. I have ways to fix it if this is indeed what's occurring, but it may not be. There is so much paranoia regarding the slightest lumbar movement that you may be infected with it.

Peter_k: Ok, but just to be clear about what would be the ideal: Is it: a) spine kept slightly arched and maintained in a rigid position throughout the whole movement, or b) spine arched as hard as possible throughout the whole movement. I'm just asking because it seems the leverage is better when the spine is "flat" rather than hard-arched (i.e. slightly curved). It also seems to take more energy to keep the spine rigidly flexed.

Mark Rippetoe: Ideal is normal anatomical position, the slight lordotic curve you assume when standing normally upright. An "over-arched" spine is neither normal nor desirable. When I squat, I think of it as the position I'm in at the top: I want my back to stay motionless in the curve it assumes while standing upright with the load as I lower and raise my ass. To do this, I have found that it helps to understand that the spinal position is maintained with ALL of the trunk muscles working isometrically to set and squeeze the whole trunk, not just the spinal erector muscles keeping the back arched. Every time I squat a rep, I think about the general set of the whole thing, not just the low back, and this seems to work well for me. If you just think about the erectors and arching the lumbar (although this might work for a novice just learning the position) you will have a tendency to over-arch the lower back while at the same time be less likely to be able to maintain a constant normal position with heavy weight.

Bend/Crease in hips as I'm doing GHR's

Stylesbjj: Doing Glute/Ham Raises (esp. floor ones) seem to be easier when you bend at the hips. I can do GHRs keeping my body perfectly straight (except for the knees of course), but it's just much easier with a slight crease at the hips. Is the slight bend ok, or should my hips be completely straight?

Mark Rippetoe: A glute/ham raise is a back extension followed by a hip extension followed by a knee flexion (let's ignore the floor version that leaves out the back extension/hip extension part). When you put a hip flexion into the movement right after the back extension, you essentially shorten the moment arm of the load the knee flexion is lifting by decreasing the distance between your head and your knees. The mass is the same, but it's arranged in a way that's much easier to lift. So no, it's not okay.

Other Squat Assistance Exercises

Alex Blonde: I had questions about two squat assistance exercises that aren't mentioned at all in either SS:BBT or Practical Programming: the overhead squat and the lunge. I was wondering what your thoughts were on the utility of these two exercises for the intermediate trainee.

Opinion seems to generally be pretty split on the overhead squat. Some people think it is a great exercise for working midline stabilization and developing the ability to apply force to objects in awkward positions. Other people think that once you have developed the core strength and flexibility to do the overhead squat at a moderate load, working them further provides very little benefit. The lunge isn't really an assistance exercise for the squat, but it is a commonly performed leg workout, especially among those who are too scared to squat. I'm not really sure what the specific benefit of the lunge is, but they do make you tired.

What are your opinions on these two exercises? Do they have a place in an intermediate training program? Obviously, that depends somewhat on what your training goals are, but in general, are these exercises useful or not?

Mark Rippetoe: Both overhead squats and lunges are interesting exercises that require balance and control. I like overhead squats (I've got a kid doing them right now, this very minute in fact) for Oly lifters. They are not heavy enough to be considered a lower-body strength movement for anybody, but rather they are used as stability work and upper-body support strength work for lots of different sports. Lunges, on the other hand, are usually done with light weights, and even done correctly so that they are not hard on the knees are still ineffective as a strength exercise because they are unilateral. Would you rather get your squat up to 405 or your lunge up to 135, and which would make you stronger? Hell, reading the questions on this board makes me tired, but I don't get to write it down in my journal. Lunges make you sore, I know, but that is not a criterion for an effective exercise.

Rebecca: Please pardon my ignorance here, but I'm very curious about your comment (...unilateral exercises are not good for strength development?) I understand that the amount of strength gained from a unilateral ex would pale in comparison to the amount gained from a bilateral, but I'm not sure that's what you mean. Could you explain why they're not effective for building strength?

Mark Rippetoe: *"Would you rather get your squat up to 405 or your lunge up to 135, and which would make you stronger?"*

This is what I mean. They are not effective for building strength relative to a heavy bilateral exercise due to the loads that can be handled.

Some questions

Pnigro: 1) Are calves worked in squats or deadlifts? What is their function in those exercises? I have tiny calves!

2) During the squats, I loosen up my abs when going down, because my back rounds so I try to hyperextend it by contracting the lumbar muscles. Then, when I go up, I contract/tighten my abs again so that my lower back don't overarch and my spine stays in the normal anatomical position. Is this how it's supposed to work? I mean if my back rounds when going down, then there is no point in keeping the abs contracting, otherwise they are going to help keep the back rounded.

3) My friend has reached the point in the program where it's very hard for him to keep adding weight to the squat. We train together, but sometimes we can't so we end up training alone. The other day he did 5-5-2. He couldn't get up in the 3rd rep of the last set, so he had to call someone to help him. He had to wait with the bar on his back at the bottom of the squat and it was painful. Is this normal? Should we always squat with a spotter? Can this be prevented somehow? We suppose this had to be some kind of problem with his technique, but we really don't know.

Mark Rippetoe: 1. Calves act during the squat and the deadlift to stabilize and "anchor" the knee angle: they, along with the hamstrings anchoring the hip angle, control the ability of the quads to transmit knee extension force to the bar by keeping the knee angle from opening in the absence of bar movement. Their function here is purely isometric, and you won't get big calves from squatting and deadlifting even though they get worked. And generally speaking, big calves are genetic. Sorry.

2. You are a crazy person. Your spine must be stable during any movement that loads it, and the function of the trunk muscles -- both abs and erectors -- is to hold it *still*. Very still. You don't want the spine to alter its intervertebral position under a load, and the muscles keep it from moving. But YOU have decided to *relax your abs on the way down*, and then *tighten* them on the way up??? Really, don't do this. Squeeze the hell out of the muscles on both sides of your spine at the top, and then keep them that way all the way down and all the way up.

3. If he's doing the same thing you are with his abs, it's good that he's stuck – less likely to kill himself. He's probably got a form problem related to this. Yes, get a spot on your work sets, if there is the slightest doubt they might not go.

Shoulder tendonitis

Philds: I have had a minor ache on my left shoulder (I'm a lefty) since about mid December last year. I finally got it checked out 3 weeks ago because it felt a bit worse lately. I have had some x-rays and an ultrasound exam done and my doc diagnosed it as an inflamed supraspinatus together with tendonitis of the supraspinatus tendon. Except for the ache the only thing that is noticeable is that when I "scratch" my back my left arm won't bend more then 90°. Which is a lot less ROM than my right arm has.

Should I listen to the doc and lay off lifting for a while and only continue squatting?
If yes, how long does it take to heal in your experience? It's been bugging me nearly 9 months now. But of course, I started pressing, and bench pressing 3 months ago, so that might have been a dumb move.

Mark Rippetoe: The doctor always wants you to lay off and let it heal. I have beaten this to death on this board: **it will not heal unless you make it heal.** You have to train through it. Have you been laying off it this past year, during which time it got worse, or have you been training it like you want it to heal?

Before you answer that let me give you the bad news: sometimes supraspinatus problems don't heal without surgery. But the good news is that sometimes they do, or sometimes you can figure out a way to train around them so that they don't bother you without surgery. I have eliminated the bench and most dips while keeping presses and chins, and mine doesn't bother me much at all, certainly not enough to cause me to contemplate surgery. Are you pressing and doing lots of chins?

Philds: Thanks for the answer: I started Starting Strength because I wanted to get to the root cause of my shoulder problem which is being a skinny fat underdeveloped 34 years old male with bad posture. (Know thyself.) So the first 4 months after the shoulder pain started I didn't do any work, and it didn't make any difference, but neither did the 2 months of SS, nor the 1 month I laid off. So since I'm damned if I do, and damned if I don't, I'm starting the program again since it's fun. I'll follow your lead for the moment and stop the dips. I'll see what happens with the bench press. If my shoulder gets so bad it needs surgery, well, it probably would have sooner or later.

One last question: Is doing lying tricep extensions in lieu of the dip worth it, or shouldn't I bother. (I know that it's an isolation exercise) If yes, would I do sets of 3x5 reps like the press etc. or do the 3x12's?

TravisRussellDC: If the problem has been going on for 9 months, then it is no longer an inflammatory condition and tendonitis is unlikely. Once you step into that chronic phase the tendon is no longer inflamed, rather it is classified as a tendonopathy and the term "tendinosis" is more suited. The tendon itself has likely started to deteriorate and dehydrate. Laying off the exercise will not help this condition. Since you are in a chronic state, you must find a way to break the nociceptive (pain reception) cycle. Stimulation of the tendon while assuming a posture of pain provocation works really well. ART, Graston, cross fiber, friction rub, etc. all work very well for working out the musculotendonous junction area to break the pain cycle and promote healing.

That being said, the majority of rotator cuff pain and dysfunction is secondary to poor mechanics of the scapula. You must fix the biomechanics of the upper extremity, including the cervical and thoracic spine, if you want to prevent further flair ups.

Mark Rippetoe: Philds: I'd be careful about doing LTEs with a shoulder injury. If you use enough weight to make the exercise useful, you'll get into problems with handling the weight safely getting on and off the bench. This would really piss you off, hurting your shoulder again with an assistance exercise.

Trav: I agree with everything in the first paragraph, but I'm afraid you're going to tell me that "poor mechanics of the scapula" is fixed with chiropractic treatment.

TravisRussellDC: Not at all. Chiropractic treatment can only release the fixations that the joints are experiencing after months of improper positioning and movement. It's up to him to put forth the time and effort to rehab the shoulder joint complex properly to ensure this doesn't happen again.

I tell my patients this all the time: being healthy and pain free is hard work. But if you're willing to put in the time and effort then I will do everything in my power to help you get there. But I can only direct the body to where it's supposed to be. The patient has to do the work to get it there and keep it there.

Mark Rippetoe: I tell everybody that good shoulder mechanics is pressing with correct technique, and that if you do that you won't hurt your shoulders, and if you can't press with correct technique you need to get to where you can in whatever way you need to.

Tiburon: This is a great thread, thanks. Can you say a little more about good scapular mechanics? I understand what to do during the press (page 162 of SS:BBT) and during the bench (page 87). But what about chinups and pullups - should my shoulders be "active" throughout the entire range of motion, for the entire set? In other words, should my shoulders be shrugged the whole time? Also, what about deadlifts - should my shoulders be pulled back (scapulas trying to touch) or are my arms just hanging there with my back in good position? And what about dips?

I think I am having trouble distinguishing - in terms of their definitions and my proprioception - between "active shoulders," "shrugged shoulders," "scapular retraction" and even the "chest up" that you talk about for the press (Fig 5-13). Any advice / references would be welcome.

Mark Rippetoe: During chins and pullups, the scapulas travel through their range of motion across the posterior ribcage as the movement progresses from hanging at the bottom, where they are abducted and inferiorly rotated laterally, to locked out at the top, where they are adducted medially. But they scapulas have a different function in the deadlift: they are the points below which the load hangs and where the force transmitted up the back is transferred to the arms and down to the bar. The traps and rhomboids connect the scapulas to the spine, and they are in isometric contraction when they are working. The bar essentially hangs from the scapulas, and thus the traps and rhomboids. If these muscles are contracted concentrically – shortened – as in a shrugged position with the scapulas medially pulled into the spine, they can be pulled out laterally with enough weight.

This means that 1.) things are moving that are best kept still, and 2.) you have placed them in a position where they are *going* to move. I'd rather put my scapulas in a place where they can stay *without* moving while they are in contraction, and that place is just plain old normal anatomical position. Don't shrug your shoulders back – just get your chest up and stay tight, and your upper back muscles will be working in the way they are supposed to while they hold your scapulas, arms, and the bar.

While the traps and rhomboids are working isometrically, the lats are too, holding the arms at a slight angle so that the load does not swing out in front of the scapulas and away from the point over the mid-foot where it is in balance. If you try to adduct the scapulas before you pull, you have to contract the lats too. If the weight is heavy enough to pull the shrug out – and it will be at 1RM – the movement can tear muscle bellies that would otherwise not tear if they don't move. It's hard to rupture a muscle in isometric motionless contraction, and relatively easier to rupture a muscle in either concentric or eccentric contraction.

"I think I am having trouble distinguishing - in terms of their definitions and my proprioception - between "active shoulders," "shrugged shoulders," "scapular retraction" and even the "chest up" that you talk about for the press. Any advice / references would be welcome."

Active shoulders is a term that recognizes the role of the traps in the press. The scapulas are the points on the torso where the arms articulate, and when the arms are locked out with the bar overhead, the load must be directly over the point on the scapulas where the humerus hooks up: the glenoid fossa or "socket" of the scapula. Since the scapulas are suspended from the traps, when the bar is overhead in this position the traps must be in contraction to hold up the scapulas. "Active shoulder" means a shrugged up shoulder actively supporting the load overhead. It has to be shrugged in the press, jerk, overhead squat, and snatch – as opposed to merely in isometric contraction in normal anatomical position in the deadlift – because the shrugged position protects against shoulder impingement, and because the force on the shoulder in this position is compressive instead of tension as in a deadlift.

"Chest up" is a cue for spinal position that really doesn't directly involve the scapulas. When you lift the chest you're contracting the muscles of the upper back and the serratus anterior. "Scapular retraction" means that the scapulas are pulled together into adduction. "Shrugged shoulders" might mean either scapula retraction or shoulder elevation, the trap contraction that makes the whole shoulder girdle – both scapulas and clavicles – move toward the superior.

SS makes you hard

firemed839: Just wanted to tell a story about how SS is helping us. My buddy who posts on here (firemedic840) has a second job on the ambulance like most of our firefighters do. We have both been doing SS and he has made tremendous gains. He is doing over 300 on all the lifts, except PC. The other day, while working on the ambulance, a guy doing about 80 mph struck the back of his ambulance while they were stopped at wreck. He struck the steering wheel with his face and was a little loopy for a few seconds. It completely demolished the back of the rig. This hardass gets out of the rig, shakes out the cobwebs from his brain and goes to treat the guy who hit him. He took the guy, who was pretty jacked up, to the hospital in another ambulance and then checked himself in as a patient. He hasn't even been sore and the only thing we can figure is that doing the SS program has adapted the muscles so much that not even a dumbass who can't see flashing ambulance lights can shock them. Thanks for the books and all the advice. Just wanted to let you know about our resident hardass.

Mark Rippetoe: Damned impressive. Pass this along to the asshats in charge of your FD PT. Maybe they'll see the value.

I a n: Impressive story, but I gotta call BS on this one. First of all, when you are rear-ended, your body goes backwards, not forward into the steering wheel. It's simple physics. Drama queens and liars out for cash settlements who are too f-in stupid to understand Newton's Law say they hit their head on the steering wheel from a rear-end impact. Second, what kind of p***y goes to the ER after getting jostled by a rear-end impact, who has no broken bones and maybe a little stiffness in his neck, much less when he is in an ambulance that weights about 5 times the car that hit him, and even better, after saying he wasn't injured? Do you really need to go to the ER because you have a little soreness in your neck? It never ceases to amaze me why people get so much more hurt and turn into such whiney pathetic p***ys when there is $$$ to be gained from it. Would this same strong weightlifting fireman need to go to the ER if got a little jostled playing a sport or with a minor accident at home, or better, if he was the at fault driver? Does he consider himself "injured" when he wakes up sore after squats, DLs, and BP? Sounds like a case of "whipcash" to me. I bet he already has an attorney, making the workers comp claim and sending him for 40 useless chiropractic treatments and some other referrals to litigation doctors, so he can get his settlement at the cost of all of us. This is why we pay out the a** for insurance. Another injured victim - when it's convenient.

Mark Rippetoe: You fucking idiot. Did you not stop to think that his fucking department might ***require*** a medical evaluation after a wreck involving a potential workmen's comp case by a fireman on duty??? Did you not stop to think that any public service employee on duty always has to be examined if they are involved in a wreck before you embarrassed yourself by accusing him of being a pussy? Did this actually not occur to you before you typed all this silly shit? Go away, you fool.

TomC: You just called a guy who you don't know, who lifts over 300 lbs on everything except power clean, and who works as a goddamn firefighter and paramedic a pussy, liar, and an opportunist. Very smooth. I'm embarrassed for you.

It also seems that your grasp of physics is as tenuous as your grasp of good manners. Let's think about what happens when you get rear ended. The vehicle in which you are seated gets hit and exerts a force on your body. In this case, that force is directed toward the steering wheel. Your body does not actually go backwards, because there is no force acting on your body to press you backward. Instead the vehicle gets pressed into your body. If your head is not supported, it will remain stationary relative to your body as it gets pushed forward, potentially causing whiplash. The next thing to happen is that the vehicle stops moving, but your body does not. It will continue to move until something acts upon it to stop its motion. In this case, that will be the seat belt, the steering wheel, or the windshield.

If you really moved backward when you were rear ended, you might expect that behavior to be seen in other systems. Last I checked, the laws of physics were remarkably consistent no matter where you are. Why when you hit a cue ball into the eight ball on a pool table does the eight ball go forward instead of rolling back towards you? The argument you presented would seem to suggest that would occur.

I would certainly believe that someone who is as strong as this man would be in less danger of serious injury due to a collision than someone who is weak. What's more, that he then got out and treated the dude who hit him while potentially injured speaks to his strength of character and devotion to helping others. I think you owe both this man and your high school physics teacher serious apologies.

Mark Rippetoe: Gentlemen, I assure you that this moron will never have the opportunity to apologize on this forum.

Rolling the bar on deadlifts...

Kiknskreem: Someone recently made the point of an object in motion wanting to stay in motion, and that even momentum in the horizontal plane can then be directed vertically...as in the kipping pullup.

Mark Rippetoe: Changing the direction of motion requires force, in the same way that changing the velocity requires force. This change during a kipping pullup is assisted by the stretch reflex inherent in the eccentric component of the down-stroke. But there is no down stroke in a deadlift. If you roll the bar toward you at the start of a pull from the floor, you are 1.) introducing a horizontal motion component that will have to be cancelled before the vertical bar path can be expressed, and we do in fact want the bar to go *up*, and 2.) pulling from a position where the skeleton cannot transfer force optimally to the bar.

George Noble: But what about the first rep of a set of kipping pullups? That isn't assisted by a stretch reflex, but the horizontal movement still makes it easier. Right? And surely if you're well practised at deadlifting in this way, you'll be able to do it without ending up out of position, like the example of Andy Bolton bringing his hips down to the start position quickly.

Mark Rippetoe: A bodyweight exercise and a 1003 deadlift are not equivalent activities in terms of their use of a bodyweight-only stretch reflex.

George Noble: I know, and I wasn't comparing the two. My first point was that the horizontal movement in a kipping pullup is not coupled with a stretch reflex when it is done on the first rep of a set, yet it still makes the pullup easier. Can this not apply to the deadlift?

My point about Andy Bolton was in reference to
"2.) pulling from a position where the skeleton cannot transfer force optimally to the bar."
But if someone is really well practised at this, then wouldn't they be able to roll the bar back and pull it from the correct start position? The comparison to Andy was from this quote in a different thread, where you said that well practised people can get away with doing stuff that would pull most lifters out of position:

"Notorious: The slight advantage it might confer is eaten up by the disadvantage of getting the bar out of position into a place where the pull off the floor is harder. If you drop your ass – unless you're good at it like Andy – you'll shove the bar forward, and then it has to be pulled back in as it leaves the floor. Straight lines make better bar paths."

elVarouza: I notice Magnusson rolls the bar toward him before he starts his pull. I don't get the point though, because strictly horizontal movement does not translate into upward movement. Maybe the bar gets slight upward momentum upon hitting the legs, but who knows. What is it that Bolton does anyway? Is he trying to get a stretch reflex out of bringing his hips up and down quickly like that?

SkinnyWimp: Newton pretty much nailed this one a few hundred years ago. It is impossible to make something move up by applying only a sideways force to it. The corollary is that when applying only a sideways force to something, it won't move upwards. This doesn't even require gravity to be true.

Mark Rippetoe: Rolling the bar back in to the mid-foot before the bar leaves the ground is indeed what most lifters do. It can be done, albeit with less exact reproducibility than without the roll. Andy does *not* roll the bar; he just raises and lowers his hips a couple of times to stretch out his hamstrings before he sets his back. But my point is that horizontal movement is not useful in terms of making the bar go up, and that since the bar is going to leave the ground most efficiently from a position where the bar is directly over the mid-foot and directly under the scapulas, why not just put it there to begin with and call *that* the starting position?

Patrick: It's a comfort thing rather than a physics thing. Tiger Woods places his feet and wiggles his ass a dozen times before he hits his drive and that's pretty much all you need to know. The optimum deadlift starts with a vertical pull. However, because humans are not machines, sometimes the feel you get from a good controlled roll is used get a good pull going. You feel the right stretches, the right symmetry, the right grip, and so on. I'd rather see a guy bob up and down into and out of DL start position with a static bar to get the same effect but the roll seems more common for whatever reason, probably because it involved movement both of the lifter and of the bar.

There shouldn't be ANY controversy that the physics makes pulling a rolling bar harder. Getting to the bottom of why it might be so common despite that is useful, and I think that's what I've tried to get at above.

Knkavo: Considering that they roll the bar back before they start to lift it, and they are in fact performing a lift, then the start position is where they start lifting. Otherwise it would be called the "Roll & Deadlift". You could get points for rolling style, with a panel of judges like in figure skating (not that I have much against figure skaters, I bet those guys can squat a ton).

Mark Rippetoe: So, knkavo, you want the start position to be where the bar starts *moving*, and I want it to be where the bar starts moving *up*. Semantics such as this have served to make things fuzzy for quite some time.

Knkavo: Semantics are dangerous. Whole schools of philosophy have been hijacked to justify fascism/communism on the basis of semantics. I can only imagine what havoc that could wreak in the weightlifting world. And for the record, I try to make the start position to be where the bar starts moving *up*, just as you say. Sometimes, I do roll it a bit... (but the bouncing has *absolutely* been cut out of my deadlifts).

Ryan: The fact that Andy Bolton holds the WR for Deadlifts, and has something like 20 years of weight training experience, means that he is able to Deadlift however the hell he likes. If he thinks that rolling it, and rocking up and down will exhibit a stretch reflex he is more than welcome to do it, as I would rather see a 1003lbs deadlift completed with a bit of showmanship, then a 1003lbs deadlift missed, as he can't do whatever the hell he wants before the pull. Also notice how the bar will start over the correct starting point, before the vertical pull is started. How many people here are confident that they can find that position 10 times of 10, or on the last rep of a set, when you should be struggling to do anything.

Mark Rippetoe: This is a terribly important point: extraneous bar or body movement prior to the actual start of the pull serves to make the correct start less reproducible. Andy does not roll the bar. But one of the talents that good lifters have is being able to do things wrong the same way every time, so that they can get very good at doing them wrong the same way and thus compensate for the inefficiency adequately. Starting at the optimum position for the pull just eliminates wasted movement and makes it easier to do the same way each time.

Deadlift vs. Squat

Rbenz: I have a friend who talks to Mark Twight (Gym Jones Owner) regularly and abides by Twight's every word. He claims that 3x3 deadlift super-setted with box jumps is more beneficial than squatting and starting strength for his sprinting purposes, for he runs the 100 and 200 meter. His reason being the increase in lower back strength keeps his abdomen contracted along with his spinal erectors throughout his strides, and I have no idea what the super-setted box jumps would provide. This sounds like a bullshit training concept. I would think that the pulling movement of a deadlift would not benefit a runner quite like a hip drive squat which is where total-body power originates. He should do both, but claims deadlift is needed and squat will lead into overtraining for he has about a 430lb deadlift at 155lbs. Basically I need an argument against Mr. Twight's program he prescribed for my buddy.

Mark Rippetoe: I don't know that I have an argument against this approach, especially if you're dealing with an athlete that already has a decent squat. Obviously leg strength plays a pivotal role in spring ability, since force applied to the track must be generated by the legs. But think of the role of the low back in this cycle: front foot strikes, hip extensors pull through as knee extends, release, repeat. What does the pull-through act upon? Low back. It serves as an anchor against the pelvis as the hip is extended. If the lumbar arch is soft, some of the hip extension is absorbed in the flexing lumbar. If the lumbar arch is hard, all of the hip extension gets transferred from track to body without any of the ROM of the hip extension being wasted as the back flexes. We have improved the 40 yd. times of 13 y.o. kids with just deadlifts and back extensions. If the squat is not strong, this is an obvious hole in the training, but don't dismiss the effectiveness of deadlifting and ground reaction training for sprint performance.

The problem I'd have here is that the guy's deadlift is already 430 at 155, this may be an example of bad problem analysis: if the only tool you've got is a hammer, every problem begins to look like some kind of nail. I don't see the whole program here, but squats and deadlifts are both a part of a good sprinter's training.

Extra back work without screwing up SS

Dana: I have herniated L4 and L5 and twice in my life (last time was about 5 years ago) have had my lower back suddenly go out to the point where I was stuck in bed for a few weeks. By being very, very patient have managed to make decent progress via SS over the past 6 months, taking baby steps on the DL. I'm 180lbs, 5'10". DL is now at 285 for the set of 5. I'm starting to get that warning feeling from the lower back, and am thinking that some extra work would be a good idea, but don't want to mess things up. What's the best move? Keep the DL the same for a while? Add RDLs? Add extra DL sets with lighter weight and/or higher reps? Something else?

Luckily the low bar back squat seems to keep my back happy, so it's really just the DL that concerns me. My Power Clean weight isn't heavy enough to cause trouble at this point. FWIW, my back feels most unstable about halfway through the DL, when the bar is just clearing my knees.

Mark Rippetoe: If I were you, I'd be content with the 285 and start adding in RDLs, SLDLs, reverse hypers, glute/hams, haltings, and rack pulls. In other words, your injury history requires that you establish a different goal for your back training than a 500 deadlift. But post a video and let me see your form, because the instability you describe might be a back angle issue.

bgates1654: I would suggest back extensions to lactic acid threshold at least 3 times a week. Don't make them jerky, just slow up/down. If you can do more than 25 reps before hitting the lactic acid threshold, slow down or add weight. If you are worried about repeated spine movement, then I would suggest good mornings instead of back extensions. Either way the point is to get the healing effects of lactic acid in your back.

Mark Rippetoe: You don't think goodmornings involve spinal movement? Loaded spinal movement? Standard goodmornings are essentially defined as flexion and extension of the spine under a compressive load. Even flat-back goodmornings take the spine from compression into maximum torque by turning the distance from the bar to the hip into a moment arm. This is not a bad thing, since it's inherent in any movement that functions as an effective back exercise, but it is hard for an injured back to counter if the moment arm is changing from 0 to maximum around the ROM of the exercise. The force is not really shear, since the bony anatomy is constructed with overlap between vertebral segments and shear is not actually possible. It is actually tension, because what you are resisting is spinal flexion, and flexion involves the pulling apart of the adjacent spinous processes. Extension is maintained by keeping sufficient tension along the posterior lumbar spine. Anyway, goodmornings are just about the last thing I'd have someone with a disc injury doing.

Rounded back lifts

TravisRussellDC: I'm curious as to what you think about some of the rounded back lifts. I know you mentioned them as an advanced exercise in SS along side a picture of stone lifting. Now, I've never performed rounded back good mornings. But I swear by stiff leg deadlifts standing on a box as the best way to train for lifting stones off the ground. Taking the barbell through a full ROM so the bar touches the tops of my shoes has helped my stone loading more than anything else. I've been able to work up to the mid 400's for sets of 5's without incident.

Now, my question comes because I had done these for years up until about a year ago. Perhaps due to my chiropractic training, I started to think that the rounding of the lumbars was a major no-no and I was just asking for an injury due to the shear force on the discs. However, the only time I ever injured my low back was coming a little too far forward with a high bar squat back in May, after not performing full ROM stiff legs for months.

I understand that rounded back lifts like these are an advanced exercise. But I was curious if you had any further opinions of them. I've always thought that if you build up the muscles around the joint to be as strong as steel cables, then the chance of injury is drastically decreased. I would never want an untrained individual to attempt to lift a heavy weight with a rounded back. But I've felt like they have kept me from having lower back issues in my many years of heavy training.

Mark Rippetoe: Really and truly, a spine cannot shear in the absence of a dynamic trauma, and the force applied to the spine by a load is compression and torque, or more correctly *moment*. I think that in light of the fact that most people lift heavy things "incorrectly" in terms of the proper extended lumbar and thoracic spinal position, that they always have and always will, and that most people are still fine having done it this way, some rounded back lifting is good practice for what will inevitably occur in the course of working with heavy objects. The back can get stronger more safely if most work is done in normal anatomical position – thoracic and lumbar extension – but some round-back work gets you strong in this position and lets you practice staying tight and controlled in spinal flexion. Since it's going to happen anyway, you might as well prepare for it.

Anterior Valsalva force

Phillipo: In Starting Strength you discuss how both the Valsalva Maneuver and the weight belt are meant to provide anterior force on the spinal column in order to stabilize it and protect it from injury due to shear or rotational force. Yet when a heavy weighted barbell is on the back it tends to cause rounding in the posterior direction of this chain as is evidenced by the rounding of the back and loss of lordotic curve at heavy weights. If the bar causes rounding in the posterior direction, why is it that anterior force is required for stabilization, not posterior force? I have an image in my head that the increased thoracic pressure created by a contracted diaphragm would push in the opposite direction of the natural lordotic curve and exacerbate the problem. Can you please clear this up for me?

Mark Rippetoe: The spinal position, meaning specifically the intervertebral relationships, is established by the posterior spinal musculature. These curves are then reinforced from the anterior by the pressure head generated by the abs, all the lateral trunk muscles, the costal muscles, and the Valsalva. The spine comes into flexion when the weight is too heavy or when control is relinquished, but this control is best thought of as spinal *rigidity*, a quantity controlled by both posterior and anterior muscular force.

Knees Out

Michael P: Is it possible to shove the knees too far out under load? I was trying to make sure of this on my last lifting day and during lighter loads, it feels as if the weight over my feet actually rolled to the outside of my lifting shoes. Not that I lifted up the inside to roll the shoe over, but I could feel the weight distribution really moving to the outside of the foot. As weight went up, I don't know if I felt this any more...as I was a little preoccupied with all of the freakin' weight on my back, but my secondary question would be...would the above scenario maybe indicate that my stance is not wide enough? All I can tell you is that the next day, my hamstrings, and inside groin muscles were ROCK'd hard. They were as sore as they have ever been.

Mark Rippetoe: "Too far" would occur if the weight distribution between your shoe and the floor changes to the point that the medial side deloads. It's more likely to happen with a narrow stance, or if your flexibility is excessive. It's very hard to do this for most people since adductor tension usually cannot be overcome to this extent.

Too much horizontal back angle during squat?

Speediskey: I know in your book and some videos you say to create hip drive during the squat, it's ok to decrease your back angle. I was wondering if your back can become too horizontal during the lift. Yesterday someone told my that I shouldn't bend over so much, but then again the same person told me I don't need to go to parallel.

Mark Rippetoe: If you think about the squat like it's a goodmorning, obviously it can become too horizontal, increasing the moment against the hip joints and making the bar drift forward of the balance point on the mid-foot. Don't do this.

elVarouza: I've been kind of curious about the distinction of 'good-morning-ing' a squat. Would it only be considering a 'good-morning' if the bar drifts ahead of the mid-foot? For example, is it "alright" if a strong hip drive inclines the back angle quite a bit, but keeps the bar over the mid-foot? An example of this can be seen in the second rep in the video of Captain Kirk's 1000lb x 2.

Chris: I leaned forward too much when I was teaching myself the back squat out of SS. I wound up getting very sore hips, which I think was due to bursitis but I am no expert. I had to go off the program and am still recovering, somewhat. When I later examined my videos and videos of Rip teaching, my "loss of back angle" was so damn drastic it was downright dangerous. I was doing 300# squats with a killer hip drive, losing tons of back angle and doing a 300# Good Morning out of the top. My hips would literally rise about 5-12 inches before my back started its ascent.

Mark Rippetoe: To begin with, I don't regard Karwoski's squat as having too horizontal a back at all, and had the bar actually been forward of the mid-foot with that much weight he would have dumped it; he didn't, so it wasn't. The man squatted a lot of weight like that with way less equipment that is used today, and it seemed to work just fine. The back angle should actually be established about 1/3-1/2 of the way down, and not change until you get back up to about the same place. The thing you see at the bottom is just enough change in position to indicate that hip drive has taken place – no more than a couple of degrees, both of which are restored to the angle immediately. If you let your chest cave, Chris, you have permitted your hamstrings to fail in their job of holding the back angle constant as the hips and knees extend. "Chest up" is the cue that fixes this, but don't confuse it with "lifting the chest", which would be a steepening of the back angle.

Patella related mechanics during squats

Ronen: The particular question I wanted to ask you relates to the relationship between the Femur/Tibia and the Patella during squats. With the amount of pressure that is applied to the three areas of the leg, is there a Grinding Effect when doing the exercise that produces pressure on the Patella against the Femur or the Tibia? If not, what are the mechanics that prevents this pressure from happening?

Mark Rippetoe: The patella is anchored in place by the patellar ligament and the retinaculum, so its relationship to the femoral condyles – the knobs on either side of the distal end of the femur – is held constant by these ligaments. The meniscii cushion the rolling action of the femoral and tibial condyles against each other, and the cartilage of the undersurface of the patella rolling against the hyaline cartilage of the femoral condyles performs the same function. "Grinding" requires a non-smooth surface, and the components of a normal knee lack non-smoothness. A healthy joint is essentially frictionless.

Question regarding deadlifts & straps

bobp718: You have spelled out in your text that the use of lifting straps isn't a good idea and in theory I agree with you. The problem is that I have these little girl hands and I can't really keep a weight that is challenging to DL in my hands, even with an alternated grip. The problem is of such magnitude that I have taken to performing three sets of five DL's as opposed to the one set prescribed in SS:BBT because the weight that I can carry in my hands is insufficient to bring about a homeostatic perturbation in response to a single set of DL's. (Or at least this is my thought.) With linear progression it's getting to the point where the bar is slipping out of my hands prematurely during the 2nd and 3rd sets now.

Do you suggest retarding my progress as the cost of developing grip strength or biting the bullet and utilizing straps on at least the last set? Should I have added the 2nd or 3rd set of DL's at all? I don't want to second guess you coach, but this is what I thought would illicit my body to respond to DL's.

Mark Rippetoe: How long are your fingers? Measured form the palmar/digital fold, my middle finger is 3 3/8" long, and with my hand around the bar the end of the finger touches the palmaris of the thumb. If they are close to this long it is a grip strength problem that needs to be addressed. If you have very short fingers you'd might as well strap, because there is no way I know of to get strong enough to hold a heavy deadlift. I had a training partner once who could pull 675 off the ground, but his PR deadlift was 518. Short fingers, fat hand. We tried everything, believe me.

Clay: My finger is only 8cm long (no idea what that is in inches) I think about the same size as yours from the tape measure though. Yet my grip absolutely sucks in deadlifts. I'm pulling 155kg and have to use an alternate grip. I even have to alternate my grip between reps. I'll do the first couple with my left hand supine and the next couple with my right, then back to left. I can do my last warm up set, 125kgx2 with DOH but not even one rep of my working set weight.

Would this be finger length stuffing me up or is my grip just pathetically weak? If the latter, what exercises should I add, if any, to my SS program to increase grip strength and assist in being able to use a DOH in my deadlifts. If the former, am I just destined to be a lousy deadlifter?

bobp718: My middle finger is about 2-7/8". Might this be the reason that I haven't had any luck applying a hook grip to the bar? I thought that I might have been applying it incorrectly but it could be my body geometry working against me?

Mark Rippetoe: 8 cm is about the same as mine, 2-7/8" is enough shorter that it is significant. But don't misunderstand my finger length comment: the issue is not merely finger length, but finger length vs. palm thickness. If your hand is not fat, 2 7/8 may be plenty of finger length. And most people do not have a pull that exceeds their grip strength until the competitive PL level. It happens frequently there, but not usually with guys that don't train for competition.

Pistol Squats - any point at all?

travelgirl1978: Is there any benefit to doing one-legged bodyweight (pistol) squats? I was thinking they just might be useful when traveling and away from a good gym for a few weeks, or something. I was also thinking that they might be a really good way to screw up ligaments and tendons.

Mark Rippetoe: They might be useful in a gymless environment, but so are high-rep vertical jumps, and they are 1.) easier on the knees, and 2.) more applicable to general strength development since they are bi-lateral.

Karpasia: Practicing pistols gave me a healthy dose of tendonitis in my quadriceps insertion that is still annoying me 2 months later.

Jefferson: What's the point of high rep vertical jumps apart from endurance?

Brad: I'm curious why pistols are hard on the knees. Not arguing, but I'm curious as to your reasoning. For the record, they HAVE always killed my knees regardless of how gently I work up to them, how careful my form is, etc. I'm a little curious if there are inherent "issues" with them.

Mark Rippetoe: It depends on how you do them, but just look at the position you're in at the bottom. When I was squatting 600 I never did them because they always felt like they were going to destroy my knee. And high-rep vertical jumps are *not* an endurance workout. Jogging 5 miles is an endurance workout. Try 20 reps for 3 sets and see what you think.

Polynomial: My guess is that to keep balanced, people sacrifice lumbar extension, disabling the hamstrings to counter the pull of the quads. I might be completely off on that, though.

Mark Rippetoe: No, that's very good. You've probably explained it precisely.

Revisiting the Trap-Bar "Squat-Lift"

fedor1: I was wondering if you had given additional thought to the aforementioned lift. In the past you have called the lift silly and not useful as a pull. You have also stated it 'makes more sense' as a squat movement. Having lifted decent weight (300+ at 190 pounds) weight using both movements, I recall form being much easier to maintain with the trap bar. It also seems like a much safer lift, as the weight is distributed around you instead of on top of you etc.

Now I totally understand your likely response ("The squat works great and isn't all that hard to learn, wtf do I care about something 'like' the squat?"), but if there is a free-weight lift as effective as the squat(?), yet much easier to learn and safer (especially for the train-alone type) don't you feel more thought on the subject should be given?

Mark Rippetoe: This part is good: *"if there is a free-weight lift as effective as the squat(?), yet much easier to learn and safer (especially for the train alone type) don't you feel more thought on the subject should be given?"* Now, why can't you see the fundamental differences between an exercise using the bar on the back and a start position that allows for an eccentric-concentric cycle, and an exercise with a bar-thingy hanging from the hands that's kinda like a deadlift but unstable at the top because the bar is not locked against the thighs? Why should things be easy to learn? How is the trap bar safer? And why in god's name do you think I haven't thought about this?

High rep DLs

Ian Kovtunovich: I was watching the 2009 CF Games NorCal qualifiers, and noticed that the workout included 22 reps of deadlifts. This got me thinking about your admonishment against doing DLs for sets across, and how that jives with some of CF's programming. I notice that "Diane," for instance, features 21-15-9 of DLs, and I've seen some other WODs that have a high number of them. Obviously you must not feel that workouts of this nature are not too foolhardy. I wonder, though, what percentage of a trainee's work set weight would you typically deem as safe for high-rep DLs? And what guidance might you give for safely incorporating DLs into high-rep and high-intensity workouts?

Mark Rippetoe: High-rep deadlifts are a wonderful metcon exercise, perfectly safe at weights you can do for 21 reps even when done wrong like most CFers do them. The current vogue is to bounce them off the floor to decrease the time and "increase the intensity", with no attention paid to the lumbar extension. It is important to recognize that the work of muscular contraction that is done when the back is set in extension between reps, although not measurable in foot-pounds, is work nonetheless. The pulling together of the z-lines in the sarcomeres of the erector spinae and the holding of this position of isometric contraction consumes ATP. That's why it's easier to go faster if you don't do it, and therefore why your intensity decreases if you sacrifice good spinal position for a faster time.

Tsypkin: Would you contend that there is no benefit to doing them faster and sacrificing form, assuming that technique is maintained at least at a level to keep the athlete safe and assure full ROM? Should it be done perfectly every time you do a WOD, or are there advantages to going faster with worse form half the time you do "Diane," or "Grace," or "Isabel," and using ideal (or closer to ideal) form the other half of the time?

Mark Rippetoe: Why don't you just go faster with an extended lumbar spine all the time? You can't, eh? Must mean there's more work to do that way. Faster time with shitty form creates holes in the final results.

Tsypkin: Actually, I've found that I can't actually go faster with shitty form. If I make my form during "Grace" 100% perfect it'll slow down, but if my form is good, say 90% of as close to ideal as I can get - i.e. lumbar extension, explosive jump, quick pull under and fast elbows, I move much faster than I would if I had a soft back/bent arms, etc. If I am doing fast deadlifts at 225#, keeping my spine in extension causes me to move faster, not slower. Assuming that I am not an anomaly, and better mechanics do in fact create more efficient (i.e., faster) movement, why do you think so many people do it poorly? Is it just too much work to invest the necessary effort into getting better at the lifts or what?

Mark Rippetoe: If you assume that the only work being done is on the bar, and that work done on the bar is the only measure of the work being done, I think you are ignoring the fact that the whole system – bar and body – has to be included in the work calculation. There is demonstrably less work being done by the spinal erectors, for example, if their constituent z-lines are not held in contraction and the spinal ligaments are being relied on solely for support. Is the work of isometric spinal position-holding easily quantifiable? No. But does that mean it is not being done? Is an isometrically-held position not consumptive of energy?

There is a weight for every lifter that is light enough that correct position-holding mechanics – the stuff necessary for the completion of 1RMs – is not a critical factor in the completion of lots of light reps, especially reps bounced off the floor using bumper plates. But 30 pulls of any type done with the spine held in extension and reset from a dead stop will always involve more ATP-consuming muscular work than 30 bounced reps done with Superball™ plates and the spinal erectors allowed to relax and the spinal ligaments allowed to carry the relatively light load. The bar moves the same distance, granted, but the harder-to-quantify isometric work done by the position-holding muscles cannot be ignored in an accurate assessment of the effort, and this extra work is easily observable in the increased time involved in the stricter version of the set.

You Know How Fond I Am of Seafood

I once ate 225 shrimp in one hour. It's actually not that difficult, mechanically at least. You get better at peeling them with practice. I used to eat a lot more than I do now, and several all-you-can-eat buffets served as a testing ground for weight-gaining techniques that are now out of fashion, what with all this idiotic misplaced concern for eating "healthy." When an athlete needs to be bigger, there are a couple of ways that work really well, despite the fact that they may be viewed with distaste by the more gentle members of society.

SS and diet for the tree-hugging fatass

SixtySix: I'm 6'5", about 290, with probably 28% BF (using the military method of calculating BF via neck/weight measurements). My lifts for 5x3 are: Squats 245, bench 205, and deadlifts 275 (5x1 on the deads). I am using the SS workout, and I'm on about week three. It's going very well, and I feel stronger, more energetic, and overall healthier. I follow it strictly, and do the workout exactly as listed in SS.

My only question is in regards to diet. I am fatter than I'd like to be (I'm not worried about abs, but I've got a 48" waist, so I could use a bit of a trim down). I'm currently eating approximately 2500 calories/day with around 225-250 g of protein. I should mention that I am a vegetarian (I know, I know...I am a hopeless gaywad and I pray for death daily). Actually, I am pretty much a vegan with the sole exception of whey protein. I take about 150-200 g of ion-exchange whey protein per day, as the rest of my diet is obviously lacking in major sources of non-plant protein.

With all of that tremendously uninteresting background aside, am I on the right track to lose weight while building a decent strength base? I know that I am in a pretty significant caloric deficit and won't be putting on a lot of mass, but I feel that if I can get rid of some of this fat over the next few months I can up my calories and look to accelerate my gains. The only reason I am fucking around like this at all is that I'm looking to join a police department and I need to drop my bodyfat.

Mark Rippetoe: The gross numbers look pretty good for sustained progress and bodyfat loss, until the vegan silliness begins to interfere with recovery when you get up to bigger weights and bigger stress loads. Until then, you'll be fine. A vegan policeman.

KSC: I guess you had no sympathy for the milk when the whey and casein were savagely torn apart from each other after spending a lifetime together, and then the whey was tortured further by having its ions exchanged.

Caloric deficit and strength gains

Brian: I was interested to know what experience Rip has with training people who are losing weight. I'm not talking obese, and I'm not talking about someone training for a bodybuilding contest. A flabby adult lifter, basically. If they're dieting (nothing too severe and assuming adequate protein intake) how does it affect their strength gains?

Do you have them make smaller jumps? Would you make any changes to their routine? There seems to be tons of information about losing weight as it relates to bodybuilding, but less for strength training. But surely some athletes are trying to lose some weight (boxers for example).

So what's a reasonable strategy for someone wanting to attain, say, a reasonable 15% body fat level while getting stronger at the same time (not bigger - I understand the difference)?

Mark Rippetoe: First, unless your body fat is only 20% right now, and depending on your age, 15% might be tough. Maybe it would be better if you told me your age, current body fat, and training history before I piss you off any more.

Brian: Yeah, I should have been more specific, especially since many people don't consider themselves "adults" until the age of 40 and it makes me sound geriatric. I'm 25, an intermediate trainee (training for a little over a year) and about 25-30% body fat. I need to lose about 30 lbs, I think. I'm currently doing the TM workout from practical programming. I don't actually have a problem losing weight, per se. I know about adequate protein, etc., and I am losing steadily (1.5-2 lb/week). I'm essentially on track training-wise at the gym as of two weeks ago, but I feel more sore than usual and it feels more taxing on my body. I'm wondering if I'm still going to be making progress in a few weeks or whether the strength will start leaking out.

I know I haven't stalled yet, but I'd rather maintain some progress, even if it's smaller rather than hit a wall early on. I'm interested to know what you've done with other people like me and how they managed.

Mark Rippetoe: If you are losing a couple of pounds a week and continuing to maintain a strength increase, that's about as good as you can do. With your training history, age, and current body fat levels, a strength increase occurring with a weight loss means body fat is coming off. If you haven't stalled, things are going well. If you're worried about soreness that is above normal, up your protein intake another 50 grams and see what happens. If this fixes the problem you'll know in 3-4 days.

Supplements for preserving joint healthiness

FROGGBUSTER: Through your many years involved in strength training, are there any standout supplements that you would recommend to preserve joint healthiness or help heal injured cartilage/ligaments?

Mark Rippetoe: Glucosamine and chondroitin sulfate work well for some people, not for others. MSM is probably a waste of money, as are blends of all three that cost huge dollars. I'd try the first two and see if they work for you.

---

nutrition for older guys

wecoyote: Should there be any difference for SS nutrition for older guys (40 and up) versus younger guys. More to the point, should I consume the same amount of milk? I will have to say that SS and CrossFit have been the best programs that I have ever used. I have four compressed discs in my lower back that hurts every day but feels much better after my SS workouts. My orthopedic surgeon encourages lifting heavy as a matter of keeping strong.

Mark Rippetoe: Unless you are in a weight-gain situation, no, don't drink all that milk. Just eat enough to train and get recovered and things will progress just fine. The milk deal works best for the young and the underweight, and it will just make older guys of normal weight fat.

Ryan: Let me piggy back on this thread. I'm 33 and 5'7 170, so I wouldn't say I 'need' to gain weight. I don't care about mass, I just want to get as strong as possible as quickly as possible. I'm on my second week of SS and I've been drinking a gallon a day of whole milk, as a matter of fact I think I'm closer to 173 now. Should I continue the milk, or will I get the same strength results with out it?

Mark Rippetoe: I think you should stay with the proven method until you have a reason to change it. Fat is easier to lose than muscle is to gain.

Billy: What do you think about whey protein shakes? I'm a fat piece of shit and can't lose weight, and still I feel like eating 250 grams of protein per day (1 gm per pound bodyweight) is difficult. Now if coffee consumption counted toward my nutritional goals I'd be fit as a fiddle...

Mark Rippetoe: You may be a fat piece of shit, but it is wrong to say that you can't lose weight. It would be more correct to say that you have yet to decide that you are going to do what's necessary to lose weight. I think whey protein shakes are useful but not absolutely necessary.

SS, milk, and a big fat guy?

Johan: I have one question, I am 6'2, 311#, 28, I am a former football tackle looking to get back in shape, and I wanted to get back down to around 245#. When I trained before and needed to lose weight, I would diet while lifting, drinking no milk or maybe some skim. My friend Rob says I should keep eating, and drink the gallon of milk to build muscle which will wear down the fat. I think this will make me gain weight. Who's right?

Mark Rippetoe: You're right. Why would an overweight/overfat guy want to go on a program specifically designed to make a skinny kid gain weight?

Danish Viking: This intrigues me. Are you (Rip) saying that this programme should not be used for people trying to lose weight? My personal experience has always been that a solid strength programme is what works for me, whether I am trying to lose or gain weight. The variable, then, is usually diet. Maybe that's what you're saying, but your phrasing kind of got me wondering.

Mark Rippetoe: I thought I was clear: people trying to lose weight should *not* be on a diet designed to make people gain weight.

Peter_k: Well, IMO you weren't very clear at first. You said an overfat individual shouldn't be on a "program" designed for skinny kids. It sounds like you were saying the SS lifting program is only designed for skinny kids, not just the associated diet.

Mark Rippetoe: The SS lifting program is designed for novices of all types. To this can be added the GOMAD diet if weight gain is desired.

Small jumps and linear progress

Peter_k: I'm pretty much at the end of my novice phase and am making small jumps of 1-2 lbs a week on BP and Press. The thing is, even these jumps seem to be too big. For example, for the new weight of 120 I'll do 1x5, 1x3, 1x3 and then the next workout 1x5, 1x4, 1x4 and then finally get it on the third workout. So I'm not exactly stalling, but making very slow progress overall. I'm eating around maintenance or slightly below now and getting enough protein (I'm already overweight so I'm not drinking the huge quantity of milk).

My question is: is being reduced to a slow crawl as bad as stalling outright? I mean, should I wait until I'm truly stuck at the same weight for several workouts before considering intermediate programming? Or, is this probably a function of reduced calories and I should just accept any progress as fine at this point?

Mark Rippetoe: Everybody will slow to a crawl before they get stuck, IF they have done the program properly, so you're okay there. But eating at "maintenance" is the problem, because you're not trying to MAINTAIN, you're trying to grow bigger muscles to help you be stronger and burn fat. Rethink.

Peter_k: When I eat a lot, my strength shoots up. But the fat also comes on. I was thinking maybe to give myself a slight calorie surplus, gain a little bit more "good" weight, and start losing once I'm in the intermediate phase. Is it generally easier for people to drop weight once they're in the intermediate stage, because they aren't gaining as much strength anyway?

Mark Rippetoe: It is easier to drop bodyfat than it is to gain strength, so you're worried about the easy thing when the hard thing ought to be your primary concern.

Milk and the midnight toilet break

Astro: I just started drinking the prescribed amount of milk with my 6 meals spread throughout the day and occasionally I have the tendency to wake up in the middle of the night to do a massive piss. I have pretty much stopped drinking water throughout the day except during training. Is there anything I can do to stop this because I'm sure broken sleep affects recovery as much as it makes me feel like shit for the rest of the day? The only thing I can think of is to take the milk from the last meal and have it earlier in the day.

Mark Rippetoe: I think you figured it out, George Jetson's Dog. Timing is critical.

Another Milk Question

Whatupdun: If you had a guy, let's say this fellow is 200lbs and stands 75 in. He's gaining 1 to 2 lbs a week on your BBT template, adding weight each time and is approaching or firmly seated in the intermediate strength standards listed in the back of PP for each of the 5 lifts (yes, he's still making linear progress, and yes, goddammit, he's doing power cleans on B days;)).

Let's say this fellow's 1 to 2 lbs a week weight gain is mostly muscle, and he notices a slight pudge as well. He's eating 3500-4000 calories on the work days and 3000-3500 on the rest days to get these gains. He's not overly concerned with gaining some fat (within reason), and he understands that simply pumping more food into his gullet won't result in more lean gains, but will instead add a little more fat than he's used to.

This handsome young man has become keen on the idea of milk drinking. Check that, he's curious about drinking a gallon a day. The thing is, since he already eats 6 to 8 small meals a day (including post-workout shake), he wonders if he can benefit from it. He already takes a protein powder that's enriched with IGF-1, and he feels like that product has helped his gains. He also knows that milk has a good amount of that same growth factor, so he wants to drink more.

With all this in mind, he's thought of a few options:
1. add the milk on top of the normal diet (he thinks this may only help him get fatter)
2. significantly alter his diet to keep a similar caloric input, but include a gallon of milk
3. alter his diet a little and add a quart or half gallon of milk a day.

He wonders:
-Since adding a gallon of whole milk on top of his already sufficient-for-gains diet will likely increase his body fat *far* more than his lean gains, is this a sensible option?
-Since he's already eating at least 100g of fat a day, including cheese, olive oil -- a bunch of good tasty foods (he's not scared of saturated fats, and understands their role in hormone synthesis) -- since he's already getting at least 100g of fat a day, could he get good results from drinking a gallon of skim milk? It's probably gonna have the same amount of IGF-1 and other beneficial elements, just with less fat (which he already gets a good amount of).
-Is it wise for him to swap out some solid food, and replace it with milk?
-If he swaps out *some* food for a quart or half gallon of milk, is this worth the effort, and would you expect his gains to improve, even with a similar caloric input?
Bonus question:
-If he were a pussy, would soy milk be a suitable substitute?

You know what, just a simple chuckle is fine for the last one, but I'm really curious about how I can best integrate more milk into my diet, which is already producing good (but can always be better?) gains. I'm getting at least a quart a day, sometimes up to a half-gallon, and it's usually skim or 2%.

Mark Rippetoe: I like this handsome, literate, undoubtedly intelligent, young raging-hormonal-beast of a man's option number 2: significantly alter his diet to keep a similar caloric input, but include a gallon of milk, which I think he would do anyway without a lot of weighing and measuring due to his vast experience with his own belly and its fullness/emptiness situation. But I am not necessarily convinced that his statement: "*Since adding a gallon of whole milk on top of his already sufficient-for-gains diet will likely increase his body fat *far* more than his lean gains*" is absolutely true. It may not be, and even if it does it would not create an unmanageable situation for THIS young man; anybody this adept at dialing in his diet will have no trouble taking off 3% bodyfat when it is necessary to do so, and will be aided in this endeavor by the slabs of muscle that have been laid down due to the anabolic conditions made possible by the extra calories, milk (Nature's Steroid!!!) and the heavy training he is obviously motivated to do since he has taken the time and trouble to learn how to do Power Cleans.

Bonus answer: Soy milk is essentially Coffee-Mate laced with estrogen, and is best left to vegans and other socialist vegetarian types that can't bring themselves to eat the completely natural-for-humans flesh and milk of our friends The Animals, but who have no trouble with slaughtering trillions of our other friends The Plants and processing – in gigantic factories run by multinational corporations with shareholders that eat meat themselves – very selectively chosen components of their poor little bodies into gooey shit that humans have never had an opportunity to adapt to digesting. Why, eating such material, with its high levels of isoflavones, touted by gynecologists as tantamount to Estrogen Replacement Therapy (ERT), will make you grow boobs, and this will screw up the clean lines of this fine young man's Under Armor. I recommend against it.

Milk it! (The Famous Very Long Milk Thread)

Butter: Howdy. I'm a big fan of drinking the good stuff, is the other types of Milks available almost as beneficial as Whole Milk?

Mark Rippetoe: I like whole milk because one of the problems in gaining weight is calories, and obviously whole milk wins on this criterion. Why would a person concerned with gaining weight be concerned with the fat content of milk?

progressiveman1: I'm concerned with the saturated fat in whole milk, which is why I think skim milk is a better choice. Saturated fat is known to clog arteries so cutting it in particular parts of your diet would probably be beneficial long-term. Per serving, there is 5g of saturated fat/150 calories in whole milk and 0g of saturated fat/90 calories in skim milk. Given that there's only that small amount more of calories in whole milk, don't you think it would be wiser to make up that difference in calories in a more efficient manner? There are plenty of foods which contain 5g of saturated fat that have several hundred calories in them as opposed to just the 60 calories difference in the milk alternatives. So if you're going to eat 5g of saturated fat, you might as well get a bang for your buck.

Mark Rippetoe: What is your concern with saturated fat? And please be specific when you detail the detrimental effects.

progressiveman1: You just made me realize that I made a stupid mistake - accepting claims without seeking proper evidence for it. I accepted the claim that saturated fats cause heart disease because it seemed like all the big health organizations tout this as a fact:

1. American Heart Assoc.
2. World Health Organization
3. FDA: I think they're the ones who create the guidelines on the food labels, which state a strict limitation on saturated fats.

Those are just the top few from doing a quick search, so I'm sure there's plenty more organizations who make the same claims.

But after digging a little deeper, it's starting to make more sense to me that eating a diet high in saturated fats (and low in processed foods) is the healthiest way to go. However, I can't say that I can make a strong claim on the issue because there are so many studies that "prove" saturated fats are unhealthy and plenty "prove" that they are healthy. It's hard to sort through all the contradictive information.

Mark Rippetoe: The deal with saturated fat is that, above all, it is not poison. No study in existence has ever shown that saturated fat causes cardiovascular disease, and its presence in a food that is useful should not prevent you from using it in your diet. No one is suggesting that you get half of your calories from the "butter" they use on movie popcorn, but whole milk for a growing young lifter is much more valuable than the fat it contains is dangerous. Milk is quite literally better than steroids for a novice lifter to grow on, and no supplement produces the same effect.

3pack: Any suggestions for a milk replacement for us lactose intolerant folks. I have tried Lactaid with limited success. It's weird - it seems to work at first and then stop working within a week or two and gets worse. I then up my intake of pills and lower my milk consumption to see where a good balance is and it doesn't help.

Mark Rippetoe: There is no substitute for milk. Sorry.

Corey: With regards to milk. I'm 36 YO. Should I be drinking milk to assist growth? I do whey protein morning and night. That and L-Glut are my only two supplements. I have been a pretty big milk drinker, but have given it up from time to time. I thought the sugar in the milk was making me fat.

Mark Rippetoe: Older adults using milk for weight gain may find that they get a little chubby on this program. This is because as growth hormone and testosterone levels diminish with age, the ability to easily build muscle on a heavy training program diminishes as well. This means that less of the nutritional input can be converted to muscle in response to stress, and consequently more fat will be deposited.

This is a rotten, shitty fact. I personally am offended every time I contemplate this. But the fact remains that older lifters cannot grow as efficiently in response to training as younger lifters can because of their inability to recover, and the efficient conversion of nutrition to muscle is a major factor in recovery.

Tiburon: With all due respect Coach, there are dozens of studies that implicate the role of saturated fat in cardiovascular disease. Here are just a couple epi studies:

-In the Nurses Health Study, for every 5% increase of calories from saturated fat, risk of coronary heart disease increased 17% (Hu et al., Dietary fat intake and the risk of coronary heart disease in women. New England Journal of Medicine 337 (21), pp. 1491-1499).

-In a study of 3500 Danes, every 3% increase in energy from saturated fat increased risk of CHD 36% in women (Jakobsen et al., Dietary fat and risk of coronary heart disease: Possible effect modification by gender and age. 2004 American Journal of Epidemiology, 160 (2), pp. 141-149).

As for the mechanisms:
-Harmful effects of saturated fat work through its effect on total cholesterol; it has been shown for a long time, in experimental studies, that saturated fat is twice as potent at raising total cholesterol as PUFA (polyunsaturated fat) is at lowering it (Keys et al, Serum cholesterol response to changes in the diet. (1965) Metabolism, 14, p. 776. and Hegsted et al, Quantitative effects of dietary fat on serum cholesterol in man. (1965) American Journal of Clinical Nutrition, 17 (5), pp. 281-295.).

-Intake of saturated fat also raises LDL, the "bad" cholesterol. For every 1% increase in energy from saturated fat, LDL increases approximately .03 to 0.5 mmol/L (Clarke et al., Dietary lipids and blood cholesterol: Quantitative meta-analysis of metabolic ward studies (1997) British Medical Journal, 314 (7074), pp. 112-117.)

-Because of reams of evidence supporting the above, the National Academy of Sciences and the Institute of Medicine recommend keeping saturated fat intake as **low as possible**. (emphasis mine) (IOM, (2002) Dietary Reference Intakes for Energy, Carbohydrate, Fiber, Fat, Fatty Acids, Cholesterol, Protein, and Amino Acids (Macronutrients). Washington, DC: National Academies Press

-As for a specific target, the National Cholesterol Education Program recommends keeping saturated fat to less than 7% of total calories, in order to LDL and reduce CVD events (Cleeman, J.I. Executive summary of the third report of the National Cholesterol Education Program (NCEP) expert panel on detection, evaluation, and treatment of high blood cholesterol in adults (adult treatment panel III) (2001) Journal of the American Medical Association, 285 (19), pp. 2486-2497.

-While it is true that saturated fat is not the only player here, or the only target for intervention (other lipids/lipoproteins, markers of oxidative stress, inflammations, insulin resistance, thrombosis, etc), it is probably *best* to get your sat fat intake as low as possible, within the context of an otherwise nutritionally adequate diet. keeping saturated fat to less than 7% of total calories, in order to LDL and reduce CVD events (Cleeman, J.I. Executive summary of the third report of the National Cholesterol Education Program (NCEP) expert panel on detection, evaluation, and treatment of high blood cholesterol in adults (adult treatment panel III) (2001) Journal of the American Medical Association, 285 (19), pp. 2486-2497.

-While it is true that saturated fat is not the only player here, or the only target for intervention (other lipids/lipoproteins, markers of oxidative stress, inflammations, insulin resistance, thrombosis, etc), it is probably *best* to get your sat fat intake as low as possible, within the context of an otherwise nutritionally adequate diet.

Mark Rippetoe: Likewise, with all due respect, I am not particularly interested in correlational implications. I said that saturated fat has never been shown to cause CVD, and I stand by that statement. SF intake level and its correlation with total cholesterol, and TC's correlation with CVD in self-reported studies on sedentary populations aren't terribly compelling and are not relevant to the folks reading this board. Do you actually think I am not aware of the body of literature on this topic? I am as capable as you are of reading them and drawing conclusions, and it irritates me that correlation and cause-and-effect are so often conflated, becoming the source of most of the conventional wisdom regarding matters of health and exercise.

EIC: I agree 100%. The idea that saturated fats are harmful is rapidly being extinguished both in society and in the scientific community. For every study cited above, there are at least 3 doctors I can think of that have had decades of success with patients by limiting carbohydrates and allowing patients to eat freely of saturated fat. Remember that when you start implicating saturated fat as "deadly," you start implicating a host of natural foods that man had ready access to in the wild: eggs and meat. Grains, the source of food that is touted as healthy by the authors of the studies cited above, only came into the picture far later.

As a purely logical matter, you should be highly suspect of any physician who tells you that man's most natural sources of nutrition are deadly. What's next? A study showing that rabbits shouldn't eat grass or that squirrels shouldn't eat acorns?

When saturated fat is consumed in carbohydrate-controlled diet, the results are nothing short of miraculous. When you eat saturated fat without any regard for carbohydrate consumption, you will wreak havoc. That is all that the cited studies show us. What they won't show you is that high sugar, low saturated fat diets cause as much, if not more damage, than high saturated fat and high sugar.

Iron4Life: For an Intermediate lifter who is bulking do you still suggest drinking a gallon of whole milk a day? Or is this more of a beginners protocol?

bango skank: Raw milk, anyone?

Mark Rippetoe: That much milk is really a novice strategy, and might make an intermediate guy chubby. Raw milk is not available but in a few states, and is hideously expensive. If you're lactose intolerant, take some lactaid.

Amu: A gallon of Lactaid (~$10 a day) is getting heavy on the bills, what do you suggest I do? I'm thinking of calling the company and asking for a commercial purchase, as long as it's not too big.

Mark Rippetoe: Use the capsules. Much cheaper.

Lylemcd: The Lactaid pills don't seem to work for everyone, they never did for me.

I've been using a product called Digestive Advantage: Lactose Intolerance Therapy that has allowed me to drink regular milk for the first time in years. it's a once a day pill containing bacteria that helps with lactose digestion along with a little bit of lactase. at places like WalMart and Rite Aid it's about $10/month which is cheap as hell compared to buying Lactaid milk. It's worth looking into for folks who have problems with milk IMO

Amu: Thank you for the advice. I recently tried the product and it seems to be working. I'll have to see how the next few days go. I'm getting it at 10 bucks for 24 pills (24 days). That saves me well over a hundred dollars a month :eek:

fat bastard: Mr. Rippetoe, some people say too much dairy can cause kidney stones so what do you think of that? They say kidney stones can form if there is too much calcium in the kidneys. Is there any truth to this? What if we drink a gallon of milk a day but we also drink a gallon of water a day. Would all that water help to flush the kidneys out and avoid this problem?

Mark Rippetoe: I am not a urologist. But I have never had a young man on my program develop kidney stones. Never.

Spur: Rip, How much milk should a boy 12 years and 7 months old drink? He weighs 68 kilos, 5 feet 6 inches tall, and is on your novice program for the last few months. Last session Squat was 48 kilos 3x5, Bench Press 36 kilos 3x5, Overhead press 20 kilos 3x5, Dead Lift 50 kilos 1x5. Thanks

Mark Rippetoe: I'd have a 150 lb. kid drinking the whole gallon, if he wants to get Huge and Powerful.

JeffreyS: I'm grateful to you for taking time to respond to folks' questions on this board, but you should confine yourself to your areas of expertise. The fact that you do not find the correlation of saturated fats and heart disease "compelling" is irrelevant to the fact that it is overwhelmingly established by the studies cited above and by numerous others. If you have conducted some kind of groundbreaking study that disproves the link between saturated fats and heart disease, you should by all means send it to a medical journal and have it peer reviewed by people with MDs--you know, the people who know what they are talking about when it comes to producing and testing knowledge about diet and health.

As far as your statement that no one has "proved" that saturated fat "causes" heart disease, well, it's not a hard statement to stand by. The only way to prove causality would be to take two subject pools, subject one to a diet high in saturated fat, restrict the intake of saturated fat in the other, and then observe them over an entire adult lifetime. Given that that kind of experiment is impossible to conduct for a whole host of reasons, I would suggest that you "interest" yourself in correlation, especially if you are going to go around dispensing dietary advice.

Mark Rippetoe: And I would suggest that you are on very thin-ass ice here. I would also suggest that since you are obviously familiar with the literature, you cite the paper that you consider shows this strong correlation between dietary saturated fat and heart disease.

I further suggest that you read chapter 11 in Nobel laureate Kary Mullis's book *Dancing Naked in the Mind Fields* that deals specifically with the topic of causation/correlation.

In your first paragraph you assert that this relationship has been "overwhelmingly established," and in your second paragraph you state that the assertion would be impossible to prove with a study. So how, in your mind, has this relationship been established, save in the style of V.I. Lenin, paraphrased: "Bad data repeated often enough becomes the conventional wisdom."?

There are numerous examples around the world of specific cultural diets that are high in saturated fats (a food humans have evolved with) and very low in refined carbs (which became common food sources only quite recently) where heart disease is essentially unknown, specifically among the Eskimos, the Tokelau, the Masai, and other non-farming peoples.

I further suggest that you read beyond the literature that espouses the conventional wisdom and broaden your knowledge base, lest you incur the awful wrath of Drs. Kilgore and Bradford, neither of whom, fortunately, are MDs, but rather are familiar with research and have conducted it themselves. I find your reverence for the judgment of MDs rather quaint, and lest you interpret my reference to Dr. Mullis as a similar *ad hominem* pleading, I have actually reviewed the relevant arguments and have not relied on the expertise of others for my conclusions.

progressiveman1: How do you know that lifters who have milk in their diet perform better in the gym than lifters who don't drink milk? Have you done or seen a double blinded study?

Mark Rippetoe: Are you seriously suggesting that a double-blind study is the only way to obtain information about the effects of a protocol? Does thirty years of careful anecdotal analysis not count? Have you done a double blind study to investigate the effects of substituting leg extensions/curls for squats? Do you think you really need to? Why do you already know you don't? And how would we do such studies? What would be your placebo substitute for milk and squats?

progressiveman1: The diet without milk could increase their quantity with the other foods to ensure the same calories and the same percentage of f/c/p. The only thing missing would be the milk.

Mark Rippetoe: No, the thing that would be missing would be the "blind" part. And I've never asked anybody to accept my authority on anything I've said. I'm just telling you what I've observed, and what I continue to observe.

progressiveman1: I'm just asking you to be more specific with your observations on the issue, so I can make an informed judgment on your methods.

Mark Rippetoe: My point is that you don't seem to understand the nature of a double-blind study. You seem to think that it just means "really good" study, when it indicates a specific investigative protocol that cannot be applied to all situations.

progressiveman1: A double-blind study means the evaluator and the subject don't know which aspect of the experiment they are taking part of. An example for a milk study could be coconut milk vs. cows milk (or/and vs. a concoction of juice, non-dairy protein powder, and an oil to match the f/c/p distribution and calories), and the evaluator and subjects wouldn't know which they are taking. I understand it now. The *randomized study* I listed above could still be a valid study too.

Now, will you be kind enough to explain how you know the lack of consumption of milk is the reason for the lack of progress in those trainees you've observed? In other words, are you sure the trainee was following *every* other aspect of your program as prescribed? If so, what difference in progress have you noted from milk drinkers?

Mark Rippetoe: You actually said this: *"An example for a milk study could be coconut milk vs cows milk (or/and vs. a concoction of juice, non-dairy protein powder, and an oil to match the f/c/p distribution and calories), and the evaluator and subjects wouldn't know which they are taking."*

Only if you could find a study population that had never tasted milk of either kind, because in the absence of this condition, the study would not be blind. Now, you might get someone to do a randomized study, but I can't even find a study that was done using correct squatting technique, so let me know when you find a university with a competent faculty that is willing to challenge the conventional wisdom. The studies you want to see do not exist, and I'm sorry about that, but not everything we know comes from a double-blind study that results in a peer-reviewed paper.

And I shall now be kind, and explain why I know the lack of consumption of milk is the reason for the lack of progress in those trainees I've observed. It is because over thirty years of direct observation has demonstrated to me that *when trainees drink one gallon of milk added to their regular diet and train in a progressive linear fashion*, they gain significant muscular bodyweight, *and those that do not drink their milk, even in the presence of progressive linear training, fail to do this*. They also fail to continue progressive linear training for the same length of time, because this is facilitated by the steady weight gain. I understand that you're asking me if I have controlled for other factors such as failure to do the program correctly, and the answer is yes, of course I have, because I am not a complete idiot. Those that will not do the program are not being considered when I make these remarks, because that would be too fucking obvious a hole in my analysis. The difference in the milk drinkers is that THEY GET BIGGER THAN THE ONES WHO WON'T DRINK THE FUCKING MILK. Please tell me that you understand this now.

progressiveman1: The only reason why I don't believe that the trainees you are considering in your judgment have followed every aspect of your program correctly besides drinking milk is because drinking milk is probably the easiest part of your program. And even more importantly you are telling me they are eating a surplus of calories (usually at least 4,000 calories for younger trainees; it's 6,000 for me) and for some odd reason they won't obey your simple suggestion to add milk in their diet? I understand your assertions, but I'm having a hard time believing they followed every aspect of the program correctly besides the milk.

Mark Rippetoe: Well, okay then.

Fluxboy: Actually, gotta disagree a little here. As someone who followed the ol' squat/milk program years back ... the toughest part of the training, for me, was the sheer quantity of food I had to consume every day. Particularly the milk. God, how I hated looking at the big gallon of milk every day, knowing I'd somehow have to consume it.

Those who have experience in the iron game training younguns can probably attest to this ... the most difficult part is getting the scrawny ass kids to consistently eat enough to make gains possible. And the more reluctant they are, the more likely they need to! It's probably even more difficult now, given the age we live in. After all, what use is thirty years in the iron game if you haven't gotten a double blind study with raspberry flavored coconut milk to back your experiences?

That all said, I'm making fine gains simply eating a meat and cheese sandwich every hour or so. However, my circumstances are unique. If I were living an active lifestyle, I'd likely just chug a litre of milk between meals. Kind of a nuisance, not altogether pleasant, but it works. However, I'm not sure if Mark's approach is really going to be embraced by the new generation. Size and strength seem to be taking a back seat to the Calvin Klein / metrosexual industry. It seems to be more fashionable to be a waif. To each his own.

progressiveman1: Just curious if you have ever examined the effects of someone drinking *more* than one gallon of milk a day; say two gallons. Did those people get better results than the one gallon trainees? Essentially at two gallons of milk the person's diet would consist solely of milk, which would be pretty awesome. I might try it just to see what happens.

Mark Rippetoe: But you would be shitting primarily cheese. Are you ready for this?

Polynomial: You can probably sell it in France, you know.

Mark Rippetoe: They eat a paste made from the livers of diseased geese, so you're probably right.

Stu: I think it'd be fairly obvious you can't get all your dietary requirements just from milk. I assume that unless you're over about 230lb your caloric intake isn't going to be so high that half of it can't be met by other food sources. A US gallon of whole milk has about 2460 calories - about half of a 5000 calorie diet? How many guys need to eat this much in a day?

Mark Rippetoe: Guys trying to get big.

Butter: How have your personal clients been chugging their gallon Mark, what is the interval secret please?

Mark Rippetoe: Nobody chugs a gallon of milk that wants to keep it down. Start with a pint twice a day, and work up to the gallon, a quart at a time, as soon as you can. Go slowly and build up to it, like a 300 lb. squat.

George_T: A trainer once told me we can only absorb 30-40g of protein at a time. Do you have any idea what the refractory period (?) would be before we can absorb more? (I realize protein isn't the only benefit of milk, but this is something I've been wondering about as I'm upping the number/frequency of my meals.)

Mark Rippetoe: That figure obviously varies with the bodyweight of the trainee, the individual capacity of the trainee, and is almost certainly trainable as well. I have no idea of any specifics regarding these details.

Peter_k: Humans didn't evolve to eat small pieces of meat throughout the day. For most of our existence, we went hungry until we killed a mammoth. Once that happened, it was buffet time. Anyway, as far as I know the body can absorb huge amounts of protein at a time without much problem.

Paul Stagg: Anyone who says such a thing has no idea what they are talking about, and can safely be ignored. Or better yet, next time, ask him:

What do you mean by 'absorbed'?
What is the effect on 'absorption' of other foods in the gut?
What is 'a time'?
Where does it go if it isn't 'absorbed'?
How does one measure this?

While you are waiting for his answer, eat a pound of beef. That way, you can be doing something productive.

Butter: Thanks Mark. Would it be best if I include those pints pre and post workout?
I hear Milk Casein 30 - 45 minutes pre-workout is very effective but whole milk post workout may not be as effective as protein with minimum fats??

Mark Rippetoe: Good God! Too much specificity. Go to **www.bodyrecomposition.com** and search for this shit there in forums or books. Lyle knows way more about this than anybody else has the patience to learn.

Cycomiko: Phillips work (that is currently unpublished) shows a mixture of casein (micellar) and whey 50:50 provides a greater benefit post workout than either 100% whey, or 100% casein. but he underpowered the study somewhat, so its not quite significant. Robert Wolfe's crowd published this one awhile back:

Milk ingestion stimulates net muscle protein synthesis following resistance exercise.

Elliot TA, Cree MG, Sanford AP, Wolfe RR, Tipton KD.

Metabolism Unit, Shriners Hospitals for Children and Department of Surgery, The University of Texas Medical Branch, Galveston, TX, USA.

PURPOSE: Previous studies have examined the response of muscle protein to resistance exercise and nutrient ingestion. Net muscle protein synthesis results from the combination of resistance exercise and amino acid intake. No study has examined the response of muscle protein to ingestion of protein in the context of a food. This study was designed to determine the response of net muscle protein balance following resistance exercise to ingestion of nutrients as components of milk. METHOD: Three groups of volunteers ingested one of three milk drinks each: 237 g of fat-free milk (FM), 237 g of whole milk (WM), and 393 g of fat-free milk isocaloric with the WM (IM). Milk was ingested 1 h following a leg resistance exercise routine. Net muscle protein balance was determined by measuring amino acid balance across the leg. RESULTS: Arterial concentrations of representative amino acids increased in response to milk ingestion. Threonine balance and phenylalanine balance were both > 0 following milk ingestion. Net amino acid uptake for threonine was 2.8-fold greater ($P < 0.05$) for WM than for FM. Mean uptake of phenylalanine was 80 and 85% greater for WM and IM, respectively, than for FM, but not statistically different.

Threonine uptake relative to ingested was significantly (P < 0.05) higher for WM (21 +/- 6%) than FM (11 +/- 5%), but not IM (12 +/- 3%). Mean phenylalanine uptake/ingested also was greatest for WM, but not significantly. CONCLUSIONS: Ingestion of milk following resistance exercise results in phenylalanine and threonine uptake, representative of net muscle protein synthesis. **These results suggest that whole milk may have increased utilization of available amino acids for protein synthesis.**

KSC: I cannot believe that there have been this many pages filled up under a thread about milk.

Mark Rippetoe: Eight now, and me too.

AaronShaf: I agree. Drink the milk and shut up. I did and I gained 15lb in 5 weeks on SS, nearly all muscle too. There isn't much to say other than "yes, that worked very well, thank you coach"

KSC: I'll try to help out with a synopsis:

Soy Milk - bad
Rice Milk - how does rice make milk?
Whole Milk - good for growth, bad if you are a fatty
Low fat Milk - still good for growth, probably better than whole if you are a fatty
Skim Milk - tasteless watery substance resembling real milk

MOOOOOOOOOOOOOO!!!

Update

Franklie: I wanted to give you an update on what your advice has done for me. About 9 months ago you helped me set up my Starting Strength program. Due to slow recovery by my body I changed the routine in order to continue to add weight to the bar. My 5x5 workout weights are rapidly approaching my 1RM from 9 months ago.

I have a complaint/ compliment from my wife. For the first time in my life I have some "junk in the trunk" and some meat on my legs. I was always a skinny guy and was told because I was an endurance runner that I would never have anything but skinny legs. I'm not sure how to put this next part, being as this is NOT Maxim or Playboy, but lifting heavy iron has also caused changes in my libido. The wife says she always knows when I have lifted heavy at the gym and she has a new appreciation for lifting heavy iron.

Since last November my weight has increased 20lb. I was told by my doctor that the physical changes I have experienced are NOT normal for someone my age because of reduced levels of testosterone to create muscle.

Mark Rippetoe: Yes, there are hormonal benefits associated with getting stronger and eating enough food.

Couple questions, Coach...

Fullpen: I just started your program two weeks ago and I've seen some excellent results already. Some background - I'm 5'6" 148 lbs. I lost about 110 lbs. in the last 18 months. I'm squatting 205, benching 140 in sets across. Deadlifting 235. Still learning my clean form.

I believe you on the milk thing. The only concern I have blends into my next... is it too much calories for a guy my size? That's almost as many calories as I eat per day. I got a physical job, so I eat a lot for a guy my size anyway. Plus, I'm 31, do I fall into the "older guy who's gonna turn chubby" category if I drink that much? Should I just work up to half a gallon to start?

Mark Rippetoe: A guy your size? My god, man, you're 5'6" and 148 lbs., not what I'd call a mastodon. Are we talking about the guy you are now, or the guy you used to be? Think about that.

Fullpen: Oh, no, not at all sir. I meant a guy as small as me.

Mark Rippetoe: A guy your size (now) is exactly who benefits from the gallon of milk program. You are who it is designed for.

Fullpen: Ok then, I'll build up to it like you've suggested in other posts. Is my age, 31, any concern for this either?

Mark Rippetoe: No concerns about age, at least not until you're really old.

SS without the gallon

Will: I was following SS with the gallon for about 3 months and saw really good gains with it. Although I had a lot of stomach trouble whilst on the gallon and some medical problems which my doc thinks was caused by it. I recently had appendicitis and had to have it out but I got complications in my operation and basically have no core strength left at all.

Would following SS again be a good way to go about increasing my strength again? I understand it wouldn't work as well without the gallon but I also want to start some ring training as well and I think the extra size would be more detrimental than beneficial at this stage. Could I have your thoughts on this please?

Mark Rippetoe: If you want to train without gaining a lot of muscle mass, don't drink the milk. It's very strange that the folklore now has it that the milk is part of the program itself, when it is really just a method of improving the effectiveness of the program for the underweight, the poor, the disenfranchised.

Spare tire

Corey: I've been on the program for about 7 weeks now, albeit with some inconsistency, i.e. a couple of missed workouts subbed with boxing. I have no doubt I have gained strength and muscle (I think), but I have definitely added some unwanted fat. The small 'dummy' spare tire around my waist has grown to a full out spare tire. Now I was not super lean to begin with. Still, I am having doubts about following through with this program. A real man follows through. I don't want to quit and I'm not a wuss with my workouts. I just need some reassurance that I won't become a stronger version of the Michelin man. I have put in many hard gut checks, semi-hernia efforts under the bar and have increased all my lifts. I just don't want to get fatter. Any advice? I realize you may cringe with a question of this type, but I feel it is a valid concern of many of your program's trainees both far and wide (no pun intended).

Please reassure me that if I stick to my guns and continue your elegantly designed program that I will eventually displace the spare tire.

Mark Rippetoe: So you've finally found an exercise program that actually produces calories, as opposed to burning them? I'm really afraid that I don't understand how my training program has made you chubby. Perhaps you've been following a diet that is inappropriate for your individual situation.

Corey: Okay, I deserve that. Wouldn't be a very marketable program, would it? Point taken, Coach. I probably have been drinking too much milk for my own good. About 1 gallon a day. Sounds like blasphemy to most. I will heed your words and modify my caloric intake accordingly.

Vitamin supplementation and the shovel approach

Drewfasa: I just read the bit in PP where you discuss vitamin supplementation and the Bill Starr 'shovel approach'. However, while I no longer need to concern myself with overdosing, I still have budgetary constraints. How many times the recommended dosage would be a good rough target for a generic grocery store multi-vitamin?

Mark Rippetoe: That depends on what's on sale. Grocery store multivitamins are not the best choice, because they're not really that cheap. Go to GNC and get the cheapest strong multivitamin they have there, and it will be a better deal for the money.

Drewfasa: I got my vitamins at Sainsbury's (big British grocery chain) because they were cheapest (£2.50 for 90 generic one a day pills). I checked the health food stores first but they had nothing for less than £19 a bottle which is to big for my student budget. I'll try and find a GNC and check there prices (they are hard to find in the UK but I think there is a least one here in London).

Anyhow, I'm taking double the recommended adult dose with these cheapo multivitamin and mineral pills. Let me know if you think this is dangerous or if I could bump it up a bit.

Mark Rippetoe: The Sainsbury's vitamins are fine; I suspect they are a version of what we call One-A-Day vitamins here. They have low levels of all the B-complex, usually 100% of the USRDA which is quite low. The only way they could be taken unsafely would be to coarsely grind them and inject them into your heart.

Nutrition

Stakehoagy: These are probably a few stupid questions but I would like to get a some things straightened out about diet. I realize how important it is to eat a lot to gain muscle and strength but does it have any negative health benefits. For example, I am sure you are aware of the studies done on rats that support calorie restriction can increase longevity. What does this mean for the strength trainer? I am wondering if the high calorie diet for gaining is in fact healthy for the strength trainer.

Mark Rippetoe: You want to get strong, or old?

Tongzilla: Are they mutually exclusive?

Mark Rippetoe: Not really, but eating for longevity will keep you from getting bigger, so as a goal eating for longevity precludes productive strength training.

Skim milk for poor people who are fat?

Drewfasa: As a financially constrained student, I have found the gallon of milk a cheap and delicious way to supplement my protein intake (meat is pricey on this side of the Atlantic). As a heftier gentleman, would there be any disadvantages to drinking skim milk instead of full fat? I don't need the extra calories, but do need the protein.

Mark Rippetoe: If you are using it as a protein supplement and not as a weight-gain supplement, skim is fine. I just hate that it is bluish.

Genetic Performance Potential graph question

Banderbe: I am looking at the graph on p. 286 of BBT and it shows the beginner stage lasting about nine months, and so on with the other levels of training. My question is regarding the effect of a hypo-caloric state on the trainee's level. In other words, if you had a trainee who spent that first 9 months as a beginner dieting down to lose body fat. They probably gained a little muscle, and trained the nervous system up well but, and I am guessing here, probably they didn't add that much weight to their lifts - certainly not weight at every workout for 9 months.

Is that person still a beginner once they return to a hyper-caloric (e.g. "bulking") phase? Presumably once they go back to eating for size they can still add weight to the bar at each workout just like a true beginner.

Mark Rippetoe: Well, a person that spent the first 9 months of a strength training program in a hypocaloric state was damn sure not doing my program. I suppose that if the fundamental recovery conditions were altered so that recovery and progress could be resumed, the lifter would go through a linear progression of some sort, although possibly a truncated one.

Clean - Hand Positioning

Jowee: I am a large man, obese, and have been doing starting strength with a lot of success, with the exception of the clean. I cannot seem to catch the weight correctly at the top and I have form issues all the way up. I know it will probably take me a bit more practice to get the correct motion down, and over my fear of letting the weight go on to my chest and shoulders. But it seems the biggest problem is being able to get my arms up to rest the bar on my shoulders and chest without the bar going into my face or throat. I am not sure if it is flexibility, arm length, or what, but I was trying to see if there are any recommendations for how to best practice to learn the catch up at the top.

Mark Rippetoe: These are the kinds of problems I'd need to be there to solve. But try widening your grip and see if that helps. If not, it will just take stretching and weight loss. If you cannot rack the bar correctly, you shouldn't do cleans until you can, and that's okay because for you bodyfat loss is a more important short-term goal than power acquisition.

Jowee: What type of lifting/exercise do you think I should do for the most EFFECTIVE fat loss? :confused: I was doing strength training figuring building muscle would help me trim down, but I think I was fighting myself because of restricting calories. I am eating 50% protein, 30% fat, and 20% carbs and having good success with that.

Mark Rippetoe: It unfortunately depends on how old you are. If you are 22, you just add some squat volume and run a couple of miles twice/week. If you are 52, you have to watch your diet closely and train hard too. Your diet sounds like it is under control, so just keep after it. You didn't get fat in a month, and you won't get lean in a month either, as you have discovered. My advice would be to keep a tight diet and just worry about your training; don't make your bodyfat loss a goal that you monitor, and your brain will be happier while you get stronger and leaner.

Weight gain

Klipsch: I've read that it is only possible to gain weight by eating more calories than you burn. However, is the reverse true? In other words, will eating more calories than you burn necessarily translate into weight gain? For a lean weightlifter like myself, it seems the body should only absorb the excess calories necessary to build muscle in order to adequately recover from stress. Will *all* of the calories beyond this necessarily go to fat or will some simply be excreted by the body?

I'm 21 yrs old, 5'9" and have gone from 135 to 148 lbs in the first 3 months of the SS program. In the next 3 months, I have gained no weight (although my squats, for example, have gone up 20 lbs). The first 13 lbs were surprisingly easy to gain (I didn't have to stuff myself every day). I'd love to put on another 10 lbs.

My second question is, will it be easier for me ("feel hungrier") to gain weight once my lifts and need for more muscle increases further as I progress through the program, or should I add another 500 calories now to my current diet to increase my performance in the lifting program?

Mark Rippetoe: You are now 5' 9" and 148. You are still what I would consider quite underweight, so whatever you're doing now is not working very well. Since you feel no hunger now, it is safe to assume that hunger will not be a reliable indicator of how much you need to eat to gain weight, and this of course means that you'll have to eat more than you want to – more than you're comfortable with. You must have missed our milk discussion.

And no, you don't excrete excess calories, because evolution didn't see fit to exterminate the species in this way. If that happened, fat people would be in zoos where they belong since they'd be quite rare.

Nutrition

Jicjac: We always hear and read about how important nutrition is to weight training, but if this is so then why do many prisoners who weight train get such impressive builds? I know genetics and possibly steroids, in certain instances, have to be taken into consideration, but they only have access to three meals per day and I'm thinking not the highest quality and definitely not the access to protein that people on the outside have. Is protein supplementation overrated?

Mark Rippetoe: Protein supplementation – the expensive kind – is obviously overrated, as are optimal training conditions in general. Doug Patterson used to drive down to Huntsville to help with power meets in the prison back in the 80's. He told me about 850 deadlifts he'd seen done by 250 lb. inmates. The best case nutritional scenario is a useful model, as is perfect technique, a two-parent family, and a nice pickup. But it is just a model, and it is often not possible. We did not evolve to require the Best Case Scenario to survive – we evolved to cope with the worst case scenario.

Juicysweet: I seriously doubt that prisoners are at a nutritional disadvantage. I've been in Florida prisons and the food was plentiful and of far better quality than that of Florida public schools. Now consider: A big caloric excess, enough protein, plenty of rest, minimal responsibilities and few distractions is a pretty damn optimal training environment. This is pretty much like the Olympic Training Center, and it wouldn't surprise me if the competitive environment and coaching is far more effective in the pen.

Rocko: From your experience, are there any protein supplements you would recommend?

Mark Rippetoe: Protein supplements? Other than eggs, milk, and roast beef, I'd just buy the cheapest whey protein you can find. Even if all that technical-mimicked advertising in the magazines is not total bullshit – and it is – it would only make a small difference in the quality of the protein anyway. And the best way to make up for lower quality is through greater quantity, made possible because it's cheaper.

GOMAD and Old Farts

RobertF: My wife really appreciates these kinds of diets. I suspect that I might be banished to the couch for quite a while. I'm hoping to start a SS type program early in the new year once I get my joints stable (I usually need 12-16 weeks of careful lifting before my shoulders are strong/flexible enough to do much without turning into another useless bout of tendonitis.)

At 40 and a bit I'm less than sure that I have the ability to turn a Gallon of Milk a Day into muscle. What's your recommendation?

Mark Rippetoe: I recommend that ***IF YOU NEED TO GAIN WEIGHT***, you do the GOMAD thing. I have ***NEVER*** recommended it for everybody. ***NEVER, EVER*** have I said that everybody needs GOMAD to do a linear strength progression. ***NEVER***. Anywhere. Read the book, not the internet, and we'll all be happier.

Overtraining during Starting Strength?

Pnigro: 23 year old male from Costa Rica, 173 cm., 147 lbs with shoes. Been on SS for 3 months but lifting for more than a year. I always had a problem with soreness. I asked you and you said most of the time it is a nutrition problem. So I started eating more and it definitely helped, but I am ALWAYS at least a little sore during each workout. I am aware there are some people that get more sore than others, but still. My squat has gone from 115 lbs to 190 lbs. My deadlift from 135 lbs to 200 lbs. My bench from 115 lbs to 155 lbs. My press from 55 lbs to 85 lbs.

Before you say "eat more", I try to eat all I can, to the point where I get a lot of gas and sometimes stomach ache and even diarrhea. I try to eat the most protein I can, I drink 1 liter of milk a day (I'm a little intolerant, can't drink too much), one scoop of 23g whey protein everyday, oats, eggs, beans, tuna, cheese, turkey sandwiches, etc. I know I probably should eat more, but I'm doing everything I can. I sleep a lot (9-10 hours per day) and I always rest 2 days at the end of the week. So I'm definitely resting enough. I gained 10lbs of muscle during the last 2-3 months.

Is this the classic example of overtraining? Should I take a week off? It's very frustrating, I started doing the program with a friend who never gets sore, and he even swims on his rest days. He weighs 165 lbs and I don't think he eats that much more than me.

Mark Rippetoe: Yes, it is a classic example of overtraining due to undereating. You are 5' 8" at 147 lbs. By any estimation you need to gain 40 pounds to be considered a lifter, 20 to be even considered fit. You have gained 10 lbs. in the past 2 months where most of my trainees gain 10 lbs. in the first two weeks. Sorry, but you have to eat more or train less.

Milk: The Evil Poison

JB1981: I stumbled upon this book in my Chiropractor's office the other day while waiting and I immediately starting to think about the Milk Diet. Basically, the book posited that the majority of the diseases in America are caused by the consumption of milk. Anyone here have any idea what book I'm talking about? Should I take any of this seriously?

Mark Rippetoe: Jesus Christ Riding a Fucking 3-Legged Burro. If you have to ask this question, how am I going to take *you* seriously???

Polynomial: Rip, I think he can figure it out on his own without reading anything. Otherwise, there's no hope.

Calorie math (?)

RobertFon: I've been thinking about the basics of diet and could use a little help if you don't mind. In order to gain weight a caloric excess is required. For example: 1 gallon of milk = 2000 calories give or take. If I were to increase my dietary intake by 2000 calories daily (assuming I'm currently eating enough to maintain my weight) while doing the SS program then will I likely turn a good 1500 calories per day of this into body mass? A pound of body weight is about 3500 calories. Over 30 days that's 45,000 or about 12 pounds of mass or around 30 pounds in 3 months. What percentage of this is likely to be fat? Does reducing the caloric excess change the percentage of fat/muscle gained and to what extent?

Mark Rippetoe: Some of it will be fat, but most of it will be muscle. Muscle cannot be acquired under the conditions in which fat is lost without Chemistry™ involved, because a caloric surplus is required for anabolic conditions. But fat is easier to take off than muscle is to put on, so worry about that later. Much later.

Fluxboy: At what point should one concern oneself with this? I'm starting to develop some love handles (oddly enough, I don't really detect any real increase in body fat anywhere else), when I tense, I can still see my abs, but ... I've gotten a little chunkier. Everyone has their own tolerances, I suppose, but for someone who wants to be big and strong, at what point should he begin to start trimming down? Or should he even not consider this until he's reached his size and strength goals?

I'm around 215 lbs, maybe a tick heavier. My goal is 250 lbs. Do I continue to bulk and fatten continuously, or would it be better to throw in a cycle of Zone eating along the way, to keep body fat at reasonable levels? I just feel a little odd right now, being a little chunky for the first time in my life.

(ps: My nifty "bio-impedance" scale says I'm at 11.8% bodyfat, but I take that with a grain of salt.)

Mark Rippetoe: The bio-impedance scale works about as well as the US Government, so disregard everything it says except what you weigh. One should concern oneself with bodyfat gain about 12 weeks out from the bodybuilding contest. You can't get too fat if you're training hard and under the age of 40.

RobertFon: Hmm... Am 41 but honestly having removed the junk from my diet I'm having a fairly tough time breaking 3000 calories a day. I'm going to see what happens @ ~3000 calories per day with a zonish 4:3 type distribution. (2 quarts) I'm a little nervous about jumping to 3500 as I haven't convinced myself that I won't turn into the butterboy quite yet. 4 quarts would put me up around 4k calories a day and I have to admit to being shocked about this kind of intake although on paper it sounds like a good idea.

Justin: I see a lot of folks around the internet doing what they can to quantify calories in, total work output, etc, etc, to make predictions as to how much weight they're likely to lose or gain over a given time period. I suppose it's impossible (or highly impractical) to measure a person's ability to actually metabolize and put to good use the amount of food that's being consumed. At some point, I assume there must be some sort of a "saturation point" where the body can't use the nutrients and the excess is passed by the body in the stool (as was mentioned in a recent post here that I can't seem to find.)

Your books and other writings often mention that you've seen many a skinny kid put on crazy amounts of muscle with the GOMAD/SS combo. I gather also that this dramatic increase is less common in older trainees. I was wondering, in your experience, is the ability of a person's body to actually digest a (relatively) huge amount of calories per day for muscle gain a "trainable" quality, especially in older trainees? Or is the ability for the body to put the nutrients to use just a hard limitation of the hormonal differences between younger and older trainees? Or am I thinking about this too much?

jwm79: What should someone do if they're really overweight? 300 lbs. about 180 lean body mass according to scales. Wait before beginning weight training or just try to maintain muscle while losing weight. If I went this route, could I start Starting Strength after more fat was lost?

Mark Rippetoe: Once again, for the 7.764976×10^{60} time, the GOMAD deal is not for everybody. It's just for gaining weight. If you don't need to gain weight, don't do it. And if you're 45, don't do it. The ability to put on muscle using this approach diminishes with age, as hormone levels change and as injuries acquired through other activities accumulate and affect stress levels and the stress response. And the ability to absorb nutrients from the gut – although trainable to a limited extent – is finite, and dependent on genetics like everything else about the human body. However, you cannot eat 10,000 calories of fat and simple sugar/day and expect that you will use what you need and shit out the rest. The older you are, the more likely you'll be to store fat as opposed to build muscle. My point is that a young man can work hard enough and has the hormonal equipment that makes him capable of gaining large amounts of muscle mass, because he can use a huge amount of calories and protein anabolically, and that this ability diminishes with age.

And thinking *too* much is like making *too* much money or getting *too* much pussy

Very Tired

Axegrinder: I've had 8 hours of sleep and a good breakfast of 5 eggs, a bowl of oatmeal and 2 glasses of milk and I'm very tired, especially my legs. I last worked out on Friday, and am still making progress on all my lifts. I had a 7 day break last week.

Mark Rippetoe: Tired is long-term. It doesn't just go away after breakfast.

Axegrinder: Oh lawd, I phrased that question (statement?) terribly. What I mean to say is I'm sleeping enough, my diet is in check but I'm very tired physically, to the point where I just want to crawl into bed, which does not feel right to me. I had done a 10 week "cycle" of SS and took a week long break, which might not have been enough as I was still tired and even a little sore on day 7. I'm still making progress workout to workout so it couldn't be overtraining, could it? I tried a multi-vitamin but it didn't seem to help. Any ideas on what the problem might be? Could my mass gainage be in danger?

Mark Rippetoe: Then your diet is not "in check" – you are not eating enough. Read the neighboring posts here about this.

John N.O: Said this a few times in surrounding posts, but this seems to be one of the more common/difficult areas for people to get 'right', and often seems to be a stumbling block.

From my calculations from that breakfast you are getting around 800 calories. What is your target calorie intake? If you are aiming for around 4k, then are you getting another 3.2k in during the day? I would suggest getting onto Fitday and track exactly what you are eating. This is very useful, and helps you hit those targets, and removes that element of doubt.

Draco: Sounds helpful, but if one doesn't have the time or patience for calculating the numbers for everything they eat each day, here's another idea: keep naughty, delicious food around. I found that when my choices were oatmeal and eggs all the time, I didn't feel so hungry. After stopping for the all-you-can-eat buffet at the Indian restaurant, my hunger was suddenly magnified after the first bite. This idea might scare some people (the dirty bulking part, not the Indian food), but it can't hurt you much to try it for a couple weeks. You just have to make sure you mind your protein intake so that all your calories don't just come from Palak Paneer and Channa Masala.

TomC: This is less than ideal, especially if you are older than 25. Eating lots of rice, pasta, ice cream, and cookies probably won't get you that strong, although it may help you get fat. Some folks can get away with worse diets than others. Need some calories? The secret has been divulged here often - whole milk and lots of it.

Mark Rippetoe: I don't necessarily agree, TomC. If a kid just can't or won't eat enough calories, ice cream is sure as hell preferable to weight loss and overtraining. As usual, it all depends.

lukeBW: Nothing wrong with rice pasta and ice cream, I try to get at least 50 % of my calories from rice and pasta the rest form meat and milk. I am 45 btw. Pasta and rice is on the menu every day for me, usually pasta in the AM around lunch and rice is for dinner.

And what is wrong with good ice cream? It's supposed to be made with eggs, milk and fruit. I say eat plenty of that, mind you I said good ice cream, not crappy stuff made with chemicals and HFCS. Actually, there are few foods nearly as perfect and complete as ice cream

Axegrinder: Calories from sugar build muscle?

Mark Rippetoe: Let's see if we can deal with subtle nuance. Luke thinks that a diet composed of 50% high-glycemic carbs is a good thing at the age of 45, and that ice cream is a Perfect Food as opposed to an occasional treat. Unless Luke is extremely underweight and therefore has a lot of room to be forgiven for shitty calories, he is wrong. A diet this heavy in sugar causes so many problems that even an underweight person would do far better with a higher fat/lower carb diet.

But Axe is equally wrong in his assumption that sugar cannot build muscle. You have to eat enough calories that you are in caloric surplus over your baseline requirements before you can build muscle, and if some sugar intake puts you over the line it can facilitate growth. Is it the preferred source of calories? Of course not. But is it preferable to catabolism? Obviously.

lukeBW: Sorry... but I am Italian. Pasta, rice and bread have been staples in my country well for over 2000 years. I was 172lb before I started SS and eating 3.6k cal a day, now 175 after a month, my cholesterol is practically perfect #s and my heart is pumping like a 25yo

My diet is not perfect for sure but it ain't bad either.

Mark Rippetoe: If it works so well, why have you only gained 3 lbs. in a month? I can take a 3 lb. shit, you know. Maybe rice and pasta are deficient in some critical nutrient involved in the gaining of muscular bodyweight? Wonder what that might be? Hmm?

GOMAD: A watered down bulk diet for the anemic

Fluxboy: So I'm talking to the big guys in the gym. The only real lifters in the gym, and one is about 6' and 300 lbs, and the other 5'6" and 215 lbs. I said I was trying to put on another twenty pounds or so, and they sorta laughed:

"You should weigh about ... 315-320 lbs."

I informed them I didn't really think that was possible, but I appreciated the thought.

"What do you eat?"

I told them about my buttermilk and trail mix. They sorta laughed. Then informed me what the smaller (?) guy ate. Three double burgers, fries, and a milkshake ... on the way to Denny's for breakfast. I was told that another hundred pounds of bodyweight would be about right, and then my deadlift would really climb. And I sorta got a sense of where Rip might be coming from when he so patiently humors us each week when people post about not making progress. I thought my 5000-ish calories a day was a good, solid meal plan, but it's not even close to what these monsters eat. The smaller guy nearly took in that much on his way to breakfast. And the big guy mentioned he can literally gain or drop fifty pounds on a whim.

I'm not saying this is healthy or anything, but this is the sorta 'relationship' the biggest, strongest guys in my gym have with food. It's such a different world that GOMAD literally comes across as barely sufficient for gains. It's almost as if it's a watered down bulk diet for the anemic. You know, lifting is lifting it's transformational potential is limited *by itself*... but doubling the food intake over and above the normal bulk diet would, literally, make me a Titan in this world of underwear models.

You too, probably. Just a thought.

Mark Rippetoe: The real lifters all recognize the intimate relationship between increased bodyweight and increased strength. But modern bodybuilding has fucked this up. Abs seem to be the primary criterion for everything to most people, including most of you guys.

I do what I can.

KSC: I can't count the number of kids I have had come to me saying "I can't gain weight no matter what I do." It has been my experience that most trainees who are trying to gain weight and can't, have no fucking idea what big eating looks like. As a general rule, I have found that most people who are overly concerned with weighing and measuring their food are not eating enough. They are most unpleasantly surprised when they realize that I ingest more calories in the hour and a half following my workout than they do all day.

elVarouza: While it's true that a shitload of calories and nutrients are needed to grow and grow big, I believe attention must be paid to eating healthy food and a clean diet. This isn't to look like a bodybuilder so much as it is to maintain your own health. While this may not be true for some people, I do strength training not only to lift heavy weights, but also to improve my overall health. Sure, you can get a ton of calories by eating at McDonalds or whatever all day and become a monster, but you can do the same thing eating healthy foods as well. While I don't have as much experience as a lot of people on this forum, I've been eating a lot of healthy food, drinking my GOMAD, and I've been making consistent mass and strength gains.

Mark Rippetoe: You really think a young man, between 18 and 35, needs to be conscious of his "health" for a year while he gains muscular bodyweight? What do you think can happen to him in a year of 7000 kcal/day eating?

TomC: Rip, there's a picture of you floating around that probably came from a powerlifting meet. You are pulling what looks like 585 and you are quite lean. Hell, you may have even been in danger of having six pack abs. Whatever the case, you don't look like a 300 pounder, yet you are moving some serious weight. In your earlier training days, did you eat as much as you recommend now?

Mark Rippetoe: If I told you how much I used to eat, you would not believe me. And the "Supersize Me" did involve absolutely no training, if I remember correctly, and is obviously therefore not an equivalent situation. You guys that worry about eating clean are actually merely bodybuilders looking for justification for your obsession with abs. You cannot get big and strong on 3000 kcal/day. And you cannot eat 7000/day and eat perfectly "clean".

JBlack: Can you please give us a glimpse of what your previous diet was like? Thank you.

Fluxboy: Hey, Rip, I think it might really help if you could give us an idea of what you used to consume (love that word). Vague approximations are fine. I suspect many people hear about GOMAD or whatnot, and assume that it is, like, a monstrous undertaking. That the sheer quantity is something they are not ready for. At the very least, something to work up to. Rubbish, I say. Aspiring Titans wanna know: What did you used to eat when you were focused on building size and strength?

Mark Rippetoe: Okay, you want to know what I ate. I'll tell you. I have eaten a dozen eggs for breakfast before, but always ate 6 with toast and milk, and 5 bowls of raisin bran was quite normal until my members asked me to stop doing that. I have eaten 11 10-oz. steaks at an all-you-can-eat steak deal – several of us went there, and the special was discontinued the following week. I have eaten 4 *very large* plates of spaghetti and meat sauce in 30 minutes. I have eaten 15 pork chops + vegetables at the Olympic Training Center back when the food was really good. I have eaten 225 shrimp in an hour. At a seafood buffet in Michigan, I ate 10 lobsters and the claws off of 10 more, in addition to shrimp, crab legs, lobster bisque, clam chowder, and bread, in 2 hours. I have eaten 7 big bowls of Mongolian BBQ. I have had a gallon of milk in less than 30 minutes. I was very expensive to feed, but I am told by reputable sources that I was absolutely nothing compared to Phil Grippaldi.

And folks, for weight-gaining purposes, "eating clean" is not a useful concept. Big Macs are.

Half and Half

Northernyogi: Was thinking of switching from whole milk to half and half. When I looked at the stats on both, it looked like I could get the same of everything with half the volume (1/2 gal of half and half vs. 1gal of whole milk). Your thoughts?

Mark Rippetoe: You looked at the stats wrong. Half a gallon of half and half has twice the fat, one third the carbs, and less than half the protein than 1 gallon of milk. If you want less volume, get evaporated milk.

GOMAD quick question

Joshua: Decided being 6`3 and 190lbs I could afford to put some weight on so going to start consuming 5000cals a day including the gallon of milk plus 3 large meals, my only question is due to the high protein from the milk and other foods do I still need a high water intake? If so how much? I'm sure I'd be pissing every 10 minutes with much more than a gallon of fluid! I'm asking primarily because I know of a fair few articles linking high protein diets with kidney issues when not supplemented with decent water intake.

Mark Rippetoe: Please post links to these articles.

lukeBW: It's only theoretical. There are no studies that back that up. Now check this out and see how stupid this is:
Quote:

HARVARD GAZETTE ARCHIVES

Too much protein may cause reduced kidney function

Researchers at Brigham and Women's Hospital (BWH) have found that high-protein diets may be associated with kidney function decline ***in women who already have mildly reduced kidney function.*** *On further analysis, the risk was only significant for animal proteins, indicating that the source of protein may be an important factor.* ***Researchers observed no association between high protein intake and decline in kidney function in women with normally functioning kidneys.*** *These findings appear in the March 18 issue of Annals of Internal Medicine.*

So unless you're a woman with fucked up kidneys you have nothing to worry about. And I didn't make this shit up; it's from the Harvard gazette.

Mark Rippetoe: That's why I wanted to see the articles. Notice that he hasn't posted any.

Ryan: Given that milk is between 80-90% percent water, drinking a gallon of milk will give you a water consumption of 80-90% of a gallon.

Joshua: To be honest I couldn't state specific references as I've come across the articles just browsing, was just clarifying as I'm not scientifically minded in the slightest so was making sure, so a gallon of milk has more than enough water content to constitute zero pure water intake through the day? Also when I say high protein I mean in the 300-500g mark.

Mark Rippetoe: Yes, there's plenty of water in a gallon of milk. If you're thirsty, drink more. And when you say you mean 300-500 grams/day, I still want to see the studies. But you can't find them because there aren't any. In the absence of kidney pathology, there is no "unsafe" protein intake level.

LCN: So while we're on the topic of milk, I guess you have an argument why we shouldn't be concerned about the high amount of saturated fat in a gallon of whole milk? As you know saturated fat is widely believed to be a cause of heart and arterial problems.

Mark Rippetoe: And the Earth is widely believed to be 6000 years old and frequently visited by space aliens from the planet Groz.

LCN: Am I wrong that that seems to be the consensus of the medical community? If they all changed their mind on that they probably should have made a more public announcement about it.

EIC: Believed, but never proven. All you will find is a heap of speculation. Indeed, all of the well-designed studies show that the opposite is true. Also, as a purely logical matter, don't you find it a little ridiculous that the sort of fat which is common in natural foodstuffs (eggs, meat) would essentially be poison for humans? This strikes me as quite nonsensical.

Mark Rippetoe: But totally in keeping with the medical consensus that pressing overhead will destroy your shoulders, that squatting below parallel will destroy your knees, that eating lots of meat will destroy your kidneys, and that drinking lots of milk will just kill you outright. Jesus, LCN, this is the wrong forum for an Appeal To Authority argument. Consensus only works in the absence of actual proof, and those forming the consensus in your case are not entitled to an opinion. I find that this happens frequently.

LCN: Relax, I never said that saturated fat caused heart disease, I said that the medical consensus seemed to state that, and asked what your response was. Who is being dogmatic in this thread? I am aware that there is a minority opinion that saturated fat is not bad, but last I heard it was just that. There is such a thing as focusing only on research that supports the conclusion you desire to be true and ignoring contrary research. I'm not accusing you and Dr. Kilgore of doing this, because I'm sure you know more about the saturated fat issue than I do.

On the other hand I think most SS people linking to a random doctor who doesn't believe in the lipid hypothesis are doing exactly that.

"Also, as a purely logical matter, don't you find it a little ridiculous that the sort of fat which is common in natural foodstuffs (eggs, meat) would essentially be poison for humans?"

Yes that would be ridiculous. However I don't think it's ridiculous that consuming something in quantities massively larger than we were adapted to consume would tend to cause health problems in humans living to ages well beyond what evolution 'intended'.

"But totally in keeping with the medical consensus that pressing overhead will destroy your shoulders, that squatting below parallel will destroy your knees, that eating lots of meat will destroy your kidneys, and that drinking lots of milk will just kill you outright."

Some topics are much more amenable to scientific study than others, and some topics have generated much more rigorous and widespread interest than others. The fact that doctors have come up with some stupid conclusions about weightlifting does not in itself cast much suspicion on their research on heart disease. Do you apply this same level of skepticism to the theory that smoking increases the risk of lung cancer?

[And for the record I'm drinking a glass of whole milk spiked with vegetable oil as I write this.]

Mark Rippetoe:

"However I don't think it's ridiculous that consuming something in quantities massively larger than we were adapted to consume would tend to cause health problems in humans living to ages well beyond what evolution 'intended'."

Now we're getting somewhere. Carbs in forms other than those we are actually adapted to eat are in fact that thing. Fats are not, unless they are of the trans- variety. There are no essential carbs, while there are quite a few essential fatty acids.

"The fact that doctors have come up with some stupid conclusions about weightlifting does not in itself cast much suspicion on their research on heart disease."

Well of course it does, because it reveals their analytical standards. They are low when they exist at all, and consensus is the usual substitute.

"Do you apply this same level of skepticism to the theory that smoking increases the risk of lung cancer?"

I did. The theory holds up well to explain the data, although not when applied to the 2nd-hand smoking issue. The germ theory of disease is similarly unassailable.

LCN: Thanks for taking my post in good spirit. I admit I was kind of stirring the pot but I also was genuinely concerned about the saturated fat issue... only knowing the arguments on one side makes it a little nerve-wracking to drink 200% of your USDA sat fat recommendation in milk alone every day.

Mark Rippetoe: Not your fault at all. If every day of your life you are told by authority figures that the Earth is flat, you will be scared of falling off the edge whether you want to be or not.

Eating to discomfort?

Stu: Is this necessary to adapt to the high caloric requirements of the program? I've found despite the fatigue from the program I can only now manage c.4500 calories a day, and that is forcing some food down - as far as I can tell, my stomach simply has to adapt to the volume of food it's subjected to. Recent lifts and progression has been:

Squat: 108kg (adding 1kg per workout)
Bench: 57kg (adding 1kg per workout)
Deadlift: 122.5kg (adding 2.5kg per workout)
Press: 42.5kg (stalled despite adding only 0.5kg per workout for the last 2 weeks)
Power clean: 58kg (adding 1kg per workout)

19/M/6'0/165

Mark Rippetoe: Improvement in everything requires adaptation. Eating is obviously no exception, especially if you don't have a big appetite to start with. You don't, or you wouldn't weigh 165 at 6'.

Gaining Fat and feeling sluggish

Blah3: I saw you touched a little on nutrition and your advice you gave me was that I wasn't eating enough fat and eating too many carbs. Since then I took on your advice and changed my diet around but am still gaining a considerably large amount of fat around my stomach and ass making my hips almost as wide as my upper back and also feeling very sluggish. I tried to calculate my daily requirements by bodyweight x 18 = 5138cals/day (I'm 6'7" 295lbs) so I went with that. Does this look like what I should be eating?

Breakdown of roughly around:
Protein: 40% - 530g
Fats: 40% - 235g
Carbs: 20% - 265g

DIET AFTER RIPS ADVICE:
Meal 1: 24g Whey + 150g Oat bran + 500mls Whole Milk + 50g Peanuts
Meal 2: 2 185g Cans Tuna + 200g broccoli + 50g peanuts
Meal 3: 220g Chicken Breast with salad with mayo + 200g broccoli + 3 whole eggs
Meal 4 (PRE): 24g Whey + 150g Oat Bran + 500Mls Whole Milk
Meal 5 (POST): 55g Whey + Water + 150g Oat Bran (should it be dextrose?) + creatine and glutamine
Meal 6: Always changes but around 220g Chicken + 10 - 30g fats + 200g broccoli
Meal 7: 24g Whey + 500Mls Whole Milk + 100g Peanuts

Mark Rippetoe: As a general rule I always stop eating as much if I find that I'm getting fatter than I want to be. If your ass and your belly are getting chubby, why would you continue to eat the way that made them chubby? Do you actually need my permission to drop your calorie intake to more closely match your actual requirements? I like the ratio and the composition, but the gross amount is obviously excessive.

Questions About Food Intake

Kyle5000: I've been on the program for a few months, and at this point I consider myself an okay lifter, but a damn good eater (too good maybe). I've never had a small appetite, and since I've been lifting, I've been consciously trying to eat a lot of food, since you tell us to. I don't measure or count calories, but on a typical day, I'll eat 6-7 eggs in the morning with some fruit, a large steak and cheese or chicken stirfry sub for lunch, and as much of whatever meat we have on the dinner table as I can eat, plus some veggies for dinner. I know it's only 3 meals, but I'm eating XL portions, plus I'm doing GOMAD (2%). I'm 22, 5'8", and when I started the program I was 165 lbs. I just weighed in at 203. I can gain 5 lbs a weak, easily, on this diet. I've just been eating as much meat + veggies along with my milk as I can, because I want to get stronger. However, today when I got over 200 lbs for the first time in my life, I got a little concerned that I may be eating a little too much, and that a lot of the weight I've gained is fat, not muscle. I regularly see you recommend 6,000-7,000 calories a day. I'm wondering, is it true that we are "burning" close to 6,000 calories on a training day if we are doing your program (squats, bench/press, deadlift/clean)?

Mark Rippetoe: I doubt you're eating more than 7000 cal/day, because it's pretty damned hard to do. But you have gained 40 lbs., and most people at 5'8" cannot continue to gain muscle at this rate forever. You didn't say how long you've been on the program, but gains do slow down over time. The caloric surplus that is most certainly necessary in the initial stages cannot be consumed forever, and maybe it is time for you to cut back to 4000 and see if your body composition improves. First thing to do is calculate where you actually are, because everything is conjecture until then.

Kyle5000: Well, truth be told, I was on the program from August 1-October 15 consistently, and went from 165 lbs to about 195 lbs in that time. Partially due to a couple of extenuating circumstances, but really due to me being stupid and lazy, I got off the program the 2nd half of October through November, and just started again Dec. 5. I stopped eating tons and doing GOMAD when I wasn't lifting, and around the end of November I was still weighing in around 195 lbs. I'm pretty sure I've put on the extra 8-10 lbs since I started the program again.
I'm 5'8, and right now my 5RM's are.....

Squat- 260 lbs
Bench- 170 lbs
Press- 115 lbs
DL- 315 lbs

I'm still making linear progress, but I think I'm nearing the end of it on pretty much everything.

When you say "calculate where you are," you mean how many calories I'm eating per day? How many calories do you think are expended in a typical SS workout? You think 4000 calories might be enough to continue to make strength gains? Since I'm cutting back on calories, does that mean I can cut back on protein and not require the 1g per 1lb of bodyweight?

Mark Rippetoe: The number of calories expended in a workout is utterly irrelevant. The caloric surplus is for tissue growth, not substrate replacement. And your numbers at that bodyweight are not terribly good, since you're not even benching bodyweight for a set of 5 yet. I think that correct use of the program will yield quite a bit more progress before you actually stall. I meant that you need to calculate your actual caloric intake, since that was what we were discussing. Keep your protein at 1g/lb. and cut your calories down to ~3500 and you will still make good progress, but your bodyweight is a little heavy now for your strength and your level of advancement.

Caloric surplus question

MMM: Say by a fluke of training you are intermediate in OHP/bench and novice in squat/DL. To put some numbers on it say you are pressing 135x5 on the Texas method, but you are only squatting 150x5 and hoping to add 5 pounds per workout. Is it possible that you could be eating with a caloric surplus that is large enough to sustain progress on the slow-gaining intermediate lifts, but too small to sustain progress on the fast improving and big muscle dependent novice lifts?

Mark Rippetoe: You think your digestive/hormonal systems understand about bodyparts?

Soy

Soonerjay: I know from reading a lot of your internet articles and diet references on here that you believe the Zone is a beneficial diet to follow. My question is what do you think about the soy that Dr. Sears recommends? I have heard alternating opinions on it (increases estrogen levels / good for the heart) and wanted to know if you think any soy protein has a place in a strength program?

Mark Rippetoe: Soy protein makes men more womanly, and makes most people fart even more than they do already. I'm sure you'll agree that these are bad things. It is a poor-quality protein, always grainy and unblendable, no cheaper than whey, and I'm damned if I see a reason to eat the nasty shit.

Exhausted After a Workout. Normal?

JB1981: I train after a day's work and by the time I am done with the major lifts I am frickin' dead. I am eating a fair amount of food, taking my vitamins and minerals and drinking protein shakes w/ milk etc. Is it normal to be this tired after a workout? I think it's the squats that are killing me. How is it possible that squats can be this taxing on the system?

Mark Rippetoe: I'm not going to insult your intelligence here by reminding you of obvious things, but I would ask you to specify your pre-workout dietary schedule.

JB1981: Pre-workout diet

Morning:
- 5 extra large scrambled eggs
- Kashi Bar
- bowl of mixed fruit

Morning Snack:
- Cup of yogurt w/ raw almonds

Lunch:
- Big salad w/ chicken and/or steak w/ veggies etc, sometimes brown rice

Lunch Snack:
- Protein shake w/ 1% fat milk

Mark Rippetoe: I think we have found the problem. You are eating like the owner of a Health Food store, not a lifter.

Drinking powdered eggs

TerriblyUsefulBlockOfWood: Check this out, lads, I made an exciting new discovery: a man can DRINK powdered eggs! It's supposedly better than raw eggs, and it's fairly easy to gag down as long as you use enough water in my opinion. (But hell I'll eat/drink anything. I've even eaten dog food and peanut butter before and it wasn't that bad either.) I make a tuna/egg/olive oil smoothie in the morning and before I go to bed. Along with GOMAD and lots of meat, fruit, vegetables, and other crap it gets me to where I need to be. The equivalent of a dozen eggs gives you an extra 84g protein and 840 calories.

Clay: I seriously doubt it could be better than raw eggs. The amount of vitamins, minerals and nutrients lost in the process of turning them to powder can only be replaced by synthetic nutrients which would be no where near as good as the real thing. Raw eggs don't taste bad anyway. I do a dozen a day.

Mark Rippetoe: Let's stop a second to consider where eggs come from: they emerge from a chicken's feathery, unkempt, unpampered ass. You'll do this until a little bit of goo remaining on a shell makes you sick as a horse for about 2 days. Then you'll stop eating raw eggs.

Kiknskreem: Ahem... actually Mark, they come from its *vagina.*

Mark Rippetoe: No, they come from it's cloaca, which for our purposes is Close Enough. You'll have to look this up, because it's now officially outside the scope of this board.

BreezerD: I cannot possibly imagine how you came to know this in the first place.

Mark Rippetoe: I have a rather extensive science education, which includes quite a lot of zoology. Old-fashioned, I know.

Kfreeman: I think that a lot of the protein in eggs gets "lost" if you don't cook them. I just remember reading somewhere that cooking an egg "activates" about twice the protein than would ingesting a raw egg. And Rip is right: eggs are just slimy gooey chickens, and chickens are unkempt and disgusting enough as adults

TPrewittMD: A tuna, egg, olive oil nightcap certifies that TUBW will, in fact, eat anything. My daily breakfast of 2-3 eggs scrambled with cheese, which is also delicious and much easier. But be sure the heed Rip's advice: the certain health risks of regularly consuming raw eggs far outweighs the uncertain, speculative benefits of raw eggs. A bad case of Salmonella can really lay you low.

Clay: I've thought about that, really, and it had me worried for a bit. But I've been eating raw eggs for about 3-4 years now and as yet I've not fallen ill.

Don't know that this would have anything to do with it, as an ass is an ass and a chooks ass would be among the fowlest - excuse the pun, but I get organic eggs and rate them highly for any strength training diet. Along with raw milk, this makes up a big part of my diet. I guess for countless generations we consumed a lot of our foods raw, including eggs, and given how long the digestive process takes to adapt, I'd imagine we're still more efficient at digesting our foods raw than cooked or processed.

Sam Crish: Quite the opposite. Cooked foods in general, especially animal products, are way easier to digest than raw. It's commonly accepted that cooking food was an adaptation that played a major role in human evolution, particularly brain evolution.

Sepandee: Not that this means everyone is safe eating raw eggs, I started having raw eggs as a kid when my mom mixed two in a blender with milk, bananas, apples, and sometimes some cocoa powder. I still make this but replace the cocoa powder with my chocolate whey. Not only is it delicious, it's never made me ill. My parents have had raw eggs too and they've never fallen ill because of it either.

While caution should be taken, the chances of getting salmonella or anything else from raw eggs is very low.

Mark Rippetoe: Damn. I've had it twice.

Sepandee: Wow. That's pretty... well, damn! Looks like the eggs produced in third world countries are much safer! When I mentioned the story about myself, my parents, and their parents, I should note that they (as well as myself) are/were Iranian and I lived in Iran until I was 16. So yeah, our president might deny the holocaust and our nuclear program might be looked upon with suspicion, but we have good eggs.

Mark Rippetoe: I think the soil in Iran may be cleaner. Until we make it radioactive for you. But you're here now, so it's okay.

Rhymer: My understanding is that salmonella used to be more of an issue with eggs than it is today, due to improved inspection and handling in the supply chain. To some extent, this may be similar to trichinosis, which apparently is virtually non-existent today but still strikes fear into the hearts of many. That said, gulping down dozens of eggs on a daily basis is hardly the diet we evolved to eat. And organic chickens are still filthy.

Mark Rippetoe: All chickens are filthy. Have you ever been around chickens? They are stupid, uncooperative, inconvenient, ill-tempered creatures. I say steal their eggs, kill them, and eat them. They get what they deserve. Fuck chickens.

The Ocho: Sports-related Stuff.

I am not really the biggest sports fan in North America. I quit watching football when Staubach stopped being the quarterback. Baseball as a spectator sport has always seemed a little slow, like watching chess. Basketball involves very tall people, and I cannot relate. I do not understand hockey, being a Texan. Soccer is more fun to play than to watch, and the huge crowds of fans always seem to be singing badly. Sumo is cool, but it's hard to obtain in this country. The field sports, fencing, wrestling, and the other interesting individual events that are the guts of the Olympics are prohibited from broadcast by the network, because they would take valuable time away from explaining how one of the swimmers' moms is winning her battle with cancer. Bullfighting and dueling are considered inappropriate for modern American audiences. And I don't have time anyway. So this section may be a little skewed.

2 questions - Specificity and Microloading

Peter_k: 1. I use microweights all the time in my workouts, and find them indispensable. However, one gym I went to didn't allow "bags," meaning that I'd have to carry them in my pockets (not even really possible) or not use them at all.

Needless to say, I didn't figure this would be a good place to come, long-term. But I got to wondering: how valuable are microplates, in your opinion, and what is their main benefit (what is different about simply increasing by 5lbs when you're ready to, rather than tiny increments all the time?) Does everyone in your gym use them, by the way?

2. About sport specificity and powerlifting. You mention in your books about how certain ways to do exercises (like sumo squats or deadlifts) are suitable for powerlifting and not for general strength. Is the opposite true, though? I realize that doing wide-stance squats is good preparation for doing, well, wide-stance squats, but wouldn't getting stronger overall be better for powerlifting, a test of absolute strength? I mean, training power cleans can help powerlifters more than deadlifts sometimes, even though they're not specific to the sport. So why wouldn't doing shoulder-width, non-suited, below parallel squats help more than geared sumo squats, in the same way?

I guess my question is this: could powerlifting be an exception to the specificity rule because it's so similar to general weight training? You don't learn to jump by doing only squats--you need to practice jumping. But I suspect you could squat at a competition without ever training wide-stance squats.

Mark Rippetoe: 1.) Small plates are useful because small muscles don't get strong as fast as big muscles. So, 1 lb. plates are useful for the press and the bench press, but not for the deadlift. It is not always possible to go up 5 lbs. on the press and make all 5 reps of all 3 sets, so when this is the case you add 2 lbs. so you can maintain your rate of increase.

2.) If you don't practice your competitive movement, you will not be as good at it as you would be if you did. There are strength specificities to the wide stance suited squat that must be addressed, but if for no other reason you have to practice them in training so you can do them in the meet to the best of your ability. In other words, yes, powerlifting is a specialized expression of strength that must be trained for specifically.

SS and Rock Climbing

M2H8M: I've read about doing some other training like CrossFit or sprinting with SS but nothing about rock climbing. Do you think that climbing 1-2 times for a couple hours per week would interfere with strength gains from your great program? I am just starting it and am 17 if that helps. Thanks!

Mark Rippetoe: I think of rock climbing as a sport or activity that strength benefits, not something that is in and of itself training. But that depends entirely on the level at which you climb. Mark Twight or Rob Miller obviously climb hard enough to produce enough stress that it would need to be taken into consideration in a barbell training program they were doing. I don't know about you; it might. You'd know more about how hard you climb, and whether it would constitute a training effect in and of itself that might interfere with your barbell program.

High Rep O-Lifting

Craigrasm: This is something I have been meaning to ask you about. One of the criticisms that I have seen about CrossFit is the use of high rep Olympic lifting and the possible dangers that can occur due to technical breakdown. I'm sure that many of us have all heard that the Olympic lifts aren't very suited to higher reps (usually no more than 5 rep sets are suggested) because of their more technical nature. I am sure that you can put this into context and I am curious to hear any thoughts that you may have on this subject.

Mark Rippetoe: I think that anyone who can do snatches or clean and jerks with high reps and enough intensity to produce a metabolic conditioning effect is obviously strong enough at the lifts that using weights light enough that this can be done is neither dangerous nor counterproductive to good form on heavier work. It is not useful to do sets of 10, or even 5, on these two lifts with weights heavy enough that the last reps are sloppy. But 30 snatches done in a short time cannot be done with enough weight that it could be considered the same problem. I think that if this is anyone's major problem with CrossFit, then that is not much of a problem.

Power Clean video – WTF?

Pear: I am new to power cleans as I've been reading SS 2nEd and practicing for a few weeks at the gym. I went to YouTube to see some videos to get some better ideas of what it's supposed to look like, and while I am not really in a position to criticize...

WHAT IN THE HELL ARE SOME OF THESE PEOPLE DOING???

To me this (and many other videos) look to be as bad a form as one could possibly do - even though this little shit and countless others with cut-off t-shirts and weightlifting gloves are tougher than nails and can probably lift more than I can... it looks ridiculous - maybe I'm wrong:

Attachment removed to keep from embarrassing a kid that doesn't know any better.

Is this seriously what's going on in the world?

Mark Rippetoe: What's going on here is the same thing that's been going on for a long time: it is in the best interest of the coach that the athlete "clean" (and "squat" and "bench" and "deadlift") as much weight as possible, and form is not important. If the coach can say that his entire defensive line can "clean 300", this looks pretty good to the AD, better than 225 done correctly. The AD doesn't know any better than the coach, and the kids suffer for this incompetence/unconcern.

This awareness can be applied to many aspects of human conduct, if you think about it.

Strength levels for OL?

navi86: How do you know when you have adequate strength relative to your OL competitive lifts. I'm guessing there is probably no set formula (i.e. squat has to be at least 150% of clean & jerk), but are there any indicators or ways to tell?

Mark Rippetoe: This question is astonishingly vague. What the hell are you asking about?

navi86: Success in Olympic lifting is a function of at least strength, speed, technique, and flexibility. Time spent on one of those elements is time you could be spending on the others. What I am asking is, how do you know if you have enough maximal strength for how much you are lifting in the competitive OL lifts? For example, if I have a 500lb. squat and a 100lb. clean, then it is pretty obvious maximal strength is not something I need to focus on for the time being. But what if I only have a 300, 200, or 110lb. squat and 100lb. clean? I'm sure everyone is different and there is no set ratio for maximal strength in the squat vs. your clean, but are there any indicators/clues that will tell you if maximal strength is or is not your problem?

Mark Rippetoe: Everybody operates at a different level of efficiency with respect to turning force production into power. Also, anyone capable of becoming a competitive weightlifter has about 95% of their technical ability developed in the snatch and the C&J by the end of the first year of training, so while it is true that training each parameter represents time that could be spent training other parameters, the real question will always be, which parameter's improvement will contribute the most to my total? Speed is largely controlled by genetic endowment, as sad as this may be, because it is almost purely a function of the efficiency of the neuromuscular system and the density of motor unit innervation; it cannot be improved much more than 25%, if that. Flexibility is developed by the exercises themselves, and while some supplemental stretching may be necessary at first for more inflexible individuals, it doesn't represent a huge investment of time and effort.

So we're left with strength, aren't we? A guy with a 500 lb. squat and a 100 lb. clean has that ratio for about a week, and then normal improvement for a person capable of doing the sport rapidly carries this ratio closer to where it should be. The real question, stated another way, is this: if a guy has a 500 lb. squat and a 300 lb. clean, is technically good at the clean, and has been stable at this ratio for several months, what will be the best way to get his clean to go up? Or, what would be the best way to improve the 300 lb. clean of a guy with a 400 lb. squat? In either case, the easiest way – and the most often neglected or overlooked way, for whatever the reason – is to increase the squat. And the deadlift, while we're at it. Because no matter what the ratio is, once it's stable it should be recognized as that individual's indicator of the strength/power relationship and used accordingly.

I know that this is not mainstream Olympic weightlifting thinking. I just think that it should be.

Sport Specificity

Jason AUS: I understand that the core lifts (deadlift, squat, OH press) are great because they are performed standing, and in most sporting endeavors, the kinetic chain begins from the floor, when the athlete is standing. I have one concern about the positioning of the individual. I understand that the body is highly adaptive, and it is highly adaptive to the exercises we do.

My question is in relation to Brazilian Jiu-Jitsu (or, just the ground aspect of wrestling). Because most of the movements are performed on the floor, either on your back or on your knees, how is the principle of specificity employed? As an example, if I performed a bent over row standing, and then in a match was called upon to pull my opponent close to me while I am on my back, how effective would the movement transfer be?

Also, have a question which might sound stupid, but here goes. In the cold, if you don't wear enough clothes and are always cold, will you be more susceptible to storing fat because your body is adapting to the cold stressor?

Mark Rippetoe: The transfer is not specific, unless you're doing barbell training for a barbell sport. Strength is a general adaptation, not a skill. The specifics of barbell biomechanics control the training, and the strength gained transfers through sports practice because the mechanics of the sport are different than that which governs barbell training. The *row* doesn't have to transfer – it can't, because you don't wrestle barbells.

The *strength* produced by training the row transfers to wrestling because you practiced it as you got stronger.

Regarding the question about training while you're cold. I assume that you have heard that swimmers store fat as an adaptation to the cold stressor, and you extrapolate this to training in your basement. Maybe you do. But really, who gives a shit about either swimmers or a little bodyfat?

Intermediate Olympic Weightlifting setup

Polynomial: I'm slowly but surely creeping towards the intermediate category. I've decided to start training for Olympic weightlifting. Unfortunately, I'm having a hell of a time setting up a 4 day routine. My short term goal is to bring my C&J and Snatch to where they should be given my strength levels. This requires doing a lot of those lifts to solidify my technique (along with some assistance exercises like drop snatches, etc.,) But I also began to have nightmares about not squatting enough and my strength progress stalling. What's your recommendation in a case like this?

I currently thought up the following basis for a 4 day program. The idea would be to work the Olympic stuff on Monday and Thursday, and do strength related exercises on Tuesday and Thursday.

Monday
C&J - Some warm-up then 10-12 singles. At this point I'm not sure if I should stick with the same weight, or slowly increase throughout the sets.
??? - some assistance exercises for the C&J?
Tuesday
Squats - 3x5? 5x5? 5x3? And should I aim improve from week to week?
Bench press/Alt with press -Same question as above
Thursday
Snatches - Some warm-up then 10-12 singles. Same questions as for the C&J.
Friday
Deadlift alt. with RDL - one set of 5 for the deadlift, maybe couple sets of 8-10 for the RDL. *Bench press/Alt with press*

Mark Rippetoe: The Olympic lifts are complex movements that require lots of practice, and that means that you need to do each lift at least twice/week, probably more. How about this:

Monday: Snatch volume, squat 1s or 2s, press, chins
Tuesday: Clean & Jerk volume, snatch light, front squat
Thursday: Snatch medium, clean medium, jerk from rack, bench
Friday: Snatch and Clean & Jerk heavy singles, squat 5s, deadlift 5s/RDLs

Polynomial: Sounds great, thanks! By the way, when you wrote '1s', do you mean 1 set or a heavy single? And I assume that doing enough snatches removes much need for overhead squats at this moment?

Mark Rippetoe: 1s means multiple heavy singles, and overhead squats will not be necessary unless there is a specific problem to solve with them.

Intermediate programming and the Olympic lifts

Kerpal: I just joined a gym with bumper plates and a platform so I was very excited to be able to do the Olympic lifts, but I wasn't really sure how to incorporate them into the program.
Right now I'm doing a power snatch because I'm too scared to drop into a full squat with a weight overhead, and a power clean & jerk because after power cleaning for so long I'm having a hard time making myself drop into a full front squat position during the clean. Any idea how I can fix this? I get the feeling your answer to the first problem is going to be "stop being a pussy", but what about the clean & jerk?

Mark Rippetoe: If you really want to do the 2 lifts, they need to be done twice a week at least. They are somewhat technical and require more practice than training – at least until you get good at doing them. In the context of your 3-day schedule, I'd snatch Monday, C&J Wednesday, and do both on Friday, with perhaps an alternation between the Monday and Wednesday lifts each week. Keep your strength base trained like you have been doing and add the 2 lifts to the program. And you'd better try to get some coaching on the more technical aspects of this project, like the full squat snatch.

Starting Olympic lifting...

Stronger: I've been toying with the idea of competing in Olympic lifting. Nothing big, just something to do and get good at. I know this isn't an Olympic board, but I was wondering if you could give me an idea of whether or not this is plausible.

Where would I start?

I am 5'8, weigh 175-180lbs. 19 years old
best 1RM (done on calculator)
Squat: 285
Deadlift: 315
Bench: 195
Press: 135
Power Clean: 135 (I've been doing these for 2 weeks, could probably rack 155-165, rough estimate)

I'm not very strong, and I started sort of late, so it might not be worth it, but I thought I'd put it out there. I will work hard though.

Mark Rippetoe: No matter what your lifts are – and they are fine for a starting point – the most important thing you can do to become a meet lifter is to get a coach, or at least some coaching. It is very hard to do this without feedback in real-time, so much so that many bad habits will be acquired that will be hard to break later.

Basketball

ben23: Just wondering what would you say was the best exercise out of the ones listed below, or one that you know of, for improving explosive strength, specific to basketball and vertical jumping?

Snatch
Clean and Press
Power Clean
Hang Clean/Snatch
weighted squat jumps

Mark Rippetoe: How much do you weigh, and how much do you squat?

ben23: Sorry, yeah should have been a bit more informative. 84kilos, and 1 rep max of 110K. I haven't started SS btw, I haven't done any major strength program, so am hoping that will increase my vertical.

Mark Rippetoe: Then in this case your primary exercise for increasing vertical jump is the squat. Increase your absolute strength and your force production goes up, and nothing more is either necessary or recommended for a novice.

Routine for fencer

Rudd: I'm a competitive fencer looking to up my strength. The last two years have been mainly a CrossFit-style workout. While my fitness is good I feel my overall strength has dropped.

You had previously provided me a copy of your excellent document "Strength and Conditioning for Fencing" (*Strength and Conditioning Journal, 22(2), 2000*). I was looking for some feedback on the programme I've constructed from it. I will be lifting twice per week. It basically just a variation of Onus Wunsler routine but with vertical jumps substituted for squats on day two as per a suggestion you sent me before.

Workout A Monday
3x5 Squat
3x5 Press
2x5 Deadlift alternated w/ 5x3 Power Cleans

Workout B Thursday
3 x20 moving toward 5 x 30 Vertical jumps
3x5 Bench Press
3x10 or 5x10 Back Extensions (unweighted)
Chin-Ups: 3 sets to failure or add weight if completing more than 15 rep

I also had one other injury related question. I have reduced range of motion in both flexion and external rotation in my right hip. This affects my squat as I go below parallel and causes it to become slightly skewed. I have had therapy and it has helped but not fully corrected the issue. Would you recommend stopping at parallel or not worrying about the slight irregularity at greater depth. I unfortunately don't have access to a video at the moment.

Mark Rippetoe: If you're serious about increasing your strength quickly, you need to squat twice/week. The jumps are useful, but do them on a separate day. As far as the injury, what caused it, and why have your squats not improved your ROM?

Brandon: I'd add some unilateral assistance work for fencing... one-legged plyo work (maybe depth jumps or something) might be helpful. Other than static strength in the stance, you really need to be able to fire quickly off of one leg.

Rudd: Thanks for the feedback. I'll move the jumps to a separate day and squat twice weekly. The hip injury was probably caused by fencing. It appears to be chronic tendinitis but I have been recommended to get an MRI in case I had a labral tear. Therapy improves but doesn't fully alleviate the issue. I've been working on my squat form and my ROM is good. However once I break parallel my left hip sinks deeper than my right and this pushes my right knee slightly further forward. Concentrating on keeping the hamstrings tight helps. but I just lack the necessary flexion on the right side. After a therapy session the ROM is better.

Squatting doesn't appear to further aggravate the issue or cause additional pain but I'm just worried about any long term issues the torsion might cause. FWIW front squats to the same depth don't appear to be as asymmetrical.

Mark Rippetoe: This question came up in response to the original article:

I read with interest the article titled Strength and Conditioning for Fencing by Mr. Rippetoe. I congratulate him on his ability to provide general information regarding the sport of fencing and the keys to a successful sports specific weight training program. I would like to point out an area which is lacking from the article - muscle strength imbalances.
Mr. Rippetoe pointed out that fencing is very unique in that the motions required are very ipsilateral in nature. The majority of weight bearing and eccentric loading is on the lead (forward) leg and explosive attacks done only with the lead (weapon) arm. In more experienced and elite level fencers these factors create the potential for strength imbalances in the quadriceps, shoulder, and forearm musculature. Studies have been done by Sapega (1) and Nystrom (2) and myself (3) that confirm this. In addition, there is evidence that statistically significant strength imbalances increase the potential for injury (4). This being said, I believe it is necessary for any fencing coach and strength coach to address this issue and instruct his/her athletes to perform exercises that counteract this. Lunges, one-legged squats and skipping/hopping exercises for the back leg and single arm pulley or dumbbell exercises for the back arm are examples of exercises that address this issue.

Thank You,
Kevin M. Casey, MA, ATC,CSCS
Director of Rehabilitation - Health and Wellness Clinic
Salt Lake City, Utah

My response:

The observation is certainly valid, but I believe that the program suggested in the article addresses the imbalances inherent in an ipsilateral sport such as fencing. Although it is true that the lunge and the position of the weapon arm and back leg produce strength asymmetries in fencers, the performance of these movements requires a small percentage of absolute strength, even in a non-resistance-trained athlete. As the program detailed in the article is implemented and strength increases in the specified exercises, the symmetrical nature of the squat, presses, and pulling movements strengthen all the muscles in a balanced way, quickly making irrelevant any strength asymmetries acquired during fencing.

A similar observation could be made regarding the performance and training of the snatch and the clean and jerk. In years past, and indeed today in many masters competitions, the split snatch and the split clean were commonly performed; the split jerk is still the usual technique. These are asymmetrical movements, and significant strength imbalances would have been produced if training excluded other exercises. This was seldom observed because of the tendency of weightlifters to train the squat, presses, and pulling movements with heavier weights than those used in the competitive lifts. Great strength in the heavy symmetrical exercises renders irrelevant the asymmetrical nature of light ipsilateral activity.

Rudd, I would suggest that when you see a hip/knee asymmetry the problem might be solved by keeping the knees symmetrical. I have found that if your knees are doing exactly the same thing (and you don't have a short leg) your hips will do the same thing too. If you make damn sure that your knees stay straight at the bottom of your squat ROM, the hips will stretch the way they should be stretched to increase the ROM.

Routine Question

Conniffj: I am a wrestling coach. Currently I have my team doing SS and am seeing huge strength gains. My goal in the "off-season" is to get them as strong and big as possible. I am not a big fan of weight cutting, our team usually loses all their weight due to the intensity of our practices. Strength training during season is always difficult. It is always a challenge to balance conditioning, technique, live wrestling, and strength training without overtraining.

We just finished our Freestyle/Greco season and I have been having them do only strength training. I am getting ready to work in some agility training also (dot drills, gymnastics and some stuff I picked up from CrossFit). Do you have any recommendations at all about how to structure a program for wrestlers? Exercises that are a must? How often to lift during season and what type of rep/set scheme? Any advice would be greatly appreciated!

Mark Rippetoe: I think they need a simple 3 x/week program of squats, presses, deadlifts, benches, cleans, and chins/pullups for an off-season lasting several months using a straight linear progression. If I were going to have wrestlers train in-season, I'd have them squat, press, and clean once a week, at a time when they had an opportunity to get full recovery before a meet.

Conniffj: This is pretty much what I am having them do right now. As for in-season, do you think If we did a heavy lift on a Monday (using the exercises you mentioned) and follow it up with a sandbag workout on Wednesday we would have enough recovery time for a meet on Friday and still be able to maintain if not gain strength? Also what kind of rep scheme would you use? We have a "trainer" who is saying high rep/low weight with only 1 or 2 sets. I think if a kid is trying to maintain if not build strength we should stick to a 3x5 or 4x6 plan. Also we want to build strength but not really size. Season is 4 months long so we have to do something to stay strong for the run at State at the end!

Jeroen: Would your advice be the same for a football player (soccer player you call it in the states) with all the running, jogging, walking, short sprints that's being done during a game and normal training?

Mark Rippetoe: My advice would be the same for both in-season sports. The sandbag workout would be fine on Wednesday, since they are high-school kids and they can get recovered since you're not one of those irresponsible weight-loss-at-all-costs coaches. And your "trainer" does not understand the rep-range continuum on page 60 of PPST2.

The Press and Competitive Powerlifting

KSC: Wondering what your opinion was on the role of the Press in a competitive powerlifter's program. Looking around at a lot of guys training it is a rarity that you find it in a lot of use, with the seated version being more prevalent or often times, no overhead work at all. In addition, in the now somewhat popularized Max Effort/Dynamic Effort styled programs, where do you find the appropriate place is to insert this exercise?

Mark Rippetoe: I think that the press is of primary value to the competitive PLer as an injury preventer, but that to get the best benefit it should be approached as another primary lift. IOW, it should be trained with the same ME/DE approach as the other lifts. In my opinion, but again, I don't train modern equipment-based PLers.

Have you ever heard of this guy?

B33k4y: 124k bodyweight and 6'4:

(Deleted Youtube links of Konstantin Konstantinovs deadlifting 885 x 2. This may be the strongest human alive today. Look him up.)

Thoughts?

Mark Rippetoe: I obviously taught him to deadlift, since he uses perfect technique.

Banderbe: I guess what constitutes perfect changes as weights get very heavy because he seems like his back is pretty rounded. But what do I know?

Jamieb: Err... Mark, was comment that tongue-in-cheek? To my untrained eye, that seems like much less than perfect technique. Isn't his thoracic spine in a much more rounded position than you coach in the CF videos? Am I missing the point because acceptable standards change when the weight becomes that heavy? Help me out here.

Mark Rippetoe: Okay, would you guys agree that an 885 double is heavy? Would you also agree that any 2RM is going to have some technical problems or it's not really an actual 2RM? And would you not agree that if you were going to have a technical problem that still allowed you to finish the second rep, a rounded upper back would be better than, say, a rounded lumbar, or the bar away from your mid-foot? Any limit attempt is going to be less that perfect – including yours – or it's not a limit attempt. The bar came up in a perfectly straight bar path from directly over the mid-foot and locked out for 2 reps, with a weight that exceeds the world records for a single in more than a few federations. Perfect form is a Model for the best use of your skeletal and muscular mechanics for the movement. But as you approach your limit, your adherence to the model will begin to deviate, until it deviates to the point that you cannot execute the movement with a weight any heavier. If you are content to never lift a weight heavier than you can move with perfect form, you will be lifting weights with perfect form that will never make you any stronger. And I'll bet that he regards his round upper back as "perfect form", since it seems to be working well.

As is so often the case, the perfect is the enemy of the good. In this case, the perfect is perhaps the enemy of the stronger.

Jamieb: Ok I think there's something worth clarifying here. Take the case of a novice trainee on SS only doing 5RMs. For the first few weeks, there should be no failure, right? As progress starts to slow, you might begin to approach failure on a set of deadlifts by the 5th rep. Do you think it's acceptable for form to deviate a little at the end of a set of 5 for a novice trainee as linear progress reaches a limit, or is it the case that form should never be allowed to deviate on a 5RM for a novice training for sports conditioning purposes?

Mark Rippetoe: Yes, there is in fact quite a bit of difference between a novice trainee and a world champion powerlifter, and I'd like to thank you for pointing that out to everyone. But at this point everybody who reads this board needs to come to grips with the fact that there are no absolutes in barbell training, or in anything else with more than about 3 variables. Do I really need to tell you that a guy training for a world record in a dangerous competitive sport might have a different perspective on what is an acceptable deviation from the mechanical deadlift model than a novice in his 3rd week of training that is still trying to learn how to keep his low back flat, or what that even means? Does Dale Jr. get to break the speed limit if he needs to catch Jeff? What is the speed limit in Florida anyway?

Deadlift vs. clean starting positions

Brandon: There have been some remarks made by a couple of Olympic weightlifting coaches about the respective powerlifting and Oly starting positions over at the CF boards. Suggests that hips lower, with shoulders back, is advantageous for the clean. Thoughts?

This is not an attempt to start inter-coach feuds... although that's always fun.

Mark Rippetoe: Sure it is Brandon, you ass-hole. So, here we go. I see no advantage to starting in a position that is out of line with the mechanics of force transfer through the skeleton. I know what is being said – look for yourself: go to youtube and look at a lot of snatches, as many as you can see from the side, and see for yourself what happens to the bar as it leaves the floor. Then look at really heavy cleans, and then heavy deadlifts. My prediction is that the heavier the bar gets (i.e. snatch to clean to deadlift) the more closely the pulling mechanics will conform to our model. Since the bar obviously hangs beneath the scapulas, as you will see, why not just start there and save the energy expended getting it there later, and the energy wasted moving it through an inefficient bar path? And if his more vertical back position reduces fatigue on the lower back in the clean and the snatch, why not the deadlift too, where the heavy weight makes pulling efficiency even more critical? The reason is that this is not how a heavy pull moves, and it is therefore not the best way to pull a lighter one either. And how is "fatigue" a factor in a movement that takes less than a second to perform?

I know what everybody does. I've watched many thousands of lifts done this way because that's the way they were taught, or they weren't taught at all, as one poster mentioned. I've seen it for 30 years. I'm more concerned with what everybody *should* be doing instead. And I'm not asking you to BELIEVE me. Try it yourself and see.

Polynomial: Would it be fair to say that a lot of lifters do a funky set up where they squat down with their hips below their knees, then start to raise themselves right before the pull, making it difficult for most people to see exactly when the bar gets off the ground?

For what it's worth, the famous Olympic lifter Tommy Kono has said that he wants the hips to be higher than the knees, because once the bar gets past your knees, you want your legs to be nearly straight, keeping your hamstrings tight and ready for the second pull.

Mark Rippetoe: It would be more fair to say that the dynamic start produces a looped bar path off the floor, and that the straight line produced by my method is more exactly reproducible every time. This eliminates an important source of variability in bar path and makes it much easier to be maximally efficient every time, in addition to all the mechanical advantages already described elsewhere. And my method produces exactly the position Mr. Kono advocates at the top, and gets it there with a vertical bar path. And I have never heard a good mechanical argument for a non-vertical bar path.

Brandon: So I hashed this out with some O-lifters and the response I got is basically that: the bar starts touching the shins, the scapulae start over the bar, the back is locked in posture, BUT the difference is that the bar actually starts FORWARD of the mid-foot. This lets the shins come forward, the knees come forward, the hips come down, and at last, the torso to become more vertical.

Argument: unlike in the deadlift, the goal is not to move the greatest possible weight, but to provide the best starting position for the second pull. The more vertical torso allows this, and this does not demand the bar starting exactly over the mid-foot. This latter, at least, seems reasonable given how many times my bar has swung forward during deadlifts due to weak traps. I'm starting to buy it...

Mark Rippetoe: When the bar is forward of the mid-foot and the knees are more forward and acute, the tension on the hamstrings is gone and the lower back is much easier to arch into lumbar extension, and this is why most lifters like to start there – it's much easier to "set" the back with the bar in front of the foot. The price paid for this is the curve in the bar path as the knees go back, the hamstrings tighten, and the bar moves back into its position of balance over the mid-foot. When you look at a lifter like Naim Suleymanoglu (find a video on youtube.com), or any other strong lifter that starts the pull with the bar over his toes, watch the bar path closely. Where is the bar just after he clears the floor? By the time it gets to his knees, where is it? The bar always heads toward the position it would have been in anyway had he started it as I suggest.

Much more importantly, notice his back angle at this point, and then look at it between there and the start of his second pull. Please tell me why you think that his back angle off the floor being "more vertical" has anything to do with his back angle at the second pull when he has clearly assumed the position that I predict he will by the time he gets the bar to his knees – a position with the bar hanging directly under his scapulas with the bar over the middle of his foot – and then changes it as he rotates behind the bar for the second pull. At the knees he is at the same position HE WOULD HAVE BEEN IN had he pulled it off the floor over the mid-foot, and since that angle was assumed at that point, his starting angle had *nothing to do* with his second pull position. *Except that he wasted a bunch of energy getting there inefficiently.* He is strong enough that this obviously doesn't matter to HIM, but saying that he does it this way so it must be right is not an analysis – it's merely an observation and an Appeal to Authority.

Would you suggest that a curved line off the floor is a more efficient and reproducible way to get the bar to your knees than a straight vertical line? Would you seriously suggest that a more physically efficient pull off the floor would be detrimental to his total? Why would it not be better to have a straighter bar path? How would a coach not appreciate the physics of the straighter pull? The reason is the same as the one you have cited here: this is the way it is done, THE WAY IT HAS ALWAYS BEEN DONE, at least until somebody does it differently. Well, Pyrros Dimas, for example, does it differently. And I'm just saying that this is not reasoning.

Brandon: I haven't played with it enough for a personal opinion, but my instinct is that the "reason" for a more vertical start position, EVEN IF you end up having to move back momentarily into the deadlift posture at some point in the pull, is that the psychological difference between:

1. Starting horizontal (deadlift) and going vertical (second pull)
and
2. Starting vertical (first pull), popping through a horizontal position for a moment, and immediately moving back to your vertical position for the second pull is significant, and lets you "feel" like you're staying more vertical the entire time. Combine that with being as vertical as possible within the biomechanical limitations of the movement (there is some room for variation here and this way you're always on one extreme) and the difference may be significant.

I think it's at least fair to suggest that plenty of weightlifters have TRIED it both ways and even if it just feels better one way, that's not really a terrible reason to do it as long as they're getting the weight up. A lot of Olympic lifting is in figuring out what weird language you need to speak to communicate the correct technique to your brain that lets you be both mechanically correct and still expressing the maximum force. "It feels better" may not be a terrific reason to do something, but the "greater efficiency of moving around less" may not be an especially important one either, as long as you're not missing lifts because of it.

Perhaps the heavier the weight gets the closer to a deadlift the first pull gets, because they become closer in function. But if it's just a mental game that hardly seems to matter, since it'll adjust itself. And in truth I'm sure there's nobody cleaning very close to their max deadlift anyway, since you couldn't generate enough speed.

Mark Rippetoe: So you're saying that "feeling" is more important than mechanics. I'm saying that the reason they do it this way is simply and only because that's the way they learned it. It might not matter so much if they were strong enough off the floor to tolerate a bad mechanical position, but they aren't. More later on this. And no, most weightlifters have not tried it both ways, because many weightlifting coaches do not even address the start position at all, and lots of the ones that do insist on the vertical back angle. And if a weightlifter misses an attempt, then he hasn't gotten the weight up, and you can't say that that lost efficiency during the bottom part of the pull wasn't the reason.

One of the hard parts about both the clean and the deadlift is holding the back angle constant until the bar gets up to the position where the back angle would mechanically need to change. It is almost as though the dynamic start is a way to rationalize around having to perform this important skill. All weightlifters miss lifts, and they always will. I just want them to make and miss heavier lifts by pulling from the floor more efficiently.

I find it ironic that the idealized situation is pulling with the shoulders over the bar and the bar as close to the body as possible – no one would argue that you are stronger with the bar farther away from the mid-foot, would they? Yet this idealized situation is prevented from occurring by allowing a poor start position. I'm just saying that this idealized situation also applies to the pull from the floor and pulling from the floor in this manner sets up this idealized situation for the remainder of the pull. Probably the most common cues given to weightlifters would stop being "over the bar", "close", "keep it close" and "finish the pull" if a disadvantageous start position was abandoned in favor of a simple recognition of the correct physical model. After all, it is not 1919 and a "clean" is now allowed to touch the body on the way up. Quote:

> *Perhaps the heavier the weight gets, the closer to a deadlift the first pull gets, because they become closer in function. But if it's just a mental game that hardly seems to matter, since it'll adjust itself. And in truth I'm sure there's nobody cleaning very close to their max deadlift anyway, since you couldn't generate enough speed.*

And you're wrong about this too, unfortunately. One of the biggest problems in the American version of Olympic weightlifting is that you have a bunch of senior international coaches running around the country telling their lifters that a strong deadlift/back squat is unnecessary and represents wasted training time. The fact is that lots – maybe the vast majority – of American Olympic weightlifters can't deadlift more than 20% more than they clean. Really. Kendrick Farris comes to mind as a notable exception, and he's one of the 2 (3?) on our team at Beijing this year. If our lifters were stronger, like all of the Europeans and Asians poised to hand us our asses, the start position wouldn't matter so much. And in fact that is what you see when you watch the European training videos of the Polish guys pulling the bar off the floor from in front of their shoes – guys that are strong enough that they can tolerate a bad mechanical position. And I promise you they are very strong, for various good reasons. Just remember this simple fact: steroids do not improve technique, yet they are deemed important enough to take to risk your career.

Weightlifting coaches seem quite content to focus on the technical aspects of the top part of the pulls, and content to ignore the start position details. At the same time, they claim that technique is more important than strength. But if a lifter is not going to focus on strength in his training, he'd damn sure better have the correct technique off the floor since he doesn't have the strength "surplus" that allows stronger lifters to more successfully do it wrong, the harder, non-vertical way. A more critical examination of this pulling model would be of benefit to these hard-working kids that deserve more from their coaches than just copying more successful coaches with stronger athletes.

SS broken up

Arlo: I only have 2 months for training before my soccer season. I really want to start SS now but I'm not sure if I can expect the same results by following the program for these two months and post-season as I would if I just followed it post-season without any interruptions. If I do start pre-season I'll try to maintain the strength gained by squatting, pressing, and deadlifting once a week (is that right?) during the season and continuing where I left off afterwards. If breaking it up will be a hindrance to any future gains I will just do CrossFit for the 2 months I have and start SS after soccer. What do you think?

Mark Rippetoe: I think that since the strength and size will benefit your soccer season, you'd better start yesterday. All the other considerations are irrelevant.

Arlo: Forgot to mention that I'm 17, about 5'8-9 and 140-150 (somewhere in the ballpark on weight and height). I read that you recommend squats, presses, and cleans once a week in season for wrestlers. Do you think this would be more beneficial for a soccer player as well rather than squats, presses, and deadlifts? My main goal is to maintain strength in season so I can continue post season smoothly. Also, should I use the same rep scheme as if I were lifting 3x per week (3x5 for squats and presses, 1x5 for deads and 5x3 for power cleans)?

Jeroen: Would you advise Squat, Press, Deadlift once a week during season or Squat, Press, Power Clean? Or is this irrelevant too?

Mark Rippetoe: Since you both asked, others will want to know too. I don't think it's that critical for a holding pattern, but if you find that you can in fact make progress during the season – and you very well might if you're a young novice – you can alternate deadlifts and cleans. You can actually train twice/week if you're still getting recovered enough to get stronger during the season. Just don't tell anybody I told you that, because it is

Heresy.

Paul: I would wager a significant portion of my monthly income that a 17 year old soccer player could continue to lift 3x a week in season using a routine like that in Starting Strength. You might need to make some minor adjustments, maybe back off a little on some days, but I honestly think we underestimate our recovery ability, especially in teenage boys, who can lift, run, chase young girls, do all the other things 17 year olds do, and still score a goal on Saturday.

Mark Rippetoe: IF you can get the little bastards to eat. It has been my experience that boys soccer in the US is plagued by hemp clothing, Hacky Sack, and a strong desire for abs that precludes eating enough to recover from any type of training.

Sorry Rip, just couldn't do it...

Fluxboy: So I think to myself: This *Starting Strength* routine worked. And I bet there's all sorts of people out there that could use a nudge. Perhaps I can do my part to spread the word.

I swing by T-Nation and bodybuilding.com and I'm horrified. Absolutely horrified. I type in "Rippetoe", and I find the most bizarre questions I've ever come across. And you should see the answers. Just weird shit that I can't even respond to. I'm mean, its so far off, it's not even wrong. Then I go to "Transformations of the month" and all I see are fat guys with their belly sticking out, "transformed" by dropping thirty pounds, sucking their gut in, tanned, bleached, and ... oiled? It's weird. And creepy. And they want to know what supplements were taken. (My first thought: estrogen?)

I was going to just put a nice post on how a simple little book called *Starting Strength* taught me how to squat, bench, deadlift, power clean and press correctly. And along the way, I put on thirty-five pounds in a few months. Fuck that. I don't want to be near a forum with oiled guys and hyper NOs vacuum pumped androgelatin. Sorry Rip, someone else will have to spread the word. I just don't have the stomach for it. I'm serious.

Mark Rippetoe: Yes, the internet is a very weird place.

h k: Here's a good quote from t-nation:

Does anyone else have a problem with this program [my note: SS]? It's an insanely low volume of work, and I've not met a single person with a decent total who's done the program. Granted, it's a program that'll get kids hitting basic exercises instead of the pec dec, but they also live in fear that some sort of Overtraining Boogeyman is going to emerge from their closet and steal all of their muscle if they even THINK about doing more than the 11 total sets (or thereabouts) that he prescribes. ***Lastly, insofar as I know, Rippetoe has never totalled decently in a meet or the gym, and looks like he's never entered a gym, leading me to think that "Starting Strength" should really be called "The Blind and Fat leading the Blind into the Squat Rack."***

Thoughts?

It's amazing how deep a critique people can give without even reading the book. Oh the internet...

Mark Rippetoe: I guess the T-Nation boys don't remember me competing in the 80s, since little kids weren't allowed in the warmup room. It would be logic of the worst kind to base the weight of one's opinions about lifting weights on one's former, or even current, total, the genetic variable being as important as it is. I was never a very good lifter, and I have never claimed to be. In my defense, it has been my experience that good athletes are usually poor coaches. And I have actually never claimed to be a good coach either. But to clear up the misconception that I was never a lifter at all, here are my previous PRs at 220:

Meet squat: 611, (622 got 2 reds, one depth and one politics)
Gym squat: 600 x 3 Both done in a single-ply Frantz suit I still have.
Meet bench: 396 on an easy 3rd attempt after my foot slipped on the 2nd with that weight. In a t-shirt. I have never been in a bench shirt.
Meet deadlift: 633 on two separate occasions.

PR Total: 1643
Won the Greater Texas Classic at 198 in 1981. Retired from PL competition in 1988.

Squatting in Powerlifting

Kerpal: Is the rule for legal squat depth in Powerlifting different from the one you present in SSBBT? I've been watching a lot of Powerlifting videos on Youtube and very rarely does it look like they are deep enough, but the lifts are usually approved anyway.

Mark Rippetoe: My depth criterion is the same that is supposed to be used in powerlifting, in that I take it directly from the old USPF rules developed by my good friend John Pettit, whose annoying craziness I miss quite a bit. Your observations are interesting, and you are not the first to make them.

Training the Dead with Pulls

KSC: I've heard you mention a few times about how Starr had you training at one point on a deadlift routine where you never explicitly deadlifted, but instead did a plethora of Olympic style pulls and cleans. I am intrigued by this concept.

Questions:
1) did you ever re instate the deadlift at any point before competition?
2) How often were you pulling? How often were you squatting?
3) Mixture of clean pulls and power cleans or one or the other?
4) Were snatches included in this type of training? Furthermore, do you see any benefit to snatches as compared to cleans when it comes to training the deadlift?

I have more questions on this fascinating subject as I seek to make myself a better coach and lifter but I know you have many many posts to get to after your rather lengthy and inexcusable absence from our board.

Mark Rippetoe: 1. The only time I deadlifted was in the warmup room, where I did 225 x 5, 405 x 2, 495 x 1, 555 x 1, then opened.

2. I was pulling 2x/week, one heavy and one light, and was squatting twice.

3. The heavy pulls were halting DL alternated w/ rack pulls, and light days were cleans, snatches, clean pulls and snatch pulls.

4. Yes, snatches were done, but less often than snatch pulls.

Sorry about my profligate fucking around.

OL in Beijing

RRod: Now that weightlifting in the Olympics has a 4 year layoff, I wondered what your thoughts were (if any) on the performance of American lifters this year. I thought it *very* interesting that the man you pointed out as using deadlifts/strength-work consistently in his training (Kendrick Farris) had one of the two best performances (placing 8th despite being in the B division and setting 2 American records). You can tell he has plenty of reserve strength (especially in his 1st pull, where he starts off like a rocket). His performance alone has convinced me that deadlifts do not "make you slow" as so many OL coaches seem to think.

There's also been a good bit of forum talk about improving recruiting for USAW, especially targeting those smaller youth who are not football/basketball material. Any thoughts on this matter?

Mark Rippetoe: Somebody posted a YouTube video of Hossein Rezazadeh from the Athens Olympics doing a 263 C&J. Anybody that saw Rezazadeh clean the 263 saw a far-below-limit front squat with 578.5 lbs. that indicates a back squat of probably 850-900 lbs., and god-knows-what for a deadlift. I feel as though absolute strength is relevant to Olympic weightlifting, since the guy that lifts the most weight is the winner. I may be wrong, but Rezazadeh shows me I'm not, and Shane Hamman tells me I'm not. It has literally been decades since the USAW's program at the Colorado Springs OTC required the resident athletes to perform a 3RM squat, or deadlift anything. Our national program is not capable of sifting through the population to select for naturally strong athletes the way many other countries do, and it does not emphasize the development of absolute strength as a part of training to compensate for this.

Deadlifts don't make you slow – failing to clean makes you slow, and failing to select your parents correctly makes you slow. The Chinese are very good at selecting your parents for you, and then in selecting you, and it shows rather clearly.

What's best for improving speed?

Axegrinder: In a discussion on another site, someone asked what they could do to improve their speed for soccer and I suggested that they do squats, power cleans etc., as that definitely improved my running, though I don't play any competitive sports. Then someone came along saying squats are a waste of time because you'll never find yourself performing a squat motion during soccer unless your headbutting the ball or something, which doesn't really make sense, but he did go on to say:

"You don't want huge quads if you're a soccer player, you need lean mass, and the way to do that is by doing resistance training and light weight high volume repetition weight training. Of course every sport team trains with weights, I'm not saying that, but weight training is not what most sport teams use when it comes to increasing speed. Go talk to the USA Olympic track and field team and see what they say, guarantee they tell you the key to being faster is running in a pool, running more often and longer, and doing the right resistance training, with the right type of weight training, not just squatting and power cleans. I have never in my life seen a soccer player do power cleans."

And now I'm wondering which would be more effective for improving speed, strength training or running in a pool, more running etc, or a bit of both? What would you recommend for someone looking to increase their speed?

Mark Rippetoe: I recommend that, in addition to getting your sprint mechanics fixed (which might not help much for soccer) making your low back stronger – especially if is untrained – will make an immediate contribution to your speed. This is because lower back strength enables the spine to stay locked in lumbar extension, and this locked lordotic curve allows for a more efficient stride. If each stride is power-dampened by a loose low-back, some of the force of the hip extension as the leg pulls through gets absorbed by the collapse of the arch. The effect of strengthening the lower back shows up fairly quickly, so you'll know if it's working soon.

zephed56: Soccer players and runners are generally clueless about weight training, don't trust them. I was once a soccer player btw.

Mark Rippetoe: So was I. At the time I was clueless.

Annoying Knee Pain

Notbuff: Last week I played basketball for the first time in a few months. The next day I woke up and my knee was kinda sore. I figured it would go away in a couple days but it's been 8 days now and the pain hasn't gotten better or worse. I feel it most when I bend my knee. It's right above my right knee cap. I know you generally recommend aggressive rehab so I've continued lifting. It bothers me on squats and deadlifts- more so on deadlifts, I think because my legs are facing forward as opposed to squats where I push the knees out. I can still lift, but not quite with maximum intensity. Is this something that will eventually go away on its own, or should I be concerned? And should I continue to lift?

Mark Rippetoe: This will teach you to avoid basketball. BB is for watching, not playing. Hell, I don't even like to watch it. But if you didn't feel it at the time, it is an inflammatory situation. Advil time. Train through it. Maybe use a wrap for a while.

Sport specific lifting

Nlbauers: I am using SS to put on around 25 lbs of muscle to be competitive in flatwater canoe racing: I think SS covers the muscle groups involved in this rowing motion. However, when I'm looking ahead to more advanced programming, do you see a need for adding in some other specific exercise for this motion? Lunges perhaps?

Mark Rippetoe: I never like to prescribe unilateral exercises for sports that are unilateral in some component of their performance, because to do so demonstrates a misunderstanding of the purpose of strength training for sports. Strength is a general characteristic, and as such is *trained* in a general way, meaning that it utilizes bilateral movements that allow the use of heavy weights so that more weight can be lifted and the athlete gets stronger in general. Strength is applied specifically in the context of sports *practice*, where the ability to utilize what has been developed generally through training is applied in the specific context of that sport's particular movement patterns. In other words, don't throw a heavy basketball – get your press stronger and practice your free throws. Don't do lunges – get your squat stronger and practice in your flatwater canoe (or paddle it, or do your mileage, or meterage, or whatever you guys call it).

Cardio while strength training for a sport

Brutorious: I have a question regarding cardio conditioning while strength training, particularly football. So far I have been jumping rope 3-4 times a week for about 15 minutes total (during this strength program). I will be playing for a local semi-pro team but practices don't start until late February so I have a little time. I will also be getting into some flag football as well, all though I'm not too concerned about my cardio for that. 2 years ago I was able to run a 4.6, so I would like to be able to hit that or possibly lower it. But what would you recommend and how often? I will be going out for the tight end position. I'm 6'3" and about 227 right now.

Mark Rippetoe: Sprints a couple of times a week should cover your needs. Start with 5 sets of 40s and accumulate more sets each week, then vary the distances and volume. But stop using the term "cardio". It is associated with health spas, long slow distance, and Richard Simmons.

Texas method for powerlifting

Rugger: I've decided to enter in a powerlifting meet that takes place on the 23rd of November. Just to give the sport a try and compete in the sub-junior category while I still can. Now this decision comes just as I've decided to transition from a linear program that was more or less SS (with 5x5 because the internet told me to, but don't worry, I replaced rows with power cleans ages ago) to the Texas method. As I'm unlikely to have to compete in the clean and press, would it make sense to drop those lifts from my program until the powerlifting meet is over? Leaving me doing something like this every week for the next 8 weeks:

Mon:
Squats 5x5
Bench 5x5
Deadlifts 1x5

Wed:
Front Squats 3x3
Dumbbell BP 3x10
Light pulling 2x10, RDLs?

Fri:
Squat 1/2/3 RM
Bench 1/2/3 RM
Deadlift 1/2/3 RM

The program I was going to try before getting interested in this powerlifting meet would have had me switching deadlifts and BP with power cleans and OHP on a weekly basis. **1.)** Is omitting the press/clean week going to have me benching and deadlifting too heavy too often and cause overtraining? **2.)** Is leaving out explosive pulling a bad idea? **3.)** Are the 3x3 front squats from the PP squat template supposed to be done heavy because of the FS emphasis on the quads and low volume? I want to bring my big three up as much as possible before the competition, but as this is my first experience with intermediate programming I'm a little wary of overtraining, and don't want to do anything stupid without realizing it. I'm 18, 185lbs, GOMAD fanatically, and get plenty of sleep. Freshly tested 1RMs for SQ/BP/DL are 390/200/420.

Mark Rippetoe: I think you're making a mistake to drop the clean before a power meet. You can use the old George Hechter method and warm up your deadlifts by doing cleans up to a max triple, and then continue on up through your deadlift warmups to your work sets. And you'd get more out of presses on Wed. than DB benches, because of the posterior stability you get from pressing. Just drop them about 3 weeks out. And I'd do low box squats on Wed. instead of front squats, because quad strength will not be an issue at the PL meet.

Notbuff: Coach, is it wise to do 1x5 deadlifts on the same day as 5x5 squats for an intermediate lifter?

Mark Rippetoe: Since you have to do them both the same day at the meet, it's wise to prepare.

Notbuff: Doesn't heavy squatting prior to deadlifting limit how much you can pull? I understand if you're preparing for a meet, but if you just want to get as strong as possible on the deadlift, would training the squat first hurt your deadlift progress?

Mark Rippetoe: Heavy squatting prior to deadlifting does produce fatigue, but the deadlift is a shorter range of movement lift that is already being done with a heavier weight than your squat sets, so it all comes out in the wash.

Training up to a meet

MilkEnthusiast: My first meet is about 7 weeks out. I plan on doing rest and active recovery for the final week, and hitting my openers on week 6. I am using the Texas Method. I read your interview on EliteFTS which touched briefly on powerlifting gear. I have a few questions about this. Is there anything else I should alter as far as training? I have already decided to focus on the Bench press each week, eliminating any tough overhead work. Should I do presses on light Wednesday, or would something bench related be more beneficial? Lifters will be wearing knee wraps, which I have never used before but plan on purchasing. Should I add these into my workouts as soon as possible in order to get used to them?

Mark Rippetoe: I think it's a mistake to take that long a taper before your first meet. I don't think you're so overtrained that you need that much rest before you lift, so I'd have you do your openers on Tuesday before the Saturday meet. Anything you use as equipment in the meet needs to be vary familiar to you, so you have to train with it *at least* 2-3 weeks before the meet. And I'd press heavy up until 3 weeks out, then cut it out altogether until after the meet.

MilkEnthusiast: Any idea, maybe a general range, about what kind of carryover the knee wraps should provide?

Mark Rippetoe: That depends on how tight you wrap them and how good you are at using them. You will see soon.

Bench Press Mechanics Question

TravisRussellDC: First of all, let me preface this by saying that I work out in a powerlifting gym. So, the majority of serious lifters in the place are training/competing in powerlifting, most of them in federations that allow practically unlimited gear. I witnessed a guy bench pressing with a piece of PVC pipe wedged under his lumbar erectors. I understand the thought process behind this of increasing the lumbar arch so it effectively cuts down the range of motion. In powerlifting this translates to higher numbers.

However, wouldn't benching with a lumbar hyperlordosis like that approximate the origin and insertion of the lat dorsi thereby decreasing its activation? And wouldn't this decrease in lat activation also decrease the amount of stability the lifter has when performing the bench press exercise? Now, I've never bench pressed in a shirt. But is the amount of stability that the lifter is giving up by diminishing lat activity equal to or less than the amount of stability provided by the bench shirt? And will that make it more advantageous to decrease the range of motion in order for less effort to be exerted on a specific amount of weight, translating into higher numbers for the lift? I'm thinking that it must, otherwise why would the lifter do this? Or is it just that the guy is a douche and I should quit analyzing what others are doing and focus on myself in the gym?

Mark Rippetoe: I've never benched in a shirt either, so I can't tell you about this with any authority. But I don't think the point is the lumbar arch, but rather the exaggerated kyphotic extension that comes with it. When the bar is in balance at the top lockout position, it is directly over the glenoid, but at the bottom it is at some point on the sternum. These two points involve some lateral distance along the sagittal plane, which represents a lever arm against the shoulder joint at the bottom position. An exaggerated chest-up position pulls the shoulders back under the chest, thus compressing the lateral distance between the two points and therefore shortening the lever arm. I think that this is the main effect of the chest up position – improved shoulder-joint leverage against the bar.

Why are elite powerlifters so fat?

Drewfasa: Why is it that the old school powerlifters, like you, and the ones in your books, had muscular and fairly lean physiques, where as all the best powerlifters of today (Andy Bolton et. al.) look like a bunch of fat asses?

Mark Rippetoe: We had our share of fat guys. But really, you can't say they're all fat. I don't go to power meets, but I suspect that you are just seeing the superheavyweights and construing from this that they are all fat. And this would be a profound logic error.

KSC: My two cents on this:

1) Leverage: lots of lifters actually feel that a big gut helps you in the hole when you squat. I actually agree. It helps even more on a high squat (not to parallel) which most heavy squats in modern powerlifting are, especially at the "elite" level. Additionally, the bench pressers (especially those who wear the bench shirts) generally touch the bar to their upper abs and not their chest, so a giant fat gut means the bar has to travel less distance. Both of these factors contribute to modern "equipped" powerlifting being somewhat of a joke, and why it will never gain credibility as an Olympic sport. I'm not saying I don't respect the guys at the elite level or that they aren't strong (because they are) but I'm sorry, a 800 lb belly bump bench press done in a multi-ply open back shirt is not as impressive as a 400 lb clean and jerk.

2) Training Methods: The old school guys simply trained harder in my opinion. They squatted, deadlifted, cleaned, snatched, pressed, benched, pulled, etc, and they did so frequently, i.e. multiple times per week. You don't see that much anymore in powerlifting. Maybe guys squat once per week, deadlift 2-3 times per month, and rarely do you see any sort of Olympic lifting. Lifters have gotten away from the full body stuff for the most part, and their training of the big lifts is low volume and infrequent. I think this probably has a lot to do with what you are talking about.

Dano: LMFAO, buddy! Your whole post illustrates that you obviously know zero about powerlifting and haven't trained with or around any powerlifters. More internet armchair CrossFit quarterbacking. My teammates and I squat and bench 2-3 times a week, often for twice in one session with total volume reaching 60-90 reps for one movement and we pull every single week. And this isn't just us, I know most lifters train this way.

As for the gear, suit up and give it a shot. Yes, it's different than "raw" lifting but it adds a whole level of difficulty. You have to be strong before you get in the gear otherwise you still get crushed.

KSC: I don't believe your wretched lies about multiple squat sessions per week. When I said many powerlifters train infrequently and with low volume, I meant it. My previous assertion applies to all powerlifters on earth with no exceptions. Furthermore, every statement I have ever made on this forum applies universally, to all lifters, with no exceptions period.

You are right, it is crystal clear from my statement that I know nothing about powerlifting and have never powerlifted, nor have I ever trained with powerlifters, and by operating a CF affiliate you are correct in assuming that CF is my only area of expertise and from now on I will stick to things I know like kettlebells, pullups, and 5K's.

As for the gear, I am not strong yet so I will hold off on "suiting up" for fear of getting "crushed".

Brandon: One question that does interest me is whether cutting some of that fat wouldn't benefit them. I mean this as a strict question of mass. If you take 10 pounds of fat from your abdomen without losing any strength, wouldn't it follow that you could add around 10 pounds of iron to your squat? You're just moving weight from your torso to the bar.

Mark Rippetoe: Why does the absence of a parcel of fat equal the same amount of potential weight added to the bar? Because you lost it from your gut and don't have to lift it there, you can put it on the bar and lift it there instead? Where would that logic stop? The reality of the situation is more complicated, in terms of the negative caloric balance necessary to lose the weight and this effect on your training.

Draco: Since most everyday males are familiar with benching, the numbers in powerlifting just look like a sham once you disclose the fact that the bench you do and the bench they do are not the same. As in "Holy Shit! That was 600 lbs! Wait, take off 100 for that top of the line shirt." If I ever considered PL, it would be raw and that's it. I refuse to pay money for bigger lifts in garb befitting Victorian women.

Mark Rippetoe: My advice would be to do more than consider it before you come to a conclusion. And it is always tempting to assume that everybody that is stronger than me is on steroids.

Weight Class question...

Tjayarmyguy: I've been flirting with the idea of competing in powerlifting. Does it make more sense to work up to the limits of a weight class and then maintain the weight and attempt to increase strength, or is it better to gain a little extra weight and then attempt to decrease body weight and maintain strength levels attained at a higher bodyweight? Granted this is all pretty hypothetical at this point, but I was just curious about your take on it. You have previously mentioned that competing is an excellent way to stay motivated.

Mark Rippetoe: Most people have had better luck training a little over the weight class and then cutting weight 3-4 days out, keeping the strength gained at the heavier bodyweight. This has been the standard approach to both WL and PL for the entire history of both sports.

Sports conditioning

Neil G: I used to be a competitive swimmer (an average competitive swimmer, but competitive none the less). I did this between the ages of 10 and 18 - I'm 25 now - and the training consisted of very long hours in the pool, a bit of running and a bit of bodyweight exercise circuit training. It didn't seem to matter what distance I was training for, the training seemed to be based on swimming as far as I could in one session. I remember the coach stating that anything less than a two hour session was no good.

Since then, having read about other views regarding training, I'm curious as to your thoughts on the following ideas: Would someone training for a skill-dependent sport such as swimming be better served spending less time in the pool and more time in the weights room? For example, a swimmer could use a CrossFit approach to increase metabolic and cardiovascular conditioning whilst increasing strength on programmes such as those described in your books. Of course, skills training would be required, but this could be done in a more limited period each week in the pool along with some kind of sport-specific conditioning.

Looking back, most of the events I used to compete in lasted from between 30 seconds and about 2 and a half minutes. It now seems silly that I had to spend long hours in the pool training for this knowing what I know now about the specificity of adaptation to stress. And this model could of course be applied to other sports: running, cycling, etc.

Mark Rippetoe: It's interesting that you regard swimming as a skill-dependent sport. It seems more like a repetitive motion-dependent sport to me, one that is learned quite quickly by any decent athlete capable of performing the motions efficiently. I don't coach swimmers, and have never done competitive swimming myself, but a few things are obvious:

1. Any repetitive motion, once learned, requires minimal skill maintenance. This is also true for sports otherwise regarded as technical, like Olympic weightlifting.

2. Fencing is a skill-dependent sport. Gymnastics, diving, downhill skiing, and boxing are too. Swimming and running, not so much.

3. Once the movement patterns are learned to the level of efficiency that the athlete is capable of demonstrating, other factors become more important to high-level performance.

4. These include anthropometry, strength, body composition, neuromuscular efficiency, and endurance capacity. Some of these characteristics are more trainable than others, and some are not trainable at all.

5. Lots of coaches in lots of sports get married to training methods that have been used for many years and that just don't work well. Good athletes excel in spite of them, not because of them.

Starting Strength: Sport Specific for Boxers & Martial Arts

Dave I: I have three questions about Starting Strength progression, two specific to sports like Boxing and Martial Arts and one specific to myself.

1) Would you, or do you, ever recommend a different programming sequence than the three-day-a-week for weight lifting novices that are involved in Martial Arts (Boxing, Judo, BJJ, etc.) that have specific needs? Specifically:

A) Would you recommend fewer SS lifting days for more focus on core work and conditioning, or just lift three days a week, do conditioning two-to-three days a week, and eat/rest as much as possible?

B) Do you still recommend SS to people who are trying to stay within a weight class for a sport but still want to increase their maximal strength, or are the goals too counter-productive?

2) If I want/need more core work for Boxing & Judo, is it o.k. to do one-armed Dumbbell Bench Presses in the novice program or should I stick to the @#$%'in program for now? You mention one-armed presses in SS and the added stress to the core sounds like it might be beneficial to somebody that is planning on taking punches to the gut or trying to squirm to avoid an arm bar or get out of a choke while grappling on the mats.

3) If I have sleep apnea, can/should I stick with SS? For my background, I am thirty-one years old, 5'9", weigh 190 lbs., and have/had sleep apnea. I have a CPAP (it blows air in your nose so your throat does not collapse in your sleep), so I breathe normally at night. I was actually a very fat 230 lbs. when I got the CPAP a few years, but lost 50 lbs. (the 10 lb. difference is from lifting and eating more the last couple of months), so I am not sure if I still have sleep apnea, but I still snore (albeit not as loudly). Just wondering if I should change anything for health reasons (I would not mind ditching the CPAP) or just keep everything the same (in other words, stick with SS or switch to metcon training & Zone to get the body fat down).

Mark Rippetoe: 1. A. It depends on whether you are a novice to strength training and have done a linear progression up through your novice strength potential. If you have, more complicating programming than the novice progression is appropriate/necessary.

B. Novices gain weight much faster than more advanced lifters, and it would be a problem for them. But if by SS you mean the novice progression, a more advanced lifter would not be doing it anyway.

2. It depends on whether you are a novice to strength training and have done a linear progression up through your novice strength potential. Novices need to gain basic strength on the bench press, while athletes that have already done so can benefit from less basic work.

3. It depends on whether you are a novice to strength training and have done a linear progression up through your novice strength potential. If your sleep apnea is associated with weight gain and you are a novice, SS will make you gain weight and might aggravate the condition.

Overhead Shoulder Position

Michael P: I had the pleasure of working with you in Milwaukee a bit ago, and at your Cert, the point came up about the Kettlebell Nazi's referring to the overhead Shoulder Position as needing to be sucked DOWN and IN. I know that when I am overhead with the press, or anything Barbell related, I need to be UP and THROUGH with my upper body, with active traps. This helps correct what I seem to remember you demo-ing, an impingement in the shoulder.

My question is that in talking to some of my RKC friends this past weekend, they are so adamant about this positioning being right and mine being WRONG, DANGEROUS, it will KILL YOU....that I need your help in better understanding this difference. The argument is that it is more stable...safe...bla...bla...bla

1. Is this difference in perspective something unique to the Instrument being used?

2. Is this just an agree-to-disagree situation and tell them to SHUT THE F%@# Up?

3. Is this "Impingement" not something they experience due to the movements they are performing?

Mark Rippetoe: 1. If they never lock out overhead, it must be. But the shoulder morphology doesn't change with the object lifted. The impingement/balance/leverage rules all still obviously apply.

2. This agree-to-disagree shit really gets old. That works fine for our favorite color, or whether we like oysters or not. But not about things for which analysis is possible.

3. They won't impinge with a KB out in front in a swing. I don't know enough about the positions in KB work to even comment on any other aspect of the training.

Brandon: My understanding as related by word of mouth is that he teaches the "packed" shoulder as a reasonable compromise -- it's safer than a loose unstable shoulder and it's easier to learn than an active shoulder, which for whatever reason he feels is too difficult to easily teach.

jep6095: These KB "experts" also preach that you must increase your Long Slow Distance "training" in order to be successful at "training", are 40-50 pounds underweight, and do not train for any kind of useful strength. But you already know that Michael, right?

KSC: Kettlebell snatches and cleans are great for building explosive power....until you realize that even though it looks cool, its still less than 100 lbs, and you're still a pussy.

– paraphrased from Jim Wendler

Mark Rippetoe: It's too difficult to teach somebody to shrug their shoulders at the top of a press? I find it difficult to believe that anyone calling themselves a coach thinks this.

Training for powerlifting

TerriblyUsefulBlockOfWood: How soon can/should we adopt an ultra-wide stance/very low bar position for the squat and sumo-style for the deadlift? That is if our goal IS competitive powerlifting rather than general strength training. Also, you teach thumbless grip (to keep the forearm straight), and downward gaze (to enable hip drive by keeping the neck in its anatomical position). The powerlifters at my gym are very insistent on thumb around the bar (for safety) and forward gaze. Not sure why on the latter, but also every competition squat I've ever seen is with forward gaze. Is that killing some of the hip drive?

And I've just been ignoring everyone's advice and sticking with the form described in SS for now because it's the only view with an articulate defense behind each detail. (Maybe when I double my squat I'll have other opinions?)

Mark Rippetoe: If you want to be a contest suit-and-wraps powerlifter, adopt the stance techniques they suggest immediately, if you have determined that sumo will work for your anthropometry. Of course you know that looking down is the stronger position, and if you are a good communicator you should be able to teach them. Even I manage to do this, and it's widely known that all I do is scream and cuss.

Skinny and inexperienced

Reactiontm: I'm training the 8th graders I coached in football this year. One thing that drives me nuts is that so many of the high school kids are using that GD "Manta Ray" or the tampon for squats. Now if I watch closely, that Manta Ray keeps the bar too high, and it wiggles back and forth, or rises forward during the bottom third of the movement. It appears to me that it shifts the bar forward of the midline of the foot. For me, I found Rip's suggested position for the bar was "like a glove" from the first try. But I'm 5'9" and 210, so I've got some fat and muscle up top there, so the rhomboids pop out and there's some meat up there at the back of the shoulder...

A lot of these kids are skin and bone, their arms are so skinny that there's no posterior deltoid for the bar to rest on, so it's just riding against the spine of the scapula and they complain about pain from the bar placement while squatting. Also, for some reason, when I get them placing the thumbs over the bar, riding low(er), and hands placed closer in with elbows up, there seems to be a reflex or something and they seem to round their backs. I've seen more kids get into position initially and completely forget how to stand up straight, much less maintain any sort of arch. Is this a normal reaction in a novice or is their something in the water here?

Mark Rippetoe: The rounding is a common thing to see in skinny kids. It seems they are of the opinion that they need to make a horizontal spot for the bar to lay on. You'll have to teach them that a close grip with thumbs on top and straight wrists, with elbows up the back, makes a shelf for the bar, and that it's trapped in place well enough that they just don't need a flat spot. They need to hear "chest up, chin down", and have their wrist/elbow position reinforced by yelling. This will require that you work with them individually with this position. I suspect you're trying to deal with them as a group, and I assure you this will not work. You have to dial in each kid separately. Sorry, I know time is tight, but there is probably no other way.

Reactiontm: Our head coach says it's just a lack of core strength. The legs are strong enough to push the weight, the torso's just not capable of holding it all together. Maybe that's why a few of them wobble, or "corkscrew" on their way out of the bottom position.

Mark Rippetoe: Your head coach, as usual, is wrong. But there you go.

Lessons from Westside

Rob18: You have mentioned in the past that Louie Simmons is a good resource for powerlifting. I have read all of his articles on their website and realized that I fell into the deep end of the pool. I also realized how hard you had to work to make this stuff sound simple (thank you). Is there anything that a guy that wants to get strong can take home from Westside Barbell?

Mark Rippetoe: The dynamic effort techniques are extremely useful for anyone wanting to get stronger. CFT benefits from their application immediately. They are an incredible tool, and in my opinion are the major contribution that Louie has made to modern strength and conditioning.

Snatch and Jerk for people with poor shoulder flexibility

XTrainer: Do you have any suggestions for trainees with shoulder inflexibility who are trying to learn/improve their snatch and/or jerk? (I'm referring to power jerk and power snatch for my purposes). I've been working on my shoulder flexibility a lot, and have made some improvement, but my shoulders are still very inflexible. For example, when I do overhead squats, I have to grip the bar collar to collar. With the grip width I use to jerk, I can only get a couple inches of knee bend before the bar falls forward. Do you have any suggestions for people like me? I appreciate your help. BTW, I'm not sure if you remember my question about my mother's knee pain, but she is back to squatting. She just turned 46, did a set of 6 strict chins the day after her birthday, and also recently pulled a 185 deadlift with a double-overhand grip. Thanks.

Mark Rippetoe: Widen your jerk grip. What is it now? And your mom is cool.

XTrainer: It's narrow, compared to what I see most Oly lifters using. Narrower than my clean grip by quite a bit, and just a hair wider than my press grip. My press grip is about as narrow as possible without having my hands/fingers in contact with my body. I feel weak when I try to go wider, but maybe it's just one of those things that feels weak because it's unfamiliar.

Mark Rippetoe: I have pretty much everybody jerk with as wide a grip as they can rack the clean with, because I prefer there be as little time possible between the rack and the jerk. Since you'll jerk with a wider grip, resetting the grip from narrow to wide adds time to the jerk prep. Sometimes it is necessary to shift grip after the rack, but this is inefficient and can usually be fixed. If you are jerking narrower than you clean, you are probably not a competitive Olympic lifter.

XTrainer: Thanks for the help. I am not a competitive lifter yet, but would like to lift competitively in the future. I think I assumed as much about grip width thing, I just didn't want to take the steps backward in training that widening my jerk grip out to match my clean grip will require. I would guess the reason that I felt most comfortable jerking with a press grip because I was indeed pressing the bar up rather than pushing myself underneath it. Hopefully a wider grip will help change that.

Mark Rippetoe: Both the press and the jerk involve applying force to the bar. But the press starts this process in the rack position while the jerk delays it until the bar has been carried off the rack position by the force generated by the hips and legs, a position that might be as high as the nose or forehead. This is why a wider grip works okay in the jerk – the leverage in the initial stages of the movement is not as critical, and you can use the wider grip to reduce the distance the bar has to travel to lockout.

Your Weightlifting background...

Kiknskreem: Rip, can you give us a little bit of your background specifically in the sport of weightlifting, as both a lifter and coach? What positions have you held, any high level athletes that you have trained? One thing I hear repeatedly hear on other boards from Oly lifters is "Rip's not an Olympic lifting coach... yada yada." If I recall, you are a level III USAW Coach in fact? Anyway, just looking for the scoop and possibly some responses to the above mantra.

Mark Rippetoe: I have doing the two lifts as a part of my training since 1979. I was a competitive powerlifter, but we snatched and C&Jed as a part of training with Bill Starr. I have snatched 82.5 and C&Jed 105 as lifts that were not my competitive sport. My best clean was 275 many years ago – power, I believe. I have been coached by Bill Starr, Tommy Suggs, Jim Moser, Dr. Kilgore, Glenn Pendlay, Angel Spassov, Harvey Newton, Mike Conroy, John Thrush, and many fellow lifters. I have never claimed to be a good weightlifter, but I have coached the lifts since 1984. I obtained my USWF Level III certification in 1988 at the OTC in Colorado Springs with Mike Stone, Harvey Newton, and Angel Spassov on faculty. I obtained my USAW Senior Coach certification in 1999 at the OTC with Lyn Jones, John Thrush, Mike Conroy, et al. I was invited, as an Olympic weightlifting coach, to the Olympic Solidarity course at the OTC in 2000. Dr. Kilgore and I taught both the USAW Club Coach course and the Sports Performance Coach course from 1999 through 2005. I have served as the president of the North Texas Local Weightlifting Committee of USAW since 2004. I have coached and participated in the coaching of James Moser, Glenn Pendlay, Dr. Kilgore, several of our national and international-level athletes, and the members of the collegiate team at Midwestern State University (still actively coaching the MSU people) and Wichita Falls Weightlifting from 1999-2006. I still actively coach the sport on a daily basis here at CFWF/WFAC, and the power clean (and occasionally the power snatch) at our seminars around the country every month. As much fun as it may be, it would be wrong to characterize me as inexperienced in these matters.

Injuries in High-Level Powerlifting

BreezerD: We've all seen the table at the back of SS that lists the very low frequency of injuries in Powerlifting and Olympic Weightlifting. What I'm wondering is, what are the most typical injuries in the squat and deadlift, and what is usually their cause?

Mark Rippetoe: For me it was back injuries, and I suspect so for most lifters. Olympic lifters have more wrist and elbow injuries than PLers, but for both sports the heavy weight and the human back interact in a way that can cause the most serious problems.

BreezerD: Okay. And is this typically caused by a deficit in the isometric strength of the muscles that maintain the back's rigid position?

Mark Rippetoe: No, it's caused by getting slightly out of position with a real fucking heavy weight.

Choosing a Weight (category)

AidenBloodaxe: Mark, as a former competitor obviously you competed in a weight category(s). Were you ever concerned with remaining in a certain group or did you simply compete in whichever category you happened to fall in when competition time rolled around?

The reason I ask this is because since starting SS I have put a tremendous amount of weight on. When my novice progression diminishes I'm planning to starting competing locally & although a naturally small skinny kid I find no problem whatsoever piling on weight(I can't see where it's coming from really) with weights & calories. I'm thinking this may be frustrating when aiming to become a good competitor in a given weight category (in the long term future that is).

Is it correct to assume that a person competing in a weight category closer to their natural weight has a larger chance at being a better competitor (in general that is)? With me being quite far away from the weight I was (some 80lbs away) I find that I'm not as strong as people that are 'naturally' closer to this weight. Maybe I'm just being too impatient what with me being quite young (18), still growing (possibly) & still only a novice?

Mark Rippetoe: I competed in both the 198 and the 220 lb. classes, going up to the heavier class when making weight became too hard to do and keep my total. Since I was never a National Threat in either class, it didn't matter that much in the grand scheme of my competitive career. But you are worrying about something that you won't have to worry about for quite some time, if ever. When you first start lifting you compete in the weight class you find yourself in on the day of the meet, since you're going to get killed anyway. The first few meets teach you about the sport; after you've become familiar with its specifics and subtleties – and if you stay in the sport – you can adjust your bodyweight to meet your competitive needs with respect to weight class. But since you have no experience in the sport, don't get ahead of yourself on this. Just train, get strong, do the best you can at your first few meets, and after that you'll be able to answer the question for yourself.

Split Snatch?

Sam Crish: I've been having knee pain problems with snatch and overhead squat recently. After reading your and Polynomial's posts in the pistol squat thread I am thinking that, due to shoulder inflexibility, I am losing my back arch in order to get depth, then hamstrings relax, knees hurt, etc. I saw that you do split snatches and was wondering if you'd recommend them in this situation.

Mark Rippetoe: Again, a split may be easier, but changing form does not fix the problem unless you know for sure that the form problem is unfixable due to anatomical issues. If you want to split snatch, that's fine, but it's not fine to want to switch to the split because you don't want to have to address an addressable form problem with the squat snatch.

Sam Crish: Fair enough. What would lead someone to choose one style over the other? For example, why do you split?

Mark Rippetoe: I split because I am 53 and anatomically incapable of performing an overhead squat, in that when I try I spend the next 3 weeks rehabbing my thoracic spine. But many people who lack the ability to effectively squat snatch, for whatever the reason, should stop beating their heads against this particular wall and just learn to split snatch. It's an effective way to snatch heavy weights that worked well for decades until the squat version became all the rage and everybody forgot how to split.

---

4 questions about application to sport

London Lion: 1) On page 124 of PP you say: "During the late novice and intermediate stage, an athlete defines the course of his career, choosing a sport to train for and compete in".
I like a lot of people who read this forum are indeed novice when it comes to strength training and want to improve our strength to improve our performance – BUT have already chosen our sports (probably because we are adults and not school/college students) and for the most part as in my case are amateurs or recreational participants in the chosen sport, we have no chance of making professional. For guys (or girls) like us would it still be "best" to follow the novice program as written without any additional work in the chosen sport to set us up for optimal performance down the line? i.e. we sacrifice playing the sport and our skill development in the sport for better results later by building our strength base?

2) If a break from the competitive season and skill work in the said sport is not possible am I correct in thinking that you advise a two day a week A/B strength workout program that we must fit into and around our sports training and matches that gives us the optimal chance of recovery?

3) From reading PP I have concluded that my chosen sport – soccer, is indeed a Power sport (I play striker, so many sprints per game) and so would benefit from strength training. However there is clearly a difference between the mass needs of different positions for football or rugby than soccer. Most soccer players exhibit the same mass profiles whereas there is difference in football and rugby dependant on the position the player plays. How do I make sure that I am not too big for my sport? Is it based on food intake or the type and amount of additional work I may do such as sprints?

4) Is the Romanian deadlift the preferred substitute for the back extension if the back extension cannot be performed due to equipment limitations?

Mark Rippetoe: 1. Everybody gets the most progress out of their initial linear progression phase. It makes no difference what the other circumstances are – until you have completed the initial phase of training that produces the quickest and most efficient gains you will ever make, all other training considerations are secondary.

2. A rank novice in strength can train the linear progression model without too much disruption of sport-specific practice, because recovery at the novice level is not yet that hard to do. You're not yet strong enough to produce enough stress under the bar that it interferes markedly with your soccer.

3. You are too big for your sport if you can't play it effectively as a result of getting bigger. When that happens, you'll know. But don't assume that just because no one on the team is as big as you that you're necessarily *too big*. Perhaps they are too small.

4. RDLs are more stressful on the hamstrings than the back at novice performance levels, usually. There are occasional anthropometric oddities that make this hard to say for sure. Do them if they help.

Head/Torso Angle on Over Head Squat/Snatch

Randle McMurphy: I am learning to full squat snatch without a coach, and doing overhead squats is a part of my training. I have noticed that at the bottom position of the OHS/snatch my torso angle has A LOT of forward lean, and that I am looking downwards with my head. As a result the bar is FAR behind my head, and the whole position resembles a low-bar squat. It feels secure however. I notice no pro's do this.

I have noticed that I am losing a little depth by doing this, and if I were to have more of a vertical torso and look forward a bit more I could get a bit more depth in the squat, like in a front squat. I notice the pro's do this. When I try and do this, the bar doesn't feel very secure overhead, as it has the capability to roll back to the 'low bar position', and because it is closer to overhead it is easier to go forward and lose the bar in front.

-What should I do? Should I keep my low bar OHS/squat snatch? Or Should I strive to have a more vertical OHS/snatch?
-What should I do to get more depth, and keep a vertical torso? Are their any cues? Or something I think about?

Mark Rippetoe: Lots of "pros" use a low-bar squat back angle to snatch, especially the very strong ones who are snatching enough weight that the squat itself requires a display of strength best accomplished by driving the hips up. The OHS is an exercise and can be done with both an upright torso like a front squat or a more horizontal torso like you do it to incorporate hip drive. Your eye gaze direction facilitates hip drive like in a squat, and if it's working to do it this way, that's why. The depth is a concern if you are using it as an exercise as opposed to a snatch recovery, since there is nothing to be gained by squatting deeper than you need to when you snatch. The bar in both forms will be in balance when it is directly over the shoulder joint, so when you use a more horizontal back angle it will seem like it is further back. If it stays in balance, it's where it needs to be.

It Hurts When I Do *This.*

I got bucked off a really rank horse one afternoon. I had ridden him previously and wasn't that concerned about him, and he snuck up on me pretty thoroughly. I was up in the air so high that I remember having time to think to myself, "You know, this is about to hurt pretty bad." Injuries are an unavoidable consequence of serious training for competitive sports, and, actually, all serious engagement with physical stuff that's fun. Dealing with pain and injury is an unfortunate reality for those of us that grab life by the boobs, and the following are some of the ways I've learned to work around the inevitable slap in the face.

Strained hamstring while squatting

Timm66: I strained my left hamstring while squatting on Tuesday. I was at the bottom of the first rep of my 5th set (sets across), and I felt a sharp pain in the back of my left leg so I set the weight down onto the rack pins. The weight was 225 lbs and I have used that weight several times before with no problems, with my 5RM being at least 240. At this point the only time I feel pain is when attempting to squat, or while in the process of sitting down or rising from a seated position.

I figure it will be a few weeks before I can squat again, so I am wondering what I can do in the meantime, and what I can do once I am back to squatting, to prevent this injury from recurring.

Mark Rippetoe: Without seeing a video of the squat, it's hard to say what happened to cause the pull. My only guess would be that your other knee may have caved a little as you were driving up, throwing an asymmetric stress on the injured side, but that's just pulled out of my ass. You say that you only feel it when coming up from a squatting position; does this mean that it doesn't hurt to deadlift? If that's true, it is probably not a hamstring, and you may not mean the "back" of your "leg".

Whatever caused it, here is the tried-and-true injury rehab method for muscle-belly injuries we got from Starr and that has worked for years better than any other method I've ever used. Wait 3-4 days until the pain starts to "blur", which indicates that the immediate process of healing has stopped the bleeding and has started to repair the tissue. Then use an exercise that directly works the injury, i.e. that makes it hurt, in this case the squat. Use the empty bar and do 3 sets of 25 with perfect form, allowing yourself NO favoring the injured side. If it's ready to rehab you will know by the pain: if the pain increases during the set, it's not ready, if it stays the same or feels a little better toward the end of the set, it is ready to work.

The NEXT DAY do it again, and add a small amount of weight, like 45 x 25 x 2 , 55 x 25. Next day, 45 x 25, 55 x 25, 65 x 25. Continue adding weight every day, increasing as much as you can tolerate each workout. It will hurt, and it's supposed to hurt, but you should be able to tell the difference between rehab pain and re-injury. If you can't, you will figure it out soon enough. This method works by flushing blood through the injury while forcing the tissue to reorganize in its normal pattern of contractile architecture.

After 10 days of 25s, go up in weight and down in reps to 15s, then to 10s, and finally to fives. During this time do NO OTHER HEAVY WORK, so that your resources can focus on the injury. You should be fixed in about 2 weeks, squatting more than you hurt yourself with.

This method has the advantage of preventing scar formation in the muscle belly, since the muscle is forced to heal in the context of work and normal contraction, using the movement pattern it normally uses. The important points are 1.) perfect form with 2.) light weights that can be handled for high reps, 3.) every day for two weeks, and 4.) no other heavy work that will interfere with the system-wide processes of healing the tear.

It is also very important through the whole process of healing the injury that ice be used, during the initial phase after the injury and after the workouts. Use it 20 on/20 off, many times a day at first and then tapering off to morning, after the workout, and before bed. Ice is your best friend in a muscle belly injury, holding down inflammation and fluid accumulation ("swelling") while at the same time increasing beneficial blood flow through the injury. But DO NOT USE ICE MORE THAN 20 MINUTES AT A TIME. More than that can cause more damage than it repairs.

This may actually be the most useful post on this entire little forum of mine, and if you use this method exactly you can save yourself many weeks of lost training and long-term problems with muscle-belly scarring. Try it and see.

Timm66: Now I'm very confused, since after four days not only has the pain blurred, it is almost gone. I guess it is not a hamstring strain after all, but now I don't know what it was. I can feel a little bit of pain if I lie on my back and pull my left knee up towards my chest with both hands (I get nothing from the right). I imagine this will be gone soon too, as I keep trying to localize the pain but this stretching is actually helping. It seems like is is more towards the inner thigh, maybe halfway around from the back, and about halfway between the knee and groin.

I wasn't sure what to do earlier today so I did my regular workout except squats, and had no trouble at all with deadlifts. I tried some squats at 45x5 and 95x5, and got a little twinge on the last few reps so I didn't want to push it, but maybe I am OK to slowly work back up.

Matt: Mark do you have any similar experiences with rehabbing lower back strains? I got loose in the hole of a squat and tweaked my back and I'm trying to find something to speed recovery as I'm meet prepping right now.

Mark Rippetoe: If Timm's pain is gone that quickly, it was not a full tear. Sometimes a few fibers get yanked and it's painful, but there is no "bruising" under the skin that would indicate a major bleed.

It has been my experience that most injuries that do not involve torn connective tissue or fractures respond well to the above method, low backs included. Reverse hypers, 45-degree back extensions, glute/hams and supermans all work well for this if deadlifts are too painful.

Pdellorto: I'm unsure what you mean by "starts to 'blur'". Do you mean the pain begins to shift from acute, sharp pain and into dull aching and soreness? Would the continuing incidence of sharp or acute pains be a sign to rest further?

I ask because I pulled or strained a muscle on the right side of my lower back doing a workout. I thought it was a mild pull but a week later I still have sharp pains although not as bad as when it first occurred. Attempting even basic exercise motions that involve the back results in sharp pains. I'd like to get onto to the business of rehabbing it. But I'd rather not get back to it too enthusiastically and too early because I misunderstood the signal to get started.

Mark Rippetoe: Starts to "blur" refers to the tendency of healing soft tissue to change from being perceived as sharp and pinpoint to more diffuse and harder to precisely localize. Your injury, however, is not of that type. You have a back injury that will not respond in the short term as described above for muscle bellies, because the vast majority of the time a back injury of this type is not a muscle belly. It is usually a facet joint, a disc, or an associated nerve root, and the pain is triggered by movement that tweaks the injury. You'll notice that it doesn't really hurt if you don't move in a way that makes it tweak. In contrast, a muscle belly tear aches all the time till it goes "blurry". You need to see a chiropractor about this, or a decent PT if you can find one.

What would you consider an injury that calls for not lifting for a while?

Irishman301: Unfortunately doctors (my doctor at least), personal trainers, and just about everyone else I know would tell me that you're supposed to rest when something is hurting. I don't consider the personal trainers at my gym worthy to offer advice to anyone (well, actually it's my old gym now since I found a little hole-in-the wall, non-crowded, 3 power rack-having gym - best gym I've ever been to!). Not like I know that much myself, but the personal trainers at the local 'health clubs' are just.....well I'm sure you know the type I'm talking about. So my question is about injuries, or what is defined as a serious injury.

Since I started lifting 'heavy' about 5 months ago, as opposed to just lifting moderately heavy, I started getting aches and pains in my joints. My knees are achy underneath the kneecaps after I squat (which I'm sure will has a lot to do with improper form). My shoulders kind of hurt, but not bad enough that I can't move them around (possibly due to rapid growth from all the heavy overhead pressing I've been doing). I had that costal cartilage injury that I posted about 2 weeks ago, which you said should be okay. All types of s*** hurts now and again. None of it keeps me from my scheduled workouts though.

None of these things hurt too badly, but I can tell that it's pain other then normal soreness. The last thing I want to do is to stop lifting or even slow progression, so I just keep lifting anyway, and I'm always very careful. Now I also know that you're supposed to 'listen to your body', but my brain says 'don't be a pussy, and just lift the f***ing weights', and that's just what I do. If I rested every time I had a little bit of pain, I would never get anywhere.

So what I want to know, are these types of aches and pains fairly typical for people that lift for strength (as opposed to a 'bodybuilder')? And, what would you consider a serious injury that would require one to do rehab? I'm just wondering. It would take a damn serious injury to get me to stop lifting.

Mark Rippetoe: I admire your balls, because if you ever want to get anything done you have to have them, and I've got no program for making them grow. As far as I am concerned, a serious injury is a fracture, a ruptured tendon/ligament/muscle belly, something that involves significant loss of blood like a gunshot wound or a bad sword cut, abdominal or orthopedic surgery, or an overuse injury that cannot be warmed up enough to train through. These things you train around, meaning you train everything else that can be trained while leaving the injury alone, so that the system receives stress but the affected tissue does not. This helps things heal. As a general rule, if you train heavy, you will have injuries. Sorry, that's part of the deal. You have to learn which ones to train through, which ones to train around, and how.

Your test is always this: what would happen if this was 10,000 BC? Because as far as the vast majority of your body is concerned, it is. If you broke your femur 12,000 years ago, you either walked on it if you could, or you died. Therefore, if you can use it, you should – that's what happened then, and it can also happen now. Using myself as an example, I trained 4 days after my appendectomy (when I was younger in 1986), 10 days after my ACL/MCL right knee (1994), 10 days after my C6-7 cervical fusion, 10 days after my hernia repair, 10 days after my septoplasty, and 3 days after a left patellar tendon repair. I didn't do anything stupid (surgery is expensive) (at least not terribly stupid) (maybe just a little stupid), but I trained.

Doctors are much more concerned with not being sued than they are about your speedy functional recovery. So it is your job to test your limits, and to take advice about why you should lay around on your ass for protracted periods of time with a large grain of salt, especially when given by people who themselves don't train.

Galapogos: On the same note, how do you tell if an injury can be trained through, or should be trained around? I have had a lower back/hip injury since early 07 that causes pain during trunk flexion, and this has affected my rows, deadlifts and to a lesser degree my squats. I have since switched to DB rows and front squats, which are almost pain free, but heavy deadlifts still hurt. It doesn't hurt enough to cripple me, and I can train through them, but I find that over a couple of weeks/months of training through them it becomes almost disabling, and I have to deload for a week or 2 with plenty of rehab work done for it to become better. Because of this my dead numbers haven't improved since February. Would this be a case where I should probably lay off heavy deadlifts for 1-2 months at least?

Mark Rippetoe: No, if a layoff hasn't worked before, why would it work now? Depending on the nature of your injury (do you have a diagnosis?) it is usually best to go through the rehab protocol I wrote about in the earlier thread regarding this topic.

Galapogos: Actually the layoff worked...until I went back and gradually increased my poundages, then the pain just came back. I've been to several sports doctors, rehab specialists and PTs, and the general consensus seems to be a referred pain from the lumbar spine. The hip, spine & SI joint x-rays came out ok, as well as the hip MRI. My current rehab protocol includes SMFR of the calves, ITB, quads, adductors, lats, piriformis/glutes, TFL, pec minor, stretching the calves, hamstrings, glutes, quads/hip flexors, pecs, ankle/hip mobility drills, glute med/max activation and core work. I've read your rehab protocol in the sticky, but it seems to be for pulls/tears and other muscle belly injuries. I'm not so sure mine is one.

Mark Rippetoe: Actually, if the pain came back when you got the weight back up, the layoff didn't work because the injury is still there. I have an idea! Why don't you try the rehab protocol and see if it works???

Modifications for crappy knees

Billy: I'm 48 years old, 50 lbs overweight and weak. A few months ago I started working with barbells, inspired by SS (1st edition) and some o-lift coaching. I guess I did too much too soon and quickly (re)discovered that my knees are my weakest link with regard to over-training and insufficient recovery. I'd like to start up again doing a stricter SS routine, but I think I'll need to lessen the volume of knee-heavy work. Any recommendations on how to do that within the context of the novice program?

Mark Rippetoe: At your advanced age (you are 4 years younger than me) and with your knee history, I'd try squatting only twice/week and see if you can tolerate it that way. Young healthy people suck, don't they?

Billy: Definitely. I hate anyone younger, richer or thinner than me. And let's not talk about hairlines. But getting back on point: in your estimation, which are harder on one's knees, the slower lifts with relatively heavier weights, or the more explosive lifts at relatively lighter weights?

Mark Rippetoe: It has been my experience that explosive lifts pose more danger to knees than slower lifts, due to the fact that the same range of motion is being covered in a small fraction of the time. There is a greater potential for control errors during the faster movement, as well as the fact that decelerating the momentum of the bar as gravity overcomes your applied force places a different quality of stress on joints and muscles than a squat or deadlift of comparable effort.

That having been said, neither is as dangerous as soccer. Or dating younger married women.

Pars/spondy

Howardw: Apparently I have a pars fracture and grade I spondylolysthesis (assumed to be congenital). Do you know of any reason these would be a problem for SS (currently 36, as far as I know they've never been trouble)? And I've done years of Muay Thai, Brazilian jiu-jitsu, etc...in other words, I haven't been a couch potato. Naturally any doctor is against squats/deadlifts anyway...so asking them is pretty much out, so I wondered what your take on it was. In fact, my primary doctor told me to take up swimming. Not going to happen. I ask because I had a lower-back issue starting a year and a half ago. It wasn't caused by lifting but seemed to be aggravated by squats (and that could be form-related admittedly). I still think it was trigger-point related since the original issue started shortly after a kickball game (embarrassing, but I kick hard).

I had a massage person do a psoas release which helped quite a bit (felt it pull directly on the source of the pain in the lower back)...though it wasn't final. But my understanding is that trigger points take multiple sessions to go away. Chiropractic was so-so...sometimes it helped, but nowhere near as much as the massage/trigger-point stuff. When I stopped squatting/deadlifting last year it went away. I did kettlebell work for most of the last half of the year and that caused no pain, but now I want to build my strength up.

Mark Rippetoe: I have a 62 year-old doctor in here who trains here with a spondylolysthesis, and who has less trouble with it now than he did before he started squatting and pulling regularly. Direct flexion/extension work for the back like glute/hams or reverse hypers aggravates it pretty bad, but as long as he just squats and pulls – keeps the intervertebral relationships constant in a normal isometric trunk – he's fine. It would be stupid to ignore the potential for this injury to really and truly fuck you up at heavy weights, but it can be trained with successfully if you are the possessor of good judgment. You mentioned that you had stopped squatting and deadlifting before and the symptoms went away, and I suspect you were training then at a level above which was prudent. You'll have to learn how to train hard with lighter weights, as I have had to do.

Hernia or strain? Your recommendations...

Matt: About last August, while doing a strength routine (a mix of a lot of things, but in this case, the injury happened on 5 x 3 back squats, and repeated on 3 x 5's at a later date), coming out of the bottom of a squat I felt a burning pain on my right hip crease, right under about the beltline (not lifting belt, I don't wear one, I mean a regular belt line). There is *no* pain at all when I'm not doing higher weight squats, the only other time I felt any discomfort was literally the other day when I was on the john.

The reason I'm asking is you mention that when you had your hernia, other things bothered it, but for me, it seems ONLY squats bother it. Basically, there's no pain when I do deadlifts, even high reps near my max, or singles working up to max for a new PR, which I've done lately. No pain during glute-ham situps, or back extensions, I've never felt pain during front or overhead squats, or doing cleans, jerks, or snatches. That's not to say those things may not irritate it eventually, but they haven't so far. I've "fixed" it temporarily before by laying off the squats for a while, coming back gradually, and it wasn't a problem. But then all of a sudden, out of the blue, it's back.

Mark Rippetoe: Sounds to me like you are in the initial stages of yanking the hernia open. Mine did the same thing. It will probably scar down for a while, and not bother you until it actually needs to be repaired. This may be the best case to be made for the subsequent use of a belt for everything above 135. Let us know what he says.

Matt: Thanks Coach, I did go to see him, and here's what he said: It doesn't seem like it's a hernia, though it could be. He says a sports hernia in a lot of cases is a non-diagnosis, basically meaning if it's nothing else, cut you open and see if it's a sports hernia. He thinks it's a muscle strain, and prescribed Physical Therapy, they're going to work on some stretching and strengthening in that area to see if that helps fix it up.

The other thing is, today at my initial PT evaluation, I asked if they'd check my squat form, and they said everything looked good, but they did say that my left shoulder was slightly lower than my right (though it didn't feel that way). I'm wondering if this caused some strain on my right side by forcing me to resist twisting on the way back up, maybe that contributed to it.

Mark Rippetoe: I think it's probably a hernia, and I think you're thinking too hard. Except when you asked the physical therapists to check your squat form.

Deadlift - abdominal pain/pressure

Ganondorf: When doing a set of 5 deadlifts I noticed there was a significant amount of pressure, like straining or something going on in my lower abdominal/adductor region. What do you think that could be? I think I may have had the bar not on my thighs on the way up; could this pressure/pain be form related?

Mark Rippetoe: This is the region typically associated with a hernia. It could very easily have been tweaked by a form problem. Have it checked.

Ganondorf: The feeling went away after about 6 or so hours. I think my issue with the deadlift and my form was that I was trying to have the knees too bent. I watched your instructional video and I noticed that if I put the bar | | from my shins when standing, that when I put my back into the right position, my knees are only slightly bent.

Mark Rippetoe: Still, get it checked. It might be nothing, but then again it might not be nothing.

Ganondorf: This was on the work set of deadlifts. I remember feeling this pressure in that area when I used to do deadlifts a couple years ago. It only happened on the heavy sets, and nothing ever resulted from it. I am guessing it is a form problem of some type, and I am just lucky to have not acquired an injury.

Also, it is common to have random bouts of achiness in your knees? I have not been doing squats continuously for any more than 3 or 4 weeks. My knees don't hurt, at rest or while doing squats, and my strength is going up. They have just been aching intermittently, but there is no actual pain. My form is correct, as I have compared it to the correct and incorrect videos here.

I have piled up a considerable amount of doctor's bills recently due to other injuries and circumstances, and since I am a full-time student I am on my father's health insurance; he is getting irritated that I am going to the doctor, for financial reasons. I do not know if I will be able to go; if the pain and pressure symptoms go away in a few days should I just forget about it?

Mark Rippetoe: Like I said, I think you may have a hernia. A hernia diagnosis is neither expensive nor terribly important to have done, so either way is fine. The early stages of a hernia usually stabilize and the pain will go away for varying periods of time, until it finally gets re-injured to the extent that it cannot be ignored. And the only situation in which it becomes an emergency is when a loop of your intestine gets injected down into your scrotum through the inguinal ring. This is an unpleasant situation for most men. You will know when such a drastic change occurs, and you will feel the appropriate sense of urgency in getting your ass to the ER. Until then, do a lot of abs, wear a belt when in doubt, and be careful about picking things up in awkward positions – this is when you're most likely to hurt it, when you're unprepared for the sudden load in an ergonomically unfriendly position.

And if your knees don't ache occasionally, you're not training hard enough.

And get your own health insurance, like a Big Boy. Unless you're 15.

Hernia??

Bobdouk: I am 37 and I have been 7 weeks in the basic S.S program. Last time I was doing squats with 55kg and I was struggle to finished the rep (I am weak) and felt a strange feeling in my abs and my colon. I had a minor sensitive discomfort at my left testile after that. Now 2 days later, after deloading 15% (I was hitting a wall for third time) I dont feel anything, or maybe I feel something at my low left abs, but maybe it is my idea. I squeeze my abs to check it. I have no protrusion. Do you think I am over reacting? I read about hernias from weightlifting all the time.

Mark Rippetoe: Hernias do not happen from weightlifting. They may occur during weightlifting in men who are predisposed to having them. They may also occur while working or while taking a dump. Sorry for the American idiom. Get yours checked by a physician.

Valsalva

Captainpicard: In Starting Strength and also in a couple threads on here you have discussed that the Valsalva is safe and should be used to prevent injuries while lifting heavy weights. It has also been shown that power production increases as much as 20% due to the intrathoracic, etc. pressure being applied. I have seen a few places where people do not bring up passing out or having a cerebrovascular accident in regard to the Valsalva, but rather say that using it makes you more likely to have a hernia. If the Valsalva increases thoracic pressure so much, this seems like a possibly legitimate argument. Thoughts?

Mark Rippetoe: Lots of predisposed people are going to get a hernia. I did. But this was going to happen anyway, since I am predisposed. It is not a matter of producing a hernia, it is a preference for not hurting your back.

Is this a hernia?

FROGGBUSTER: Hey mark, I've read your discussion of hernias before. I think I may have one. The area to the left (right side above is fine) and above my genitals and below my waistline feels a little tight. I can walk just fine, and I only feel it a little when I stand up. I don't see anything coming out thru the walls of my stomach, it looks normal. I've felt something weird in that part of my body for a week now, but it just became a lot more apparent today (I think deadlifting yesterday may have something to do with this?). What do you think? Thanks a lot.

Mark Rippetoe: I think that instead of asking me what I think, that you should go get it checked. Look, boys, I know that it's no fun to have the doctor handling your nads, but an inguinal hernia is a potentially bad deal. It's not life-threatening, and it is probably not an emergency now, but it can in fact get that way if you inject some of your colon down through the inguinal ring into your scrote.

So, no more hernia questions. No cancer questions either. I know a little about orthopedic injuries, but if you have a pain in the area of your crotchline, just go get it checked by somebody that can tell you what you need to know.

Squats and scoliosis

Win: I am just beginning the Starting Strength program. I am 43 years old and have had scoliosis since I was about 16. Have you had experience with trainees who have scoliosis or similar spinal structure issues? If so, are there any special considerations such as supplemental exercise I should consider, or should I just start at a manageable weight, squat with correct form and let the squats take care of themselves? I already wear an orthotic in my left shoe since the root cause of my scoliosis is a leg length discrepancy.

Mark Rippetoe: If you are properly shimmed, you should be fine. But not all cases of scoliosis are caused by asymmetric leg length. Does the curve diminish with the shim?

Win: I believe the curve is pretty constant. The orthotic in my left shoe helps put my hip bones on a more horizontal plane, but the curvature in the spine seems to remain whether I wear it or not. I've had some doctors say heavy weights might worsen the curve, while others seem to think strengthening the muscles might help provide better support. I hope the latter is true, because I want to continue to squat and deadlift.

Mark Rippetoe: There will be a weight with which you can work safely and get strong using more advanced techniques. You may not be able to do heavy 1RMs, but unless you are a competitor you don't need to.

Win: Thanks for your response. Is there a good way for me to determine what weight would be safe and which advanced techniques would be most helpful?

Mark Rippetoe: The safe weight will be the heaviest one you can use that doesn't hurt your back, and you'll have to titrate that yourself. The advanced technique I'm thinking of would be the Westside method of explosive squats with a lighter weight, detailed elsewhere.

SS & Golfer's Elbow

Brad: I just finished reading SS and am going to start the program. Just a little background: 37 year old, decent competitive PLer in my early 20s, intermittently worked out and sat in front of a desk from 25-35 and started following CF and then a CF-like program for the last couple of years. Now I want to switch gears and work on strength, which is my biggest weakness. I'm healthy and ready to go except that I gave myself a case of golfer's elbow in both arms last July by over-reaching on towel pullups and weighted fat-bar pullups. No pulling exercises since then. At this point the pain is only about half as when I noticed the pain. In other words, it's healing VERY slowly. I can't grip the bar for DLs or cleans, but appear to be able to squat, bench, and press with no pain.

My question is how to adjust SS for this. Should your method listed in the sticky thread be tried first? (Not sure if it's applicable to golfer's elbow.) OTOH, should I go ahead with squats, bench, and press and simply wait out the golfer's elbow?

Mark Rippetoe: Golfer's elbow (medial epicondylitis) is a bastard sometimes. If you're loaded up on ibuprofen already (and if you're not you should get that way for about 5 days) you'll just have to do as much of the program as you can tolerate. Sometimes a hard friction massage helps, sometimes it hurts. Deadlifts with a hook grip or straps should allow you to train your pulls. Straps can get you through chins. Don't do any more rope or towels for a couple of years, and respect them when you do start again. It will eventually heal, and as it does use less and less grip assistance, until you're back to normal. But be aware that this may take a while, like 6 months to a year.

Ryan: How I cured my golfers elbow: Got a 5 lb dumbbell and did reverse wrist curls 100 rep each hand, 5 days a week. Went to ironmind.com and bought a set of hand expanders, basically rubber bands of varying widths and started with the lightest one sets of 20, then started moving up. After about month pain was gone, now I can do all pulls including weighted chins or pullups with no pain. Yours may be worse than mine was so take it slow. At one point in my right hand it hurt to hold a dinner plate.

Brad: Ryan, thank you for chiming in. How do reverse wrist curls work the muscles affected by golfer's elbow? Did you have tennis elbow instead?

Mark Rippetoe: Reverse curls don't work that area. That's the tennis elbow side. Golfer's elbow is medial epicondylitis, the flexor side.

Ryan: My pain was Golfer's, on the inside of my elbow. So basically I worked the opposite muscles. It hurt to grip so I worked the extensors. I couldn't even think about doing regular wrist curls, so I did reverse. But I believe one of the biggest causes of Golfer's elbow or Tennis, is an imbalance. I know in my case I never ever worked the extensors, but I worked the crap out of the flexors. After bringing up the strength of the flexors I've not had a problem since. Good luck!

Jeff: This is an old blacksmith trick. They get "golfer's elbow" from using a hammer so much. The thinking is that this is an imbalance in the flexion and extension muscles of the forearm. If you think about it, most of the things we do in life require you to grab and pull in and we hardly ever work the extensor muscles. I've used this same combination of exercises with my patients that have medial epicondylitis with great success. Good call.

Mark Rippetoe: This is an approach I have not tried, but it makes sense if you consider the fact that it is really not possible to completely isolate the extensor and flexor functions of the forearm from each other. Chins are thought of primarily as flexor work because of the position of the fingers in maintaining grip, but the extensors are antagonists to this work and are heavily involved. Deadlifting likewise. I healed up a very bad dose of tennis elbow on my left arm by inundating it in submaximal grip stuff like chins and sledgehammers. I had assumed it was the direct work to the extensors that occurred as they functioned as antagonists, but maybe not. I know it works, but I'm not sure about the exact mechanism.

Brad: Have you tried the rehab method in the sticky thread for golfer's elbow? Do you have even a wild guess as to the chances of success for golfer's elbow? I figured it was worth asking before taking a couple weeks off SS to give it a try. I am able to DL with straps and power clean with a hook grip, BTW.

Mark Rippetoe: One of the only things the Sticky Rehab doesn't work well on is small tendon overuse injuries. I am told that actual tennis elbow involves some necrosis, and I've never had golfer's elbow so bad that it got to the point of needing this level of attention. So, ice, hard massage, ibuprofen, careful rehab work, and that's about all I can suggest.

(Subsequent input on this by several folks indicates that, contrary to the conventional wisdom, ice may not be nearly as effective as heat for this type of tendon issue. Try both and see which works best for you.)

Shoulder flexibility?

XTrainer: I notice that most good lifters, heck most lifters period, can lock their arms out overhead even with their ears or perhaps even further behind their head. When I raise an arm overhead, my flexibility only allows me to raise my arm so that it (at the elbow) is about 3 inches short of vertical, with some effort. I first took notice of this problem when I started doing overhead squats, and as you can imagine, OHS are quite difficult when you're holding the weight slightly in front of you rather than vertical or even slightly behind the head (as most Oly lifters do). What causes the flexibility issue, and how can fix it?

I don't know if this means anything, but I'm pretty flexible otherwise. I'm long-legged but I can still reach down and grab my toes without bending at the knees, I squat ATG routinely, I can lay on my back and touch my knees to the ground next to me ears (it's a stretch we do for jiu-jitsu) and I can kick to the head in martial arts training as well...but I can't even raise my arm to perfectly vertical.

Mark Rippetoe: Sounds to me like your shoulder ligaments are tight. Mine are too, and I have a little stenosis in my upper back, so I can't do OHSs either. Just for reference purposes, overhead squats are just like squats and presses in that the bar will be in a vertical relationship with the scapulas and the mid-foot, so that the bar is behind the head at the bottom.

Fixing it is another matter. If conventional stretching hasn't helped, there are talented PTs that know how to release the joint capsule with a stretch they can apply to your shoulder. You just have to find one that knows how.

XTrainer: Thanks for the reply. I think it's great how you help all of us out. Can you explain what you mean by "releasing the joint capsule?" What, physiologically, happens?

Mark Rippetoe: Best I can tell, the single session stretched out my capsular ligament to the point that I can now carry overhead in good lockout on the side I had done, while the un-worked-on side is still short of lockout. I have to assume that the change is in the ligament itself. Don't know how, but the genius behind this is Dr. Kelly Starrett, my buddy in San Francisco who uses the "Maitland" technique.

And thanks for thanking me. Many people think I am harsh.

XTrainer: Wow, that's very interesting. Looks like I need to do some reading. Is there any particular reason you still have an "un-worked-on" side? Is there some sort of undesirable side effect to this operation?

Harsh? You're helping people out for free, who are they to complain?

Mark Rippetoe: I have an un-worked on side because Dr. Starrett lives in SF and I haven't had time to go get the other one done yet.

My harshness is in lieu of pay.

Groin/ Adductor Problem

Anthony D: Last year around early July I injured my leg playing Ultimate Frisbee. The pain radiated mostly in the adductor region on the most medial part of my upper leg. The pain worsened and I eventually had to sit out for the rest of the season. The injury as I know came from sprinting—and groin strains are fairly common during that motion (if only I was doing squats with a wider stance at the time).

I've been active my whole life and being injured was not new territory, so I took it easy for a day or two. Squatting hurt a lot despite me doing close stance high bar squats at the time. However, I still was progressing on them for a week or two after being injured. So I kept squatting, but then after the third week the pain was too much and I stopped doing them. So in summary, to treat the injury I basically did nothing for it (stupid I know, but I didn't come across your/Starr's rehab protocol at the time).

After about a month I started squatting again (no other exercise aggravated it), building my way back up slowly. I lifted weights regularly until this year but the problem was always nagging, but not enough to prevent me from lifting. A few months ago I really thought the problem went away. I had no pain while squatting. I started up with martial arts again and the problem came back but only when doing a stiff leg deadlift/good morning. I did some high rep work after my main workout and the pain went away after about two weeks.

So Monday I ran the 300 yard shuttle and the same area hasn't been feeling too good the past few days. I would start the rehab protocol however there isn't any exercise that really 'hurts' or targets the area injured. Do you have any experience with using the rehab method with an exercise that doesn't necessarily 'hurt' as you explain it in the sticky topic? I think I'm just going to wing it with SLDLs or squats and see how it goes.

Mark Rippetoe: I really think that what you have in the afflicted area is a bad scar that needs some work. The injury healed during your layoff, but did so in a way that has restricted the function of that tissue, making it less extensible and quite prone to re-injury. It needs to be broken up so that you can get it working right when you resume rehab after this therapy, which will amount to a new injury. This will not be fun, especially in this particular area, but you need a friction massage performed by a therapist that knows how to do it correctly. Have a couple of beers before you go.

Strength Training and the Immune System

Tiburon: Since I started lifting heavy about 9 months ago, I have had some health issues that are possibly related to a "weakened immune system" - a case of shingles, a nasty MRSA infection, and a six-week bout of bronchitis. I am young (30), otherwise healthy, strong, eat well, sleep well, drug-free, etc. This could simply be bad luck. Or there could be some underlying problem (Docs have ruled a lot out). My question for you - could this be related to overtraining? My understanding is that in the long-term, exercise is probably good for the immune system. In the short-term, however, the intense stress possibly depresses the immune system.

p.s. - When you are in Boston, check out the beers at
The Publick House
1648 Beacon St
Brookline, MA 02445

(We did. Best beer bar with the best kitchen and the most interesting menu I've ever seen.)

Mark Rippetoe: Overtraining will indeed depress the immune system. You don't happen to be running along with your strength training, do you?

Tiburon: I've subbed in the occasional CrossFit metcon workout (Barbara, Michael, Cindy, Fight Gone Bad), but have never been at the gym more than 4 days a week. Maybe that is too much and I need to scale back a bit….

Mark Rippetoe: Sounds to me like you are a good candidate for 3 x/week training, at least for a while.

Muscle Tears

Baldr: Coach, I'm curious as to what causes muscle tears, and if they are inevitable (due to genetics/lifting heavy) or can be prevented? I've seen some pretty disheartening images of pec tears, scary enough that I have to know the root of the cause.

Mark Rippetoe: Muscle tears are ultimately caused by an instantaneous loading of the muscle belly beyond its tearing strength, and can occur due to a strength imbalance between the agonist and antagonist muscles of the movement. This is why they almost always occur in an acceleration/deceleration context in muscles whose primary job is producing rapid movement around a joint. Shoulder, hamstring, and quad tears are the most common in athletics. Pec tears are peculiar to bench pressing, and they occur at peak force production levels across the broad muscle belly of the pec/delt where a small tear starts and the lifter cannot get away from the load to stop it from progressing further. Genetics has nothing to do with it, and they are an inevitable consequence of the change from training for fitness to training for competition.

Stomach virus

naf7: I've been on the Starting Strength program for a few weeks now, making pretty good progress. I recently reset on squats to 165 after I stalled at 190 (which I later discovered was due to not eating enough, which I fixed). I got up to 180 last Friday, and it felt pretty good. Although I got about 3000 calories in that day (my current target amount), I got a stomach virus that night and threw up a lot. On Saturday, I got about 400 calories, Sunday, I managed to eat 1000, and on Monday, I got around 2500, feeling better towards the end of the day. Tuesday I went in to the gym and I decided to stay at 180 for another day, since my diet was bad over the weekend. However, I couldn't complete all 5 reps on the last 2 sets. Should I have dropped the weight? Should I drop the weight next workout?

Mark Rippetoe: By next workout you'll be fine. There is always a short period of time after a sickness that keeps you from eating and dehydrates you, to the extent that your strength will be down. Overeat and overdrink until you're back to normal, which will be your next workout.

Helping/preventing arthritic knee problems

Piratejon: I got an x-ray on my leg (motorcycle related, nothing permanent) and the doc noted "early stages" of arthritis in my knee. I'm 33. There's no pain or range of motion problems. I had no idea it was there. I'm not currently being treated for it, but I've setup an orthopedic consult to see what should be done. I'm worried the answer will be "never squat". What changes (if anything) would you make for this fact in your trainees? All I can think of is extra warmups.

Mark Rippetoe: What were the specific indications of "early stage" arthritis? There was an interesting study done shortly after the MRI was developed on a large population of asymptomatic middle age people that showed degenerative changes in the lumbar spine. And I know of an x-ray study done on a large population of horses that showed a very large percentage of asymptomatic navicular disease. The upshot is that lots of people have lots of shit "wrong" with them that never causes any actual problems. Take this into account before you schedule your prophylactic knee replacement.

ACL reconstruction, long term health

Chris P: Ok, so I made it to page 11 of SS:BBT, and I have my first question. Do you think the squat is key to long term knee health, post ACL surgery? I had my ACL done back in 1996, and since then have remained fairly injury free after picking up bicycling. I have yet to find anything written on long term knee health/maintenance, post ACL surgery. I want this thing to last the rest of my life, and so far, your explanation of the squat would make me think the squat is the best thing I can do for my knee. My cycling experience(mid-level amateur racing 6+ yrs) proved to be a very risky time sucking activity. So I wanted to get your thoughts on maintaining knee health with the full squat, by properly developing the legs function.

Mark Rippetoe: Well, I don't have an ACL in my right knee, having ruptured the repair graft some years ago after the surgery. I partially ruptured it playing soccer (I know, don't tell me, I don't want to hear it...), and finished it off stepping down off a tall horse onto bad footing. The squats have never hurt it, either when I had the graft or after the second rupture, and the other knee is fine. I have used squats to rehab several knees that I had the opportunity to work with, with excellent results. Done correctly, the squat is an ACL-neutral movement, one that provides balanced strength anterior/posterior, unlike any machine-based program of rehab or exercise. But you can rupture an ACL or an ACL graft despite your correct rehab if you engage in ACL-risky behavior. You just can't rupture it doing squats correctly, and they will keep your leg strength in balance to reduce the likelihood of it happening.

Shoulder pain during bench

Banderbe: I have an interesting little issue going on. When I begin my warmup sets for the bench press I start with the empty bar. As I begin the push up to the top (eccentric?) almost immediately I feel a slight pain in my left shoulder, where the delt and bicep meet in the front if that makes sense. It's not bad enough to stop the workout.

Here's what's odd to me. The second empty bar set still hurts a little but not as much. As I put more weight on the bar, the pain becomes lesser still. By the time I am at my working weight the pain is gone. This has happened two bench workouts in a row now. Is this anything to be concerned with?

Mark Rippetoe: As long as it's warming up like that, it won't be a problem. It's obviously a little soft-tissue inflammation, and I don't know that's even necessary to know more about it than that. These will be with you the rest of the time you are training, so you might as well learn to enjoy it.

Bad deadlift form and hyperextended knee

QSAle: I did deadlifts yesterday, and while concentrating on breaking the hip-angle before the knee-angle (on the way down), held the former too long, and ended up with a heavy bar away from my body and locked knees. I had no immediate pain from it, but soon after the workout and today I have some pain and stiffness in the pocket behind one knee ("popliteal fossa" according to med journals). I think the damage is all ligament, as I can massage the two tendons back there really well with no pain. From what I've looked up, it sounds like a hyperextended knee. The only increased pain comes from locking the knee, and swelling is minimal.

Program changes during recovery:

- I plan to go ahead and squat tomorrow, and just not extend to lockout where it becomes painful. I think the knee is stable up until that point.

- I wont need to sub for cleans, because I'm still doing bent-over rows till my deadlift form is perfect (obviously still isn't).

- Do partial deadlifts (up to knees and back down) for two weeks, or until back to normal.

Does this sound like a good workaround to you? Any other changes you can suggest to keep me on track?

Mark Rippetoe: The longer you sub assistance work for basic exercises, the longer it will be until you learn how to do the basic exercises. Deadlifts are just not that complicated, and I can't imagine how you pulled this off. Your plan sounds fine and the knee will heal quickly, but it very well may be that the bar-in-the-air-out-in-front position you have become accustomed to while doing your rows is the movement pattern that got you in trouble when you deadlifted. If you keep the bar smashed into your leg from the ground up, there is just not much of a way to hyperextend your knee.

I sincerely wish you guys would get less infatuated with the barbell row.

George: Question: to me it seems that doing barbell rows – which teach an early elbow bend off the floor – as a means to learning cleans seems contradictory, especially for a novice. Is this as significant a deal as I think it is, in that it would compound the problem of early elbow bend which lots of novices already have?

Mark Rippetoe: You're right, anything that teaches people to lift the bar with bent arms or by using an arm bend will make it harder to teach those people to clean and snatch with straight arms. Upright rows and to a lesser extent barbell rows have fucked up many a clean before it even had a chance to get learned.

Tendinitis in the foot

JeffreyS: After experiencing increasing pain in my left foot over the past three months, I was recently diagnosed with tendinitis. The injury is an overuse injury related to the amount of uphill walking I have had to do for work, but unfortunately it also tends to be aggravated by squats and deadlifts. I can do those exercises without excruciating pain, but I have to drop the weight, and I often feel stiffness, tingling, and some significant pain along the 2nd metatarsal when I do them. Also, doing squats and deadlifts causes me to feel pain later in the day after I sit down. I have stopped the uphill walking.

My doctor suggested ibuprofen and said I should come back if the pain is not cleared up in 30 days. I was wondering if you might be able to help me construct a routine that will allow me to recover from tendinitis. Should I discontinue the Starting Strength workout for a certain period of time? Is there a modification of the workout I can perform in order to rehabilitate my left foot?

Mark Rippetoe: I had plantar fasciitis several years ago from working on a ladder for several months while remodeling the gym. I tried all kinds of clever ways to rehab it, none of which worked. So I just trained through it and when I got through with the job it gradually went away. Take away the stressor, train anyway, and it will heal, at least in my experience. And make sure that your squatting footwear is sufficiently supportive.

Broken pinkie toe!

Cmdrfunk: Rushing out the door to work today, I stubbed my pinkie toe against my bathroom door. I got it x-rayed when I saw it start to swell I went for an x-ray, and yup, it's broken. I've been using the Texas Method lately. Things were going great. But what can I do for legs now? Should I still squat? I think I actually could if I lift my toes up, but I'm worried about the heavy day on Friday and walking the bar out. Maybe I could try speed squats on Friday instead? Or perhaps change to other leg exercise(s) until this toe heals that I'd be able to do and would help my squat/deadlift the most. I'm sure you've trained guys who have broken toes before.

Mark Rippetoe: Broken little toes are not an excuse for missing training, and really are no reason to waste money and health care resources to x-ray. Just tape the fucker to the one next door and train. If you can't train through a broken little toe you can't train hard.

Cmdrfunk: Well since then I've had 2 PRs on squats and deadlifts. Actually I've gone for 1RMs with 5-10 lbs more than my last 1rm attempt and ended up getting 2 or 3RMs instead. This Texas Method stuff is great!

Mark Rippetoe: See there? Not the end of the world after all.

Shoulder/Rotator Cuff Problem

Baldr: I've had a shoulder problem off and on in my right shoulder, before it was only affecting my bench. It seems to have presented an entirely new problem now, manifesting my press and squat. During the first work set of squats, it feels as if the bar is slipping down on my right side. By the last rep, I only have one finger on my right hand left on the bar (the left side is fine). When I rack it, my external rotation flexibility on my right shoulder completely and immediately diminishes. I try to rotate both elbows upwards, but I try as hard as I can and my right elbow won't raise more than 45 degrees. I feel no pain during the squat, but I do feel pain (the good pain) in my right shoulder when I am benching or pressing - it only presents itself when I do either heavy weight or many reps.

Mark Rippetoe: Damn, that's really weird. It sounds neurological, but I can't tell you more than that. Better get to the chiropractor first.

Baldr: Unfortunately, I don't trust chiropractors, especially the ones in my area. Also, I don't want to go to a doctor. I have no idea what I'm going to do. I think I'll just continue working out and hope for the best.

Mark Rippetoe: Well, the good news is that everything heals eventually. Usually. The bad news is that occasionally you have to go to the chiropractor, or maybe even the doctor. I don't like it either, but what are you going to do – build your own car?

Arthritis, atrophy and squats

JasonLeC: I spent most of the last year "chair ridden" due to an unusually severe bout of Reactive Arthritis caused by salmonella poisoning further complicated by peripheral neuropathy in the feet. Medication has recently made it possible for me to do wonderful things like walk for more than 100 feet and bend my joints. Two and a half weeks ago I restarted the program using the exercises detailed in Starting Strength (switching Rows for Power cleans). I'd done one of the net variants of the program before getting sick and loved it.

My question is about squats. Two and a half weeks ago I could not do a single body weight squat. Today I did 4x5 Body weight squats with a broom handle for a bar. It was difficult. My plan is to take myself to 5 x 10 with the broom handle before moving to 45lb bar for 3 x 5 and adding 5lbs per day from then on. Would this be too aggressive or too conservative in your view? Any recommendations?

Mark Rippetoe: The only thing I see that I don't like is the jump from the broomstick to the 45 lb bar. This is a rather arbitrary jump caused by equipment limitations that it may be necessary to rectify. I think you'll be better off trying to find an intermediate jump, which you can do by hanging something on the stick. Other than that, I think that the program is sound. Conservative or aggressive is only answerable by you: did I push as hard as possible today, within the only confines of being able to do it again tomorrow? A conservative approach to rehab for a pre-geriatric patient is a waste of time and life.

Groin Injury

j5coleman: I'm new to barbell training and began SS about two months ago. Aside from time lost due to traveling, I'd been making linear progress until two weeks ago when my right adductor(s) "popped" on the way back up in a squat -- nasty pain, and I had to bail out. Since then I've followed your injury protocol and made decent progress. (I've gone - at age 42 - from just about puking from pain from air squats 10 days ago to where it now takes something more than 100 pounds to make my thigh feel like it's going to split.) Still, I'm thinking it'll be additional weeks before this starts to get right again. I'm conscious of allowing the body to focus resources on the offending part, but I read in the book about using a narrower stance to allow for squatting while protecting an injured groin, making me think that I might not need to wait until things are completely healed to get back to business. So, my question: at what point would you recommend adding additional (non-squat) work back in, given it might be a LONG time until I could get things fully back on track. Just not sure how to think about the trade-off.

Mark Rippetoe: It doesn't really take that long. Once upon a time in the 80s I squatted 600 x 3 on the Monday before a meet, and pulled my gracilis out on both sides right up against my pubis. I obviously couldn't squat at the meet, and my deadlift was also affected to the point that I think I remember that I just benched. The next Monday Starr made me start back, squatting 95 x 25 x 3. I was not pleased with the sensation. But I had no say in the matter, and I squatted every day for 2 weeks, then cut back to 3 days/week, and at the end of 3 weeks I couldn't feel the injury. What was so painful that I couldn't even walk effectively was essentially gone in 3 weeks with the constant work. This is why I have no patience for people who manage to nurse an injury for months in their attempt to avoid the discomfort of rehab. So, to answer your question, you will be fine soon, and as early as possible – like tonight – add a set or two of narrow stance squats to the light weight/high rep sets you're using for rehab.

What about horse liniment?

nisora33: I've talked to football players who've used horse liniment to ease sore muscles during play. They've also told me that the pain-masking effects are dramatic compared to Biofreeze and Bengay. My concern with the liniment would be that it's so numbing as to be detrimental to proprioception -- I wouldn't know, because I've never used it myself. Farmer's co-ops and tractor supply companies sell a kind called DMSO (or Dimethylsulfoxide). Had any experience with this or other kinds of horse liniment?

Mark Rippetoe: "Horse liniment" means Absorbine. It doesn't do anything that any other mild counterirritant doesn't do too; if it did, the horse would kick you. Biofreeze is for female massage clients, and Bengay is for elderly male massage clients. There are more powerful counterirritants based on capsaicin and nicotine that can divert your attention from a compound fracture. DMSO is different in that it actually penetrates the skin and goes into the tissue underneath, carrying with it anything dissolved therein. You'll have to decide whether this is a good thing or not.

ITBS and Squats

J_Hendrix: I had a training question regarding iliotibial band syndrome that I was hoping you might be able to weigh in on. I hit a PR of 185 on my squats last Saturday (up from barely 135!) in sets of 5, but ever since then my knee has been bothering me pretty severely. I have a lot of noises in my knees that can best be likened to rice krispies at times, but this doesn't hurt so much as it just sounds bad. But I believe I have ITBS and the squats seem to be exacerbating the symptoms to the point of having to stop doing squats. Deadlifts and power cleans feel fine. The point that it begins to be a problem is when I get to at least approximately parallel to the floor. In fact, I almost lost my balance going around the turn on the stairs to my apartment due to a sharp pain from the movement after my workout this afternoon. Assuming this is ITBS--which I have reason to believe it is--do you have any recommendations on how to rehab my situation?

Mark Rippetoe: IT band problems are always best resolved with a friction massage, where the tendon is broken away from the underlying fascia to which it is scarred/adhered. This usually produces immediate relief from the symptoms, and if done correctly only needs to be done 2-3 times for a complete fix. Now, in the interest of full disclosure, an IT release is among the most painful experiences a human being can endure. It's like childbirth condensed into a little joyous 90-second bundle. And if doesn't make you hallucinate it was not done correctly. Just to let you know.

Pain in right quad

Ace: Since last Friday I've had a pain in my upper right quad, around my pants pocket area, when squatting. I can feel it when I start to warm up and it hurts more the more weight I do, eventually becoming quite painful on my last set. I've been lifting for about half a year and had the same problem when I first started, but it went away. As far as I know my form is pretty close to perfect. What should I do?

Mark Rippetoe: It's not your form. It's probably an old scar around which the adjacent muscle tissue has become inflamed. Get thee to a vicious massage therapist.

Ace: I've lifted two more times and my quad still hurts. What will the message therapist do, and how many visits will I have to make before the problem is corrected?

Mark Rippetoe: The massage, if done correctly, will actually begin to break the scar tissue down, and break it away from the healthy muscle tissue so that it can function in its normal contractile capacity. It is way more painful than just training around it, but if you don't get it done you will have continual problems with this injury.

Orthopedist visit...seeking advice

Jicjac: I went to see an orthopedic surgeon today to diagnose a problem I have had with my right knee for years. Long story short: after his examination and a few x-rays, he diagnosed my knees as having **lateral patella maltracking**. I'm sure you've heard of this before, but in layman's terms, my knee caps track toward the outside of my legs. For some reason only my right knee seems to be affected with any noticeable ache or pain during extension. In addition, he says that this condition also affects my feet to the extent that I place my weight toward the outside edges of my soles when I walk thus wearing out the heels of my shoes in an angled way.

He recommended stretching the quads and the hamstrings before weight lifting. He also said that squatting any lower than 45 degrees put tons of stress on the knees (I was very dubious of him at this point, but didn't want to debate). He recommended the use of an over the counter knee brace for the pained knee. After his squatting advice, I took everything with a grain of salt. I was even more disturbed when I learned he played football in college and strength trained with the team. So, I know you're not a medical doctor, but what do you think of his diagnosis and recommendations?

Mark Rippetoe: I have heard of this diagnosis many times. In my opinion – I am not a doctor – it is a bullshit diagnosis, the result of these weekend sports medicine seminars they often attend. Tight piriformis syndrome is the same type of thing: sounds cryptic enough to dazzle, but when everybody with knee pain leaves the office with the same diagnosis, the pattern comes from something other than the patient demographic, perhaps one of the presenters at the CME meeting. If your patella maltracks laterally, it involves a rupture or luxation of the medial retinaculum (look it up). Mine is ruptured on my right knee and scarred down poorly, but I track just fine. You probably have a tight IT band, and a massage therapist can fix this quickly.

Training Around Finger Fracture

od1: Wondering if you have any thoughts/experiences: I have a distal tuft fracture (right ring finger) that will require 4-6 weeks of healing. I was on a good novice progression at the time, and am trying to figure out how to salvage my current state of strength while allowing the bone to heal and not interrupt a speedy recovery. Making a close fist is not possible, so I was thinking I could do a program of squats, presses, and bench presses. No cleans, deadlifts, or pull-ups. I'm not even sure if I can do the presses/bench presses safely. Should I bother? I'm perfectly fine with taking four weeks off to drink beer, chase women, etc, but it would be nice to maintain some of the gains I acquired.

Mark Rippetoe: I think you can press and squat, and do a bunch of back extensions, and preserve most of your gains without taking time off for a 4-week party. But the primary thing here is that you will make the bone heal faster this way than if you lay off. Movement makes bones heal faster than immobility.

Pec Tear - Rehab Protocol Question

Atcq: About 2 weeks ago I suffered a partial pec tear while doing BB floor presses. A couple of years ago I cut off full ROM benching and switched to floor presses/board work as I found these exercises to a bit kinder to my shoulder which already had a SLAP tear before my latest accident occurred.

Anyway, after resting a few days and plenty of ice I began the rehab protocol stickied here in this forum. I initially chose to use the floor press as my exercise but then about midway through I decided I should probably be using a full bench press as it does a better job to make the area 'hurt' (after a few days the floor press stopped hurting) and if the goal was to get blood flow to the area than it seemed like bench press would be the better choice as it uses more of the involved muscle. Things were going great up until Day 8. Pain was decreasing each day and ROM was improving each day. On that 20th rep on Day 8, it kinda felt like I worsened the tear. I could just be paranoid but it sort of felt like a small rip when it happened (nothing near the magnitude of the initial injury though). It wasn't really painful or anything afterward but it was a bit more sore than usual the following day. Normally I wake up feeling a bit better but on Day 9 (today) it felt a bit worse.

Did I do anything glaringly wrong in my setup? If I had to guess, I would say that I loaded a bit too aggressively. I tried to follow the example posted where you used squats as the rehab exercise and I didn't really take into consideration that the jumps on squats might be bigger than the jumps for bench press. Any tips on how I should proceed going forward? Like I said, I think this protocol worked absolutely amazingly initially, but now I feel like I'm treading a very fine line between rehab and re-injury. I really want to be cautious and not screw this thing up anymore then I may have already.

Mark Rippetoe: Your setup was fine, textbook actually. What you did wrong was dropping the full ROM bench 2 years ago and then changing back to full ROM bench presses in the middle of the rehab. Since you already started back on them, back up to your Day 3 and use the full ROM.

Kazzin: Quick question about 3rd degree muscle strains. I'd assume that a complete rupture of the muscle would always require surgery to fix, but a casual glance on articles regarding the subject suggest that they only 'usually' need surgery. How is it even possible that a complete rupture would ever be able to heal itself without surgery? Given that all the tension on the muscle is completely gone, I don't understand natural mechanism (or any mechanism save surgery) would be able to stretch it back to its attachment with the tendon.

Atcq: Thanks for the help. I agree - switching midway was probably not wise. I was unsure about it at the time, I wish I would've checked in with you here first before making that decision. If I had asked before starting the rehab, would you have recommended the floor press or the bench? And just to clarify your comment, I take it you were not in favor of my decision to ditch the bench for floor/board work (in addition to plenty of pressing and OH stuff)? Also, if the area is still sore to the touch (the pec-shoulder tie-in and bicep both are) on day 11 of the rehab....would you say that's indicative of me screwing up the rehab?

Mark Rippetoe: There are several criteria for surgery, among them the ultimate usefulness of the procedure to the patient. If your grandmother falls face down, catches herself on the way down and ruptures her pec, what might the considerations be? Does she really need a functioning pec so bad that she needs to have surgery to fix it, considering that the surgery will be at least as much trauma as the injury?

And a rupture of the rotator cuff that involves a substantial part of the muscles will in fact not heal for the reasons you cite. The muscle belly pulls away from the tendon to the extent that the two ends are not in contact and therefore cannot heal back together. A thicker muscle belly that suffers a partial tear can heal, but any time a muscle is completely separated from its tendon it cannot heal, and you're then in a surgical situation. And for strength training purposes, a full ROM exercise is always preferable to a restricted ROM exercise. The injury may very well be tender to touch for quite some time.

Atcq: In reference to surgery....FWIW, I actually took a trip to the orthopedic surgeon and he said I'd be fine and no surgery was necessary. He said it would heal on its own in several weeks. And I hear you on the full ROM being better Mark, but I didn't think I had much of a choice. It was either partial work or nothing. I actually find floor presses to be a GREAT strength builder. At this point, I'm pretty uncertain whether I'll be doing partial bench work let alone full ROM ever again. As much as this injury has sucked, it could've been a billion times worse. Seems like a full tear would be inevitable (feel free to correct me if you think this line of thinking is stupid).

Mark Rippetoe: Floor presses, and many other partial movements, are a great strength builder *for the range of motion they involve.* The problem with them is that they leave so much other stuff out. But regarding your current injury situation and benching in the future: you might want to consider just doing presses and chins/pullups as your primary upper body work, with an occasion set of dips thrown in after things heal in a few months. Along with your pulling movements, presses and chins provide a complete approach to the shoulder girdle, unless you're one of these guys that think his pecs need to be hyooge, and once you get started with pec tears they tend to recur.

LCL pain??

Chris H: Do you have any ideas how I might be putting too much strain on my left LCL from doing squats? If it's already in SS I'm sorry for asking, and please don't rip on me too bad, although it is to be expected.

Mark Rippetoe: A correct squat is a ligament-neutral movement. So, either what you have is not a ligament injury, or you are not squatting correctly.

(BTW, this is paraphrased from a response given to me by the COO of Eleiko when I wrote him about a bent bar. He said that since Eleiko bars do not bend, what I had could not possibly be a bent Eleiko bar.)

Chris H: So what kind of squat faults would put strain on a ligament? Knees pushing in? Toes pointed too far out? Could it be my IT?

Mark Rippetoe: There are several threads here that reference IT band issues. It could be, yes. Ligaments get strained when squatting if the form used does not produce balance across the joint, like knees-in, toes-forward, etc.

IT band Issues and squats

BIGGUY6FT6: I am in my 4th week of SS and have been making really good progress. I have been doing fine except this last week. I have been getting some bilateral thigh soreness I have never had. It originates at about 3 inches lateral and 5-6 inches distal to the ASIS on both thighs. If my memory serves me right it is painful at about the area of the Tensor fascia lata insertion on the IT band. Either way, today I did the squat warm-up sets as Rx'd, then on my first work set at rep 4 when I was coming out of the hole it felt like I pulled/tore the lateral side of my left thigh in the same area as I mentioned above.

So I did a walk around the track then tried it again and the same thing happened. It was pretty painful. So I pulled about 20% off the bar, told myself to quit being a pussy and lift the damn weight. It was still painful but manageable. I then checked my form with my coach and he said it was good as far as he could tell.

I have severe DDD at L4-L5 and L5-S1 bad enough that at age 32 an orthoprick wants to shove 2 artificial discs in.

3 questions:
1. Could I be compensating and trying to use my quads more?
2. Would that show up form-wise?
3. Should I just continue with SS as Rx'd on other lifts (I was able to do my PC's...some pain but I sucked it up and refused to puss out) except use 20% less on squats and concentrate on strict form and work myself back up?

Mark Rippetoe: 1. You could be compensating for the back issues by keeping your back angle too vertical, and thus using more quad in the wrong way. I suspect you are not really keeping your knees out like you should be, and that this may be causing a small problem, but certainly not enough to account for an acute injury to your lateral thigh. After all, most people squat wrong and never have problems like this. Your height may make the situation worse, but I still doubt this explains the situation. And the area you describe may actually be the origin of the vastus lateralis and not the IT band. But they're close enough together that it won't matter much to the therapist – get an ITB release ASAFP, and see if this helps. If it does, you probably had an old injury there that was trying to un-scar itself.
2 Yes, with knees-in, and front squat-looking diagnostic angles.
3. Yes, if the ITB torture does not help immediately like it's supposed to.

Shoulder pain from squats

Pluto's mom: Rip, I just completed your cert in Longwood, FL and have been trying to adopt the correct form on the squat. Our gym did a CrossFit total yesterday and most of them got the form with the bar below the scapula ridge with elbows up. When it became my turn, I was extremely uncomfortable with my shoulders in that position. I sucked it up at the cert. but it was unbearable yesterday when I tried 185. It feels as though I have no flexibility when it comes to placement of the hands, elbows and position of the bar. How do I fix this or is it just practice makes perfect? By the way GREAT time at cert. Pluto misses you guys.

(Pluto is her doggie. He is a good little boy.)

Mark Rippetoe: Pluto's my buddy. It may be that old injuries and tight soft tissue could be the problem, since probably half the population over 40 has this problem to some extent. You will eventually stretch it out, but the fastest way is a vicious massage of the anterior and posterior shoulders, one that does not feel good at the time done by someone you don't want to be your friend. If this doesn't work, you could try bourbon before you squat.

Terrible pain in right leg

Ben00: I was squatting last Wednesday and I got a terrible pain in my right quad on my third rep in my last set. Being the hardass you trained me to be I finished my set, then deadlifted, all the while in bad pain. The next day I could barely put my underwear on; I am able to now. I skipped squats on Friday and managed to power clean without much difficulty. Today I was unable to squat the bar; the pain was unbearable. I was also unable to deadlift, not necessarily because of the pain, but because it seemed my right leg had no strength. The pain is pretty much all over my upper right quad in the pants pocket area. What should I do? Who should I see? When will I be able to train hard again?

Mark Rippetoe: See what you get for wearing underwear? Sounds like you have a torn quad. I am assuming you had enough sense to ice the damn thing 20 on/20 off. Has the blood showed up down the leg yet? I'd wait a couple more days to test it, and then start trying to run it through the range of motion unloaded. You should be ready to do the rehab in the sticky by Friday.

Kyle5000: How can I avoid this happening to me? It sounds like it really sucks.

Ben00: Damn. No I have not used any ice, I'm sorry, I'm an idiot. I thought it was just another pain that happens from lifting weights. What do you mean by the blood showing up? My leg has shown no visual signs of being injured. I feel sick now knowing that I'll be living with an injury that will inhibit my entire lifting career. I only just got my squat to 200 pounds.

Mark Rippetoe: Calm down, Ben. Everything heals. You just don't want it to heal wrong, so that's what the rehab is for. The blood will be from the tear in the vascular muscle belly (they bleed when they tear), and will look like a bruise on the skin. And Kyle, the only way to make absolutely sure this never happens to you is to quit lifting weights.

On Starr's rehab - continued pain?

Connor Mc: As it were I've had to stop progressing recently - I did an ugly set of squats a few weeks ago, and after continued sharp pain in my lumbar area, I realized I had to do something. I stopped lifting as I had before and started doing the rehab you list up at the top of this page - I've followed it more or less to the letter for these two weeks. I always feel better after doing the sets, and I'm almost back at the stage of doing sets of 5 again, but each day before I do my sets, I feel roughly the same pain I did before I started... I want to chalk this up to a kind of soreness (although it doesn't feel like a muscular pain in the way I'm used to) but I also don't want to be wrong, since my sports season (wrestling) is fast approaching and I can't afford to miss any practice or competition time.

So - is this normal? Should the pre-WO pain have subsided, or is the point of doing it every day for two weeks to MAKE the area feel this way?

Mark Rippetoe: It depends on the nature of the injury. A torn ligament takes a long time to actually heal, and will hurt long after it has become well enough to use. Inflammatory problems can persist for quite some time too. The bad news is that your back may hurt for quite a while after you've finished what rehab can be accomplished, but athletes learn how to deal with pain. The good news is that this lesson has a lot of carryover.

Injury that hasn't healed in almost 2 years

PowerTricks: I got the injury from doing acrobatics into a sandpit and my back and hips weren't strong enough to take the extra foot or two of height. The next day my lower back was really sore and has been sore ever since. Before this summer, I went to a physiotherapist and they said it was because one of my hips slipped a little higher than the other, causing the lower back pain (usually mostly on one side or the middle). He gave me light exercises to do and I did them for as long as he said and they seemed to help. But when I was done with the physio, my back started to hurt again.

So I went to a chiropractor a month later and my back started to heal more but still very slowly. After about 15 sessions he said that I didn't really need anymore chiropractic stuff and that I can start to strengthen my back. I decided to use one of the routines from your book that my friend has. When I do the workouts, my back doesn't get much sorer during the workout (sometimes it will) and even sometimes feels better towards the end. But most of the time it will hurt a lot about 30 minutes or more after the workout and then it will be sore for the rest of the day and following day. Would this be classified as rehab injury? I would really like to do plyometrics as soon as I get my lifts 1.5 my bodyweight but my injury has been keeping me from what I really want to do for almost two years now.

Mark Rippetoe: I think that plyometrics is a really stupid idea with this type of pain, something that I'd get an MRI done for. I'd suspect a disc injury, and I'm surprised that neither of the therapists has recommended a better diagnosis. I'd want one, if I were you.

PowerTricks: I kind of thought plyometrics wouldn't be that smart but I just wanted to make sure. I really would like to get a better therapist but my parents are tired of taking me to the physio or chiropractor and my dad thinks that I should be healed and done by now but my mom is saying that these injuries take a lot of time to heal.

Oh and about the MRI, before I went to the first physio, I think I had one or something very similar. Nothing showed up on the images so they determined that it was a muscle and hip problem (both of which the physio and chiropractor determined also). I'll try really hard to convince my parents for yet another and better therapist but how do I know which ones would give me the best diagnosis?

Mark Rippetoe: The only types of pain that persist this long are ligament/joint inflammation and disc problems. That's why a diagnosis might be important. But the type of therapist you go to for a diagnosis may have a bearing on the type of diagnosis you receive. This is just the rotten truth. So it's always best to start off with the guys who will usually give you the least invasive treatment for a given diagnosis and then get more invasive from there, i.e. therapist → surgeon.

What would Rip do?

Onemanroadcrew: Got any advice on rotator cuff injuries?

Mark Rippetoe: Quit benching if it hurts your shoulder. I had to, now it's your turn. Unless you want to have surgery.

OITW: Alright, you say that DLs are expendable, but here you say benching is. I've had shoulder pain following benching in the past, but no actual rotor cuff damage. Now I'm seriously into month two or three of SS at age 46, nothing broken or torn so far, and you're telling guys to lay off benching if they don't want to end up on the surgeon's table. Granted my bench numbers are weak, but I hoped to make them respectable. Now, I don't know.

Mark Rippetoe: Do you have a history of rotator cuff injuries? My advice applies only to those who do and don't want surgery.

OITW: Good copy, just note the original poster didn't say he had an injury, either.

Mark Rippetoe: If nothing is wrong with your shoulders, benches are fine. But when someone asks me about rotator cuff injuries, I assume they're not asking for their cat.

Shoulder Problem

BigMIKE: When I do the press motion with my bare hands both of my shoulders makes a clicking noise. Also when I keep my arms straight and at my sides and raise them sideways all the up, like when making a snow angel, it makes a clicking noise. The funny thing is that when I'm at the gym and doing the press with a empty bar and with weight on it, my shoulders don't make the noise.

I had a problem with my right shoulder a year ago, and everything is alright with it now, I don't worry about the right one because it always seemed to do it. I never had a problem with my left shoulder till now; this is the one I worry about. The clicking noise on the left is a louder one and I can feel it click more. The right one is a low click and just seems regular. The problem does not affect the press in any way. Before, during and after a workout it doesn't hurt. The right one doesn't hurt at all but after a while of doing the press motion with my bare hands, when I practice the motion, my left one pains a little.

Mark Rippetoe: Noises do not constitute problems. They are merely telling you that they are pissed off about being older. And who isn't pissed about that? Better than the alternative, I suppose. Tell them to shut up, ignore them unless they hurt, and quit worrying about this, because most everybody else's joints are noisy too.

Major quad injury

Dagfin: I tore my left quad muscle in a work-related accident and had to have it surgically repaired. It'll be many weeks before I can even think about working out. The doctors tell me I'm in for a long, slow rehab.

I fell straight down with my left leg bent underneath me, so my full bodyweight slammed down on the leg. The quad muscle tore completely off above the left knee. In the ER, you could see the bottom of the quad was 2"-3" above the knee in a lump. The surgeon told me he drilled four holes in the kneecap and used some kind of cord to "lasso" the muscle, pull it back down and anchor it to the kneecap, then used a couple of more cords horizontally to reinforce the whole thing.

He also told me I'm looking at 3-4 months of recovery time. Am I going to be able to squat again? What's been you experience with quad tears\ruptures?

Mark Rippetoe: Tendon ruptures are tricky. They have to heal unloaded for a few weeks until they regain some integrity, and then they have to be loaded like a muscle belly injury but without the frequency. More like every other day instead of every day, but with the same linear progression from a very light weight and high reps.

My buddy Cardell completely ruptured his patellar tendon at work a few years ago, and was back to a 315 x 5 squat in 5 months this way. The bottom line is that everything heals, and if the surgery was done well, it will heal faster than the surgeon thinks it will.

Diagnosis sore leg

one_one_six: Meralgia paresthetica, lateral femoral, cutaneous neuropathy, 79 year old male. Got into SS about three months ago, did a few workouts and developed this problem. Did do a few workouts and right upper thigh (quad) acted up and worried I might exacerbate the thing. Waited for it to just go away on its own, it didn't. Went to an orthopedist: not bone, ligament, etc. Finally yesterday to a neurologist, receiving this diagnosis. He prescribed Lidoderm lidocaine patches and Ibuprofen as needed and a visit to a PT to learn appropriate stretches. Asked him if squats would be okay, he said "no way".

I would really like to get going with SS. It does NOT hurt when I squat. Please, what is your opinion? Thanks.

Mark Rippetoe: Here is the description of this condition:

Meralgia paresthetica is the term that describes a painful mononeuropathy of the lateral femoral cutaneous nerve (LFCN). It is an entrapment neuropathy (pinched nerve) that develops as the nerve passes through the inguinal ligament. It may be due to direct trauma, stretch injury, or loss of blood flow to the nerve. The clinical history and examination is usually enough to make the diagnosis. The LFCN is a purely sensory nerve and is responsible for sensation of the anterolateral thigh. The LFCN has no motor component.

I assume you have not had this area massaged, but this might help with the entrapment at the inguinal ligament, if this is palpable to your therapist. Your doctor just told you not to squat because you're older, and that is the reflex reaction of The Doctor. If squats don't hurt, do them; you're capable of making this decision without his permission.

Runner's Knee and Squats

Hystikal: I've been diagnosed with patellofemoral pain syndrome (runner's knee). I don't run much at all any more. I did make a PT appointment, but there's no way in hell I'm doing partial squats. Plus, it's not a muscle imbalance issue, as I follow crossfit and your advice on lifting form to the T. Likely, my hamstrings and/or IT band is tight. Did full ROM 3RM squats the other day and they went fine. Knee did feel a bit full the next day but nothing big. However, tried to do push presses yesterday but couldn't. There would have definitely been pain issues. Besides my PT appointment, do you have any advice?

Mark Rippetoe: Sure. Cancel the PT appointment. It's a waste of time, and you already know this. Get your IT band released and get some ART on the area. Use the money you were going to give to the PT.

TravisRussellDC: The IT bands, quads and hamstrings are usually the first place I look for issues when my patients come to me with knee problems (assuming there's been no direct trauma to the area). However, with my runners, I also check the hip joint and the foot/ankle complex. When you run, you can put anywhere from 3-10 times your bodyweight of force through your foot and ankle. Plus, this force travels through your body at approximately 200 miles per hour. The next joint in line to deal with this impact stress is the knee. So, if there's anything going on with the foot/ankle complex, that can contribute to the knee pain.

I'm willing to bet that the IT band release and hamstring work will provide quite a bit of relief for the knee pain. But, if it doesn't seem to get everything, then I would suggest having the feet/ankles checked out.

sasquatch989: Or you can get a foam roller, do some myofascial release on yourself, and take all the money you've saved and buy gold, commodities, a firearm, or just save it.

Mark Rippetoe: Trade the foam roller for a piece of 3" PVC, if you insist on doing this to yourself. The foam is in fact too friendly.

Deadlifting and shoulder impingement

Isis: I am now just realizing that another one of the major exercises is helping one of my orthopedic problems. For as long as I can remember my right shoulder has been less flexible reaching up my back than the other one, and prone to getting sore for no obvious reason. I really aggravated it earlier this year and saw an orthopedic surgeon who diagnosed me with posterior capsule tightness leading to impingement and bursitis. He said it looked like what baseball pitchers get from too much throwing. He prescribed me PT, where I learned some stretches, which have been helpful, and some exercises, which as far as I can tell were designed to keep me sore enough to keep coming back to PT until my insurance ran out. Fortunately for me that happened quickly.

The PT thought it was actually biceps and supraspinatus tendinitis instead of bursitis but either way my symptoms were crunchiness and pain from reaching for anything over shoulder height. Doing the PT's stretching program has made it manageable and I find I can do the overhead press if I warm up, thoroughly stretch, and roll on a tennis ball on the outside edge of my scapula. And concentrate on form and stretch and roll more between sets. At least most days--some days my shoulder just says No Thank You to the press no matter how much I stretch. Anyway I'm up to 30 pounds, after starting with a broomstick, and making slow progress. Bench press doesn't bother the shoulder and my bench is at 70 pounds, up from 20.

The point of this story is that my deadlift has gotten heavy--160 lbs (I'm female, 42, 140 lbs) and after my last two deadlift workouts my shoulder has felt amazing, which is to say normal and pain and crunch free, for two days. But I'm only deadlifting once every two weeks and there's no way I could deadlift every two days and recover. So I have been reading your section of BBT about partial deadlift movements, even though I know you don't recommend them for novices. But if I keep the weight down under my actual deadlift work set weight, and the reps low, and use these exercises to work the part of the movement that fixes my shoulder, do you foresee me having problems? Or maybe you have other suggestions for my shoulder issue.

Mark Rippetoe: I'd say that if the deadlift is helping the shoulder through some mechanism (that neither I nor you and most assuredly not the PT, understands), then you need to keep doing them, and doing them more frequently will help enough to justify using them in a way not usually employed in a novice progression. I'd do them every other workout, and alternate between your normal heavy set of 5 and a lighter workout of 3 sets of 5 with about 85% of the heavy day weight. And I'd press every workout too, using the weights you need to use to make this possible. If the bench press doesn't bother the shoulder, chances are it's not going to make it heal either, so I'd cut it back to every third workout for a while, done after you press.

Numb Thumb

Qwooldridge: While coaching a game recently I noticed that my left thumb had gone numb, and remains in a pins and needles state. A doctor friend of mine thinks it could be carpal tunnel and recommended I switch to a thumbless grip on bench because I had expressed that at times I squeeze the bar so tight that my fingers leave imprints in my palm and the knurling also leaves tracks. Other than never speaking to the doctor friend again because he recommended the thumbless grip, what advice could you have other than stop squeezing the damn bar so tight? Ever hear of this before?

Mark Rippetoe: First, is the guy a plastic surgeon? Maybe he needs your business and actually wants you to drop the bar on your face. Second, see if you can get somebody to adjust your wrist a few times. This may relieve the symptoms. Third, numb thumb should be accompanied by a numb or tingly index and middle finger as well as the inside of the ring finger, if it's actually carpal tunnel syndrome/radial nerve stuff. This may not be what it seems.

Justinbass: It is your duty as a human to give your friend a beating for suggesting a thumbless grip on the bench. People get their rib cages crushed from this.

Qwooldridge: No index or middle finger numbness involved. There is a trigger point on the palm side of my thumb at base, and any pressure to this area recreates the electric pulse to the end of my thumb. Really no restrictions on what I'm able to do, for instance on Tuesday was able to complete Squat/Press/Deadlift day with regular weight and no complications. Just hoping that this issue is not lifting related and will not get in the way of my only hobby. That's why I have enlisted the thoughts of those smarter than I, or at least so I thought until the thumbless grip was recommended.

Mark Rippetoe: Your grip is probably the problem. I'll bet the bar is back in your hand, away from your wrist making a lever arm out of your metacarpals. You can keep the bar over your wrist without a thumbless grip by pronating your hand when you set the grip and then squeezing it tight the way you've been doing.

Muscle trauma

Phillipo: Recently I was involved in an accident in which resulted in a 3-4cm deep cut on the front/side of my leg that partially severed one of my quadriceps muscles and did some additional damage to my IT band. I couldn't put any weight on it for a few days but it has been about a week and I am slowly starting to lose my limp.

How does the injury sticky apply to this situation? The ER physician said to be careful of calcification of the muscle, or myositis ossificans, which can be caused by returning to activity too soon. At the same time, if I remember correctly, in your cert you said that often they get myocardial infarction patients moving around the same day as the MI to try to apply a moderate stress to the heart muscle to return function as soon as possible. I guess my question is what is the difference between rehabbing a lacerated muscle vs. a muscle injured through training?

Mark Rippetoe: The difference is one of degree. A lacerated muscle belly has more initial healing to do before the stress will not make it bleed, but after this has occurred it needs work to keep it from scarring. The injury sticky still applies, but you have to wait a little longer and go up a little slower. The principle is still the same.

Phillipo: Thanks Mark, I appreciate you getting back to me. I'm starting medical school in the spring and am looking forward to seeing the similarities and differences in what is currently being taught on such subjects vs. what has been fleshed out through real-world experience. I know that the information you've given me will help me to cast a critical eye on what I'm being taught and will also help my future patients through exercise/rehab protocols. I'm looking forward to it.

Mark Rippetoe: I hope your good attitude remains intact. Good luck.

Shin splints, what to point the finger at?

Harry: I followed the Starr method over summer with Simmons' speed box squats thrown in on Fridays and achieved great results. At the start of the university rugby season I was obviously running and sprinting a lot more. I also did some short road runs for a couple of weeks. This was in addition to singles on the squat and power cleans, including some done barefoot (don't ask why, I wouldn't recommend it). After a week I developed shin splints down the inside of both shins which got worse over about a week until I stopped the running altogether. 4 weeks on it is still troubling me.

Do you know if performing large volumes of lifting and then returning to rugby without conditioning the body to run (enough) has caused this? Will the non-impact lifts and cycling have impede my recovery? Perhaps muscle imbalance in the lower leg has caused this injury?

Mark Rippetoe: Weight training does not cause shin splints. Running causes shin splints, although barefooted cleans are incredibly stupid. Shin splints are caused by trauma to the periosteum of the tibia, not muscle imbalances. Did you do the road work in your cleats?

Harry: Yes, running outside of training was on the road. Shall I steer clear of the tarmac in the future?

Victorc: I'm curious as to why you think barefoot cleans are incredibly stupid? I'm asking because I do all my lifting barefoot. Is it the possibility of dropping plates on your foot or some other reason?

Mark Rippetoe: No, Harry, were you wearing your cleats when you ran, as opposed to squishy shoes? Pose runners don't usually have shin splint problems, even on pavement. The fastest way to get them is to run on pavement in shoes designed for turf, like cleats, with poor technique. Barefoot cleans are obviously very hard on your podiatry, since the foot bones are unsupported during the impact with the ground. If you do all your lifting barefoot, you are doing some of it wrong.

Pectoral strain/tear and Starr rehab method

Bill: My question is regarding the injury sticky and my situation. I strained my left pectoral muscle about 2 years ago. It got better with time, but still would bug me from time to time in the way of stiffness. I also aggravated it again last year, but it didn't keep me out of commission for too long. Now, I've aggravated it again last week doing dumbbell bench presses. Out of the 3 times I've strained it this is the second worst in terms of pain. I have been able to do some pushups without pain the last few days, and just read the injury sticky and am considering using it. Do you think the Starr rehab method would be a good idea for me after almost 2 years have passed since the original injury?

Mark Rippetoe: No, the rehab protocol is for a fresh tear. The old injury has scarred long since, and will probably be a source of trouble for the foreseeable future. If you continue to experience problems, and I am sure you will, you should consider becoming a press specialist and only do the bench as a moderate assistance exercise. Sorry, but that's my advice.

Swollen Knee

samGwin: A week or two ago my right knee started to get sore, it wasn't exactly painful but it felt and still feels swollen and kind of stiff and pops and cracks more than before. I'm not sure what has caused it. My squat seems to be in pretty good shape from what I can tell of your other squat critiques. I keep my knees tracking over the toes, my knees don't drift forward at the bottom, but I did notice that on my heaviest workout around when I started to notice the injury, I only squatted to parallel instead of below. Would this be enough to cause an injury like this? I reset to a lighter weight and continued on squatting and made sure I was well below parallel, yet the knee still feels swollen and stiff. Should I just continue to squat or take a break? Should I take an anti inflammatory? Will muscle gains continue if I have to take a break but can eat even more, and I'm still lacking sufficient mass?

Mark Rippetoe: A swollen knee usually (but not always) indicates a cartilage problem. One high set of 5 is seldom a cause of anything bad, although bad habits can accumulate into injuries over time. But it might have been enough to irritate a pre-existing problem. Take an anti-inflammatory, wrap the knee, ice it, lay off a couple of workouts, and then get back to it with good form. The vast majority of meniscus tears require no surgery. If it does not improve markedly this week, get it looked at.

Gman: It could also be a Baker's cyst

Mark Rippetoe: It could also be cancer. But it's probably a meniscus tear. And it will probably be fine without surgery.

DJD and dextrascoliosis in lumbar spine..deadlift therapy?

Bethany: I am 45 years old and have moderate degenerative joint disease and dextrascoliosis in my lumbar spine. My max DL is 215. I have had significantly increased lower back pain in the last 6 months and much more noticeable muscle imbalances in my spinal erectors. All the medical community has to offer me so far is "sit on your ass and take narcotics". I'm not going to go down that road just yet. Interestingly, lifting or any of the CrossFit stuff I do does not cause me pain. Vacuuming, doing dishes, and standing around cause pain. I know, I know...you just think I'm trying to get out of the housework!

My questions...Is continuing to do this stuff exacerbating my problem? Is there a way to moderate the lifts to correct the muscular imbalances? I'm wondering if I set up for my DL and then consciously try to straighten out my back (so I would actually be rotating my right hip down and forward) and then lifted if this would potentially be some sort of "DL therapy" at lower weights?

Mark Rippetoe: If doing so produces normal muscular soreness on the atrophied side of your back, I'd say it was certainly worth doing. I have no personal experience with scoliosis, but everyone I've trained has reported that pain is much more easily managed if training involves deadlifts. Doctors with no personal experience may find this hard to believe, but the loading of the deadlift decreases the effects of the loading encountered in submaximal tasks encountered daily. The question is which component of your program has exacerbated the problem. The way to find out is to selectively eliminate metcon, barbells, and endurance, or the components of each that you feel most likely to be the problem, and see what happens.

Bethany: Thank you for the quick reply! I absolutely agree that the days that start with heavy DL or squat go much better ;). I have eliminated running except for races because I find that does increase the back pain...probably d/t the impacts on the arthritic joints. While a great deal better than the alternative...aging still sucks!

Rehab for a Broken Rib

Traktor: About six weeks ago I strained/damaged the cartilage somewhere around the connection between my 7th rib and my sternum (guessing - didn't see the doctor at that time). I hurt myself on a light warm-up set of squats after I had already warmed up on the rowing machine. My stomach was unusually bloated after a big lunch and little too much milk in the afternoon. I felt a little pop in my rib cage. That night it was smarting pretty good but I didn't think it was that serious given the way I had injured it.

So when the rib hurt I just trained through it for 2 weeks and it didn't get better. I hadn't found Strengthmill.com at that time so I hadn't seen your post on rehabilitating injuries. I took two weeks off went back and dropped 10 kg. After two more weeks of training I was just past the amount I had been doing when I hurt myself. I still hurt a bit but I felt strong. I attempted deadlifting 165kg but on the first rep I felt a really good pop from the same place in my rib cage as I was about half way through the rep. It hurt but I locked out the rep and finished out the next 4 to complete the set. Within minutes it hurt so badly I could barely breathe. When I got home I tried laying down but it hurt too much. At this point I decided to see a doctor.

The doctor made an educated guess (no x-ray) that I may have further damaged the cartilage connection to the rib cage and perhaps cracked it near where it connects to the spine. Regardless of what is going on there something isn't right and it hurts to sleep. I just turned 40 and I don't seem to be recovering as quickly from injuries as I was ten years ago and it irks me a bit. I have been under the impression that most of the time I could punish my body back into shape in direct proportion to my pain tolerance. But this last attempt didn't work out so well and I have wasted a lot of time and pain for nothing.

Mark Rippetoe: Costal fractures are the quickest-healing fractures in the body because of the fact that the fracture cannot be immobilized. It literally *has* to heal while it's moving, and the movement along the fracture plane provides a great incentive for the bone cells to repair the fracture. A costal chondral fracture is the same type of thing, and it heals rapidly as well. Even at 40 it will heal very quickly. Follow the instructions from your pain, but train as much as you can stand it without doing any deadlifts for a while. It may be useful to put a knee wrap around your chest during your squats and presses, or even when you're trying to sleep. The injury sticky won't apply here, since the ribcage is involved in every single movement you do and there's no way to pick an exercise. This whole thing should be over in 2-3 weeks, so just be patient.

Delayed onset & prolonged back pain after deads

Hystikal: Last Monday (over a week ago) I was doing 5x5 of 295s. I didn't finish all the sets, partly cause the gym closed sooner than I expected, but I felt great doing them. No form issues whatsoever. Thinking back though, if anything, maybe I was hyperextending my back. Anyway, I felt 100% before, during and after the workout. Woke up Tuesday and had a lot of pain in the middle of my vertebral column, around the lower lumbar/upper sacral segments. It was confined to that area. No radiating pain. I'd experienced muscle strain a few months back, but I knew it immediately during the workout and I stopped. The pain subsided a few days later. The pain I have now still persists, although it has gotten much better. I did a full-on metcon workout Sunday which went fine and today was the first day of using Starr's rehab method with the high rep, very low weight squats. Felt good during them. The soreness is still there afterwards, but certainly no worse than before.

So I guess my 2 main questions are, can injury manifest itself relatively long after a workout? In my case, ~ 10 hours. And can strain of muscles/ligaments (which I assume I have) persist for over a week? I'll be continuing Starr's method for the coming weeks.

Mark Rippetoe: Delayed onset of pain is usually the case in an inflammatory situation, and is frequently the case in connective tissues and discs/meniscii. All types of injury can persist for long periods, especially inflammatory problems, which can persist for months longer than even fractures. The injury you describe is likely an overextension injury, and you have probably mashed your facet joints or even pinched the stuff between the spinous processes of L4-5. It will heal, as everything does. But fix your form and quit doing that pelvic thrust at the top of the pull. Just lift the chest to lock out the deadlift.

Can I squat after this type of injury?? How can I strengthen it and here's doc note...

logged101: A friend got injured about 8 months ago while playing basketball, sum1 landed on his ankle awkwardly and he was out for about 5 months. He went to the doctors and this is what is in the doc's note:

"NO bony injury is noted. The talar dome is well preserved. A mild tibiotalar joint effusion is noted. A small soft tissue swelling is noted over the medial malleolus."

Well it's been 8 months and he still feels some pain when doing a certain flexibly drill and also when applying some pressure. He was walk without pain but other then that he still feels it a little. He pretty much can't jump and all these things like he used to. So what can he do?

Mark Rippetoe: I guess he could get one of those Hoveround power chairs, As Seen On TV. A guy that crippled can't be expected to endure any more pain than he's no doubt already suffered. I mean, there ARE limits to the ability of a human to endure the agony of an ankle injury that involved no fracture and a little swelling.

Gman: If he is really that worried about it, he should get a repeat x-ray done to make sure they did not miss a small hairline fracture or stress fracture.

logged101: Not cool guys not cool at all.

Mark Rippetoe: Gman was trying to be helpful. I was trying to be not cool. Unless there is something actually wrong with "your buddy's" ankle, he has long delayed his rehab by being a pussy about the pain.

Calf Muscle injury rehab

Pdellorto: During my MMA training last week, I injured my right calf. My doctor diagnosed it as a class I/borderline class II injury of the gastrocnemius. Nice little bruise right behind my knee and the calf is yellowed all the way down. My MCL hurts, but it's not injured, just suffering from the off-loaded pain.

I was thinking using the Starr rehab routine once it's healed enough to start into that. I'm not sure what exercise would be best. My first thought was just calf raises - directly hits the muscle, easy to load. Obviously I'm also going to be walking around so the calf will get some work from that too but I'm worried it's not sufficient to just walk it off. Would that work as rehab or is there a better exercise?

Mark Rippetoe: I tore the shit out of my calf about 12 years ago, the day before I left for an overseas trip where I had to walk every day. It healed well and made the trip interesting. You could do it like that, or you could use the calf raises. I suspect the walking would be better since that is the normal function of the muscle, and calf raises are not. But try a little of each and let me know.

Pdellorto: What a coincidence - I just hurt my calf, and I'm going on an overseas trip next week where I'll be walking all over the place. As the calf feels better I'll start in on the calf raises and report back.

JonnyPrimal: I have done both of my calves (not at the same time) a couple of years ago. I wouldn't do the calf raises - every time I tried that it would cause problems again. I suspect the calf raises contributed to the problem in the first place.

Mark Rippetoe: Makes sense to me. Any exercise they had to invent a machine to do is not a normal human movement pattern.

Question on Starr's Hamstring Rehab Strategy

RayKin: I am 47 years old, and 3 days ago I sustained a probable Grade 2 tear in my left hamstring during a 225 deadlift (1st of the day). Lot's of mistakes on my part: not enough of the right kind of warmup, inflexible hammys to begin with, 6:00 AM with inadequate hydration, etc. My quads & glutes can get it going, but my hammys are weak in comparison. I was ignorant of the role of the hamstrings in that lift, and I bit off more than I was ready to chew. I just bought your books, and I will be going back to square one the hard way.

I will not know my MRI results for a few more days (that will be day 7 post injury). Is that too long to wait, or should I just wait for the official results? I am trying to avoid as much scar tissue as possible while also avoiding making things worse. I am meeting with a massage therapist today to talk about what he can do to help me as well. Also, my so called "sports med doc" was gonna send me home without an MRI to rest.....forever. He finally caved on the MRI. I will probably find another doc. I want to get into some sports PT ASAP to get going on the light stretching and some strengthening very soon. I would like to start the Starr plan in another week or so. Does that sound like a plan?

Mark Rippetoe: I agree with your doc: what the hell is an MRI going to tell you that you don't already know, and if you're not going to have surgery (you're not) why do you care what the MRI says? You know you tore it, you know you have to rehab it, so why waste the money and time on an MRI? If you're just starting, the rehab will work, just use it conservatively. The important thing is to get a lot of lactate in the area as often as possible. Massage is helpful if the scar has already formed, but not until then. Stretching might have helped prior to the tear, but not on a fresh injury. Just start doing something that makes your hamstrings burn at about 20-25 reps for about 3 sets everyday. It might be more useful in your case to use the back extension bench.

Numbness in heel

Blades: A couple of days ago I woke up with numbness in my right heel, lateral side. Today the numbness feels a little less and I feel it more on side of foot, below ankle. I've been following the program for about 2.5 months. I'm 60 years old. My wife says she found on the Net a reference to a link between lifting weights and foot numbness, attributable to compressing force of the weights. Recommendation was for stretching after lifting. If this doesn't go away soon, I will see a doc. Have you come across this type of thing? Assuming you think I should see a doc, who would you look to see? I'm thinking neurologist.

Mark Rippetoe: If you're going to see a doc, a neurologist is the specialty. I have had numbness is isolated spots over the years, and while it is irritating and worrisome, it is most usually insignificant and associated with a superficial dermal nerve. But on the off chance it isn't and you're worried about it, get it looked at.

Bergie: Since numbness is a loss of feeling, is "numbness feeling a little less" the loss of even more feeling? :)

Mark Rippetoe: Believe it or not, there are actually degrees of numbness. And dumbness.

What to do once you stop

Dana: Thanks to your program, I'm about 15lbs. away from a 2x bodyweight deadlift at 180lbs. I know this isn't special, but it's amazing for me as I used to throw my back out lifting 135lbs. off of the ground. Given my age and needs (40, non-athlete, herniated L4 and L5) I don't know that there's good risk/benefit to proceeding much past 360. I have tweaked my back slightly on some of my recent lifts, though it's always recovered within a few weeks.

So what to do once I hit a 360lbs. deadlift (an arbitrary goal, but one I'd like to hit)? Just maintain it and work on other things. Work on micro-increases? What's the best programming for maintenance? I've definitely found the increased deadlift useful in daily life, so don't want to let it go.

Mark Rippetoe: Good question. I think that with a history of back problems there may be good reasons not to do the deadlift at all past a certain point. They are very hard, are hard to recover from, and with a bad back they can hurt you if you get out of position with a heavy weight. Unless you're going to a powerlifting meet, you don't need to deadlift at all past the point it has served your purposes as a novice. You can rack pull and do haltings, as I have described in the book, and which got me to a 600+ deadlift. Or you can do RDLs, reverse hypers, and other assistance work. If you decide not to pull heavy, your squat will probably stop progressing too, and this may fine too, depending on the context of your training. If you have a herniated L4-L5 then your injury must be figured into any training decisions.

Sprained Ankle

Blah3: I have badly sprained my ankle which means I won't be able to squat but *may* still be able to deadlift, press and bench. What should I do? Continue with my program without squats and do the exercises above as I usually would do or lay off for a while and recover?

Mark Rippetoe: You don't know what you can't do until you get under the bar. It may be that you can squat just fine, but will have trouble unracking/racking the bar. Test all the exercises before you decide what you can't do. I have squatted with so many ankle injuries that I can scrape up very little sympathy for your situation. Just go train. Wrap the ankle if it makes you feel more Whole. You'll be fine.

Yet another knee problem

Jereth: Started SS two weeks ago and while my unacceptably pathetic squat strength has gone up about 50lbs, I'm having some knee problems during the warm up. During the warm ups (and if I squat down to pick up something outside of the weight room) I get a very sore feeling where my tibia meets my knee. The pain is gone by the work sets but it seems to increase a bit with every workout.

I do the programme on Mon/Wed/Fri so I had the weekend to recover and yesterday the pain wasn't even there during the warm up sets. I have used the search function and following some advice offered in a similar thread, I concentrated on keeping the knee's well out during the squat but the stiffness and pain is back today. Have you had any experience with this...?

Mark Rippetoe: Have I had experience with knee pain? I have never had an experience without knee pain. But I cannot help you from here, beyond the trillions of posts that have already appeared on this board.

Jereth: Is there any chance this pain might just subside after a week or two...?

Mark Rippetoe: Of course there is. That's what it usually does. Everything heals. You'll be fine. That's how the species persists. Especially when the species uses correct squat technique.

Strengthlifting to Rehab Knee

Andrea: I had arthroscopic knee surgery to repair a torn meniscus about 12 years ago and my knee healed really well after that. I then had to have a second surgery in the same knee about two years ago at the age of 45, but the results weren't as good this time, because the surgeon (a different one) may have fucked up the surgery and/or my natural recovery abilities are not as good as they were at the time of the first surgery. Due to a significant amount of pain after the second surgery, I was not as diligent with post-op physiotherapy, in that I did not push through the pain as much as I should have. Also, I did not have access to proper strength training and rehab techniques back then like I do now, after my husband bought BBT, PPST, and the BBT DVD, all within the last year.

I have since attempted to use the back squat to help me with my knee rehab, but I can only get down to about four inches above parallel without feeling a blinding pain in my knee that I'm not able to push past. I have a decent amount of hamstring and low back flexibility, so I do not believe this is a flexibility issue. I understand that squatting high would be counterproductive, so I am unsure where to go from here. I am able to deadlift without any pain, but I don't know if deadlifting alone would help me. Equipment-wise, I have access to an Olympic barbell set and a power rack.

Mark Rippetoe: Make very sure that you are squatting correctly, i.e. that you are shoving your knees out to the side enough. Enough meaning as much as you can with a correct stance. This may be the only thing wrong; menisci are sensitive to this when they are tender. Deadlifts are important as well, to get the meniscus used to bearing weight, but the squat is the key to the full use of your knee again.

Andrea: That's exactly what the problem was. I increased the angle of my feet and exaggerated the knees out cue, which then got me down to parallel.

Press and fucked up neck...Help!

Tongzilla: I warmed up for my presses in the usual way, by doing reps with the bar then gradually adding more weight, etc. On my second working set, when the bar just about to be pushed up above my chin, I felt an acute strain in my neck/trap muscles. I immediately stopped and put the bar down. My neck fucking hurts now. It hurts when I look up/down/left/right. My I lie down with my back on the ground in a sleeping position, even the thought of trying to lift by head up (e.g. to get out of bed) hurts like fuck. Also, when I look in the mirror I noticed my shoulders have become even more lopsided than before. My family noticed that my neck is really tensed and unnatural. They can tell I'm in pain. Is this the end of my lifting career as I know it? What should I do? See the doc?

Mark Rippetoe: Sorry it took so long to get to your post, I was out of town. Is it better yet?

Tongzilla: I saw a doc the next day, someone who specialists in spinal disorders. Did an x-ray scan, nothing wrong according to him. Sent me to the physio. Physio told me to move my neck around and stretch it...which really hurts. Physio did some weird ultrasound thing on my neck and put a sticker on my neck. Not much help. I saw a Chinese doc the next day. He violently snapped my neck. According to him, one of the discs on my neck is out of place, which I was surprised because the other doc didn't mention anything even with the x-ray scan. I immediately felt less strain and regained some of my lost range of motion in my neck. He also did some "cupping" on my neck/back area. It's now 3 days after the accident and I feel ~50% better. I fear lifting heavy weights.

Mark Rippetoe: Shit like this occasionally happens and it's not always possible to determine exactly why. Sorry, but this is the way of the Universe. Address your fear. But wait till Thursday.

Tikuane: I think the same thing happens to me. Constantly re-pull a muscle on the back of the neck while struggling through the last reps of an OHP set. It now always pops and buckles when I finger it.

FWIW, my uncle, a nurse, told me a story about a guy herniating a cervical disc pressing 185 overhead.

Mark Rippetoe: Everybody's uncle has a story. My cousin's best friend had this other friend who knew a guy in the army whose brother benched 1000 lbs.

Eyeing the Prize Some People Call Manly Footwear

Get some weightlifting shoes.

Elevated heels

Baldr: Received the 2nd Edition of SS today. I'm just wondering, in almost every illustration the person demonstrating the exercise is wearing weightlifting shoes, with elevated heels. I remember you saying you yourself wear them in the deadlift (I think it was because it helps you with glute activation?) for whatever reason. Personally, I deadlift barefoot. What are the exercises in which wearing shoes with elevated heels can add difficulty to the movement?

Mark Rippetoe: In my opinion, heels don't add difficulty to any movement we do for general strength and conditioning purposes. The purpose of a little heel lift is to throw the knees forward enough that the knee angle is a little more acute, providing more quad range of motion available for use at the start of a pull from the floor. They help in the squat the same way, and in all lifts provide a stable, non-compressible connection to the floor. Modern powerlifting uses flat shoes in the squat and the sumo deadlift because the stance is wide to best use the suit and does not depend heavily on quads. The thinking on not using them for conventional deadlifts is that the heel adds extra distance to the pull -- and it does, true enough, but not enough to offset the benefit of a stronger knee extension off the floor. I deadlifted better in my 5/8"-heeled squat shoes than in wrestling flats.

I don't allow barefoot lifting in my gym, because I don't want your nasty feet all over my place, and in the event that plates get dropped there is no HepABC/HPV/syphilitic/KJD infected blood to clean up.

Squat shoes

Howardw: I have another question. I believe you said that putting a plate or block of wood under the heels because it forces the weight towards the ball of the foot (not counting the stability issue). Why is this different than what squat shoes do since they have a heel (as compared to chucks or even bare feet)?

Mark Rippetoe: A block of wood or any other heel block leaves the piece of your foot in the middle unsupported. This is not critical at 135. It may become important at 405.

Lifting Barefoot

Stu: I know you advocate wearing weightlifting shoes, but assuming one has no foot problems (sunken arches etc), is it not acceptable to train barefoot? I'm actually wearing Vibram Five Fingers to the gym. The Sprint version also has a strap that goes over the top of the foot. Any thoughts on these?

Mark Rippetoe: Training barefoot is not allowed in my gym. I don't need your DNA all over the room if you stub your toe or drop a plate. The Vibram things are fine as long as they contain your fluids. But I don't see why you people are so defensive of your Right To Train Barefoot. There's a good reason why everyone that is serious about barbell training trains with both barbells and weightlifting shoes.

Uneven leg geometry?

Kazzin: Many years ago (8 then, 21 now), I severely injured my right knee in an accident. Without getting into all the unnecessary details, the final result compromises the following:

1) No PCL in the right knee (either completely torn, or detached from the bone, I don't recall which).

2) About 3/4" difference in length of the legs. Perhaps 1/4" of this comes from my inability to completely lock the right leg at 180°, the other 1/2" due to the right femur being physically shorter (growth plates got damaged in the injury).

Throughout my youth I obviously favored the 'better' leg, and a significant muscular imbalance between the two legs developed. I've been squatting for 2 years now, pain free– SS has greatly improved my technique; only my hip drive needs minor adjustments– and I figured this would even out the legs both in terms of strength and size, but the imbalance persists (excepting the hamstrings).

Could this perhaps be due to the uneven geometry of my legs, resulting in less load on one leg than the other? I already shim the right leg when I deadlift (I just stand on adjacent 5lb plates), should I do this when I squat? Even so, shimming still won't change the fact that the femur itself is shorter. And finally, judging from a previous post I've seen you make I find it doubtful you'd consider my PCL injury a danger to squatting, but perhaps you could confirm this?

Mark Rippetoe: I have a guy in here with a similar asymmetry, and we had a weightlifting shoe built up to take out the 3/4" when he squats, presses, and pulls. This severe a leg length discrepancy needs to be corrected or back problems will generally come along quickly. The short femur cannot be helped, and your knees may track asymmetrically, but at least your pelvis will be level and your back protected while you train. The PCL is no big deal if your form is good, and even if it's bad I've never seen a squat that would result in posterior tibial translation; quads keep that from happening.

Kazzin: How might one go about getting a weightlifting shoe to correct the difference in length, and have you any suggestions on how to get the legs more-or-less on par strength and size-wise?

Mark Rippetoe: Buy a pair of weightlifting shoes, take them to a shoe shop, have the rubber sole removed, have a the correct shim added, have the sole put back on, and pay the man his exorbitant fee. The corrected geometry will balance out the asymmetrical strength/size issue to the extent possible.

Win: I have a similar leg length discrepancy, and scoliosis as well. My doctor measured the difference in my legs and wrote a prescription for an orthotic. I took the prescription to a recommended shoe guy and he made an orthotic that I can take out and put in whatever shoe I need to wear. When I change shoes I simply swap out the orthotic.

Mark Rippetoe: But a 3/4" orthotic will change the ankle angle position significantly, thus affecting the knee angle on that side. I know about orthotics. That's why I recommended shimming the whole shoe.

Weightlifting Shoes (Elevated Heels)

Deadmaster200: I have a question about your explanation on weightlifting shoes. In SS, you talk a bit about using a block of wood under the heels to make the squat easier. You specifically state that this becomes just a crutch that does not deal with the root cause of the problem. You then talk a bit about how important it is to have weightlifting shoes citing the elevated heels as one of the benefits. This struck me as slightly contradictory. Could you please elaborate on this?

Mark Rippetoe: There is a tremendous difference between a 1 1/2" thick 2x4 under the heels, which provides load on 2 places against the foot, and a weightlifting shoe with a solid wedge sole 5/8" thick. The 2x4 allows a lifter with tight hamstrings to not stretch them out since the board plus your heel thickness amounts to at least a 2" lift, while the shoe provides a little better knee position for use of the quads at the bottom as well as a stable interface between the foot and the ground.

Toes wider than 30 degrees?

Cskolnick: When would a trainee want/need (if ever) to have his or her toes pointed out more than 30 degrees with a shoulder width stance? I ask because the other day I exaggerated my toe angle to what I believe is past 30 and when I dropped into the whole I felt for the first time the "bounce" from my hams and adductors. It was also the first time I felt my knees traveling inwards and having to spread my knees apart to resist it. What is going on here or what have I been doing wrong up to this point?

Mark Rippetoe: Do you normally stand duck-footed? People whose feet are attached so that they point out generally need a little extra toe point to compensate. This means that the 30-degree rule is not really a rule.

Squatting/deadlifting with a fallen arch

Cley: I noticed a fallen arch on my left foot and it's starting to affect my left hip on heavy deadlifts. What do you recommend?

Mark Rippetoe: Weightlifting shoes. The metatarsal strap supports the arch, among other things. I am continually amazed by the number of people I have to argue with about this. Do you have to have spikes to play golf? Do you play basketball in sandals? Tennis in heels? Why is this conversation necessary every week?

Your thoughts on Vibram Five Fingers as weightlifting shoes?

Justinbass: Do you recommend weight lifting shoes because of their lack of heel give/flex compared to sneakers, because of the raised heel, or both? I workout with a few people that swear by their Vibram Five Fingers for lifting (and no, they aren't filthy hippies.) I imagine they would be good for deadlifting, since it is so similar to barefoot deadlifting. But what do you think of them for squats and pressing? For the Olympic lifts?

Mark Rippetoe: The Vibram shoes are designed for pose running. Very fashionable for that. But the stomp involved in performing a clean or a snatch doesn't sound like something I'd want to do in my socks, even if they do have little toes on them and are covered with rubber on the bottom.

BradD: I'm actually a little surprised by this, Rip. Weightlifting shoes are VERY hard, to provide more stability, right? I would've thought that "no shoe" would be even harder. Now, I do understand the problem with dropping a plate on one's foot.

Mark Rippetoe: You're surprised by something I've been saying in print since 2005? And on this board for a year? In lengthy, verbose, protracted explanations? I'm surprised you have not found the search function. Frankly, I'm shocked. *SHOCKED*. Think about it like this: which of the two, barefoot or WL shoes, would you rather have on if you were standing on little pointy rocks? The shoes *are* harder, eh?

Patrick: Bare feet, in my experience, are more stable than sneakers... sure. But imagine you could make your feet, exactly as they are now, wider. That'd be more stable, right? A good lifting shoe lets you strap in really tight so you don't wobble, and is wider at the sole than your bare foot. This is about the same as widening your foot in that it provides the extra stability that comes with width, and it seems unlikely that the straps are there to ensure that stability merely by coincidence -- it seems like this is what they're meant for. Add to that the fact that you get a little heel elevation to make the geometry of your lifts nearly universally better and you've got a pretty solid product.

Weightlifting shoe size

TravisRussellDC: Quick question for you regarding sizing of different brands of weightlifting shoes. Since I don't have the option of trying on weightlifting shoes before buying, I was wondering if you knew of how some brands run compared to dress shoes, sneakers, etc. I normally wear a 10 wide or 10 1/2 depending on brand. I've heard that some weightlifting shoes run big and some run small. Do you have a recommendation for brands and sizes to look at for my weightlifting shoe purchase?

Mark Rippetoe: I don't buy them or sell them, but the people that do say that most brands run true to street shoe size, as opposed to athletic shoe size.

Shoe question...

McKirdyP: When I go heavy doing squats or deadlifts in a pair of Adidas Ironworks II my feet kill me the next few days. They feel fine to move the weight in but then the next day my feet are killing me. The shoes seem like they fit fine, but I do have wide and thick feet. The pain usually is on the very outer edge, but still feels like a plantar thing...

This doesn't happen when I squat in a pair of Chucks. With Chucks on I have no flexibility issue, I can pretty much go ATG, or as far below parallel as my legs will bend with no problem at all. Should I just ditch the Oly shoes and continue with the Chucks or should I man up and endure the Oly shoes until my feet get used to them. Try a different pair possibly?

I have also been doing foot drills now every workout trying to eliminate any possible foot weakness, and it seems to have helped except when I use the Oly shoes.

Mark Rippetoe: If you have a foot any wider than a C, Adidas will not fit you. I have D/E width foot and I cannot even get my foot in an Adidas WL shoe. This is the only problem, so get some wider shoes ASAP.

McKirdyP: Aye, keptain. Rogue Do-wins for wide feet?

Mark Rippetoe: Yeah, ducks can wear them. The heels are too high, but you can have them cut down.

(I have just received some new shoes from Rogue with a ½" heel. They are just right.)

Suede vs. leather weightlifting shoes

pats fan: I jumped on the sale price of the VS Athletics suede weightlifting shoes...and am curious...what is your opinion of the durability of the suede vs. leather shoes?

Mark Rippetoe: Last I heard, suede was leather.

pats fan: Shows you how little I know about leather...thanks

Drewfasa: Some leathers are more equal than others. I skateboarded for years as a teenager and nice, hard leather shoes tended to outlast suede ones by at least double or even triple the time. I wore holes through a number of suede ones, but usually wore out the soles on hard leather ones before the leather wore all the way through. That said, I don't imagine that weightlifting shoes wear out very fast at all, considering how little friction they are exposed to (unless one wears them out dancing on weekends). How often do you have to replace your weightlifting shoes,

Mark?

Mark Rippetoe: I've had my Safes for about 12 years now, I think. Not suede.

Squats Form deterioration

Tjayarmyguy: I have noticed that as the weight is moving towards PRs every workout, my form is getting progressively worse. I think this might have something to do with my improper footwear. Yesterday I ordered some weightlifting shoes. Will these help to correct my squatting? I definitely just feel way too unstable with squishy shoes on. I'm almost certain that that's my biggest squat problem.

Mark Rippetoe: Anybody who is having squat technique problems in squishy shoes will have fewer problems in appropriate training footwear. This is not to say that squat shoes fix all squat problems, but you already knew that.

Squat - elbows up

NastyNate: Sometimes when I do heavy squats my elbows come up almost parallel with the floor. Sometimes it causes my arm pain in the brachiallis/elbow region. My form is good other than that from what my spotter tells me. Any ideas on how to correct this?

P.S. just got my weightlifting shoes....I want them to have my children.

Mark Rippetoe: Yes. Stop raising your elbows that high. And I'm happy for you. Clean the shoes after each inappropriate use.

The heel and the squat (once more)

JayvH: I have started barbell training last March and have improved it since I read SS 2nd. But I am still unsure concerning the role of the heel in weightlifting shoes. So I will try to devise my questions as good as possible.

1. As I recall everybody who knows something about good squats says that you shouldn't cheat, when you have flexibility issues but work on your flexibility. Alright, why isn't using a heel under your feet cheating? Putting a wedge or small plates under your feet seem to do the job although they are insecure.
2. I found a post on a German board, where the author – a physiotherapist – explains why it's easier to balance yourself with weightlifting shoes. But then he is describing where he sees the problem and I will try to translate that as well as possible:
   Because of the small feed your knee joint is also moving forward. So the pressure behind the knee caps increases. Permanent use of weightlifting shoes and hence increased stress would (after years) result in increased wear in the cartilage behind the knee caps. The quads are more trained but the hamstrings, glutes and lumbar spine musculature is more important for the powerlifter.
3. *Those muscles are more activated when using flat soles as when using weightlifting shoes. The use of heels implies therefore less stress for the back but more stress for the knees.*

I know from reading the book and your postings here that you prefer a heel. You say that you have discussed that, but I can't find the medical reasons to squat with the heel and why it's not dangerous for my knees.

Mark Rippetoe: There at least 20 posts on this board regarding weightlifting shoes, so I'm not going to repeat myself again. However, this is an interesting passage because it is essentially a series of false statements:

Because of the small feed your knee joint is also moving forward. So the pressure behind the knee caps increases. Permanent use of weightlifting shoes and hence increased stress would (after years) result in increased wear in the cartilage behind the knee caps. The quads are more trained but the hamstrings, glutes and lumbar spine musculature is more important for the powerlifter. Those muscles are more activated when using flat soles as when using weightlifting shoes. The use of heels implies therefore less stress for the back but more stress for the knees.

How is it that when the knee moves forward the pressure behind the patella increases, especially when the hips are moving back at the same time? I have been training for 15 years in weightlifting shoes with a 1" heel and my patellar cartilage is just fine. The quads are only more trained if you don't know how to squat correctly, shoes or not. Likewise, lots of people manage to leave out their posterior chain in Chuck Taylors. And the *correct* use of "heels" implies that the lifter knows how to squat correctly, thus distributing the stress of the movement evenly across knees, hips, and back, no matter what shoes are worn.

And why is it that the Germans always seem to sound so authoritative even when they are completely full of shit?

Mistakes

Exercise is so closely associated with running in the minds of both the medical community and the general public that the two are often indistinguishable. The "exercise physiology" people are not doing much to help either. This, and the silly-ass "inhale on the way down and exhale on the way up" dogma together contribute to a lot of people not getting very strong.

Cardio?

Fknabe: Read SS and am currently experiencing wonderful strength gains!! I have searched through most of the Q&A and have not heard your take on the amount of cardio one should be doing.

Mark Rippetoe: By "cardio", most people mean long, slow distance. I don't recommend it at all unless your cardiologist tells you to do it, in which case I stay out of the way. For cardiopulmonary conditioning, I recommend high-intensity met/con-type training, but LSD is terribly catabolic and counterproductive to strength training.

Fknabe: How many times per week and for how long? (Met/Con) The last thing I want to do is be counterproductive. Seriously.

Mark Rippetoe: Start with one per week for a couple of weeks, add one more per week until it screws something up, and then back off one. This is what is referred to in chemistry as "titration", where one variable is manipulated while the others are controlled, and is a valuable concept for lots of applications.

Tomfitzyuk: What is a long distance considered? I cycle to and from campus every week day which is just under 4 miles each way, and this takes me 15-20 minutes, so I'm not particularly fast. How detrimental do you think this would be to my training (I'm on the standard basic routine described in SS)? Though I enjoy cycling (and it's cheaper), I would be willing to start using public transport. Would it be worth me reading more about HIIT and applying that to my cycling? I hear that isn't as catabolic as slow long distance cardio.

Mark Rippetoe: A long distance really means a long time, and that means more than 30 minutes. Your 4 mile trip is not significant in terms of its effect on your strength training, and I don't want to be the cause of your taking a bus anywhere. Buses are dangerous places.

Flexing abs

Baldr: One concept I am confused about is the issue of abdominal pressure. For all the exercises I just suck in a big breathe of air into my stomach at the start of the movement and don't flex my abs. Am I supposed to also flex my abs during the lifts? SS mentions "abdominal contraction" in addition to raising the chest. Does this refer simply to getting a big breath of air by pushing out the stomach at the beginning of the movement, or "flexing" the abs? Should the abs be pushed "out" throughout the entire exercise?

Mark Rippetoe: You seem to be confused about an important piece of anatomical information. The air goes into your LUNGS, not your stomach. Your lungs and your stomach are separated by your diaphragm into your thoracic and abdominal cavities, respectively. The big, held breath (the Valsalva maneuver) increases the pressure in the thoracic cavity only. Contracting your abdominal muscles increases the pressure in your abdominal cavity at the same time, and allows this increased pressure to be applied all along the spine from bottom to top, not just the part that lies behind the lungs. The abs are not pushed "out" when they are contracted; they just get shorter, meaning they pull the pubis and the ribcage closer together while the spine stays in extension. This effectively increases the pressure against the spine from the front – the anterior – side and reinforces the curve that has been established by the back muscles. Pushing "out" refers to a way to think about using your belt to help increase this pressure, but this is just a way to think about contracting against the belt, and is not what actually happens, especially if you don't have a belt on.

Baldr: I've never worn a belt, and don't plan on wearing one. The "pushing out" must only refer to when a belt is worn, and since I don't wear a belt, I will forget about doing that and focus on tightening my abs instead.

Just to recap:
1.) Should the abs should be contracted **after** the back has gone into extension?
2.) I see that there are two different ways of breathing. I've been taught that during the correct way of breathing, the belly (stomach) should be expanding and condensing (diaphragmatic breathing), instead of your chest coming up and down. Which is the correct way for the exercises? Also, should the chest be raised before the breath is taken?

This is from Dave Tate:

"Secret #7: Learn to use your belly!

I've caught more shit over this than any other aspect of training. But the truth is that every big squatter I know has learned how to use his abdominals while squatting. You must learn how to breathe into your belly. You want to pull as much air as you can into your belly, then flex and force your abdominals out.

Walk over to a mirror. Take a look at your shoulders and take a deep breath. Did they rise? If they did, then you're pulling all the air into your chest, not your belly. You need to learn how to breath into your belly. This is how we teach everyone to squat. For the squat, we advise the use of a weight belt worn one notch loose. This is to teach you to pull air into your belly then push out into the belt. The belt acts as a great training aid to push against.

As a side note, we use the same technique for all of our max-effort work, but don't use the belt in that situation. This is one aspect of our training that has been misunderstood for too long. We use the belt to teach how to use the abdominals for the squat, bench, and deadlift, and do not advocate its use for anything else unless the lifter feels it's needed. Many in the gym have worked up to 600 and 700 pound good mornings without any adverse effects and have been doing them this way for over ten years.

This brings me to the next point. We've been told breathing and using the abdominals this way will lead to back injuries. Louie Simmons has been coaching this for the past twenty years at Westside and hasn't had any lifters with these problems. Learning to use the belly has made a profound difference in all of our squats, especially for those who've never tried it. I've seen squats increase by 25 to 50 pounds on this aspect alone. Now that's what squatting big is all about.

Filling your belly with air will also create a larger torso and give you a bigger base of support from which to drive. Ever wonder why those with bigger waists squat so much? Think about it. We want as much tightness and support as we can get from the gross muscles of the spinal errectors, abdominals, and obliques."

What Dave describes is the way I have been doing it - sucking air into my belly, and pushing my abs "out". Help a noob out; I'm just getting confused. I would greatly prefer your word over Dave's.

Mark Rippetoe: I don't know that preferring my word over Dave's is that brilliant an idea. I think it might be more productive to figure out how we might be telling you the same thing, since neither you nor I can squat the weights Dave has handled while breathing "wrong".

It is a demonstrable fact that air stays in the lungs, and since this is the case Dave is describing the movement using different terminology than I do. There are two sets of muscles involved in breathing: the diaphragm pulls down into the abdominal cavity to produce the negative pressure that causes air to enter the lungs upon inhalation, and a full deep breath always involves a maximal diaphragmatic contraction. And the ribcage, or "costal" muscles in synch with the abs and other torso muscles produces the positive pressure which causes exhalation. An inefficient type of inhalation often seen in respiratory disease patients with compromised lung function involves raising the ribcage using the upper back and serratus muscles to get a more full breath.

I think that by pulling air into the "belly", Dave is increasing the pressure in his thoracic cavity without allowing the ribcage to expand upward as much. It might very well be that an unexpanded, unelevated ribcage can be pressured more effectively than a ribcage that expands upward during inhalation. His cue to "force the abdominals out" is the interesting part. If the abs are not allowed to expand outward it would not be possible to get as big a breath with the diaphragm as it would be if the abdominal cavity made room for it with this cue. So I think that forcing the abs out actually makes room for the air, and then an ab contraction follows. An abdominal contraction involves shortening the rectus abdominis – applying isometric tension between the ribs and the pelvis. If the abs were not contracted, intra-abdominal pressure would be lower rather than higher, so some ab contraction must occur after the deep diaphragmatic contraction.

Different cues work better or worse depending on the circumstances under which they are used. I am not sufficiently familiar with Westside methods to criticize them in a public forum such as this. I am pretty good at teaching people how to do the 5 lifts. But I am familiar with Louie's, Dave Tate's, and Jim Wendler's abilities with regard to making people strong, and they are better at that than I am by far. I shall always exercise caution when examining the methods of people who have demonstrated that they can produce results.

Cardio again

Kuzushi: I scanned ahead in the book, but I do not know if you write about incorporating cardio conditioning for more wind and endurance in your book. I train in MMA and BJJ and I get winded after rolling for only a short time.

Mark Rippetoe: It may have touched on at one point, but what the hell. Long, slow, distance is not a useful way to condition for a sport that does not itself involve the low intensity provided by long slow distance. LSD is easy, BJJ is not. So to condition for BJJ and MMA the best system is the metabolic conditioning provided by high intensity glycolytic workouts.

Aerobic exercise less than optimal for gaining mass?

Sgtmattbaker: If I did 10-15 minutes of progression type running on my non-lifting days would it hinder my ability to gain mass? What I mean by progression type running is starting out at a slow jog and working up to a sprint over a period of 1-2 minutes and maintaining that sprint for 20-60 seconds. After that a break of a minute is taken and the process is repeated.

Mark Rippetoe: It would depend on your recovery ability, i.e. how old you are, how much you eat, how well you sleep, and how big your balls are. Some guys can recover from lots more work than other guys, so this just depends on you.

Sgtmattbaker: You said in your book that the cardiovascular system along with all of the other tissues in the body adapts to lifting, so is it even necessary for health to do exercise like jogging in addition to lifting (and by lifting I mean doing squats, deadlifts, presses, bench presses, and power cleans; the reason I say this is because it is far more common to see people who do not do lower body exercises at all, or either they just do leg presses)? Thanks.

Mark Rippetoe: The only time LSD (long slow distance) is necessary is if you're going to compete in a sport that requires it. It is far inferior to high-intensity glycolytic exercise for producing an increase in VO_2 max, it interferes with power and strength production, it can be quite catabolic and immune-suppressive in high doses, it destroys muscle mass, and the people that do it usually wear silly clothes.

Question (rather lengthy unfortunately) about Valsalva maneuver

solidsnake123: After reading the section on breathing in the squat section of Starting Strength I am thoroughly confused on whether or not to use the Valsalva maneuver. It is not that you did not make it clear that it was an essential technique in the weight room, but I have a few questions on the matter. I apologize for the length in advance; I am just trying to present all the necessary information. Here are the points made in the section regarding the safety of the maneuver.

- The likelihood of a cerebrovascular accident is overplayed in regard to the Valsalva maneuver

- The likelihood of an orthopedic injury is greatly downplayed in regard to the Valsalva maneuver

- The pressure applied by the Valsalva maneuver is a natural response to heavy exertion, as the opposing forces being applied to the cerebrospinal fluid and the cardiovascular system in the trunk are in balance.

- The process of inhalation increases pressure in your thoracic cavity, which provides support to the surrounding abdominals, obliques and spinal erectors.

- The Valsalva maneuver is used by fighter pilots to keep blood in the brain in momentary high-G conditions to prevent a blackout.

- The cardiovascular system adapts to resistance training just like all the other tissues and systems in the body.

- It is a good practice to take and hold the biggest breath you can before every heavy rep.

However I wonder if the positive effects of the Valsalva maneuver are good enough reason to use the technique considering the possible negative implications such as syncope, stroke, blown aneurysm or death. I assume that these possible implications are the result of heightened blood pressure. I do not know how common these occurrences are, and how closely they are linked to the health of an individual. For example, the NASM Essentials of Personal Fitness Training says for those with hypertension to avoid Valsalva maneuvers. Hypertension is obviously something to take into account when discussing exercise methods.

The other thing to consider is blood circulation and oxygen deprivation. According to that source, a prolonged Valsalva maneuver during a *static* exercise that involves straining lowers the heart rate, and thus reducing venous return and blood pressure. The negative side effects of this lowered heart rate diminish blood supply to the brain, which can produce dizziness, "spots before the eyes" (same thing as stars?), or syncope (otherwise known as passing out). I have heard that many older people die because they are straining on the toilet or otherwise. I guess those are conditions in which they are not in good health in the first place though. I have definitely had a headache after heavy deadlifts before and have most definitely seen stars after a set of squats. Were those occurrences a result of the Valsalva?

It would be nice if the book told the reader how long a prolonged Valsalva maneuver is. It could be a couple seconds, or a minute, but we do not know because the only description is "prolonged". Since the Valsalva maneuver involves holding ones breath, doesn't that restrict oxygen flow to the brain and muscles (which would be counterproductive)? I assume that a Valsalva of sufficient length to cause lightheadedness, syncope or poor oxygen circulation to the brain and muscles is being performed for way too long, longer than one would use the maneuver for a rep.

By the way, you said in your book to hold your breath during each of your heavy reps, but I have heard differing opinions on the matter. I have heard the ever common "inhale as you go down, exhale as you go up", "only use the Valsalva for 2-3 seconds as your go through your sticking point", and "do not consciously think about breathing or the Valsalva during exercise as it will come naturally". When you say deep breath, how deep do you mean? A truly deep breath can take a few seconds which would throw off your timing during reps, wouldn't it?

You seem to have an impeccable reputation when it comes to matters regarding strength training, but on a subject with so much controversy and possibility of injury (orthopedic injury without/fainting, lightheadedness, even death with) I would find it very helpful and reassuring to have other sources that back up your very clear stance that consciously applying the Valsalva maneuver during weight lifting is a good, safe idea in which the good effects outweigh the possible negative effects.

Mark Rippetoe: Several things are interesting about your post. First: *"However I wonder if the positive effects of the Valsalva maneuver are good enough reason to use the technique considering the possible negative implications such as syncope, stroke, blown aneurysm or death. I assume that these possible implications are the result of heightened blood pressure."*

The incidence of training-associated cerebrovascular accident (CVA) in the weight room is so low as to be statistically unmeasurable. We have done a thorough search of the literature and there is a complete absence of any documented case of stroke due to hemorrhage during barbell training. There are, however, lots of back injuries. Which eventuality would you rather prepare for? As for a blown aneurysm, you first have to have an aneurysm to blow one out, and THAT is always just plain old bad luck (despite the fact that the incidence of weight training-associated aneurysm dissections is also statistically insignificant).

Second: *"I have definitely had a headache after heavy deadlifts before and have most definitely seen stars after a set of squats. Were those occurrences a result of the Valsalva?"*

I don't know. But headache and death are certainly two unrelated phenomena. I've had lots of headaches that were associated with Guinness, during the consumption of which no Valsalva or deadlifting occurred.

Third: *"By the way, you said in your book to hold your breath during each of your heavy reps, but I have heard differing opinions on the matter. I have heard the ever common 'inhale as you go down, exhale as you go up', 'only use the Valsalva for 2-3 seconds as your go through your sticking point', and 'do not consciously think about breathing or the Valsalva during exercise as it will come naturally'".*

Which one do you think Andy Bolton used during his world record 1003 lb. deadlift? It makes absolutely no difference what the NASM, the ACSM, the NSCA, AFAA, ACE, IDEA, the YMCA, or Pat Robertson thinks about how one *ought* to breathe during exercise. The fact is that every heavy deadlift that has ever been pulled off the floor was done with some form of a Valsalva, and the death toll fails to mount. What does this tell you about the safety of the Valsalva for your workout this afternoon? The last remark about the Valsalva coming naturally is correct, but a 1003 deadlift is not "natural" in the commonly understood sense of the word, and the Valsalva that accompanied it was not "natural" either – it was deliberate, thorough, and lasted for the whole deadlift. The inexperienced, lawyer-spooked fools at the certification organizations can issue any position papers they like, but the fact remains that as long as heavy weights are being lifted, people will be holding their breath while they do it, and everybody will be just fine if they don't hurt their backs or pull a hamstring.

Furthermore, Mr. Bolton was adapted to both a very goddamn heavy deadlift *and* a deliberate, thorough, and long Valsalva maneuver, because he'd trained for it. He didn't just wander in off the street, and neither have you. Since tissues adapt to stress, the stress of a Valsalva is adapted to by whatever structures are subjected to the stress as the intensity of the load accumulates, just like the spine, the ligaments holding the spine together, and the muscles that keep the spine straight have that make the deadlift possible. This fact – that adaptation occurs in response to exercise in all affected tissues – along with the fact that lots of people have lifted heavy weights with no known incidence of stroke, even in the absence of an explanation for why, should provide solace and balm for your furrowed brow.

big pull: Blood pressure typically rises significantly during heavy lifts, regardless if you employ the Valsalva maneuver, or not. The protective increase in intrathoracic pressure is definitely beneficial, and I've personally noticed a boost in strength when I hold my breath, and bear down. You would be more likely to have a syncopal episode (fainting/near fainting) due to the vagal response, which lowers your heart rate, while you bear down. If you don't currently take prescribed beta blockers, which lower your pulse rate to control high blood pressure, you should have no issues. Like Coach Rippetoe advised, the potential risks are practically nonexistent.

Polynomial: I was once one of the spotters for a 40-some year old man who did 405 lb box squats for 16 reps. His lips were purple by the end, and he took a whole 5 or so minutes to fully recover, but he's alive, well, and damn strong.

As a fun exercise, try exhaling with a decent amount of weight over your head. When you're done, please don't sue me.

Mark Rippetoe: And as an added treat, here is the abstract from a paper presented in 2005 at the American Society of Exercise Physiology National Conference

The Valsalva Maneuver: Risk or Risk Management?

Becky Kudrna, Lon Kilgore, and Mark Rippetoe

Within the clinical community, the major risk associated with the Valsalva maneuver is cerebrovascular accident. The term cerebrovascular accident can refer to stroke, aneurysm, or hemorrhage of the blood vessels of the brain. It has been suggested that the extremely high, although transient blood pressures created when an individual utilizes the Valsalva maneuver are simply too high for the vessel walls to handle (Linsenbardt et al., 1992). Thus conventional wisdom states that the Valsalva maneuver causes cerebrovascular accidents by raising blood pressure beyond a safe level.

There have been documented cases of cerebrovascular accident occurring while weightlifting. Haykowsky et al. (1996) reported three case studies of subarachnoid hemorrhage in otherwise healthy individuals during weight training. These authors noted that all of the individuals recovered and returned to normal activities within 3 months. Cayen & Cullen, report an additional case of cerebral hemorrhage during resistance exercise in 2002. A fifth occurrence was reported in an anabolic steroid user who suffered both a myocardial infarction and cerebral hemorrhage during resistance exercise, (Kenedy et al., 1993). This individual died as a result of his injuries. In deceased populations, one case of a cerebral hemorrhage occurred in a preexisting brain tumor during resistance exercise, (Goetting & Swanson, 1987). Finally, one case of an effaced lateral ventricle and one case of a subdural hematoma were reported in two males performing sit-ups with the Valsalva maneuver (Uber-Zac & Venkatesh, 2002). It is important to note here that of all the reported cases of CVA in both healthy and diseased populations only one resulted in mortality.

Whereas Narloch & Brandstater (1995) and Uver-Zac & Venkatesh (2002) interpreted the cause of the cerebrovascular hemorrhage in two male recreational lifters as transient vascular hypertension caused by the Valsalva maneuver, Haykowsky et al. (1996), attributed the three cases of subarachnoid hemorrhage in resistance-exercised individuals to preexisting, but undetected aneurysms. Haykowsky (1996), and McCartney (1999) suggest that the few incidences of CVA that do occur with resistance exercise may be linked to undetected cerebral aneurysms and thus are not entirely attributable to resistance exercise or the Valsalva maneuver. According to McCartney, approximately 1% of the population has cerebral aneurysms and the response of such individuals to the transient stresses of weightlifting should not be viewed as the normal or typical response. With millions of people participating in resistance exercise daily, the small number of reported CVA events actually represents a frequency that is statistically insignificant.

When considering exercise induced CVA it is important to understand that aerobic exercise, an exercise modality that is not associated with the Valsalva maneuver is also associated with a small number of CVA incidences, (Cayen & Cullen, 2002).

Not all researchers hold that the Valsalva maneuver during resistance exercise is dangerous. McCartney (1999) and Hughes et al., (1989) acknowledged that the Valsalva maneuver is an instinctive response and should be used particularly in lifts above 85% of 1 repetition maximum. Further, there is compelling evidence suggesting the Valsalva maneuver actually prevents catastrophic cerebrovascular injuries rather than causes them.

The work of Haykowsky et al. (2003) suggests that elevated vascular pressure is only dangerous to the delicate vascular walls of the brain if intracranial pressures remain low, and thus transmural pressure is high. Essentially, if the pressure surrounding the vessel increases and pushes back against the vessel wall, the blood pressure within the vessel will not be transmitted across to the cranial tissue, meaning that transmural pressure is low. The measure of the difference in pressures between vascular pressure and intracranial pressure should therefore be a better indicator of the stress the vessel walls are under and thus be a better indicator of the danger of cerebrovascular accident. Haykowsky et al, (2003) found that performing the Valsalva maneuver decreased the pressure differences across the cerebrovascular wall, theoretically decreasing the risk of aneurysm or hemorrhage. This finding corroborated the much earlier and ignored work of Hamilton et al. (1944). These studies strongly suggest that performing a heavy lift without the Valsalva maneuver places individuals at greater risk of CVA than performing the same lift with the Valsalva maneuver. This is directly contrary to the conventional wisdom.

The mechanism through which the Valsalva maneuver raises intracranial pressure is theorized as follows: (1)The Valsalva maneuver directly increases thoracic pressure by attempting to force air through the closed

glottis. (2)This elevated thoracic pressure is transferred to the cerebrospinal fluid in much the same way that thoracic pressure increases abdominal pressure. Because the cerebrospinal fluid surrounding the spinal cord is continuous with fluid of the subdural space in the skull, intracranial pressure also rises. The rapid nature of fluid pressure transfer within this system means that arterial pressure and intracranial pressure rise at the same rate, yielding a balanced transmural pressure from the beginning to the end of the lift. Thus the lifter is protected throughout the entire lift so long as the Valsalva maneuver is performed.

solidsnake123: So let me get this straight, according to your book, you take a deep breath before you begin the rep and as you are doing the "work" portion of the rep, e.g. pushing up for a squat you hold that breath until you get back to the top and then exhale and breathe in again? I watched the video of Andy Bolton doing his world record deadlift and he holds that breath the entire time. However, that is a 1RM.

A book that covers some stuff from the NSCA says that pressure can be created without the Valsalva, although many competitive lifters choose to do that if they accept the risks, and know not to use it so long as to produce the risk of passing out. Would it be just as effective as Valsalva to only use it through and maybe a bit after the sticking point and then start to exhale, or just to slowly exhale as you go up? I read a study that said the same 1RM was done by the same people with slow exhalation and Valsalva and the only thing that changed was blood pressure increases.

Dude, really sorry for these posts. I am frankly just quite anxious and frightened to use the maneuver since nobody has come to the same consensus about the matter.

Mark Rippetoe: I don't care about blood pressure increases. I'm adapted to those. I don't care about the statistically unmeasurable risk of CVA. I've never seen or heard of it happening. I don't care about internet articles (this is not a study) that say things like this: "*The reason for this type of research were some cases of acute stroke in otherwise healthy weight lifters".* without substantiation. I really, really, REALLY don't care about 35 year old female personal training clients doing 3 lb. alternate dumbbell presses on a Swiss ball. I care much more about not hurting my back. I care even more about your observation that Andy Bolton had enough sense to hold his breath during his 1003, and that he – quite significantly – managed to get off the platform without being entirely dead. Is this fact meaningless to you? Is the fact that everybody that deadlifts heavy holds their breath while doing it and that nobody has had a stroke when they did meaningless to you? Is the fact that all record cleans, jerks, snatches, squats, bench presses, and deadlifts have been done with a Valsalva somehow not relevant? We do it this way because it works better, and because it keeps us from hurting ourselves. And as your strength increases your ability to withstand the stress of a Valsalva does too. It's a part of the adaptation to lifting weights, and heavy weights cannot be lifted safely without it.

Brandon: I wonder if the extension of this is that someone attempting a vastly post-max lift (a novice trying to pull 800lb, say) could actually spike their blood pressure past their trained tolerances and have a CVA – despite the fact that the weight won't move.

Mark Rippetoe: If it could have happened, it would have already. I know plenty of stupid people who have done that with a squat, a far more likely place for such an accident than a deadlift, and they're just fine, although no smarter. Deadlifts that are too heavy to pull generally don't take very long; the bar just kinda lays there. So if trying to move immovable objects was dangerous from the standpoint of stroke, the history of the human race would be littered with stupid people's corpses.

Metcon and strength training

Captainpicard: Yesterday my roommate said to me, "I just don't get the point of weight lifting. I mean sure, it works your muscles, but you could run or ride a bike and live longer." I suppose he is saying that lifting weights is just for muscles and one would be healthier if they ran or biked instead, as they work the cardiovascular and respiratory systems.

This brings me to my question. I prefer to lift for strength, i.e. heavy sets of 5s, and after the novice stage possibly 3s, 2s, 1s. I know that "cardio" and metcon workouts help increase your VO2 max, etc., but while training for such strength levels are not as high. For general cardiovascular and respiratory health (improving those systems as well as keeping them active and healthy), is it necessary to do any exercise in addition to training for strength (e.g. 3 day novice workout shown in SS:BBT)? I wonder what your response would have been to my roommate's comment.

Mark Rippetoe: My response would be same to him as to you: how does increasing VO_2 max increase longevity? And likewise, how is it dangerous for a person who has not sprinted (as opposed to an untrained person) to begin a sprint training program?

Captainpicard: So you are saying exercise other than strength training isn't necessary for respiratory and cardiovascular fitness, correct?

Mark Rippetoe: I am saying that unless respiratory or cardiovascular fitness is compromised by some pathology, strength training provides enough improvement in VO_2 max to provide all the cardiopulmonary work a healthy person needs, as well as strength and peripheral metabolic conditioning that LSD absolutely fails to provide.

Grunting

Scott: The other day I struggled on my deadlift work set. I only got 3 reps, and was feeling kinda unmanly about it. I debated calling it a day but instead I threw a little more weigh on the bar and demanded two more reps of myself. In doing so I found myself grunting louder than usual and filed a note in the back of my brain to try grunting again in the future, but it occurs to me that doing so would diminish the valsalvic pressure, theoretically to the detriment of the lift.

I plan to experiment with grunting as a technique regardless, but I'm curious to hear your take on it. I'd imagine there's a lot of grunting in the powerlifting community. Does the good outweigh the bad? Does it function as a CNS escape valve, of a sort?

Mark Rippetoe: A vocalization produces a momentary spike in valsalvic pressure, and is useful for focusing support at a critical place in the movement. Like the ki-ya (however it's spelled) in martial arts, it provides more pressure instantly than a simple Valsalva will. But if the noise is loud and of long duration, as it might be if you yelled like a fool during the entire upward phase of the squat, it amounts to an exhalation – a release of pressure instead of a way to momentarily increase it.

Ryan H: That makes sense if the grunt is caused by the valsalvic pressure overcoming the body's ability to contain it for a brief moment, thus resulting in a grunt. It is kind of like you are closer to 100 % efficient by going over at peak effort than by trying to maintain 100 % exactly. It is almost always better to hit something harder than you think you need to rather than exactly as hard as you think you should.

Mark Rippetoe: It is not that the pressure exceeds your containment capacity. Not at all. Is that you have decided at that instant to produce a sound, which requires that you force air out of your glottis at that instant, which causes the pressure to increase at that instant. It is you timing the noise, and thus the pressure increase, not that you have exceeded your ability to contain the pressure which, after all, would not be time-able.

KSC: I just entered a thread on a weightlifting forum about grunting.....my journey towards complete meatheadedness is now complete.

Ryan H: Is one creating a grunt my increasing valsalvic pressure or decreasing glottis constraint? Guess what I was thinking is that it wasn't the grunt that increased pressure, but rather the conditions that right before, that led to the grunt. Then again the only grunt I have had lately is my first BM post hernia surgery!

Mark Rippetoe: The "grunt" is created by both. I hope the other grunt was successful.

Aerobic exercise?

RobertFont: I think I'm mostly with the program at this point. Outside of the workouts I am as sedate as my cat. I'm thinking about adding an hour walk to my day. Not exactly met-con I know, but is the addition of easy cardio helpful, detrimental, irrelevant to strength improvements if calories are added to make up for the effort?

Mark Rippetoe: Walking for an hour is not exercise. It's shopping. If you count it at all, in any way, as part of your program ...well, I'll be disappointed.

Lifting for a Female Cross Country Runner

Stronger: I have a female friend who wants to get stronger for her sport, where strength is apparently at least somewhat beneficial. She goes to a major university which has her lifting on a program that I don't think is terribly productive. She is lifting on a 4 day plan with legs 1-2 week, including squats, ad/abduction machines, quad extension, leg press, and any other type of machine. Everything is done in 3 sets of 10. They also do bench, rows, and arms in various exercises.

Now, I've been advocating strength training programs that you and Starr etc. teach, so it's essentially a battle of her team's idea of a good program, and your knowledge of the best way to get strong. I know you're not an expert on the specialized needs of the sport, but she simply needs to get strong. Since it is currently season, the in season training must be done with races every weekend.

Here is what I have proposed:

A.
Squat 3 x 5
Deadlift 1 x 5
Press 3 x 5
(pullups?)

B.
Squat 3 x 5
Press 3 x 5
Row 3 x 5 (Obviously Power cleans would be desirable, but that might have to come later)
(hypers?)

Perhaps this could be done 2-3 days per week. I included deadlifts (which she had not been doing) because I read on these boards that a stronger back will help sprint times. Seems good enough. She is a fairly strong girl who has done weight training in high school. At average height, 125lbs with a bench at 85lbs x 5 and squat 135 x 10+.

Mark Rippetoe: Your proposal is a good simple program for an athlete playing another sport in need of a strength base. It is infinitely superior to the ridiculous waste of time she is doing now. The smartest people are sometimes not found in colleges and universities.

Johnbr: Quite an interesting and certainly valid comment about Universities and Colleges. I have a flatmate studying Sports Science, and I took a little look at the books she's bought for the course (which cost over a hundred pounds, ridiculous I know), and the exercises they condoned were laughable. All isolation exercises (leg extensions etc) and don't even get me started on nutrition. She says she eats around only 1000 calories a day during season.

Seems the mentality of even the supposed 'most learned' establishments is pointless isolation exercises, long distance cardio, and ludicrously low calorie intake. Our halls of residences gym is just packed full of useless machines, treadmills, cross trainers, leg extenders, etc, but fortunately the campus gym has some decent equipment, although only like one power pack and few benches that nobody seems to use.

Stephen: Stronger, looking at the weight training you have your friend do, I'm curious to see if her interval times drop, as you can't judge times on a cross country course because of the different style course. To me, the weight training your going to give her with the normal running she is doing seems a bit much. Her legs are probably trashed from races on the weekend, weekday intervals, and if she is still doing a long run. Post her progress if you don't mind. Hope she improves, but to me it's too much. The running is enough. Ease into new weight training after the cross country season, and that should help her before track season starts.

Mark Rippetoe: Stephen seems to think that long slow distance constitutes enough stress that adding even a minimal amount of non-LSD stress would be counterproductive. I disagree, and I'd like to know upon what logic or experience you base this recommendation. If running is enough and a little bit of full-ROM resistance training will induce overtraining, I'd say that her nutritional situation is completely inadequate. It probably is, and if so you might be right.

I'm Workin' on His Mind.

Psychologically.

Power clean hard on traps/shoulders?

Brian: I've finally decided to start doing power cleans. Never had an objection to doing them, per se, but I was worried about messing up my shoulder joint. For some reason my shoulders don't take well to things like shrugs and upright rows; I did heavy shrugs once and really strained one of them. I always avoided cleans because I figured they were kind of like an explosive shrug/upright row. I know it's more complicated than that after reading SS, but I'm wondering if it still might be risky.

Just to clarify, my shoulders/traps are perfectly healthy but are really sensitive to abuse. I do rotator cuff work and it seems to have helped, but I don't want to undo my progress of making them stronger and the joints tighter. Would power cleans likely screw them up if done in bad form (which will inevitably happen at least a couple times)? Is there a way to minimize the danger? And would you ever decide general joint laxity is a reason *not* to do them at all?

Mark Rippetoe: I am sorry about the sensitive nature of your traps and laxity of your shoulder joints, and the danger posed by performing cleans. It has been my experience that starting light and then adding more weight as you get stronger usually renders even the scariest of exercises less intimidating for most timid novice trainees such as yourself, and provides a way to obtain the benefits of exercise without the excessive risks that normally make barbell training such a famously lethal activity. Very light weights make even terrible form both safe and unproductive; safety is the most important thing in the Whole Wide World, and a lack of productivity is indeed a small price to pay for it.

Heavy shrugs weren't the best choice of things to do with untrained shoulders, and upright rows are just plain old stupid. But cleans – *my god, man*, they can be as dangerous as a dose of Spinal Meningitis! I'll bet you personally know dozens of lifters whose shoulders were destroyed by doing cleans incorrectly. I recommend that you ask your physical therapist for a safer exercise that can be done with the same dumbbells you've been using for your rotator cuff exercises.

Novice Clarification

Scott: 1) I see many videos with people throwing the weight down after completing a lift. It would seem to me that a better way to do this is lowering the weight onto the rack. Are there benefits to the throwing I am not understanding?

2) Is a possible, good programming strategy to incorporate your idea of squatting, bench pressing, and deadlifting in a workout with other exercises that would promote aesthetics?

Mark Rippetoe: 1.) Are they throwing it down after a snatch or a clean/jerk with bumper plates? If not, they're kicked the fuck out of my gym. I don't need the members that bad. Don't know about yours.

2.) The basic program promotes aesthetics better than any other program in the history of mankind, because bigger, stronger people are aesthetically pleasing to other normal humans. Skinny people with quad separation are not.

Press and chins

Pamparius: Would increasing my vertical pulling strength (weighted chins, pull-ups) help my press? And if so, how?

Mark Rippetoe: Chins and pullups heavily work the triceps, as well as all the other upper body muscles one way or another. The rotator cuff muscles and upper back are stabilizers for pressing, and lockout depends on stability. I actually get pec-sore doing high volume chins. If you cannot chin yourself a respectable number of times, you have a strength imbalance that should be addressed.

Adas75: What is regarded as a respectable number of chins?

Mark Rippetoe: Well, I can do 18, and I'm 53 and I weigh 210. So you have to beat me or you're a pussy. And if you do beat me, you're probably using drugs. See what questions like those get you?

Baldr: Mark, this is kind of an off-topic question, but do you ever see yourself giving up the iron? Assuming no injuries are acquired, is there any physical or health reason to not lift weights when one reaches his 70's or older?

Mark Rippetoe: Tommy Suggs came in my gym in 2006, 9 months after two total knees, and squatted 275 x 5. He was 70. And he's stronger now. I'll train until I cannot train.

Hesitant to move forward in squats

Irishman301: Hey Mark, I was wondering if this thought ever occurred to you: You're underneath the loaded bar ready to squat, and you go all the way down. When you complete the 1st rep you fear that the next rep may rip your quad open or your hamstring may explode. You do the next rep anyway, and you survive, but you fear that the next rep may be your last - maybe your back will give out, and your spine will snap in half. Again, you complete the next rep, and you survive. You complete the set of 5, but before every rep you were afraid that it may be your last for a while. Then you still have 2 sets ahead of you, but you do them anyway, no matter how scared you are that you may get injured, but you survive.....

I'm at that point now. I'm not going to say what weight I'm at, but it's heavy enough that they are HARD. I don't mind putting the work in, but I feel like it's possible that my leg muscles may not be able to handle the load one of these times if I keep adding weight every workout. Basically, I haven't stalled yet, because I'm still completing all 5 reps for 3 sets, and I am warming up adequately, but I don't want to find that weight that I stall at because it may possibly hurt.

I feel like my form is pretty decent, and it's only squats that I'm scared of hurting myself with. I'm thinking that it may be time to start adding in a front squat day, and only back squatting two times a week, and only increase the weight once a week instead of every workout. However, I will continue to increase the weight in all the other main lifts EVERY workout since I feel like I can. Does that sound like a logical thing to do?

Mark Rippetoe: Training at limit intensity will sometimes involve an injury, but not usually and certainly not often enough to spook a young male. It shouldn't, anyway. If your squats are legitimately slowing down to the point that intermediate programming is needed on them but not on the other lifts, then do so. But don't confuse desire with necessity – you may want to ease up a little, but if you don't really honestly need to you're wasting training time. If you have had a bad squat injury, most often a back injury caused by getting out of position, it can indeed make you think hard about the next hard rep. This is where balls gets acquainted with good judgment.

People and stupid statements

Robert: In my total 3 years experience of lifting (broken up a year or two in between my 3 training periods) I have had a total of 3 injuries. None of them serious, though the shoulder deal has been time-consuming and is requiring some orthopedic help. The ortho business being the case I have had a fair amount of doctor's visits in the past months.

My 3rd one (sustained a few days ago) means another trip to the doctor. My parents said to me today "Why do you do something that you know is going to cause injuries? Only an insane person would do that. Why don't you just do some exercise like walking or running or just lift light weights? You always overdo it and hurt yourself. I just don't think you can take weight lifting." Essentially they are saying that lifting heavy is not safe, and I am a fool for doing such a dangerous method of exercise. I said I would rather lift hard and get a few injuries every now and then than be the people who go in and screw around and lift the pink hand weights for their "exercise".

Also, if one would like to train hard, e.g. a competitive lifter, is it expected that when you are older your joints will be shot? In the short-term joints get strengthened, but I have noticed several statements by older lifters saying that they should have taken it easy when they were younger. If you wanted to train as hard as you can to get as strong as you can but not have terrible joints later, would there be a point where it would be advisable to level off the intensity? I am confused, lifting hard and with correct form produces stronger everything in the short-term, so why does that translate into ruined joints of older lifters?

Mark Rippetoe: If you are going to be a competitive lifter, you are going to have injuries. Training hard enough to beat other people who are also training hard enough to beat you is not conducive to long-term health, and it is different from training for fitness. Handling your parents aside, intense training for competition requires a willingness to train with injuries, and the willingness to train hard enough to get them. Now, if you are not training that hard and you are still getting hurt, you are doing something wrong.

Robert: Hmm. I want to follow the guidelines in Practical Programming and just get as strong as possible, so regardless if I actually compete or not I will be training *like* a competitive lifter. I really like training hard; getting stronger is really the only thing that makes it fun. Otherwise I would just be lifting for some vague ideal of "fitness", which isn't a definable goal and doesn't really make me any different from anyone else at the gym doing bicep curls and bench press machines. Is it possible to train that hard if I want to be "healthy" when I am older, i.e. having joints that don't ache abnormally all the time? Seems like I am in a catch 22 right now...

Tongzilla: When weight lifting at a high level, are injuries caused by incorrect technique, training too frequently or training too heavy? What are the most common causes for injury at the competitive level and why is your opinion that it is not possible to intelligently train to avoid these injuries? After all, weight lifting is not a contact sport like football or judo.

Mark Rippetoe: It is a sad fact that unless you are training for a meet you are actually going to lift in, you will not train as hard as if you were. If you are not an actual competitor, you will not be lifting the weights and receiving the stress that a competitor does. Enter a meet and see for yourself what happens to your training.

Another sad fact is that the weights handled by competitive lifters, especially competitive powerlifters, are hard on the joints of most people. Spines, knees, and shoulders get pretty beat up, and bony changes usually occur to all but the most genetically freaky. There are old lifters that are still in very good shape, but I'd say that most of us show signs of our previous exposure to heavy weight.

Robert: I am not interested in competing, at least with anyone other than myself. I just want to see how strong *I* can get, and could care less about anyone else. I want to get as strong as possible with the main lifts, i.e. squat, deadlift, power clean, power snatch, press, bench press but specializing to a specific area like powerlifting routines wouldn't be very interesting to me. Is there an age or point as someone gets closer to their genetic potential that they should just lift for maintenance? For instance, once you get to the point where you have exhausted intermediate programming, don't move up to advanced programming unless you want to be a competitor.

It seems so lame to me that if decide to compete you are likely to have old, worn-out joints later. You have spent years training to get progressively stronger, but the hard earned result of that is having joints that hurt routinely and you have a hard time doing what you spent so many years trying to adapt to :mad: ! This being the case I don't understand the reasoning behind competitive lifters; why do something that will hurt you in the long run?

Maybe this is why doctors think weight training is bad for the joints, because *competitive lifters* often end up with poor joints. They just fail to understand that competitive lifting is drastically different than a normal strength training program.

Mark Rippetoe: Powerlifters typically use much heavier weights than most weightlifters, and the spinal loading can be quite high. But weightlifters load dynamically, which can be just as bad if not more so. Hell boys, alls I know is that me and all my buddies are pretty beat up.

There is no concrete line beyond which you should not go, obviously, because everybody will achieve a different percentage of their genetic capacity at a different cost, and this is of course also controlled by genetics. There are lots of former national champions running around today that are fine having lifted very heavy 20 years ago, but the fact that they were genetically freaky enough to have been that strong is likely also responsible for the fact that they're still fine today. I'm as sorry as you are that I'm not in that elite group of athletes, and I never was. I had to train very hard for the tiny bit I accomplished, and I have paid for it for years. Only I can assess the sense this makes, and you'll have to do the same based on your individual priorities and values. Kinda like getting that tattoo on your neck: it may seem like a good idea now, but let's wait a few years and check back with you.

Tongzilla: How ironic that something you do to make yourself stronger can make you less able-bodied as you get older. Sort of defeats the initial purpose doesn't it.

MadDwarf: Tong, you're missing the point. Yes, if you lift very heavy weights, you will have sore joints when you get old. If you lift moderate weights, you will have sore joints when you get old. If you sit on your ass watching game shows and eating Cheese Doodles, you'll have sore joints when you get old, plus bedsores from all the times the hospice nurse was too lazy to roll you over. If you practice hot yoga daily and eat only organic vegetables, you'll be limber and full of energy when you get old. Wait, no, that's a lie - you'll still have sore joints and wake up grousing about the weather, and for some inexplicable reason, your lawn.

Found the common denominator yet? Getting old sucks, sorry. Using the probability (certainty) of your body breaking down when you get old as an excuse not to use and enjoy your body while you're young requires a distinct lack of male genitalia. I can't think of anything you would regret more when you're older, unless it's something overwhelmingly ridiculous like avoiding sex for fear of it interfering with your training.

As for when you should slow down and change focus? You'll know. Nobody accidentally becomes an advanced lifter. That's as silly as people who tell you they don't want to lift weights because they don't want to start looking like Arnold. The only way to get there once you outgrow novice and intermediate programming is careful manipulation of diet and training, with specific goals that span months. At some point, assuming you reach that level, the ever-diminishing gains from that programming will no longer seem worth the ever-increasing effort, priorities will shift, and you'll train more simply with the intent of keeping and enjoying what you have for as long as you can.

Mark Rippetoe: And MadDwarf thus wins the post prize of the week.

KSC: Like many other things in life, it is a trade off. For some guys the back, hip, and knee pain is worth the joy of winning, for some it is not. Everybody is different, and we all have different reasons for competing or not competing.

I would also like to agree with Mark, that there is NO WAY you will train as hard on your routine now then if you were preparing for a meet. Not if you are a competitor at heart.

Robert: Once someone reaches the level where they would need to use advanced programming to progress, that does not automatically make them a competitor. I do not see any reason why someone who was serious about training and did not settle for anything less than hard training could not train as hard as a competitor without being one.

Being a competitive lifter requires a lot of motivation, but I don't think it is impossible to have similar motivation if you are only competing against yourself. It is a competition to see how much stronger you can be than your previous self, instead of doing it just to do better than other people.

Mark Rippetoe: Robert is wrong too. Any advanced lifter is a competitor by definition. That level of training never occurs in the absence of a competitive stimulus. Perhaps he can give us the name of an advanced non-competitor.

Robert: If you have trained to the point where you need advanced level training, it is surely possible to do advanced level training. If I followed the Starr model accurately until I couldn't get any stronger off of that, I would be advanced. The advanced level of programming refers to how close you are to your genetic potential, whether or not you decide to go to meets with that or not. It just so happens that people that dedicated to going that far with training are often competitors. That doesn't mean that there aren't any people who train that hard just because they enjoy improving themselves.

Nobody can name any advanced level lifters who don't compete because if there are any that do lift that hard and don't compete, they probably don't care how much stronger they are than anyone else but themselves and lift in their basement instead of bringing attention to themselves by going to competitions.

Mark Rippetoe: Okay guys, help me out here. I feel a sore growing on my head, from the wall.

Polynomial: We know what advanced means. Actually, some guy here might have written a book about that. We also know that it's possible to have advanced lifters who don't compete. What's being said here is that this is highly unlikely. So unlikely, that it doesn't happen. I've trained around some strongman, powerlifting, and weightlifting competitors, and out of the whole set of people who might be intermediate/advanced, there was only one guy that didn't compete. But even he would take 2-3 weeks off and switch up his routines constantly due to boredom. He was damn strong, but I'm not sure that he was anywhere near advanced-strong on any lift.

So yes, it is possible that there are advanced non-competitors out there, much like it's possible that I'll become a rock star one day. And besides, a lot of competitors are still at the intermediate stage, so if you see your numbers soar beyond meet records, as an advanced lifter would, you probably start to think about going in and showing what you got...

What the hell have you done to me?

Sigix: Last time I had strep throat, I was a whiny little thing, holed up in bed bitching about how much it hurt to swallow. This time I'm going to work as usual, swallowing my horse pills of amoxicillin, and continuing to go to the gym to lift heavy objects repeatedly.

I guess stronger people *are* more useful in general (and less annoying to be around).

Mark Rippetoe: This is merely the way all self-employed people behave when they are sick. Glad you've grown some balls. I'm proud.

Radosuaf: Don't know your case but it might turn out in a few years it might have not been the best of ideas... Going to extremes is usually a bad idea.

KSC: I guess I am an exception to this rule. When I get sick, I send all my clients down the street to Gold's, lay in bed and revel in the fact that I can stay at home without cutting into my vacation time because I used up a couple of "sick days" allotted to me by my employer. I also enjoy this arrangement during dove and deer season.

Mark Rippetoe: I guess rado thinks that competitive athletics is a bad idea. Or a gallon of milk a day. I don't like your approach, rado. Way too many people think this way.

Radosuaf: I would say competitive athletics is a good idea. Provided you have abilities and possibilities to compete at some level. If you know you're going to be mediocre, better look for something else. I believe a gallon of milk is basically a bad idea if you can smooth out your diet and get protein from meat leaving lactose aside. There are healthier fats as well - mackerel is a better choice than full milk, almonds or olive oil are as well. Sure it's easy and self-explanable to tell someone to eat as he used to and add a gallon of milk ton top of that. But, if we're in the area of competitive athletics, I s'ppose no professional athlete is on such a diet.

Anyway, I surely agree my approach doesn't guarantee best results. Far from that. But it's safe and easy-going. I like it that way.

Mark Rippetoe: Yes, it's quite average.

Attitude change

Windcliff: The man I was even two or three years ago would not recognize the man I am today. I've been sick for the past couple of days, strep-throat, and I'm on antibiotics. Two years ago, I would've been in bed staring at the ceiling, feeling sorry for myself. Yesterday night, I was in the gym squatting, pressing, and rowing. Tomorrow, if I'm ambulatory, I'm going into deadlift. Even during 'good' weeks, there're days my joints ache, but I'm still at it.

Just reading SS and PP has really affected my attitude towards taking on challenges and enduring through pain. I can't say I properly execute or understand everything I've read in SS or PP, but I'm going to re-read them and eventually I will. Thank you, Coach.

Mark Rippetoe: Very cool. The brain/barbell barrier is breached with hard work and tenacity, which it also teaches. You're not just stronger now – you're a better human.

Steroid Usage on the Beginner Routine

Amu: Certain teenagers are bent on using anabolic steroids with SS. Since advice over side effects doesn't work well, I was wondering whether you think they'll even be effective. I don't see how steroids would be wise when you're already progressing in a linear manner. Your advice is valued and would help many of those looking into steroids. I apologize if this question is inappropriate for this section.

Mark Rippetoe: It's perfectly appropriate, and I think you for the opportunity to answer this question on the record. Novices progress in a linear manner. Novices on this program are frequently accused of using steroids, most usually by people that are unfamiliar with the capacity for human adaptation when training, food, and rest are optimal in people who have previously not adapted to them. This adaptation can result in bodyweight and strength increases in novice trainees that are far in excess of what can be obtained by more advanced athletes using steroids. It is not uncommon for novices to gain 40 lbs. of bodyweight and 300 lbs. of squat strength on this program. Anyone who thinks that steroids can improve upon this is inexperienced with both this method and steroids. I have had quite a bit of experience with both. Therefore when I tell you the following things, you can believe me:

1. Nothing works better for a novice than a linear progression on heavy squats and 1 gallon of whole milk per day. Nothing.

2. Novices who insist on using steroids are lazy bastards who want a shortcut where there is none. The fact that they want a shortcut means that they are not willing to do the work that is actually necessary EVEN IF YOU DO TAKE STEROIDS.

3. There are no shortcuts. The fact that a shortcut is important to you means that you are a pussy. ***Let me be clear here: if you'd rather take steroids than do your squats heavy and drink enough milk, then you are a Fucking Pussy.*** I have no time or patience for Fucking Pussies. Please tell everyone you know that I said this.

Self Critical in the Weight Room

XTrainer: I beat myself up a lot (mentally) in the weight room. For example, I can do 19 chins. Having hit this number several times, I really wanted to get a PR of 20. When I attempted yesterday, I knew by rep 16 or so that I wasn't going to get it. I, for whatever reason, started the long set out holding my breath and I think that did me in. I gripped wrong as well. But the reasons didn't matter, all I could think about is my failure.

Anyway, I was so angry at myself for missing the attempt. This is very common for me: When I miss weights or reps that I expect myself to get, I become extremely angry with myself. It gets to the point where I really can't do anything useful for awhile after I come home from the gym because I just feel so *sick* about my performance. I *know* it's stupid to get that worked up about a bad day in the gym, but I do nonetheless. It's detrimental to my training and my well-being as a person. I certainly don't like letting my gym performance determine my mood for the next 24 hours. Have you ever trained athletes who have these same issues? How did they get over them?

Mark Rippetoe: Most people grow out of this. It is a matter of perspective. I assume you're a very young guy with limited life experience, and the fact is that until something really bad happens to you, you don't actually have a handle on what *BAD* really is. If you judge yourself based strictly on your weight room performance, it also indicates that you're probably not trying really hard in any other area of your life, and that maybe an adjustment could be made here as well.

XTrainer: Well, I'm a definite type A, a perfectionist in almost every aspect of my life (a lifestyle and mentality which I wouldn't recommend to anyone). I guess it's not just a weight room thing because I have the same issues with school stuff, for example. But as far "bad" things not happening to me, you're probably right there. For example, no one *really* close to me has ever died. Thanks for the input. You've given me some things to think about.

Clean question!

Killiansred: I've just completed the madcow 5X5 and was going to do the Texas method next and just wanted your input of where I should work in some power cleans. I played college football and we lived on power cleans I haven't done them for a while, but after reading your book and reading some of other peoples post I got jacked about doing them again. Here is the Texas method I'm going to use, please feel free to critique it and tell me where the best spot to fit in the cleans. I love doing deadlifts so I don't want to replace those.

(He lists here a bunch of silly exercises that omit the power clean and include the barbell row.)

Mark Rippetoe: You should obviously do them instead of barbell rows, a relatively useless exercise compared to cleans. But how do you plan to know when to add weight? How will you know when it is "possible"?

Killiansred: I will try to add weight every week, if I can. Once I stall on adding weight for the majority of the exercises I will reset back 10% and start working up again. Is this what you would do??

Mark Rippetoe: Think with me here: "Try to add weight" means what? You'll try to add plates to the bar and see if they actually go on? "If you can" means what? How will you know "if you can"? Wouldn't it be more productive to add it first, and then see "if you can" lift it?

Question about squat days

Ark: 5'5, 34yr. female, 119 lbs. I am currently using a 4 day upper/lower body split. My goal is to maintain for the next two months before I start trying to gain again. In the past year, I've gained 10-12 lbs. Here is my new routine. Please critique :) One of my goals is to perform a chinup/pull up unassisted. I currently use the machine to help or I perform the fat man pull-ups on the smith machine.

Monday (heavy quad/light ham)

squat 5x5
hyperextension 3x10
step-up 3x10
calf raises 3x10
weighted ab work 3x10

Tuesday: (heavy horizontal push/pull - light vertical push/pull)

Bench press 5x5
Seated cable row 5x5
dumb bell press 3x10
chin-ups 3x10

Wednesday: off

Thursday: (heavy ham/light quad)

cdl 5x5
Bulgarian split squat 3x10
hyperextensions 3x10
weighted abs 3x10

Friday: (heavy vertical push/pull - light horizontal push/pull)

Chin ups 5x5
barbell press 5x5
push-ups (elevated) 3x10
seated cable row 3x10

Mark Rippetoe: Are you sure you've posted this on the right board? What are you trying to "maintain", as opposed to "improve", and why? Why are you doing seated cable rows, squats only once/week, no deadlifts, no barbell presses, and no cleans? Have you done a linear progression through the end of the novice phase? Do you know what the Novice Phase is? Have you read the books?

Peter_k: I think what she's getting at is that she finds gaining weight a bit of a chore and wants a break from it before she "bulks" again. Conventional wisdom holds that people cannot gain much strength unless they are gaining weight at the same time. From what I've seen, for women this can be psychologically hard as well as physically hard. Many women don't like the idea of putting on 20 lbs to drive their strength gains.

I have to admit, I don't quite understand myself what the procedure should be after the novice phase. Take any novice who gains a couple dozen pounds, gets a lot stronger, and generally works themselves into good shape, whether thin or fat to begin with. When they start on an intermediate routine, they still try to make steady progress, but gaining another 20 lbs in a few months will make them fat, whether or not it gets them stronger.

Mark Rippetoe: Peter, this is all wonderful stuff, but what does it have to do with a bodybuilder chick that hasn't read the books, thinks 5 x 5 squats is about "heavy quad/light ham", and has been training a year at a light bodyweight without a getting pullup?

Ark: Yes... I know my questions aren't your "typical" questions... but I figure why not ask? I am maintaining at the moment because I am trying to "adjust" to adding more weight. As Peter said " *From what I've seen, for women this can be psychologically hard as well as physically hard. Many women don't like the idea of putting on 20 lbs to drive their strength gains.* "...... rings 100% true for me.

I definitely want to improve, but I need this "down" time to come to terms w/ the gain. I most definitely want to improve strength and build more muscle. It may not make sense to you, but hey… I'm trying ☺ I was a gymnast for many years, but after I quit, I had a lot of issues w/ food, body image and so on…. I lost a lot of my muscle and now I'm trying to build it back in the most mentally healthy way for me… one small step at a time. I plan on building again in the fall. I am currently doing seated cable rows 2x a week.. one on a light day and one on a heavy day. I do have barbell presses and dumb bell presses. As for cleans…. I have never performed them before and am looking for a trainer to help me. The trainers at my gym are not very good. As for squats, I only have them in my program 1 day, because I'm using the heavy quad/light ham, heavy ham/light quad set up.

If I'm performing the heavy/light set up for quads/ham…. would you suggest adding squats to my light quad day…. possibly using a 3x12? Or do you feel I should do heavy squats and deadlifts on the same day? I don't mind it… just *thought* it was a no, no from other readings. I've read the books, along with several others (I believe this is why I'm confused).

I am definitely not a bodybuilder chick….. just a mom trying to look the best I can, realizing that all the cardio/light weights I've done in the past wasn't getting me where I wanted to be. I have read the books along with several other books…..trying to learn as much as I can… I understand I am not following your routines, but have learned a lot from your books/YouTube demonstrations on form and figured I'd ask you. Just trying to put together a routine that will get me where I want to be in my strength and appearance. And I attempted unassisted pull-ups today and performed 2. It was tough, but I did it ☺ I underestimated myself… haven't tried one in a few months until today.

Mark Rippetoe: I seem to have misinterpreted your posts, and for that I apologize. I may be misinterpreting now, but here's the deal:

"I definitely want to improve, but I need this "down" time to come to terms w/ the gain. I most definitely want to improve strength and build more muscle. It may not make sense to you, but hey… I'm trying I was a gymnast for many years, but after I quit, I had a lot of issues w/ food, body image and so on…. I lost a lot of my muscle and now I'm trying to build it back in the most mentally healthy way for me… one small step at a time. I plan on building again in the fall."

Since you're anonymous here, I'll go ahead and say that this is probably the type of thing that someone recovering from an eating disorder says. On one level, I am amused by your constant references to bodybuilding-think with this heavy quad/light ham sets-of-12 shit, and this indicates that you have spent more time – and I mean *way more time* – with books other than mine. You're thinking in body parts and muscle groups rather than movements and performance, and your program has been designed accordingly. These things I can address, and I believe I have done so in my books and articles. But sadly, the things I cannot address are your issues with food and appearance, and they comprise the bulk (if you'll excuse the expression) of your questions. I could tell you to quit thinking about how you look and start concentrating on what you can *do*, and that this will have a more positive impact on your appearance as a side-effect than any appearance-based bodybuilding training can. But I don't think you are equipped to listen to that right now, so I'll just wish you good luck with your training.

Frustrated

Sdds: Sorry about this rant but I have had enough of this shit: Its come to that point now, if I want to progress in training I need a place where I can do it in peace. I get criticized for your low bar squats over and over, a hardcore gym is a nice place to train but if you don't do what others agree with… well you get the idea

Basically a chap tried to make me move from low bar to high bar squats today telling me my form was all wrong, he said you have too much of a horizontal back when squatting, the result, apparently would be a major back injury but looking up and not going to parallel is the way to go! He was around 250lbs lean and I am 165lbs…. have worked my way up to squat 117kg which am pleased with…

I just can't take this bull any more. I have the option of leaving and trying to find a new gym which will be commercial or rent somewhere and build my own gym…. I live on second floor flats so really cant train a home. I am just frustrated with all this, I want to train and progress, that's it!

Mark Rippetoe: There occasionally arise situations in which major changes are necessary to facilitate progress. Assuming you are unable to get away with telling irrelevant individuals to ShutTheFuckUp, this appears to be one of those situations. Keep us posted.

Tiburon: Just wear headphones. And really tight, high, cut-off jean shorts. No one will bother you.

Size and strength vs. gym bunny

Fluxboy: So I've been a little bummed over the past few weeks because progress is slowing, everyone looks bigger, no one does squats, power cleans, or deadlifts, yet … everyone … looks … bigger. Perhaps some of you can relate to this.

Anyway, I saw a real weightlifter in my gym today, 250 lbs, 6'5", push pressed 225 lbs for a few sets, and I was reminded why I adopted Rip. A genuinely strong man steps in the room, and you notice. Instant respect. Even the muscles *appear* different, if that makes any sense. They just look thicker and smoother without that watery, inflated look to them. Talking to the cat, I got the impression he could tear me in half.

I just thought I'd mention this because I know sometimes I get lulled into wondering if some cosmetic bodybuilding wouldn't be in order … then you meet someone with real muscle, capable of driving hundreds of pounds overhead repeatedly, and they look so much better, and command so much more respect than the 'iPod, abs & guns' crowd, there simply is no comparison.

So Rip, I seriously need another forty pounds of bodyweight, and the strength to match … any suggestions? Experimental is fine. Faster is better.

Mark Rippetoe: You fool, you're doing everything right, you're gaining weight, getting stronger, and you're bitching about your progress. What ambitious young trainee wouldn't be impatient? So here's your test: do you have the gumption to do your homework and stick to the program in the face of the temptation to try something that supposedly speeds things up? This is when the lazy bastards try to find steroids.

Will you pass the test?

Press, Power Clean and Squat troubles

speedster101: I have been doing Starting Strength for a few weeks now, and I am very impressed with my results in the bench press and dead lift, although I am having trouble with the press, power clean, and squat. I have listed my starting weights for the press and power clean which have not been increased at all. I have increased my squat, but with problems coming with it. I have read all of the sections on these lifts many times, and very thoroughly, but I seem to be having struggles with all of these lifts particularly when I do them all on the same day. I would post videos of my attempts at them, but my gym is one of those stupid ones that will not let you have a video camera or cell phone anywhere in the gym. I have searched to see if anyone else has similar problems, but I couldn't find very much. Here are the problems I am having:
press- 60lbs: When I do these, it fells like I should be able to do a lot more weight on the first rep or two, but as I get to the end, it feels like my muscles quit early, and something is locking up preventing me from pushing up. The same also occurs when I even try to do just the bar for 5 reps, and it feels ridiculously hard to push up at the end. I have not upped my weight at all since I started.

Power clean- 75lbs: When I try these with up to 75lbs, I can get my technique working good, with the bar staying on my legs until the jump. When I get to the rack with light weights though, it feels like I am almost pulling the bar down to rack it, because it shoots up high after the jump. However, I have tried these with heavier weights (From 85-95lbs) and I have a lot of trouble keeping contact wit my legs, and I end up digging up my shins. Since there is hardly any thigh contact, maybe just a small bump at the jump, the bar has little upward motion, and it looks like a messed up jump shrug. I really want to do these, so this is starting to get frustrating.

Squat- 135 start- 155 now: This used to be my favorite lift pre- Starting Strength, but I am running into lots of minor difficulties with these. First off is the low bar position that I have switched to after reading SS. I was comfortable with the high bar position before, but the low bar position seems very hard to get into, and seem to dig into the scapula bones that the bar is supposed to sit underneath. I try to keep it in the right spot, but it really hurts, and when it starts to slip my wrist angle changes, and my hands take some of the weight of the bar. I also cannot keep my wrists straight, and have my fingers wrap around the bar. The only way to keep the straight is to have only the bottom part of my palm on the bar, which feels very unstable. The last thing with squats is that my stupid gym has mirrors everywhere, which causes me to get distracted very easily, making me lose focus, and forgetting about some things, mainly the Valsalva maneuver, and keeping my eyes focused on a point. This also seems to mess up the bottom of my squats, because I have a bad habit of looking how deep I am in the mirror, which is very hard to tell. This makes it look like I am not going deep enough to myself, which makes my upper body want to compensate for by leaning more forward, which the makes my butt not go as low, as it does not feel like below parallel. This may sound weird, but it is very hard to control.

Mark Rippetoe: Ah, such helplessness is seldom associated with adult males. It seems as though every line of your post is a statement of a form problem or programming issue that you need to correct, and that is addressed in the book. I kept waiting to hear that you have *diverticulitis* too. Here are a few selections:

"I have listed my starting weights for the press and power clean which have not been increased at all."

You picked the weights wrong. Lighten them up so that you can make a small increase.

"I seem to be having struggles with all of these lifts particularly when I do them all on the same day."

If you're tired, you're not eating enough. If you're not gaining weight, you're not eating enough.

"My gym is one of those stupid ones that will not let you have a video camera"

Change gyms.

"press- 60lbs: When I do these, it fells like I should be able to do a lot more weight on the first rep or two, but as I get to the end, it feels like my muscles quit early, and something is locking up preventing me from pushing up."

That's the way warm-ups are supposed to feel. If the last sets are too heavy to do for 3 sets of 5, you picked the wrong weight.

"I have not upped my weight at all since I started."

You fool.

"Power clean- When I try these with up to 75lbs, I can get my technique working good, with the bar staying on my legs until the jump. When I get to the rack with light weights though, it feels like I am almost pulling the bar down to rack it, because it shoots up high after the jump. However, I have tried these with heavier weights (From 85-95lbs) and I have a lot of trouble keeping contact wit my legs, and I end up digging up my shins."

Have you tried 80 lbs.?

"Squat- 135 start- 155 now:"
If you jump even 5 lbs. per workout, 6 workouts has you past 155.

"I was comfortable with the high bar position before, but the low bar position seems very hard to get into, and seem to dig into the scapula bones that the bar is supposed to sit underneath."

Put the bar underneath the "scapula bones" where it belongs.

"I try to keep it in the right spot, but it really hurts, and when it starts to slip my wrist angle changes, and my hands take some of the weight of the bar."

Try harder to keep it in the right spot.

"I also cannot keep my wrists straight, and have my fingers wrap around the bar. The only way to keep the straight is to have only the bottom part of my palm on the bar, which feels very unstable."

This is where the bar is supposed to be, on the bottom part of the palm. This is where it is the most stable. If you cannot keep your wrists straight, you have to fix this, for lots of good reasons.

"My stupid gym has mirrors everywhere, which causes me to get distracted very easily, making me lose focus, and forgetting about some things, mainly the Valsalva maneuver, and keeping my eyes focused on a point."

Are you indentured to this facility? Can you not leave? How is it possible to be this goddamn silly? You are supposed to be looking at the floor anyway.

"This also seems to mess up the bottom of my squats, because I have a bad habit of looking how deep I am in the mirror, which is very hard to tell."

Yes, looking in the mirror is bad. I am sorry that you are apparently not in control of your central nervous system, or precious little else.

"This makes it look like I am not going deep enough to myself, which makes my upper body want to compensate for by leaning more forward, which the makes my butt not go as low, as it does not feel like below parallel. This may sound weird, but it is very hard to control."

Yes, when your upper body leans forward you can't go as deep. Your upper body does not *want* things – it just does what you tell it to do, or what you allow it to do. Weird would not be my choice of description.

Unless you're very, very young, it is just *wrong* of you to even type this shit.

Hips Rising Too Quickly in the Deadlift

Seamanseau: One of our clients has a fairly common problem with his deadlift: his hips come up too quickly as he breaks the bar off the ground. We've pointed out the problem, he's aware of it, but nothing we've tried ("Lock the back angle in", "Lead with the shoulders") has helped him fix it. Can you suggest some more effective coaching cues?

Part 2. He's a strong guy, with a back squat 2RM of 350lbs, but he is unable to DL over 315. Part of it, I am sure, is anxiety due to a previous back injury. Today we had him try lifting sumo-style; the more vertical torso made him feel safer, but he was still stuck at 275lbs. This guy is a ferocious athlete, so it's not a matter of telling him to man up or stop being a puss. Given his squat (and a power clean of 225, with only a few months' training), he certainly has the potential to DL over 400 pounds. He just has a mental block. Have you noticed that the DL tends to cause more fear in athletes (especially the previously injured) than other movements? How do you help them past it?

Mark Rippetoe: The hips rise first in the deadlift because the hamstrings fail to anchor the back angle. This is discussed in BBT with illustrations that I cannot reproduce here, so refresh your memory there. We have had very good luck with more experienced lifters by just telling explaining the biomechanics of the error, and then yelling at them to keep the hamstrings tight before the bar leaves the ground. This usually works better than cueing the chest-up.

As for the fear, it is there, certainly. I have it myself after more back injuries than I can count. Depending on your sport, it might actually make sense to curtail heavy deadlift training after a couple of back injuries indicates it will be a problem. If you're a competitive lifter, you just have to not care that you might get hurt. I know this is not satisfying, but it is necessary.

Working a more physical job = bad?

Fisch: Hey Coach, I have a question about working a more physical job. I'm 16, and just about to do SS (well, restart it at least) and I'm looking for a warehouse job. The thing is, I'm not sure if this would hurt my progress. The most important thing in my life right now is to get strong, so a lot of decisions I make will be based on that. Right now I work at a department store where I stand all day, doing nothing. Would getting a job where I have to lift, push, pull, carry, etc. be bad for my progression? I would more than likely work on the off days. Any advice?

Mark Rippetoe: I mowed yards in North Texas in the summer while I was competing as a powerlifter. If you can't train and work in a warehouse at the same time, you probably have ovarian cancer. Consult your gynecologist.

Pussies

Tongzilla: Mark, you frequently use the term "pussy" to describe people who train/live like pussies (e.g. those who don't squat, and if they do squat they don't go deep, and even if they do go deep they use pussy weights, etc.). My question is, what's the equivalent term for female athletes? Thanks. I'm looking for a term that embodies the same essence of the word without being overly derogatory.

Mark Rippetoe: So you want to find a nice way to call women "pussies"? That's very considerate, but I think you've missed the point, as you often do.

How do YOU stay motivated?

Tiburon: I've been training my ass off for a little over 2 years now. I've been on and off for 6 years before that, but the on/off crap doesn't count. So I can honestly say that I've been actually training for 2 years now (not 8). I sometimes feel my motivation slipping though. I tell myself not to be a pussy, and I just man up and hit the gym anyway. I've only skipped workouts in these past 2 years when I TRULY could not make it (except this last Friday, where I had the opportunity to have sex with this chick, so I skipped for her, but that was the ONLY time).

Anyway, I'm trying to keep that same motivation that I've had for these past 2 years, and stick with it for the rest of my life. Is there any motivating yourself techniques you have other than telling yourself to stop being a pussy and just do it?

Mark Rippetoe: I train out of habit now, because I feel like shit if I don't. When I was in your situation – the 2-years-into-training one, not the getting-laid one, which I never had to miss training to do – I was competing. Competition motivates training better than vanity or a desire for fitness. Enter a meet. That's how I did it.

Charles Staley: I'll second that. Rip took the words right out of my mouth: give yourself a *reason* — above and beyond aesthetics — to be training. In fact, this is what differentiates an exerciser from an athlete. The word "training" implies a purpose for that training. So get out there and put yourself on the line, and I think — actually, I *know* — you'll be pleasantly surprised by the outcome.

Training lessons outside the gym

Jamie J: So I have a decent squat, I haven't replaced cleans with rows, I don't sneak out of the gym on deadlift day and I'm generally not a pussy. In the gym. How do you take that with you after your shower? How do you take the lessons you learn in the gym to the rest of your life?

Mark Rippetoe: When you finally get around to trying a heavy set of 20 squats with a weight you previously thought was a 10RM, you will understand how our weight room lessons apply elsewhere.

Strength training for beating depression/anxiety?

Gordon Bombay: I swear strength training has helped ease the anxiety that I've had throughout my life. I got pretty depressed last year, truth be told, and hitting the weights and focusing on getting a good diet has seemed to have changed me into a completely different person. I don't think I'll ever stop lifting due to the positive impact it's had on my life this past year.

Have you got any thoughts on this yourself? Obviously you're in a position to have witnessed scores of kids take up training… do you ever sense an increase in their confidence levels?

Mark Rippetoe: Many lessons are learned under the bar, if you allow it to teach you. Stress can be adapted to, and this is the premise of training. It should be no surprise that the ability to adapt to physical stress is something that helps with other types of stress too. It's saved many of us over the years.

KSC: A good weight room is a sacred place.

Mark Rippetoe: Amen.

Headshrinker: I make my living treat people with depression, anxiety, etc. (thus my forum handle). What has kept me on an even keel, especially recently? Getting stronger. I think Mark starts one of his books with "Nothing is more important in life than strength." I love that quote because it gets at the point that ultimately we are physical beings in a physical world - and all else being equal being strong is a very good thing. I always suggest to my patients that they get more active as part of their treatment, but that is very hard to do. The few that have invariably find it to be of great help.

Dinosaur Training

Galapogos: I've briefly skimmed through *Dinosaur Training* by Brooks Kubik, and there's a section on rounded back lifting that I didn't like. Have you read this book?

Mark Rippetoe: Yes, but what do you not "like" about rounded back lifting?

Galapogos: Well specifically when you lift anything with a non-neutral spine you're placing it at risk of injury. You've written about this before too in your analysis of the deadlift and in SS.

Mark Rippetoe: How about when you're in a burning building rescuing an unconscious person? Or if you're in full kit on a battlefield, picking up a wounded buddy while they're shooting at your ass? Or if you have to load another 75 lb. bale on the trailer? Or your PR deadlift? What happens when you're in a situation in which improper spinal mechanics will be used whether you like it or not? Does it make sense to prepare for this eventuality by occasionally training round-backed, or should we pretend that we will never lift anything with incorrect spinal mechanics because we've read *Starting Strength: Basic Barbell Training*?

Gordon Bombay: The first two examples are obviously worth risking injury for, the other two aren't. Does it make sense that training round-backed might lead to injuries that render the person unable to perform any of the activities you mentioned? I thought one the indirect purposes of barbell training is to provide the trainee the knowledge to apply good lifting form to real life situations?

Mark Rippetoe: The last 2 examples: *"Or if you have to load another 75 lb. bale on the trailer? Or your PR deadlift?"* So, nobody gets to haul hay or do PR deadlifts? Are you being serious about this? Think harder, please. Hay can't be picked up with perfect spinal mechanics due to the size of the bale, and we have talked before about form breakdown at PR-level intensity. Correct spinal mechanics should be practiced in training so that 1.) it carries over *whenever possible* to real-life lifting, and so that 2.) when it is not possible you're strong enough to not get hurt.

SS For the Morbidly Obese

DoctorLoomis: Hey Coach...I have a friend who wants to begin SS. He is 34....6'0 tall....weighs 340. He is morbidly obese. He wants to someday be 185lbs and in good shape. Obviously a caloric surplus for him is not correct. My question is if we start him on say 2500/3000 cal/week, wont there come a time that his progression will stall because of a lack of ability to recover due to the caloric deficit. How should we cater his diet to achieve what he desires?

Mark Rippetoe: Surely "per week" is a typo. And 185 looks like typo too, if the height is correct. He doesn't need to set his bottom weight right now, because he may be fit at 245. He can do the program as written for the ROM he can manage, and probably do it well on the Atkins diet for several months.

This is all academic, of course. Chances are very high that I have just wasted 3 minutes typing this, because if he had enough self discipline to train and do a ketogenic diet (actually the easiest way to eat to lose weight), he wouldn't be morbidly obese.

OITW: Have a little faith, Rip. There's a guy in my gym, probably at least 100 lbs overweight (closer to 150, probably, but he's been losing), who beats the Hell out of himself for about two hours every time I'm in there. Bike, every damned machine, pulleys cables and even some dumbbells. I watch him max half the damned ab crunch nautilus machines--every plate! So I asked him, what are you going to do now? His reply--do more reps. I've tried to get him to shift to free weights as being more effective, but he doesn't understand the difference in metabolic impact, and he's sticking to what the trainers gave him on that little card. Ignorant or stupid, not sure, but it's not lack of focused work that's keeping him back.

Mark Rippetoe: There isolated examples of fat guys who get it fixed. These are anomalies, and are statistically insignificant across the fat population as a whole. The overwhelming majority of fat people have fat people's brains, and cannot stay away from the carbs that make them fat. This is why one quarter of the US population over 20 now has impaired fasting glucose tolerance. What a favor the dietary fat-is-poison shitheads have done for us, huh?

Jon: I think the part I'm most annoyed about is how much bacon the fat-is-poison shitheads prevented me from eating. Well, I still ate my share. I just felt slightly bad about it. No one should ever fuck with your enjoyment of bacon.

Dave M: Right on, Rip. I like your diagnosis of "fat people's brain". An associated symptom with that particular disorder is dismissing automatically any fitness routine that seems like it would *actually* be hard. After all, why is this man attracted to a program that builds nothing but strength? Is an undiluted barbell training program best for preventing the heart attack that will kill him at 50? Is it the program that would be best for improving his ability to do normal life tasks? I'd argue that no, it isn't. So why be attracted to a SS program? I'm guessing it's not because he wants strength more than he wants overall health and mobility: It's because he wants an EASY program.

Now, I'm not saying that your program, properly executed, is easy--or that there would not be overall health benefits to doing it--but there are lots of very strong people with a lot of fat, so that goal of "fat + strong" seems a lot easier to shoot for than "not fat," which is what I think most of us would agree he needs to be shooting for right now.

Mark Rippetoe: My point is that that it doesn't matter what kind of program is best for him. He is a morbidly obese fat guy, and he is statistically unlikely to do it or anything else he ought to do. It is all academic until he shows up one day having been training/eating better by himself for several weeks without anyone else knowing about it.

I'm feeling bad.

Barbeque: Well, first of all, thanks for everything. My strength and lifts have increased, and so has my weight. The thing is, something really bad happened yesterday. I'm really sad and my chest hurts, and yesterday was a horrible day. Today was supposed to be my training day, but when I went into the gym (I go in the morning, and I didn't eat breakfast, I would have puked), it was weird. I failed reps in ALL the lifts I had to do today. (Squat, Press and Deadlifts). So I was thinking, while I'm recovering from this shitty experience I'm having, I'll lower the weight in all my lifts and focus on improving my technique like a fine-tuned machine. Let me show you:

Squat: From 240 lbs to 200 lbs.
Press: 115 lb to 90 lb.
Deadlifts: 260 lb to 220 lb.
Power cleans and bench press will stay the same, or if I fail them later I'll reduce them by 30-40 lb.

I don't like to do this, but I rather have a less effective training for a while than quit, which I felt like doing today, I felt frustrated at my uselessness. I just don't know, coach, you think I'll get somewhere with this? Can one's mood influence his strength? I'm confused and anguished. Thanks a lot for reading this.

Mark Rippetoe: What happened?

Barbeque: My deadbeat dad came back after years of absence and tried to act as if nothing had happened. We kicked him out, but for some reason I was really depressed. I'm still a bit shaken, but I think I've recovered. Mom was really sad. I think THAT was the thing that got to me the most. I sound like a total pussy, sorry coach.

Mark Rippetoe: You don't sound like a pussy at all. You sound like a normal human being, just like me, who thankfully has a barbell to keep him sane when things get shitty. They always will from time to time, and many of us have our training to thank for our continued existence. Things will be better, my hugs to your mom. Just understand what is happening next time you are distracted during training, work through it if you can, and realize that one workout out of thousands does not affect your overall progress. Training is a process, not the events of one day.

I need to gain weight but...

Poisonhearts: Okay so I use to weigh 210 lbs at 5'11", I've since dieted down to 140 lbs. I did very little to try and stop muscle loss so I'm now fucking skin and bones. I want to gain some weight but I'm wondering if jumping straight into a calorie surplus would be good in my situation since I've just stopped dieting to lose weight only a week ago and my body's metabolism might be a bit fucked up.

Any experience with situation similar to this? I guess I'd have to be in a calorie surplus if I wanted to see any gains, but any idea if it would be best to go a while at maintenance caloric intake then up it from there?

Mark Rippetoe: No experience with it at all, as I am not a psychologist.

Poisonhearts: Someone had recommended that I take the calories easy while having only recently come off dieting. He mentioned that my metabolism might be a bit out of whack and that jumping straight into a calorie surplus would not be an appropriate course of action and might possibly only induce substantial fat gains. It looks like I might ignore this advice and eat a surplus of calories and drink my gallon of milk like you suggest in your book. I believe my body will adapt quickly to the change.

You are suggesting that I have some sort of psychological problem solely based on the fact that I went on a diet and lost some weight? Sorry if my assumptions are wrong. I merely went about my dieting foolishly because I felt the need to loose weight for a future career in law enforcement.

Mark Rippetoe: You didn't just lose some weight, PH. You lost 1/3 of your bodyweight and a huge amount of muscle. It will have no effect on your ability to do the metabolic work necessary to regain it, but I have to wonder about the motivation to go from a useful bodyweight at 5' 11" to what can only be described as emaciated, under voluntary circumstances.

Am I way wrong on cleans?

Mr. okiebjj: I am a 34 recreational athlete that loves to lift. I was taught what some call a traditional hang clean in high school (catch and drop in to a front squat versus a power hang clean. Although I read the reasons why you like the regular clean because it helps the deadlift, but I feel much more comfortable with doing hang cleans. Should I keep trying to get better at the clean from the ground or just keep doing hang cleans.....and does it matter if I "catch" it in more of a power fashion (quarter squat) or can I keep doing it the way I was taught?

Mark Rippetoe: It is important to always stay within your comfort zone. This prevents having to subject oneself to the inconvenience of learning something new and potentially useful.

Hypertrophy - looking bigger

UnBalanced: I know that you are not a bodybuilder and both skeeve and scorn their behaviors (dieting, shaving, oil, tanning, prancing in underwear, beauty contests, etc.). However, I am sure that you appreciate the work that goes into obtaining the hypertrophied physique, and the concurrent gains in strength that occur. After all, I think it was you who said that a larger muscle is a stronger muscle and that a stronger muscle eventually grows into a larger muscle. Also, I feel confident that you will agree, that women who appreciate a man's muscular physique are making the better decision than those who seek the flat-chested, narrow shouldered and chicken legged (all other things like money being equal). Therefore, I am confident that you have a considered and learned opinion on how to best develop the aesthetic attributes in addition to the strength attributes of muscle (in other words, even though you have not cast yourself as a trainer of muscular appearance -i.e. bodybuilding - I'll bet you have some strong and interesting opinions on the most efficient way to effect an increase in muscular bodyweight and appearance).

So, if you were to give advice to someone (like me!) who was trying to increase the aesthetic appeal of his physique through hypertrophy (not for the purpose of winning public contests in front of other men, but for the purpose of participating in private contests before a single woman), what changes, if any, would there be to your recommendations? I understand Starting Strength is a beginner program and that hypertrophy considerations are not yet ripe for a beginner. But as my strength gains through linear progression begin to taper down, what programming specifically enhances hypertrophic gains? Of course, as I indicated earlier, the pursuit of a stronger and stronger body will lead to an increase in muscle mass and an increase in muscular appearance, we all understand that. But what precise methods (programming or exercise selection) will speed the hypertrophy process even if it means a slight loss in strength? Further, in your opinion, does pursuing hypertrophy necessarily come at a price to strength and/or strength increases?

Educated and intelligent opinions on this subject are rarer than hens' vaginas, so your input is desperately needed. I know that many who follow your advice do not care to look "big and muscular" (that seems to be part of the same disorder that leads CrossFitters and their ilk to spurn bench pressing, which you quite correctly identified as being an overreaction to the bench pressing masturbation at commercial gyms) but there are many of us who do want to look as big as we are strong; we do want our shoulders to appear noticeably wider than our waists; we do want women to touch our arms, coo and squeeze; we do want a thick chest; etc. So for those of use interested in looking big while being strong, what advices do you have?

Mark Rippetoe: *"But what precise methods (programming or exercise selection) will speed the hypertrophy process even if it means a slight loss in strength?"*

The confusion stems from the fact that the level of training advancement of the athlete is seldom considered when answering questions of this type. That is discussed in PPST at length. The easiest way to answer this is to remind you that for a novice – with the ability to gain anywhere from 25 to 50 lbs. of muscular bodyweight in from 4 to 8 months – the best hypertrophy program is the novice progression, and for more advanced guys the best way to gain mass is to do a combination of 5s and 10-12s on the basic exercises while adding in a limited amount of assistance work, all on a diet that will support continued growth.

"Further, in your opinion, does pursuing hypertrophy necessarily come at a price to strength and/or strength increases?"

This is a much more important question. Pursuing hypertrophy as a primary goal comes at a much higher price than the sacrifice of strength. It means that you have traded the ability to DO for the APPEARANCE OF BEING ABLE TO DO. Now don't get me wrong: most people that start training and stay with it did so *at first* because of a concern for their appearance. Nobody actively seeks to physically look like shit. But most people grow out of this as a primary motivation pretty quickly, as soon as they have to deal with actual competitive bodybuilders and their odd neuroses. Think about it just a second – why would a normally adjusted person train that hard and diet that hard for the sole purpose of showing other people a particular version of their appearance? One that is transient, unnatural, and incompatible with a useful physical performance? Wanting to be bigger is perfectly natural for men that aren't big, because they know that bigger is stronger and stronger is better. But to make hypertrophy the sole purpose of training is to demonstrate an obsession with the perceptions and reactions of other people.

I saw a guy last year in the Columbus airport after the Arnold with his fitness chick girlfriend. The guy – big guy, 6' 3", ~285, very lean – was wearing a skinny black tanktop, black lycra knee pants, white gym shoes with ankle socks, tanned and I swear to god oiled, carrying his gym bag. **In the middle of the airport in March in Ohio**. He wanted me and everybody else in the building to see him and his big muscles. I was embarrassed for him, because he completely lacked the sense necessary to be embarrassed himself. And for a second I was embarrassed to be in this business. Just for a second.

Today at the gym.

the_junk: So today in the gym I was squatting 170# 3x5. When the biggest and definitely strongest guy in there comes over to me to give me some wisdom.

He says "Not many people squat like that."

I said "Most people are pussies, I'm doing Coach Rippetoe's Starting Strength and....."

He cuts me off and says "Oh, of course. Well, your form is perfect"

Then he goes back to where he was to finish deadlifting what I can only refer to as basically a small car. (A shit load of weight.)

I don't care if the UnderArmour wearing bodybuilder types or disco dancing squirrels give me weird looks when I'm doing my power cleans. Because I know soon that I will be able to break them in half, and that makes me feel good. Thanks Rip.

Mark Rippetoe: People actually criticize me for fucking with bodybuilders, you know.

sushi362: Why is that?

Mark Rippetoe: I might do so on occasion.

UnBalanced: I have tangled with Coach Rippetoe on the concept of hypertrophy in the past. Good times. I argue that pursuing hypertrophy (becoming stronger and looking bigger, better, more masculine and more muscular in the process) is laudable while bodybuilding *per se* (wearing silk panties and lubing your body) is just plain gay. Coach tends to automatically equate a desire to improve one's physical appearance and performance through barbell training with bodybuilding.

I barbell train to get stronger, be healthier and look better. Rippetoe trains (and advocates) barbell training to get stronger and be healthier. To Coach, looking better is only a douchebag's errand.

That being said, I predict that, much to his chagrin, 10-25 years from now nobody will have done more to advance/further the development of bodybuilding than Rippetoe, simply because his coaching (unlike therecommendations in the muscle comic books) effectively produces muscular results. As per the tenets of capitalism, what works succeeds. Eventually, Rippetoe will produce more bodybuilders than Joe Weider! Just my opinion.

Mark Rippetoe: I appreciate the kind words as always, but please don't mischaracterize my position. I understand that appearance is an integral part of most people's motivations when they begin training. It certainly was mine, and only a fool denies a desire to be perceived more favorably by other humans, as well as oneself. This serves as motivation for beginning to train, and once a person achieves a modicum of improvement in strength and physique, a normally adjusted individual moves beyond the aesthetic as the primary motivator and becomes interested in the various aspects of performance. My position is that when the aesthetic-improvement aspects of training are retained as the primary fascination with it, to the extent that a person wants to show everybody else what he looks like so badly that he enters a "competition" venue designed specifically for this purpose – or prepares himself for this purpose whether he enters the physique show or not – then he has become a fucking weirdo. The oil, brown paint, silky underthings, shaving one's ass, bizarre stage behavior, and questionable juxtapositions with one's fellow weirdos onstage are merely the trappings of such weirdness.

Such behavior is tolerated well when displayed by women, since our culture seems to appreciate such things. And the defenders of the IFBB/NPC may therefore claim that they are the leaders in the transformation of society, the fellows who are at the forefront of the push to objectify both sexes. Fine with me, boys. But it has been my experience that men who so desperately wish to be thought of as being muscular/defined/massive/Herculean that it becomes the sole focus of training, that it carries over into dietary practices that effectively isolate them from normal social interaction with family and friends, and that it finally leads them up on stage in their oil, paint, and underwear to show other men their muscles, are fundamentally different than I am. Better or worse is something we may disagree on.

The Advice of Physicians Regarding Training, and Other Gibberish

"I'd hate to see you jeopardize your career in athletics by doing a bunch of weightlifting." This was the actual statement by a pediatrician to one of my trainees, a big 15 year-old kid with a 7" vertical. For the 30+ years I have been in this business it has been my experience that the advice of doctors regarding exercise is approximately as useful as that which would be given by their nurses. The advice of physical therapists is, on balance, probably worse than that...

Question on cleans/rows, also, general questions on the Texas method

Richie_Awesome: I read that you recommended athletes start doing cleans. Is there any way I can do cleans and barbell rows in the same week? I am progressing greatly on barbell rows and would rather not remove them, unless they are absolutely for the best. I am getting stronger from them and my biceps are responding greatly to them. By the same token, more explosiveness for lifts and improved technique on cleans would be great as well.

I was going to do this:

Monday
Squat 5X5
Bench Press 5X5
5x5 Bent over Row
3x8 Decline weighted situps

Wednesday
Front Squat 3X3
Press 5X5
a1 4x6 Pullups weighted

a2 3x15 cable crunch
b1 3x12 leg raises
b2 3x12 external rotation
b3 3x12 hip adductor

Friday
Squat 1X5
Bench Press 1x5
1x5 or 2x3 deadlift
a1 3x8 glute ham raise
a2 3x20 decline situps
a3 3x8 external rotation
a4 3x8 hip adductor

Where could glute ham raises go at? I do not want them interfering with deadlifts. Please do not think I'm a noob trying to cram in every exercise possible without giving the program a chance, also please know that external rotation and hip adduction are for injury prevention and to stop imbalances. They are very easy on the CNS and will not lead to fatigue. Also, I believe the ab exercises will only cause direct fatigue and won't add to CNS fatigue, but please tell me if I'm wrong.

Mark Rippetoe: I guess all this depends on how much you're squatting and deadlifting now. That looks like an awful big mess of assistance work to me. You can certainly row and clean the same week, but I don't see cleans in the workout you've listed. I do, however, see exercises that "are very easy on the CNS and will not lead to fatigue". If they are easy, why do them? Why do you think the program you are doing will lead to imbalances? And how will exercises that do not produce fatigue correct them? And why would ab exercises that only cause "direct fatigue" be preferable to exercises that work abs during the performance of their normal trunk stabilization function?

I don't think you understand the concept of the program. It doesn't need any help from assistance exercises because it leaves nothing out, and it causes no imbalances that need to be corrected. "Muscle groups" are components of systems, and when the systems are worked, so are their components.

Richie_Awesome: My squat 1 rep max is around 310, my deadlift 1 rep max is around 430, I can tell I need to catch my squat up and I'm working on it. I was training them with a 1 day per week frequency. For the cleans, I was going to ask you where they could fit in my workout. Would Friday's max intensity day be best, or Monday's volume day? A good rep scheme for cleans? I read somewhere that you should not go over 3 reps on cleans as form breaks down due to fatigue. As for the imbalances, I read an article titled "Waterbury Rules". He said he's never seen anyone with adequately strong Wrist Extensors, External Rotators, and Serratus Muscles and that everyone could benefit with training them, the same applies to hip adduction and hip abduction. At this stage, do I not need to do individual training for those muscles?

bango skank: I can't speak of the other assistance exercises, but the external rotation for the rotator cuff seems to address a muscle weakness that is otherwise neglected in full body routines. I have notoriously weak rotator cuffs and this has hindered my progression in the Press. Exercises like pull-ups, push presses, push jerks, and snatches can make my shoulder subluxate, so I have to be very careful when doing them and use light weight. And forget about arm wrestling. I've been doing the RC rotations to try and correct the imbalance, but it's very slow going. Can you offer any insight into RC weaknesses and why it is so underdeveloped despite my history of compound shoulder strengthening movements?

Mark Rippetoe: Now, here's the deal. All this shit about having to separately strengthen the wrist extensors, the internal and external shoulder rotators, the serratus (both groups), the hip ab- and ad-ductors, is bleed from physical therapy. All these muscles, believe it or not, work during complex movements in ways that contribute to those movements WITHOUT being isolated into their physical-therapist-5-lb.-dumbbell individual exercises. Presses strengthen the external rotators because all those muscles contribute to stabilizing the lockout position in isometric contraction; they don't just externally rotate. The wrist extensors get lots of work when you chin, hold heavy weighs overhead, deadlift, clean, snatch, bench, and work with fat bars, sandbags, tires, sledgehammers, and farmer's walk weights. But an arm trainer might not know that; they are very dumbbell/mirror-oriented. The squat works adductors and abductors because they have an important role in the movement that is not necessary to supplement with isolated physical therapy elastic band bullshit. Same with serratus muscles (look them up and see what you think they might be doing in a heavy press), the shoulder rotators, all the abs, all the little muscles in the hips and back, and anything else it's real neat to know how to isolate with a chrome dumbbell or a therapy band. All the muscles necessary to do presses, squats, or pulls are trained by presses, squats, and pulls, and if you think that muscles are somehow getting left out of your workouts, you may not be using enough weight or using correct technique.

You can train effectively your entire life without ever doing a single isolation exercise if you use barbell exercises that make you squat, press, and pull from the floor, and do other functional exercises like chins and stuff that looks like work. But you have to use textbook form, challenging weights, and common sense.

Squatting with Osgood Schlatter?

Dschenck: I have 15 year old two sons. One of them is in the middle of SS, and making great progress. The other plays basketball, and has a pretty bad case of Osgood Schlatter's disease, which of course the basketball makes worse. He loves playing, however, and so he basically just plays through the pain, and ices his knees when they get really bad. He's had it for over 18 months now, and it doesn't seem to be getting better. He'd like to get stronger for basketball.

Do you have any experience working with kids with OS? Do you think squatting and deadlifting could help him, or would you advise keeping away from knee work until the OS clears up? Any other recommendations you have for him?

Mark Rippetoe: I have had several kids with OSD, and every one of them has benefited from correctly performed full squats. We kept one kid out of a scheduled surgery because he responded so well. Quad-dominant activities like jumping (basketball), knee extensions, and half-squats produce/aggravate OSD symptoms, while posterior chain stuff like the low-bar deep squats we use in SS, and pulls like RDLs tend to re-balance the knee and allow it to heal while still getting stronger. Your orthopod/pediatrician will "disagree". But you already know that.

Strength Training and Hypertension

od1: This is a question I am going to bring up with my doctor in a couple of weeks, but I was wondering if you had any feedback based on your coaching experience: I'm a 35 year old male diagnosed with mild hypertension, but had it under control prior to beginning the Starting Strength program. Now, a few months into the SS program, I noticed that my blood pressure and pulse readings have risen considerably.

Obviously, I don't know for sure if the training routine and diet (addition of 1 gallon of whole milk per day) are the cause, but it's likely that my doctor is going to tell me to stop. It's disappointing if I have to stop because I'm on a good linear progression and had the specific goals of a 300 pound squat, 400 pound deadlift. After hitting those marks, I was going to switch to a CrossFit or Olympic weightlifting program.

Here are my stats:
Male
35 years old (36 on Jan 25)
When I began SS, I weighed 173, I am now at 187.
These are the numbers where I'm training at now and require 4 to 5 minute rests between sets:
Squat : 3 sets of 5 at 220 pounds
Deadlift : 1 set of 5 at 258 pounds
Press : 3 sets of 5 at 132 pounds
Bench : 3 sets of 5 at 198 pounds
weighted chins, pull ups, dips; doing cleans at 60kg, but need to find coach
Systolic/diastolic/pulse
prior to SS : 132/70/46
today : 149/80/58

I'm thinking the BP may have gone up due to the weight gain. I don't have measurements, but any eye can see that I have more fat around the mid-section now than prior to the program.

So, I was thinking that I could try to stay on the SS linear novice program, and just halt or reverse the weight gain (reduce milk intake, or use lowfat variant), but this seems to go against the principles of the program. What do you think? I'd hate to have to stop and reduce myself to some enduro-runner homo, but I guess it's better than the alternative.

Mark Rippetoe: There are about 900 reasons why this is of absolutely no concern. To wit:

You've only gained 14 lbs., and you did it on a weight-gain program with a strength increase.

149/80 is not terribly "hypertensive".

What size cuff did they use when they measured your BP?

How tall are you? You'd have to be shorter than 5' 6" to be considered overweight. Your strength doesn't look like that of a short muscular man, so I assume you're fairly tall, and therefore not "overweight".

On how many separate occasions have you been checked at 149/80? Have you been checked by several different testers/nurses/doctors and have been consistently hypertensive?

Is there hypertension in your family, and have you had problems with it before? Would this cause you to be apprehensive about having your BP checked?

Do you realize that a RHR of 58 is still below average?

Had you been in pain before the test/were you nervous about the potential results/were you pissed off about something/were you tired or overtrained/had you trained in close proximity to the test/had you drunk a bunch of coffee or taken any medications or supplements that might affect BP/were there any other explanations for a transient elevation in blood pressure?

Why do you think belly fat elevates blood pressure?

If you want to lose some weight, go ahead. Certainly not everyone needs to be drinking a gallon of milk/day, and not everybody needs to gain weight. I think you're overreacting to this, but then again, I'm not a doctor. However, I would say that anybody that diagnosed you with hypertension without evaluating the above questions is not much of a doctor either.

Arthritis in knees-advice please

Kuzushi: I am 48 years old and the Dr told me I have psoriatic arthritis. My fingers, the bottom of my feet, and my knees hurt. I am on a prescribed steroid drug to treat the pain and swelling. The drug works pretty well. I am on your SS routine. Doing squats SOMETIMES hurts when I get about ¾ of the way down, but it is not too bad. I asked my doctor about continuing my workouts and she gave some general advice like "exercise is good but watch that stuff," and the ever popular "don't do too much." My ex-rays show that my knee joint has "narrowed," but there is not a lot of damage. Based on your expertise am I okay to continue? When I do the squats using your protocols my knees actually feel less tight and the pain subsides a little after I am done.

Mark Rippetoe: I can't offer advice on a specific medical question like this. The tragic thing is that neither can your doctor. I've had no experience with psoriatic arthritis, and she's had no experience with barbell training. So this means it's your call. It's ultimately your responsibility to decide what to do with your body, and you are in a better position than either of us other two to decide what works, what's good, and what's necessary. If an exercise hurts more as you do it than it did when you started, quit. If it makes an injured area feel better, chances are quite good that it's helping. You are your own best prescriber, if you equip yourself to be.

Deep squats and meniscus

Robert: I work in the athletic training room at Santa Clara University and started doing the Starting Strength novice routine recently. One of my bosses in the training room saw me doing deep squats and was all upset and said it looked so painful. I tried to explain to her about how deep squats activate the hamstrings and keep balanced force over the knee and help prevent ACL injuries but she responded saying that some studies have shown that is questionable and that going below parallel in squats puts a ton of stress on the meniscus. Not wanting to argue with my boss too much I left it at that and kept doing my deep squats because I do not think she is correct.

Since then I have tried to look up studies on Olympic lifters (overhead squatters and snatchers) and meniscus tears but have found little. I also searched this forum and found little on the subject so I figured I would post and ask you. Do lifters going below parallel have increased incidence of meniscus tears? What do you think about this argument?

Mark Rippetoe: Well, I have several tears in my meniscus, none of which occurred while squatting. Furthermore, deep squats do not bother either my torn meniscus or my absent right ACL. In my 30 years of doing this, I have never observed a single example of deep squats tearing a meniscus. Ever. I've seen it happen once or twice on cleans and snatches that got in a bad position, but never squats or deadlifts. As for actual data, I don't have that, but I do know that she doesn't either. I do, however, have experience and logic on my side, while she has merely her preconceived perceptions and conventional wisdom.

Hip arthritis and deep squats

Cmn: Have you had experience training anyone with osteoarthritis of the hip? My brother-in-law, who is an orthopaedic surgeon, insists that squats are going to damage my hip further. In my experience, the only time my hip feels good is when I'm using a program of fairly heavy squats and deadlifts.

There is very little information available on osteoarthritis of the hip for people who want to keep training. Most of the advice tends towards water aerobics and gentle stretching. I don't personally know anyone with as much experience in the gym as you have, so I'm hoping you've seen someone keep training successfully under similar conditions. And, fwiw, I'll never stop lifting. I stopped several years ago and was miserable. I've been back at it for a while now and feel great.

Mark Rippetoe: You know the answer already. You typed it in your post. Squat, and if you need a new hip eventually, get one. What are you supposed to do in the meantime, according to your BIL MD? Heal up doing water aerobics and gentle stretching?

Stance width and uneven quad development?

Canoscan: My physiotherapist (who I'm seeing for my hip, which I have a problem with that nobody seems to be able to figure out) told me that squatting with a "wide stance" as per starting strength, puts more emphasis on the outer quads which after a long time can tighten to the point where it can start pulling the patella out of place. He further pointed out that because my quads stick out more on the outer side (which it has done since I can remember, even before I started weight training) this is the reason, and that I should either switch to a narrow knees straight ahead stance, or at least to do squats like that sometimes. Is there any truth to it, or is it silly bullshit?

Mark Rippetoe: As is usually the case, your physiotherapist is full of shit. Our stance is not particularly wide at all. The only way a "wide-stance" squat can cause patellar tracking problems is if the femur and the tibia are aligned wrong, i.e. your feet are not in line with your femurs. This means that the wider the stance, the wider the toe-point must be. If this alignment is respected, all the quadriceps work evenly to extend the knee. The advantage of my "wide-stance" squat is that it also works the adductors and the external rotators, left out by close-stance squats. Does your physiotherapist know that adductors and external rotators are involved in the squat?

Question about worn out joints, specifically shoulder joints.

Captainpicard: I noticed on this forum that you commented that "your knees sound about like mine do" to someone who was having knee trouble. In your books you say that not only muscles are strengthened by weight training, but also tendons, ligaments, and many other bodily tissues. I spoke to a doctor recently and he said that you should not train overhead pressing or shoulder activities too hard, as a core upper body exercise in training, as it is hard on your shoulders and you have to live with your shoulders for the rest of your life. He also commented that the shoulder joints just were not made to press such heavy weight like people do, and in comparison to other muscles that people train, the shoulder muscles are tiny. He gave an example of a muscle group that was more suited for heavy exercise and that was the pectorals. I thought heavy training made joints stronger, not wore them out? :confused:

Mark Rippetoe: I am an old, retired competitive lifter that has been bucked off of lots of horses. I did not train for fitness, and I have not lived my life for either comfort or longevity. Do not take my personal example as one that is reflective of the short-term results of a strength training program.

Now, the doctor you talked to is not entitled to an opinion about overhead pressing movements, having never done them himself and having never been trained in their correct execution. In the same way that you would not allow me to remove your appendix or adjust your psych meds, you must not allow untrained and inexperienced people to define your exercise habits.

Older Guy, Dead Lift and Back Pain

Harry: After a short 35 year break in my weight training I have begun anew with your SS program, hoping of course to find the fountain of youth before I completely melt away. I'm two months in and progressing nicely. In the beginning I experienced a good deal of back pain from the squats and deadlifts. Close attention to form adjustment has resulted in pain free squats but the deadlift still results in increased lower back pain. Today's weights were 170 for the squat and 185 for the deadlift. I'm sure I could do 200 or more for the deadlift. Right now there is a new dull numb pain in my lower back that began during the deadlift exercise. If the pattern stays the same, it will begin to fade later today and I'll be back to normal by tomorrow evening.

I'm 6'6" 250lb and back pain has long been a way of life for me. If I stand in place for more than a few minutes my back hurts. If I kneel over my back hurts. If I sit and lean over my back hurts. After 7 hours in bed my back hurts. Four or five times in the past 30 years I've managed to throw my back out by doing nothing in particular, and I'm disabled for six weeks or so. To tell you the truth I'm hoping this weight training will take this burden from me.

Yesterday I went in for my physical and spoke with the doctor about all this and he really didn't have much to say except that he was pleased I was lifting weights. He showed me a picture, pointing to where the strain was during the exercises, but really had nothing else to say except that when he was doing it, he went with 20 reps instead of 5. What would you suggest?

Mark Rippetoe: Well, I sure as hell wouldn't do a set that is so long that it almost guarantees that fatigue will compromise your form, at any weight. Doctors are not, as is obvious, trained in even the rudiments of exercise science. But it is very good that he recognizes the value of the work. He's unusual in this respect.

I think you're doing fine, and I think you should try to add some back extensions and some reverse hypers to the program for direct lower back work. This will help your particular situation so much that if you don't have this equipment I'd advise to do what is necessary to obtain it. The bottom line is that for many years inactivity didn't seem to help, so let's try something else. You'll be fine, much better very soon.

Runner's knee

lakers16: My orthopedist diagnosed me with bilateral runner's knee and recommended that I do quarter squats (to angle of 135 instead of just below parallel) and to lower weights in favor of doing higher reps (going from 5 reps to 15). Should I listen to his advice and do more reps at lower weights and give up squatting? Or is this really the manifestation of some sort of form problem that I can fix? I am 23 yrs old, 6ft, 180lbs. I've been doing starting strength novice routine for about four and a half months. I've been experiencing knee pain especially after doing power cleans and a little after squatting. The pain was at its worst last week after I played basketball (one day after lifting) and I've had swelling in both knees.

Mark Rippetoe: My advice:

1. Quit going to doctors for sports "injuries".

2. Quit listening to doctors about training.

3. Don't ask me about cancer, although I know more about it than the doctor does about lifting weights.

4. Quit running for quite a while. Quit playing basketball for a couple of weeks too.

5. Fix your squat form so that your knees can heal.

6. Gain about 40 lbs. so that your lifting mechanics can improve.

About kidneys and diet

Dan F: I'm a 46 years old man from north-east of Italy (sorry in advance for my English), I started strength training after reading SS 2nd edition and PP in mid January (2008 of course) and happy with it: my first question to you is not a technical one but medical. I've now only one kidney ('cause a problem I had in 1991): have you experienced training persons in this same condition?

My concern is in particular about diet: doctors say to eat low protein meals not to stress kidney function but I think if I train for strength I need some more protein than a sedentary person in an equal condition to progress and that will not badly influence my renal function. In the past years I had no problems training "cardio", slow cardio too but in particular interval sprinting and GPP drills for time: the real problem was that strength, upper body strength in primis, flied away... leaving me with shoulders pain, low back pain etc. What are your thoughts about this? (Actually my one kidney function is ok, normally hypertrophic after so many years alone). Thanks.

Mark Rippetoe: What caused the loss of the kidney in 1991?

Dan F: Surgery, after that a doctor accidentally found with echography that my right kidney was functionally dead. This was due to a particular type of slow and pervasive calculosis caused in the years by a congenital narrowing of the upper part of the right ureter. The cause was bad anatomy and it seems, by medical tests, that I'm not particularly prone to normal calculosis or other kidney problems.

Before kidney surgery I was an amateur soccer player and a decent track athlete without any symptoms of a problem. Doctors said this is not uncommon with that particular kind of calculosis. My interest in strength training now is because after years of mixed sedentary/low activity or more intense cardio training I really need to improve strength (or contrast its decline in years) in primis for general health I think and also for improving my mountain biking. I don't aim to begin very big and very strong like a master powerlifter or similar (I believe my genetics are not for that) but, after reaching the novice plateau, to improve strength/BW ratio as intermediate trainee, in particular upper body strength that actually is not only absolutely but also relatively weaker than lower body.

So I don't think that some more grams of proteins each day for building muscle could be dangerous for a kidney that, today, is in perfect health. Some doctors are with me, others not and so your thoughts and eventual experience on this will be very appreciated by me: last decision is obviously on my own.

Mark Rippetoe: Provided that no pathology exists that would predispose to problems with the other kidney, my expert staff tells me that a higher than normal protein intake is of no concern at all. If your GFR is normal, there will be no load on the kidney. This is probably an example of CYA medicine. I'd proceed under the assumption that you're going to process protein like everybody else does unless they can show you why you won't.

Dan F: Yes, my GFR is normal (so are creatinine levels) and I check them regularly. Actually I have no renal insufficiency at all. The one kidney is normally hypertrophic and working good. What's the meaning of "CYA" acronym?

Mark Rippetoe: CYA = Cover Your Ass. Refers to the best way to avoid getting sued out of existence. It is the cause of many silly recommendations uttered by medical professionals who actually know better.

I think you will find this somewhat amusing.

Sgtmattbaker: After my visit with a P.T. today, I am thoroughly convinced he is very misinformed about weight training in regard to skeletal/muscular anatomy. He thinks my shoulder issues are mainly AC joint related; I should modify my normal routine (your novice program) for a while. When he said these things, I thought "err, Rip would disagree":

Use sets of 10s (excluding squats) for a while. Use a weight that isn't really difficult near the end of the sets. Less than 10 reps is hard on your joints, and for someone with/or predisposed to a joint injury that is bad.

Having a back that horizontal puts a lot of shear on your spine and will wreck it (my back was more horizontal than vertical in the deadlift).

Sub rows (or machine rows, DB rows) for deadlifts. Deadlifts don't work the back muscles enough to provide necessary muscular balance for avoiding rounded shoulders.

Sub incline presses for overhead presses for a while because they are not as hard on the shoulder joints.

Power cleans are ok because they start with a more vertical back angle than my deadlift. He seemed to talk as if he did not think there was a shrugging motion at the top of an overhead press, like the shoulder blades were not working in their full range of motion of something.

Mark Rippetoe: If you accurately recounted his advice, not one single thing he said was correct. This is why I do not perform brain surgery; I know as much about it as the PT does about barbell training.

Rotator cuffs.

Ganondorf: If someone sustained a rotator cuff injury not serious enough to require the use of an arthroscope or similar tool, and/or internal/external/whatever strength and range of motion is decreased in one of their shoulders, they should just do the Starr rehab using overhead press correct? Should any resistance band exercises for internal/external/whatever rotation be used in addition to the press?

A lot of people seem to think they need to work their rotator cuffs independently, and a lot of therapists and doctors think that these exercises are helpful for healing them. I'd like to know the truth.

Mark Rippetoe: It is my opinion that muscles should be rehabbed the same way they are used, so that they heal in a way that prepares them for normal function. The rotator cuff muscles do not work in isolation, and therefore I like to use presses to fix shoulders.

Ganondorf: Ok, makes sense. I am under the impression that none of the major lifts other than chins and pullups directly work the rotator cuff. Bench might do so as people often hurt their cuffs doing it, but they could be failing to keep their shoulders back (as is with correct form). I got from SS:BBT that the rotator cuff wasn't directly worked during the overhead press, but was only used somewhat as basic stabilization if needed.

Mark Rippetoe: This impression comes from a misunderstanding of the function of the cuff muscles. You have been taught by the PTs that the real function of the external rotators is isolated external rotation, and that's just not the case. Shoulder stability is their primary function, and they perform this function by applying tension that can also produce external rotation when they are isolated. But just because the PTs discovered that you can move a 2 lb. chrome dumbbell up and down while lying on your side with your arm against your ribcage does not mean that this is the primary function of the muscle. In fact, my recent personal experience with a rotator cuff repair was that the first exercise to come back to full strength with no pain was chin-ups, at about 8 weeks post-op. My presses were slower to respond, and more painful, but the entire rehab has been accomplished without a single rep of any RC isolation exercise.

Press Question

XTrainer: This question was prompted by someone's comment about training the press (specifically, that we shouldn't :eek:), and while I'm not about to stop lifting heavy stuff over my head because of something a mortal said, I want to know where the argument is coming from. Does pressing shove "the humeral head up into the glenoid fossa," what does that mean, and what are the supposed consequences?

Mark Rippetoe: Oh. My. God. Only if the heavy barbell fails to shove it back down. Heavy weight, gravity acting perpendicular to the floor, all that shit. This is from a PT who thinks that everybody trains with 3 lb. chrome dumbbells, right? What the hell is wrong with these people? Why do they not want anybody to get strong overhead? Have they never heard of Ken Patera?

KSC: First guy to press 500 lbs right? I think I still have his WWF wrestling figurine in my attic somewhere.

Training with Ankle Sprain

JoshL: I started doing SS and eating once I found out about it over the summer, and put on 20lbs of bodyweight and 90lbs on my squat. I follow the program strictly, eat a downright painful amount of food and get an ok amount of sleep. A few days ago, I played some pickup basketball and sprained an ankle (mostly ligament, but a tiny crack in bone). It hurts to walk, I am using my crutches and boot, and doc has told me not to put weight on the foot for 2 weeks. I'm real pissed off that I cannot continue progress in my squat, deads, and things. What should I do about my training?

Mark Rippetoe: I'd go ahead and train. But then again, I'm stupid: I squatted 4 days after my appendectomy. You have already put weight on the foot, haven't you? And you know that you'll heal faster if you continue to do so at as quickly-increasing a level as you can stand, don't you? Because you know that if this were 30,000 years ago the hyenas would eat you if you didn't, right? So you be the judge, not the doctor. Rehab it aggressively as you can possibly stand, because that's the only way that really works. You know this already, because it's in your DNA.

Statins and Muscle Damage

KSC: Been hearing reading a lot in the media lately about the possible links between statin drug usage and muscle soreness and muscle tears. Even the Lipitor website has some info on it about this possible danger. About two weeks ago this was all over the news and that was the first I had ever heard about it. Wanted to relate to everyone on the board who either takes statins or trains those that do that I can attest to this side effect first hand.

About a week ago I had a client suddenly yell out in pain during a set of air squats during a workout I was taking him through. He grabbed his hamstring where it inserts at the knee joint and has had a lot of pain in this area since that time. This particular client is well adapted to regular back squats and high repetition air squats as a part of his program and had no problems with his form so I was baffled as to the problem. He revealed to me today that he has been on Lipitor for about 6 weeks and the light bulb went off in my head about the possible connection between his mysterious hamstring injury and his Lipitor usage. I then researched it some on the internet and found a lot of data on the subject making the link.

I then did a run through of all of my clients information charts that have ever experienced an injury while training with me. I had two other injury cases over the past year. One guy had a really severe strain/tear right around his hip flexor region during a set of walking lunges with no added weight. The other guy had a strain/tear in his groin during a set of lightweight thrusters. I went back into their folders today and guess what - BOTH OF THESE GUYS ARE ON LIPITOR TOO.

It was just so weird to have three different clients, all of which were very well adapted to the exercises they were performing, were using perfect or near perfect form, were properly warmed up, and were using little to no resistance suffered similar mysterious injuries and all are on the same meds! Take it for what it is worth but I believe the connection.

Mark Rippetoe: I'll see if I can get Dr. Kilgore and Dr. Bradford to both post on this extremely relevant topic. It would behoove everybody taking statins on the advice/insistence of their GP due to a slightly elevated serum cholesterol to do their own homework and carefully weigh the costs/benefits of this usually unnecessary prophylaxis.

Lon Kilgore: Putting someone on anti-cholesterolemic drugs after one test that shows a marginally above normal result is wrong. A series of tests separated by weeks is required to truly establish the presence of hypercholesterolemia. When hypercholesterolemia is authentic then diet and exercise behavior modification should be the first prescription. If those turn out to be ineffective over a period of a few months, then prescription therapy should then be considered.

I also find it interesting that in a huge number of clinical laboratory tests, the results need to differ from "normal" by two standard deviations in order to be considered a medical problem. I'm pretty certain that this is not the case in cholesterol measurement.

High cholesterol is associated with premature death over time, it is not an emergency condition that any research I know of says will kill you tomorrow. That means a GP and someone with mild to moderate hypercholesterolemia has time to address the situation properly prior to prescribing statins.

Dan F: I was a pharmaceutical representative of Merck & Co. in north-east Italy for many years and promoted simvastatin in the nineties. With that kind of drugs muscular soreness and muscular damage, going also to rhabdomyolysis, is not frequent but a well known problem. A statin from Bayer, Lipobay (cerivastatin), was retired from commerce some years ago (perhaps 2001), because there were about 50 known deaths (I think about 30 in USA), the majority of them took together the statin AND gemfibrozil (drug for triglycerides), a thing absolutely not to do.

It is real that some people have muscular soreness taking these drugs, it is also real that some types of intense training could cause a lot of soreness, so the result of muscular damage adopting the two in the same time could be real. I completely agree with Dr. Kilgore: the statin would be the last thing after tried other methods (diet and exercise) to lower cholesterol levels. If I'd try to lose weight through intense training (with CrossFit or other methods) I wouldn't take statins, and I'd test my cholesterol levels no less than 6 months after starting training.

Mark Rippetoe: The problem is that physicians placed in a "gatekeeper" role often treat a slight elevation in cholesterol as a treatable disease situation. They have been trained to merely respond to stimulae: cholesterol = > a certain number/treatment = statins. With no more understanding of the lipid biochemistry involved in the situation than their nurses have. I have a good friend whose *18 year old daughter* with no family or personal medical history of heart disease was put on Lipitor after one blood test showed a serum total cholesterol of 218.

Dan F: The pharmaceuticals companies have to get their target profits... But it's not so simple: there's an intricate network of interests between industry, medical doctors and public expectations (patients). In some sense the situation resembles that of fitness industry where, like a beginner, you go in a gym for better shape and they put you in a program with machines and cables and a X times a week split routine. The problem is also what public expects: a shortcut to health, or what resembles "health": low cholesterol in blood in the first case and in the second case a pleasant ripped look (with 6 pack?) like models.

The keyword, I think, is "shortcut" that very often is not the better way but equally often is the most convenient for someone.

Dr. Stef Bradford: http://www.nhlbi.nih.gov/guidelines/cholesterol/ataglance.pdf
Standard treatment guidelines.

Not followed closely in actual practice as the bias is strongly in favor of adding drugs due to CYA. Notice how this is mostly when to start drugs. And that for LDL (their main focus) the benefit is a 5.5 to 30% reduction. What this means then is that 1.) goals aren't reached and/or 2.) multiple drugs are used. And #2 means much better chances of adverse effects and side effects. "Weight management" and "physical activity" for 3 months -- 3 MONTHS @!@#@!!???, of low-end ACSM-type recommendations. Slapping on cholesterol-modifying drugs intended for very long term use after 3 months of minimal ineffective exercise is ridiculous. 3 months isn't a good timeframe for dietary modification either, not in the kind of population group you'd likely be having this conversation with -- overweight, sedentary, lazy and accustomed to doing whatever feels easy and good. It takes a while for someone without any skills, who's gone for a long time without giving a shit, to learn to live in a better way. The first problem is that these guidelines suggest that the underlying problem is lipids/LDL instead of inappropriate exercise and diet and rest. None of these drugs are magic pills that can make up for the neglect of physiologic realities. An obsession with LDL or triglycerides or whatever marker you choose is missing the big, giant (extremely giant in the case of many health professionals) point.

So 3 months is as silly as novice kids adding steroids after 3 months of a foolish training program. Come to think of it, if doctors were pushing strength/size this is probably exactly how they'd add Dianabol. 3 years would be more appropriate than 3 months.

Gman: A few points I wanted to address.

"Not followed closely in actual practice as the bias is strongly in favor of adding drugs due to CYA"

While I agree that medications are often overused, using such a broad generalized statement without any actual clinical experience is akin to saying "All chiropractors are quacks", or "All physical therapists suck". There are bad apples in every field, but don't forget about all those good apples as well. Not all physicians want to simply CYA and throw pills at people. But it is very hard when a patient comes in demanding a mediation he saw on TV for XXXXXX ailment. Most of these people have no interest in anything but taking a pill. Sad but true. Blame the Big Pharma companies for that one.

"Slapping on cholesterol-modifying drugs intended for very long term use after 3 months of minimal ineffective exercise is ridiculous."

Just because you start a medication, there is nothing that says you can't stop it if the patient continues to progress and improve with their diet, exercise and weight loss. Medications do not always have to be long term, but the hard truth is most people are lazy and not at all motivated to improve themselves, and would be much happier taking a pill a day than worrying about exercising every day and watching their diet. My clinical experience is that while the vast majority of people will be motivated in the short term to exercise and lose weight, less than 5-10% of people will last longer than 9-12 months. Also, keep in mind that most patients seen with elevated cholesterols who are treated are not the teens or 20 something year olds that show up on this board. They are older people, usually with other medical problems that place them at a higher risk for MI/CVA, etc. A LDL of 160 in a 22 year old is very different than one in a 55 year old with hypertension, diabetes and who smokes.

"The first problem is that these guidelines suggest that the underlying problem is lipids/LDL instead of inappropriate exercise and diet and rest."

This article is how to deal with elevated lipids, but I did not see anywhere where it stated they were the problem. They are the result of many things, including genetics, diet and lack of exercise, addressed (poorly in my opinion) in the article. As far as missing the point, couldn't agree with you more, but this is only a guideline for lipid management. There are others out there that deal with obesity and poor nutrition.

The sad fact is that we used to have our high risk patients meet with a certified nutritionist and counselor on a regular basis for 45-60 minutes at a time, and at the end of the day, "surprisingly", there was very little difference in improvement with folks who we saw every few months.

Dr. Bradford: Quote:

> *...using such a broad generalized statement without any actual clinical experience*

My comments are based on clinical experience. And a broad generalized statement was put in to sum it up. I stand by them and would point out that they are a very mild, cleaned up version of my thoughts on this subject. Too many are conditioned to think of medicine as a field that encompasses and contains Health, when medicine is really a small, specialized practice area that rubs up against big, giant Health from time to time. It is unfortunate that Medicine is deluded about itself, and has leveraged itself a controlling interest in so many things outside its actual purview.

www.quackwatch.com & chiropractors

nisora33: Rip, I'm still having a tough time trusting chiropractors after having some bad experiences with them. Since then, I've read some pretty damning stuff about the profession in general, most of it on a website called Quackwatch. I'm not saying that there aren't legitimate uses for chiropractic and honest, effective practitioners out there, but in a market so saturated with chiropractic, imagine the desperation of some of these guys and gals to distinguish themselves and meet their bottom line. Walk into a lot of offices (those in the Tennessee area, at least) and just look at all the horseshit supplements some of them are pushing.

Mark Rippetoe: Yes, there are bad chiropractors. We have some amusing ones here in town. But need I point out that there are bad surgeons, attorneys, plumbers, barbers, hairdressers, and PTs, all of whom are licensed by some governmental entity which supposedly assures the public of quality in practice? Chiropractic as a whole is a useful approach to many types of problems, even if they are a bit fuzzy in terms of what they are actually doing and why. I like Dr. Homola's comments about "defining the proper limits on chiropractic" and "support[ing] the appropriate use of spinal manipulation but renounc[ing] chiropractic dogma". But they are less expensive than most other treatment modalities (if you know how to deal with their office people) which makes the good ones the default first-in-line for most common back injuries. This is why the MDs don't like them; this, plus the fact that they get to be called "Doctor" with a lot less time in school than the mainstream medical professions require.

How to diagnose a muscle belly injury?

GavinL: I want to make sure I diagnose my injury correctly before I do the rehab in the Sticky. I have pain in my left-side lumbar back just above the glute. It's on one side so I don't think it involves my spine, but sometimes I can feel the through the hamstring or further up the back (such as after sitting for long periods of time) so I wonder if maybe a nerve got damaged or something. I felt it happen after I tried to put down the weight after a heavy Power Clean, versus just dumping it (no bumpers.. foolish, I know). I got the weight down and felt a strain and within a minute, I was stiff as a board and called it a day. The next day I could barely get out of bed. Ice helps a lot, contrast showers too (but I do only cold for the first 2-3 days, then cycle cold/hot). In the mornings it's hard to move, but once I get warmed up, the pain fades considerable and ROM is back to normal, but I feel the strain at extreme ranges, such an an ATG squat.

So I figured it was a muscle issue and I had intended to rehab it starting with Back Extensions and BW Squats. The more reps I did, the better it felt such as 25 reps, 3 sets, but after I cool down it tightens up worse than before and the next morning is even worse, so that's where I am confused.

- Do nothing? Sometimes staying off an injury lets it heal, but I hope that's not the answer. There has to be a better, faster way. I'm 21 and quite fond of things healing quickly but this back issue is stubborn.

- Or restart that same rehab protocol? Is the stiffness and pain to be expected or does it mean I am doing it wrong? I don't want to dig the hole deeper before I climb out of it and time away from Squats, Deads, Cleans, Snatch, Rows, and everything else worth doing is killing me.

Mark Rippetoe: This a classic example of a job for a Chiropractor. It is not a muscle belly tear, but rather a facet joint or an intervertebral ligament injury. It is very common, you will have it again, and you'd better get used to the idea that you 1.) don't go to the doctor (MD-type) every time you tweak your back, and 2.) you are going to train through and around it, which you're doing well now. Traction is very helpful for these things, so get some ab straps that you hang from in the rack and learn to use them. Reverse hypers are usually good for this injury, along with back extensions, and the pain you're having now after it goes away when you train it will be helped with traction and will subside very soon as the thing starts to heal. This is an unfortunate part of training for some people, myself certainly, and you'll have to learn to cope. A chiropractor can help, if you can find a good one. I know one here that thinks that "the gravity is pulling back and to the left today", so he wouldn't work out well.

It might also behoove you to figure out what might have predisposed you to this injury. It's very often hamstring flexibility.

Osgood-Schlatter's & squats

Stevo: One of the consequences of playing football in high school 20 years ago was developing O/S in my left knee. The sports doc I talked to advised, take a guess, DON'T DO SQUATS. She's a hefty old bag & probably hasn't exercised most of her life. Anyhow, my guess is that your response will be, "...continue to squat until you're dead. Next?" But if there is anything else you may know about this condition to look out for, please tell me. I've done research online, but it's not as good as learning from someone with actual experience.

Mark Rippetoe: The treatment of OSD is poorly understood by most orthopods, who all nonetheless seem to have a favorite method of doing the surgery. We have had several kids over the years heal it up with full squats after it was aggravated by leg extensions. My best advice is that you don't talk to "sports medicine" people about sports medicine. They have had poor training – all of which assumes that "sports" means running and riding your bike – and little professional experience with it, and usually no personal experience that might temper the silly things they have been taught. The sports med guys are usually only good if they've trained with weights themselves. Some have, most haven't.

Jshreck: I am glad you clarified that about the sports medicine people. Yes, some are good, and you will find some bad. You will find that with any profession.

Mark Rippetoe: Jerry, let me further clarify: it is my position that some are good but that most are very bad. Most of them.

ACL reconstruction

Kazzin: A friend of mine is having ACL reconstruction surgery shortly, and was told by his doctor that he would need to be on crutches for 4-8 weeks, and no exercise for the next 6 months! This seems excessive enough to me that I'm sure it comes down to a combination of CYA+stupidity, especially since the stress on the ACL in a proper squat should be minimal. I understand that there are varying methods of repair, and degrees of injury, but on average how long should it take an individual to recover enough to start squatting again? 3-4 weeks or so?

Mark Rippetoe: Your friend urgently needs another surgeon. This is the silliest thing I've ever heard. If he is not confident in his repair to the extent that he doesn't want it loaded for 8 weeks, then he is not a competent surgeon. And he knows absolutely nothing about rehab. Seriously, get another opinion.

Robert: I am working with a friend of mine who had an ACL replacement. He was off crutches in less than a week. Doing PT from a couple days post op till 8 or so weeks post op. And I had him doing weighted squats 5-6 weeks post op. And I was probably being too conservative. 8 weeks on crutches is ridiculous.

Mark Rippetoe: If it helps, I was never on crutches, did partial squats 14 days post-op, had full passive ROM back in 32 days, squatted 225 x 5 legal in 9 weeks. At the ripe old age of 38.

Jshreck: I would expect that your friend is having a more extensive surgery than just an ACL repair. My guess is he probably is getting his MCL and Medial Meniscus repiared as well. If his Doctor stitches down the meniscus then there would be a non-loading period of a couple of weeks. I do agree with Rip in getting a different opinion, because he should be starting exercise the next day after surgery (non-weight bearing) (isometrics) and then progress forward. Our staff will typically have our athletes with ACL surgeries squatting within 4-8 weeks post op. I have NEVER heard of NO Exercise for 6 months. The scar tissue would be so excessive he would have difficulties the rest of his life.

Acromioclavicular arthritis

Jordanwashington: I'm a 6'0", 27, 200lbs male. I've been having worsening shoulder pain since the spring of this year, and first noticed it after squatting with the bar too low as I described in another post. I went to an orthopedist, had a shoulder MRI, and was diagnosed with AC arthritis. He said that at my age, this is uncommon. He told me that this injury won't go away on its own and that I should get surgery whenever I want it to go away. I asked him about the cause, and he said the squats probably contributed to aggravating it. I'm wondering if you have any thoughts on this diagnosis/injury/surgery. I'm thinking of going through with the surgery after I get a second opinion from another ortho. And was wondering what to expect post-op as far as getting back to squatting.

Mark Rippetoe: I am always suspect of diagnoses that involve blaming commonly-practiced activities not normally associated with problems for said problems. I didn't invent the low-bar squat, you are certainly not the first person to take my advice and do it that way, nobody else that does them has A/C arthritis, and so I doubt very seriously that your brilliant MD has stumbled upon the cause of the injury. He listened to you say "squat", thought to himself "Yeah, those are bad," and blurted out an etiology. Since bony changes take time to occur, it's much more likely that it is the result of kid football, an activity that orthopedists seem to hold in high esteem. Why, if I were cynical, I'd say they feel this way for commercial reasons.

If the damn thing is really screwed up, have it fixed. But I'd sure get someone else to confirm this. It will affect your training for at least a couple of months, so make sure it's necessary.

Why the Hate for Overhead Pressing?

EIC: Sometime ago, I saw an orthopedic surgeon for my persistent shoulder pain, which continues despite (or because of) a Bankart repair I had years ago for a torn labrum. The MRI revealed a small tear in the labrum and a small tear in the rotator cuff. Neither is worth operating on. When I asked him for advice, he cautioned me to absolutely avoid dips and overhead pressing.

Initially I dismissed this as the same sort of misguided caution to avoid full squats. But more and more I've been seeing a persistent trend in strength trainers advising clients to avoid overhead pressing of any sort. Most of these people write for T-Nation and advocate such things as single-leg lifts, planks and similar static abdominal exercises rather than sit-ups, lots of "prehab" work for the joints, and so on. The common theme seems to be that overhead pressing is a bad idea for shoulder health, which is exactly the opposite of the view espoused by accomplished individuals like you, Bill Starr, J.V. Askem, et al.

Again, I can dismiss the advice of the surgeon, but I cannot so easily explain away the views of these younger strength trainers who, unlike the surgeons, believe that full squats, deadlifts, etc. are good. Do you have any idea why the overhead press is getting so much hate lately? My instinct tells me that these trainers are misguided, but I must concede that some of their arguments against overhead pressing are superficially enticing.

Mark Rippetoe: Strength coaches and personal trainers who advocate against the press are trying to obtain the approval of doctors and PTs for various professional reasons. They feel that being in the medical club confers legitimacy upon their opinions. That, or they have absolutely no experience with the exercise done correctly. Their arguments are not enticing to me at all, because I've never heard one that made any sense.

Sternum pain from benching.

Robert: I've been going at the SS program with good results for approximately three months. The pain started after approximately two months. I've been seeing steady gains in each lift. Unfortunately, there's a lot of pain in my sternum while doing dips or any stretching that has some resistance to it. I've been able to pinpoint the pain to benching. I'm wondering if the sternum hasn't strengthened enough for the weight that I'm doing. I'm guessing that I should also lessen the shoulder blade "pinching" that I've been doing.

Mark Rippetoe: If I was a betting man, I'd bet that the dips were the offending movement, not the bench. The sternum strengthens along with the muscles, tendons, and ligaments, but the dip is a considerably more severe bottom position than the bench press, so I'd tend to think it was the problem. Try laying off the dips for a few weeks and see what happens

Robert Weagle: Thank you for the advice about the dips. Looks like I'm taking a break on them. I went to see my doctor a few days ago. He was saying it may have something to do with a condition he called "Pectus excavatum". He explained that due to the sternum being basically "off centered" then there would be more stress on the one side of the sternum bone. And so if I was using heavier weights, that this condition would be amplified and may "have potentially" stress-fractured the sternum.

Mark Rippetoe: Looks like he pulled this out of his ass. Search that term on google: I doubt seriously that this is you. The sternal area is just one of the thousands of things that will get irritated when you train heavy. You'll have to learn to ignore most of this shit or you can't train.

sergeant_81: Coach, if I may... I too have pectus excavatum, in fact a very extreme case (all the docs wanted to completely reconstruct my chest when I was younger, thankfully my mother refused). For most of my skinny life the xyphoid process and upper right half of my sternum stuck out nearly a full inch from my chest (the x-rays are pretty neat). As I grew older it corrected itself somewhat, but was still very noticeable.

Since I began SS several months ago and put on a good 30 pounds, the condition has corrected itself even further, to the point where I can no longer see it in the mirror and have to go feeling for it. I am of the opinion that proper benching, if not completely correcting the issue, has at least contributed to reducing its severity.

Not sure where I'm going here, but I would tell your doctor that pectus excavatum is not an issue. Whatever you do, don't let them talk you into cutting you open and reconstructing your rib cage.

Mark Rippetoe: Doctors often feel as though they need to provide an answer, even if it's wrong. This is part of the moral hazard of overcharging for your opinion.

Weightlifting & Varicose Veins.

Maximuspita: I have varicose veins, not the spider ones but the really ugly ones, and I would like to start weightlifting. I've checked what some medical sites say about the matter and they say I should avoid strenuous exercise like weightlifting but I would like your opinion the matter.

Mark Rippetoe: What is their reasoning on this, since the venous return blood flow is under no pressure?

Maximuspita: Well, I checked around again to be sure and it seems that the medical community is divided on the issue. The best I could come up with was this: Quote:

> *While you may like the way your legs look due to weight lifting or long-distance running, a strenuous exercise program might result in legs that are aching, throbbing, or restless after the exercise period stops, cautions D. Brian McDonagh, Vein Clinics of America, Schaumburg, Ill. Based on treatment of patients, he believes certain types of exercise exacerbate varicose veins.*
>
> *[...]Through the use of duplex ultrasound to study the diseased vein, physicians have observed that, when individuals with varicose*

in time, will worsen the condition of the varicose veins."[...]

I did some heavy lifting this last week and my calves started cramping up around halfway through the workout. I'll just wear compression stockings and see how that works.

Brandon: Can you clarify what you mean by this? If venous blood were under no pressure, it wouldn't go anywhere.

Mark Rippetoe: Yes Brandon, I'd be happy to. Venous blood is under no systolic/diastolic pressure, since it's already been through the capillaries. The pressure it's under is balanced between that provided by muscular contraction as it compresses the veins and the force of gravity. It is at maximum in the feet and lower legs and drops with proximity to the heart. And I assume the good doctor means that after the set starts your venous flow becomes retrograde from the right atrium back down the venous bed. I'd *love* to see this study.

Zarsky: I personally have noticed a reduction in the severity of varicose veins. Mine weren't very noticeable but had started right on cue at 40. I hardly see them now after just 2-3 months of lifting (and ending the long slow distance running ;)

Brandon: Okay. Not to overstep my pay grade (lowly EMT here), but in my understanding: Cardiac output is very much a factor in venous pressure insofar as the heart has to pump to "drain" the venous system; think of it as a potential bottleneck in the system. So it would make sense that under Valsalva, where intrathoracic pressure increases, and cardiac stroke output commensurately decreases (heart can't expand as much), less venous blood would be pumped and more would "back up" in the queue. The aforementioned pressure would also decrease compliance of the vascular system and make "less room." Either way (more blood on one hand, less compliance on the other) you have a higher venous pressure and in someone with varicose veins that's not what they want. Your mileage may vary, I'm not a cardiologist, etc. etc. But it does make some sense.

Mark Rippetoe: But this pressure change is balanced by the pressure head produced by the contracting muscles, and because the blood flow through the tissues drops significantly as a result of the central and peripheral effects you describe. And how long would a set have to be before pressure from this cardiac effect backed up enough to affect varicose veins in the leg?

I'd prefer that we worried more about the effects of not training than training.

TPrewittMD: Cardiac output, per se, is not exactly an issue with varicose veins and venous stasis disease. These problems are due to either obstruction of the veins in the legs due to a prior deep vein thrombosis, or more commonly, incompetent valves in the veins. This causes pooling of venous blood in the legs. Legs swell in patients with congestive heart failure, a state where one has lowered cardiac ejection fraction and therefore lower cardiac output. But this swelling is fluid in the soft tissues of the feet, ankles, and lower legs, not venous stasis disease.

Anything that increases intrathoracic or intra-abdominal pressure will decrease venous return to the heart, i.e. a valsalva maneuver. But that is a transient phenomenon and does not create venous stasis problems. There are reasonable surgical treatments for varicose veins, and graded compression hose fitted by an experienced provider are often helpful for venous stasis problems.

But I'm with Rip. Simply telling a patient to not lift weights seems pretty ridiculous to me. A few moments a week of increased decreased venous return related to heavy lifting is easily trumped by good ole constant gravity. And Rip, I would be shocked to see if anyone has done anything approaching a scientific review of venous stasis disease and lifting.

This is a fact: we tell patients to do all kinds of things that we can't prove.

Mark Rippetoe: You're a good man, Dr. Prewitt.

Venezuelan Strongman Hugo Chavez Squats 1353 lbs. Raw

If this isn't a headline yet, it ought to be. One of these assholes should conform to OUR definition, don't you think? After all, what's 615 kg. to a godlike figure like Hugo?

Work, squat depth

Colnago: Hallo mr Rippetoe Excuse my english I am from Holland. I have manual labour 5-6 days a week 8 hours a day, I am a gardener,.which means that there are days that I stand bend over and digging in the earth for hours. Or pulling heavy (for me) plants out of the earth and dragging them around for 20 meters all day long; just 2 examples. I am 35 years old.

I have followed your novice routine (fun!) for 5 months now and I am still adding weight altough it is only 1 kg at a time ; 85 kg 5 rep squat. 72 kg bodyweight. So so far so good but before problems might occur:
Questions: Will my labour stand in my way of development (injuries)? Wont I grow/get very much stronger because I wont rest enough? Do you have any recommendations, reassurance for my situation?
Breaking parallel in the squat: Is half an inch enough? (page 8 in the new book landmarks a and b)
Thank you for writing such a detailed book and answer most of our questions.

Mark Rippetoe: Your English is as good as that of anyone from North Texas. If you have had your job for longer than a few weeks, you are already adapted to it and it merely serves as background activity, provided you are eating and sleeping enough. Breaking parallel in the squat just means that your hip joint dropped below the top of your kneecap. Deeper is fine as long as proper lumbar extension is maintained, but depth at the expense of form is not useful.

Assistance Exercises

Duck: G'day Mark. I'm currently in a 4-week strength phase (just finished the 2nd week) to improve my, funnily enough, strength and better my CrossFit WOD performance. I'm using something along the lines of the Texas Method from Practical Programming as follows:

(Various sets, reps, percentages, exercises, etc. listed…)

My stats are 31 yrs, 6 foot (183cms) and 187lbs (85kgs)
Current PR's as of this morning
Back Squat - 145kgs (319lbs)
Bench - 100kgs (220lbs)

Deadlift - 150kgs (330lbs)

My short term goals (for this phase) are 150kg Squat, 170kg Deadlift and 105kg Bench. Ultimately I'm after a 170kg Squat, 130kg Bench and 215kg Deadlift.

After that long winded intro, my question is this: what value are assistance exercises such as Pull-throughs, GHR's, Reverse Hypers, Weighted Dips etc, in improving my strength on the big 3 and overall? Should they be included somewhere, maybe in another phase or should I just keep it simple and squat, bench and deadlift more?

Mark Rippetoe: I think that under your specific circumstances the best assistance exercise for you is drinking milk. Bodyweight will help you toward your goals better than anything else right now, and the core program looks very good to me. The assistance exercises you mention are good, but with your stats weight gain will help more than anything, and adding workload if the intensity of the base program is good enough might keep the weight gain from occurring.

Duck: Ok. I haven't been actively trying to increase bodyweight but was thinking of trying to get up to 90kgs (200lbs). I have been up there before but it took eating a truckload and drinking heaps of milk and protein shakes. Then I stopped eating and drinking so much and dropped down to my present weight which seems to fluctuate between 85 and 87kgs. I'm also a 3rd generation Aussie and we tend to be naturally wiry and lean. Built for speed, not comfort!! Being a law enforcement officer, it is always handy to be a little bigger just for sheer presence in situations! What weight do you think I should be aiming for? Or should I not worry about that and just eat/drink/lift/shit/sleep, rinse and repeat.

Mark Rippetoe: Just get bigger, and don't worry about how much. And your theory about Australia making people small is very interesting. Texas doesn't seem to have that effect.

High Bar Position for Squats

Amu: I was wondering how less beneficial it would be to have the bar on your traps (right below the neck) for squats as compared to a lower bar position? I feel I'm more comfortable with a high bar position. However, if it NEEDS to be changed for the benefit of my body, I'll go ahead and lower the bar position.

Mark Rippetoe: There is an extensive discussion of this in BBT (pp 221-227). A low bar position dramatically increases hip drive and hamstring involvement in the movement, and allows a greater weight to be used and adapted to. This is why we treat the high bar variant as an assistance exercise, except in those who are limited by shoulder flexibility or injury problems which prevent a low bar squat from being used as their primary strength building exercise.

Markus: Mark, what are you referring to as a low bar and high bar position? I tend to use what I think is high because that is the spot in which the bar feels weightless.

Mark Rippetoe: The high-bar position is at the top of the traps, and the low bar position is just under the spine of the scapulas at the base of the traps, on top of the posterior delts in contraction with the elbows up. If the bar feels weightless on top of your traps, check to be sure you have added weights to the bar.

Amu: Thanks for the feedback. I have SS but I'm still having trouble finding out where the bar is supposed to be on the back. Page 33 of SS 2nd Edition: The picture on the right is similar to my own bar position, so I'm a bit confused as to the position.

Mark Rippetoe: The picture on the right is the correct position, so I don't understand your confusion. It goes right below the bone on your shoulder, at the base of the traps, on top of the posterior delt when contracted with the elbows up.

Amu: I guess there is no way to know the exact position without face-to-face instruction. I'll try sliding the bar down 2 inches from my traps and see how that feels.

Mark Rippetoe: I think the position I described is fairly exact. Pray tell how I could be more precise.

Amu: You can't be more precise. It's my fault that I hate learning lifts via the internet.

Mark Rippetoe: That's one reason I do these seminars. Save up and come to one.

Khoan: When will you give a seminar in Sydney/Australia? :D

Mark Rippetoe: When the planet shrinks a little so that the plane ride is more affordable.

"Two workouts on one or more days per week"

FROGGBUSTER: I was re-reading PP and came upon this little gem that you wrote:
Quote:

> Dr. Keijo Hakkinen *(a Finnish guy)* has shown that strength gains may be more efficiently produced by dividing up a day's training volume into two workouts instead of one.

I'm thinking of doing this in the summer (nothing to do except lift, eat, and sleep).

When you say dividing the training volume into 2+ workouts, do you mean for example squatting in the morning and benching/other exercises later in the day? Or do you mean for example (Texas Method volume days): **Morning**: Squats 3x5, Bench 2x5; **Afternoon/night**: Squats 2x5, Bench 3x5

Perhaps you could even provide your own template on how this type of training would lay out to look like (for an intermediate-level trainee)?

Mark Rippetoe: I think he was referring to splitting the work into two workouts, not doing the work twice. But if you can get recovered, and it sounds like you can since you are apparently not productively employed, try it the first way for a while and then gradually add some duplication in to see what happens.

Butter: Interesting, Mark, is the first way you mentioned to try the example with squatting in the morning and benching/other exercises later in the day?

Mark Rippetoe: I was referring to splitting the exercises, but both ways are viable. The Bulgarians often repeated exercises several times/day and got what you would have to call good results. They were, of course, cheating in important ways, and had the benefit of genetic freaks as athletes, but it will be good for you to see how Bulgarian you are.

Why people don't do cleans

Jamie J: There have been a few people over on (another) board saying they aren't going to clean until they find a coach, they don't want to hurt themselves, it's too hard to learn and so forth. They said that you had said that it's too hard to learn to power clean on your own and that you should sub something instead. I wanted to bring this to your attention since it seems somebody has misquoted or misinterpreted you. You probably have heard of this, but it really pissed me off, just one more excuse to something difficult yet highly effective.

I mean, why don't people just do the clean? Shit, people learn how to do planches and front levers from books, why not the clean? As much as I value the input of coach, just do it. It won't be perfect, and a coach would make it better. But you aren't going to die, break anything, or get so screwed up you won't heal. And if you do, good riddance you uncoordinated, illiterate bastard, and hopefully you haven't reproduced yet.

Mark Rippetoe: If I didn't think you could learn how to clean without a coach, why would I have put the goddamn things in a book the sole purpose of which is to teach you how to do the lifts without a coach?

Dan F: Touché! I was one of those thinking not to do PC without a good coach present: I changed my mind now that I tested myself doing them and understood that, yes, are more difficult than bench but no more difficult to learn than many things we learn without professional coaches present! Plus we have The Book in which they are deeply described: from written page to real practice is not a joke but with some "trial and error" and patience I think every one could do a not so bad PC. (Plus: like every explosive movement they are fun!)

My experience says that is better in this way than with a pseudo-professional coach with no real knowledge of these kind of exercises. If in USA good coaches in barbell lifting are not so many, in Italy they rare like white elephants... Yes, you have invaded us not only with Hollywood films but also with a bunch of shining gym machines!

Mark Rippetoe: I apologize for the machines, Dan, from the Americans to the entire Italian race.

Dan F: Accepted. I apologize too for the not so good wine we sometimes sell you at not so low prices...

Speaking of machines: about 2 years ago I visited the gym where make their muscular training athletes of a professional soccer team. The team ranks usually in the first 10 in Italy, where soccer is first religion - catholic church the second, so nothing is amateurish in their training I thought: but I don't remember one Olympic barbell or plate there, only enormous "stations" of machines. From photos I've seen it seems this is the same for the majority of other professional teams. Could this be in relation with the high frequency of muscular injuries of these athletes?

I don't talk of injuries from violent contacts but of hamstrings rips and ligaments and tendons problems at knee level that very often happen when the player simply sprints or kicks alone: all them are the most common injuries.

Mark Rippetoe: Dan makes a damn good point about the state of the art in strength training for sports, especially European sports and especially "football". Soccer has the highest injury rate of any sport in the world, by far, and the bulk of these injuries are ACLs that do not result from impact trauma. Think about what the ACL does in the knee – it prevents the forward translation of the tibia relative to the femur, among other things. You think maybe the fact that they don't squat or deadlift has a bearing on this matter?

Which brings up another point: why don't they know this? Why don't professional level S&C coaches, whom they obviously employ, know these things? Why don't D1 and professional S&C coaches in this country know any more than they often do (with certain quite notable exceptions)? Could it be that a guy whose only experience is working with the genetic freaks that D1 recruiters and the professional sports system place before him – most of these guys come out of college programs and go straight into college-level S&C – might well be of the opinion that his HIT program on Hammer Strength machines actually improves athletic performance? Quite possibly, because in a situation where all you train is guys who are strong *already*, you may very well be unaware of the process by which they got that way. And you may be unaware of the fact that for some of them that process is still in its early stages. You may also be unaware of the fact that some of them can get one helluva lot stronger with a program more suitable to their particular level of training advancement – yes, a certain percentage of the ultrafreaky will actually be novices or early intermediates, depending on the program from which they were recruited, athletes who could get even better were they trained in a manner appropriate to their level of training advancement. And you may have lost sight of the fact that squats, presses, deadlifts, and cleans are always your most useful tools for developing strength, since your HIT/Hammer Strength program *seems* to be working so well. If all you work with are elite athletes, you may either be really good at working with elite athletes, or be being carried along by the already considerable strength of the athletes in your program, and have a lot left to learn.

Wide legs while doing press...

Shaodw: I'm 6"4 and the power rack at my gym is too short for me to stand how the book describes without hitting the bar on the top of the rack before locking out. There is also no room outside the rack to even power clean and then press (I've tried once in a walkway where there was some room but people were getting pissed because it's near the water tap). So as of now I spread my legs to the width of the rack, lock my knees out and press with just enough room to not hit the top of the rack. I was wondering if this is ok, or by doing this am I losing core strength from lower back / abs keeping steady because my feet literally touch the side of the rack to get enough room.

My membership in the gym doesn't run out for another 6 months so after that I'll be definitely finding one with a bigger rack / lifting platform so I don't need a rack.

Mark Rippetoe: It is indeed unfortunate when equipment limitations interfere with optimal training. But the exercises do not change form based on the equipment; rather, it is always the equipment that must facilitate the movement. You'll have to get a better gym, and the sooner the better.

tscw1: Brisbane has quite a few gyms, but they are all what you would describe as health spas. Is there such a thing as the ideal gym?

Mark Rippetoe: Wichita Falls Athletic Club.

Shaodw: I'm still awaiting your reply to visit Australia haha.

Mark Rippetoe: Please describe the flavor of wombat meat, and kangaroo while you're at it. My curiosity about this may be the deciding factor.

Trip to Kansas

Fluxboy: You are in Wichita, yes? Hmm ... according to Google maps, you are exactly 2571 kms away from me. Not an insurmountable distance in this day and age. Might be a good adventure. I've never been to Kansas. Are the girls pretty? I'll give your book a few more readings and see if I can sort this out. If not, I may wander on over. Come to think of it, I believe there may be an Apache somewhere in Kansas that I wanted to learn some knife fighting from. Might make for a good weekend.

Mark Rippetoe: Well, I am in Texas, in Wichita Falls. If you go to Kansas, the girls look like they are from Kansas, not Texas. And the Apaches are all in New Mexico now since we sorted them out a while back.

Mark: I was born in Wichita Falls. The year I was born there was a F3 tornado, and the year I left there was a F5. Coincidence? Yeah, probably.

Mark Rippetoe: Funny thing, we haven't had a tornado in Wichita County since then. Coincidence? I think not.

Sciatica - GONE!

Scbowley: I started squatting and deadlifting a few months ago with CrossFit. I then came across your Starting Strength program. I've only just started, and started light, but really like the program and now love lifting. The BIG side effect, though, is that my sciatica has gone! Physios, doctors etc... couldn't do anything, and actually made it worse sometimes. Squats and deadlifts have fixed it.

PS: Coming to the UK soon?!

Mark Rippetoe: We hear this all the time, often enough that I'm surprised that the British National Health Service has not begun sending me money. Glad we could help anyway.

Gaining too much fat

Blah3: I'm not sure if this is supposed to happen because I know that you are meant to be gaining weight but I feel that I am not gaining any muscle. I just feel that I'm just gaining fat, I constantly feel flabby and soft. Is this normal? What could be causing this problem?

Mark Rippetoe: It may be that you are actually flabby and soft. Are your lifts going up?

Blah3: I'm 6'7 about 285lbs. I never really felt like this until I started SS. (I did bodybuilding routines for a while till I realized I needed some solid strength.) I know it sounds really stupid asking the question about gaining too much fat but I thought I would see if there was anything wrong. My lifts were going up but I have stalled at 105kg squats, which I think for my weight + height I shouldn't be stalling this early. This true? Nothing else is stalling.

Mark Rippetoe: If there is sufficient training stress to cause an adaptation, this most usually prevents getting fat. Not every time for every body. I suspect you're one of these guys that are not doing the program out of the book.

Blah3: I haven't been able to get the book; its really expensive to get over here in Australia but did manage to get the first edition off a friend so I have just been going off that and what I have seen on the internet.

Mark Rippetoe: The book is not any more expensive in Australia than it is here except for the shipping, which is what you get for living in Australia.

Deadlift, Rack Pull, Halting - How often?

Jason L: From what I understand, rack pull and halting are not accessory work you do in addition to the deadlift. Rather, they are meant to take the place of the deadlift. Is that right? If so, do I just stop deadlifting altogether for awhile or would you recommend keeping it in the rotation (something like: power clean - rack pull - power clean - halting - power clean - deadlift)?

P.S. I signed up for your barbell cert in December. What's Wichita Falls like? I lived in Dallas for twenty years and have never been up there. The only thing I know about the place is from a clip from King of the Hill …Go Sooners?

Mark Rippetoe: Rack pulls and haltings replace the deadlift. Don't do them all at the same time or you'll break something.

Wichita Falls is not the most exciting place on Earth. But we'll have a good time anyway. And we regard *King Of The Hill* as a documentary.

Fractured hand, no lifting for 6 wks

Jimike: I was on the SS novice programme and a gym veteran, as is often the way of things it seems. Was loving all the squatting especially but then disaster struck. I fractured a bone in my hand (the so called "boxers fracture" beneath my ring finger) and was told by the lady in A&E that I would be unable to do any barbell training or putting much pressure on it for at least 6 weeks. This has obviously thrown a spanner in the works. I get out of my plaster cast in 14 days if all goes to plan and I'm reluctant to stop strength training but now my options are somewhat limited in regards to following your programme. I feel I may have to dust off my dress and start using the instruments of Satan, otherwise known as resistance machines again – leg press, pec flyes along with high volume air squats and so on – that I can do without involving my hand. Do you give me your blessing for such an unavoidable use of machines?

Mark Rippetoe: Precisely where is the fracture, and how did you do it?

Jimike: It was below the first knuckle of the ring finger. Sadly I got it in a bar fight 2 days ago when some drunk aggressive random idiot of the highest order managed to drag his friend into a fight with my friend after this idiot half-nutted my friend and threatened him with a empty beer glass in a bar. Which then caused me to get involved to even the numbers up. Caused a fairly big scene. There was probably a few bruises and black eyes but I think I was the only one that needed to go to the hospital after hitting his forehead or some other solid mass a couple of times with my fist. My first fight I've been in since I was 14 just about. I'm 27 now. I really couldn't have avoided it.

AidenBloodaxe: Fourth metacarpal fracture? You could use the very heel of your palm to support the bar when squatting

Mark Rippetoe: That's it: we'll let the Scots teach the English how to fight, and the English can teach the Scots how to train. History repeats. *(Aiden is English.)* But don't hit people with your hands anymore. At least not that way.

Jimike: Yes, It is the fourth metacarpal fracture, having just googled it. I don't know how I would really do that safely with my palm to be honest. I'm sure at some point I'd get a bit of a wobble in the bar mid-lift or something then revert to my original grip or a more secure one. And Rip, you are indeed right no more punching. If I had employed my hometown's Glasgow Kiss I would likely have injured nothing, it wouldn't have been the same for the other guy though.

You also forgot to say that we also teach the English manners, as you American's did yourselves back in the day ;) Sorry Aiden, I couldn't resist a wee dig. I'm sure you'll retaliate by calling us all miserable drunkards. Which is quite unfair as we're all fairly cheerful mostly.

Mark Rippetoe: I'll bet you can figure out a way to back squat with some tape and a grip adjustment, maybe going very wide with the bad hand. The English (actually, their silly government) can't be taught manners. They have fucked up everything they have touched for the past 1000 years. But, the people on both sides of the wall are very cool. I enjoy my time there immensely. We'll need a description of the Glaswegian Kiss.

Jimike: The Glasgow Kiss is an affectionate greeting people in Glasgow have for meeting strangers. Or so it seems sometimes. (it's also a head butt) I'm glad to hear you enjoyed yourself Rip. Did you need to hire a translator for your trip?

Mark Rippetoe: No need for a translator. I have more trouble with Yorkshiremen than I do you Glasgow boys

---

Maintaining my strength on a very tight schedule.

Enzian: I'm about to start working 13-hour shifts for an indefinite period. That does not leave enough time to keep training but I do not intend to become weak ever again. I can get in one full workout every week on my day off but that's it. So fitting something into my long work days is very important.

Here are my resources:
At home: The only equipment is a variety of dumbbells going up to 20lbs.
Gym: I got a power rack that hardly anyone else ever uses, an assisted pullup/dip station, back extension benches, and concept2 rowing machines.
Time: I have 30-35 minutes free every day at best. A round trip to the gym eats about 10 minutes of that total, so I do not have enough time to warm up properly and do 3 sets across for any major lift. I could probably do one work set, or maybe just warm up and go home.

My current plan isn't very creative. Warmup lifts 4 days a week to practice form and keep from de-training, 1 day on the rowing machine at high intensity for glycolytic metabolism, and one day of rest after my heavy lift day. Does that sound effective? Would swapping in some assistance exercises work better? Anything else I haven't thought of would be helpful.

Mark Rippetoe: I really hate to be this way, but the fact that your schedule is going to prevent you from doing the program just plain old-fashioned means that your schedule is going to prevent you from making the progress that the program provides. You may be able to maintain on your abbreviated schedule of one heavy workout and the rest warmup and C2, but until this changes I'm afraid you'll have to settle for suboptimal results. There will no doubt be good advice offered by others here, and I hope I prove to be wrong.

Franktae: I suspect you might be a medical resident. If you are not, there is absolutely no reason for having 13 hour shifts. I highly recommend reading Timothy Ferris' book "The four hour workweek." If you are planning on doing 13 hour shifts for tons of money, the book definitely gives advice on how to automatize things, eliminate unnecessary work and even on how to deal with your boss so he does not only approve but give you a raise for working less. It also has funny examples on how to even outsource parts your personal life to a Virtual Assistant. That way, you will find SOME way to actually work around your schedule and make way for progression on training.

Mark Rippetoe: Frank, you're a decent poster here, but you are just too damned European. You people suffer from a high unemployment rate because you apparently want it that way. Any self-employed person in the US works 12-hour days ALL THE TIME, because we have to and because we want to. You don't know this because far fewer people in the EU are self-employed; this is because your government has fixed things up so that they can't be. I guarantee you that this asshat Ferris works more than the title suggests, that you do too, and that he is full of shit (you, I don't know about). Things are about to get shitty everywhere, and they are not going to get un-shitty if everybody thinks that less work is okay.

Shouldn't I be sore?

Bluecheese: Shouldn't I be sore? I am starting my second week of SS, and have followed the recommendations for increasing weights for every workout. I have PR'ed on the deadlift. I figured I would be experiencing some sort of DOMS. But, all I really have now is a little soreness in my glutes and lower back, and a little twinge in my shoulders. Will I begin to get more sore when my lifts get heavier? It's not that I'm looking forward to crippling soreness. I'm just concerned that I may be doing something wrong.

Mark Rippetoe: Soreness is never a reliable indicator of anything other than that you have just changed something in your training, and even that not always. You have started light enough that you didn't get sore in the context of your present conditioning level, and since your increases will be slow and uniform you may not get sore for quite some time. That's why the numbers are your indicator of progress, not the perceived effects of each workout. Bodybuilder-think is pump/soreness = progress; strength training-think is force production increase = progress.

Bluecheese: Thanks for the reply Coach. I should have known that that my lifts going up should have been the indicator of progress. I was really expecting the crippling DOMS I get from CF. So I figured I'd shore up some strength deficiencies with the SS program. I have not been disappointed. I'm hoping that eventually a barbell cert will happen somewhere relatively close to New Orleans.

Mark Rippetoe: You should have come to Spring, TX in November. It may be awhile before we get back.

Bluecheese: Bah! Driving through Houston! I drove through Houston one time on the way to San Antonio. The interstate there was a labyrinth, and I half expected that some locals might toss bombs at my truck. They love to attack vehicles, which are a symbol of progress, I guess.

Mark Rippetoe: Houston is not my favorite place either. But then again, a guy from New Orleans has got very damned little room to bitch about Houston.

Bluecheese: Touché

Taking Matters into Your Own Hands

Several years ago when I was leaving my girlfriend's apartment on Christmas Eve, after enjoying a nice evening of fellowship and cheer, I noticed that my car was gone from the place I had parked it. Turned out that the apartment manager had called the tow truck about 10:30pm to have it moved. It was not parked in a marked space, it was not blocking any other car (as confirmed by the later-helpful tow truck driver); it had been towed because the manager thought it was too close to a no-parking space.

I was pissed. I tried to do the right thing, so I went through the courts, sued them, won, obtained a judgement, and had it served. And the bastards had by that time declared bankruptcy, although they continued to operate the apartments. So I arranged for a gallon of oil-based aluminum paint to find its way into their pool. It was chickenshit, but it made us even.

How to make a hardcore gym commercially viable?

Johnkuc: I just wanted to know how you made WFAC commercially viable while still keeping it hardcore and basic. Nowadays most commercial gyms seem to be health spas not real gyms. How did you appeal to the average person and how did you retain them without selling out and turning into a front for muscle & fitness?

Mark Rippetoe: The viability of a black iron gym like WFAC depends on the size of the market. A bigger city with enough people can support an actual gym like this one if it's marketed correctly. If they know you're there and they know that you're serious, with usable equipment and a good coaching eye, they will find you. I hate to say this, but WFAC is not viable in this 100K market. Since we moved in 2001, the amount of commercial gym space in this town has doubled, leaving us in a situation where the only members we have now are serious trainees, and there are not enough people like this here to keep the bills paid. The average person has no interest in work this hard; they'd much rather walk on the treadmill and watch TV, and I have never figured out how to turn an average person with average expectations and an average level of commitment into an athlete. I'm not sure that any black iron gym has ever made what you would call Real Money. In fact, the gym business as a whole – big box and small local – is not a particularly profitable business. That's why corporations have entered the market, so that relatively small margins can be aggregated into what are cumulatively viable earnings.

I have hung on this long because I am very good at not spending money, which comes in handy if you're not very good at making it. I know how to keep my overhead down, and book sales have helped. If you want to try it, my advice is to start very small, and build your business as you grow your membership. Don't try to do it the other way, because that's how used commercial equipment dealers – the guys you'll be buying stuff from – stay in business.

Online Training: Good or Bad?

PMDL: Just for curiosity's sake and as part of an on-going informal survey of mine, if you were given the opportunity to train/coach people across the internet, would you do so? Why or why not? There's an abundance of people that seem to think this is an effective way to do things; I mostly thinks it's garbage and a way to con people out of money, but I'm interested in your thoughts.

Mark Rippetoe: I have been invited to do it by folks you would know, and have declined. I don't see how anyone can effectively coach someone without standing there, watching, giving feedback to what is seen each rep, making decisions about sets and reps based on the previous sets, correcting errors as they occur, asking direct questions and getting answers, changing things up as necessary, making suggestions about the next workout – you know, *coaching*. I know that good money is made this way, but I don't want any of it.

Vicjg: With that said. If someone was to travel to you, and want to spend a week being coached, is that something you do or would consider doing? I was always curious about that, I even went so far as to look at tourist info in the Wichita Falls area to convince my wife and kids that it would be the perfect vacation spot.

Mark Rippetoe: I would consider doing it that way, or you could attend one of our seminars in what would be a more scenic location. If you can convince your wife that the Falls is a tourist destination and then continue to stay married to her afterward, you should consider a career as an elected official, because you'd have what it takes.

Sentinel: But if u claimed to only be a program designer (glorified) is it still unethical?

Mark Rippetoe: If you claimed to be a program designer only, then you have fully disclosed the nature of your services, and the buyer can better decide what to do with his money than anyone else. After all, if you're not free to waste money, you're not truly free.

But it is unethical to abbreviate "you".

General coaching and technical lifts question - best way/place to learn?

Peter_k: If someone wants to learn a technical lift like the power clean but finds it difficult to do so using only the book, or just wants a decent coach to look over the form and correct it immediately, what's the best way to find such a trainer? Is there a straightforward way to find coaches that will train someone in the fast lifts, for more or less recreational purposes (as in, to novices or intermediates not affiliated with a sport of any kind)?

I might not be looking hard enough, but it seems that since 90% of the fitness market is Nautilus commercial gyms, people that teach the basic weightlifting that's been done for years are pushed out of sight. I've been a member at several gyms over my lifetime, and have never seen a trainer teach someone to do a regular deadlift, let alone a clean. I've also never seen bumper plates or an OL platform at any gym in my life; and I think I'm not alone here.

I live in a city of about 2 million and even then I'm not sure where to start looking. Do you have any general tips for people living in American/Canadian cities to find coaches? Mark, you do a better job than 99% of the coaches in this world, IMO, but it's crazy how much of a rarity you are... I think we're emerging from the fitness dark ages now.

Mark Rippetoe: As usual I appreciate the kind words. You have articulated the basic problem with the fitness industry, the problem created by Arthur Jones in the 1970s, the one that enabled the industry to grow so much in the ensuing years.

Here's the deal: the fitness industry doesn't want you to train the lifts. They don't want you to deadlift, clean, snatch or do anything else noisy or hard. They don't want you to train AT ALL. They want you to sign up, pay, and go away. If you must come in, please just do some curls and ride the treadmills, and *then* go away. This represents the best use of their time and money to make money off of you.

Finding a coach is tough, but get online and ask about good people in your city. Somebody will know.

Infiltration of Physical Therapy into S&C

KSC: Mark or anyone else who cares:

Wondering what your opinion was, or if you had an explanation for the rise of physical therapists and physical therapy driven training modalities within the S&C world, and particularly within organizations such as NSCA & NASM. I've always known that NASM was founded by PT's but I am increasingly aware of the presence of physical therapy in NSCA material, which disturbs me since this is who I am certified through. I'm seeing terms like "scapular stabilization", "glute activation", "core strength" being tossed around quite a bit, along with a tendency to go outside of our scope of practice away from S&C and into PT. Is this just a new trend to sell a bunch of inflatable crap to personal trainers?

Mark if you have any opinions/explanations/comments/thoughts about this trend and how and why it came about, I would love to hear them. Thanks

Mark Rippetoe: Nice observation, one made repeatedly within the serious S&C community over the past few years. It is why the college and pro strength coaches formed their own organization several years ago, and why I and several other strength coaches whose names you'd know dropped our memberships in the NSCA. At this point, I am about ready to drop my CSCS credential -- one I have held since I was certified with the first group to take the test in 1985, and which makes me one of only 37 people with the potential to have been certified this long -- because I don't see it as particularly applicable to my profession at this point.

I am not that familiar with the NASM, except that they are famous for "assessing the kinetic chain" instead of teaching people how to do the exercises correctly, but I have never seen any of their material other than that. The NSCA publishes the most embarrassing "peer-reviewed journals" I have ever seen. The PTs have in fact taken over, and it has been a very long time since the NSCA was concerned with making anybody strong or conditioned. For example, they have entered into an agreement with Gold's Gym to provide discount rates to Gold's Gym employees who wish to become certified, and that sounds to me just like it sounds to you.

At this point in the history of the strength and conditioning profession there exists a market for a legitimate certification. I hope someone steps forward to fill it soon.

NSCA Cert Question

Robert: I recently finished my undergraduate career and am currently taking the steps required to apply to medical school but will have at least a year off before I start. I was an athlete in college and have been CrossFitting for about a year now and have decided to do personal training while I deal with applications. I have been looking into becoming NSCA certified so I can have some credentials for being in the training business. I recently took the NSCA practice test and had a few questions I thought you could help me with since you have been very involved with them.

There were two questions I missed that I was confused about. One was concerning breathing during a heavy lift. In Starting Strength you recommend the Valsalva maneuver which says to hold the breath through the sticking point, but the NSCA test said you should exhale through the sticking point. The second was concerning 1RM testing, essentially it asked what was an unsafe exercise for 1RM testing and the correct answer was shoulder press. How is an intermediate/elite athlete supposed to make a workout without knowing his 1RM?

Is the NSCA wrong? And should I just answer them wrong to get it right on the test? Or is something else going on?

Mark Rippetoe: The NSCA is wrong about these two questions, and about enough other shit that I am no longer a member and will either be dropping my credential or just letting it expire, depending on my mood between now and the end of the year. Their journals are an embarrassing mess, they are run by physical therapists, and they don't think you should press heavy or squat below parallel. Many years ago they were a very reputable organization, but at this point I cannot recommend that you associate with them. I see little going on there that distinguishes them from AFAA, IDEA, ACE, or any of the other certifying bodies.

(I formally relinquished my CSCS credential on July 27, 2008.)

USA Weightlifting

Wecoyote: From older posts, I know your opinion about the NCSA. What is your opinion about USA Weightlifting and their coach certifications, specifically the USAW Sports Performance Coach's certification?

Mark Rippetoe: I think the SPC course is a waste of time and money. It lacks detail, is overly broad, and is full of irrelevant doodoo. That's why Lon and I quit teaching it. The Club Coach course is much better.

Canada

Hiravaxis: Your books don't seem to have good distribution in Canada. I was unable to purchase them via the websites chapters.ca or amazon.ca. Do you intend to distribute them to Canada?

Mark Rippetoe: We sell to Canada every day, but only to people who order from us at our website.

Hiravaxis: I think you'd sell more books if they were available in Canadian stores and Canadian websites. This would be a very good thing to me. In terms of getting better information out to more people. I admit I know nothing of book publishing or distribution or anything like that or even if you could make any money doing it. I do know it was an impediment to me getting my copy of SS:BBT.

Mark Rippetoe: But nobody lives in Canada. It's a frozen wasteland with an inefficient postal system, probably suffering from a shortage of sled dogs. And we're not in bookstores anywhere. Not even in Texas.

Irishman301: Yeah, tell me about it. I went out to 3 different stores trying to find Practical Programming. After sorting through hundreds of books on how to get ripped fast and how to get huge biceps, I realized that the bookstores don't sell your books. I had to order online, then wait a week for it to come. Bookstores suck.

Mark Rippetoe: Let me tell you about the book business. We are on Amazon because of a program they have called Amazon Advantage, which enables small publishers to sell directly to Amazon. The retail book business is obviously dominated by the companies you cite: B&N, Borders, and their subsidiaries, and these companies will not enter into a wholesale relationship with any publishing company that represents fewer than about ten titles, like us. Small publishers typically go through an aggregate wholesaler. We will not deal with these rapists, and therefore we are not in stores, and will not be for quite some time.

But I believe that we may be the highest rated independent title on Amazon, with BBT having reached 613 at one point in early January. We are frequently ahead of Arnold's book, usually ahead of NROL, and all of the Human Kinetics titles except Delavier's anatomy book, even considering the fact that we are twice as much money. And for that, I thank you guys. The success of SS is completely and totally a function of the internet, which means that every copy we have sold has been the result of a purchaser specifically looking for it and deciding that it was valuable enough to wait for. I am indebted to you.

(Since this was written, BBT has been as high as 138 on Amazon's total sales ranking, pretty good for an independently published barbell book.)

Gym Etiquette?

Keenan: When is it appropriate to intervene when individuals are giving out poor training advice? (If ever?) Case in point: Individuals at my YMCA are teaching squats to 14-15 year old boys only on the smith machine because "they are easier and you can add more weight" was the exact quote I heard. Another was "You do not need to go below parallel to perform a good squat." It makes me cringe to watch these kids be taught unbelievably poor habits. I grew up with the same problem and had to unlearn everything at age 22, which was a humbling experience. Any opinion would be appreciated.

Mark Rippetoe: Neither you nor I nor any other member of this forum is going to solve the problems of the world. YMCAs are famous for harboring fools on the staff. That is the Y's problem, and it is up to them to solve it. Even though you know better, it is not your job to teach anyone anything you have not been asked to teach them, any more than it is my job to teach Hillary Rodham Antichrist about economics until she hires me to do it. Walking up to the staff of a gym and inserting yourself into their business is absolutely wrong, despite the fact that they are fucking up. The client or member has entered a voluntary business relationship with the club and their staff, of which you are not a part. It is up to that member to decide who to hire for advice, and when you get hired you can give it.

Now, *you* have also entered into a voluntary business relationship with the YMCA, and maybe it's time to do something about that, because *your* relationship with the Y is very much your business. If you don't like the way their instruction is being conducted, with good reason, you should say something to the person in charge. If you are sufficiently dissatisfied with the response, then end your membership and find an actual gym. But interfering in staff instruction activities – no matter how stupid, wrong, unprofessional, idiotic, unscientific, ineffective, ugly, and dangerous you think they are – is not only bad gym etiquette, it's likely to get you in trouble. It would here. Because you might be wrong.

Tiburon: Is it appropriate to intervene if there are unsafe practices going on, and there is no staff in the weight room? For example, there is a group of high school kids who lift at my gym, and they clearly have little understanding of form, and often little regard for safety. I have seen them randomly walk up to heavily weighted bar in the squat rack and pull it out backwards. Or they will not use clips and end up losing weights while doing curls or triceps extensions. As an "older, wiser" guy at the gym, should I say something in these situations?

If the above situations warrant comment, where do I draw the line? Do I say something to a kid using a thumbless grip for a bench press? Do I talk to a kid who has a very rounded back in a deadlift?

Mark Rippetoe: If they are doing unsafe stupid shit, go get the gym owner or management. But no, it is not your place to give free advice in someone else's gym, no matter how badly it needs to be given. You can help if there's a wreck. You can even ask if you could point out something. But you don't walk over and make a correction unbidden.

Hockmasm: As a side note. I have been seeing people use the Smith Machine to do a Squat that has their feet about 2 feet in front of them. They are squatting like their back is against a wall and they are sliding down it. Is that even a real exercise????

Mark Rippetoe: No, it's a real Smith Machine exercise, which is not the same thing we do.

Dave Van S: I have run into this same problem at both of the places I lift. It's a tough one but I try to employ the rules of home ownership:

1.) Clean up your own backyard. Lead by example. Be an absolute technician with your own form. People recognize skill when see it.

2.) Know your neighbors. Get to know the trainers on at least a friendly conversational basis. People are not ignora on purpose (not usually). If you have a relationship with them it's a lot easier to ask them why they teach in a certain way. As a big plus, you may learn from them and they from you. Side benefits ensue: a trainer at my gym lets me keep my kettlebells there.

3.) Buy a fixer in the best neighborhood you can afford. Quit your gym and go lift someplace where people are smarter and stronger than you. It's profoundly unhealthy to be walking around thinking you're the only one who knows shit. Most people don't get better unless pushed. Empty your cup and go someplace where you can learn, not where you feel the need to teach.

Mark Rippetoe: Thanks Dave. Damn good post.

Barbell lug size?

Corey: After dumping my Olympic barbell on the floor many times during my last workout I noticed the bar started sounding "broken". I know nothing about the construction of these bars, but I noticed that the lugs on either end of the bar were very loose. I tightened as best I could without the proper Allen wrench. Do you know the size of the tightening wrench? Should I be taking the bar apart from time to time and greasing or oiling the roller component?

Mark Rippetoe: The Allen key size varies. There is no standard. Furthermore, bars using an Allen bolt sleeve assembly are usually shitty bars. I have the only good one here in my gym I have ever seen. All the others were bent.

Working in a commercial gym

Damien: I remember hearing you talk on the CrossFit radio and you mentioned about dealing with some members in the commercial gym setting. I recently took on a position as gym manager in a gym and we have refurbished the place just last week.

I have undergone a barrage of abuse about the lack of mirrors in front of the squat rack and removing the leg extension machine. Mirrors are easily fixed, buy some although I see it as an unnecessary cost. But do you have any advice for trying to provide a more productive gym environment in a commercial setting and trying to balance the two?

Mark Rippetoe: That depends entirely on the type of gym you're hired to work for. You and I and the rest of the guys on this board realize the value of doing things the way that you have indicated you want to, but if you have been hired to run a standard industry-model facility, this will not work.

We are still years away from a paradigm shift in the public perception of fitness, although several things seem to be hastening this, like the rise of CrossFit, the proliferation of sports-performance facilities like Velocity, and the internet. Until that time, Gold's/Powerhouse/24 Hour/Bally's will continue to be what most people think of when they join a gym. I'm not saying this is right; I'm just saying that this type of shit is what these fools paid for, and it is what you are probably going to be expected to provide.

I just took a bunch of silly equipment out of here, but then again, I'm not a standard industry model club, and I'm less dependent on new members than I used to be. So, what you have done may be fine, but it might not be so fine. If you want to function in a transitional context between commercial gym and black iron gym/functional training-type facility, the best thing to do would be to have all the things you need for both. This way, nobody gets pissed when you take things away; they just get happy when you provide new stuff. Put the leg extension back, and get two squat racks – one with a mirror and one without. Eventually, you may have worked hard enough that the members will ask you to take the mirrors away.

NASM certification enough to have a decent job?

solidsnake123: Is certification for personal training by the National Academy of Sports Medicine enough to have a decent job or is other school past high school required or highly recommended in order to make enough doing personal training to pay the bills?

Mark Rippetoe: The only thing required to make a decent living doing personal training is enough clients to make a decent living.

solidsnake123: Ok, thanks. I was wondering if it was necessary to have any other certification or school beyond high school in order to be able to legally have clients. I guess if you have the certification the answer is no, with the exception of the certifications that are a pre-requisite to the NASM certification.

Mark Rippetoe: As far as I know, there is no state currently regulating the personal training market. But things change, sometimes rapidly.

Good/Bad Trainees

KSC: I'm not sure how much one-on-one training you do or have done in your career (i.e. what one would consider personal training), but of those that you are training or have trained what percentage of them actually get the results they wanted or the results that you had wanted for them when you designed their program?

I was thinking about it today after a conversation with a friend, and probably the vast majority of people I have ever trained did NOT get the results they wanted or that I wanted for them. 99.9% of the time this occurs because trainees/clients consistently cancel appointments, don't follow dietary instruction, skip workouts you assign them to complete individually, etc, etc.

Looking back over my past client files I realized how few of them actually listen to what you tell them, show up to all of their sessions, eat what you tell them, do extra work on their own, etc. I also realized that the ones that do listen to what you tell them have done well so it made me feel a little better about my performance.

What is your experience with this conundrum in your many years in the industry? Any interesting observations or comments?

Mark Rippetoe: I can tell you with certainty that EVERY SINGLE ONE of my clients and members *that did what I told them to do* got good results, to a degree directly corresponding to how closely they followed my program. I have done personal training and coaching of my members for as long as I've been in the business, 30 years now, and I've had people behave along the entire spectrum from hanging on my every word to completely ignoring me while I was standing right there.

The problem most of the time is very simple, and doctors figured this out a long time ago: you have to charge more money than the service is actually worth, more than you're morally comfortable with (if you have any morals), or your clients will not value your information or take your advice seriously. This is why doctors are regarded as authorities on exercise, and everything else. It costs so goddamn much money to see one that you feel cheated if you *don't* believe them. I wish it were not this way, but it is.

Randy T: This is very interesting advice. I am not used to being in a position where I can ask people to pay me a lot of money for my services.

Mark Rippetoe: I understand your point. It's a fine line to walk, especially when starting out. But even when you're new to any business you have to establish some rules for yourself which will govern your professional limits. There will be a price below which training someone would be a waste of time you could be using more productively. As you get better, that price should go up. If you set it unrealistically high, you will be broke, and if you set it too low you will be aggravated all the time.

Regarding power cleans in a typical gym

Kajota: Simple question. Without the access to bumper plates, would it be wise still to just drop the iron O weights on the barbell to the ground in a typical LA Fitness gym from shoulder height? My concerns are not weird looks, but starting this up only to be told on the first day that I cannot drop the weights from that high up for liability reasons or whatever excuse they come up with. Basically my point is, if I get told once I can pretty much kiss my chances of doing it at that same gym goodbye. I have also heard that it is not good to take the bar from shoulder height and, while still gripping it, dropping it down to knee height, and then placing it on the ground, as this produces a lot of stress on the back. Thoughts?

I have considered maybe taking 2 thick towels to place the O weights on and standing on a very small platform so that I'm still equal but have something soft to drop the weights back down on.

Mark Rippetoe: No, you don't get to drop iron weights on the floor in anybody's gym. This tears up things that do not belong to you, and two towels under the plates will work for about 3 reps before it resumes destroying the floor. If you have to clean with iron plates, and we all do at one time or another, you will figure out that you can catch the bar against your thighs while you decelerate the drop with your traps and knees.

Home Training?

Joshua: I live on a small island in the UK and as such only have access to one gym. I signed up yesterday and was given a briefing of all the equipment etc and the trainer said he would write me a program, when I told him I wanted to be doing the novice program outlined in Starting Strength here are some of the things he told me:

It's far too low volume and intensity to build muscle.

I shouldn't be lifting heavy weights because I'm so skinny and it could cause dislocations or tiny fractures in my bones.

Using heavy weights is only optimal for powerlifters.

If I want to gain weight I should eat loads for a few months till I gain about 10lbs of fat then go to the gym and turn it to muscle.

Only experienced trainees can use the racks.

He then went on to give me a program consisting of a circuit doing 15-20 reps on each station, i.e. leg extensions, pec-deck, lat pulldown, curl machine, press machine and dumbbell curls followed by 30 minutes on the treadmill. Now, being completely new to all this should I follow his advice? Or alternatively I could invest in some Olympic weights, a bench, and a power rack and workout at home; would this be safe and worthwhile?

Mark Rippetoe: It seems to be a primitive little island. Was he wearing a loincloth with "Trainer" embroidered on it? Honestly, if you have to do what he says, you can't train there, and you'll have to get some equipment.

KSC: You should write "experienced trainee" on a white t-shirt and go start using the racks. Then no one could dispute you. We need a serious purging of the personnel in the fitness industry. Perhaps we could use Joshua's small little island to hide all the bodies.

Mark Rippetoe: I'll provide the ammo.

Kettlebell training?

DMcK: What is your opinion of kettlebell training? I don't have a lot of time to train in a gym with regular weights (dumbbells and barbells), and so have started to train with kettlebells. I find that they fit my schedule and give me some decent strength and endurance, which I find very useful in my practice of martial arts.

Mark Rippetoe: Kettlebells are an excellent adjunct to barbell training, but they are not a replacement for it. Kettlebell training – as I understand it, and I may be understanding it incorrectly – is an endurance activity wherein volume is the primary parameter that is manipulated. It does not lend itself to lower rep incremental increases in strength at the 5RM level as barbell training does. For this reason, it would be considered an assistance method for intermediate or advanced athletes interested in competing in non-barbell sports. Quite useful for some things, not terribly applicable to an initial acquisition of absolute strength.

DMcK: I understand that kettlebell exercises are not a replacement for barbell exercises for absolute strength. For me, at least, they seem more versatile, since I can obtain a good combination of strength and endurance and power at home in a short amount of time. I practice martial arts, so most of my free time is spent on that and the kettlebells are a good compliment that I can fit quite easily into my routine.

Mark Rippetoe: They have been used successfully for this purpose for a long time.

Nosebleeds

Powerhawk: Every once in a while I get a nosebleed, and I think it's related to lifting. Usually it happens after deadlifts. Is this something worth fretting over?

Mark Rippetoe: Never fret, my child. Many people have nosebleeds when lifting, and it is not usually associated with leukemia or any other life-threatening situation. They will usually get less frequent with time, unless you're doing something to aggravate the situation, like living in Arizona. If it is a problem for much longer, get your nose looked at by a ENT specialist, not your GP who will just tell you to quit lifting weights.

Draco: Powerhawk, This may or may not be relevant to your condition, but if I've had FAR too much caffeine before training, I am sometimes prone to nose bleeds. "Far too much" is somewhere in the range of 9 - 15 shots of espresso. For me, a faster-than-usual heart beat and a lower-than-usual amount of energy are precursors to a bloody nose while training. Interestingly, as I have gotten stronger and accrued more time under the bar, this issue has disappeared. Just keep training hard, and if the problem doesn't stop, make sure you clean up. And don't point to it and ask people if they think it's cool, too. They don't.

Mark Rippetoe: The gym owner will not think it's cool.

Advice for someone who wants to own a gym

Drewfasa: So I've finally finished university here at LSE and am now having sessions with the careers advisor. We've decided that I need to own a gym. I think a first step on what will probably be quite a long journey will be to get some kind of coaching certification. Which of these options do you think would be the best:

USAW
BWLA - (British Weightlifting Association) offers a powerlifting and weightlifting cert.
Your cert (probably involves flying out to USA, unless you are still planning on coming to London)
NSCA, IDEA. AFAA, etc.

Am I correct in thinking that a coaching cert is the logical first step? What other advice can you give to a young Padwan who wants to follow in your footsteps?

Mark Rippetoe: My advice for someone who wants to own a gym is to get a thorough psychiatric examination. It's a fine business if you aren't interested in money and don't care what happens to your own training. Really. With this economy, rethink this idea. It will be an excellent way to lose your ass, especially if you are concerned about training people correctly.

Drewfasa: Well, I don't need the psychiatric exam, that's one certification I already have. But the gym scene in London is so incredibly poor that I've decided the only way to fix it is to start my own. There isn't a single proper barbell gym in all of London, and there's probably more Americans and Canadians here (myself included) than in some smaller states and provinces. I work at my university gym and many people come in asking about CrossFit and Olympic lifting and bemoan the crappiness of English fitness facilities.

My mind is made up! And my psychotic monomania shall be devoted to opening a usable gym here in London, hopefully around Elephant and Castle.....if I build it, they will come!

KSC: First of all, if you are going into the business for yourself, don't worry about certifications unless it's important to you. You can waste a lot of money here. The only caveat might be that having a certification can lower your insurance premiums which you definitely must have if you are going to train people. I let my USAW cert expire and am letting my NSCA cert expire at the end of the year.

As a gym owner, all I can tell you is to start small and don't get in over your head with a bunch of loans, etc. The worst thing you can do is to get into a situation where your overhead costs are real high and you can't afford to pay yourself. I started off with a minimum of equipment, which was all used, and I have slowly upgraded to better and better stuff. I have financed nothing and I rent a space for a very reasonable rate.

Draco: He might have some success opening a machine-only facility, with Pilates/Yoga classes and an entire room filled with Swiss balls, located directly across from your gym in Wichita Falls. He'd get all the bored housewives and kids who live to concentration curl.

Mark Rippetoe: That place is already here. The Powerhouse Gym is just around the corner. They can have all that business. They are involved in the standard business model: 24-month paper sold to a finance company, a floor consisting of 55% cardio, "trainers" that they certify themselves for a fee, etc. God help them. My entire overhead is half of their electric bill. And I have never tried to do it this way because it is unpalatable to me, having worked in that type of club when I was first starting in the business. I have always had a black iron gym, and it has always been very hard. But if you have no one using this model in big market like London, it might just work very well.

New job, new ideas

Matrix2012: I've recently applied for a job as a gym manager within a corporate setting. As it is a small team, I get the impression I would nearly be alone at this site. My responsibilities are the usual jack-of-all-trades from personal training, class instructing, membership retention, cleaning etc. and all that entails managing a gym. Having had previous experience, the job itself is nothing I'm not familiar with. I've been for the 1st interview and after talking with the area manager about functional compound lifts, barbells, and met-con, his eyes started to glaze over like I was speaking Martian. He then proceeded to tell me about the company classes that included crunch time, ab blast and a whole load of sure-fire ways to waste a perfectly good hour in the gym. I know that his main priority is to keep the corporate client / investment people happy and they, who no fault of there own, believe it will actually be more beneficial to them than squatting. I will try and get them to see the light, one person at a time if need be. He then asked if I planned to continue my studying in any form, which I replied that although I am aware of the Olympic lifts, I would like to go on a course or get some training which really teaches me the ins-and-outs of the lifts.

I did mention the idea to him that once qualified, I would be interested in introducing more productive training methods to the class, which would be a new experience for the clients, would be varied and interesting, and would deliver results (and he would get his member retention). He didn't say no to any ideas but also didn't say yes and I could tell that it seemed more important that he get someone in that wouldn't 'rock the boat' and just play ball. My 2nd interview is secured on my knowledge of LSD 'cardio' and 'resistance guidelines' and nothing to do with what I know that works.

Here is my question: when I attend the 2nd interview with the same guy and the client, do I explain that if I become manager of the facility there will be a few things that require expanding i.e. Olympic weights, racks, and somewhere we can install a multi-pullup bar (as none are currently present). All for the purpose of delivering a first class service for their employees. Or do I sit back and nod at the right moments and try and implement my ideas when I have been offered the position. I will need to know how much control I have with purchasing and decision making if I'm the gym manager and I would hate to be offered the job, only to find out that crunch time and the smith machine is the company's idea of thinking outside the box. My thinking is to speak up now so at least I would know where I stand and could decide whether or not to accept the position.

Mark Rippetoe: I guess it depends on how bad you need the job. Unless it is your own place, you'll have to work within the parameters set for you by your bosses. Duh. But the question is: do you tip your hand as to your intentions at the interview, or do you just sneak things in a little at a time after you're hired? You can do the latter more productively. Why don't you just get the job, especially if you need the job, and then get as much good stuff done as the format permits, with an eye towards changing the format over time? You may also find that they have some things to teach you as well, things that might be handy for you to know about the business later.

FLETC

JSHADE: I am currently using an intermediate three day a week program. Alternating press and bench. In December I will leave FLETC to attend the Criminal Investigator Training Program. From what I have heard, it is generally run, push up, set up, run some more, sort of stuff. The last time I was there they had some cross fit stuff going on, but I don't know how much of it has drifted into the CITP pt program. My question is do I just continue to follow my three day program and hope that the FLETC run, run, and run a little more doesn't hurt me too bad? I am 45 years old.

Mark Rippetoe: You may have to cut back to twice/week barbells to make sure you get recovered, or even once/week if necessary. I don't know how quickly the FLETC people are going to be in catching up to the more modern aspects of training, and you have to get through the course.

Historical question

sergeant_81: Out of sheer curiosity, I've been wondering how the standard US pounds olympic barbell plate weight progression/system as we know it came to be. Is the 2.5-5-10-25-35-45 lb. system the result of the conversion from kilogram plates or vice-versa? Or did somebody along the line (Bob Hoffman is probably a good candidate) just say "this is how it will be?"

Mark Rippetoe: I suspect pounds were first, but I can't say for sure. I'll ask Starr next time we talk.

(Bill tells me that when Hoffman bought the barbell company from Alan Calvert in 1935, the plate diameter and weight had been in their current format for years. Calvert started the business in 1902, so sometime between then and 1935 the specs had been worked out. The plate diameter was to facilitate clearance between the bar and the ribcage in the event of a fall with the bar, and the weight was a conversion from the Europeans, who had conducted the first modern Olympics weightlifting competition in kilos in 1896.)

Strength and conditioning coach

Painholic: For a person trying to be an S & C coach, would you recommend earning a masters degree+ ?? I really don't want to learn more than I need to. I intend to major in exercise and sport science at UNC. I wonder if this is enough. My dream is to become a knowledgeable coach like you. Any suggestions?

Mark Rippetoe: Get a science degree, and then learn how to make your training and coaching conform to those standards. There are no college strength and conditioning programs that I am aware of that can teach this material as a science should be taught, and no college programs that I am aware of that can effectively teach the coaching of strength and conditioning. But it disturbs me that you don't want to learn any more than you have to; this is not a productive attitude for anyone.

BIGGUY6FT6: I have a BA in Kinesiology with an emphasis in Exercise Physiology and I can honestly say that if I wanted to continue in the EP area a Master's is the only way to go. Otherwise it is completely worthless. It did get me into my Radiology career though so I am not complaining.

Mark Rippetoe: You'd have to be damned picky about where you did that masters, and I'm not entirely sure that you'd find a good program at all.

Painholic: Thank you for the replies. I know Penn state has the best kinesiology program in the nation. Anyone know about this school? Anyway coach, it seems like you taught yourself everything about training (am I wrong?). How did you study? A major in geology doesn't seem that much related to training.

Mark Rippetoe: Here is Dr. Kilgore's input:

Preparation to be a PE teacher is mired in individual state, county, and individual school regulation. That means that you have to meet the educational requirements of the state that you plan to teach in. That may be difficult to do from the other side of the world. Also know that current efforts in PE are focused only on health, not on fitness. School PE is soft and fluffy and does not make kids fit, it is intended to prepare them for a lifetime of engaging in "healthy lifestyles".

To be a good professional trainer, you are already on the right track. Take human anatomy and physiology, physics, and maybe some biochemistry and then think about how to apply what you learn to training. Taking physical education or exercise science courses may or may not help you along the way as most teach only health and physical activity concepts, not fitness and exercise (there is a large difference). The lack of relevant and practical information on training people available to fitness trainers was the reason Greg developed CrossFit and why Rip and I put out Starting Strength and Practical Programming. None of us have degrees directly relevant to fitness, it is through patient practice and unceasing efforts to learn more that made us "experts". You can do the same thing we did. Until the fitness industry actually gets an accepted standard of fitness trainer education that is actually sound scientifically AND practically, individual effort might just be the best way to get good at what you want to do.

TravisRussellDC: My BS in Kinesiology with an emphasis on Exercise Science and a coaching endorsement from the University of Illinois didn't do anything for me in the realm of strength. In fact, I already knew more than my instructors back then. And I was an idiot compared to what I know now. And in another 10 years I'll look back at what I'm doing now and want to kick myself in the ass. The classes that helped me the most were the anatomy, physiology, and advanced biomechanics classes I had in my doctor of chiropractic program. Other than that, I read everything else on my own. Unfortunately for me, the best teacher has been trial and error.

Anthony D: I currently go to the University of Pittsburgh and am majoring in, 'exercise science/health and physical activity'. I've shadowed the strength coaches and I am interning with the football team. Really, everyone in the business tells you "do something else." This field isn't respected enough yet and as Rip stated, it's probably more practical to get a shitty cert that costs a lot less money.

Buying a Belt

wc33: Any recommendations on where to buy a good-quality belt from?

Mark Rippetoe: I just bought one from www.elitefts.com

Toddmr: I was thinking about ordering from elitefts, as I've heard lots of good things about their goods. But then I saw that they offer their belts in "Pearl White" and am rethinking. What color makes you lift best?

Mark Rippetoe: Mine is green, about the color of bile. Makes me happy to remember that I haven't had the dry heaves in 15 years. I got the cheap, thinner suede one. A belt that tapers in the front was designed by people who don't know how belts work, or for people with not much room between ribs and pelvis. I like single prong because they are easier to get off quickly.

Howardw: It's weird how much I like my belt. I feel like a hoss once I put that bad boy on. I mostly use it for squats and presses. I don't like it for deads for some reason.

Mark Rippetoe: It's hard to get in a good start position with that much belt. I prefer a thin velcro job for lighter stuff, and a plain leather single-ply belt for heavier deadlifts.

GHD or Reverse Hyper

j5coleman: Coach -- If you could only have one or the other, would it be a GHD bench or a Reverse Hyper machine? (Not just a hypothetical -- I only have room for one!).

Mark Rippetoe: I'd get the GH bench. You can do more stuff on it. Always defer to broader use.

How do I bail out of a squat?

Ltgrady: I just started the program and it's my second week. Things are going well enough, but today when i went to do my squats I bumped up and on my last one I had a hard time getting the weight up. I did, everything was fine.

Then I realized, what would I have done if I couldn't? The only gym near me is a Retrofitness, not exactly strength training nirvana. The rack isn't a power rack but the half rack that angles upward? If I get stuck down there, do I lean forward into the rack trying to get the bar onto some hooks? Should I try to heave it off my back and catch the large rails at about thigh height? Is there a proper way to do this and anything I should be careful not to do (like the first day I tried squats, before your book, when I was standing in the rack backwards and would have cracked my skull had I fallen forward :eek:)

Mark Rippetoe: In my gym, you get spotters, you safely dump it backwards loaded with the *bumper plates*, or you learn how to accurately judge your ability. If you dump the bar on rails or pins or anything else in here, I will beat the cum out of you with the remnants of the bar.

Heather: Why is it bad to leave the bar on the safety rails? I ask because I've had to do it a couple of times--I set the rails just high enough so if lose it and can't get out of the hole I can relax my hamstrings and sink down a little and the rails take the weight. I don't make a habit of it, not least because it's embarrassing as all getout, but I didn't know that it was poor practice too...

Mark Rippetoe: Heather darling, he said *heave it off his back onto the rails*, which means it's falling through the air for some distance and which destroys even the best bars. Heaving off the back requires bumper plates and an empty spot on the floor.

Conflict w/ Other Powerlifter

Gary G: I have a PL buddy with lots of experience and big numbers. He has trained with the strongest and the best and he has helped me a great deal in the couple of months that I've known him. Of course, he disagrees with most of what I've taken away from your books. Highest on the list right now is looking down on the squat, but I don't care because it works and I understand why it works.

Next is the programming. He is not happy with me squatting heavy more than once per week. Indeed I did overtrain horribly for the last six months by pretending I was an Eastern Bloc professional with chemical assistance. Now I want to do an "Advanced Novice" program that will turn into Intermediate in a couple of months. That's a heavy 3x5 Tuesday, easy FSQ Thursday and another heavy 3x5 Saturday; later it will be a heavy 5x5 Tuesday, easy Thursday and heavy x3, x2 or x1 Saturday. He says this is too much and that a simple 5x5 on Monday or Tuesday with a light day three days later is perfect.

Of course, really strong people with years of experience (like him) wonder why skinny and relatively weak people (like me) don't just accept the offered advice. Why do we read books and internet articles and think we know it all? Granted, most books and articles are either crap or don't apply to the majority of trainees. I'm sticking to my guns on the squat form I learned from you, but I am a little unsure about the programming. If my buddy were to read your books (he won't), he'd probably insist that my squat and pull we're advanced (like that damned chart says) and required more advanced programming.

My bench and press are "intermediate", but I still think they could both use a little novice planning before switching to less frequent training, especially my press. I know you don't train powerlifters, but I think at my level there is more I can take from your books. This gets complicated when someone with tons of experience and a big total is trying to help. Like you've written: I want to be more coachable...but that can get a little complicated.

Mark Rippetoe: I appreciate your position. A pair of experienced eyes is a valuable addition to your training tools, and when you can get the help you should take it. More coachable is better; I got yelled at a lot about that myself. The problem is that this guy doesn't appreciate the fact that athletes at different levels of development respond differently to training. If he's not interested in learning anything – from you or me or anybody else – he is of limited use since he can only coach what he knows right now.

Linear progress is always faster progress than more complicated programming provides. Do the arithmetic. Use it as long as possible before you get unnecessarily complicated.

Technique vs. tonnage

Svenskefan: A while ago I decided to get more serious about training and bought SS and PP. I then headed to the local powerlifting club and started working out. Pretty soon I got some comments regarding my technique from what appears to be a very knowledgeable gentleman. Fine I thought, I am more than willing to accept guidance and coaching from somebody who knows what he is doing. I seriously believe that I have benefited greatly from his technical advice, however when it comes to programming I don't agree with his principles. Since I am a novice I try to use sets of 5 across for my working sets. The coach keeps telling me to keep the weight considerably lighter than what I can handle, and he insists on my doing 2 or 3 reps (instead of 5) for my working sets.

I think he sees my technical shortcomings and doesn't want me to use inferior technique just to get the weight up, but I am also pretty sure that he really doesn't know what he is talking about regarding the process of gaining strength. The coach does have an attitude of "Mr. know-it-all" and really isn't open for discussions regarding programming.

So, the question really is: What is preferable, let him decide according to his knowledge and theories about technique and programming, or just use him for technical advice and keep the programming for myself. Or stated another way: Is the risk of using non-optimal technique when using heavier loads enough to warrant going at a much slower pace than what is possible?

Mark Rippetoe: So the question is really about gym etiquette: do you accept the coaching of a guy – for free, I assume, correct me if I'm wrong because it's germane to the question – about your technique and then reject what he says about programming because you're sure (and you are probably right) that he doesn't know much about programming. Good question. It would depend on the relationship you have built with the guy, and the relationship the guy has with himself. If he'd be amenable to some reading, you could ask his opinion on some programming stuff I've written, and the conversation could be productive. Hell, we might all learn something. But if the guy is convinced he knows everything there is to know, and that learning something from somebody else – you, for instance – would prove to him that he doesn't, well, some guys just won't go there.

If he won't "let" you try the more conventional sets-of-5 programming, I'd thank him for his help so far and just do it anyway. You are grateful to him, but you are only responsible to YOU. It's your training, your time, your gym dues.

Thinking of starting my own gym

LG1: I am thinking of starting my own gym in NY. What advice would you have for someone new to the business? What's a good point of reference for someone like me who wants to open a no-nonsense old school style gym geared towards people who want to train with free weights, use chalk and not the AM/Lunch/PM work crowd interested in cardio, yoga, spin classes, machines etc...

Mark Rippetoe: First, determine whether you can tolerate being broke most of the time. Second, decide whether or not you can tolerate destroying your own training. Third, understand that the momentum in direction you want to go is now with CrossFit, and that they are making more difference in the changing opinion about what the gym business is about than any other development since Arthur Jones shoved Nautilus up our asses in 1984. You'd probably do better with them than on your own.

LG1: Thanks Rip. Your feed-back is sincerely appreciated. If I do go the gym owner route... I will def. invite you to come up for a guest seminar. In your experience, where is the best place to purchase quality used gym equipment?

Mark Rippetoe: There are companies that specialize in selling used commercial gym equipment. These businesses are predicated on the following true facts: 1.) the average lifespan of a commercial gym is about 18 months, 2.) the vast majority of the equipment in them is new and bank-financed, and 3.) the banks have no use for this shit once they repo the floor. These guys come in and buy the whole floor for $0.10/dollar, haul it to their warehouses, refurb the stuff/wipe it down nicely, and sell it to YOU and ME for $0.40-0.50 depending on how good a trader you are. There are at least 3 of these companies in Dallas/Ft. Worth, for example.

LG1: I was thinking of trying to go after clients who are hard-core and well versed in DB and BB training. Not really looking to cater to the cardio/machine crowd.

Mark Rippetoe: Everybody like us thinks of going after that market. It's not big enough to sustain your entire business. At least not yet.

KSC: Hardcore lifters who are well versed in sound training methods will most likely not be looking for a full time trainer unless he is somebody with an unbelievable rep like a Mike Burgener/Louie Simmons or something and specializes in a specific niche. Who knows, maybe you are the next Louie Simmons. If you build the right type of gym, you might attract some of these guys as members but if you are going to be a full time personal trainer then your market is the cardio machine crowd. Then you have the rewarding but sometimes difficult task of introducing them and teaching them about barbell training and other productive methods.

Zach: Opening a gym is a stupid idea... but, if you're like me, knowing that won't dissuade you from doing it. I had a nice little CrossFit gym in Reno for 2.5 years that was profitable to the tune of $50K per year, when I sold it. Not bad, but not good enough for a family of 4. Here's what I learned:

1. Training other people, in a facility you own and are responsible for, is rewarding for about 6 months... then it becomes a royal pain in the ass.

2. If the only source of income for your gym is training other people (one-on-one or in groups,) you will never get a break.... this seems okay looking at it from the outside, but 6, 7, 9, 14 months into it, you will be going out of your mind.

3. If I get a chance to do it again (and I do intend to), a gym will not be the primary source of income for my family.

4. Go cheap on everything you can.

5. Be 100% prepared to close the gym.... don't follow it to the bottom of your bank account... it is better to cut your losses and spend some time refining your concept for another try.

I would highly recommend spending some time around 1 or 2 SUCCESSFUL gyms that look like what you want... I've been training at Metroflex, here in Arlington, for the past 3 months, and it has been very instructional.

LG1: Thanks for the info. Zach. I don't plan to train... only provide for others to workout.

Mark Rippetoe: You're not going to train?? Yourself?? Are you currently a shoe salesman that just likes the idea of owning a gym? Or are you going to quit training in favor of the glory of being a gym owner?

LG1: I will train in the gym myself but I will not be training others. I like the idea of being a gym owner.

Mark Rippetoe: So you are going to own the gym, but not control what happens in it. You're going to just open the doors every day and merely bask in the glory of gym ownership. You're not going to train clients because the money will be so good from your dues line that you won't need to. And you're not going to teach your members how to train. My god, man, if you are really this foolish, you will learn several things very quickly that may eventually improve your wisdom levels.

Construction Work Hinder SS

Projectaero: Hey Rip I will be starting construction work soon and wanting to know will that hinder my results or would I have to change my workout accordingly or the time I do the workouts?

Mark Rippetoe: You'll be tired until you adapt and learn to eat more and rest better. But all the guys reading this that have construction jobs are laughing now.

Trends

MatV: I am currently enrolled in a class that is primarily interested in the way that society, and particularly those in positions of power, portray "deviance" or "the other". My main piece of assessment is a research essay in which I plan on exploring the way in which the development of "health clubs" and 24 hour takeaway fitness centres have changed the contemporary image of masculinity. I figure that I'll find that the perceived ideal body shape has changed from being about big, barrel-chested, big legged functional strong men to lean, athletic, 6 pack-but-not-much-more looking blokes.

So my question is: Since you've been involved in the industry, how has what people want to look like changed? Could there have been a link between the way that men have been portrayed in the media with the increased spread of Health Clubs, etc.? If you've got any input, it'd be fantastic. I'd love to hear from somebody that's been involved for 30 years and seen all sorts of trends.

Mark Rippetoe: By far, the most important trend amongst general public-type health club members is abs. Thirty years ago, men that joined a gym had the idea that they wanted to be bigger and stronger, but Mr. Weider, 3000 infomercials, and the media at large have changed the perception to the point that size is a thing to be feared if obscures ab definition. Young guys are especially infected with this virus, and you see it on this board all the time.

We are doing our best here. Your support is appreciated.

The Rippington Post

The vast, overwhelming majority of the time, government is the problem.

Question re: reference to communist-bloc physical education in Practical Programming

Twotubman: I was looking at the previews for Practical Programming when I saw this sentence:

The U.S. high school student of today does not have the general fitness and movement skills developed by the programs inherent in communist systems, programs in which children learned how to move effectively and began developing base fitness at age 6, long before they entered sport-specific training.

That's very interesting. Could you elaborate on that a little? What were these "movement skills" that the Soviet kids had that contemporary American kids don't have? Under that system, what sort of fitness would have been normal for 14 year olds with average genetic potential, for the kids who wouldn't have been channeled into the elite sports system? Where did you learn about this? What are some good sources for further reading on the topic of East Bloc physical education?

Mark Rippetoe: This is, unfortunately, a question for Dr. Kilgore, who wrote that part of the book. But I suspect that one of the features of a society that directed everyone's private lives to the extent of the Soviet Union was a regimented pedagogical approach to PE at a young age. Unstructured play might, after all, breed dissent, with its selfish emphasis on personal happiness.

Smoking and strength training

Drewfasa: How detrimental to training is smoking cigarettes, in your experience? For some reason I get the urge to smoke in the summer and usually smoke about a pack a week of roll-ups. I imagine you've probably trained smokers in your 20+ years of coaching, how do they stack up against non-smokers?

Mark Rippetoe: How do *you* think it affects athletes? It is, of course, detrimental. How much varies with the individual. But I have always regarded sucking on round things as blowjob practice.

Drewfasa: Just wondering, you didn't seem to have anything against mixing strength-training with alcoholism (earlier post). So I thought that moderate amounts of smoking could not be as bad as that

Mark Rippetoe: Drewfasa, are you unable to distinguish the differences between breathing smoke and drinking a normally metabolizable carbohydrate-like nutrient given to us by the Gods?

Jamie J: Guinness, unlike cigarettes, has protein.

Gordon Bombay: It hardly has any protein, maybe a couple of grams per pint. Not any more than your average lager. I don't know who started the myth of Guinness being some sort of calorie-dense high protein substance, but it's bullshit.

Tongzilla: Another perspective is the following. If you decide to smoke and have made up your mind, you will still be healthier doing basic barbell training. If one enjoys smoking so much, then doing appropriate exercise will prolong one's effective life (effective meaning physically self-sufficient) so they can continue smoking for longer.

Mark Rippetoe: I don't think anybody treats Guinness as a protein drink. But it has more nutrients than tobacco smoke, wouldn't you agree? And I have never heard barbell training recommended as a way to prolong your career as a smoker. That is damned innovative.

McKirdyP: I'll adapt one from Rip: There are few things graven in stone among them are that you either have the hardened discipline to follow intelligent alteration of path or you are a pussy. This goes for all types of criticism and general illumination that elucidates more efficient path in contrast to the human bullheaded notion to continue being a moron.

Experience, data, intelligence, knowledge, wisdom and ultimately common fucking sense dictate that smoking is counter productive to becoming a strong and thus more useful (more from Rip) carbon-based life form. Thus if after concretely knowing this you fail to stop smoking, you are a pussy. However, you can decide and act at any point to become at the very least previously a pussy. If it helps get angry and hate me, if it leads to your discontinuing smoking then I am glad to be of service.

I am presently still only previously a pussy, but I am still working hard to become an all-around strong carbon based life form again. This is why I am an expert on this subject matter. You have the information, act on it. There is no second way.

Jamie J: Drew, did you really have to ask someone if smoking was bad? Seriously dude. What did you think he was going to say? "I use cigarettes to time my breaks between squats"?

Drewfasa: It's quite funny how moralizing everybody gets when smoking/tobacco comes up. The anti-smoking lobbies have really done their work well - smoking a cigarette is now considered the moral equivalent of spraying children with machine-gun fire. In earlier posts when someone asked whether heavy-lifting was detrimental to longevity, he was bombarded with replies saying 'live fast, die young, pussy!' However, if someone wishes to smoke the occasional cigarette, they are told that to do so is cowardly because it might shorten life-expectancy (a truly inverted logic, I must say). I smoke only rarely, but I enjoy the company of many chain-smokers. They have decided that life is too short to deny oneself simple pleasures. They also seem to have a much better handle on their own mortality and are more interesting people - I have never had a stimulating conversation with a vegan long-distance runner. All my heroes smoked - R.L. Stevenson, Mark Twain, Bertrand Russell, Edison, my grandpa (and please don't tell me that smoking suddenly became 'wrong' when people 'discovered' tobacco was 'bad', its adverse effects have long been known).

Anyways, all I wanted was anecdotal evidence from Mark's experience. Ever since the whole "smoking kills everyone around you" campaign, I find it hard to separate fact from fiction regarding smoking, and since I know a good many superb athletes who smoke with apparent impunity (including my training partner), I thought I'd draw upon Mark's vast experience in training high-calibre (and not so high-calibre) athletes.

Mark Rippetoe: Drewfasa, just so you'll know, I hate smoking. My parents smoked and I remember being a powerless little kid in the back seat unable to breathe. It stinks, it creates trash that I seem to always have to pick up, it causes health problems (which of course are your own business unless the fucking government makes me help pay for them), and it adversely affects performance. I grew up with people that smoked, and I think that the VAST majority of people who smoke started because "their friends were all doing it", and that the VAST majority of people who still smoke do so because they are pussies who cannot make themselves quit (I'm sure that there are ex-smokers here that will have an opinion about that). I had to watch my father die of COPD because of smoking, having been rendered rather useless for several years prior. Nobody hates it worse than I do.

The ONLY thing I hate worse than smoking is the government telling me that I can't, in whatever form this coercion may take. If you want to "enjoy" your tobacco, go ahead. "Enjoy" it wherever you want to and wherever the owner of the private property allows you to. And God Damn to Hell the busybodies who want to make laws that tell me how I have to use my property that I paid for and pay taxes to keep. The post office and the municipal building are one thing, but local bars and restaurants, and even my gym, are quite another.

I realize that this is a different discussion, or that at least it should be, but don't confuse my hatred for your bad habit with a desire to keep you from doing it. I just wish it killed you faster so I didn't have to smell it as long. But I would NEVER use the power of government to make you act like I wanted you to.

Hip Replacement

JWarkala: I'm 53 and have been training most of my life, but just started training smart after the 1st edition of SS came out. On 4/15, I was squatting and felt a pull in my hip. For once, I acted my age and stopped what I was doing to assess the problem. I did the normal sports injury routine and after 6 weeks with no progress, I went to see the orthopedist. After about 30 seconds of manipulating my leg and a couple of x-rays, he said basically that my hip was severely arthritic and shot and I needed a hip replacement. So, as I wait for a second opinion, my questions to you are;

1. Did you ever hear of someone being asymptomatic (I never had a problem with my hip before) and then BAM, all of sudden having severe arthritis needing surgery? I always thought that there was a gradual onset to arthritis.

2. Do you know or work with anyone who continues to train with a hip replacement ? My so called "sports" doctor said my squatting career was essentially over. (And then the guy said, "But you can do these" while making a curling motion with one arm!)

3. And finally, if I am unable to squat or DL, does this blow the BB cert in Boston out of the water for me?

Mark Rippetoe: 1.) No, that is certainly as hell not a normal presentation.

2.) I have a guy in here now that just deadlifted 600 at 253 on two new knees 9 months post-op. I have trained people with new hips, but never heavy like that. You can certainly squat with new hips.

3.) It depends on whether you decide to have a hip replacement based on one very odd opinion. Did you see the pictures yourself, and why have you not gotten a second opinion? Doctors are consultants; hire another one, or two, and if the consensus is surgery go get it done now. But I am far from convinced.

JWarkala: Thanks for the quick answer. I haven't gotten a second opinion yet. I literally wrote my post 1 hour after seeing the 1st Dr. I called a PT I know who is also an Olympic lifter and runs some local strongman competitions and he referred me to a REAL sports doctor (one who trains). He also thought the diagnosis was somewhat unusual.

I know you've talked about this in your books but why do all these orthopods have to put "Sports Medicine" on their resume' when they don't know a barbell from a bar stool?

Flying Fox: Quote:

> *I have a guy in here now that just deadlifted 600 at 253 on two new knees 9 months post-op. I have trained people with new hips, but never heavy like that. You can certainly squat with new hips.*

Really? Wouldn't that shorten the life span of the prosthesis?

Mark Rippetoe: Why do 'orthopods' all claim to be sports medicine specialists? To make money, you fool. And as far as the lifespan of the prosthesis, the best way to extend that is to get the surgery and then remain in a supine position on your back for the rest of your life. This will ensure that you die with a shiny new prosthesis.

Flying Fox: In other words, you have no idea what squatting would do?

I have avascular necrosis in my hip and will need a hip resurfacing or hip replacement sooner or later. *(Note: Flying Fox is from Belgium.)*

Mark Rippetoe: Taken as a whole, American doctors are far better than Belgian doctors. Our system is superior in many ways, such as not having to wait 5 months for an appendectomy. The Canadians will back me up on this. They'd better anyway. Maybe you should come here to have it fixed.

And squatting will shorten the life of the prosthesis, certainly. You missed my point.

Philds: As a Belgian I can only say BLAH. Our healthcare system is one of the best in the world. At least as good (if not better) as that of the US. We have national insurance that protects all citizens with private hospitals who compete for the money from said insurance. Best of both worlds.

Mark Rippetoe: What happens to a person in Belgium that has a carotid cavernous fistula?

Philds: Ah, those patients just get shot. :) But I'll bite: You'd go to your GP, or have him come to you (at a slightly higher price). You can choose which one you want since all GP's have a private practice. He'd do some tests and/or refer you to a hospital. Here also you can choose which ever one you want. A doctors consult would cost me about 5$, the rest of the fee will be paid by social security. (the small fee is there to stop over consumption.) The quality of healthcare is top level. (One of Belgium's big industries is pharmaceutical. Many of the big international companies have major research centres over here.) Anyroad, I'd just wanted to correct the view you had of my country as if it were an underdeveloped nation. But who cares anyway. I'm happy to live here and I'm sure I'd be happy to live in the US. Except for Texas of course, because we know how backwards they are over there. ;)

Sorry, the penny just dropped. I thought that it was a made up disease. I just googled it and found out it's real. I'd me more then happy to find out for you if you want me to.

Keenan: Don't you have a tax burden between 55-60% to pay for this? My libertarian ideals cringe at the thought. But I have to say that your country produces some of the finest ales in the world.

Mark Rippetoe: I suspect you will find that your initial response was correct. But let me tell you what happens here: they are flown to the finest hospital the free market can build, cared for by the finest surgeons in the world operating in a free market, using the finest technology the free market can provide, and thus have the best opportunity in the world to survive. All thanks to the free market, or at least the remnants of the free market that have been left us by the government operating Medicare and Medicaid, and mandating what coverage the private companies must or cannot provide. And this is true despite the fact that the person may be underinsured or uninsured. The same thing happens to an underinsured person with an aortic aneurysm that requires millions of dollars of resources and technology that can only be provided by a system such as ours. The present electoral climate has renewed the call for European-style health care in the US, and I sincerely hope that it never happens. And if it does, I sincerely hope that the craven dog politicians that vote for it for the purpose of retaining their offices are afflicted with the aforementioned conditions, which will be left untreated in a timely manner or not at all in the US Public Health Service.

I'd agree with Keenan. And his observation about your fine beer culture is especially relevant since the beer producers operate in a free market, or at least the remnants of the free market left to them by the fools that run the EU and the Belgian government.

Drewfasa: I'm going to go ahead and ask the obvious question, if the health care currently available in America is so great, then why are voters so keen on social health care? It is also pertinent to point out that many of America's great technological inventions were developed with government subsidies - because the free market did not offer sufficient conditions to make them profitable (The internet is a fine example - developed by the pentagon. In fact a great portion of America's technological superiority is due to government spending on research and development).

Also, I think European politicians compare rather favourably to George Bush, Dick Cheney, Donald Rumsfeld, et. al. America's economic position at the moment does not warrant much smugness (and you can bet the 'free-market' fundamentalists in Washington are going to start pumping money into the economy like there's no tomorrow). You have rigged elections, weak currency, sluggish GDP growth, FEMA, watery beer, and George Bush. Europe has robust growth, good health-care, less fat people, more beautiful women, and much better beer.

America's a great country, but not nearly so great as to warrant any smugness on her part.

Philds: That our government is run by fools, I can gladly agree with. What you are describing happening to patients is the same as here. I was not arguing for socialized medicine. I was just pointing out that Belgium is a bad example since we have comparable healthcare to you guys. Our system is not the bad one the UK uses and who now ship over patients to our hospitals because of the lack of waiting lists and the advanced treatment they can get here.

Regarding the beer: yep it's tasty and plentiful. (Though I must admit I'm not a big drinker.)

I now have to go because I need to harvest some beets. I must reach the quota stipulated in the 5 year plan.

Mark Rippetoe: Let me do this a piece at a time:

"I'm going to go ahead and ask the obvious question, if the health care currently available in America is so great, then why are voters so keen on social health care?"

Because the poor things have been told it will be "free". And people like free shit. Like that toaster they used to give you when you opened a new checking account. They fail to realize that you Europeans are paying for your "free" health care with an incredibly high tax rate, what amounts to rationing of the access, the complete lack of the ability to treat certain exotic ailments, and a lack of choice in who you see when you finally get in. And our craven dog politicians will say absolutely anything to get elected. ANYTHING.

"It is also pertinent to point out that many of America's great technological inventions were developed with government subsidies - because the free market did not offer sufficient conditions to make them profitable (The internet is a fine example - developed by the pentagon. In fact a great portion of America's technological superiority is due to government spending on research and development)."

This is pretty funny. Would you care to name one great technological innovation that does not involve killing people that came about because of government subsidy? And the internet was not "developed" by the Pentagon any more than the airplane was.

"Also, I think European politicians compare rather favourably to George Bush, Dick Cheney, Donald Rumsfeld, et. al. "

This is like comparing your turds to my turds.

"America's economic position at the moment does not warrant much smugness"

America's economic position is still the strongest in the world.

"(and you can bet the 'free-market' fundamentalists in Washington are going to start pumping money into the economy like there's no tomorrow)."

There hasn't been a free-market fundamentalist in Washington since Barry Goldwater. The pieces of shit that comprise the Bush administration wouldn't make a wart on a "free market fundamentalist's" ass. *(And the subsequent Obama administration is blatantly Marxist.)*

"You have rigged elections, "

This is farcical. We have a stupid electorate, and so do you, but our elections are not any more *rigged* than yours.

"weak currency, sluggish GDP growth, FEMA"

All the result of the above-noted absence of free-market fundamentalists.

"watery beer,"

Given.

"and George Bush."

He'd make a fine Prime Minister somewhere.

"Europe has robust growth, good health-care, less fat people, more beautiful women, and much better beer."

Europe has had sluggish growth for a very long time, very high unemployment (except for Ireland and some of the newer EU members who have learned their Hayek), good health care if you don't really need health care badly or soon, a growing number of fat people, more beautiful women except for Texas, and better beer if you only consider Coors Light and Bud; we do have some very damn good beer here if you care to buy it. And we are not subjects – we are Citizens with the right to defend ourselves. Looking at the math, I'll stay here.

A question of politics

sasquatch989: In my various readings of Coach Rip I've come across a number of startling facts.

1) You quote Heinlein a lot
2) You don't like seat belt laws and other 'nanny state' BS
3) You listen to Coast to Coast AM
4) You are from Texas

My suspicion is that you have libertarian leanings, maybe even you are a Ron Paul man? Tell me it is so... I understand if you delete this and ban me for life.

Mark Rippetoe: I have Ron's bumper sticker over my office window. I am a libertarian. I voted for Bob Barr. I listen to Coast-to-CoastAM for amusement and Mike McConnell for most other purposes. Robert Heinlein is an important writer and you should read him too. And I am from Texas.

(Mike McConnell has become unavailable since this was written, and has been replaced by Mike Church as my preferred talk show guy.)

Does blood donation adversely affect strength training?

LCN: And if so can you avoid or minimize this by timing your donation for a particular day if you're doing a MWF SS routine?

Mark Rippetoe: I don't donate blood, because I'm usually using it all myself. You are too – that's why it's all there. You don't have "extra" blood. If you want to donate, you must realize that the loss of a pint takes time to recover from, will be a stressor in addition to that administered by your training, and will have to be allowed for over more than one workout.

Gman: Sometimes you have to think about priorities.......donate blood, possibly help save a life, and have 1 or 2 less than optimal workouts every 2-3 months, or don't donate. Choice is yours.

Mark Rippetoe: How much does the Red Cross charge the hospital/patient for the blood I should donate free? Just out of curiosity...

Gman: Great question as I assumed they were a non profit organization. Here is the contact info, let me know what you find out.

American Red Cross National Headquarters
2025 E Street, NW
Washington, DC 20006
Phone: (202) 303 5000
Donation Hotlines: 1-800-REDCROSS (1-800-733-2767) / 1-800-257-7575 (Español)

Mark Rippetoe: Great news!! Here's your answer: they told me that they make more off of it than I do. It's like recycling – we are told that the stuff is valuable, but the market does not/is not allowed to reflect this Truth.

SMN: "Crowding Out in Blood Donation: Was Titmuss Right?

Abstract: In his seminal 1970 book, The Gift Relationship, Richard Titmuss argued that monetary compensation for donating blood might crowd out the supply of blood donors. To test this claim we carry out a field experiment with three different treatments. In the first treatment subjects are given the opportunity to become blood donors without any compensation. In the second treatment subjects receive a payment of SEK 50 (≈ $7) for becoming blood donors, and in the third treatment subjects can choose between a SEK 50 payment and donating SEK 50 to charity. The results differ markedly between men and women. For men the supply of blood donors is not significantly different among the three experimental groups. For women there is a significant crowding out effect. The supply of blood donors decreases by almost half when a monetary payment is introduced. There is also a significant effect of allowing individuals to donate the payment to charity, and this effect fully counteracts the crowding out effect."

Mark Rippetoe: This is an awfully weird paper, for several reasons. Not having the original Titmuss reference in front of me, they do a piss-poor job of explaining the premise here: that offering monetary compensation for an action perceived socially as altruistic actually reduces participation. It is certainly not immediately apparent why this might be so. And I don't know about where you're from, but where I'm from a $7USD payment for an hour's time – training effects not even considered – would not act as an inducement to me to do much of anything (unless we project the current economic situation forward into Mr. Obama's third or fourth year).

My point is that blood donation is detrimental to heavy training, and under the current system that treats blood as though it was not a commodity I have no real reason to give blood to anybody unless I personally wish them to have it.

The Universe Doesn't Care About *Why*. But We Do.

This is some physiology stuff, more of the kind of things that – from a strictly practical standpoint – are a waste of thinking time to most coaches. However, it amuses me, and perhaps it will explain some things you've been wondering about, if you're a wondering kind of person.

A few questions for Rip

Protobuilder: (1) Rumor has it you can add 100 pounds to any able-bodied man's squat. Have you seen a difference in the speed and amount of linear progress possible between, say, a "good" and "not-so-good" trainee? If so, what factors play into it? Does it just come down to coaching (e.g., there are no "not so good" trainees, just poor programs)?

(2) Some have questioned the hypertrophy recommendation in Practical Programming of multiple sets of 15. Care to elaborate/defend? I ask because many tout 5x5-style training as a "guaranteed" size builder, the thought being, you simply can't expect big muscular legs until you're squatting 20x315, 5x495, etc.
(3) How do you define "hard work" in training terms, and what role does it play in week-to-week training?

(4) Do you have thoughts on how much time a trainee should spend in the 50-70% range? 70-80%? 80-90? Etc. (using whatever percentages or guidelines you use, if any). What factors play into this?

Mark Rippetoe: 1.) There are huge differences in genetic/psychological potential between people. Some have good levers, some have a short attention span, some have lots of time and no job to finance their protein habit, and some want it worse than others. A shitty program might work much better for a gifted athlete than even the best program would for me. It might come down to coaching, but lots of people get strong without a coach. It usually comes down to the individual.

2.) It is well established that higher reps build hypertrophy better than lower reps. That having been said, or typed I suppose, 5s pull up the weight that can be used on 15s, and 15s contribute hypertrophy that improves the leverage for the 5s. But you're right, big legs are a function of big weight, no defense necessary.

3.) "Hard work" is the kind of work that committed lifters do all the time – week to week, day to day, month to month, and year to year. Rah-rah. Think of a more specific question.

4.) I guess that would depend on the program, the contest being trained for, the level of advancement of the athlete, and the time available for preparing for the meet.

Lylemcd: 2) - No it's not, Rip. An old myth that refuses to die is what it is.

Behm (or is it Sale) has unpublished data showing that progressive triples build size just as well as higher reps. And, if anything, PL's are often more muscular than bodybuilders despite using a predominantly lower repetition range (IU realize that most use a mix of ranges). Many OL'ers have legs that bodybuilders would KILL for despite high reps being multiple sets of 5. What higher reps do is give a greater acute effect due to pump and glycogen storage. But heavier weights give better MU recruitment and training effect. at 80% 1RM (5-8 RM or so), you get full MU recruitment from rep 1 and plenty of metabolic work without wasting time moving around pansy weights for sets of 15.

Blowdpanis: The most hypertrophy actually occurred in the lowest rep group (~5 RM) compared to the intermediate (~10 RM) and high rep (~20-28 RM). Intermediate was just about the same, but yah, the "strength" group grew as much/more than anyone else when total volume between groups was similar-ish.

This is also the source of confusion on rep range and hypertrophy potential, imho, NOT holding total volume constant in one's comparisons. A lot of literature out there comparing stuff like 1 set of 3 RM to 1 set of 10 RM, finding 10 RM makes you grow better. Except that 10 RM is > 300% the total volume of 3 RM. What happens if you compare 10 RM to 3 sets of ~3 RM? Magic.

Mark Rippetoe: A very good discussion, yes. My take: First, anecdotal reports of various guys that train with weights mean almost nothing at all. Yes, Kurlovich had nice legs, and lots of other weightlifters, like Alexiev, didn't. There are lots of very muscular powerlifters and weightlifters, and then there were Mike McDonald, Lamar Gant, Jeff Michaels, Nicu Vlad, Bob Peebles, and Gary Heisey. But I don't think Lyle means that they do; I think he means that you have to get strong to get big legs, and that getting strong makes your legs bigger.

Second, the vast majority of published studies are shit. SHIT. Anybody that tries to draw a conclusion about different training modalities based on controlled studies of untrained 18 year-old boys that are not capable of producing a 1RM, a 5RM, or any RM in an exercise or bunch of different exercises they don't know how to do and who will get stronger by simply doing the tests because they are so completely unadapted to any type of exercise and who can make their squat go up by riding a bicycle is either 1.) unaware of how humans adapt to training, 2.) publishing to keep a job, or 3.) both.

For instance, the Springerlink study cited had the following comment in the abstract: "Maximal strength improved significantly more for the Low Rep group compared to the other training groups, and the maximal number of repetitions at 60% 1RM improved the most for the High Rep group. In addition, maximal aerobic power and time to exhaustion significantly increased at the end of the study for only the High Rep group." Now, this is not terribly surprising, given that untrained kids would in fact get stronger *using heavier weights*, and that the maximum number of reps improved more *for the group doing higher reps.* Fucking DUH. Note that the study authors concluded that their work supported the rep-range continuum standard model, but I say it doesn't support anything, except that untrained kids will adapt if they train, they won't adapt if they don't train, and the adaptation will not be terribly specific until an initial period of non-specific adaptation has elevated the gross fitness level substantially.

Now, PPST discusses rep ranges and objectives as a continuum (p114) and gives general ranges: 90% 1RM low reps (1-3), strength end, ~65-80% 1RM "higher" reps (8-12), hypertrophy 50-75% 1RM for moderate reps (3-5) with maximal velocity, power. Reps vs. types of hypertrophy is also discussed p. 86-88. Glycogen storage at higher reps is examined as a contributor here also.

There's a lot of slop in those numbers because "1RM" and the %RM of a particular rep range mean very different things depending on the training experience, motivation, talent and mental abilities of the lifter, something that studies of this type are incapable of taking into account and that prove nothing without doing so. And the relationship of reps to %RM depends on the exercise in question as well; bench presses and deadlifts respond differently to changes in volume and intensity for most people. Working in the 80-95% range is pretty typical for the general hypertrophy range listed above for lots of people on lots of exercises. Higher reps don't necessarily mean small weights (although they probably do for untrained, college-age males), and particularly for people who have adapted to working within a particular rep range.

Separating out reps per set, total reps, and total tonnage and how these interact hasn't been performed in any kind satisfactory way in studies I've seen. So the best evidence I have is not comparing the legs on lifter A with those of lifter B, but observing changes in the same lifter with different training. And what I see is lifters training hard with low reps at high %s (e.g. lots of heavy singles, doubles) gain size when they switch to periods of higher rep work. How much higher? Total reps? Total tonnage? Time between sets or density of the reps? It all depends. But everybody is right when they say that pussy weights don't make big legs, and studies done on kids that can't lift anything but pussy weights can't come to valid conclusions.

I maintain my position that for more experienced trainees capable of producing heavy effort that approximate true 1-3RM and 15-20RM ranges of effort, the higher rep ranges produce a more voluminous sarcoplasmic hypertrophy and the lower rep/heavier weight ranges produce more contractile protein-dominated lower volume hypertrophy. And personal experience must temper your application of these general rules.

---

3 sec rest

Colnago: Getting close to my 5RM I find myself resting for about 3 seconds after rep 3 and 4 in order to complete the set of 5 reps. Am I fooling myself and should I rest shorter (just lockout and descend) and not make it to 5 reps that day and try again next workout ?

Mark Rippetoe: Time between reps does not matter, unless it is extremely protracted, in which case the next rep will be shit anyway. If all 5 reps are technically correct, the set is good. In our strength acquisition model used in SS:BBT, we are primarily concerned with getting all the reps of the set, not so much with how long it takes.

Supercompensation curiosity

Polynomial: I understand that many of the figures in PPST are meant to be descriptive rather than quantitative, but here's something that piqued my curiosity: Figure 2-2 on page 30 makes it seem as if supercompensation occurs in a very specific time period which depends on the training program and the athlete. I'd like to know how this works in practice in the following sense: suppose that I'm doing something based on the Texas Method (which I am), and that the peak of the performance vs. 1RM curve for me is on Monday at 5pm. How slowly does this curve decay around its maximum? Are we talking hours or days? This probably matters a lot more for advanced athletes, but what about intermediates?

Mark Rippetoe: You are trying to make precise that which is in reality a squishy thing. It varies widely with experience, previous week's work, rest, diet, genetics, and all the other things about your life which control your recovery, and I don't know how you have determined that 5pm on Monday is the magic hour. I suspect that no one has that degree of control over this information.

Weight to Strength relation

progressiveman1: In the last chart in PPST, you guys estimate strength levels according to bodyweight. I couldn't help but notice that at the heaviest end of the spectrum the strength levels were very much higher than the lowest end, even in untrained people. Is this solely because a surplus of calories drives strength progression, or is there another function derived from bodyweight that relates to strength levels?

Mark Rippetoe: Your question is unclear. What do you mean by "heaviest end of the spectrum"?

progressiveman1: The heaviest end of the spectrum in the charts in your book; i.e., the heaviest bodyweight compared to the lowest bodyweight. For example, in the Squat chart the heaviest bodyweight you list is 320 and the untrained strength level for that weight is 147. The lowest bodyweight you list is 114 and the untrained strength level for that weight is 78. Basically, my question is: Why does an untrained person who weighs more have more strength than someone who weighs less?

Mark Rippetoe: I was afraid that's what you were going to say. The answer is: because his muscles are bigger, and bigger muscles produce more force than smaller muscles.

progressiveman1: 1. So the answer to my first question would be, "Yes, the reason a heavier untrained person is stronger than a lighter one is solely because eating a surplus of calories drives strength progression."?

2. For trained people, I don't understand how you can make an estimation for strength based on bodyweight without making a distinction between bodyfat percentage. For example, based on the charts an intermediate man who weighs 220 has an estimated 301 squat, and a man who weighs 198 has a 185 squat. If a man is currently at the former stage and decides to rid 20 off his bodyweight to reach the latter bodyweight, he wouldn't lose 15 off his squat if he continued training, would he?

Mark Rippetoe: 1. No, the answer to your first question is in my second reply.

2. Our chart says the intermediate man has a 285 squat. Given that typo, it is understood that these are averages, and that an average 198 lb. guy that is squatting 285 does not have 30% bodyfat anyway. Average bodyfat for that level of advancement is assumed.

Brandon: I think a better question would be the opposite; why are the strength-to-mass ratios LOWER at higher bodyweights? That is, it appears that a very light lifter is able to lift RELATIVELY more than a very heavy lifter at the same level of training. Why is lower bodyweight associated with greater pound-for-pound strength?

Mark Rippetoe: Finally, a sensible question. This is because strength is related to the cross-sectional area of the muscle mass, not its total mass. The contractile mechanism of muscle depends on the total number of fibers in a cross-section, not the length of those fibers, and a short guy will have the same cross sectional area as a taller guy, while the taller guy will have more muscle mass due to the fact that his muscle bellies are heavier because they are twice as long at the same cross-sectional area. Therefore, taller/bigger people have more muscle mass per unit of cross-sectional area than do shorter/lighter people. So on a pound-for-pound basis, shorter/lighter people will be stronger.

Why are squats so uniquely effective?

Robert B: I'm curious about why squats in particular are so effective at building mass & strength in novices. I had assumed that any really heavy lift would have an effect similar to squats – especially deadlifts, which have a similar range of motion (at least in terms of bar travel) and typically use even more weight than squats. Yet you recently made a post suggesting that subbing deads for squats would appreciably lower mass gains. And of course there is the fact that your extremely successful SS program includes 6 squats for every deadlift. Please understand that I'm not challenging your observations about squats; I'm just curious as to the hows & whys of their unique efficacy.

Mark Rippetoe: I'm not sure I can provide a deeply satisfying answer to this, because I really don't know. It's come up often, and it's obviously one of these things that ex.phys. types don't deal with. I THINK that it has to do with the fact that the stretch reflex aspect of the movement and the long range of motion causes so much stress on so much tissue, and this coupled with the fact that the bar is sitting on you so that your entire frame is loaded for the whole set produces a stress event that results in a system-wide hormonal response. The deadlift doesn't do this same type of loading, because it starts in the concentric position, doesn't use the full range of motion, and if it's trained using multiple sets it gets so damn hard that it beats you up enough that you don't recover. The squat is harder in more friendly ways, so to speak, and can be trained hard but recovered from more easily.

But really, I don't know.

Possible cause for my damn shoulder pain

Irishman301: I'm taking a break from the SS novice program is mainly because of these shoulder pains I've been having. I was just wondering what the possible cause could have been so I can avoid doing this again in the future. Basically, my shoulder started hurting after I started attempting to increase my press linearly. I started at 95 lbs., and I added 5 lbs. per week until I got to 135 lbs. It was right around the 120 lb. mark that I started to experience the pain in my right shoulder (and even a little bit of discomfort in my left shoulder too). I sucked it up anyway, until I hit 135 lbs. I then decided that I was either a.) doing the press with bad form, or b.) increasing the weight too quickly, and not allowing adequate adaptation. It was bothering my just to take the loaded bar out of the rack at that point.

The pain is right in the side head of my right shoulder (I think it's called the lateral head), and I feel it 1.) when holding the bar in the low-bar position for squatting, 2.) when I reach behind my head and touch my left shoulder, 3.) when I squeeze my shoulder blades together, and hold it for a few seconds, like a double biceps pose like bodybuilders do, and 4.) when I do overhead presses. It's not a serious pain that stops me from being able to move my arm in every direction, but it's something that bothers me enough to know something's not right.

I'm thinking that this was caused from pressing without pulling my shoulder blades back and not sticking my chest out as described in SS. I'm also thinking that when I start back up on the program, I may start the press at 75 lbs. (or less) and increase in 5 lb. increments from there, then once I hit 120 lbs. I will start increasing by 2 lbs or so. I was just wondering what you think may have been the possible cause of this, what it may possibly be (rotator cuff?), and if my method of trying to fix it seems like the right way to go about it?

Mark Rippetoe: This could be either a bicep tendon or a supraspinatus (rotator cuff) injury. If it came on gradually – as opposed to a sudden trauma, like a pop – it's probably some inflammation that will heal with either a correction of form or a short layoff and a reset. But it will not be necessary to start back over at the bottom and run up in 5 lb. jumps again since you are stronger now that you were when you started.

But let me clarify something: YOU HARD-HEADED FOOLS THAT WON'T USE THE SMALL PLATES ARE JUST ASKING FOR AN INJURY LIKE THIS. Smaller muscle groups cannot get strong as fast as larger muscle groups, and if you do not allow for this when planning your progression, especially after I have TOLD YOU THIS IN THE FUCKING BOOK AND ON THIS BOARD SEVERAL TIMES, then I hope you get hurt and have to have something amputated.

Brad: Am I missing something? It seems like he was only increasing his press poundage by 5 lb per week. :confused:

Mark Rippetoe: You're correct in noting that he was not doing the program correctly. You're missing the fact that he was adding 5 lbs. at a time, no matter how infrequently he was doing it, and 5 lbs. is usually too big a jump for smaller people's upper body musculature. Now, learn that the object of the program is to NOT stall until it's absolutely unavoidable. That way, you don't have to get unstuck. Very slow progress for 2 years is preferable to very rapid progress for 2 months, no?

Coldfire: That makes sense, but why do you think it might cause an injury? Wouldn't you just fail to lift the weight if you made a too big jump?

Mark Rippetoe: Especially for the press, when we try really, really hard to lift a weight that is too heavy – perhaps even just a tiny little bit too heavy – we get in positions bad enough that things occasionally get hurt.

Speed development ROM carry-over

Brandon: You've mentioned that one reason you use the power clean in SS is to train force generation in pulls from the floor, which carries over to slow-but-maximal deadlifts and similar max efforts. However, the power clean is usually taught -- by you as well -- with the critical explosion occurring at the second pull, very far indeed into the lift, with the initial pull from the floor being mainly about positioning and often done more slowly. So if the main "power" movement happens near the top of the ROM, can we expect to see improvements in muscle recruitment and speed generation at the bottom when we're trying to initially budge the bar in a heavy deadlift?

This question is about the power clean/deadlift dynamic, but I'm interested in the generic issue as well, because it bears upon speed training in general. We know we need to train for strength in the full ROM (well, within a handful of degrees) that we want to be stronger in; do we also need to train for speed in the full ROM we want to be faster in, or does it work differently?

Mark Rippetoe: Once the clean is learned correctly, with the explosion occurring at the top, and heavier weights are attempted, the bar will have to be accelerated off the floor. In other words, the bar leaves the floor slowly in correct position and then gets faster as it gets higher, culminating in peak velocity at the second pull. So it leaves the floor and immediately gets faster. The slow pull off the floor is only a learning cue, and is not preserved in the final technique. So really, the whole ROM is being trained explosively.

---

20 rep squat routine

Ursus: In your book you mention 20 rep squat routine, and my impression was that it was done with respect. As I understand this routine was developed by Strossen for gaining mass. I did two cycles of it and must confess that there are few workouts that may compare to it in terms of effort of the will needed to complete the set. My question (finally) is, in your opinion, does 20 rep squats contribute to strength training? My goals are increase in maximum strength in squat and deadlift. How would you incorporate (if at all) this routing into overall training. Doing it once a week? Or doing it for 6 - 8 weeks exclusively then going back to 5x5 or whatever the main methodology is? I am 45 and my recovery ability is not that great anymore and I am cautious not to overtrain or get injured.

Mark Rippetoe: The 20-rep squat program has been around a lot longer that either me or Randall Strossen, PhD. Peary Rader wrote about it often in Iron Man decades ago, and I'm quite sure he didn't invent it. They may be the hardest thing in the weight room, so most people will never do them. They don't contribute to strength, in the strict 1RM sense of the word, since any weight that can be done for 20 reps is not heavy like a 1RM is heavy. But they do make your legs grow, and bigger legs make for stronger legs by improving leverage. The biggest problem with 20s is that they burn you up after just a few weeks, so they can't be used more than a couple of times a year.

The Skin Fold Test

Spur: Besides body building, is this test really necessary for a player in field sports? Is the lower body fat percentage more an appearance requirement than a sporting one? Instead of the guys with higher fat percentages trying to reduce it by dieting and aerobic/anaerobic work, is it not better to focus on gaining functional strength with BBT instead? I mean the player with an est. 20 percent body fat who can squat and dead lift twice his body weight obviously has better functional strength for his sport (and therefore move efficiently on the field) than a weaker player with say 12 percent body fat?

Mark Rippetoe: The process of gaining functional strength while on a diet appropriate for one's individual needs will take body composition in the correct direction for each athlete. As a general rule, most strong athletes in their 20s that train hard and eat clean will be closer to 12% than 20% anyway. At 20% bodyfat, an athlete that needs to move will be carrying around a load that doesn't contribute to performance, but really, honestly, I've seen very few athletes who were actually training hard and eating correctly/not partying too much at 20% bodyfat. In other words, the process of gaining the strength to squat 2x bodyweight x 5 and obtaining the conditioning to APPLY it on the field most usually precludes a bodyfat level of 20%. But aside from that, there is no physiologic reason to assign to bodyfat percentage the role of an important indicator of athletic performance.

Your thoughts on taking weeks off?

solidsnake123: I have heard that it is a good idea to take a week off every 6 to 8 weeks in order to let the CNS take a break and get some rest. Is this accurate, or should breaks (optimally) never be taken if you are not doing excessive workouts and/or volume?

Mark Rippetoe: If you need a break, take one. But don't stop training just because you've heard you're supposed to. There are few things graven in stone, except that you have to squat or you're a pussy.

Cold weather garage lifting

Sandbagger: Does cold weather (I live in Jersey) have a significant effect on heavy lifting performance? If so, would a proper warm-up be enough to counter any negative effects? Is hot weather/humidity more of a detriment?

Mark Rippetoe: Lots of people have trained in the cold for a very long time. Clothes and warmup are a very effective solution to this problem. Heat is much less fun, because you can't take off enough clothes to make a 107-degree weight room comfortable. The heat is friendlier to joints, connective tissue, and muscle bellies, while the cold is friendlier to sweat glands and my general demeanor. Given the choice, I suppose I'd rather not get hurt as easily, so I'd take the heat, as much as I hate it.

"Advanced" SS alterations

bango skank: Instead of resetting or microloading once I've plateaued on a lift, could I instead alternate it with an accessory exercise? For example if I stalled out on the Press, could I do:

Workout B:
Squat 3x5
Press 3x5 / Handstand Pushups 3 sets (alternating)
Power Cleans 5x3

or if I maxed out on the Bench:

Workout A:
Squat 3x5
Bench 3x5 / Dips 3 sets (alternating)
Deadlift 1x5

Would these adjustments allow me to progress due to the reduced frequency of the exercises? (This assumes the other lifts are still progressing on their own.)

Mark Rippetoe: As a general rule the reason you plateau is because you have adapted beyond the ability of the stress imposed by the workout to continue to produce an adaptation, coupled with the fact that the magnitude of this stress now requires more time in which to recover. This is the difference between a novice and an intermediate lifter. Therefore, if a stress reduction like you propose works, it means that inadequate recovery, and not an inadequate stress level, was the reason you were stuck. Try it and see, and make corrections to your program based on what you find out.

Stalling and Next Step

Tca: I have been doing a 5x5 3 day per week program for about 10 weeks. I was injured and had to start over completely with squatting, deadlifts and power cleans. I was doing them all wrong, and your book really helped me. I am still only working with very light weight on these exercises to nail down the form. However, on the overhead press and bench press, weighted dips, pullups/chinups I am just about at my limit. I'm at 5 sets of 5 for 130 on the overhead, and 5 sets of 5 for 225 on the bench and 3 sets of 5 for 55 on the others. My question is, how do I change the program from here to keep gaining strength if I can't keep adding weight? Would you suggest 3 sets of 5 rather than 5 sets? If so, what is the big difference in 3 sets or 5 sets in general? I'm a little all over the place, but my basic question is, what is my next step?

Mark Rippetoe: You're making two mistakes: First, you're waiting for something cool to happen to you that will suddenly permit your squats, deadlifts, and cleans to be treated like the smaller upper body exercises in your program. Just go ahead and make the damn things get stronger every workout like you're supposed to. Waiting to add weight to the most important exercises in your program is terribly unproductive; when will you know to start going up? Who will tell you it's okay? If you have form problems, fix them and get busy.

Second, the fact that you have not made the bodyweight gains that are facilitated by the squat, deadlift, and clean have contributed to your being stuck on the upper-body stuff. This will take care of itself when you start doing the program correctly.

Tca: Wow! Now wait a minute. I ripped my groin to the point that I could not even bend my knees. I wasn't able to do anything with my lower body. I just recently am starting to feel better, and I have been trying to get the form down perfectly. That's why I haven't done squats, deads and cleans. I would rather do them than any upper body exercise. That's the whole reason I am even lifting weights. I was devastated with the injury, but stuff happens. I worked a lot on stretching, and the only thing I could do was upper body. Now I'm stuck. I just ordered your other book, so maybe there's something in there to help me with being stalled.

Mark Rippetoe: I'm not assigning any value judgment to the fact that you are not training your lower body, and you didn't say what your injury was. I've had groin injuries and I understand how bad they can be. I pulled both my gracilis origins loose during a heavy squat triple once, and had to start rehab on them 4 days later. To say that it hurt badly is a pathetic understatement, but nonetheless the rehab took place.

But it doesn't matter what your injury is. What I am saying is that this is probably the reason your progress has stopped. The universe doesn't care about *why* – it only cares about *what*. Goddamn universe. The program is set up the way it is because it works that way, and the fact that you can't do it that way is the reason it's not working. Why is irrelevant.

Partial squats

Brandon: I know you're not big on squats that don't break parallel, but it occurs to me that they might have some value for certain things. The main benefit, just like for most partial-ROM movements, would be that greater weight can be used. You don't get strength over the full ROM, or the same systemic effects, but the movement used in, say, a quarter squat seems very much like that used when jumping, dipping for a push press or jerk, or many other athletic movements. Lifting in this ROM with the highest weights possible would seem to yield certain athletic benefits beyond what full ROM squatting with lower weights would produce. Thoughts?

Mark Rippetoe: If lifting heavy weights for partials were of any benefit for sports, Gold's Gym would be fielding the majority of the 2008 Olympic team. They don't really help with jumping because they are so slow that the stretch reflex recruitment is different, and they are so hard on the knees that they get you hurt. The jerk is its own partial squat and doesn't need any back squat partial assistance work. And the better mechanical position at the top of the squat has been nicely addresses by the chains and bands used in the Westside method.

Variation for relative strength athletes?

Mmafan: Hey coach I was just wondering if you would change anything for an athlete not looking to gain much size but mostly strength and power. I'm a grappler and compete in submission wrestling and would like to get stronger and more powerful with minimal weight gain.

Mark Rippetoe: Don't eat to gain weight, and you should be fine.

Mmafan: Thanks coach. Are their any specific exercises I should do besides the squat, dead, press, clean, chin-up, and row for my goals?

Stakehoagy: I was thinking about the same thing. Suppose I want to run 100 meters for track next season. If I don't eat all the food required to gain some mass, how would it affect my strength? Would my linear progress stop quicker? i was planning on taking .9 grams of protein per pound of bodyweight. Double that in carbs, 4 or 5 fruits and 4 or 5 vegetables with 4 glasses of skim milk per day. But it seems that is close to what you recommend anyway except for the skim not whole milk.

Mark Rippetoe: As is usually the case, your barbell training should reflect the level of training advancement you have achieved in barbell training. IOW, if you are an experienced grappler that has never trained with weights before, you train with weights as a novice and your novice program is just the six exercises.

And a novice progression in the absence of a way to gain muscular bodyweight as rapidly as the program with the normal novice diet provides will plateau earlier that it would if the lean body mass had increased.

Dan F: Once this plateau has been reached is it possible, changing to intermediate program, to gain anymore some strength without gaining muscular bodyweight through diet? And if possible is that new strength only from neuromuscular improvement (apart from improvements in form of exercises)?

I ask this somewhat theoretic question because sometimes I read here or there that gains in strength are possible, not only in a novice period, without gaining muscular bodyweight: I always thought it's impossible if we speak of "absolute" strength and not strength relative to bodyweight. But I'm often wrong in many things...

Mark Rippetoe: There will be a point at which all the neuromuscular/technical improvements that can be made have been made. At that point some muscle will have to be grown. Normally these two processes proceed together, and that's why novices normally gain weight. If you restrict calories to the effect that muscle cannot grow as it normally should and will, you restrict most of your progress to that which is possible with neuromuscular/technical improvement.

Impact of age on progression rate

Patrick: Recently I've been wondering about how one factors age into strength training protocol. I found the discussion in another thread about the response to milk and exercise to older lifters. I also took your pointer and read your article in the CrossFit Journal and I recall a brief mention of the role of age in stress adaptation in Practical Programming. So while I get the big picture – it's a multi-variable process and everything goes to hell as you get older – but I'm wondering if you have any rough mile markers when you train someone.

For instance, at what age do you think the GOMAD scheme does more to add fat than facilitate strength gains? And is there an age where one's rate of progression begins to drop off more rapidly than before – in other words, how does the fifteen year gap between 15 and 30 compare to that between 30 and 45? And more generally, when can one expect to begin factoring age into training protocol as a valid reason rather than an excuse not to work hard?

I'm in my mid-20's and aside from the accumulation of some minor injuries I don't notice that I've slowed down since high school. But every time an older friend of mine gets excited about lifting and tags along to the gym here's what happens: we spend some time learning lifts and determining starting weights – nothing really to beat up the body. He leaves excited to come back. Then, two days later, I find him complaining of aches and pains, refusing to return to the gym. These guys are in their early to mid-30's and to me it just seems like they're allergic to work and discomfort and I've learned that those are not good lifting partners or even lifting company. So I've been telling them that they're just paying the price for being lazy and it'll get better in a couple of weeks when their bodies are used to moving again. Is that wrong – is 30 really the new 90?

Mark Rippetoe: No, 30 is not the new 90, or even the new 40. There are no mile markers, only general trends. You know the fish diagram in chapter one of PPST? The asymptotic line that represents training progression serves as a good model for lots of trends through time, and the effects of age are one of them. As you get older, the effectiveness of your response to training, your ability to recover, your ability to tolerate stress in general and unaccustomed stress in particular, your ability to train on little rest or bad diet, the perception of the pain and significance of injury, your willingness to push through a rep you may hurt yourself doing, and 80 other things fall off like that curve describes. It is a highly individual variation, but it will always conform to that curve in a general way. So, according to the curve, the gap between 15 and 30 is waaaaaay less significant than the gap between 30 and 45. Just think what it's like to be in the middle of the next one.

Can stretching hurt performance?

QSAlexander: My 4th workout on SS: During my squats yesterday, I forced my hands and the bar into your recommended positions. It wasn't painful, just felt like a really good stretch in the shoulders. So I kept it through the sets. When doing the press next, I had nothing. Had to drop 10 lbs. off the previous work set numbers, and felt like all I had working for me was triceps. Could the stretching have caused this? I don't think I overstretched and caused any injury, as my shoulders aren't really sore at all.

Mark Rippetoe: All the studies have shown that stretching prior to either strength or power work diminishes performance. Even given that most studies are shit, I know enough lifters that have told me that stretching prior to squats makes them fell "loose", meaning that it detrimentally affects their power out of the hole. That may have been what happened. The real question is whether you keep doing it, and the answer is yes, you have to so that you can squat better, and when you don't need to stretch anymore – when your shoulders are flexible enough to get under the bar correctly – you can stop, because at that point you won't need to anymore.

Sawol: Specifically, I'm wondering if it's okay to stretch my hamstrings before deadlifting. I've found that keeping my back "rigid" is easier after some stretching. Is this okay to do?

Mark Rippetoe: I do it, because my hamstrings are tight enough that I have to before I can get in a good position to pull. Stretching for athletes that are already flexible enough is a waste of time and may be detrimental to power production, but for someone who needs to stretch before a correct position can be achieved it is essential. And if you are so inflexible that your lack of ability to get into position hurts your power production, you need to stretch despite the fact that stretching diminishes power production. But if you are sufficiently flexible, don't stretch before a power-dependent workout.

Training to failure

Killiansred: I read that training to failure is an old training philosophy and nobody should do it anymore. That got me thinking, say you doing 5X5's of Bench Press on volume day of a Texas workout, should your last set of 5 not be all you can do? Once I reach my last set I'm dying trying to get that last rep. Would that not be training to failure? Maybe they meant going to failure on every set, I don't know. I was hoping you could shed some light on the subject.

Mark Rippetoe: You believe everything you read? Okay. Wichita Falls is the Scenic Capital of the United States. Our mountains are beautiful, our rivers are clear, our weather is the best in the country, and there are no fat people. Better get in the car now.

Killiansred: So you are saying that training to failure is the correct way to train? Please enlighten me. Or you agree that your last set of 5 across is training to failure.

Mark Rippetoe: Training to failure is not incorrect. It is just not my program. You are supposed to train according to your numbers that the progression you are doing calls for, and this varies with your level of training advancement.

O-lifts for sports conditioning

Jamieb: I'm interested to hear your thoughts on the usefulness of Olympic lifts for sports conditioning. There appears to be much debate over this on the net. I saw a previous post where you indicated you may write about the subject one day.

Mark Rippetoe: The controversy seems to be over whether form can hold together the length of a long, light set of snatches or C&J, right? The fact that the set is very long means that it is done with a weight which by definition is not hard in terms of the lifter's 1RM. The set is being done for the conditioning effect provided by explosive multi-joint long ROM movement, not to improve 1RM strength. So the question is actually whether or not a very low % of 1RM 20-rep set has the potential to adversely affect the technical ability of a lifter capable of a much higher 1RM, and the answer is that if it can then the lifter is not very experienced. The ability to separate the two types of work – technically correct heavy weight low reps from technically unimportant very light weight high reps – is an ability any decent lifter possesses, or can develop this afternoon. So yes, I am in favor of using snatches and C&Js for conditioning work.

"Winged" scapula

Peter_k: I realize I can't rely on Internet diagnoses, but it seems I have what is referred to as a "winged" scapula in one of my shoulders. Basically the left scapula sticks out too far, making some lifts more difficult and occasionally resulting in swollen joints. I realized that when I bring my shoulder blades together to bench, one of them is out more than the other, resulting in an uneven platform. It also seems to affect presses to some degree.

Ever trained someone like this? From what I've read, it's either due to a weakness in the Serratus anterior or nerve damage. I doubt very much it's nerve damage, so my question is: do you know a way of strengthening the serratus anterior to prevent this? You've scared me off physical therapists so I figured I'd get your take.

Mark Rippetoe: I very much doubt that it is SA weakness, because this corrects itself with training rather quickly, and why would it just be one side? If you've been training the major exercises for any length of time at all and you still have a wing, it's probably neurological. The question is then: what, if anything, do I do about it? Can I isolate the SA? And the answer is, of course, sure, all the PTs have lots of ways to do this. But even if you could that's not the way the muscle actually works, and isolating it doesn't fix the neurological problem. If the motor units will not fire, you cannot work them. You just keep training the major exercises that normally work the SA and the improvement that can occur will.

Teaching trainee with MS to squat

CokeNaSmilee: I was wondering if you have ever trained any clients with MS? I have one very determined 61 year old individual that I train who has MS and very much wants to barbell squat. I have him doing air squats damn near perfect now, and with this his confidence has gone WAY up. Do you know of any techniques or cues that might help me give him better instruction? I know there is nothing I can do no matter how much the MS effects his balance, but I was thinking in your day you might have had some success training an individual with MS and if so any advice you could pass off to a young coach would be great.

Mark Rippetoe: Just train him like he doesn't have MS, and pay very close attention to his recovery. This is the only problem he will have that other trainees don't experience to the same degree. It may be necessary to adjust training frequency down and to schedule light days more often than for other folks, but training with free weights is absolutely the best thing he can be doing, both for his body and mind.

Powerflifter48: I know MS symptoms are different for each and in 2002 I was told I might have possible MS but since have been free of any symptoms but always fear they will return.

Mark Rippetoe: MS is coming to be understood as a chronic condition that can be managed up to a point, but I don't know where that point is. I know that training can preserve function where function might otherwise be lost. I know that training can preserve immune system function, and with a good diet, good recovery, and an emphasis on doing everything possible to stay as healthy as possible (i.e. not smoking, not getting terribly drunk too terribly often) you can give yourself the best possible chance at a life free of symptoms. Six years is a long time to be asymptomatic, I believe. How confident are you in the 2002 diagnosis?

PaulS: PLer48: I have been diagnosed with MS. I had optic neuritis about a year ago. That's often associated with MS. I decided to go with MRI to see if there were any other signs, and there were. I have three small lesions on my brain consistent with MS. I didn't go with a spinal tap, because I see no reason to have someone stick a gigantic needle in my spine to tell me "maybe". My original Neurologist wanted me to start drug therapy (Avonex) because a study showed good results (no episodes for 2 years) in people with my exact situation. After two other opinions, however, I decided that the odds of not having an episode in 2 years were pretty high, regardless of drug therapy, and the side effects didn't excite me. So, for the past year, I have had an MRI every 3 months. So far, no change, and no additional symptoms. I'm going to 6 month MRIs now.

At the time of the optic neuritis, I was under a great deal of stress (work), was drinking every night, and more than just a beer, although I was not getting drunk most nights, I had gained some weight, had started smoking after not habitually smoking for years, and hadn't lifted for a good 18 months. The diagnosis woke me the fuck up. After researching the impact of healthy living for MS patients, I figure my best shot is to live healthy. That's certainly a focus now.

As far as training goes, I'm training harder than I have in years, setting PRs, and preparing for a meet in December. I'm not going to set any records, but I'll probably hit Class III, and my long term goal is to total Elite as a Master (I'll be 40 in 2 years). There's no reason at all to worry about training unless you are having issues. My docs all agree, lifting can only be a good thing. There is some concern with stress and heat for people with MS, but it is far outweighed by the benefits of getting strong and being healthy. So far it hasn't hurt me.

I also understand (anecdotally) that there are lots of people in my position - one episode, indications of MS being there, and then virtually no impact on life... no more episodes, or episodes so minor they are not noticed or very low impact. These people never have to go on drugs. Many of them are athletic/active. Might be a connection there.

Don't get me wrong, the diagnosis scared the shit out of me. I saw a life I did not want to live while undergoing treatment for the optic neuritis (I had a fucking home health care nurse come to my house to hook me up to an IV. I was 37. Only old invalids need home health care.) I wake up every morning happy I can feel my feet. Every time my arm falls asleep, I wonder if this is it. But I'm healthier than I've been in years. I've made huge changes to how I manage time, reduce stress, and actually got more productive. If you've gone 6 years, I'm even more encouraged. Hopefully we'll talk in another 5 or 10 years and wonder what we were worried about.

Mark Rippetoe: It would be very good if a lot of people read Paul's post above. See what you people can do about that.

GPP-General Physical Preparation

StuH: Paraphrasing heavily, you mention in SS that the people who will make the best gains on the novice program are well-fed young men on sports teams. These athletes will of course have better GPP than a sedentary male at the same weight and training age. In addition, their mobility/flexibility is likely to be far improved versus the previously sedentary trainee.

So, with all other factors unchanged (GOMAD, lots of rest, three full-body workouts a week, no fucking about with the program) have you found it beneficial in your experience to hold off on the increasing poundages while a sedentary trainee adds some form of metcon and mobility work on the off-days? Or can the novice begin both the three days of lifting AND extra work to raise GPP as their capacity to create fatigue with the barbell exercises is initially very low?

Mark Rippetoe: A novice trainee with no background level of GPP will obtain conditioning while doing just the 3 strength workouts per week, because strength training provides some improvement in VO_2 as a side-effect of getting tired during the workouts. Will it produce the levels of conditioning that a program based on metcon will? No. Will it produce the levels of conditioning that a 3-day strength program with a 4th day of metcon will? No. Can a novice recover from either of these? Certainly. But a 3-day strength program will produce better strength and muscular bodyweight gains that either of these 2 other options when followed through the end of the ability of the 3-day program to generate linear progress. I have not found it useful in terms of time spent trying to bring the level of GPP up to a higher level than presented before getting strong, because getting strong can always progress in a linear fashion irrespective of the starting point, and doing so would waste time that could be spent getting both strong and fit using the strength program. It all depends on the trainee's priorities and goals.

Peter_k: Actually, I have a GPP-related question I thought I might add under this thread, as it's somewhat relevant to the topic. For an "advanced" novice in the position to add some GPP/Metcon: is this generally easier to recover from than doing SS with a caloric deficit? I'm finding the latter difficult to manage and was toying with the idea of adding a day or two of metcon. Not as quick to drop fat that I suppose, but perhaps I could make better strength gains in the long run.

Mark Rippetoe: It is hard to recover from anything in a caloric deficit. It is also hard to recover from a lot of metcon added to SS, especially if it is very long higher-volume metcon. If you want to add metcon, just add one day and train it a few weeks before adding a 2nd. If you are worried about your bodyfat, tighten up your carbs. But it's best not to worry about your bodyfat now.

Increasing vertical jump?

Sawol: I am 5' 6" 205lb. Yeah, let's say I'm not built for basketball, but I cannot help it. I love the sport. I can jump and hang on the rim, but I've been told you need to be about 6-8 inches above the rim to be able to dunk. I deadlift 425 and squat 365, but I settled for rows for Starting Strength (which I am still on), leaving out power cleans. Will simply increasing my squat/deadlift and beginning to power clean allow me to get those extra few inches to dunk or should I follow a plyometrics program?

Mark Rippetoe: Vertical jump is one of those physical parameters that is largely controlled by genetics. Like calves, you either have them or you don't. VJ can go up maybe 25-30% and that's all. It's impossible to improve without improving absolute strength, and this is why practice-based programs that simply apply plyometrics and jumping always fail if they don't include squats. If you're confident that most of your easily-available squat strength has been developed, and that you have then exhausted the potential for plyometric training to turn strength into explosion, the only thing available to you is the Olympic lifts. Cleans and snatches will be the tools that allow an already-conditioned jumper to make a little more increase.

Phil Stevens: At 5'6" 205 I am not convinced that just getting a bigger squat isn't going to help you jump higher. I'd say attack that squat some more. We have a client that's your same height and yet 45 lbs lighter then you. Fairly new to training the right way and his squat is not far behind. You have in no way, IMO reached the full potential of your leg strength, which will damn sure transfer to a higher vertical.

Squat, and concentrate on getting the loads up over time and making the move CRISP; get some POP to it and practice your plyos a bit, as well as just learning how to do the vertical jump test correctly. You can easily add 4-5 inches to a client's test by just showing then the right way to do the test.

Mark Rippetoe: Phil: True, if the guy has never tried the test before, and has not developed his squat. But if all the easy squat increase has been achieved, and the test has been practiced, all the easy vertical jump increase has too.

Phil Stevens: Very true sir. Then like you said, Oly lifts, or one better get a time machine and ask for new parents.

Jacob: Plyometrics. I have "crappy genetics" (I'm pretty much the average American Joe, 6'1", always slightly pudgy, etc) but my dad, who is built almost identically to me, was a high school and collegiate diver. His programs for that sport included a **lot** of plyometrics, even if they didn't call it that back then. His vertical at its peak was nearly 50% better than mine at my peak (38-42" vs. a dismal ~ 24" for me when playing football). I guarantee you he never squatted 400+ in his life, either, which is about where I'm at right now. I sure can't dunk.

Depth jumps of various sorts, done FRESH, with lots of rest between reps (these are not a metcon), a couple times a week, will add a couple inches to anyone's vertical. But at 5'6" and already hanging on to the rim...another 6-8" is asking for a lot.

Mark Rippetoe: And I'll bet you a lot of money that a collegiate diver didn't have a 42" vertical jump. I never had more than about a 22" vertical with a 600 squat, so strength is not necessarily indicative of power, but true 42" verticals are so very rare that I feel safe saying that his was not measured in the standard way. If I am wrong and they had a VERTEC and a good tester and a flat-footed start, I apologize.

Phil Stevens: Very good points. You have limb length, being built for the activity, etc., but the argument is valid that if one gets stronger the potential to create power is greater, is it not? It surely isn't going to hurt to flat out get stronger. I mean, hell, my fat ass has a 28.5" measured on the Vertec and that was with a bum knee my first time doing it.

Mark Rippetoe: Certainly. I had a better vertical squatting 600 than I did squatting 400. But my point is that strength alone won't ensure a big vertical. And your point is that the best way to increase the vertical is to increase strength.

Training while having a cold...

Willsnow: I have just caught a lovely 'summer' cold. It's pretty heavy. I've read in a few threads on other forums to stop training and recover then carry on or the recovery will take much longer and the symptoms may worsen. Is this your opinion also? Bare in mind that I work out at home so wont be risking infecting other people at a gym. What about training more lighter for a while untill I recover?

Mark Rippetoe: My general rule has always been: train though a cold, which only affects your nasal tissues, but lay off for the flu, which is systemic. It's always worked for me.

Anthropometry and bar speed.

BIGGUY6FT6: As you can tell by my name I am a fairly tall guy. 6'6" 265 26% BF. All of my lifts are coming along nicely in the 7th week of SS. One thing I have started to notice is that the heavier the lifts get the bar speed slows down. I have always had a hard time with bar speed. Especially on Squats, Bench, and DL. PC's are new to me so I don't have a reference. I know that, obviously, this is going to happen due to the weight but was wondering how much anthropometry has to do with this. I have long ass forearms and femurs (40" inseam). How much do long limbs affect these particular lifts? What should I do to counteract if any (i.e. 2 inch box to elevate the bar for PC and DL)?

Mark Rippetoe: I have never noticed that bar speed has anything to do with anthropometry at all. It has more to do with the genetics of neuromuscular efficiency, motivation, hormone status, and recovery status. There are lots of very explosive tall guys with your anthropometry in the NBA.

SkinnyWimp: Hi Coach, I'm coming from more of a long-distance training background (triathlon, half-marathon, etc). I find I'm slow to get out of the hole when squatting, no matter how explosive I intend to be. Do you think my muscle fibers are either mostly slow-twitch, or are mostly behaving slow-twitch-like (i.e. I've trained my fast-twitch fibers to behave like slow-twitch)?

Mark Rippetoe: It is not unusual that a distance runner would lack explosion. You have spent years teaching your muscles to shut up, sit down, and repeat quietly. It will take a while to turn things around. In order that this progress more quickly, treat all your warmups as though you are trying to throw the bar or jump off the ground, so that your neuromuscular systems begins to understand what your new list of demands are.

Advice for 12 year old

BIGGUY6FT6: A co-worker of mine has a 12 yr-old that wants to bulk up. He is 5'9" 100 pounds and a really good wide receiver in football. He wants to add weight and strength and learn how to lift. His Father has asked me to help out. I was thinking the SS to a T and work up to GOMAD. Also would coach strict form and be cautious with the amount of weight. Is this reasonable? Any advice?

Mark Rippetoe: The novice progression works well for kids that age, BUT the increases are much smaller between workouts because of their limited hormonal response and subsequently blunted ability to recover from large training loads. Make sure he eats and sleeps well, and don't hesitate to give him breaks in training when you think it's necessary.

Women and overtraining

Heather: From PP:

"As a practical matter, if daily, weekly, or monthly programming models are used to increase strength or power, some modifications are required for women since the intensities used are based on the individual 1RM, and women can work with a higher percentage of this 1RM for reps. [...]if increased mass is the goal, a relatively larger amount of high volume work over a longer time at a slightly higher intensity would be needed."

So women have to work more, harder, and longer to get results. My question is, in light of this, are women in general more resistant to overtraining?

Mark Rippetoe: An interesting question. Women, in general are more resistant to overtraining because women, in general, are resistant to training anyway. The neuromuscular differences between men and women allow for higher percentages of 1RM to be handled for reps, which means that each rep represents a lower percentage of absolute strength. So women are less likely to overuse the things that lead to overtraining. But women may suffer from a muted recovery ability from the work they *can* do by virtue of the same lower testosterone levels that contribute to the diminished work capacity. What is your impression?

Heather: I've only got my own experience as a guide, so I'm not sure how easily or often men overtrain. I don't know that I've ever been truly overtrained, but a couple of times in the three years I've been lifting I have gotten to a point where my performance started going downhill, and then an overuse injury would pop up and force me to back off for a few months. These days I am trying to find a balance between working hard enough and often enough to make appropriate progress, and not working myself to the point where I end up hurt. I hadn't thought about the effects of testosterone (or lack thereof) on recovery; but in my case it seems "muted recovery ability" may be something to consider in my programming.

A question about growing old...

Drewfasa: I would like to hear about how your attitude to training has changed as you've gotten older. Particularly since you were a competitive powerlifter as a young man, I don't imagine you set PR's anymore in these lifts. I should imagine you have been a lot closer than most people to your genetic strength potential for most of your life, and have therefore been more aware than most of the limiting factor of growing older upon training. I'm not particularly old (26) but I recently started weightlifting training at the national sports centre here in England, and being faced with the fact that - in terms of elite athletics - I am older. In a word, what kind of goals does one strive for when setting new PRs is simply no longer possible? At this point does one try to compete against their peers?

Mark Rippetoe: At 26, you are not yet in your prime for the strength sports. Not at all. But as for me, and for lots of former competitors, the accumulation of injuries is the primary limiting factor for training. So our training goals need to be focused on things other than PRs in what was once our sport. This is not hard to do.

Ben00: What age, on average, do you consider a person to be in his prime in strength? It seems to me that most 50 year old men who don't train are a good bit stronger than most 18 year old men that don't train. Am I correct in the idea that men naturally get stronger as they age? Up to a certain point of course. I believe some people refer to this as old man strength.

Mark Rippetoe: If I remember correctly, Larry Kidney squatted 722 when he was 62. I'd say most strength athletes peak in their mid-thirties and hold it for several years before injuries start to kill them off. And I am well past that, just training to stay alive. I do some light strength stuff and a little metcon. No running.

TPrewittMD: I have to call BS on your comments above. I saw you flipping that tractor tire and wailing away at it with a 16 lb sledge hammer a few months ago. And as I recall, we check your pulse at one minute intervals, or close to it, and you had recovered after maybe 3 minutes. So, this "light strength" and "little metcon" stuff is grossly understated.

Mark Rippetoe: Well, all right then.

Shaky legs on Deadlift

Fullingm: First the whine - I have made three attempts at 405 in the last 6 months and have not been able to get it - (major profanity). This last attempt, I got the bar to my knees then my legs started wobbling like a new born calf! WTF! Obviously something is wrong with my form and or I am not keeping something tight.

On a second note, I use the standard grip – both palms facing towards me I believe this grip is referred to as the overhand. I don't seem to have a problem with the grip, but everyone at the box says if I use the alternate grip – one palm facing forward – that I would get this weight. I dunno.

Mark Rippetoe: It is quite common to miss a heavy deadlift at the knees with this type of tremor between the quads and hamstrings. You'll see it at every power meet. I don't have the neurological explanation for it, but it actually might have something to do with your grip. When you lose your double overhand grip, the bar starts to uncurl your fingers. The body has a "feedback" protection mechanism installed that prevents you from pulling a weight you cannot hold on to, and you will perceive this as a deadlift too heavy to pull. If the grip loss starts to occur at this place (the knees) on the way up, it might be contributing to the start of the tremor. It may be that you are having a grip problem that you do not perceive this way, and that if you switched to the alternate grip for your next attempt at 405 the problem might not appear. Then you would know for sure.

Light squats x 10 for technique

Knkavo: I seem to have some kind of mental block with squats. My technique is shit. As much as I think "knees out, lower back arched, chest up, head down, drive with the hips, lean forward to keep knees back", I still do pretty much the opposite for most of these. What drives me really crazy is that after struggling at a max of 120lbs/55kgs for a long time (sometimes even failing at that), about 1 month before Xmas, for one beautiful workout, something clicked in my mind and it all came together. So on the second workset I put on an extra 5 kilos and squatted 60 with ease, and for the 3rd I added 7.5 kilos and still had no problems.

So yesterday I tried something new and not approved in SS. I squatted only 42,5kgs trying for perfect technique. For the first time since that workout mentioned above it seemed to be working. I felt the stretch in my hamstrings, and the bounce. Knees stayed out. Back stayed arched. However, I found I was able to do 3 sets of 10 reps with no real effort (I ran out of breath a bit, and felt a bit wobbly right after, but it was easy nonetheless). What would you think of my continuing this (3x10 with low weight), for a couple of weeks max, until I feel I have my technique down and ingrained as habit? I'll add weight to the bar every workout too. All other lifts will remain 3x5. As soon as possible, I'll go back to 3x5 on squats too, with the corresponding weight increase.

Mark Rippetoe: And then when you really, really have it down with a nice light weight that's easy to do for sets of 10 (since 10 is more than 5 and that kinda makes it almost like the same thing, hard, you know?), you'll just go back to a heavier weight that's actually heavier and everything will stay the same? Maybe you should be involved in the Middle East Peace Process, because the same logic seems to be getting applied there.

5x5 - physiological basis

Dissection: I was sent here by a friend that could not answer this question. He is a fan of the 5x5 training system and said in his experience it is superior to other programs in terms of gaining muscle mass. Actually I am a bit more into the physiology behind strength training and out of my view it is suboptimal for gaining muscle mass. I really would like to hear the opinion of an expert about this.

To my knowledge the physiological basis for muscular hypertrophy can be basically seen in microtrauma, thus the strain on musculoskeletal apparatus is determinant of the amount of mass gain. As I understand the physiology, most gain in muscle mass can be achieved when the amount of force on passive muscular elements (the sarcolemma) is maximized by time which is maximizing the TUT *(time under tension – he assumes you, the reader, know this)*. It is to note that the actual force on the sarcolemma is important for the hypertrophic response and this is increased with muscular failure due to shortcomings in energy supply (ATP) / loss of intra/intramuscular coordination. This is the reason why most of the hypertrophic response gets generated in the eccentric phase of the movement with declining ability of the sarcomeres to counterwork the forces on passive muscular elements.

It is very popular to assume a "hypertrophy" range of repetitions at 15-20 reps, normally done in 3 sets. I know that these models of maximal strength, hypertrophy and strength endurance training do not represent the physiological basis very well, but until recently I thought I know, why these subjective experiences are in line with the physiological basis behind it. I also know that one cannot reduce optimal training to one training regimen because keeping one regimen is equal to keeping the challenge similar - which according to the SAID-principle is not desirable.

To my understanding the aim in gaining muscle mass as said before is maximizing the time under tension. Maximizing the effect on hypertrophy considering the physiological basis mentioned before therefore means having a load sufficient enough to challenge the muscle on the whole while keeping the time under load maximal to exhaust it. According to Hennemann's size principle I want to achieve a full activation of all motor units plus keeping the **time** under tension maximal. If you look into the literature you can see that the point of full recruitment of motor units is at a load 60-85% of 1RM which perfectly fits into the "hypertrophy rep range" mentioned before. The 5x5 system has its weaknesses in causing optimal hypertrophy because in my opinion it is too conservative in terms of adaptation to different stimuli (SAID again, when training only 5 reps your body only adapts to 5 reps)

The second, main point I see is that it disregards the "time" factor in TUT, keeping the time under tension in one set very low. Maybe I am wrong with my current understanding of the basic physiology of strength training. Is it correct you experience optimal gains with this program? To my recent understanding it could not be that simple. I would really like to hear your opinion about this.

What is the determining factor in causing hypertrophy? How to implement it into training? To keep it simple - would the best hypertrophy regimen be doing 45 sets with 1RM instead of 3 sets with 15RM, if this could be managed by the nerve system? I thought that 5 reps mainly lead to neural adaptations, disregarding the hypertrophic effect.

P.S.: English is not my native language, I think its readable, if you discover mistakes you now know where they´re from ;)

Mark Rippetoe: Your English is better than mine. But your understanding of adaptation is not. First, I don't care about hypertrophy as a primary goal. I care about strength, which always has hypertrophy as a side-effect, especially for novice-intermediate lifters. Second, all this HIT nonsense ignores the fact that the adaptation to any program is dependent on the adaptive history – and thus the adaptive ability – of the trainee. If a novice is subjected to a linear increase in loading, he will get stronger in a linear fashion, and this is always facilitated by a gain in lean mass along with a little fat. The question for him is what kind of program makes him strong the fastest, and that program uses 3 x 5. Five sets has proven to be too much volume for rapid recovery, and one set isn't enough.

The thing your high-rep-to-failure dogma ignores is the fact that you can't do it with significant amounts of weight relative to 1RM, and thus can't get strong doing it. And if you can't get strong, you can't get big. Strong = Big, if you eat enough to continue to improve your strength. If you don't, your gains stop. If the mechanism for hypertrophy was simply microtrauma acquired during time under tension with loads of 60-85% of 1RM, programming would be ridiculously easy and everybody that did this would be ridiculously hyoooge, which they aren't. And there would be no way to explain how everybody that eats correctly and goes through a linear progression with 5s gets big and strong, which they do. If we start a novice on light weights and high reps to failure, they will not grow, as thousands of guys reading this board will attest.

The bottom line is that muscular growth is a complex phenomenon that is accomplished through several adaptive mechanisms, but it is always a result of a stress that requires the body to be bigger, such as a linear increase in weight done in a rep range that permits both myofibrillar and sarcoplasmic hypertrophy, and a method of adequate recovery that permits the adaptation to occur. And that is best accomplished with sets of 5 and lots of food and rest.

Gravitron

JimF: I've seen the Gravitron disparaged in several places vis-à-vis using bands, but almost never with any explanation. I can see how the band might provide for more natural body movement b/c you're not wedded to the platform, but is a band really that much better? Seems like essentially the same idea to me only one uses the flexibility of the material and the other uses pneumatics. Plus, the Gravitron would seem to allow for more measured progressivity if you reduce the assistance each time. I'm certainly not a Gravitron partisan -- I'm just curious whether the bias against it (vis-à-vis bands) has merit.

Mark Rippetoe: If nothing else, they're a lot cheaper and take up less room. The machine is a crutch, and having the thing under you seems to discourage progress away from it in some way that bands do not. Some psychological deal. If you have access to a Gravitron on one of the plate-loaded versions thereof, I'd be interested in knowing if you had a different experience. But I've never seen anybody get off the damn thing when started on it. That's why I gave mine away.

Power cleans vs. speed deadlifts

Kerpal: What is your opinion on power cleans vs. dynamic effort deadlifts for improving one's deadlift? Power cleans are obviously a great exercise for athletic performance, but I've been thinking about it and it seems to me like speed deadlifts are more specific to actually deadlifting. Here's my thinking: with a clean, the first pull is very similar to a deadlift, but it's supposed to be "slow and controlled". You don't "explode" until the 2nd pull, when the "deadlifting" part of the lift is already over. But on a speed deadlift, you can just do the same exact movement fast with a light weight, which may be better for "teaching" your body to deadlift explosively.

Also, what do you think about pulling against bands for speed work? I do power cleans now and they're a great exercise, but I've been thinking about incorporating some speed deadlifts too, and speed deadlifts against bands seem quite popular with the powerlifters at my gym. In fact, I'm the only person there I've ever seen do cleans and snatches.

Mark Rippetoe: Do both. Cleans cannot be done slow, and once you learn how to do them they will definitely be moving faster through the middle part of the pull than the comparable range of motion for a DE deadlift, or even a clean hi-pull. The commitment to getting the bar up on the shoulders makes a huge difference in the way the pull is approached, and a lifter that is advanced enough to use DE deadlifts should already know how to clean well enough that the bar is accelerated off the floor, moving faster at the knee than a deadlift of any type. And the deadlift stops at about the place where the bar will reach peak velocity in a clean, so it is impossible to avoid slowing it down before this point if you're not going to rack it. But I see no reason for an advanced lifter not to be able to use both in his training.

Contrast showers

quack23: What are you're thoughts on contrast showers? Any benefits to doing them post workout?

Mark Rippetoe: They work, but they are stressful, expensive, and shrink your nuts pretty badly during the "cold" part. They are not possible in North Texas or the southern latitudes during the summer because the cold water is not cold. If you are not paying for the hot water it is better.

Question

OITW: Other posters have described having to leave out certain exercises because of time / equipment limitations. I do that with chins, GHRs and sit-ups, and less often with power cleans, and I know the price I pay doing that. When time is pinched, is there a value to doing (for example) squats and press one day, and power clean the next to catch up (not routinely, but maybe once every other week), or would the power cleans in this case interfere too much with the adaptation to the previous day's stress? Using the same hypothetical exercises, would it be better to do the two more stressful lifts (squats and PCs), and save the press to the catch up day? Or is this just altogether a bad idea?

Mark Rippetoe: The program as written is optimal, and anything else is less-than-optimal.

OITW: Copy. To quickly follow up: I probably phrased it poorly--which is the worst sub-optimal, playing catch-up with some lifts during recovery days, or not doing the lift at all during that workout cycle (ex. PCs, done once a week, so not done again until the next week)? If catching up is the best of two bad options, should one prioritize certain lifts with less of a CNS stress like benches/presses for the catch-up days? Just trying to figure out the best of two bad options often faced.

Mark Rippetoe: If you leave things out of the program, you don't get the training stimulus from the omitted exercises. If you arrange things so that recovery is sub-optimal, the training stimulus is not adapted to optimally. I don't know which you'll decide on, but probably the second option is marginally better.

Nearing the end of novice progression...a couple questions

sergeant_81: I am nearing the point where linear progression characteristic of a novice is slowing considerably, and recovery is becoming a critical factor. GOMAD faithfully throughout, average 4500-5000 calories per day. Sleep has been an issue, as I am not a good sleeper and am very inconsistent with hours of sleep on a daily basis. I drink nearly a half gallon of black coffee a day (much of it during my training sessions).

Question: My bodyweight seems to have stalled at 190. I have added another half-gallon of chocolate milk to my diet for the past week, but am not seeing further bodyweight gains. Is this a matter of simply eating more, or do eating requirements become more "complex" the more advanced a lifter becomes?

Mark Rippetoe: Dietary intake cannot increase infinitely or indefinitely. If you are getting enough chow growth will continue, but more slowly as you reach further toward your genetic potential. At this point programming becomes more important than dietary manipulation in ensuring continued growth and strength improvement.

Horrible Discrepancy between pushes and pulls?

XTrainer: I'll try to keep this brief. I am 19, 6ft 180lbs, been training seriously for perhaps 3 years (though I did a number of stupid things in the weight room, on the soccer field, etc. before that :)). I have strong pull ups/chins (Well over BW+100lbs maxes, +90lbs for 3, etc., and yes, they're legit reps) and OK power cleans and deadlifts (235 and 470) for my size and experience level. However, I still do not have a bodyweight press (@ 170 now) and my bench is nothing short of embarrassing (235). My push presses and jerks are similarly embarrassing.

There's an obvious discrepancy between my pushing and pulling strength. It seems my pulls respond well to just about any way I choose to train them. My press and bench press, however, are stubbornly unresponsive to everything I try. Have you ever had trainees with this strange discrepancy, and was there a particular approach that helped them?

Mark Rippetoe: There is a possible discrepancy between your upper body strength and your lower body strength. You did not list your squat so I cannot be sure how serious it is, but if your squat is about 400 your lower body is good. The 235 bench is not great, but the 170 press is not horrible and I think you have just spent more time chinning than benching. But the push/pull concept is rather arbitrary and artificial: there are no "pulling" or "pushing" muscles, there are just lots of muscles that get used in different ways. You already know this, and I feel bad that you're embarrassed now about having stated it this way. It's fine. Everybody has an occasional lapse.

Mixing training methods in the same session

Férreo: I've read that eccentric, concentric and isometric training has different motor recruitment patterns. This also happens with slow heavy lifting and explosive lifting (both can be performed in concentric, eccentric and isometric). My question is if one should avoid to mixing explosive lifting and heavy lifting in the same session (which, by chance, it's what do WSB guys) or eccentric and concentric training in the same session, to avoid sending confusing stimulus to the CNS.

Mark Rippetoe: In other words, should one never do heavy clean & jerks? They combine concentric explosion, heavy eccentric deceleration, and isometric position control. As do heavy snatches.

Férreo: So the answer is "no problem", I guess.

jtorres3: How are you supposed to separate eccentric and concentric training?

Mark Rippetoe: You'd have to pull a sled or ride a bike, and then do a bunch of negatives. Seems like a lot of trouble to my lazy ass. I'd rather just squat.

My Cousin's Best Friend Had this Other Friend Who Knew a Guy in the Army Whose Brother Benched 1000 lbs.

If I had a nickel for everybody who has recognized me from the gym in a bar and made me sit there while I'm trying to talk to Tucker and listen to his shit about "yeah, man, I'm going to get back into lifting, I'll be there Monday. You get there about what time?" and some guy he actually KNEW that could bench waaaay more than I can, well, I'd have a big pile of nickels.

And another thing: do you have any idea how many tall fat guys there are in North Texas that think they can be Professional Wrestlers if I'll train them? There are quite a few.

What's wrong with your program?

Irishman301: Ever since I started following your program with the squatting 3 times a week and doing power cleans along with the other major compound lifts with gradual, yet continuously increasing weights I have found myself getting much bigger and stronger then I ever was before in my whole life This never happened to me when I used to try and do "bodybuilding" routines. What gives????

Mark Rippetoe: Hell, I don't know. Sounds like the steroids have kicked in. You are taking the steroids, right?

Jamie J: Apparently, Irishman is the only person on the planet for who this program works since everyone else has to screw with it.

KSC: You mean that adding 100 lbs to your squat and 60 lbs to your bench in a six week period got you bigger than supersetting leg extensions and leg curls or triple drop sets on the pec deck?

RedSpikeyThing: Hey Coach, just thought I'd check in. In the 4 weeks I've been following this routine I've grown an appetite and gained 5 lbs :) I'm happy, but ma's grocery bill isn't too thrilled haha. I pulled my previous deadlift 1 RM of 375 for 5 reps and my bench and OHP have been going up as well.

Mark Rippetoe: It's unfortunate, but sometimes getting stronger requires getting a job to help pay for the groceries. Try to get one at a place where they throw away a lot of food.

How long should lockout be held...

Baldr: ...for the press (and bench press) specifically? Should the elbows be locked out and held for a full second, rather than immediately descending right after the elbows have locked out? What about for the squat, deadlift, etc.?

Mark Rippetoe: Just lock the bar out. No official time will be kept. This is true for all exercises that involve lockout.

Wish I had this damn book years ago

Gleko: Hi Coach, just a quick thank you for the books, Starting Strength and Practical Programming. I started lifting almost twenty years ago and had some pretty okay progress, but have been off and on for the last 10 years or so and nothing the last 2 years. I started back training in March and got your book only a couple of weeks ago. I have been on BB.com trying to figure out your program and have set my program as close to yours as possible given that the gyms here in Malaysia are not conducive to strength training. My training partner and I actually have to be members of two gyms as one has a squat rack (not a safety rack) and the other lets us deadlift. Since changing my bench style to your recommendations I have jumped 25lbs in 3 workouts and this morning on the overhead press did my best weight ever.

My weights are no where near what I would like them to be but really since using your explanations in your book everything feels so much better. So basically this is just a thank you for a great book and the best explanations on exercise I have ever read, and believe me over the last twenty years I have read lots of explanations, most of which made things more confusing afterwards. Bench press explanations along the lines of "if you track the vertical movement along the horizontal axis concentrating on moving the weight in a linear fashion towards peak overhead natural contraction you will note that the movement is linearly opposite the concentric definition of the elbow peak". Or some such other gobbledeygook. Anyway, just a thanks for a great book.

Mark Rippetoe: Quote:

> *"if you track the vertical movement along the horizontal axis concentrating on moving the weight in a linear fashion towards peak overhead natural contraction you will note that the movement is linearly opposite the concentric definition of the elbow peak"*

I really like this.

Losing the arch in the lower back at the bottom of the squat

Redivote: hey coach rippetoe...
here is my squat:
(YouTube link)
as u can see, i lose my arch in the lower back...
how can i fix this???

and tell me plz, how critical is it to keep this arch?? i guss that if i get round during a big 5-6rm squats its pretty dangerous??
tnx

Mark Rippetoe: u shud luk hear at my anser to thez guise, wut i has already rote:

(*StrengthMill link*)

Now, please try to improve your typing.

Redivote: thanks, and sorry

Mark Rippetoe: That should read: "Thanks, and sorry."

Standing presses

Penske: Unfortunately I work out in my basement with a low ceiling. Its about 2" or 3" too low to do a standing press to full extension. I have been compensating by standing with my knees bent and a little wider stance so that I can extend my arms completely. This results in quite a quad workout (especially after doing squats), but I feel that its not letting me get the most out of what the workout should. I am not getting stronger as quickly with the presses as with other exercises.

Is it a big deal or just a mental problem I am having? Do you feel that the slight bending of the knees and/or the wider stance changes anything with the exercise? Would you suggest changing to seated barbell/dumbbell press?

Mark Rippetoe: You will obviously not get strong as fast in an exercise that involves smaller muscles. But no, you have to use correct form on the exercise, no matter what the reasons might be for doing it wrong. Sorry about your basement, but if you want to continue to train there effectively it will be necessary to cut 2 plate-shaped holes in the ceiling above the platform. Make sure that you space them apart at the same width that the plates load on the bar. I make these types of mistakes with saws all the time, so I'm just sayin'.

EIC: Don't forget to cut them a little wider to accommodate a second--or even a third--45 on each side. Since this is strength training, you'll want to be sure that the ceiling can accommodate progressive resistance.

Dave76: But that might affect the aesthetic or structural integrity of the ceiling. I'd cut the hole big enough for 1-45 lb plate and then use 35s for progression.

bango skank: I'd dig a man-sized hole down into the foundation. That way no one will trip over the plates brimming up through the first floor. Just don't dig so deep that you can't lower the bar down to your shoulders.

RWatkins: Alternately, the plates can be carried from the basement to another suitable area as a pre-workout warm-up. Be sure and use good form while carrying things up stairs.

Prilepin's Table

Craigmeister: What do you think of using Prilepin's table, quoted so often in Westside related literature, for the basic lifts? Should it only be applied to the low and high percentage ranges, or ignored for everything but the Olympic lifts?

Mark Rippetoe: Once again, you have stumped the band. Do not assume that I am widely read. I am merely very smart. I do know, for example, that Avogadro's number is 6.02×10^{23}.

No spotter or power cage

progressiveman1: I can't find a workout partner and no gym around me has a power cage. Will you be my workout partner? Actually I'm just curious, given a squat rack and bench press station, how can I still hit failure without getting stuck in the bottom position?

Mark Rippetoe: I currently have memberships available for a reasonable monthly fee. But if you have to squat heavy alone with stands, you'll have to learn to dump the bar behind you safely. This means that you will have to practice it before you have to do it the first time, and you'll have to fix up the platform area so that you do not destroy anything that does not belong to you. Best to squat under these circumstances with bumper plates.

progressiveman1: I take it you wouldn't recommend the Smith machine? Earlier I figured that I shouldn't even mention it, but I'm mentioning it now.

Mark Rippetoe: You shouldn't have mentioned it.

Richie_Awesome: I've read a lot about stabilizers and I didn't see anything that was a must in free weight squatting vs. smith machine squatting. What else is there? (I ask in a non-sarcastic manner)

Mark Rippetoe: You don't actually see the difference between having the load stabilized for you in two of the three axes through which it can move vs. having to control them yourself?

Roger Clemens' Squat Technique

Tiburon: For the last few days of ESPN's coverage of Roger Clemens, they have been showing a brief video of Clemens and Andy Pettitte working out. The video shows Clemens and Pettitte doing quarter-squats on a Smith machine. Now, I respect these two strong guys for being at the top of their craft for so long. But I can't help but lose some respect for them when I see them doing quarter-squats on a Smith machine. Should I give them a break?

Mark Rippetoe: No, let's don't.

How to fix early arm bend?

Smolandski: Am trying to teach my son how to do Power Cleans, he is one of those early arm benders. He has a problem getting the "don't bend your arms early". Do you have any thoughts or advice on how to fix this?

Mark Rippetoe: I usually just yell, since he's not really paying attention to you. If you can get him to listen, have him use his triceps to squeeze his elbows into extension, and then tell him to keep them that way until he jumps. If that doesn't work, I'd hit him with a board I keep here for this purpose.

Humility, Age, & PPST

Pear: 1) Have you ever had to deal with someone you trained that started to get a little too large a head for their own good ("I squatted 405 so my shit no longer stinks") and if so, how did you deal with it? I'm trying to reestablish some focus on future goals.

2) I have kids 4, 5, 6, etc that want to learn how to lift - any experience with this or anyone you recommend that has dealt with this before?

3) I am reading SS 2nd and am interested in PPST - I have done the MadCow/Starr 5x5 on several occasions and feel like I have stalled on it now. From what I've seen of the Texas Method, they look very similar in principle.

Does PPST explain:
A) what to try after completing the Texas Method, or
B) allow an individual to create their own methods using principles the book describes which prevents stagnation?

Mark Rippetoe: 1. The way to deal with someone who is cocky about having squatted 405 is to load the bar to 415.

2. I have taught children to lift for many years. The objections to lifting for kiddos are addressed at length in the last chapter of SS 1st edition. Basically, if proper form is used, they are doing an almost infinitely scalable activity, and the resistance used can be precisely matched to their strength and skill levels. Contrast this with soccer, where uncontrolled full-speed collisions between 8 year-old kids is the norm and the injury rate is the highest for any organized sport. Isn't it amazing that doctors never object to soccer, but will still tell you that weight training for children is Dangerous. DANGEROUS.

(This chapter is available for free download at www.aasgaardco.com.)

3. PPST explains all this, both a. and b., and more. PPST explains everything.

Breasts and bench

Mladen: What is the modification of the bench press for women with, how should I say... bigger boobs? The lower bottom position (to the start of the abdominal muscles with upper arm close 60deg to torso) hits the boobs, so a) its uncomfortable and b) it prevents full ROM. Should more higher bottom position be used instead (when upper arm create greater angle to torso)??

Mark Rippetoe: I think I'd better see a picture, so that I can give you an accurate, professional answer. Or maybe a video. Yes, that would be better.

Cracked skin from milk drinking?

Stu: I've noticed in the last few weeks that the skin on my hands seems to be more prone to cracking. This might be coincidence, but is there a possibility that the milk is inhibiting the absorption of some nutrients? Or might I be simply drinking a lot of milk at the expense of getting enough of other food groups?

Mark Rippetoe: Unless you're in Australia/New Zealand, I'd bet your skin is cracking for the same reason mine is: it's winter. It's dry and cold, and that's what happens to skin in the winter.

Max-Stimulation

Tomo_1: I've started to train PL (few months ago), before my goal was gaining mass (training: MST) it works very good for mass gains. Actually I need strength gains, but rather I don't want to leave Max-Stim (cause still important thing for me are mass gains). Is any good way for me? Maybe 5x5 with M-times like MST?

Mark Rippetoe: I don't know anything about the MST program. Sorry.

Tomo_1: Max Stimulation = MST
in few words about MST: "M-Time. The Max Factor . M-Time is the time between each rep, after each rep the weight should be racked or set down and gotten completely out of your hands for the duration of the M-Time. This time can be manipulated as advancing fatigue ensues, IE first few reps use 3-5 seconds, next 5 to 10 - use 7 seconds, during the last 5 use 10 seconds. The starting time is usually going to be dictated by your own recovery from repetitive contractions and the intensity you are using." You are training 4 times/week, each bodypart 4 times per week. One set with 20 reps, you're adding weight weekly.

Mark Rippetoe: I'm sorry that I wasn't really clear. I am not interested in the MST program.

Tomo_1: Thanks for replies. Could you write more about SS? If you think it's better (or the best ;)) for me, I'll want do that program. Yes, I think to put my brain on autopilot is the best way for me, could you help me? btw In

April I'm going to start in competitions (for getting experience, not good place) and I'd like to have good strength with that system (as good as possible).

Mark Rippetoe: You want me to write more about *Starting Strength*? I already wrote *Starting Strength*, and it's a whole book long. Why don't you just buy it? It will be cheaper than your first entry fee to that competition you're in.

Teenage son -what age to start

Bfoley: Hello. My son is 14 years old and is 5'11" @ 155 lbs. He broke his collar bone recently and the ortho recommended that he start weight training to put on some mass. I was wondering if Starting Strength is an appropriate routine for someone his age. Thanks.

Mark Rippetoe: Yes it is. It is appropriate for any age kid that can accept coaching and be disciplined with a program.

Bfoley: Thanks Mark. As soon as the ortho gives him clearance, I'm going to have him start training.

Mark Rippetoe: And if the ortho doesn't give him clearance? Like what will happen if you tell the ortho he'll be doing squats? This is like asking your Mormon plumber if it's okay to take your showers while you're drunk at 3am.

Milk And Cycling

STEVE: Read all the posts about how good a gallon of whole milk a day is, and how it puts on weight and builds strength. Will it help a cyclist get stronger? I'm 6' 145# and race. Don't imagine I'll gain weight... don't want to. Too hard to climb with the extra pounds. Will drinking the milk help my cycling strength? Any pointers will be much appreciated.

Mark Rippetoe: Cyclists are a hard-headed bunch. Can't seem to understand that a bigger motor doesn't slow the car down.

STEVE: Thanks for the reply on cycling and milk. At 53 and still racing the pro 1-2 category, I always look for any edge I can get. It's very hard hanging with the 20-30 year olds. Bike racing is like doing 2-3-4 hours worth of squats. It really hurts. Well, I'm going to start drinking whole milk, and build up to a gallon a day. I sure hope this give me a bit more strength. I read your reply, and it sounds like your answer is "yes," that drinking milk will give me more strength and power on the bike. Is this correct? How long before you see the power gains?

Mark Rippetoe: No, riding the bike is NOT like doing squats, not at all. And milk will not give you more strength and power on the bike – getting bigger and stronger will give you more strength and power on the bike, and that requires squats as well as milk.

STEVE: Thanks for clearing that up. I totally understand about squats. I do know that cycling and squats are totally different, and my point was that both hurt. A heavy set of 5 reps on the squats and a 3 hour race. Different muscles and in a different way, but they both hurt. I just have to try to incorporate squats into my weekly training schedule. These last few years of cycling, (I'm 53) I want to try something new. A new way of training. Been hearing all my cycling life from cycling coaches that squats do nothing for the pedal stroke on the bike. (Specific training is what they preach.) I always heard that if big strong legs make you a better cyclist, than Arnold and his gang would dominate at cycling. You're to do on-the-bike strength work. Example: hammer in a huge gear. Cycling's "squats on the bike training" ...but I will try regular squats and see how I do.

Mark Rippetoe: Yes they both hurt, but so do burning your hand and burying your bulldog. The differences are actually quite significant.

The trouble with cyclists is that their training establishment keeps reinforcing the silly bullshit that all recreational athletes want to believe: at some point, all serious athletes go outside their sport-specific work to improve, and recreational athletes just want to play their sport and wear the clothes.

KSC: I think I remember seeing something on YouTube or somewhere else that was a video of you training a cyclist with a high rep squat session or something similar...not sure if I am remembering correctly or not....I think I also heard somewhere (or read) that you and Dr. Kilgore did quite a bit of work with some cyclists...am I correct or am I thinking of something else?

STEVE: Mark what do you recommend me doing to improve my power and strength on the bike, so I can be faster? If squats, or any other leg work, what kind of workout would be good to do? I train 6 days on the bike now, race sat, long ride Sunday, recovery ride Monday, off Tuesday, hard intervals wed, recovery ride Thursday, recovery ride Friday with a few short efforts getting ready for Saturdays race. Where do I put in the leg work you recommend so I get stronger and faster? All help is appreciated.

Mark Rippetoe: We have worked a little with a track cyclist, Aaron Kacala. He's a phenomenal athlete, and one of the best guys I've ever trained. Hard working, coachable, appreciative, very talented, and a Man under the bar. He will eat you and shit you out.

Steve, man, I don't know where to put any extra work into that schedule. You and I seem to have some different ideas about how to train, and anything I could say about this program would be interpreted as critical of the training methods of a sport I have had no personal experience with. I have never had good luck training road cyclists, so I probably don't know what I'm talking about anyway. Just enjoy your time outdoors and have fun on your bike.

Dizziness, blackouts and squat racks

Corey: I have two quick questions. I realize by asking them I am setting myself up for one of your brilliantly humorous comebacks, but I appreciate your sense of humour.

1. Is there a way to minimize the dizzy, semi-blackout feeling at the rack position of the clean? I read in the book about why it happens, i.e. the bar being too far back and too close to the neck. Perhaps, it's just dizziness, because I think I catch the bar on my front delts. Sometimes I have to stop for a moment in the rack position and let my head clear and get my balance before lowering the bar to the floor

2. I'm thinking of constructing a homemade squat stand. Am I a fool to even consider it?

Mark Rippetoe: 1. The little white flies you see when this happens tell you that blood flow to the brain – specifically your optical areas – has been adversely affected. It's not "just dizziness" unless dizziness is normal for you, in which case I'd recommend another activity. Keep the bar away from your carotids and You'll Be Fine.

2. What are you going to make it out of? This is a rather important consideration.

Corey: I made an error in asking my first question. It's during front squats that I start to see stars. The clean is not really a problem since I lower the weight quickly after power cleaning. I'm doing heavy front squats and practicing lighter back squats until I get a stand or make a stand. That leads me into clarifying what I'm making the stand with. Sorry about that small omission!

I was thinking of two 4x4s with rugged and wide wood/ steel base and horizontal connection between the two 4x4s. For the catches, I was thinking of drilling holes in each 4x4 on an upward angle from back to front and then placing some type of bolted rod/pipe in the holes. I would have the catch at mid sternum. As for a rating on this thing, I'm thinking 300lbs max. That would keep me going until I happen to start squatting above 300. That won't be anytime soon.

While I have your attention I'll ask a couple quickie questions.

1. The strength standards published in PP. Are they for 1RM or 3x5, 5x5?

2. Finally, why is it my deadlift is 340 (above intermediate) but all my other lifts are classified as novice?

Mark Rippetoe: I recommend against a wooden squat rack, for much the same reason that I recommend against a wooden car.

1. The strength standards are for 1RMs. If they were for something other than 1RM, it would have been necessary to specify whether it was 3, 5, 10, 20, etc. Since this wasn't specified, it would be logical to assume they were for 1RM.

2. Because you have a weak squat, bench, press, and power clean.

Abdominals

Billy: Is there a particular abs exercise you feel has the greatest carry over to the lifts? I'd like to go as far as I can without needing a belt. I'd also like to feel more stable in the hole, particularly on the rare occasions when doing squat cleans and snatches.

Mark Rippetoe: I like weighted situps, knees-to-elbows, and L-pullups. These 3 cover all the bases.

Simeon: Could all three of those ab exercises be incorporated safely into SS as part of a warm up? Or maybe one Monday, the next Wednesday etc? Also, would the L-Pull ups double as a good biceps exercise once one wants to add a biceps exercise to the program?

Mark Rippetoe: Absolutely not. Never – and I mean NEVER – try anything that someone in authority, like Me, has not specifically approved in advance. This is not allowed, and is specifically prohibited, because if you do this irresponsible thing – this Trying Things For Yourself – you might learn on your own, and again, this is PROHIBITED.

Recovery

Whiterabbit: I wonder how you feel about the usefulness of the following as recovery aids:

* stretching
* myofascial release (foam rolling, The Stick, etc)
* yoga

Please feel free to add in anything else you feel is a useful recovery aid.

How much sleep do you recommend, and on what might it depend (age, weight, training history?). Forgive me if you've covered this in PPST; I have only SS:BBT. I've read the first edition and am making my way through the second.

Mark Rippetoe: I would be interested in knowing how, stretching, myofascial release, and yoga could possibly aid recovery. I mean, why would you specifically ask me about these three? Stretching is what you do when your range of motion needs work, myofascial release is what you do when injuries cause your range of motion to need work, and yoga is rolling around on the floor pretending it's exercise. But how could they possibly affect recovery from heavy training?

Weekly strength schedule

STEVE: Come on mark, give me a weekly strength workout to do so I won't get eaten up and shit out (what you said Aaron would do to me). Let's hope so he is 30 years younger....
Don't know if your busy or you forgot or gave up on my original post. It was on "cycling and milk." Per your post to me, you told me to go outside the regular way of bicycle training and do more strength in my workouts, so I'm

waiting and wanting to see a weekly workout plan I can follow, cause I don't want to get eaten up and shit out like you told me Aaron would do to me. Hell, I'm coming to you to get better. Give me a plan.
thanks, Steve

Mark Rippetoe: Steve, buddy, the plan is in the fucking book. That's what the book is about. That's why I wrote the book. This is a Q&A for people who are already using the plan IN THE FUCKING BOOK. Get it, read it, and use it. Really, the book is too long to post here. Get the fucking book.

"Onus Wunsler" Workout?

Robert: In SS:BBT you have a photo of a typical training log showing one Onus Wunsler's workout plan and first couple of weeks of training. I never gave it much thought until bango skank posted it alongside your other workouts on another forum. Then all of a sudden it looked like a legitimate alternative to your novice workouts in SS:BBT and PP.

My question: In what case would you recommend the Onus Wunsler plan rather than one of your other novice plans? Is it a matter of anthropometry or goals or starting fitness level or what? I ask because I'm a big tall noodle of a guy prone to back problems, and I hear (anecdotally) that back extensions are good for folks w/ recurring back problems.

So: how do I know if the Onus Wunsler Workout is right for me?

Mark Rippetoe: You try it and see, tall silly person. You learn about this like you do everything else you actually know to be true.

Squatting in front of a mirror

Tursunov: Would it be safe and beneficial to squat with my eyes closed? My gym has mirrored walls unfortunately.

Mark Rippetoe: Have you read any of the posts critiquing squat form where I yell and scream about looking down? Have you read my book, which yells and screams about looking down? Apparently not. No, do not close your eyes – you'll need them for balance. Look down.

Tursunov: Thanks for the reply. Your book (I only have the first edition unfortunately) has helped me a lot. The squat rack in my gym is right in front of the mirror, and yes I have read that one is supposed to keep his chin down and look at a point about 6 feet in front of me. The point is, the mirror is quite close (3 feet) in front of where I squat. If I follow the guidelines in your book, does that mean that theoretically I should be looking 3 feet inside the reflection?

Mark Rippetoe: Tape a piece of paper of sufficient size on the mirror at the right place and see if that helps. If it doesn't, just look at the junction of the floor and the wall. My rack is positioned like yours, and I look at the floor/wall corner most of the time when I squat.

And no, I'm not going to squat any weight with my eyes closed for any reason. If you want to do a few bodyweight warmups like this to sharpen your proprioception, that's fine, but it only takes a second to lose your balance weighted, and the benefits are far outweighed by the plastic surgeon's fee. This assumes that your appearance is worth salvaging.

Deadlifts and the glutes

Baldr: I just re-read the deadlift section in SS:BBT and I'm not sure on one thing; at the top, right when the bar passes the knees, should you squeeze your asscheeks, as if you were pinching a coin between them, to finish the movement to lockout?

Mark Rippetoe: No, we never consciously squeeze our asscheeks in the weight room. It's not a valuable biomechanical cue, and it might get misinterpreted.

Bodybuilding

Captainpicard: I have seen that you seem to be quite against the idea of "bodybuilding". Out of curiosity, may I ask why? Does it have to do with the isolation exercises that produce commonly non-functional strength? Or does the sport do something else like promote unhealthy eating habits (for the long term, meaning constantly bulking and cutting) poor form or exercises that in general are not very safe and/or good?

Mark Rippetoe: Yes, all that shit, plus the fact that bodybuilding is men on a stage in their underwear wearing brown paint and oil having shaved their asses and showing other men their muscles. It is training for appearance only, and at the contest level requires a degree of vanity, narcissism, and self-absorption that I find distasteful and odd.

Missing pages in SS:BBT

Drewfasa: I was just wondering, are all the copies of SS:BBT missing pages 206-207, or is it just my copy? From near as I can tell it is just numbering mistake, is this correct? (I'd hate to have to send mine back to Amazon across the Atlantic again for two pages.) Aside from this trivial issue I'm greatly enjoying it, having already read the 1st edition for coaches.

Mark Rippetoe: Page numbers 206-207 were offensive to us, for numerological reasons we'd not care to discuss, so we omitted them and indexed around them. No material is missing, just the 2 most horrible, sickening, disgusting, revolting, baby-killing, maggot-infested, sorry, rotten, substandard numbers in all of mathematics. And good riddance, I say. Fuck 206 and 207, both of them.

Gyromike: Thank God someone has taken a stand on this. Those numbers have been pissing me off for a long time!

Mark Rippetoe: *Courage* will always be the watchword of The Aasgaard Company.

kaipo1: My copy of Practical Programming has a page 206 *and* a page 207. Should I tear them out for safety and/or aesthetic reasons?

Mark Rippetoe: Your copy of *Practical Programming* was printed before The Enlightenment I recently experienced about the evils of 206-207. I'd hang on to it, if I were you. The next printing shall be purged.

Irishman301: Ya, I'm a math guy myself, and the numbers 206 and 207 are basically large pieces of shit. They do nothing but fuck everything up. Good call in getting rid of them. I'm glad someone else finally realized this.

I kinda don't feel right saying this, but 368 pretty much blows too.

MadDwarf: Kaipo1, I recommend you do what I did - blot out all of the page numbers from 205 on with a black Sharpie marker, then renumber them in the proper enlightened fashion.

This seems to have worked for the majority of the pages that just needed to be incremented, but proved to be insufficient for the core pages printed with the actual tainted numbers. For those pages, I've burned the numbers out and printed the replacement numbers below the char line. I've been keeping a close eye on the book, but so far it appears to show no signs of corruption.

Deadlift issue

b33k4y: I almost shit myself while I was deadlifting last week. You didn't touch upon this issue in your books at all. I was wondering if you have ever experienced this happening to someone in your gym.

Mark Rippetoe: No, shitting yourself when you deadlift was omitted from BBT. The best way to avoid this is to not deadlift when you need to shit. Planning is the key here.

Back extensions

Captainpicard: How much is too much for back extensions if due to an injury you cannot deadlift or power clean? I have been doing the 3x a week SS routine but instead doing 3x10x25 lbs. back extensions every workout.

Mark Rippetoe: What's the injury, and why would a novice do any exercise for two weeks at the same intensity?

Captainpicard: Shoulder injury, pain while doing deadlifts and power cleans. Well, I have been doing back extensions, but I moved from 15 to 20 to 25 over roughly a two week period. My back has been sore/sharp pain

Mark Rippetoe: So you have a shoulder injury AND a back injury?

Captainpicard: I suppose so. I do all the warmup stuff verbatim, and make sure my form is good. Oh well.

Mark Rippetoe: What have you been doing to accumulate these injuries?

Captainpicard: I think I hurt my back doing deadlifts.

Mark Rippetoe: Why might that have happened?

Captainpicard: I don't know. I think my form was fine. I guess I am just too old for this. Maybe all those people who say weight training isn't safe are right and I should just stick to the cycling.

Mark Rippetoe: I think that was my original recommendation for Steve.

Powerlifters at my gym use the look up cue for deadlifts

Robert: Many powerlifters at my gym seem to think a useful cue for the deadlift is head up. I am not talking about head up to keep the hips down, i.e. looking at a spot on the floor 10 feet in front of you, but part of their pulling motion involves pulling their head back to look up at the ceiling almost. Looks pretty dangerous to me, I don't want to do that and hurt my cervical spine...

Mark Rippetoe: Then don't do it. They aren't being mean about it, are they?

Sex detrimental to progress?

Tongzilla: Does sex/masturbation have a negative effect on gaining strength? Does it decrease the amount of protein your body has? Or is all just an old wives tale?

Mark Rippetoe: Yes, it does. Never do either. Ever. Not if you want to be strong like bull.

Tongzilla: Ok, I believe you (because you are Mark Rippetoe), but please give me some scientific and anecdotal evidence.

Jamie J: I'm guessing this is one of the reasons you stopped competing.

Mark Rippetoe: It is the ONLY reason I stopped competing. And it's damned sure too late to start back now. Do you have any idea how much protein I lost???

And as for the science, ask yourself this question: do I know any porn stars that squat 600? No, my friend, you don't. And there you have it.

The use of Vitamin I

Danish Viking: I have read through the different posts on elbow-ligament issues (golf/tennis elbow etc.), and seen that you mostly recommend the usage of ibuprofen, ice, massage etc. - except for one post where you mention taking a month-long layoff. I was wondering, if one were to be suffering from some elbow pain caused by the standard bad arm position during squat, and were to try to work through this (with better form, obviously), how would one go about dosing the ibuprofen? Would you recommend a stable intake of say 6-800mg 3-4 times a day for a given period, or to use it primarily to treat symptoms - i.e. when pain arises (post-workout fx)? I have primarily used the last version (symptom-based), but it doesn't seem to be getting better (nor worse) at this point - it's been hurting on/off for a few weeks.

Mark Rippetoe: I've got exactly the same elbow shit right now, for the same reasons. Ibuprofen therapy for this would be 800 mg x 4/day x 5-7 days, no longer than that. I've been doing lots of chins to flush it, and it always feels better to me after I chin.

Tongzilla: You mean YOU (out of all the people) have bad arm position for squats?

Mark Rippetoe: The point of doing the chins is specifically to inflame the damn thing more, the theory being that "a rising tide floats all ships" so that the thing will go ahead and heal. Sometimes it works, sometimes it doesn't.

And isn't it fascinating that EVERYBODY 1.) fucks up occasionally, 2.) needs a coach to see problems, and 3.) is forced to be patient with fools even when we'd rather not be?

Squats & farts

Stevo: Serious question about a serious problem...drinking that whole milk may "do a body good" but my system seems to produce lots of hideous gas to go along with it especially during squats. I deal with it by nonchalantly walking a good distance from the squat rack & cutting a rat near the guy(s) who wear the "wife beaters", are covered acne & smell of steroid fumes.

Is there a better time to drink milk that may lessen the gas attacks? Morning or night? I don't have a schedule but just drink it throughout the day. My girlfriend & dog would greatly appreciate your thoughts on farts as well.

Mark Rippetoe: Your technique, when done silently, is referred to as Cropdusting. It makes me happy when this is done in the proper context, and your judgment here seems to be sound. You'll get used to the milk, and if you don't you'll still have hours of fun in your new sport. I am unaware of any diurnal flatulence variability. Worry not about this, and get some weightlifting shoes.

Drewfasa: When I first started squatting and deadlifting heavy I would do explosive farts. I work out in a small gym at my university, usually it's just me in the small weights area and then a few pretty girls on treadmills. There's something distinctively character-building about learning to shrug off ear-shattering farts done in front of attractive women.

Tongzilla: I find drinking milk slowly helps. Just sip it. Also eating slowly and chewing your food thoroughly helps too.

Mark Rippetoe: Tong sounds like a fun guy.

Polynomial: Perhaps similarly to grunting, a controlled explosive fart can increase pressure and help with the lift. But only if you fart in chords.

Mark Rippetoe: I strongly advise against intentionally farting whilst moving heavy weights. Sometimes – especially under those circumstances – farts have a solid center.

Bench vs. Press

Mmafan: Which exercise do you believe has more carryover for a grappler?

Mark Rippetoe: I don't know for sure since I don't train any grapplers, but you should do both anyway because they are both valuable. That's like asking me which is better, steak or lobster. Is it a contest?

KSC: I do train some grapplers and they all press and bench. And steak is better than lobster.

Mark Rippetoe: Yes, I think it is too. But if you're buying, I'm eating both.

Abs

Sun tzu: What is your preferred ab routine after your SS workouts? How many exercises would you suggest and what should the sets and reps be on these exercises?

Mark Rippetoe: I don't really have a preferred ab routine. I think you should just do a few sets of weighted situps and add more weight every time, just like we do with everything else. In other words, don't endurance-train your abs while you strength-train everything else.

MadDwarf: If your abs are secure at all points, you are sufficiently prepared. If they are superior in strength, avoid training them. If your abs are temperamental, seek to irritate them. Pretend they are weak, that they may grow boldly. If they are taking their ease, give them no rest. If your abdominal strength is united, isolate it. If abs, hips, and back are in accord, put a rest day between them. Attack them where they are unprepared, train when it is not expected.

TomC: Ha! Nice adaptation of Mr. Sun Tzu's work.

Mark Rippetoe: MadDwarf again wins the Post of the Week award, but he's already won it once and has all the books. I'll have to buy him something nice.

MadDwarf: Luckily for me, I'm fairly sure Rip uses the same definition of "something nice" that I do – alcoholic and tasty. That definition may occasionally get me in trouble with the missus around Hallmark Holidays, but never with my gym brothers.

Why more than 5 reps with chin-ups? And are pull-ups necessary?

Lu36: Last month I started on your program for beginners at page 300-1 of SS.
Since I am fit (36 y.o, 64 kg, 7-8 % body fat) and I already owned a dips belt, I started right away with weighted chin-ups in sets of 5 (after a BW warm-up set of 3). That's hard but I am highly motivated and I progressed quickly up to 5x3 with +12.5 kg! Now I received the second book of yours (PPST), where the program includes pull-ups too; why need I alternate pull-ups to chin-up?

Mark Rippetoe: You don't need to alternate pullups and chinups if you don't want to. I don't do any pullups, just chinups. Because I'm a gym owner and I'm required by law to have massive arms. Have you seen my arms? They are Hyoooge.

Slow progress with squat compared with presses, am I overtraining it?

Lu36: After a month plus on the SS program I could lift (5 reps):

deadlift: 86 kg
squat: 66 kg
bench: 56 kg
clean: 41 kg
press: 31 kg
(and chin-ups +12,5 kg (c:)

Recently I started having the ugly feeling that my legs might give up in the bottom position (how often does it happen?). I train anyway, but now I wonder if training squats 3 times a week may be overtraining for me, because I am 36 and never trained with heavy weights more often than twice a week before.

Mark Rippetoe: Without your height and bodyweight this is just a guess, but I'd bet your squat technique is the problem.

Lu36: I'm 5 feet 8 inches tall and weigh 138 pounds; I have a 28 inches waistline.

Mark Rippetoe: Then your emaciated little body is the problem.

Quad weakness?

Dan F: A 48 years old woman friend of mine, a little overweight, can't do a full squat with a broomstick, apparently for weakness in quads (she has flexibility in hamstrings and other muscles more than me!). Doing back squats she has a tendency to lean too much forward with shoulder/trunk without lowering the butt enough (a sort of good morning): she says quads don't permit her to go down. Is it plausible?

If so, what kind of exercise she has to do to reinforce them before starting SS? No leg press and machines, she trains at home. I was thinking of lunges or step-ups on a chair. She has also a cyclette. Or better starting anyway with (partial) back squats?

Mark Rippetoe: It's quite likely that she's correct. I have trained many overweight women who could not do a bodyweight squat, and they are the only reason I kept my leg press machine, because it's very handy for producing a linear increase in leg strength up to the point at which squats can be done. In the absence of a leg press, she'll have to do increasingly deep bodyweight squats starting at the depth she can manage. The problem with this is quantifying the depth and making sure it increases a little each workout. You'll have to keep careful watch over this to assure an increasing range of motion as she progresses, or she will not progress.

The sad fact is that fat women usually are not disciplined enough to train for any length of time (this is why they are fat), so the question is probably moot.

Banderbe: Gotta disagree on that one. I know fat women personally who have achieved a great deal professionally, and climbed the corporate ladder so to speak with stunning agility. I have talked to one in particular about her weight, and she told me "I hate exercising".

Mark Rippetoe: Banderbe seems able to differentiate between physical and intellectual/industrial laziness. Perhaps we should too. On the other hand, "I hate exercising" can be interpreted only one way, so I think you have to say that the fat girl is at least *physically* lazy. It is good that she has come to grips with the effects of her policies and located a dressmaker that can decorate her for the trip up the corporate ladder.

Weight gain?

Brian S: I am about 5'10" and weigh about 170 lbs. I have been doing SS for about 3 weeks or so and gained 5 lbs by not changing anything in my diet. I eat around 2500-3000 calories a day. I am not able to drink the GOMAD since I am still a minor and my parents do not buy that much milk but am still able to drink around 1/4-1/2 a gallon a day. My question is if I need to gain weight or not, and if I do, what should I be?

Mark Rippetoe: I am not aware of laws that prohibit minors from buying milk, unless possibly the UK has recently enacted such legislation to protect the cardiac health of their admittedly fragile population. Do your parents have to buy everything you eat? Do you have a job or other way to acquire your own money? Yes, you need to gain a lot of weight, and it should be your responsibility to ensure that this happens. To that end, grow up and grow bigger.

Brian S: No I don't have a job. But there is other food that we have in excess besides milk. Should I just make it my priority to consume more calories than to drink more milk?

Mark Rippetoe: No, you should get a job, acquire the money, buy the milk, and drink it. For reasons you'll understand later. Much later, perhaps. Ask your dad to explain it.

Early reset on squat?

KC7: I'm 29/6'2"/179/11% body fat. I was 172/11% body fat when I started SS two weeks ago. My BS progressed from 185-195-205-215, but then I failed at my third set of 225 twice and have since gone back and looked at video for form issues. My deadlift has continued to progress to 315, press is up to 105, and bench is up to 150; all for 3x5's.

My question is this: Did I start with too high of a weight considering my form was incorrect? Now that my form is better should I reset at 135 and work up by 10 lbs per workout or should I reset at 175 and work up by 5 lbs per workout (either one will get me back to 225 in 10 workouts)? I feel like starting over at 185 and going by 10 lbs might be too much, or am I just being a pussy? I'm eating 4000-4500 cal a day including the milk, getting 8 hrs of sleep, and I'm not doing any other exercise that would inhibit proper recovery.

Mark Rippetoe: You either started too heavy, or more likely didn't rest long enough between your sets. Pray, how long were your inter-set periods?

KC7: I'm resting anywhere from 3 to 5 minutes. At 225 it was closer to 5. If you think the rest was adequate what weight would you recommend that I start again with? Thanks.

Mark Rippetoe: I think it was probably the rest, because you shouldn't be stuck this quickly. It is not uncommon for lifters to take 10 minutes between work sets, especially with relatively heavy weights. But 3 minutes is definitely too quick.

pnp_pc: When resting 5 to 10 minutes between work sets, are you supposed to be just sitting, stretching, or doing chins or some other ancillary work?

Mark Rippetoe: I'd just rest, drink your coffee, and brag to your buddies about all the pussy you get.

MadDwarf: Crap - what about the other 4-9 minutes?

Neither book describes a complete novice program, but I need one!

Lu36: You are no doubt the best strength coach I know of, but unfortunately your messy writing keeps me scratching my head: after going through both your books Starting Strength and and Practical Programming for Strength Training (which I bought expensively overseas) I still cannot put together a complete novice schedule that I can use for my training without stressing guesswork. Talk about "practical" programming!

The closest thing to a complete workable routine in either book is the "typical beginner's program" at page 300-301 of SS, which is obviously insufficient. In particular I could not find details about the reps and sets of the "ancillary exercises", such as:
-a sound explanation of why chins/pulls are to be performed at higher reps than barbell exercises, apart from "tradition" (page 253 book 1), and why "failure should happens at 5-7 reps" when weight is added (page 163 book 2)

-the number of bodyweight chinups/pullups before adding weight:
you wrote "12-15" (page 259, book 1), "more than 15" (page 155, book 2) and "over 10" (page 169, book 2). Please pick one. :mad:

-a clear example of how to alternate weighted and unweighted chin/pulls (as mentioned at page 163 book 2): I find it impossible to alternate both chinups and pullups AND weighted with unweighted "every other workout" at the same time. See by yourself: chin+ pulls- chin- pulls+ (doesn't work); chin- chin+ pull- pull+ (doesn't work either). :mad:

-how many reps and sets for the abdominals, and when to add weight:
the "typical beginner's program" (page 301 book 1) shows
2/14 Situps BWx20, 2/16 Situps BWx5 & 10lbs.x12, 2/19 Situps 10lbs.x13
Why BWx5 to "warm up" the abs, and only the first time? :confused:

-how many reps and sets for the back extension, and why:
you wrote "any other assistance exercises should be done after the basic program exercises, and then for no more than three sets" (page 163 book 2). It may seem that you meant 5x3, but that's clearly not the case: in the beginner's program (page 301 book 1) are shown 10x5 back extension, while for the advanced they would be 20x3 (page 219 book 2). And back extension is clearly listed as assistance exercise (page 219 book 2), while abs are not!

Can you see what I mean? Someone can pass me a complete novice routine for a few months, please?

Mark Rippetoe: **Yes, you're absolutely right, the books are so disorganized as to be all but unusable, especially in the absence of the ability to exercise one's own judgment and apply a bit of common sense. Please e-mail me your mailing address and I shall refund all of your money, including shipping, you fucking idiot. And with your refund I will throw in a free ass-wiping, since you obviously want me to do that for you too.**

Lu36: I thought you would either not post my message or respond in a civilised and useful manner. My intention was not to offend you, I seriously look forward leaving out the guesswork from all my training. I'm presently looking for a weight lifting coach in my area. It makes me sad that you are such a bitter person, obviously you don't have love in your life. When it's weight time I put my "105"% into it. It's in between trainings that I wonder how I should rather train the next time.

Anyone would post for me a complete novice schedule? Or send me the link inside the forum? Also references to pages in the books are OK, I do not wish the authors to lose profits.

RWatkins: It's a busy world. Not everyone has time to do this sort of thing, and not everyone can take that step to make such a difficult decision about training. I understand. This is the really awesome thing about the Basic Barbell Certification. Those of us who HAVE it, can set up a program for someone. My first copies of PP and SS are well annotated, underlined, highlighted, etc, (I was glad for the fresh copies at the cert), and while the information does require a lot of thinking, I feel quite confident that I can set up a great novice program for you. For $25 a session, three times a week, I will set up and help you through a novice progression, including auxiliary exercises, and tell you exactly how many reps you need each time. Afterwards, I can work out any kinks in your muscles for $55 an hour, with or without hot stones.

I love my work. ;-)

Shahala: Here you go..
OK, this is the resolution for your issue.
You will need the following items in front of you:
1. Yellow Marker
2. A pen - either gloomy black or attention seeking screaming red.
3. SS:BBT - the book.
4. Nude women on a card of some sort.

Now we can begin.
1. Open page 289 of SS:BBT.
2. Using your yellow marker, highlight table 8-1.
3. Using your gloomy black or attention seeking red pen draw an asterisk near the table.
4. Draw an asterisk in the bottom of the page.
5. Write this adjacent to the asterisk: "Please do the goddamn thing."
6. Place the card in the gap between pages 288 and 289 - close the book.

Gant Grimes: Specialized novice program:

A day:: Punch yourself in the face until you pass out. Alternate hands.

B day:: Kick yourself in the face until you pass out. Alternate legs.

You can do this every day, every other day, twice a day, whatever. You don't even need to warmup, and B day takes care of any flexibility issues.

PS: Drink a gallon of milk directly before working out.

WOD to accompany SS

Taleb: I've been doing this self-designed WOD once a week in addition to the basic program in SS:BBT. Let's call her "Heidi".
Max rounds in 15 minutes:
5 pull-ups
10 hanging leg raises
5 dips

Do you find this circuit useful and supporting SS, if one can recover properly?

Mark Rippetoe: It's just wonderful. But if you do it once a week, it's a WOW, not a WOD.

My balls hurt after I squat

Alx: That's the short of it. The long of it is that I did Starting Strength (which is amazing of course) for about 6-7 months, on top of over a year of weightlifting I had already done before that, with no problems whatsoever, having great progress and a great time. Then one day I woke up with a dull pain in my testicles, rushed to urgent care and was told that I may have inflamed my epididymis. The doc said it's nothing to worry about, and that after a bit of rest it should subside and I can work out again. But, he told me that it may simple be a case of one thing always leading to another, and that has been the story so far. The main aggravator is the squat, after which I get discomfort for 2-4 days, even after doing 80% of the load I'm capable of doing.
Is this just my fate? Have you seen anyone with the same experience? Info on this is very scarce on the web, but I can't believe I'm such a special case.

Mark Rippetoe: Alx, buddy, you're on your own here. My balls haven't hurt since 1973, when I learned how to finish what I started.

Dumbbell Bench

Hockmasm: What is wrong with using DB bench? In the practical programming book didn't rip mention in a sentence that the DB are actually better than the BB, but since this is a barbell book he will stick with the BB bench?

Can you tell me why linear progression cannot occur with DB? If I bought magnet weights could it? And try to go up 2lb increments a week? I prefer the DB (because not to sound weak) but getting heavy under the BB without a spotter makes me nervous. With the DB I can just drop them when they get too heavy for me. With BB I have a mental block I feel of getting too strong on it. I have had times where I have had to put all my strength to get the bar back up to the rack, and thought it might not make it on the 5th rep.

Mark Rippetoe: The DB Bench is a fine exercise, and I suppose it could be used as a core exercise ***IF*** it can be loaded in a way that supports a linear progression, and ***IF*** the dumbbells can be handled safely when the sets of 5 get really heavy and ***IF*** you can get competent spotting on a heavy limit set of 5 and ***IF*** you can avoid tearing up the room and the equipment when you fail with your last rep on your last set of 5, which you ***will*** eventually do. ***IF*** you can manage to satisfy these rather common-sense requirements, get busy on the DB benches and let us know how it works. But I think you can see that there will be problems.

Hockmasm: So I switched to BB bench today. I read online that you can use DB at 90% of your BB so I used 170lbs.

It looked liked this
170x5
170x5
170x5
170x4
170x2

Seems like I am still stuck at the same weight for 3 weeks now? What should I do since my last two sets sucked?

Mark Rippetoe: Use a lighter weight.

KSC: Yes, you should drop the weight, as Mark has already stated.

I had this awesome routine when I was a sophomore in high school. I wanted to be able to bench 315 so Monday thru Friday I would walk into our high school weight room and put 315 on the bar and try to lift it. Surprisingly, I failed 5 days per week. Sometimes on Saturdays I would go to our local Gold's gym and try the same thing, also failing. Eventually I pulled my head out of my ass and lowered the weight by about 100 lbs to something I could actually work with productively.

Hockmasm: I did 3 sets 5 across. The 4th set I did 4 reps and the last set 2 reps. It's not like I was doing one rep for 5 sets you know. So should I drop down to like 165? Or go lower to like 160 for a week, then 165, then 170? Should I reset like that? To take 3 weeks to get back up to it? Or just go down a little?

I don't think I am going that far "having my head up my ass."

Mark Rippetoe: I think you're right up to the ears, Hock.

Bench question

harmony72: I am an extreme loner and very anti-social. I will not talk to anybody in the gym nor will I ask for a spot. In the power rack in my gym, if I set the pins to one set of holes the barbell is about an inch and a half above my chest. If I set it to one set below that, it is well below my chest. So my question to you is, can I start the bench with the barbell on the pins that are 1.5 inches above my chest? I think these are called "bottom position bench press in power racks"?

Mark Rippetoe: No, you can't and still call it a bench press. Our little idiosyncrasies sometimes cause us inconvenience, don't they?

Stretch Reflex

Chris SP: After reading SS I've been incorporating the stretch reflex into most of my lifts. I wanted to ask why you don't suggest it for pullups. Is it because you need to breathe at the bottom from a dead hang? I tried using it today (slightly, not a full bounce) and found it helpful. I also wanted to ask if there's any problem using the stretch reflex in upright rows.

Mark Rippetoe: I never said you had to dead-hang all your chins and pullups. I use a stretch reflex when I do them too. It is very helpful. On the other hand, don't do upright rows. I remember saying something about that.

Gordon Bombay: Would you be willing to expand on that? I did a search and couldn't find anything.

Mark Rippetoe: I expanded on it in the book.

Chris SP: Are you against Upright Rows because they could interfere with learning the Power Clean (trainees could try to 'upright row' the weight)?

Mark Rippetoe: Upright rows teach an arm pull, which is perhaps the single worst habit a weightlifter can have and perhaps the most common error made by everybody learning the clean and the snatch. Bodybuilders do them. And they are not good for your shoulders. And they don't do anything that presses don't do better. And they look stupid.

Rips program?

ChrisLain: Hey Rip, what's you current workout schedule look like?

Mark Rippetoe: It varies a lot with travel, but I try to train 3-4 times a week, with a mix of metcon and strength. No pattern at all, just trying to stave off death.

AidenBloodaxe: So tell us what you have written down on paper from your last workout. Do you squat every time you train like you make us (not that we don't love it)?;) We are nosey fuckers aren't we?

Mark Rippetoe: I eat basically "Paleo", because starchy carbs make me fat and I like meat. Steak, venison, beef, ham, pork, bacon, cabbage, greens, salad stuff. Good wine, a little good beer, good whisky and whiskey. No bread, potatoes, rice, sugar in the house, but maybe a little when traveling for certs. I do metcon, squats, deadlifts, lots of chins, pull the sled, presses, clean & press, snatches occasionally. I deadlift in the low 300s for reps, squat in the high 200s for reps, press about 185, chin my bodyweight x 16-17. These numbers are good when I haven't recently had surgery. Now, run along.

Strong Enough Pic

TexasAg: What's up with the pic on page 101 of *Strong Enough?*, the one with you on your horse dressed up in Viking outfit? There's got to be an interesting story behind that one.

Mark Rippetoe: It's the way I normally dress and move about. You got a problem with that?

TexasAg: Negative. Just didn't know there was a Ye Olde Tunic Shoppe in Wichita Falls.

Mark Rippetoe: This is a hotbed of tunic activity.

KingOatmeal: It's funny that TexasAg asked this question because I've always wanted to ask you the same thing. After my girlfriend saw that picture while I was reading the book she almost flipped out and questioned my reasoning for reading your stuff.

Mark Rippetoe: You need a more interesting girlfriend.

Weighted vest while squatting

Markll: Might wearing a weighted vest while squatting create a more effective load than squatting alone? I realize the vest wouldn't stress the body in the same proportions as the bar, but it seems possible that the scattered distribution of small weights over the sides, back, chest and waist wouldn't infringe much, (if at all), on what can be lifted on my back.

Mark Rippetoe: How about putting the weighted vest on the bar instead? That way, you get to use a fashionable piece of modern/retro strength and conditioning association/PE/Athletic Training-major equipment *AND* get something actually accomplished at the same time! Be sure to use one vest on each end.

Pyramid model and more exercises

Science: Dear Mark,

@Mods:
Are my posts lousy-they never get published on this section-can u please tell me why?

I will hold me short: Regarding the pyramid model in your book of PPST:

I grap the concept.I want to ask to how many exercises is this scheme limited?
I have favourite lifts i want to bring up:
squat,deads but also bench,press,row and chins.
So I wonder if its not too much,to absorp all exercises on the same day.
My idea would be,to skip the recovery day and make A and B sessions 3x the week:

A:dead bench row
B:squat chins press

But remain of course the loading phase and peaking phase. What falls out is the recovery day-BUT session B can be also seen like the "Texas method recovery day",where you also include press on Wednesday cause the weight is lighter as when benching- as you mentioned.

On my B day-all exercise weights are lighter than the weight used on Monday.
So it can also be seen as a "recovery day" It would be more time efficient but will it still work?

Other ideas for an advanced athlete who wants to bring all this lifts up is welcome!

thanks-in case the post is published;) -- science

Mark Rippetoe: I have approved this so that you know I'm reading them. But since I have read it 3 times and still have absolutely no idea what the hell you're talking about, I cannot provide you with an answer. This is in lieu of deleting your post, so it was in fact appropriate to express some type of gratitude.

Limbs extension doubt on 4 exercises

Diogoo: I will start to do the Starting Strength program and I have these doubts: Do you complete extend your legs while squatting/deadlifting? Do you complete extend your arms while bench pressing/military pressing?

Mark Rippetoe: Yes, you do. This is what your knees and elbows do for a living.

What should my ideal weight be on Rippetoes?

JBlack: I am 6'0 and weigh ~205lbs. (32years old and ectomorph, if that matters.) I really enjoy training hard and enjoy your program, etc. According to most online calculators, my "ideal" body weight should be around 180lbs??? LOL, I'm well over that now, what should my ideal body weight be for this program? Have you made a table for this, or what do you recommend?

Mark Rippetoe: Your ideal bodyweight as an ectomorph at 6' 0" will be 214.378 lbs. There. Happy? And if you lose or gain *a pound*, I will have you killed. It is important to be ideal.

JBlack: Thanks Coach, I appreciate it.

Mark Rippetoe: Sure, J. Anytime. Glad to be of help.

Pooping pants while squatting

Drewfasa: Have you or any of your trainees ever had this problem, Mark? It only started happening recently as I've been approaching 140kg worksets and eating like a pig (three McD's double-cheeseburgers for lunch everyday). Nothing disastrous so far, but I still have to run to the toilet between sets. Could it be a result of wearing a belt too tight? Any suggestions? I poop before working out, but when I'm coming out of the hole (no pun intended) something always squeezes out.

I'm sorry to address something so vulgar, but I don't believe you are very priggish about these things, and you also have that great American commodity: a sense of humor. Your help is appreciated.

Mark Rippetoe: Jesus, Andrew, I could have gone a long time without having to hear about this. The obvious fix is to take a newspaper into the bathroom and not to come out until the whole thing is read. Just before you train. Works for me every time.

Quintus: He might not have covered this with respect to squats, but it's already been handled for *deadlifts*. Would you really have expected the advice to be significantly different for squats? Reading from the book of Rip, Chapter 7, Verse 12. Quote: "*...The best way to avoid this is to not deadlift when you need to shit. Planning is the key here.*"

Scott Ro: What would I do if this were me? Well that "Depends." Could you please make this a "sticky" so as to prevent it from ever being asked again?

Drewfasa: Think it must have had something to do with the new belt I've been wearing, but everything seems to be okay now, the necessary adaptation must have occurred to prevent this rather awkward side-effect.
Nope, it's not sorted out actually, happened worse than ever today. Oh well. Sacrifices need to be made if one wants to get strong. And the "Depends" idea might not be so ridiculous after all, as long as they have the elastic areas for mobility like Huggies.

Mark Rippetoe: Except that I don't let anybody wearing Depends train in my gym. I think this is actually a very good policy for gyms to have.

Sex, not with you...

4non: I was wondering if sex before a workout be beneficial or detrimental. My girlfriend always asks "so how was that workout", referring to my actual time in the gym and not in the bed. Sometimes I can say, "wow it was outstanding," sometimes it has been awful? Should I steer clear before a workout?

Mark Rippetoe: I guess that depends on how it was approached. If you PRed the poke, you might have to adjust your other numbers down a little.

Do I cut or maintain?

Potatoface: I've made a topic before about not being able to squat, you told me to go to a doctor. The doctor didn't know what was wrong and sent me to a physical therapist. From what I can understand, I have muscle imbalances and that's what he's helping me fix. In the meantime, he told me to lay off any barbell movements that require the hip. In short, I can't do the novice program to cut, like I had hoped. The only time I spend in the gym now is to retain my strict press/bench press numbers and improve my grip strength. I gained ~50 lbs in my first 5 months of the program so I have a lot of fat to cut. Would not doing squats/deadlifts mean I'd have poor results when cutting or should I just cut with minimal lifts and cardio? If you're interested in the muscle imbalances, my quads/lower back overpower my abs/glutes/hamstrings which cause my pelvis bone to tip forward, this causes my lower spine to arch more than normal. Also, my left leg is weaker than my right leg.

Mark Rippetoe: This is a highly unusual volume of gibberish for even a BB.com guy.

Potatoface: If I try to lose weight without doing anything important like squats, deadlifts, power cleans, will I lose a lot of the muscle I worked for?

Mark Rippetoe: I sincerely hope so.

Ski squats

Radosuaf: Unfortunately, I'm going through serious reactive arthritis... I'm afraid the only way to have some leg exercise is now stiff-legged deadlift or ski squats. What would be the best way to perform ski squats?

Mark Rippetoe: Maybe do them on skis?

Radosuaf: Well, maybe I used an incorrect name. It's the squat with back against the wall.

Mark Rippetoe: Why does a diagnosis of serious reactive arthritis (?) mean that you have to train ineffectively?

Radosuaf: Because my knees hurt so much that without back support I'd fall on my back with the first squat. I have to support myself with hands to get off the toilet. But there is no physical damage to the joint. So I guess this wouldn't be the worst idea...

Mark Rippetoe: What wouldn't be the worst idea? Squatting in a way that places all the stress on your knees and none on your hips? Or learning to balance without a wall?

Radosuaf: OK, Smith machine then? There is no way I could make a normal barbell squat. OK, this was stupid. How about the box squat?

Mark Rippetoe: You're killing me here.

Chest impact

Golfer: I read an article that says a small impact on the chest has a small chance of causing a heart attack. I do a small bounce off my chest on bench press if I'm really straining on the final 1-2 reps, so is that ok? I don't want to sound like a kook who believes everything he hears but I'm just wondering if this applies.

Mark Rippetoe: Yes, it applies: you are apparently a kook who believes that an event with a high level of statistical improbability is nonetheless worth posting about. You're much more likely to be eaten by pigs. If this affects the quality of your sleep, sorry.

Deadlifting in power rack - Lowest hole puts plate 2 inches off ground

JBlack: To make it easier to change plates, and get the proper bar height for warmups, I am deadlifting inside the power rack, with the bar on the pins. But the lowest pin is set so that the 45 plate is exactly 2-inches off the floor. Is this too high to start from, or should I be okay?

Mark Rippetoe: Convenience is very important in barbell training. In fact, if I were you I'd just set the bar in the rack at the level of the hole in the plate when it's hanging from your arms with your elbows straight. This way, you don't have to actually bend the elbows to get the plates on the bar, and that's even more convenient than the way you're doing it now. Good luck with your training!!

r_graz: This is a great idea. I tried it today and immediately added 300 lbs to my deadlift. It must be because I saved so much energy in changing plates. I guess another approach would be to put the bar on the floor, and roll the innermost plate onto a 2.5 lb plate to add or remove weight, but that would certainly not be as convenient.

JBlack: Hi - If you could give a serious answer that would be much appreciated. Other than getting out my drill or risk cracking my hardwood floors, would it be detrimental to dead starting with my 45s 2inches off the ground? Would the entire point of the exercise be lost - or is this difference in starting height trivial?

Mark Rippetoe: What would you do with your drill? And why wouldn't you just get some rubber mats for your floor?

JBlack: On page 110 of SS it says to get the correct deadlift starting height (for warmups) you can either

1- Build up a stack of plates
2- Use the proper hole of a power rack

This was a pretty good idea so I extrapolated it to regular (over 135lbs) deadlifts which made it a lot easier to load and remove 45s - since the bar is off the ground I can just slide on extra 45s as needed. But due to the construction of the rack, the lowest hole is about 2 inches taller than standard 45lb plate height, thus the drill. Since I value your opinion I would like to ask: is it really bad to pull deads starting from 2 inches off the ground?

Mark Rippetoe: So you want to know if it is okay to do a 2" off-the-floor rack pull instead of a deadlift because it's easier to load the plates that way. Basically, how critical is the first 2" of the pull, is your question. Since it's the hardest 2", I think it's important enough to do it.

Hip extension in coitus

Brandon: In your professional opinion, should the glutes or the hamstrings be the dominant muscles used for pelvic thrusting during sex? This is obviously completely ridiculous, but now that it's occurred to me I can't stop freaking wondering about it...

Mark Rippetoe: I find it quite hard to believe that this could possibly be relevant to your situation, Brandon. You're obviously just interested in this from a theoretical standpoint. It has been my experience that the glutes and hamstrings work together quite well, in just about every situation.

Tangential Materials

Occasionally our focus drifts.

Specialty training advice

Urdcr: I play an unknown sport called freestyle footbag (you're no doubt familiar with the brand name Hacky Sack) and I was hoping you could advise me on adjustments I'd like to make to my training regimen.

Footbag is a finesse game, by which I mean the winners and losers are determined almost totally by technical proficiency rather than fitness, as opposed to sports like football or hockey where relative strength and size are huge factors. Fitness in footbag is important mainly for injury prevention and to allow frequent hard training. My experience lists the following priorities for my training:

1) Ankle stability
2) Knee stability
3) Shin splint avoidance
4) Hip ... Not stability exactly, more like integrity. I'm often (and currently) sidelined by hip strains.
5) Lower back stability and flexibility.

I'm about three and a half months into your starting strength program, and I feel like issues 2 and 4 have been well served, and 3 hasn't personally given me much grief in the past year or so, so no worries there. But as I mentioned, I'm currently nursing a hip strain (specifically my right hip flexor is sore, and has actually prevented me from squatting for about two and a half weeks as well), and I wanted your opinion about adding some isolation exercises to my workout. I've been thinking about doing a 4th day on Sundays (on top of my t,t,sat) which includes that crazy hip adduction/abduction machine, calf raises (1), hamstring curls, and weighted hanging leg raises.

Do these seem like appropriate exercises for me to be doing? Will a fourth workout be a major detriment to my regular training? If you have anything to suggest, I'm all ears. The level of play in footbag has exploded over the past decade, and the entire community is hurting for some good cross training advice. Young, fit men are being felled by shin splints so severe as to cause stress fractures. The US champion recently had to take three months off due to a vertebral stress fracture, at 19 years of age!

Mark Rippetoe: I shall not stoop to the disparagement of the noble sport of footbag, although I am tempted mightily. Suffice it that I merely observe that soccer players formed the ranks of most Hacky Sackers back in The Day. Your statement that "Young, fit men are being felled by shin splints so severe as to cause stress fractures." just flies in the face of my admittedly limited exposure to the, hmm, activity. I am exposed enough to know that soccer players do not eat enough, so stress fractures are not a terribly surprising result.

That having been said, it sounds to me like you are a bit overtrained. If this is correct, the fourth workout is out. And as for making it up from machine training, you should know why I might make fun of you for that. Hip flexors are better trained by roman chair situps, knees-to-elbows, L-sits, and L-pullups. The quick external/internal femoral rotation and its attendant lumbar flexion is probably the problem movement, and since this is not terribly normal to human hip function I would expect it to be a continuing source of problems for anyone playing the sport. If you figure out a way to train it, or invent a Hackysack machine, let me know, but this is out of my bailiwick.

Hypothetical question

Coldfire: In Practical Programming the advanced athlete is defined as someone who is competitive in the barbell sports and weekly progression does not work for him. Which means he needs periodization. What do you think a non-competitive (in any sport) athlete, who trains just for balanced strength should do when approaching the stage where he needs periodization? Should he just maintain his current physical state, or try to advance to the next stage?

Mark Rippetoe: Unless you are a competitor in a barbell sport (or at least are lifting weights that a competitor in a barbell sport would be handling), you will not be approaching the point where you would need periodization any more complicated than intermediate-level programming. Really. It's very hard to get this strong, and you wouldn't have done it without a good reason. A meet would be that good reason. And that makes you a competitor. No meet = no competitor = not an advanced athlete. In other words, I don't think non-competitors ever approach this point.

Coldfire: So, if a non-competitor doesn't ever reach the point of periodization what happens to his training? Shouldn't he stall somewhere? And if he does, what happens next? I'm just trying to understand how someone can train his whole life without ever reaching the point he needs more than weekly periodization.

Polynomial: In your definitions of novice, intermediate, and advanced athletes, are you assuming that diet, rest, and other factors aiding recovery are kept at an optimum? Could it be the case that a non-competitive lifter could recover from a properly induced overload event within a week, but that his or her lifestyle requires two weeks for recovery and supercompensation? I'm venturing a guess that the answer is no, since an intermediate would have to be on a really shitty diet and sleep schedule to take two weeks to recover from what should take only one week.

Mark Rippetoe: My point here is that anybody training hard enough and long enough and intelligently enough to eventually need very complicated programming to get a new PR every 6 months is not the type of person to do the PR in their garage. Such a focused person is a competitive lifter that goes to meets. I suppose it happens occasionally, like maybe twice a year in the entire country, but you are asking me questions about a person that essentially doesn't exist. Theoretically, the sun can explode, or all the air molecules in the room could end up on the ceiling, but they probably won't. People that need to program their training months in advance are not doing it just so they can write about it on the internet or tell their buddies at the bar.

Typical gains in other lifts?

Stu: You mentioned in the steroid thread that it's not uncommon for young guys on SSBBT to up their squat sets by 300lb. What would be an achievable gain in the other four lifts for your typical young trainee (18 years old, 150lb say?)

Mark Rippetoe: We've had young guys put 350 on their deadlift, 150 on their bench, and 75 on their press. But most will not do the program, so it doesn't happen often.

mick in mpls: What do you mean by this? I'd give my left nut to train at your gym.

Mark Rippetoe: Bless you, my son. But it is a rare occasion when a trainee of the right age, height, and motivation shows up at my gym here in Wichita Falls. You probably haven't processed this yet, but the vast majority of the human race consists of lazy slobs that will not work to complete a task that involves something physically or intellectually hard. You guys are the tiny minority, and I'm proud to be associated with you.

SS and guzzling alcohol

Peter_k: In PP you pretty much say that consuming alcohol in moderation isn't such a big deal in terms of athletic performance. But what about large amounts of alcohol? It seems to be generally accepted that this is bad, but the explanation for why it is bad usually deals with the short term (e.g. it dehydrates you). What about long-term?

I guess your forte is training kids (under 21, by definition) so it's not much of an issue with them. But can you offer any insight into how well a heavy drinker does on SS? I mean the drinking 6 pints on St. Patrick's Day, not the drinking a bottle of vodka every morning type. In short, if someone gets hammered several times a month, will this screw up his progress?

Mark Rippetoe: I know lots of very strong alcoholics. Heavy drinking becomes a problem primarily when it interferes with the rest of the nutritional situation. It is certainly not optimal, but it certainly has been done by many people I know well, and I'd be a presumptuous, sanctimonious asshole if I told you that you shouldn't drink heavily. You know better than I do what you can get away with, and if your drinking becomes a problem for your training you'll either fix it or you won't. But you'll be the first to know as long as you're honest with yourself.

Coffee?

DYNAMICSENICAL: Mark, I did a search and didn't find too much about coffee..... I'm wondering what you think of drinking coffee to give you a boost for your workouts. I have been eating a lot more to help get bigger and stronger in my weight lifting program but I ran into the same problem I always do when I'm eating a lot for weight gain...I get sluggish, slow, and lazy when I eat like this. But I find coffee a very good tool to get me out of that lackadaisical state to get my worthless ass under the weight and stop fing around. I used to drink green tea in the morning but with all the food I've been eating it's just not enough anymore. Do you drink coffee? Do you get that lackadaisical mental state when you're eating a lot?

Mark Rippetoe: I find that a lackadaisical mental state comes very easily without any special preparation. Coffee is your friend; use it to train. Ask anyone in Seattle and you'll find general agreement with this.

Dave76: Rip is being modest. His knowledge of coffee is exceeded only by his knowledge of weight training. If you enjoy coffee, it's worth a trip to his gym to drink his coffee. No joke.

Off topic question about R.A. Heinlein

Drewfasa: I recently read Starship Troopers (in large part because of your recommendation) and really enjoyed it. Would you consider this the best Heinlein novel? Which one should I read next? Are there any other SF novels you are particularly fond of? Your recommendations are appreciated.

Mark Rippetoe: Wildly off-topic, but I'll indulge. *Starship Troopers* is one of my favorites, along with *Glory Road*, one of the most fun books I've ever read 20 times. But there are more important works, like *The Moon Is A Harsh Mistress* that other people who I'm sure will be posting after this could suggest. RAH was one of the most important writers of the 20th century, irrespective of genre, and it is one of my greatest disappointments that I never got to meet him.

Tuesday: Drewfasa, if you like Heinlein, you'll probably like Ayn Rand as well. The Fountainhead is a good place to start. Don't take her too seriously, though. Not as serious as her critics take her, and certainly not as serious as she takes herself. I think Heinlein's best book was *Stranger in a Strange Land*, though *The Moon is a Harsh Mistress* is excellent as well.

Alpha Zulu: I've read most of Heinlein. Oddly enough, *Stranger in a Strange Land* is one that I haven't read, but that is often given as one of his classics. The two Mark mentions are great, although *Glory Road* is not sci-fi if that is what you are intent on reading (its more of the wizards and beasts type). Another solid bet is *The Puppet Masters* but my favorite is *The Door Into Summer*. Some of the young adult ones are also very good, if you want to read those.

Robert: Coach Rip, have you read much Ayn Rand?

Mark Rippetoe: I've read *The Fountainhead*, *Anthem*, and as much of *Atlas Shrugged* as I could stand by reading every third paragraph.

Drewfasa: Thank you all for your replies, and Mark for tolerating the thread. I think I'm going to read *Stranger in a Strange Land* next, and then *Glory Road.* I just started *Ender's Game*, and so far, so good.

Tuesday: *Atlas Shrugged* is indeed a monster. I had to buy it as an audio book and listen to it at double speed to get through it in a reasonable time. It still took me a month of commutes to finish it that way. Galt's speech toward the end went on for days. Literally.

Mark Rippetoe: *Glory Road* is about the most fun I've ever had reading a book. I'm not a huge fan of Rand, but I am prepared to admit she is one of the most positively influential authors of the same century as RAH. And I'm also a little skeptical about Objectivism, simply because they are such assholes about libertarianism. I read an interesting comment about it one time: Objectivists don't explain, they *italicize*.

SS for a dangerously underweight individual

Jshininger: A friend of mine recently came to me expressing the desire to gain weight and muscle mass. He is, in my own opinion, dangerously underweight-he is 6'2 and weighs approximately 125 pounds, and vegan to boot. I want to suggest SS to him as a means of developing both mass and strength, but I am concerned that the program may be too intense for him (he is basically anorexic). Would you recommend SS, scaled to what would be appropriate for him, or should he try to get to a more normal weight via a regular diet before he attempts any kind of weight training?

Mark Rippetoe: This guy has more problems than a weight training program can fix. How do you plan on getting a Vegan to gain weight, even if you do convince him that the Universe would like him to be bigger?

Jshininger: My mistake, coach-he informed me he's vegetarian, not vegan. He can eat eggs, milk, and soy (don't kill me! His words, not mine). But I gather that would be beside the point...it sounds like weight training may not be for him right now. Thank you for your help.

Mark Rippetoe: Both veganism and vegetarianism are blatant denials of human nature. They can only be accepted in others in the same way religion is: uncritically. If you wish to do this to yourself, please do. But please do not inflict such mind-numbing stupidity on helpless minors in your charge, because doing so creates a sane argument for state intervention, a thing to be abhorred.

LegsLegsLegs: It's not hard to gain weight (or muscle) on a vegan diet, if you eat the right things---just like on a normal diet. Moreover, it is not hard to be an national level power athlete on a vegan diet (I am, and the diet was neither a hindrance nor a helper). I'd venture to say that it is beside the point as long as you make sure you do the research. I do not try to persuade other people to follow my lead or argue about it. It is a personal choice. Anorexics will be anorexics regardless of diet.

Axegrinder: In a lot of cases vegans and vegetarians are that way because of disgust with the meat/dairy industry.

Mark Rippetoe: Look, if you guys want to mount your own little assault on the Plant Kingdom as some kind of statement of discontent with the meat industry and their vicious treatment of our friends the cows and the piggies and the chickens, go ahead. I didn't say that you couldn't gain weight being a Vegan or a vegetarian. I just said it was a denial of human nature. Let me say now that I think it is also stupid.

Old broad puts her glasses on...

Rtzptut: ...and sees that woman on pg 82 in Strong Enough is an old woman, not a child. In my defense I can read the nice big old foggy print just fine without glasses and without them she looks just like my sister did at about 12, so I just got it in my head it was a kid. So next time I go back with glasses, geeze this must be his freakin' teeny tiny almost 80 year old Mom? And look at that card, (previously unreadable) 1916 OMG? I am a little younger than you, she a little older than my Mom so - that's my guess. It's your Mom. Correct me if I am wrong again. I searched, found nothing regarding this picture. I would love to know when she started training and how long she kept it up. I feel like a spring chicken now and also like there's hope for me if her tiny self could do it. That is just too cool, that she was doing that at her age.

I found a trainer - finally so should be getting some help for my too deep squats and miserable cleans. When I get better and you come somewhere over here I will come to a cert. Looking forward to it. Then maybe I can start up a barbell club at the senior center.

Mark Rippetoe: That's my mother. She started lifting in her mid-seventies, and came to the gym 3x/week. I was very proud of her, as I will be of you if you continue to train and live your life to your physical potential. You'd be welcome at my seminar anytime.

This is as SERIOUS, question... life and death.

Kiknskreem: Are you a trekkie Rip? Be honest: *Let me clarify: those of you with WL shoes with extremely high heels like the several versions of DoWins floating around under several different names will have trouble deadlifting in them. The heels are so high that the bar literally cannot be pulled from a position over the middle of the foot. These shoes are not usable for DLing, and they'll need to be cut down to about 5/8" heels. When they are, they work much better than CTs or barefoot, because a little heel helps with the use of the quads off the floor.* ***Locutus of Borg remembers correctly.***

Mark Rippetoe: I watch the show, yes. Okay, fuck you. I am one of the proud folks who, at the age of 9, 10, and 11 were privileged to watch the first series in its entirety every week without missing a single episode. Mr. Spock raised me, Captain Kirk taught me about women, and Mr. Scott is responsible for my malt whisky habit. I have not watched TV hardly at all since about 1980, but I did see all of the *Next Generation* shows. I have no use for *Deep Space Nine*, *Voyager*, or *Enterprise*. Once again, fuck you.

Kiknskreem: Oh, how you misinterpret my question Rip! I too have seen every episode of both the original series and TNG.... only I caught them all as reruns on sci-fi and such.

KSC: I didn't think they could do any worse than the female who played the captain on voyager until they outdid themselves by casting Scott freakin Bakula as the captain on *Enterprise.* I don't think that is what Gene had in mind.

TravisRussellDC: YES!!!!! Although I'm too young to have seen the original series when it first aired, I grew up on the original movies and The Next Generation series. As a side note, I just rented Wrath of Kahn and Search for Spock this past weekend because I hadn't seen them in a while. My wife was getting irritated when I was reciting the lines along with the movie. Star Trek RULES!!!!

Trip: Ha! There is no shame in this (as long as you are not our age and going to Trekkie Fest), it was Montgomery Scott who made me want to be an engineer.

Stevo: Star Trek = Gay

Mark Rippetoe: Stevo = Irritating Asshole.

the_harbinger: Star Wars > Star Trek.

There...I said it.

Mark Rippetoe: Opinions are like phasers – everybody ought to have one.

My balls are rockets

Stevo: Quick note of thanks for your tutelage in all things barbell related. I bowl in a league & my fat flabby friends have noted the ferociousness of the punishment the pins receive with my newly acquired strength. Granted it doesn't get me laid much more than a Star Trek fetish, or wearing a tunic, but nonetheless...

Mark Rippetoe: See what I mean? Stevo = Irritating Asshole.

b33k4y: Are you sure that your friends aren't the ones punishing you with the pins?

Weightlifting shoes for my woman

NastyNate: So I am trying to find a pair of WL shoes for my girlfriend who has been training with me for a few months now. Are there any models that are better for women, considering her foot is somewhat narrower than my flat, wide, man foot? Also, I'm concerned with heel height since deadlifting is the only thing that she sometimes struggles with. Any input would be much appreciated. The shoes will be a Christmas present so I'd rather not do any ripping and planing.

Mark Rippetoe: Get her some Adidas. They are lasted narrow, look cool, and have a low heel.

SkinnyWimp: What do you think of the idea of getting bowling shoes and having a non-slip sole put on them? Saves dollars. Ever known anybody who used these and heard feedback on how they perform?

And btw, I see what you mean about Stevo.

Mark Rippetoe: Bowling shoes would be cheaper, and I'd always thought of using them for WL shoes. You lose the metatarsal strap, and you'd need to have the sole made flat, but if the bowling alley would sell you a used pair you can afford to do it.

Best Burger?

Tomwood: I'm loving SS so far and really enjoying eating whatever the hell I want. I have to ask, what is your favorite fast food burger? I don't know if you have IN N OUT down in Texas, but I've been eating a 4x4 at least every other day since starting the program. I've dabbled with the triple bacon cheeseburger from Wendy's and the new Sirloin burger at Jack in the Crack, but I always end up coming back to the 4x4.

Mark Rippetoe: In 'n Out, by far. And it is the official burger of *The Big Lewbowski*. We don't have them here, but I get around.

Tjayarmyguy: If you're ever anywhere near suburban Philadelphia you owe yourself a trip to Chee-burger Chee-burger. They make a 20 oz burger that if you finish it they take your picture. Awesome.

KSC: No love for Whataburger??

KingOatmeal: I like In 'n Out too but I think Five Guys Famous Burgers and Fries is better. I'm curious, have you had their burgers before? There are a few in Texas but most of them are around the D.C. area.

JMT: The In-N-Out 4x4 is indeed a solid post-training choice, although I personally prefer two double-doubles, one with onions and the other animal style. The only real downside of In-N-Out is that the fries suck, although my girlfriend thinks they are great.

I should note that the local In-N-Out once made a 666x666 for some Caltech students back in the late 90's. The burger was so big, the students who ordered it had to weld up a steel trough to hold the thing.

Mark Rippetoe: Every time I eat a fucking Whataburger I smell like a Whataburger for about 2 days. Like eating menudo. Something funny in the meat, maybe.

KSC: I rather like the smell of Whataburger

Mark Rippetoe: That worries me, Andy. It means you rather like the smell of me after I've eaten a Whataburger.

Squats & 'roids...hemmoroids

Stevo: Yeah yeah yeah, laugh it up, but this is a serious inquiry! Developed a mild case of, um, persistent swelling in a certain sphincter...enough so to go see Dr. Jellyfinger. His questioning went like this...what do you eat & what is the consistency of the output? I say, lots of meat & milk & the deuces are the consistency of concrete pipes. He replied that the tissues were most likely irritated due to far too much milk which acts as a "binder" in the bowel. Second question, what type of strenuous activities do you engage in? I repeated the SS program. His response? (not joking, either) "Continue this program & you will blow out your knees along with your asshole! You wanna wear a diaper forever?"

I expected the reaction to the work-out but not about the other tissue issue. I would venture to say that other elderly lifters such as myself have hit this same conundrum. Advice? Keep lifting & tempt the Huggies fate?

Mark Rippetoe: Hemorrhoids are largely a matter of your parents handing you bad anal genetics. Your doctor is an asshole, and a stupid one at that. On the other hand, you are a stupid guy for letting your turds get so hard to pass. Fix this obvious problem and you may find that the symptoms go away. If not, get them fixed. Jesus, Stevo, *goddammit* but you are a weird bastard.

Angel Spassov

matt9: You mentioned Angel Spassov in the acknowledgments in Practical Programming. I know he presented to the NSCA some years back and some articles he wrote in the NSCA journal are still available online. These scraps of information must represent a miniscule amount of the total knowledge a man with such extensive scientific and practical experience in the field of training athletes has. I was wondering if you could let us in on any lessons you learned or interesting tidbits of information you picked up from him?

Mark Rippetoe: I met him in 1989 at the OTC in Colorado Springs at my USWF Level I certification. I have the greatest respect for Coach Spassov. But the things I learned from him 20 years ago I have long since incorporated into my own coaching to the extent that I cannot tell you specifically what they were. I can tell you that he may be the most neglected and underappreciated coaching resource in the country. And I can tell you that he appreciates a hoppy ale. He's a damn good guy. I wish I saw him more often.

Kids and the natural squat

BIGGUY6FT6: Both of my kids love to go to the gym with me. Yesterday I had my 3.5 y.o. son take some pvc pipe and perform some squats with it. He did 5 squats all with perfect form; feet about shoulder width (maybe a little more) and knees out, feet angled out, head slightly down, perfect back and pipe followed a straight path in the coronal plane etc.

My questions:

1. Are we all born with natural correct squat form?
2. For whatever reason do we "unlearn" the proper technique?
3. Or should I be training my son for the 2020 Olympics?

Mark Rippetoe: 1. Probably not. We're not *ALL* born with anything.
2. Movement patterns change over time. Ask any Olympic lifter about this.
3. Why do you hate your son? Have you got something against a normal childhood?

Coffee

Kayno: gday rip, I know you're a fan of coffee, do you have any experience with the pros and cons of drinking it between sets?

Mark Rippetoe: I have no experience with *not* drinking it between sets, if that helps.

Spud: I drink tea during my training,:eek: can't stand coffee,:(

Cheers Spud

Mark Rippetoe: That's wonderful, Spud.

What is an athlete?

TPrewittMD: Rip, how do you define an athlete? Do we declare ourselves to be athletes, or do we earn that designation?

Mark Rippetoe: An athlete is a competitor, one way or another. With others in a sport that has a quantifiable way of beating another competitor in a contest whose outcome is determined by a physical effort (bodybuilding doesn't count), or perhaps in a similar contest with one's self, one becomes an athlete.

Gary G: Athletes are what Coach Rippetoe said, but I humbly add that they should be considerably better at their chosen exertions than the average person would be. Until one is demonstrably stronger/faster/nimbler, then one is simply training in hopes of one day becoming an athlete. It's sort of like trying to figure out exactly "when" one becomes a carpenter or a musician or a scientist. There are grades of skill as well as designations bestowed in recognition of a level of proficiency.

Mark Rippetoe: But who gets to decide how much better, Gary?

Kfreeman: This is becoming some serious Tao-type Socratic dialogue. Perhaps the most important thing required of an athlete is a desire to **truly** push himself. This would be the thing that sets the naturally gifted and lazy apart from the normal person who kills himself to get under, over, or past, whatever his sport requires of him... Eventually the true athlete stops "doing" his sport and starts to live it in everything he does.

TPrewittMD: What would be the standards for proficiency? Do standards vary from sport to sport? My 14 year old daughter is a great skier and skied the Birds of Prey downhill at Beaver Creek (home of world championship a few years ago) at age 10. She is much faster than most adults on the slope. But she has never raced or been timed. Is she an athlete?

My son, age 15, began wrestling just this past year. Compared to the other kids here in wrestling country (Stillwater, OK), he was way behind. Nevertheless, with a lot of work, he actually won one match at the varsity level and a few at j.v., but lost much more than he won. Is he an athlete?

Is the 52 y.o. overweight smoking golfer who does no exercise other than hit range balls but wins the club tournament an athlete?

When John Kruk was an All Star first baseman for the Phillies, he would smoke in the dugout and was famous for being portly. In an interview, he was asked about professional athletes and smoking. His response was, "I am not an athlete, I'm a professional baseball player." Is Kruk correct?

Rocko: I read an article by Charles Staley where we described the importance of training like an athlete. What if you trained this way, always challenging yourself to beat your previous records as if you were in a competition with yourself. Would that make you an athlete?

Steve in ATL: *It's sort of like trying to figure out exactly "when" one becomes a carpenter or a musician or a scientist. There are grades of skill as well as designations bestowed in recognition of a level of proficiency.*

Those designations are already taken care of. Many athletes show up to competition. There is 1 winner (in individual competition) and 3 medalists. But they are all athletes.

Kfreeman: Does any of this matter? Really?

Mark Rippetoe: It does to athletes.

Kfreeman: I was more talking about the need for someone else to confer their blessing on/to you on what an athlete is. I wasn't saying that being athletic or competitive (inter or intrapersonally) doesn't matter. In honest this just seems like one of those topics like sexuality or favorite ice cream flavor... Cause you know, chocolate is the best flavor... it's scientifically proven.

Gary G: *Athlos*: ancient Greek for contest. At base an athlete is one who competes (as Mark has already told us).

Ye ole Greeks were referring to the contestants in track and field events. I think the general impression is that "athletics" starts somewhere in track and field and sports where there is a lot of running around, jumping, catching, throwing, shooting, etc. Golfers, bowlers, curlers and the like can fit under the broad understanding of "athlete", but the epitome are those who compete in things like track and field, football, rugby and maybe soccer. "Athletic events" are sort of like art or porn; you just know when you see it.

Who decides? Well, I can sight-read really fast and bang out songs on the piano with limited dexterity, but I have no "ear." I wouldn't call myself a musician, though some would call me a musician that just happens to be really shitty. Personally, I'd rather not be called a musician at all. So anyone can be an athlete, but most of us would be fairly shitty ones. The fact that we show up with the intention of doing better--than our competition or better than we did last time--is what really counts. So, Dr. Prewitt, both your children are indeed athletes. So was the reluctant John Kruk.

One Laura Moncur says it nicely: "An athlete is the one who white knuckles a rest day because she wants to get out on the road and run, even though her body needs a break. An athlete practices to be better. An athlete is out there competing, even though she knows she'll lose. Even though she knows there's no stadium full of people." So win or lose, it's the preparation and the showing up that gets you the label.

JLascek: Regardless of how you define what an athlete is, that definition must be quantifiable and not left to subjective interpretation. Without thinking very hard, I would pose this definition:

"An athlete is a person who trains and competes in sport."

I'm debating with myself whether or not the "training" aspect needs to be included in my definition. However, for my definition to make sense, I need to define "sport";

"An activity in which one or more people compete against one another in which that activity is A) requiring exertion from said competitors, B) requiring skill from said competitors, C) has a standard yet quantifiable way to achieve victory, and D) a sanctioned set of rules and regulations that are standardized across all competitions in said activity and subsequently competition."

This means that auto racing is not a sport. It is a motor sport. This means that darts, chess, spelling bees, and poker are not a sport, and need to get the hell off of ESPN (not that I watch anyway). This means that horse racing is most definitely not a sport, at least not for humans.

TPrewittMD: I appreciate your, and everyone else's, thoughts on this. Despite the "Taoism" of this discussion, I do think it matters. And it seems at least as interesting as one more dude asking Rip how much milk to drink.

I believe firmly that how we think and believe has very much to do with how we function and perform. Take an untrained, out of shape 32 year old man. Follow him as he works SS. He eats right, lifts 3x5 per the protocol, sets PR's weekly, gains 45 lbs and in a couple of years, after a program change, is able to squat 1.5 x bodyweight, deadlift 2 x bodyweight, and press 1x bodyweight.

He must believe more about himself than to think, "I like working out." I think this individual deserves to consider himself an athlete. Otherwise, he is no different than some guy with a pedometer counting 10,000 steps in a day.

Questions...

BreezerD: Hey Rip, what is your favourite type of question to answer? It's pretty clear that your least favourite questions are Squat Form checks, stupid questions debating your opinions which you have already provided reasoning for, or questions about modifying SS, but what DO you like to answer?

Mark Rippetoe: Oh, questions like this! Which amount to your girlfriend asking you, "Honey, what are you thinking about right now?"

Zach: Honey, (Rip) what are you thinking about right now?

Mark Rippetoe: Zach, what do you WANT from me??

Zach: I knew it....You think I'm fat.. sniff... and I disgust you... sobs hysterically…

Mark Rippetoe: Zach, I love you just the way you are.

Mom wants to use barbells

MikeD: Hey Coach, my mom wants to start building herself up again due to neck/spinal problems she's had. The 5th and 6th disks in her spine are herniated (toward the neck). She's gone to physical therapy and they had her doing various exercises, the lat pulldown being one of them (went up to about 60 lbs I think). She was doing well and feeling better, until the insurance ran out that is. She's 50 and not really afflicted by the herniated disks day-to-day, but any heavy lifting or pulling is uncomfortable. Would it be safe for her to do the basic BB exercises prescribed in starting strength?

Mark Rippetoe: Help her, you fool. Start her off light, get the special equipment you need, and be a good son for once in your life. The other older guys/gals that read this board won't forgive you if you drop the ball here. Funny how the business end of PT works, huh?

Yoga for Strength

LudwigVan: I've been hearing lots of folks mention "Yoga builds strength and muscle" as one of its supposed benefits. I'm skeptical of this claim but not terribly interested in trying it for myself in order to find out, so I was wondering if you had any knowledge or opinions about the effectiveness of yoga as a form of strength training.

Mark Rippetoe: How is it possible that an activity that incorporates no progressive loading against an external resistance could be considered a strength program? Or maybe I'm missing something about yoga.

LudwigVan: My thoughts exactly. Maybe we're both missing something, but I suspect not, in which case my girlfriend and I will continue to covertly sneer at the Yoga freaks from the safety of the squat rack.

Robert: Gymnastics has progressive loading through increased difficulty in moves by using leverage. Is it possible that one could do the same thing with Yoga?

SKURLAND: Doesn't have to be external, right? Some asanas are harder than others? Like a pistol instead of a deep knee bend; external resistance didn't change....

Mark Rippetoe: I am thrilled to hear that some asanas are harder than others. Some types of running are harder than others. Certain ballroom dances are real bastards. Tennis can make you very tired. There are board games of varying degrees of difficulty. But they do not constitute a strength program.

elVarouza: My biggest issue with yoga is the crazy positions that the lumbar spine has to be contorted into to do some of the movements.

Harry Munro: Yoga rocks. It makes you flexible and teaches testosterone pumped dudes to calm down once in a while.

SKURLAND: I'll leave the board games and dancing to you; I'll note that the hard running and hard asanas will increase strength in most people, albeit not in advanced trainees, and try hard not to conflate increasing strength with something so formal and grandiose as a 'strength program'.

Mark Rippetoe: Harry wrote this while experiencing an abnormally heavy menstrual flow. And SKURLAND, you are just stupid. That is to say, you know as much about this as the "trainers" at Gold's. In a completely untrained individual, hard running and Asanas will increase strength – for about 2 weeks. So will the programs recommended by the ACSM, and picking your nose. This is because anything harder than sedentary activity acts as an adaptive stress in a sedentary individual. You should read up on this stuff.

Harry Munro: It's an awesome accompaniment to strength training being at the opposite end of the exercise spectrum. Really. I'm not gay.

Mark Rippetoe: Right, Harry. And Keystone Light is an awesome accompaniment to prime aged beef. I don't know what makes your wood work, but you have a poor understanding of effective strength training.

Harry Munro: It doesn't take a muppet to realize you can't get strong with yoga, not what I was saying. That's not to say there isn't a lot to learn from it.

JLascek: Unfortunately this is not a matter of opinion. I'm not quite sure why any of you are attempting to validate any of aspect of yoga for improving strength. Here's some debunking of the silliness in this thread.

1. "Muscle imbalances" are eradicated through barbell training.
2. The "core", or in reality referred to as the trunk, is strengthened through things like the squat, press, and deadlift.
3. Flexibility, and the increase thereof, is a normal and integral part of barbell training.
4. If anyone hasn't noticed, the strength training described in these books or on this board exists to provide the greatest functionality in life or sport. This is why comparing a person doing yoga and a power lifter is entirely irrelevant to this discussion since a power lifter is concerned only with the amount of weight on the bar.
5. The calming effects of yoga are not relevant to the discussion either. There are far more effective methods for calming than isometric balancing positions.

BoatApe: Yoga can get better results for anyone who is into working their mind instead of their jaw or their glutes. But it's not going to build big muscles.

Mark Rippetoe: I suppose that if you do your differential equations homework while you're doing yoga, it would be working your mind. But the BoatApe seems to think there is something inherent in the holding of an isometric contraction in an awkward position for waaaaaay too long that is thoughtful.

The most important thing in life

Phillipo: I want to hear you defend your position that "Physical strength is the most important thing in life." I have read and re-read your opening chapters (and all of the other chapters in your books, I own them all) and the arguments have provoked my thought but not swayed me in their direction.

I whole-heartedly agree in the benefits of weight-training. It pushes personal boundaries, is a source of confidence and pride, and provides various metabolic and psychological benefits on a molecular biology level. I think the most motivating argument for me is that is shows people not only what they are made of, but what they can be made of, and the realization that one's limits are self-imposed is a powerful lesson to learn. Yet these arguments and the ones you present in the text are from the weight-lifting side of view. The alternative positions have not been presented and if we're talking about the most important thing in life I think that some discussion of the other side is warranted.

You state that your physical strength "determines the quantity and quality of or time here in these bodies." Surely physical strength has a positive impact on both but is that to say that it has a greater influence on our lives than our mental state? At the opposing ends of the spectrum one may consider a prison inmate with immense physical strength and a paralyzed father who supports his family on a moral level and maintains his fight for dignity despite no physical strength at all. This may not be a fair real-world example but it may illustrative. Would we care if the father were physically stronger? Has the inmate's strength caused him to be a better person?

I can say that I have known many men with very little physical strength who have held the highest levels of my respect for the way they lived their lives. And to the other side I have known many strong men that I would not trust with anything I held dear. I have also known many strong men who were inspiring and amazing individuals as well and I feel that this helps rather than hinders my point. It is not the strength level that separates these proud, honorable men from the others but the decisions they made on how to live their lives. And though these choices may be influenced by one's experience with strength training the path of an honorable life is open to all.

I guess my point is that many things improve our life from weight training, to sex, to whiskey. And the extent of that influence of each of these is quantitatively different for each individual, most likely with weight training leading the way (unless you're from Kentucky, then it's whiskey). But what are we trying to improve? What is the goal? If it is our self-respect, our benevolence, or our ability to improve the lives of others these conditions may be met in the absence of these supporting factors. It may be more difficult but my observations tell me it is certainly not infrequent. If we consider one's physical utility in the world to be the most important goal then certainly strength training is the ultimate precursor to that end and could be considered "the most important thing in life." But how high do we hold this utility?

I train. I squat below parallel. I may not be immensely strong but in the gym I give it all I have and can do 235 for sets of 5 across which is stronger than I have ever been. And it feels good. I want you to know that I am not commenting purely theoretically regarding the training side of the discussion. I know that physical strength adds to the quality of my life, but that is not what we are talking about. We are considering the accuracy of your statement that it is the most important thing in life. And I would like to hear your thoughts on this matter.

Mark Rippetoe: This is a thoughtful post. Here: *"Surely physical strength has a positive impact on both but is that to say that it has a greater influence on our lives than our mental state?"* It is precisely the effect that the physical has on the mental that is of concern. For instance: *"At the opposing ends of the spectrum one may consider a prison inmate with immense physical strength and a paralyzed father who supports his family on a moral level and maintains his fight for dignity despite no physical strength at all."* I don't care about the prison inmate (unless of course he was framed). My concern is for the father: let's give him his strength back and ask him what he thinks. Such a man would serve to demonstrate my point well.

It is true that not everyone who is strong is good, but this is completely unrelated to the fact that it is better for everyone to be strong than to be otherwise.